OXFORD THEORETICAL PERSPECTIVES IN LAW

Series Editor

ALEXANDER TSESIS

Professor and D'Alemberte Chair in Constitutional Law, Florida State University College of Law

The Collective-Action Constitution
Neil S. Siegel

OXFORD THEORETICAL PERSPECTIVES IN LAW

The *Oxford Theoretical Perspectives in Law* series publishes works that explore a diversity of topics pertinent to jurisprudence, statutory review, constitutional principles, substantive entitlements, procedural justice, legal history, and policymaking. The series is committed to intellectual diversity.

Books in this series parse, critique, expand, and elaborate theoretical approaches to broad ranges of legal topics. Authors' works explain the principles, priorities, sensibilities, perspectives, traditions, or social conditions that drive evolution of law. Authors write of how sovereignty, wealth, connection, privilege, culture, and popular discourse influence legal concepts, rules of decision, procedural justice, and substantive fairness. The series further examines how law impacts sociology, politics, traditions, and culture and, in turn, how they impact precedents, policy priorities, administrative tactics, separation of powers, and representative governance.

Oxford Theoretical Perspectives in Law offers a forum for pursuit of contested matters in legal theory that impact contemporary society. Approaches range from empirical, to normative, to positivist. The basic concept may be said to articulate core, rule of law principles in subjects that range from constitutional law to property law.

Authors in the series advance fields of knowledge by elaborating, parsing, analyzing and criticizing text, history, norms, doctrines, and structure. They thereby provide readers with substantive and structural frameworks to be used in research and teaching. Comprehensive studies, enable authors and readers to explore challenges facing a variety of current affairs. A dive into legal theory, ultimately and perhaps idealistically, seeks to evaluate and effectuate fairness and justice.

RECENT TITLES IN THE SERIES

Due Process as American Democracy
Martin H. Redish

The Collective-Action Constitution

NEIL S. SIEGEL

David W. Ichel Professor of Law
Professor of Political Science
Duke Law School

OXFORD
UNIVERSITY PRESS

Oxford University Press is a department of the University of Oxford. It furthers the University's objective of excellence in research, scholarship, and education by publishing worldwide. Oxford is a registered trade mark of Oxford University Press in the UK and certain other countries.

Published in the United States of America by Oxford University Press
198 Madison Avenue, New York, NY 10016, United States of America.

© Neil S. Siegel 2024

All rights reserved. No part of this publication may be reproduced, stored in a retrieval system, or transmitted, in any form or by any means, without the prior permission in writing of Oxford University Press, or as expressly permitted by law, by license, or under terms agreed with the appropriate reproduction rights organization. Inquiries concerning reproduction outside the scope of the above should be sent to the Rights Department, Oxford University Press, at the address above.

You must not circulate this work in any other form
and you must impose this same condition on any acquirer.

Library of Congress Cataloging-in-Publication Data
Names: Siegel, Neil S., author.
Title: The collective-action constitution / Neil S. Siegel.
Description: New York : Oxford University Press, 2024. |
Series: Theoretical perspectives in law series |
Includes bibliographical references and index.
Identifiers: LCCN 2023058776 (print) | LCCN 2023058777 (ebook) |
ISBN 9780197760963 (hardback) | ISBN 9780197760987 (epub) |
ISBN 9780197760970 (updf) | ISBN 9780197760994 (digital-online)
Subjects: LCSH: Constitutional law—United States.
Classification: LCC KF4550 .S49 2024 (print) | LCC KF4550 (ebook) |
DDC 342.73—dc23/eng/20240117
LC record available at https://lccn.loc.gov/2023058776
LC ebook record available at https://lccn.loc.gov/2023058777

DOI: 10.1093/oso/9780197760963.001.0001

Printed by Integrated Books International, United States of America

Note to Readers
This publication is designed to provide accurate and authoritative information in regard to the subject matter covered. It is based upon sources believed to be accurate and reliable and is intended to be current as of the time it was written. It is sold with the understanding that the publisher is not engaged in rendering legal, accounting, or other professional services. If legal advice or other expert assistance is required, the services of a competent professional person should be sought. Also, to confirm that the information has not been affected or changed by recent developments, traditional legal research techniques should be used, including checking primary sources where appropriate.

(Based on the Declaration of Principles jointly adopted by a Committee of the American Bar Association and a Committee of Publishers and Associations.)

You may order this or any other Oxford University Press publication
by visiting the Oxford University Press website at www.oup.com.

For Ruth Bader Ginsburg
—Mentor, Friend, Hero

The friends of our country have long seen and desired, that the power of making war, peace and treaties, that of levying money and regulating commerce, and the correspondent executive and judicial authorities should be fully and effectually vested in the general government of the Union: but the impropriety of delegating such extensive trust to one body of men is evident—Hence results the necessity of a different organization.

It is obviously impracticable in the foederal government of these States, to secure all rights of independent sovereignty to each, and yet provide for the interest and safety of all . . . .

In all our deliberations on this subject we kept steadily in our view, that which appears to us the greatest interest of every true American, the consolidation of our Union, in which is involved our prosperity, felicity, safety, perhaps our national existence. . . .

> —Letter accompanying submission of the US Constitution from George Washington to the Confederation Congress (approved Unanimously by the Constitutional Convention on September 17, 1787)*

---

* 2 THE RECORDS OF THE FEDERAL CONVENTION OF 1787, at 666–67 (Max Farrand ed., 1911).

Contents

Acknowledgments	xi
Introduction	1
The Constitution's Primary Structural Purpose	1
A Brief History of an Idea	6
Plan of the Book	12

PART I THINKING CONSTITUTIONALLY AND COLLECTIVELY

1. Foundations: *McCulloch*	25
Introduction	25
Constitutional Purposes and Pluralist Interpretation	27
Negotiating Conflicts among Modalities and Purposes	36
Democratic Legitimacy	39
Implied Powers, the Necessary and Proper Clause, and Collective Action	43
Parsing Marshall's Reference to a Pretextual Purpose	49
Democratic Illegitimacy	50
A Cautionary Tale	52
Conclusion	56
2. The New "Science of Politics"	57
Introduction	57
Definitions and Behavioral Assumptions	58
Categories of Classic Collective-Action Problems	62
More Complex Strategic Interactions	72
Solutions to Collective-Action Problems	79
Collective-Action Reasoning as a Justification for Federal Power	89
Conclusion	92

PART II A COLLECTIVE-ACTION THEORY OF THE FEDERAL STRUCTURE—AND ITS LIMITS

3. The Roles of the States and the Interstate Compacts Clause	97
Introduction	97
Preliminary Distinctions	98
Values of Federalism	99
Pre-ratification History	102

viii CONTENTS

The Constitution	105
Historical Practice	111
Congressional Consent in Theory	113
Congressional Consent in Practice	117
The Practical Difficulties of Relying on the States	122
Conclusion	127

4. The Necessity of Federal Power: Taxing, Spending, and Borrowing — 131

Introduction	131
Structural Problems with the Articles	132
The Constitutional Convention	137
The Constitution	142
Taxing	146
Spending	156
Borrowing	167
Conclusion	169

5. Interstate Commerce, Foreign Commerce, and Related Principles — 171

Introduction	171
The Interstate Commerce Clause	172
The Anti-commandeering Principle	205
The Dormant Commerce Principle	208
Foreign and Indian Commerce	217
Preemption	223
Conclusion	227

6. National Security, Positive Externalities, and National Uniformity — 229

Introduction	229
Positive Interstate Externalities: National Security	230
Positive Interstate Externalities: The Postal and Intellectual-Property Powers	235
The Virtues of Uniformity: Naturalization and Bankruptcy	247
More Uniformity: Standards, Currency, and Counterfeiting	254
Not Just Administration: Lower Federal Courts and Federal Enclaves	261
Necessary and Proper, Again	264
Conclusion	264

7. Executive Energy, Judicial Authority, and Federal Supremacy — 267

Introduction	267
Article II	268
Article III	278
Article VI	306
Conclusion	310

CONTENTS ix

8. Races to the Bottom, Interstate Coordination, and Territorial
Empire — 313
Introduction — 313
Giving Full Faith and Credit — 314
Extraditing Alleged Criminals — 330
Enforcing the Fugitive Slave Clause — 335
Regulating Federal Territory — 341
Admitting (or Not Admitting) New States — 345
Conclusion — 353

9. Constitutional Rights, Collective Action, and Individual Action — 355
Introduction — 355
Collective-Action Rights Protected by the Collective-Action
Constitution — 357
Individual-Action Rights Protected by the Reconstruction
Constitution — 374
Individual-Action Rights Protected by Both Constitutions — 388
Conclusion — 390

PART III PERFECTING THE COLLECTIVE-ACTION CONSTITUTION

10. The Collective Costs of Strict Supermajority Requirements — 395
Introduction — 395
Ratifying the Constitution — 397
Amending the Constitution — 401
Concluding Treaties — 423
Preventing Presidents from Undermining Solutions to
Collective-Action Problems — 430
Conclusion — 444

11. The Problem of Congressional Gridlock — 447
Introduction — 447
Bicameralism — 449
The Separation of Powers — 452
The Overbroad Veto Power — 455
Subconstitutional Rules — 463
Partisan Polarization, Sorting, and Dislike: Bitribalism and the
Separation of Parties — 466
Power Shifts and Partial Workarounds — 472
Congressional Regulation versus State Regulation — 479
Conclusion — 480

Conclusion — 483

X CONTENTS

Postscript on Methodology	489
Index of Constitutional Provisions	493
Index of Cases	495
General Index	497

Acknowledgments

This book integrates, deepens, and extends into new territory much of what I have been writing about the US Constitution for the past twenty years. I wrote the book amid the personal isolation of divorce and chronic pain, and the shared isolation of the COVID-19 pandemic, which brutally underscored the necessity of effective federal power if contemporary American society is going to meet the formidable challenges facing it. The work kept me company, and in doing so it enriched my life. I hope that the book will inform the work and enrich the lives of those who read it, whether today or many years from today.

This book is a product of the love, support, and education that many people and institutions have offered me during my life. My dear Aunt Ida loved me completely and showed me what it means to care about other people. My mother, Sharon Siegel, was my first teacher; she instilled in me the importance of learning. My father, Steven Siegel, first exposed me to the Declaration of Independence and the Constitution, and he piqued my interest in law and history. My middle-school social studies teacher, Seth Heaton, and my high-school social studies teacher, Gloria Sesso, deepened my interests in American history and government. Throughout my adult life, my brother, Paul Siegel, has been my cheerleader, counselor, and friend. Craig Green has been my devoted friend and favorite interlocutor on all matters legal and historical. My relationship with Maria Siegel has changed over the years, but our friendship has endured.

Duke University and the University of California at Berkeley educated me in political science, economics, and law. I especially benefited from the teaching of Craufurd Goodwin, Jesse Choper, Robert Cooter, Sanford Kadish, Herma Hill Kay, Paul Mishkin, Robert Post, and Eric Schickler. The Justice for whom I clerked, Ruth Bader Ginsburg, taught me much about what it takes to be a good, careful lawyer. She also taught me that heroes are heroes in part because of how hard they work on behalf of people who deserve it. I am grateful for her friendship and support since my clerking days, including by taking an interest in the lives of my daughters.

During my years at Duke Law School, I have been blessed with three deans—Katharine Bartlett, David Levi, and Kerry Abrams—who have always supported my scholarly aspirations, including by giving me time to write this book. I first wrote about collective-action federalism with Robert Cooter, and our joint thinking is partially reflected in the pages that follow. Many colleagues and friends have read and commented on parts of the manuscript: Kerry

xii ACKNOWLEDGMENTS

Abrams, Jack Balkin, William Baude, Lawrence Baxter, Stuart Benjamin, Joseph Blocher, James Boyle, Curtis Bradley, Aaron-Andrew Bruhl, Guy-Uriel Charles, Katherine Mims Crocker, Deborah DeMott, Charles Dunlap, Benjamin Eidelson, Katie Eyer, Bridget Fahey, Richard Fallon, Nita Farahany, Daniel Farber, Barry Friedman, Brandon Garrett, Jonathan Gould, Jonathan Green, Ariela Gross, Tara Grove, Laurence Helfer, Roderick Hills, Aziz Huq, Vicki Jackson, Andrew Koppelman, Genevieve Lakier, Margaret Lemos, Sanford Levinson, Joshua Macey, Jonathan Petkun, Jedediah Purdy, Shitong Qiao, Arti Rai, Barak Richman, Stephen Sachs, David Strauss, Alexander Tsesis, and Ernest Young. Matthew Adler, Craig Green, Toby Lester, Darrell Miller, Ryan Park, H. Jefferson Powell, and Steven Siegel went above and beyond for me by reading the entire manuscript and providing valuable feedback. Jane Bahnson of the Goodson Law Library at Duke Law School skillfully tracked down many sources; none were too obscure for her to find and help me format.

I am grateful to H. Jefferson Powell for urging me to write this book and to Alexander Tsesis for inviting me to do so as part of his series, Oxford Theoretical Perspectives in Law. I thank Guy-Uriel Charles for hosting a book workshop for me at the Harvard Law School and Jack Balkin for inviting me to discuss the book with participants in the online constitutional theory salon that he cohosts. I am indebted to workshop participants at Duke Law School, the University of Chicago Law School, and William & Mary Law School, where I presented drafts of select chapters.

My thinking about the US Constitution has been shaped by too many scholars to name here. I am especially indebted to Akhil Amar, Jack Balkin, H. Jefferson Powell, Reva Siegel, and David Strauss.

My daughters, Dylan Ida Siegel and Sydney Madison Siegel, are the loves of my life. They have encouraged me from start to finish, and they have made me laugh and have some fun along the way. Sydney also designed the cover. Although I dedicate this book to their dearly departed friend, Ruth Bader Ginsburg, I have written it for them and for the future I pray they will know.

Introduction

The Constitution's Primary Structural Purpose

The struggle to tell the story of the US Constitution—to explain what it is about and for, and therefore how it should be interpreted—has existed for as long as the Constitution itself. Americans debated this question when they were deciding whether to ratify the Constitution in the late 1780s, and they continued doing so during subsequent periods of American history. As in times past, answers to the question today are deeply contested, and they matter because they impact government's ability to help address pressing problems.

One long-standing vision of the Constitution views it as imposing significant limits on the powers of the federal government to protect the authority of state governments and the liberty of individuals. For example, the Patient Protection and Affordable Care Act, known as the "ACA" or "Obamacare," has aimed to significantly increase the number of Americans who can afford to purchase health insurance and so obtain adequate health care.[1] The statute regulates the health-insurance and health-care markets, which constitute roughly 17 percent of the US economy. The states would face serious obstacles if they tried to solve "the problem of the uninsured" on their own, as Justice Ruth Bader Ginsburg, in one of the most important opinions of her career, wrote in 2012 for four Justices in *NFIB v. Sebelius*.[2] Only Massachusetts had tried to insure all its residents when Congress passed the ACA. Nonetheless, five Justices concluded that Congress could not require financially able Americans to purchase health insurance using its power to regulate interstate commerce, and four of them concluded that the entire law was beyond Congress's powers to enact.[3] As a result, Congress probably cannot generally require people to get vaccinated to combat the COVID-19 pandemic, which has killed more than one million Americans as these words are written. These potentially life-or-death decisions—during this pandemic and future ones—are thus left to state governments, regardless of the effects of their

---

[1] Patient Protection and Affordable Care Act, Pub. L. No. 111-148, 124 Stat. 119 (2010) (codified as amended in scattered sections of the U.S. Code).

[2] NFIB v. Sebelius, 567 U.S. 519, 595 (2012) (Ginsburg, J., concurring in part, concurring in the judgment in part, and dissenting in part).

[3] *Id.* at 558 (2012) (opinion of Roberts, C.J.); *id.* at 646–49 (Scalia, Kennedy, Thomas, and Alito, JJ., dissenting).

The Collective-Action Constitution. Neil S. Siegel, Oxford University Press. © Neil S. Siegel 2024.
DOI: 10.1093/oso/9780197760963.003.0001

2 THE COLLECTIVE-ACTION CONSTITUTION

decisions on Americans in other states and regardless of whether states acting individually can effectively address the crisis.

This book tells a different story about the purposes of the Constitution. This story recognizes the states' regulatory authority and various constitutional limits on federal power, as must any plausible constitutional theory (in contrast to a normative political theory). But this story begins with and emphasizes the fact that, without exaggeration, the Constitution was established primarily because of the widely recognized failures of its predecessor, the Articles of Confederation, to address problems that have the structure of the one above. They are "collective-action problems" because the states would need to act collectively, not individually, to solve them, and they would often struggle to do so. "Congress' intervention was needed to overcome this collective-action impasse," Ginsburg wrote in *NFIB*.[4] And even the four Justices who would have invalidated the ACA wrote that Congress "can assuredly [remedy the problem that the best health care is beyond the reach of many Americans who cannot afford it] by exercising the powers accorded to it under the Constitution."[5] So, the debate was not over whether the national legislature can legitimately address the problem, but how. Congress's general authority to solve collective-action problems for the states, and the states' general lack of power to undermine these solutions or cause such problems, is part of the Constitution's structural DNA. Thus, any faithful account of what the Constitution is for and how it should be interpreted must include this primary structural purpose. In a fundamental sense, the US Constitution is the Collective-Action Constitution, and the sobering problems facing America today cannot be adequately dealt with by government if Americans do not recognize this truth.

These problems are legion. Millions of Americans lack health insurance. The COVID-19 pandemic has been a human, economic, and governance catastrophe, and future pandemics may cause equal or greater devastation. The ruinous effects of the pandemic on economically vulnerable Americans in both urban and rural America have underscored the thinness and holes in the nation's safety net. Pollution and climate change wreak increasing havoc on the environment and the quality (and quantity) of life, as a marked increase in extreme weather events causes enormous human and financial harm. Income inequality is vast and growing. The nation's infrastructure is crumbling in much of the country. Opioid addiction has reached epidemic proportions. Gun violence, including mass killings, is part of daily life. Decades of unlawful immigration have produced serious humanitarian, economic, diplomatic, and domestic political

---

[4] *Id.* at 595 (Ginsburg, J., concurring in part, concurring in the judgment in part, and dissenting in part).
[5] *Id.* at 646 (Scalia, Kennedy, Thomas, and Alito, JJ., dissenting).

INTRODUCTION 3

consequences. Globalization and technological changes have caused severe economic dislocations at home and abroad. Foreign powers interfere in US elections and invade or threaten the territory of US allies. Nuclear proliferation poses an existential threat, as do domestic and international terrorism. The news brings continual reminders that racism and race relations remain the nation's most enduring domestic crisis. Other forms of bigotry and political extremism abound.

State governments individually have an important role to play in addressing aspects of these problems. The states are the basic, default regulators in the American constitutional system, and they can handle many problems entirely or partially on their own. Such problems include most crimes, most police and fire protection, sanitation services, traffic laws, mass transit, parks and recreation, many issues of public health, and significant parts of education and family law. States also have a role to play in financial and environmental regulation, among other kinds of regulation. But states acting individually cannot succeed in solving the problems listed in the prior paragraph, and they cannot fully succeed in addressing some of the problems listed in this one. It does not matter how sound their governance structures are or how effective their political leaders are. The problems are too large—their scope transcends state borders. To solve them, at least to the extent government can do so, the states must also act collectively, not just individually.

Some states may succeed in acting collectively, at least to some extent, by creating interstate compacts or less formal arrangements if they can unanimously agree.[6] There are contemporary examples of even many states acting collectively. In general, however, it is increasingly likely that states will fail to act collectively as the number of states that must cooperate or coordinate rises, and the number of states required to act collectively increases with the scope of the problem. Moreover, even when some states do act collectively, they may harm other states or the federal government, and they may trigger disagreements over whether they are solving or causing a collective-action problem.

As noted above, this is not the first time that the states have needed to act collectively to overcome daunting challenges. Under the Articles of Confederation, the nation's constitution of sorts before the US Constitution, the Confederation Congress had no dependable source of tax revenue. It also lacked the powers needed to protect the states from commercial and military warfare waged by European powers and Native nations, and from commercial (and potentially military) warfare waged by one another. The states proved largely unable to solve these difficulties on their own. They mostly acted individually when they needed to act collectively, and the most influential and insightful of the Constitution's Framers—including James Madison, Alexander Hamilton, James Wilson, and

---

[6] U.S. Const. art. I, § 10, cl. 3.

4 THE COLLECTIVE-ACTION CONSTITUTION

George Washington—concluded from experience that the states could not reliably achieve an end when doing so required two or more of them to cooperate or coordinate.

The solution they proposed was to establish a more comprehensive unit of government—a national government with robust authority to tax, regulate interstate and foreign commerce, raise and support a military, conduct foreign relations, perform other vital functions, and act directly on individuals, not indirectly through the states. The Constitutional Convention of 1787 thus instructed its Committee of Detail, which met midsummer to draft constitutional text reflecting the decisions of the Convention, that Congress would possess the power "to legislate in all Cases for the general Interests of the Union, and also in those Cases to which the States are separately incompetent, or in which the Harmony of the United States may be interrupted by the Exercise of individual Legislation."[7] Called "Resolution VI" or "the Bedford Resolution," the Committee took this language and produced Article I, Section 8, home to most of Congress's legislative powers. The Convention accepted Section 8 without much controversy.[8] Enough state ratifying conventions would eventually make Section 8, and many other constitutional provisions and principles that share its basic purposes, "the supreme Law of the Land."[9]

None of the Framers or ratifiers who supported the Constitution used the phrase "collective-action problems," but they came close, including by referring to "all Cases for the general Interests of the Union" and "Cases to which the States are separately incompetent, or in which the Harmony of the United States may be interrupted by the Exercise of individual Legislation." More importantly, they knew such problems when they saw them. When certain activities spilled over from one state to another, nationalist Founders recognized that the uncooperative or uncoordinated actions of individual states produced harmful results for the nation as a whole—the definition of a collective-action problem. In the system the Constitution created, the federal government is designed to be the smallest unit of government that fully internalizes the effects of these spillovers. Because the federal government can internalize their effects, and because it operates through some form of majority rule rather than unanimity rule, it will often be structurally better situated than the states to solve collective-action problems caused by interstate spillovers.

---

[7] 2 THE RECORDS OF THE FEDERAL CONVENTION OF 1787, at 131–32 (Max Farrand ed., rev. ed. 1966).

[8] As Chapter 4 explains, most of the language originated in the sixth resolution of the Virginia Plan, which the Virginia delegation introduced at the outset of the Convention to set the agenda. The resolution took final form when the Convention approved a proposal by Gunning Bedford of Delaware to add additional language.

[9] U.S. CONST. art. VI.

INTRODUCTION 5

Such collective-action problems take three basic forms. First, cooperation problems arise when all members of a group of states prefer that every member cooperate rather than that every member not cooperate, but some or all group members prefer to achieve their most desired outcome without in effect paying for it—they prefer not to cooperate while others do. The Prisoners' Dilemma, a famous example of this kind of collective-action problem, captures situations in which states "free ride" off the contributions of other states to collective action or "race to the bottom" because some states disadvantage themselves relative to others by regulating businesses or individuals in ways that other states do not.

Second, coordination problems arise when some or all states would need to coordinate their behavior to solve a problem but there are multiple possible ways of doing so and there may be disagreements about how to do so. A famous example of a coordination problem is deciding which side of the street to drive on. To avoid accidents, all drivers prefer coordination to noncoordination regardless of whether certain drivers prefer to drive on one side or the other. Similarly, creating and maintaining national networks of transportation and communication would require the states to coordinate their regulatory behavior.

These classic collective-action problems of game theory can be called "Pareto collective-action problems" because all states would be better off by their own estimations if collective action succeeded. Given the number of states in the United States and the extraordinarily demanding requirement (called Pareto optimality) that all states be better off or at least not worse off, Congress would almost never be able to act if it were authorized to solve only Pareto collective-action problems. By contrast, a third category of collective-action problems, which this book will call "cost-benefit collective-action problems," refers to certain situations in which some states would regard themselves as better off if collective action succeeded but other states would regard themselves as worse off. Almost all multistate collective-action problems in the history of the US federal system are of this variety, as illustrated by Rhode Island's boycott of the Constitutional Convention. Congress, as the government institution in the nation in which all states and (almost) all individuals and interests in states are represented, is authorized to resolve disagreements among states over whether collective action should succeed if, but only if, Congress rationally determines that its intervention would help one group of states more than it would harm the other. This requirement is called cost-benefit optimality. When this book refers to multistate collective-action problems, it means to include not only the two kinds of Pareto collective-action problems but also cost-benefit collective-action problems.

This book's core claim is that the primary structural purpose of the US Constitution is to empower the federal government to solve collective-action problems for the states and to prevent states from undercutting these solutions or

6   THE COLLECTIVE-ACTION CONSTITUTION

generating collective-action problems. This is not the Constitution's only structural purpose, and this book will honor the additional purposes of preserving state regulatory authority and separating and mixing federal powers to make the exercise of federal authority safe for state autonomy and individual liberty. Vindicating these purposes requires constitutional and practical limits on federal power, and this book will endorse many of them. But when constitutional meaning is uncertain and there are conflicts among these purposes, the Constitution's collective-action objective should generally prevail. To a significant extent, it bears repeating, the US Constitution is the Collective-Action Constitution—both because a collective-action account possesses significant descriptive power originally, traditionally, and today, and because it is normatively attractive. The main goal of the Collective-Action Constitution is not to vindicate a conception of economic efficiency but to create and maintain political and economic union.

A Brief History of an Idea

Something like this idea—or a narrower, more implicit, and more intuitive version of it—has been around for a long time and has been articulated in many places. At the Philadelphia Convention and state ratifying conventions, and in public essays and private correspondence, Madison, Hamilton, Wilson, Washington, and other prominent nationalists emphasized both the need for federal power in cases of general interests, separate state incompetence, or disuniformity and the need to stop states from creating interstate problems. The Constitution was drafted and ratified mainly to accomplish these goals, not to limit federal power or to protect state power or individual liberty. Future Chief Justice John Marshall was at the Virginia ratifying convention, and collective-action reasoning supports—and appears to have informed— canonical federalism decisions of the Marshall Court, particularly *McCulloch v. Maryland* (1819),[10] which upheld implied federal power to create a national bank and prohibited states from taxing it, and *Gibbons v. Ogden* (1824),[11] which upheld federal power to regulate navigation under the Interstate Commerce Clause.[12]

Over the nineteenth century, federal courts helped entrench a political and economic union by policing state economic protectionism. Collective-action thinking supported and likely influenced their invalidation of state laws under

[10]   17 U.S. (4 Wheat.) 316 (1819).
[11]   22 U.S. (9 Wheat.) 1 (1824).
[12]   U.S. CONST. art. I, § 8, cl. 3.

INTRODUCTION 7

the so-called dormant commerce doctrine, which today limits the extent to which the states can harm sister states by passing protectionist legislation or otherwise burdening interstate commerce. In the early twentieth century, the federal government made (and the Court rejected) collective-action arguments in important federalism cases, including *Hammer v. Dagenhart* (1918),[13] which struck down a federal ban on the shipment in interstate commerce of goods produced by child labor, and *Carter v. Carter Coal Company* (1936), which invalidated the Bituminous Coal Conservation Act of 1935, including its regulation of wages and hours.[14] A distinguishing feature of the Court's federalism jurisprudence during the Republican Era, which spanned the late 1870s to the 1930s, was contempt for the idea that multistate collective-action problems partially justify federal power. By contrast, in *Missouri v. Holland* (1920), Justice Holmes's memorable interpretation of the Treaty Clause and congressional power to implement a migratory bird treaty leveraged two logics of collective action by states—and, intriguingly, by nations.[15]

Informal expressions of the collective-action concept ramped up during the New Deal and Great Society. Robert L. Stern, a lawyer for the federal government, authored a stunning law review article that presaged modern theorizing about the relationship between the Interstate Commerce Clause and the regulation of multistate collective-action problems.[16] Stern graduated from Harvard Law School magna cum laude in the early 1930s, but anti-Semitism limited his employment prospects. He nonetheless found work at a small firm before joining the US Department of Justice, where he "participated in many of the major cases of President Franklin Roosevelt's New Deal era that defined the federal government's power in regulating interstate commerce."[17] Certain Supreme Court briefs filed by the federal government during the Great Depression

---

[13] 247 U.S. 251 (1918).

[14] 298 U.S. 238 (1936).

[15] 252 U.S. 416 (1920).

[16] Robert L. Stern, *That Commerce Which Concerns More States Than One*, 47 HARV. L. REV. 1335 (1934). *See* Robert L. Stern, *The Commerce Clause and the National Economy*, 1933–46, 59 HARV. L. REV. 645, 645–46 (1946) ("When the people began to suffer as a result of the unrestrained freedom of enterprise . . . [t]heir call [for help] was addressed to the national government rather than to the states, since the problems of an integrated nationwide economy were obviously not remediable by state action.").

[17] Noreen S. Ahmed-Ullah & Tribune Staff Writer, *Legal Scholar Robert Stern, 91*, CHICAGO TRIBUNE (Feb. 2, 2000), www.chicagotribune.com/news/ct-xpm-2000-02-02-0002020109-story.html, on file with author at https://perma.cc/3QYV-AWW7. Stern eventually served in the Office of the Solicitor General from 1941 to 1954, arguing almost sixty cases before the U.S. Supreme Court and coauthoring *Supreme Court Practice*, the definitive reference on litigation before the Court. He later spent several decades as a partner at Mayer, Brown & Platt in Chicago. *Id.*; *see* Statement of Robert L. Stern of Mayer, Brown & Platt, Chicago, IL., *Nomination of Justice William Hubbs Rehnquist: Hearings Before the S. Comm. On the Judiciary*, 99th Cong. 400–06 (1986), https://perma.cc/MV3R-EFVN. The treatise "Stern and Gressman" has endured. *See* STEPHEN M. SHAPIRO ET AL., SUPREME COURT PRACTICE (11th ed. 2019).

8 THE COLLECTIVE-ACTION CONSTITUTION

reflected Stern's research and thinking.[18] Perhaps relatedly, collective-action rationales seemed to inform several transformative federalism decisions of the Court during the constitutional crisis of the New Deal, just after "the switch in time" that saved nine in 1937: *NLRB v. Jones & Laughlin Steel Corporation*,[19] which broadly construed Congress's interstate-commerce power in upholding federal regulation of labor relations in the steel industry; *Steward Machine Company v. Davis*,[20] which broadly interpreted Congress's taxing and spending powers in upholding the federal unemployment-compensation system created by the Social Security Act (SSA); and *Helvering v. Davis*,[21] which broadly interpreted Congress's taxing and spending powers in upholding the SSA's old-age pension program, which had been funded exclusively by federal taxes.

During the long post–New Deal era that reoriented constitutional law, the Court invoked the logics of collective action in justifying Congress's power to regulate interstate commerce. Examples include *United States v. Darby* (1941),[22] which overruled *Hammer v. Dagenhart* in upholding federal minimum-wage and maximum-hours regulations of manufacturers of goods shipped in interstate commerce; *Wickard v. Filburn* (1942),[23] which validated Congress's attempt to raise the price of wheat on the interstate market by upholding the Agricultural Adjustment Act's wheat-production quota as applied to a farmer who exceeded his quota but used the excess wheat for home consumption and livestock feeding; and *Hodel v. Virginia Surface Mining & Reclamation Association* (1981),[24] which upheld federal regulation of environmentally destructive practices of coal-mining companies. The Court also implicitly used collective-action thinking in continuing to invalidate state laws under the dormant commerce doctrine

---

[18] *See, e.g.*, Brief for the United States, A.L.A. Schechter Poultry Corp. v. United States, 295 U.S. 495 (1935) (Nos. 854, 864). The federal government argued that the states were separately incompetent to deal with the problem at hand:

> Nor could the situation have been met by separate action of the States. It would have been impossible to obtain prompt and uniform action by the individual state legislatures. The intense competition among the States for the national or regional market in numerous industries had been perhaps the most powerful deterrent in the past to state legislation dealing with minimum wages, maximum hours and other elements in commercial competition.

Id. at 93–94. The government canvassed the drafting history of the Interstate Commerce Clause, beginning with Resolution VI of the Virginia Plan. Citing Stern's 1934 article, *supra* note 16, the government reasoned that because this clause "is the only one of the enumerated powers in which Congress was given any broad power to regulate trade or business," the Constitutional Convention "must have understood that it was granting through the commerce clause wide powers over trade and business which would enable the national government to provide for situations which the States separately would be unable to meet." *Id.* at 94 n.41.

[19] 301 U.S. 1 (1937).

[20] 301 U.S. 548 (1937).

[21] 301 U.S. 619 (1937).

[22] 312 U.S. 100 (1941).

[23] 317 U.S. 111 (1942).

[24] 452 U.S. 264 (1981).

INTRODUCTION 9

in such cases as *H.P. Hood & Sons, Inc. v. Du Mond* (1949).[25] The Court there invalidated a New York law that prevented a company from building an additional depot for receiving milk. The law had the effect of retaining more milk for consumption in New York at the expense of consumers in Massachusetts.

Similarly, although this may come as a surprise to some commentators, collective-action reasoning, combined with long-standing judicial deference to rational congressional judgments about whether there is a cost-benefit collective-action problem in need of solving, supports the Court's decisions upholding the Civil Rights Act of 1964 just after it was passed.[26] This is (of course) not because collective-action problems impeded the ability of all states, Southern ones included, to champion racial equality and facilitate the interstate mobility of African Americans. Rather, the Court's decisions were lawful because Southern racism impeded the ability of most other states to protect interstate travel by African Americans, and the Interstate Commerce Clause lets Congress settle disagreements among states about whether collective action is warranted in the commercial sphere—and to pursue this objective when achieving it would benefit the rest of the states in the Union more than it would harm majorities of the electorate in Southern states.[27] To act, Congress need not first prove empirically that all states have been trying and failing to pursue the regulatory regime in question; like in *Darby* and *Wickard*, it suffices that the states face a cost-benefit collective-action problem.

The current era, which began in the 1990s, saw an increase in use of the collective-action idea on and off the Court. In *United States v. Lopez* (1995), the Court likely sensed the absence of a multistate collective-action problem within a reasonable time horizon. For the first time since the New Deal, the Court declared a federal law—specifically, a ban on firearms possession in school zones—beyond the Interstate Commerce Clause.[28] In 2000, in *United States v. Morrison*, the Court did so again, this time invalidating a private civil-damages remedy for victims of gender-motivated violence.[29] The Court later seemed to offer a collective-action rationale in *Gonzales v. Raich* (2005),[30] which held that Congress can use its interstate-commerce power to prohibit the local cultivation and use of marijuana in compliance with state law authorizing such use. The Court also appeared to use collective-action reasoning in *United States*

---

[25] 336 U.S. 525 (1949).

[26] Heart of Atlanta Motel, Inc. v. United States, 379 U.S. 241 (1964) (upholding application of the Civil Rights Act of 1964 (CRA) to a motel); Katzenbach v. McClung, 379 U.S. 294 (1964) (upholding application of the CRA to a restaurant).

[27] As Chapter 5 explains, what it means for a problem to exist "in the commercial sphere" is contested.

[28] 514 U.S. 549 (1995).

[29] 529 U.S. 598 (2000).

[30] 545 U.S. 1 (2005).

10 THE COLLECTIVE-ACTION CONSTITUTION

v. Comstock (2010),[31] which held that Congress could use the Necessary and Proper Clause to authorize the Department of Justice to civilly commit mentally ill, sexually dangerous federal prisoners after the completion of their federal sentences, if no state would accept custody of them.

Turning from judicial opinions during the current era to contemporary legal scholarship, collective-action reasoning has explicitly appeared in the writings of an ideologically diverse group of constitutional law scholars, judges, and attorneys, most of whom have focused on the Interstate Commerce Clause. Prominent examples include writings by Professor Michael McConnell in 1987,[32] Jacques LeBoeuf in 1994,[33] Professor Donald Regan in 1995,[34] Professor Richard Levy in 1997,[35] Judge Robert Bork and Daniel Troy in 2002,[36] Professor Maxwell Stearns beginning in 2003,[37] Professor Akhil Amar in 2005 and 2021,[38] Judge Stephen Williams in 2009,[39] Professor Jack Balkin in 2010 and 2011,[40] and Professor Andrew Koppelman in 2013.[41] Professor Robert Cooter and the author of this book expanded the scope of the analysis from the Interstate Commerce Clause to Article I, Section 8, as a whole in articles written in 2010 and 2012,[42] and this author continued the work for the next decade.[43] Professor

---

[31] 560 U.S. 126 (2010).

[32] Michael W. McConnell, *Federalism: Evaluating the Founders' Design*, 54 U. CHI. L. REV. 1484 (1987) (book review).

[33] Jacques LeBoeuf, *The Economics of Federalism and the Proper Scope of the Federal Commerce Power*, 31 SAN DIEGO L. REV. 555 (1994).

[34] Donald H. Regan, *How to Think about the Federal Commerce Power and Incidentally Rewrite United States v. Lopez*, 94 MICH. L. REV. 554, 554–59 (1995).

[35] Richard E. Levy, *Federalism and Collective Action*, 45 U. KAN. L. REV. 1241 (1997).

[36] Robert H. Bork & Daniel E. Troy, *Locating the Boundaries: The Scope of Congress's Power to Regulate Commerce*, 25 HARV. J.L. & PUB. POL'Y 849 (2002).

[37] Maxwell L. Stearns, *A Game Theoretical Analysis of the Dormant Commerce Clause Doctrine*, 45 WM. & MARY L. REV. 1 (2003); Maxwell L. Stearns, *The New Commerce Clause Doctrine in Game Theoretical Perspective*, 60 VAND. L. REV. 1 (2007); Leslie Meltzer Henry & Maxwell L. Stearns, *Commerce Games and the Individual Mandate*, 100 GEO. L.J. 1117 (2012).

[38] AKHIL REED AMAR, AMERICA'S CONSTITUTION: A BIOGRAPHY 107–08 (2005); AKHIL REED AMAR, THE WORDS THAT MADE US: AMERICA'S CONSTITUTIONAL CONVERSATION, 1760–1840, at 171, 189 & n.3 (2021).

[39] Stephen F. Williams, *Preemption: First Principles*, 103 NW. U.L. REV. 323 (2009).

[40] Jack M. Balkin, *Commerce*, 109 MICH. L. REV. 1 (2010); JACK M. BALKIN, LIVING ORIGINALISM 138–82 (2011).

[41] ANDREW KOPPELMAN, THE TOUGH LUCK CONSTITUTION AND THE ASSAULT ON HEALTH CARE REFORM 39–44 (2013).

[42] Robert D. Cooter & Neil S. Siegel, *Collective Action Federalism: A General Theory of Article I, Section 8*, 63 STAN. L. REV. 115 (2010); Robert D. Cooter & Neil S. Siegel, *Not the Power to Destroy: An Effects Theory of the Tax Power*, 98 VA. L. REV. 1195 (2012).

[43] Neil S. Siegel, *Four Constitutional Limits that the Minimum Coverage Provision Respects*, 27 CONST. COMMENT. 591 (2011); Neil S. Siegel, *Free Riding on Benevolence: Collective Action Federalism and the Minimum Coverage Provision*, 75 LAW & CONTEMP. PROBS. 29 (2012) (Issue No. 3); Neil S. Siegel, *Distinguishing the "Truly National" from the "Truly Local": Customary Allocation, Commercial Activity, and Collective Action*, 62 DUKE L.J. 797 (2012); Neil S. Siegel, *Collective Action Federalism and Its Discontents*, 92 TEX. L. REV. 1937 (2013); Neil S. Siegel, *The Necessary and Proper Clause and the Collective Action Principle*, NATIONAL CONSTITUTION CENTER, INTERACTIVE CONSTITUTION

INTRODUCTION 11

Stephen Calabresi has written several articles on this subject over the years.[44] Formal treatments of constitutions or federations in economics and political science have included analyses of interjurisdictional collective-action problems, but they have not focused on the US Constitution or constitutional law in particular.[45] Ideas related to collective action also play a role in the law and scholarship of the European Union, which uses the term "subsidiarity" to describe the basic concept.[46] So, even judging from this incomplete sketch of the role of collective-action reasoning in American constitutional thought over the past two-plus centuries, it seems fair to describe this idea as important, enduring, and, at times, influential.

It is revealing that collective-action thinking has a history; if it were entirely novel, it could not provide the basis for a persuasive structural theory of the Constitution. To date, however, the idea has not been examined rigorously and comprehensively. As suggested above, past discussions have been relatively casual, implicit, or intuitive. Or they have lumped collective-action problems together with other concepts, such as interstate externalities, without specifying the analytical relationship between the two. Or else they have focused on specific constitutional provisions, especially the Interstate Commerce Clause.

This book leverages conventional legal and historical materials, as well as concepts and methods from economics and political science, to examine the extent to which collective-action logics illuminate the US Constitution as a whole—the document, its Founding history, the structural principles that underlie it, and its evolving interpretation outside and inside the courts. The book's general conclusion is that a collective-action account of the Constitution has

---

(2016), https://perma.cc/6MD3-59PX; DANIEL A. FARBER & NEIL S. SIEGEL, UNITED STATES CONSTITUTIONAL LAW 85–93, 125, 155–61, 171–75 (2d ed. 2024).

[44] Professor Calabresi has emphasized the role of the federal government in solving multistate collective-action problems, but he has mostly leveraged economics and other arguments to defend state regulatory power and judicially enforced limits on federal power. *See* Steven G. Calabresi & Lucy D. Bickford, *Federalism and Subsidiarity: Perspectives from U.S. Constitutional Law, in* NOMOS LV: FEDERALISM AND SUBSIDIARITY 123–79 (James E. Fleming & Jacob T. Levy eds., 2014); Steven G. Calabresi & Nicholas Terrell, *The Number of States and the Economics of American Federalism*, 63 FLA. L. REV. 1 (2011); Steven G. Calabresi, *Federalism and the Rehnquist Court: A Normative Defense*, 574 ANNALS AM. ACAD. POL. & SOC. SCI. 24–36 (2001); Steven G. Calabresi, "A Government of Limited and Enumerated Powers": In Defense of United States v. Lopez, 94 MICH. L. REV. 752 (1995).

[45] ROBERT D. COOTER, THE STRATEGIC CONSTITUTION (2000); JENNA BEDNAR, THE ROBUST FEDERATION: PRINCIPLES OF DESIGN (2009).

[46] *See, e.g.*, Calabresi & Bickford, *supra* note 44 (discussing subsidiarity and emphasizing its relevance to the U.S. Constitution); Stephen Gardbaum, *Rethinking Constitutional Federalism*, 74 TEXAS L. REV. 795, 812–14, 831–36 (1996) (arguing that the Necessary and Proper Clause should be interpreted in light of a principle like subsidiarity). *But see* Vicki C. Jackson, *Subsidiarity, the Judicial Role, and the Warren Court's Contribution to the Revival of State Government, in* NOMOS LV: FEDERALISM AND SUBSIDIARITY 190, 192 (James E. Fleming & Jacob T. Levy eds., 2014) (explaining that "[i]n Europe, subsidiarity ... goes not to the scope of the power but to the permissibility of its use in particular instances").

12 THE COLLECTIVE-ACTION CONSTITUTION

significant explanatory power descriptively and normatively, but that it also has limits. Identifying the limits of the theory is just as important as identifying its promise, because the limits help define the idea of collective action more sharply and give it greater explanatory power where it does apply. The book shows the great extent—previously underappreciated—to which the Constitution empowers the federal government to solve collective-action problems for the states and prohibits states from thwarting federal solutions to such problems or generating them. The book also clarifies the contexts in which other rationales are required to justify federal power, especially the protection of most constitutional rights. Even regarding rights protection, however, collective-action reasoning plays a role.

Plan of the Book

Part I discusses interpretive and analytical tools from constitutional law and social science that Parts II and III will use. Chapter 1 identifies the kinds of constitutional arguments that will appear in this book. Just as importantly, this initial chapter explains why they will appear and how they relate to originalist and nonoriginalist theories of constitutional interpretation. For example, originalist argumentation and evidence will frequently appear, and this book has much to offer originalists, but not because it offers an exclusively originalist account. Rather, original intentions, meanings, and purposes, like structural inferences, customary political-branch practice, and judicial precedent that developed and endured long after ratification of the Constitution, inform how we should understand the Constitution's purposes and thus how we should decide interpretive questions when its language is not fully determinate or does not fully cover the case. Chief Justice Marshall used this approach in *McCulloch*, the most important structural decision in US constitutional law. Marshall's pluralist methodology, which he deployed to discern the Constitution's primary structural purpose identified in this book, is challenged now by the rising influence of relatively strict versions of originalism. As constitutional historian H. Jefferson Powell has written, however, Marshall's approach has always been "the constitutional mainstream" in the United States.[47] Marshall's methodology provides the interpretive foundation upon which the book will rest.

McCulloch provides critical guidance in additional ways. Marshall develops a theory of the superior democratic legitimacy of the federal government over individual states that justifies federal authority to settle disagreements among

---

[47] H. Jefferson Powell, Targeting Americans: The Constitutionality of the U.S. Drone War 25–26 (2016).

INTRODUCTION 13

states over whether there are cost-benefit collective-action problems in need of solving. He also offers a broad interpretation of the Necessary and Proper Clause that advances the Constitution's collective-action objectives in several respects.[48] Finally, he identifies an enduring democratic-process failure that justifies constitutional limits on state authority to impede federal solutions to collective-action problems or cause such problems.

Chapter 2 introduces concepts and methods in economics and political science that inform subsequent chapters. This chapter defines Pareto collective-action problems and uses simple 2 × 2 matrix game theory to sort such problems into two categories—cooperation problems and coordination problems. The chapter then discusses potential differences between 2 × 2 matrix models and many kinds of interactions that arise in life. Complexities include increasing the number of agents whose cooperation or coordination is required for collective action to succeed, which helps explain and evaluate the Framers' skepticism that the states would (and should) address their own collective-action problems and the Framers' optimism that the federal government would be structurally better situated to offer solutions. These complexities do not generally change the number or nature of the collective-action problems that occur, but the complexities can affect the likelihood that collective action will succeed.

In addition, Chapter 2 identifies potential solutions to collective-action problems, some of which are better suited to certain such problems and environments than others, and each of which may face significant challenges. Finally, the chapter distinguishes the classic, Pareto collective-action problems studied by game theorists from the cost-benefit collective-action problems that typically occur in the US federal system. As noted, these problems involve disagreements among states about whether there is a collective-action problem in need of solving. With cost-benefit collective-action problems, fewer than all states would be better off from their own perspective if collective action succeeded, and the benefits of successful collective action to them would exceed the costs to the remaining states.

Part II develops the theory of the Collective-Action Constitution. Chapter 3 begins with state governments. Legal scholars and judges have offered many accounts of the main functions of the states in the federal system, but commentators have not tended to recognize the states' potential role in solving collective-action problems that arise for them. Chapter 3 examines this possibility, which states can attempt to realize—and have realized to some extent—by forming interstate compacts and other agreements.[49] The chapter also explains, however, why the constitutional text (if not the Court's doctrine to date) presumptively

---

[48] U.S. CONST. art. I, § 8, cl. 18.
[49] U.S. CONST. art. I, § 10, cl. 3.

14   THE COLLECTIVE-ACTION CONSTITUTION

bars interstate compacts and requires congressional consent to overcome the presumption. Proposed compacts may undermine federal supremacy or harm sister states, and different groups of states may disagree about whether a compact solves or causes a collective-action problem. The Constitution does not compel one answer to such questions, which are also historically contingent and normative, not just scientific or technical.[50] Rather, it assigns the main responsibility for deciding them to Congress, where, as Chief Justice Marshall explained in *McCulloch*, all the states and all the people are represented. Because the Constitution privileges Congress's view, it does not have the structural purpose of preventing Congress from causing collective-action problems for the states. A cost-benefit collective-action problem is not whatever Congress says it is—the concept has a certain objective structure. But amid disagreements among states, the Constitution privileges Congress's rational view of whether the costs being externalized by some states exceed the benefits that these states are internalizing.

In addition to potentially raising normative concerns, interstate compacts are difficult to form. Many parties within a compacting state must approve, and compacts require unanimous agreement among the compacting states. Moreover, impediments to collective action tend to increase sharply with the number of states that must act together. In general, if the proposed compact must encompass many states to accomplish its purposes, free rider, holdout, and disagreement problems are likely to paralyze it. This is a lesson of early American history and subsequent experience, and it helps explain why, according to this book's arithmetic, compacts usually involve few states and why only around two hundred exist today.

Because nationalist Founders did not expect the states regularly to be able to act collectively, the Constitution empowers the federal government to solve many multistate collective-action problems. As Chapter 4 explains, the constitutional text and structure reflect the conviction that the federal government operating through majority (or supermajority) rule will be more likely to find solutions that elude states trying to cooperate or coordinate through unanimity rule. Professor George William Van Cleve writes in his history of the Confederation period that the Constitution ultimately emerged from "the states' and sections' willingness to confer fundamental new powers on the national government and to permit them to be exercised by majority vote."[51] Thus, the eighteen clauses of Article I, Section 8, where most of Congress's legislative powers are found, mainly authorize Congress to address collective-action problems for the states that are caused by state incentives not to cooperate with other states no matter what other

---

[50] RICHARD TUCK, FREE RIDING (2008). Chapters 1 and 2 discuss this book.
[51] GEORGE WILLIAM VAN CLEVE, WE HAVE NOT A GOVERNMENT: THE ARTICLES OF CONFEDERATION AND THE ROAD TO THE CONSTITUTION 286–87 (2017).

INTRODUCTION   15

states do, or by coordination difficulties for states, or by cost externalizations by states that exceed internalized benefits.

Chapter 4 also analyzes the collective-action dimensions of Congress's powers to tax, spend, and borrow. Among other things, this chapter includes a theory of federal taxing authority that the Court largely adopted in *NFIB*, as well as an account of psychological externalities that helps justify the broad scope of federal spending authority to provide for the "general Welfare."[52] Chapter 5 turns to the federal powers to regulate foreign, Indian, and interstate commerce—as limited by an anti-commandeering principle that is narrower than the Court's doctrine, and as amplified by a dormant commerce principle that is sounder than some justices believe. In partial contrast to the Court, this chapter reads the Interstate Commerce Clause textually and structurally as authorizing federal legislation where Congress has identified a multistate collective-action problem caused by interstate spillovers that produce economic (as opposed to the psychological) effects. Chapter 5 also discusses the constitutional principle that valid federal law supersedes conflicting state law (preemption), which flows directly from a collective-action account of the Constitution. Chapter 6 examines the rest of Section 8, whose clauses mostly authorize Congress to internalize positive externalities (national defense, the post office, and intellectual property) or to impose national uniformity (bankruptcy, naturalization, standards, coinage, and counterfeiting). Even the powers to establish lower federal courts and to govern federal enclaves are partially justified by collective-action rationales.

Chapter 7 extends the book's gaze to other parts of the Constitution that are illuminated by the logics of collective action. Federal statutes that aim to solve multistate collective-action problems would have little impact without their enforcement against states and private parties that violate or seek to undermine them. Likewise, constitutional or congressional prohibitions on state legislation that undermines federal solutions or causes collective-action problems for the states would be largely meaningless without enforcement of these prohibitions to ensure the supremacy of federal law. Articles II and III create independent executive and judicial branches and authorize them to enforce federal law.

Article II also empowers the president to energetically conduct diplomacy and national-security operations—functions that the states and members of Congress alike could not perform without overcoming daunting collective-action problems. Article III gives the federal judiciary its own responsibilities in the areas of foreign relations and national security, as well as in the realm of domestic peace. By umpiring disputes with international or interstate dimensions, including when attempts to form interstate compacts fail, the federal courts solve or prevent collective-action problems for the states. The federal judiciary

---

[52] U.S. CONST. art. I, § 8, cl. 1.

16   THE COLLECTIVE-ACTION CONSTITUTION

also plays this role when it ensures the uniform interpretation of federal law. Article VI's Supremacy Clause and oath requirement for state officials advance the same supremacy objective as Article III by (1) helping ensure the efficacy of the solutions to collective-action problems provided in the Constitution itself, federal statutes, and treaties; and by (2) reinforcing the prohibitions on state conduct that compromise such solutions or generate collective-action problems—for example, in Article I, Section 10, dormant commerce doctrine, and several provisions of Article IV.

Chapter 8 turns to the Constitution's underappreciated role in helping define the constitutional relationship among the states themselves. The two initial sections of Article IV contain provisions that either limit what states may do or empower Congress to act. For example, the Full Faith and Credit Clause requires each state to give "Full Faith and Credit" to "the public Acts, Records, and judicial Proceedings of every other State." The Effects Clause, which immediately follows and which this book interprets in novel, collective-action terms, provides that "Congress may by general Laws prescribe the Manner in which such Acts, Records and Proceedings shall be proved, and the Effect thereof."[53] The Extradition Clause requires each state, upon request, to extradite individuals who have been charged with a crime in a sister state if the individual fled from justice in the sister state and was found in the state receiving the extradition request.[54] These provisions aim to secure political and economic union by preventing collective-action problems for the states. Distressingly, the same could have been said of the Fugitive Slave Clause, which required the return of enslaved human beings who had fled to sister states.[55] The collective-action rationale for exclusive federal power to enforce this clause underscores the significance of constitutional rights as a firm limit on what the federal government can do, and what state governments cannot do, to solve or prevent collective-action problems for the states.

The third section of Article IV turns from the movement of persons across state lines to the control over territory. The Territory Clause gives Congress exclusive power to dispose of and regulate federal lands and other property,[56] and the Admissions Clause gives Congress exclusive power to admit new states into the Union.[57] These clauses both empower the federal government to solve collective-action problems for the states and prevent states from causing them. Their placement together in the same section may reflect an original expectation that federal territories would eventually become states. This has not always

---

[53] U.S. CONST. art. IV, § 1.
[54] U.S. CONST. art. IV, § 2, cl. 2.
[55] U.S. CONST. art. IV, § 2, cl. 3, *superseded by* amend. XIII.
[56] U.S. CONST. art. IV, § 3, cl. 2.
[57] U.S. CONST. art. IV, § 3, cl. 1.

happened, however, which raises troubling questions about the democratic legitimacy of the contemporary American empire.

Chapter 9 turns to a primary role of the Constitution in modern America, although not before the twentieth century: protecting individual rights against infringement by states. Collective-action reasoning helps explain some important constitutional rights, including those secured by the dormant commerce principle (which individual businesspeople, corporations, and consumers can invoke); the Full Faith and Credit Clause (which litigants who have won court judgments in sister states can invoke); and, disgracefully, the Fugitive Slave Clause (which slaveowners once could invoke). Chapter 9 identifies several additional rights that not only protect individual liberty or equality but also prevent states from causing collective-action problems. They can be called "collective-action rights" because they help prevent collective-action problems for the states; as a result, collective-action reasoning helps define their scope. They are the rights protected by the Privileges and Immunities Clause—which, this book will controversially argue, should be subject to congressional override[58]—and the rights protected by the Republican Form of Government Clause,[59] as well as the right to enter and leave another state. Certain rights in the Bill of Rights must also be protected for Americans to be and feel safe exercising the right to travel to and through sister states.

Enforcement of most constitutional rights does not, however, primarily reflect the logics of collective action. Most importantly, the main structural achievement of the Reconstruction Amendments (and several that followed) was to empower the federal courts and Congress to regulate the internal policy choices of states on certain subjects regardless of collective-action problems facing the states. Most constitutional rights can be called "individual-action rights," meaning that they exist principally to protect people from unconstitutional individual action by their state governments, not to prevent states from causing collective-action problems; as a result, collective-action reasoning does not help define their scope. The parts of the Constitution that protect individual rights against government at all levels can be called the Reconstruction Constitution. Although the Collective-Action Constitution does not offer a primary explanation for most individual-action rights, a collective-action theory helps account for those individual-action rights that protect the integrity of the democratic process at the state and national levels. A democratically legitimate national political process justifies giving Congress, not individual states, the authority to decide whether there are collective-action problems in need of solving when states disagree, and the legitimacy of the national process is significantly

---

[58] U.S. CONST. art. IV, § 2, cl. 1.
[59] U.S. CONST. art. IV, § 4.

18 THE COLLECTIVE-ACTION CONSTITUTION

affected by the legitimacy of state processes. The Collective-Action Constitution also provides a secondary justification for constitutional equality rights, which must be protected to make meaningful the right to travel through sister states for members of racial and other minority groups.

Part III turns from interpreting the Constitution to perfecting it by making it easier for congressional majorities to solve collective-action problems for the states in modern times. With this goal in mind, this part assesses the wisdom of certain constitutional provisions and subconstitutional rules, given historical practice, modern developments, and contemporary political conditions. Using Article VII's sensible two-thirds requirement for ratification of the original Constitution as a baseline of comparison, Chapter 10 discusses other supermajority voting rules that must be satisfied before important powers may be exercised. These rules include proposing and approving constitutional amendments, a two-part process that overrepresents the states, effectively letting them vote twice. These rules also encompass concluding treaties, a procedure as difficult for states in Congress to use under the Constitution as it was under the Articles of Confederation. There is a tradeoff between facilitating collective action by states and preventing the exploitation of a minority of states by the majority, and the Constitution typically negotiates this tension by allowing federal powers to be exercised by majority vote, the Constitution's default voting rule. These two supermajority requirements have made use of the associated powers increasingly rare and have prompted the development of workarounds: the accomplishment of constitutional change almost always through judicial interpretation and state building by the political branches instead of constitutional amendments, and the overwhelming use of executive agreements instead of treaties. Although collective-action logics cannot identify the right voting rule, they can illuminate the tradeoffs involved and raise questions about where the Constitution sets the threshold for collective action by states. Further, the development of workarounds and other considerations suggest that these supermajority rules are incompatible with the perceived needs of modern American governance.

Two other supermajority voting rules in the Constitution empower presidents to undermine congressional solutions to multistate collective-action problems. If presidents conclude that Congress is encroaching on their office, they can respond by following the Framers' plan and vetoing the offending bills. This is the primary reason why presidents were given the veto power. By contrast, if Congress concludes that a president is encroaching on its authority—for example, by legislating via executive order or acting despite what Congress views as a valid congressional prohibition—it can pass a bill to address the situation, but it will almost certainly be vetoed by the president, in which case the bill will not become law unless two-thirds supermajorities in each house vote to override the veto. The Framers did not anticipate that presidents might abuse their power vis-à-vis Congress and not just be the victims of such abuse, and so the Framers did not worry about the difficulty in this situation of overriding a presidential veto by meeting strict supermajority requirements. Nor did the Framers anticipate dramatically expanded executive power and political parties, let alone polarized, antagonistic parties, extreme partisan gerrymanders, and a closely divided polity.[60] These developments make it extraordinarily difficult both to override vetoes and to remove an impeached president by securing the support of two-thirds of the Senate. These two supermajority rules likely make collective action by members of Congress—which helps protect federal statutes that solve collective-action problems for the states—too difficult to accomplish in modern America.

Chapter 11 examines the operation of the Constitution's system of separated and interrelated powers in contemporary times. It is one thing to argue that the Constitution was intended, and is designed, to render the federal government operating through majority rule more likely to solve multistate collective-action problems than the states operating through unanimity rule. It is another thing to show that this is generally true in practice. As George Washington implied in his letter to the Confederation Congress that begins this book, to protect state autonomy and individual liberty, the Framers created a bicameral legislature and a separation-of-powers system, both of which make it more difficult to legislate than in a unicameral legislature and a parliamentary system. But the Framers did not imagine that the availability of veto threats would come to dominate the policymaking process in situations having nothing to do with perceived encroachments on the presidency or bills that the president thinks unconstitutional. Nor were the Framers responsible for modern subconstitutional "veto gates" in Congress, especially the Senate filibuster, which makes it even harder to legislate. Finally, as noted, the Framers did not foresee the polarized nature of contemporary American politics.

These developments have meant that bicameralism and the separation (and interrelation) of powers often do not merely qualify Congress's ability to legislate. The horizontal structure and contemporary politics likely make it too hard for Congress to do so, particularly given the magnitude and geographic scope of the problems facing the nation and the extent to which Americans look mainly to

---

[60] On partisan polarization, see NOLAN MCCARTY, POLARIZATION: WHAT EVERYONE NEEDS TO KNOW (2019); and Keith T. Poole & Howard Rosenthal, *D-Nominate After 10 Years: A Comparative Update to Congress: A Political-Economic History of Roll-Call Voting*, 26 LEG. STUD. Q. 5 (2001). On partisan animosity or "affective polarization," see Shanto Iyengar et al., *The Origins and Consequences of Affective Polarization in the United States*, 22 ANN. REV. POL. SCI. 129 (2019); and Shanto Iyengar, Gaurav Sood, & Yphtach Lelkes, *Affect, Not Ideology: A Social Identity Perspective on Polarization*, 76 PUB. OPIN. Q. 405 (2012). On razor's-edge elections, see FRANCES E. LEE, INSECURE MAJORITIES: CONGRESS AND THE PERPETUAL CAMPAIGN (2016). Chapter 11 discusses polarization and related phenomena.

the federal government, not the states, to solve them. The Constitution's greatest defect in modern times is probably that Congress often cannot execute its legislative responsibilities in the constitutional scheme. A result has been power shifts from Congress to the executive branch, the federal courts, and the states. The main workaround for congressional gridlock has been more frequent unilateral action by the executive, which is less enduring and far reaching than legislation, and which poses risks of democratic deficits and backsliding that congressional power does not. Other partial and potentially worrisome workarounds include efforts by federal courts to "update" the meaning of federal statutes and greater exercises of state authority. Sufficient solutions to the problem of gridlock may not exist any time soon, given the practical impossibility of amending the Constitution, the unlikelihood that veto practice will become more restrained, and the long periods required for political realignments to occur. Ending the legislative filibuster in the Senate by majority vote would, however, have the likely salutary (but not cost-free) consequence of changing the typical voting threshold in this chamber from a three-fifths supermajority to majority rule.

Although it is likely too hard to legislate in the current era, the constitutional structure still has much to commend it relative to the alternative of relying on the states to act collectively outside Congress. When problems are national or international in scope, the relevant comparison is not between Congress's ability to combat a problem and one state's ability to do so, but between the ability of the political branches to act and the ability of the states to act collectively through unanimous agreement. Collective-action problems would almost certainly be more severe if the federal government were dissolved and states had to unanimously agree to protect the environment; regulate interstate and foreign commerce; build interstate infrastructure; conclude international agreements; contribute revenue to a common treasury and troops to a common military (or coordinate separate militaries); disburse funds held in common; respond to economic downturns; provide a minimum safety net; and handle pandemics, among many other things. Congress still legislates today, and it does so much more frequently than most (let alone all) states form interstate compacts.

The conclusion identifies key takeaways of this study and different audiences that stand to benefit from accepting the central claims of the book. Constitutionally conscientious legislators and executive-branch officials, both federal and state, may better execute their responsibilities if they are more mindful of the collective-action logics that explain and justify much of the Constitution. Similarly, concerned citizens may reorient elements of their civic participation—what they demand of different levels of government—if they bear these logics in mind. Moreover, because this book privileges breadth of coverage of the Constitution and constitutional law over depth, there remains room for scholars to examine more closely the collective-action dimensions (or not) of specific clauses, sections, principles, decisions, and ideas—including those neglected here.

Finally, the book cautions the Supreme Court and other federal courts—both of which can be quite assertive—not to substantially restrict federal power in the years ahead, whether through constitutional-law holdings contracting congressional power or administrative-law decisions diminishing agency power. The nation will continue to face pressing problems that spill across state (or national) borders, so federal action will be needed to address them effectively. In general, the federal government has the authority to act. And given the horizontal structure and the era of partisan polarization and animosity in which Americans will continue to live, there are already major impediments to the ability and willingness of members of Congress to overcome their own collective-action problems and legislate. Especially in modern times, legal doctrine should reflect, not reject, the Constitution's main structural logics—its collective-action objectives.

PART I
THINKING CONSTITUTIONALLY AND COLLECTIVELY

1

Foundations

McCulloch

Introduction

It is widely agreed that the Constitution gives Congress implied powers, whether via an expansive interpretation of the enumerated powers themselves or via the grant of authority in the Necessary and Proper Clause "[t]o make all Laws which shall be necessary and proper for carrying into Execution" the other federal powers granted by the Constitution.[1] These implied powers are the constitutional basis for almost every federal law creating the machinery of government and for a broad range of substantive statutes, including national security laws, antidiscrimination laws, labor laws, criminal laws, securities laws, and environmental laws. Both historically and today, however, the scope of Congress's implied powers has been controversial. What kind or degree of connection with an enumerated power makes a federal law necessary and proper for carrying this power into execution? In the 1790s during the Washington administration, and again almost thirty years later in the US Supreme Court, attempts to create or reauthorize a national bank to aid the country's finances produced competing views of the kind or degree of connection with an enumerated power that renders a federal statute a permissible means of implementing this power.

The Court gave its answer to this question in *McCulloch v. Maryland* (1819),[2] which began as a lawsuit filed by Maryland against James W. McCulloch, the cashier of the Maryland branch of the Second National Bank. Maryland sued in state court to collect a $100 fine, which was the penalty for circulating a bank note without the required Maryland stamp. The penalty could be avoided if the bank paid a $15,000 annual tax to the state.[3] *McCulloch* became a test case for the constitutionality of the bank. Moreover, if the bank were declared constitutional, *McCulloch* would also be a test case for the authority of states to tax branches of the bank within their borders.

Chief Justice Marshall's magisterial opinion for the Court in *McCulloch*, which broadly upheld Congress's power to create the bank and categorically barred

---

[1] U.S. Const. art. I, § 8, cl. 18.

[2] 17 U.S. (4 Wheat.) 316 (1819).

[3] Daniel A. Farber, *The Story of* McCulloch: *Banking on National Power, in* Constitutional Law Stories 33, 44 (Michael C. Dorf ed., 2004).

The Collective-Action Constitution. Neil S. Siegel, Oxford University Press. © Neil S. Siegel 2024.
DOI: 10.1093/oso/9780197760963.003.0002

26 THE COLLECTIVE-ACTION CONSTITUTION

states from taxing it, has justly been called "the greatest opinion written by the single greatest figure in the history of constitutional law."[4] It commends occasional reexamination by judges and constitutional law scholars who are open to learning from it, because each encounter offers fresh illumination. Consulting multiple "modalities" of constitutional interpretation, Marshall concludes that the US Constitution embodies a fundamental belief in "the overriding importance of national union as against the centrifugal forces of state parochialism," and he interprets the Constitution in light of this purpose, in conjunction with other modalities, where its language permits. He thereby models how, in cases that cannot be decided simply by consulting the constitutional text, we are to interpret the Constitution—"how we are to think constitutionally."[5] Leveraging his pluralist approach, Marshall explains why, as a matter of democratic principle, the federal government is supreme within its sphere of action and why, if an end is within Congress's sphere, it has a wide choice of means to accomplish the end. Marshall also explains why, for the same democratic reasons, the states may not interfere with the functioning of the federal government.

For five reasons, *McCulloch* is foundational to the collective-action account of the Constitution developed in this book. First, Marshall's understanding of the main structural purpose of the Constitution can be stated in collective-action terms, and the book adopts his pluralist approach to interpretation. Second, Marshall articulates a theory of the democratic legitimacy of the federal government that is critical to justifying federal authority to settle disagreements among states about whether there is a collective-action problem in need of solving. When problems transcend state borders, the federal government enjoys superior democratic legitimacy over individual states because federal institutions— especially Congress—are where the interests of all states and all Americans are represented. Third, Marshall's broad understanding of Congress's implied powers advances the Constitution's collective-action objectives in several ways. Fourth, a collective-action problem is at the root of the democratic-process failure Marshall identifies as cause to conclude that states may not tax federal instrumentalities. This democratic deficit reappears in much later cases and legal scholarship, and it helps justify constitutional restrictions on state authority to cause collective-action problems.

Finally, and unfortunately, the implications of Marshall's reasoning for Native Americans offers a sobering reminder. A collective-action theory, like any structural theory, cannot ensure that the nature and scope of the powers it justifies will always be used in morally defensible ways. There are historical and

---

[4] H. Jefferson Powell, Targeting Americans: The Constitutionality of the U.S. Drone War 23 (2016).

[5] *Id.*

contemporary reasons to believe, however, that American society will be better off on balance, morally and otherwise, if the account offered here is adopted instead of one that would severely restrict federal power or impose no structural limits on it—especially if a collective-action theory is constrained by vigorous protection of constitutional rights.

For all these reasons, this book begins with *McCulloch*, not with the Founding history mentioned in the Introduction and discussed at length in subsequent chapters. Although the presentation is thematic, not chronological, in this instance there is little tension between the two. Marshall's opinion borrows heavily from Hamilton's reasoning decades earlier, and both capture essential truths about the Constitution as revealed first originally and then in relatively early practice.[6]

Constitutional Purposes and Pluralist Interpretation

This initial section has two objectives. First, it examines the main structural purpose that Marshall attributes to the Constitution. Second, it analyzes Marshall's approach to interpreting the Constitution. Marshall's method guides the structural theory offered in this book.

The Primary Structural Purpose of the Constitution

In considering whether Congress can incorporate a national bank even though no provision expressly authorizes it to do so, Marshall underscores the nature of the legal instrument that the Court must construe. "A constitution, to contain an accurate detail of all the subdivisions of which its great powers will admit, and of all the means by which they may be carried into execution, would partake of the prolixity of a legal code, and could scarcely be embraced by the human mind." "Its nature," he writes, demands "that only its great outlines should be marked, its important objects designated, and the minor ingredients which compose those objects, be deduced from the nature of the objects themselves." He infers that the Framers had "this idea" in mind not only "from the nature of the instrument, but from the language." In deciding the issue presented, he thus insists, "we must never forget that it is a constitution we are expounding."[7] Marshall here argues that the distinctive nature of a constitution requires interpreters to pay closer

---

[6] ALEXANDER HAMILTON, *Opinion on the Constitutionality of the Bill to Establish a National Bank (Feb. 23, 1791), in* CONTEXTS OF THE CONSTITUTION: A DOCUMENTARY COLLECTION ON PRINCIPLES OF AMERICAN CONSTITUTIONAL LAW 544–70 (Neil H. Cogan ed., 1999).

[7] *McCulloch*, 17 U.S. (4 Wheat.) at 407.

28 THE COLLECTIVE-ACTION CONSTITUTION

attention to its purpose than to the purpose of other legal texts. By attending to its purpose, Marshall implies, one does not dishonor its text; on the contrary, one respects it by registering that the most appropriate rules for interpreting it depend on the kind of text it is.

It is not clear, however, why the nature of every federal constitution, no matter the circumstances out of which it arose or the precision of its language, requires the powers of the national government to be interpreted broadly. Indeed, in the next paragraph, Marshall clarifies that he is not really offering an account of the nature of federal constitutions generally, but of the US Constitution specifically. "Although, among the enumerated powers of government, we do not find the word 'bank' or 'incorporation,'" he acknowledges, "we find the great powers, to lay and collect taxes; to borrow money; to regulate commerce; to declare and conduct a war; and to raise and support armies and navies." Generalizing, he writes that "[t]he sword and the purse, all the external relations, and no inconsiderable portion of the industry of the nation, are intrusted to its government."[8] In his view, the Constitution's basic purpose is to authorize expansive federal power to accomplish important ends.

Also in Marshall's view, however, Congress is not granted limitless authority. "This government is acknowledged by all, to be one of enumerated powers," he writes. "The principle, that it can exercise only the powers granted to it, would seem too apparent, to have required to be enforced by all those arguments, which its enlightened friends, while it was depending before the people, found it necessary to urge; that principle is now universally admitted."[9] Here, Marshall agrees that the principle of enumeration—of federal powers that are not limitless—is also part of the constitutional design. Scholars who criticize "enumerationism"—the idea that the Constitution creates a national government of (internally) limited, enumerated powers—have insufficiently appreciated the significance of this acknowledgment by Marshall.[10] His concession is compatible with his robust view of Congress's implied powers (discussed below) in part because the primary textual source of Congress's implied powers—the Necessary and Proper Clause—is one of Congress's enumerated powers, as Marshall noted a few years later,[11] and not every conceivable federal law falls within its scope. Even if, by construction, Congress would have the same incidental powers without the Necessary and Proper Clause as this clause gives it by express grant, the enumeration principle

---

[8] *Id.* at 407.

[9] *Id.* at 405; *see id.* (conceding that "the government of the Union" is "limited in its powers" in arguing that it "is supreme within its sphere of action").

[10] *See* David S. Schwartz, McCulloch v. Maryland *and the Incoherence of Enumerationism*, 19 GEO. J.L. & PUB. POL'Y 25 (2021); *see also* Richard Primus & Roderick M. Hills, Jr., *Suspect Spheres, Not Enumerated Powers: A Guide to Leaving the Lamppost*, 119 MICH. L. REV. 1431 (2021); Richard A. Primus, *The Limits of Enumeration*, 124 YALE L.J. 576 (2014).

[11] *Gibbons v. Ogden*, 22 U.S. (9 Wheat.) 1, 187 (1824).

FOUNDATIONS   29

would be defeated only if any possible federal statute would fit within Marshall's understanding of incidental powers. There is scant reason to think that this is true or that Marshall thought as much. Indeed, as explained below, Marshall distinguished incidental from nonincidental powers in *McCulloch* itself.

Marshall explains that the Constitution has the purpose of granting expansive, albeit not limitless, federal power because "[t]he exigencies of the nation" require it. His reasoning, which will require unpacking, warrants extensive quotation:

> [A] government, intrusted with such ample powers, on the due execution of which the happiness and prosperity of the nation so vitally depends, must also be intrusted with ample means for their execution. The power being given, it is the interest of the nation to facilitate its execution. It can never be their interest, and cannot be presumed to have been their intention, to clog and embarrass its execution, by withholding the most appropriate means. Throughout this vast republic, from the St. Croix to the Gulf of Mexico, from the Atlantic to the Pacific, revenue is to be collected and expended, armies are to be marched and supported. The exigencies of the nation may require, that the treasure raised in the north should be transported to the south, that raised in the east, conveyed to the west, or that this order should be reversed. Is that construction of the constitution to be preferred, which would render these operations difficult, hazardous and expensive? Can we adopt that construction (unless the words imperiously require it), which would impute to the framers of that instrument, when granting these powers for the public good, the intention of impeding their exercise, by withholding a choice of means? If, indeed, such be the mandate of the constitution, we have only to obey; but that instrument does not profess to enumerate the means by which the powers it confers may be executed; nor does it prohibit the creation of a corporation, if the existence of such a being be essential, to the beneficial exercise of those powers.[12]

Marshall deems it unfaithful to the Constitution's letter and spirit to impose semantic straightjackets on the means available to Congress to meet national "exigencies."

Marshall makes several specific points. First, one must accept the controlling authority of clear constitutional text. If "the words imperiously require" a particular answer to a question, he writes, "we have only to obey." It does not matter whether such words prevent the full accomplishment of a constitutional purpose, even the Constitution's most fundamental purpose. Second, however, the language of the text does not limit Congress to choosing only means indispensable to the exercise of an enumerated power. He observes that "there is no

---

[12] *McCulloch*, 17 U.S. (4 Wheat.) at 408–09.

30 THE COLLECTIVE-ACTION CONSTITUTION

phrase in the instrument which, like the articles of confederation, excludes incidental or implied powers; and which requires that everything granted shall be expressly and minutely described."[13] In contrast to Article II of the Articles, "[e]ven the 10th Amendment, which was framed for the purpose of quieting the excessive jealousies which had been excited, omits the word 'expressly'" before the term "delegated" in declaring that powers not delegated to the federal government or withdrawn from the states are reserved to the states.[14]

Third, because the language does not compel the Southern constitutionalist conclusion espoused by Maryland, questions about the scope of Congress's powers "depend on a fair construction of the whole instrument."[15] The Constitution gives Congress "great powers" to meet "[t]he exigencies of the nation,"[16] Marshall reasons, so one can confidently infer that Congress can create a bank as a convenient means to executing several ends enumerated in Article I, Section 8. One need not rely on the Necessary and Proper Clause (discussed below). As Professor Charles Black observes, Marshall invokes this clause only after concluding that the bank is permissible and only to confirm his "general reasoning."[17] Marshall's invocation of "great powers" to meet national "exigencies" echoes language from the Preamble and the opening clause of Section 8: Congress can provide for "the common Defence and general Welfare."

Fourth, the manner in which Marshall seeks to discern the purpose of the Constitution when the text is not dispositive reflects his interpretive approach, which is methodologically pluralist, meaning that he uses multiple kinds of constitutional arguments. Notwithstanding the significant influence of originalism in modern interpretive debates, Marshall's approach has always been dominant.[18] For example, self-described originalist justices and scholars today, although they rely on originalist methods more often than their nonoriginalist colleagues, use

---

[13] *Id.* at 406.

[14] *Id. See* ARTICLES OF CONFEDERATION of 1781, art. II ("Each State retains its sovereignty, freedom, and independence, and every power, jurisdiction, and right, which is not by this Confederation *expressly* delegated to the United States in Congress assembled" (emphasis added.).).

[15] *McCulloch*, 17 U.S. (4 Wheat.) at 406. On Southern constitutionalism, *see* Farber, *supra* note 3, at 63 (viewing "*McCulloch* . . . as part of the battle over states' rights that began with the Virginia and Kentucky Resolutions and ended at Appomattox Courthouse"). Southern constitutionalist commitments, some of which were espoused by Jefferson, Madison, Virginia judge Spencer Roane, and John C. Calhoun, were the state compact theory of the Constitution, the insulation of state courts from appellate review by the U.S. Supreme Court, state interposition against the federal government, state nullification of federal laws, and state secession. *Id.*

[16] *McCulloch*, 17 U.S. (4 Wheat.) at 407.

[17] *Id.* at 411. *See* CHARLES L. BLACK, JR., STRUCTURE AND RELATIONSHIP IN CONSTITUTIONAL LAW 13–14 (1969).

[18] Stephen M. Griffin, *Pluralism in Constitutional Interpretation*, 72 TEX. L. REV. 1753, 1768 (1994) ("The pluralism that characterizes the Supreme Court's jurisprudence has deep roots in the nature of American constitutionalism: American lawyers and judges began using the multiple sources of American law to illuminate the task of constitutional interpretation from the very beginning of the Court's jurisprudence.").

FOUNDATIONS   31

most or all "modalities" of constitutional argument that participants in American constitutional practice have long invoked in interpreting the Constitution.[19] Many originalist commentators distinguish constitutional interpretation, which focuses on the original meaning of the text, from constitutional construction, which takes place when the text is unclear.[20] For example, Professors Randy Barnett and Evan Bernick advocate consulting the original "spirit" or purpose of the Constitution as part of constitutional construction.[21] This book's use of the term "purpose" overlaps with that of Professors Barnett and Bernick because the book builds its approach to constitutional interpretation from its description of the Constitution's main original structural purpose. Because this book nonetheless offers a nonoriginalist account, it is important to the project that the original purpose is also the Constitution's primary traditional *and* contemporary structural purpose. The book would not endorse this original purpose as both descriptively accurate and normatively attractive if it had proven over time to be damaging to the country. But quite the opposite is true.

Pluralist Constitutional Interpretation

As noted, Marshall respects and invokes the constitutional text, including by identifying rules for interpreting this kind of text, as textualist arguments do. He also references the presumed intentions of the Framers of the Constitution, as certain originalist arguments do. For example, in the long quotation above, he writes that it "cannot be presumed to have been their intention" to thwart the execution of federal powers, and he asks rhetorically whether we can "impute to the framers of that instrument" a contrary interpretation. He does not, however,

---

[19] For discussions of various modalities of constitutional interpretation, *see* PHILIP BOBBITT, CONSTITUTIONAL INTERPRETATION 11–22 (1991) (discussing historical, textual, structural, precedential, ethical, and prudential modalities); JACK M. BALKIN, LIVING ORIGINALISM 4–6, 341–42 n.2 (2011) (endorsing all modalities but privileging original semantic meaning, which he deems often under-determinate); Jack M. Balkin, *The New Originalism and the Uses of History*, 82 FORDHAM L. REV. 641, 659–61 (2013) (offering a more expansive list); and Curtis A. Bradley & Neil S. Siegel, *Constructed Constraint and the Constitutional Text*, 64 DUKE L.J. 1213, 1239–43 (2015) (adding purposive argument to Bobbitt's list, distinguishing historical practice from judicial precedent, and distinguishing pre-ratification history from post-ratification history).

[20] BALKIN, *supra* note 19, at 3–6, 341 n.2; KEITH E. WHITTINGTON, CONSTITUTIONAL CONSTRUCTION: DIVIDED POWERS AND CONSTITUTIONAL MEANING 5–9 (1999); Randy E. Barnett, *Interpretation and Construction*, 34 HARV. J.L. & PUB. POL'Y 65 (2011); Mitchell N. Berman, *Constitutional Constructions and Constitutional Decision Rules: Thoughts on the Carving of Implementation Space*, 27 CONST. COMMENT. 39 (2010); Mitchell N. Berman, *Constitutional Decision Rules*, 90 VA. L. REV. 1 (2004); Lawrence B. Solum, *Originalism and Constitutional Construction*, 82 FORDHAM L. REV. 453 (2013).

[21] RANDY E. BARNETT & EVAN D. BERNICK, THE ORIGINAL MEANING OF THE FOURTEENTH AMENDMENT: ITS LETTER AND SPIRIT 15 (2021) (arguing that "recourse to the original spirit [or purpose] is the *best available* means of implementing the original Constitution when the text runs out").

32   THE COLLECTIVE-ACTION CONSTITUTION

insist that every word or phrase in the Constitution must be understood in light of its original semantic meaning, or how the Framers originally expected it to be applied, or how it was originally understood by the ratifiers. This may be because, unlike Jeffersonians, Marshall views the Constitution mainly as empowering the federal government, not as limiting it, even as he understands that it does both.[22]

Instead of adopting a narrow, "clause-bound" textualism or originalism to constrain federal power, Marshall uses multiple methods of interpretation.[23] First and foremost, he is a structuralist and so is deeply interested in the purpose of the Constitution as a whole or in important part, especially Section 8. Structuralism seeks to discern the purpose of part or all of the Constitution, but structuralism is a different modality from purposivism when purposivism is used to describe an emphasis on the purpose of a specific constitutional provision, in contrast to the semantic meaning of its language. Purposivism in this latter sense is clause-bound in a way that structuralism does not tend to be.[24] Marshall aims to understand how the constitutional system is supposed to function by drawing inferences from how the Constitution allocates and limits regulatory authority among different government institutions (here, vertically) and from how a group of provisions serves a common purpose (here, those in Section 8). He interprets the Constitution, and Section 8 in particular, as a whole. His structuralism drives him to discern the purpose of the Constitution when the text is not enough to settle the matter before him.

In addition to the text, pre-ratification history, and constitutional structure, Marshall looks to historical practice as a source of illumination. He begins his opinion with the customary practice of the political branches, emphasizing that the question presented is not novel. On the contrary, he underscores, there were high-quality debates in Congress and the executive branch concerning the constitutionality of the first and second national banks, and almost three decades of historical practice inform his conviction that a bank is within Congress's powers.[25] He concedes "that a bold and daring usurpation might be resisted, after an acquiescence still longer and more complete than this."[26] But he insists that historical practice warrants significant weight in constitutional interpretation,

---

[22] POWELL, *supra* note 4, at 22–26 (distinguishing Marshall's purposivism/structuralism from Jefferson's "rigorously text-bound thinking" based upon their disagreement over whether the primary purpose of the Constitution is to empower the federal government or to limit it).

[23] Professor John Hart Ely coined the phrase "clause-bound interpretivism" and rejected it as impossible. JOHN HART ELY, DEMOCRACY AND DISTRUST: A THEORY OF JUDICIAL REVIEW 11–41 (1980).

[24] Bradley & Siegel, *supra* note 19, at 1239–40.

[25] *McCulloch*, 17 U.S. (4 Wheat.) at 401 ("The principle now contested was introduced at a very early period of our history, has been recognised by many successive legislatures, and has been acted upon by the judicial department, in cases of peculiar delicacy, as a law of undoubted obligation.").

[26] *Id.*

FOUNDATIONS   33

at least when considering structural issues (as in *McCulloch*), as opposed to individual rights.[27] Supporting Marshall's distinction between structure and rights is the potential peril of arguing that individuals or groups should be denied protection from government action just because they have long been denied such protection. In the rights context, what is customary is more likely to be oppressive than in the structural context.[28]

Giving weight to historical practice is often called the "historical gloss" approach to constitutional interpretation, based on Justice Frankfurter's discussion of the idea in his concurring opinion in the *Youngstown* steel seizure case.[29] "It is an inadmissibly narrow conception of American constitutional law," he wrote, "to confine it to the words of the Constitution and to disregard the gloss which life has written upon them."[30] There are several reasons why historical practice might matter, especially regarding structural issues. First, from a Burkean consequentialist perspective, long-standing practice may evidence an arrangement that has worked reasonably well; the practice may reflect the realities of American governance and changes over time in the perceived needs of such governance, and deferring to it may serve reliance interests, expectation interests, stability of governance, and settlement.[31] Second, there may be limits on decisional capacity if other modalities of interpretation do not offer much guidance, so the practice may offer interpreters the most objective decisional material. Third, in line with departmentalism,[32] interpreters (particularly judges) may credit the long-standing interpretations of the political branches—especially when Congress

---

[27] *Id.* ("[A] doubtful question, one on which human reason may pause, and the human judgment be suspended, in the decision of which the great principles of liberty are not concerned, but the respective powers of those who are equally the representatives of the people, are to be adjusted; if not put at rest by the practice of the government, ought to receive a considerable impression from that practice.")

[28] Curtis A. Bradley & Neil S. Siegel, *Historical Gloss, Madisonian Liquidation, and the Originalism Debate*, 106 Va. L. Rev. 1, 37–39 (2020) (explaining why resort to historical practice is generally more problematic and less necessary in individual-rights cases than in structural cases).

[29] Professor Curtis Bradley and this author have argued that, to credit historical practice in constitutional interpretation, three requirements must be met: (1) governmental practice, (2) long-standing duration, and (3) acquiescence, which requires at least reasonable stability in the practice. The third requirement demands that the practice have existed for a significant number of years without producing continued interbranch contestation, but it does not demand interbranch constitutional agreement. *Id.* at 17–31.

[30] Youngstown Sheet & Tube Co. v. Sawyer, 343 U.S. 579, 610 (1952) (Frankfurter, J., concurring). In this case, the Court declared unconstitutional President Truman's executive order directing his secretary of commerce to seize and operate most of the nation's steel mills, thereby maintaining steel production amid a labor dispute during the Korean War.

[31] Burkean approaches to constitutional interpretation emphasize long-standing understandings and traditions. *See, e.g.,* Cass R. Sunstein, *Burkean Minimalism*, 105 Mich. L. Rev. 353 (2006); Ernest Young, *Rediscovering Conservatism: Burkean Political Theory and Constitutional Interpretation*, 72 N.C. L. Rev. 619, 664 (1994).

[32] Departmentalism, in contrast to judicial supremacy, "is the theory that each branch of government has the power to apply its own interpretation of the Constitution to its own actions." Daniel A. Farber & Neil S. Siegel, United States Constitutional Law 29 (2d ed. 2024).

34 THE COLLECTIVE-ACTION CONSTITUTION

and the president agree—to moderate the counter-majoritarian aspects of judicial review, which can be especially strong when unelected judges overturn the established constitutional views of elected officials.[33]

An additional reason for consulting practice is especially relevant here. It can inform one's understanding of the purposes of the Constitution, in whole or in part. By analogy to a machine, if one wants to understand how the constitutional system is supposed to function, it makes sense to investigate how the system has in fact functioned. As Frankfurter wrote in *Youngstown*, "The Constitution is a framework for government. Therefore the way the framework has consistently operated fairly establishes that it has operated according to its true nature."[34] Put differently, historical practice may inform structural interpretation, either by reinforcing or by limiting the structural inferences that one might otherwise draw. Along similar lines, judicial precedents such as *McCulloch*, which are often available, may inform structural interpretation, even if relevant precedent was unavailable when *McCulloch* was decided.[35]

Marshall also makes prudential (or consequentialist) arguments of a limited sort. In the long quotation above, Marshall defends broad federal power by invoking "the happiness and prosperity of the nation," "the interest of the nation," "[t]he exigencies of the nation," and the need to avoid interpretations that would "clog and embarrass" the execution of Congress's powers or "render [governmental] operations difficult, hazardous and expensive." These references are consequentialist, but they do not reflect a freewheeling consequentialism, which would compare the overall social costs and benefits of alternative interpretations. Marshall evaluates the consequences of alternative interpretations in light of the purpose he ascribes to the Constitution. He asks whether a proposed interpretation would help accomplish this purpose or thwart it. This is a different inquiry from a utilitarian one into whether an interpretation would make the world better from various perspectives, such as economic growth, distributive justice, the tenets of a particular religion, or a certain conception of human flourishing. It is also true, however, that Marshall is reading the Constitution in part so that it makes practical and political theoretical sense for the short term and the long term. This necessarily means that his own normative commitments partially inform his interpretation of the Constitution.

---

[33] For discussion of these justifications for consulting historical practice, see Bradley & Siegel, *supra* note 28, at 23–26. For the initial statement, see Curtis A. Bradley, *Doing Gloss*, 84 U. Chi. L. Rev. 59 (2017). On "the counter-majoritarian difficulty," see Alexander M. Bickel, The Least Dangerous Branch: The Supreme Court at the Bar of Politics 16 (2d ed. 1986) (1962).

[34] *Youngstown Sheet & Tube Co.*, 343 U.S. at 610 (Frankfurter, J., concurring).

[35] Professor David Strauss's "common law constitutionalism" is the leading theory that commends incremental interpretation of the Constitution in light of judicial precedent and tradition. David A. Strauss, The Living Constitution (2010); David A. Strauss, *Common Law Constitutional Interpretation*, 63 U. Chi. L. Rev. 877 (1996).

FOUNDATIONS 35

Finally, in the long quotation, Marshall makes a subtle ethos argument. Ethos arguments tell a story about national identity. They interpret the Constitution in light of certain understandings of the meaning, character, or destiny of the nation—its most fundamental commitments and values.[36] As Professors Jack Balkin and Sanford Levinson observe, when Marshall references the movements of American tax collectors, troops, and treasure in every direction—"from the St. Croix to the Gulf of Mexico, from the Atlantic to the Pacific"—he describes national borders that do not exist when he is writing.[37] He declares the (manifest) destiny of the country. His contested conception of the American ethos informs, although it does not exclusively determine, the purpose that he ascribes to the Constitution.

The arguments in this book are built on the interpretive foundations laid in *McCulloch*. Another way of describing the main purpose Marshall attributes to the Constitution is that it authorizes the federal government to solve many kinds of collective-action problems that would arise for the states if they sought to accomplish various objectives, including and especially in the areas of taxation, spending, borrowing, interstate commerce, foreign commerce, and national defense. In addition, the book supports its interpretations of the Constitution with methodologically pluralist arguments. It closely attends to the text, and it often uses originalist argumentation and evidence. But it does not offer a solely originalist account. Rather, original intentions, meanings, and purposes—like historical practice and judicial precedent that developed and endured long after ratification—inform how we should understand the purposes of the Constitution today, and thus how we should decide interpretive questions when the text is not fully determinate or does not say enough to decide the issue.

Relatedly, also like *McCulloch*, this book pays special attention to the constitutional structure. It conceives of this structure as conferring broad but not limitless federal power to solve multistate collective-action problems, and as preventing states from undermining federal interventions or causing collective-action problems. The book relies on other modalities, including historical practice and judicial precedent, as evidence of the soundness of these structural inferences. And it examines the consequences of alternative interpretations for the maintenance of this structural arrangement, which was designed to enable the Constitution "to endure for ages to come, and, consequently, to be adapted to the various *crises* of human affairs."[38]

The conception of the American ethos that informs the account offered here is partly nationalist and partly pragmatic. Both parts are contestable and partially

[36] Hanna Fenichel Pitkin, *The Idea of a Constitution*, 37 J. LEGAL EDUC. 167 (1987).

[37] Jack M. Balkin & Sanford Levinson, *The Canons of Constitutional Law*, 111 HARV. L. REV. 963, 987 (1998).

[38] *McCulloch*, 17 U.S. (4 Wheat.) at 415.

36 THE COLLECTIVE-ACTION CONSTITUTION

aspirational. The nationalist part views most Americans as generally committed to political and economic union over the pursuit of local, parochial interests. Americans are not always nationalist in their political vision; they—and their state legislatures—can be parochial. But a nationalist conception of collective identity views most Americans as identifying less as citizens of states and more as, well, Americans—although they may identify as both. Put differently, if "no taxation without representation" is an original component of the American creed, most Americans would oppose being taxed without being represented in the legislature doing the taxing, and they generally respect that they must refrain from taxing fellow Americans who are unrepresented in the body levying the tax. As discussed toward the end of this chapter, state parochialism essentially taxes Americans who are not residents of the state.

The pragmatic conception of the national ethos animating this book views Americans as a relatively practical people who look to government to help solve serious problems, even when they disagree about what those problems are, how they should be solved, and how much government intervention is appropriate. True, Americans believe in the vertical division of authority between the federal government and the states, and in the horizontal divisions of authority among the states and among the branches of the national government. But on a pragmatic account of the national ethos, Americans today, like Americans past, tend to care less that government power be bound by formal limits to protect liberty and more that problems be addressed by the level, branch, or agency of government that can do so most effectively.[39]

Negotiating Conflicts among Modalities and Purposes

Most often, the modalities of constitutional interpretation are used, like strands in a rope, to strengthen one's overall argument.[40] But it is also true that, depending on the issue, different modalities can point in conflicting directions. Marshall does not fully acknowledge this truth, but later chapters identify when the Constitution's primary structural purpose should be qualified by other modalities and structural purposes. It is well understood from debates over statutory interpretation that the language of a legal text can encompass several potentially conflicting purposes. It is thus unsound to interpret such a text,

---

[39] Professor Jerry Mashaw emphasizes the existence, from the beginning of the national government under the Constitution, of a pragmatic Congress and Executive that focused on effectively solving problems of governance by leveraging whatever tools were available and inventing new ones along the way. JERRY L. MASHAW, CREATING THE ADMINISTRATIVE CONSTITUTION: THE LOST ONE HUNDRED YEARS OF AMERICAN ADMINISTRATIVE LAW (2012).

[40] For a defense of this interpretive practice, see *Richard H. Fallon, Jr., A Constructivist Coherence Theory of Constitutional Interpretation*, 100 HARV. L. REV. 1189 (1987).

including a constitutional text, as requiring the pursuit of one purpose regardless of its language and the consequences for other purposes.[41]

That said, the primary structural purpose of the Constitution is to enable the federal government to solve collective-action problems for the states and to disable the states from undermining federal solutions or causing such problems. The Constitution was created mainly to achieve this purpose, not to limit federal power. The Articles of Confederation had rendered central authority subservient to state authority, and the Articles were abandoned for precisely this reason. Moreover, the United States would not have become a world economic and political power—for better from a US perspective—had structural constraints routinely prevented the federal government from responding to "[t]he exigencies of the nation," which, to repeat, is how Marshall described the Constitution's fundamental purpose.[42] And the problems facing American society today cannot be solved, as far as government is capable of solving them, if the accomplishment of this purpose is significantly undermined.

Even so, protecting state regulatory authority is a second structural purpose of the Constitution. In contrast to purely nationalist accounts, this book honors this purpose by endorsing constitutional constraints on federal power, including limitations on the Necessary and Proper Clause, the Taxing Clause, the Spending Clause, and the Interstate Commerce Clause—four of Congress's most important powers. The limits endorsed in subsequent chapters may not satisfy constitutional skeptics of federal power, but recall that a collective-action account regards the states as the basic units of structural analysis in the American system. Moreover, one can accept the basic theory while disputing its application to certain questions.

A third structural purpose of the Constitution is to separate and mix federal powers among the branches of the national government. Creating a separate executive and judiciary helps enforce federal solutions to collective-action problems and constitutional or congressional restrictions on state power to cause them.[43] But the separation and interrelation of powers also make it harder for Congress to act. This part of the constitutional architecture has its advantages; for example, it protects individual liberty from federal imposition. This book honors this purpose too, even as Part III argues that, given modern developments and contemporary political conditions, the Constitution makes it too difficult for the states to act collectively in Congress.

---

[41] ANTONIN SCALIA & BRYAN A. GARNER, READING LAW: THE INTERPRETATION OF LEGAL TEXTS 57–58 (2012); William N. Eskridge, Jr. & Philip P. Frickey, *Statutory Interpretation as Practical Reasoning*, 42 STAN. L. REV. 321, 335 (1990).

[42] *McCulloch*, 17 U.S. (4 Wheat.) at 408.

[43] *See* Chapters 4 and 7.

38 THE COLLECTIVE-ACTION CONSTITUTION

There are not always clear conflicts among these three structural purposes. For example, as just noted, the separation of powers also advances the Constitution's collective-action objective; it does not just thwart it. Moreover, in the area of horizontal federalism (or interstate relations), preventing one state from causing collective-action problems can protect the authority of many other states.[44] When accomplishing these purposes does not involve tradeoffs, and when constitutional meaning is otherwise uncertain, it is important to bear in mind the Constitution's primary, collective-action objective.

It is also generally important to maintain focus on this fundamental purpose when there are conflicts among the three purposes. Vertical and horizontal structural limitations on the constitutional authority or practical ability of Congress to act were never meant—and are not best understood—to erase Congress's capacity to effectively address collective-action problems for the states. Rather, these limitations exist to qualify the accomplishment of this primary structural purpose. "While the Constitution diffuses power the better to secure liberty," Justice Jackson wrote in his canonical opinion in *Youngstown*, "it also contemplates that practice will integrate the dispersed powers into a workable government."[45] Thus, when constitutional meaning is uncertain, vindication of the Constitution's collective-action purpose should generally prevail over the other two. By contrast, as later chapters discuss, several constitutional limits that certain originalist advocates of states' rights—both on and off the Supreme Court—would impose on Congress would threaten near erasure, not qualification, of federal power to address many multistate collective-action problems.

The qualifications in the above paragraph are important. First, the focus here is on the constitutional structure, not rights. Rights—including federal power to enforce them—trump collective-action goals.[46] Second, for the above prioritization of structural purposes to matter, constitutional meaning must be uncertain. For example, the president may not effectively pass a statute by executive order just because Congress fails to act and the president deems the collective-action problem severe. (What may be contested is whether the president has done so or has instead permissibly relied on power lawfully delegated by Congress or granted by Article II.) Third, this framework imposes a presumption, which can be rebutted. For instance, certain federal actions may so deeply threaten state autonomy that the state-power purpose identified above should prevail over the collective-action objective. An example might be an attempt to federalize state criminal law by proffering a race to laxity or severity in punishments among the states. But these are qualifications, not the rule: solving and preventing

---

[44] *See* Chapter 8.
[45] *Youngstown Sheet & Tube Co.*, 343 U.S. at 635 (Jackson, J., concurring).
[46] *See* Chapter 9.

collective-action problems is a more basic commitment of the Constitution than protecting state power and impeding federal legislation. Again, it is instructive to ask why the Constitutional Convention took place.

Skeptics of federal power may reject the above analysis of how to negotiate tradeoffs among the Constitution's structural purposes. If so, this book still has something to offer them. As noted above, tradeoffs do not always exist. Further, when constitutional meaning is uncertain, it is helpful to register that one important objective of the Constitution, reflected in its text, history, and structure, is to help the country address multistate collective-action problems by empowering Congress to solve them and barring states from interfering with federal solutions or creating such problems. Regardless of how often one deems constitutional meaning uncertain, and regardless of how one trades off the collective-action purpose with others, this insight cannot persuasively be dismissed as "mere" political science or economics rather than constitutional interpretation.

Democratic Legitimacy

One key structural principle Marshall invokes is that "the government of the Union, though limited in its powers, is supreme within its sphere of action." He first reaches this conclusion though "reason" about the "nature" of the federal government, after which he consults the Supremacy Clause of Article VI to confirm the soundness of his reasoning. His structural argument for federal supremacy invokes democratic theory, American-style. According to Marshall, the federal government is supreme when authorized to act because, compared with states, it possesses superior democratic legitimacy. And it possesses greater democratic legitimacy because it derives its powers from all the people, in contrast to each state, which derives its powers from only some of the people.[47]

Marshall is unclear about what, exactly, his theory of popular sovereignty is. On one hand, he writes that "[t]he government of the Union . . . (whatever may be the influence of this fact on the case), is, emphatically and truly, a government of the people. In form and in substance, it emanates from them. Its powers are granted by them and are to be exercised directly on them, and for their benefit."[48] In this passage, Marshall seems to suggest that the Constitution derives its authority from the state ratifying conventions, which represented all the American people as a national political community, not from the state governments. On the other hand, Marshall concedes that "[n]o political dreamer was ever wild enough to think of breaking down the lines which separate the states, and of

---

[47] *McCulloch*, 17 U.S. (4 Wheat.) at 405–06.
[48] *Id.* at 404–05.

40 THE COLLECTIVE-ACTION CONSTITUTION

compounding the American people into one common mass." "Of consequence," he continues, "when they act, they act in their states."[49] In this passage, Marshall can be read as acknowledging that each state ratifying convention represented each state political community, not the American people as a whole—although, as Professor Daniel Farber points out, this language "can also be read to mean that the state Peoples retain their own identities and provide a forum for action even though a unified American people *also* exists."[50] Whatever, exactly, Marshall's theory of popular sovereignty is, he clearly and correctly rejects the notion that the state *governments* created the federal government.[51] This position is difficult to reconcile with Article VII's identification of state ratifying conventions, not state legislatures, as the bodies deciding whether to approve the Constitution. And, factually, state ratifying conventions did decide.

Democratic legitimacy is a difficult subject, as is the functioning of different government institutions. As noted above, Marshall's account is not entirely clear, and it would need to be clarified in other ways to be maximally persuasive. For example, if a problem and regulatory solution affect only the people of one state, the federal government would not obviously be in a superior democratic position to address it. Marshall must be assuming that the problems federal powers are conferred to address affect "more States than one," as he would explain several years later in *Gibbons v. Ogden* in interpreting the Interstate Commerce Clause.[52] This seems implicit in his statement in *McCulloch* that the federal government has been entrusted with "[t]he sword and the purse, all the external relations, and no inconsiderable portion of the industry of the nation."[53] If a problem and solution affect the people of only one state, various "values of federalism" such as accountability and responsiveness weigh heavily in favor of state control.[54]

---

[49] *Id.* at 403.

[50] Farber, *supra* note 3, at 54. *See McCulloch*, 17 U.S. (4 Wheat.) at 403 ("But the measures they adopt do not, on that account, cease to be the measures of the people themselves, or become the measures of the state governments.").

[51] *McCulloch*, 17 U.S. (4 Wheat.) at 402 ("[T]he counsel for the state of Maryland have deemed it of some importance, in the construction of the constitution, to consider that instrument, not as emanating from the people, but as the act of sovereign and independent states."). Judging from Wheaton's report of the oral arguments, however, counsel for Maryland was not arguing that state governments, as opposed to state peoples, created the Constitution. *See id.* at 363 (quoting Maryland counsel Walter Jones as describing the Constitution as "formed and adopted" by "the people of the respective states"). Nor was it essential to Southern constitutionalism that state governments, as opposed to state political communities, created the Constitution. In the Report of 1800, a resolution adopted by the Virginia General Assembly that Madison drafted in opposition to the Alien and Sedition Acts, Madison noted the multiple potential meanings of the word "States"; defined it as "the people composing those political societies, in their highest sovereign capacity"; and wrote that "in that sense of the term 'States,' they are . . . parties to the compact from which the powers of the Federal Government result." James Madison, Report on the Resolutions (1800), *in* 6 THE WRITINGS OF JAMES MADISON 341, 348 (Gaillard Hunt ed., 1906).

[52] Gibbons v. Ogden, 22 U.S. (9 Wheat.) 1, 194 (1824).

[53] *McCulloch*, 17 U.S. (4 Wheat.) at 407.

[54] *See* Chapter 3.

Even stated relatively crudely, however, there is much truth to Marshall's argument. His point is that the interests of (almost) every American are substantially more likely to be at least somewhat represented in the federal government than in a single state government. The institutions of the federal government are where all these interests are most likely to be considered and weighed before decisions are made that determine winners and losers for the time being. Moreover, the interests of the states themselves are more likely to be represented in Congress than in any state legislature. This key point may help explain why, as noted above, Marshall expresses uncertainty about the stakes of his disagreement with state-compact theory by remarking, before expressing his position, "whatever may be the influence of this fact on the case."[55]

Marshall's comparative argument holds up regardless of the combinations of federal institutions that the Constitution empowers to make different decisions. Whether institutionally vested in the House of Representatives, the Senate, the Executive, all of them jointly, or some of them jointly, decision-making by the federal government is more likely to represent all the people and all the states than decision-making by one state.[56] Marshall's argument also holds up notwithstanding the vulnerabilities of these institutions from a contemporary democratic standpoint. For example, if one views democratic legitimacy as inhering in the will of the American people, then even though a Senate majority will often not reflect national majority sentiment on an issue, it is still more likely to approach national majority sentiment than the legislature of a given state.[57]

The superior democratic legitimacy of the federal government primarily entitles it, when otherwise acting within its powers, to resolve disagreements among states about whether there is a multistate collective-action problem in need of solving. When states disagree, the technical tasks of identifying the existence, scope, and significance of a multistate collective-action problem, and

[55] The issue may have mattered at the time because of what St. George Tucker—a Virginia judge, law professor, and states' rights Jeffersonian—in 1803 called the "maxim of political law" that a sovereign state can be divested of its powers only if it expressly consents, and such consent must be interpreted narrowly. It followed that if Maryland was correct that the states were sovereign, Section 8 should be given "the most strict construction that the instrument will bear" in favor of the retention of power by states. H. Jefferson Powell, *The Original Understanding of Original Intent*, 98 HARV. L. REV. 885, 931 (1984) (quoting Tucker).

[56] This is not to deny that state governments are better represented in Congress than in the Executive. For state governments, a gridlocked Congress is cause for concern, not just relief. As Chapter 10 explains, power flows to where it can be exercised, and in the United States it flows from Congress not just to the states but also to the president. The latter power flow arguably undermines the regulatory autonomy of state governments because it circumvents the political safeguards of federalism. *See* Margaret H. Lemos & Ernest A. Young, *State Public Law Litigation in an Age of Polarization*, 97 TEX. L. REV. 43, 63–64 (2018).

[57] For discussions of political branch counter-majoritarianism, see SANFORD LEVISON, OUR UNDEMOCRATIC CONSTITUTION: WHERE THE CONSTITUTION GOES WRONG (AND HOW WE THE PEOPLE CAN CORRECT IT) (2006); Corinna Barrett Lain, *Upside-Down Judicial Review*, 101 GEO. L.J. 113, 144–57 (2012).

42 THE COLLECTIVE-ACTION CONSTITUTION

of determining how likely the affected states are to solve the problem on their own without harming the federal government or other states, are not only scientific exercises. They also require historically contingent, normatively contestable value judgments. As political theorist Richard Tuck argues, beliefs about when collective action is rational or likely are historically contingent and so can change over time.[58] Relatedly, even at a given time, reasonable minds (and states) may differ over whether the absence of cooperation or coordination by states is a good thing or a problem—and, if it is a problem, over its seriousness and scope.

Thus, to say that the federal government can use certain powers to solve certain collective-action problems facing the states is to say that the federal government can decide that the absence of collective action by states is a problem (such as the views of Americans today about a collective failure to ban child labor), as opposed to a good thing (such as the views of Americans today about a collective failure to enforce slavery).[59] It is to say that the states gaining a competitive advantage, or otherwise going their own way, should not be permitted to do so. Such judgments can change over time; for example, the use of child labor and the rendition of allegedly fugitive enslaved people were once controversial issues. Further, disagreements can erupt at a given time. States and sections of the nation often disagreed during the 1780s; among many examples that appear in this book, Rhode Island boycotted the Constitution Convention. Earlier in the decade, Rhode Island, Virginia, and New York infuriated other states by rejecting proposals for a revenue-raising federal impost and by continuing instead to impose their own. States disagree today over whether collective action is warranted to, say, combat climate change, provide universal health care, or impose a national mask mandate during a pandemic.

To identify who gets to resolve disagreements, one must consult Marshall's theory of democratic legitimacy, the Constitution's language, and long-standing judicial deference to congressional determinations of fact and of the geographic scope of problems. If the federal government is otherwise acting within its powers, then during any given period, it is entitled to decide whether there is a multistate collective-action problem in need of solving and how to solve it. This grant of authority to Congress helps explain why the constitutional text requires congressional consent before states may form interstate compacts or other agreements.[60] And Congress is better positioned than states or the Supreme Court, both democratically and institutionally, to determine whether federal spending is for welfare that is "general"[61]; whether commerce "is among the several States"[62]; and whether certain state violations of the dormant commerce

[58] RICHARD TUCK, FREE RIDING (2008).
[59] *See* Chapters 5 and 8.
[60] U.S. CONST. art. I, § 10, cl. 3 (discussed in Chapter 3).
[61] U.S. CONST. art. I, § 8, cl. 1.
[62] U.S. CONST. art. I, § 8, cl. 3.

doctrine should be permitted because they are unlikely to cause a collective-action problem in need of solving.[63] Congress, as the government institution in the nation in which all states and (almost) all people are represented, is authorized to resolve disagreements among states over whether collective action should succeed if, but only if, Congress rationally determines that its intervention would help one group of states more than it would harm the other.

Note, however, that many problems cannot rationally be viewed as multistate collective-action problems, and Congress lacks power to act based on contrary assertions. Pure majoritarianism in Congress has no limiting principle and has nothing to do with collective action. The logics of Pareto and cost-benefit collective-action problems have objective content,[64] which can be policed by the judiciary with appropriate deference. The point is instead that cost-benefit collective-action problems require comparisons of externalized costs and internalized benefits. Given its enormous costs to many countries, global warming still poses a multination, cost-benefit collective-action problem even if some nations are unconcerned about climate change or more concerned about economic growth. Raising the price of wheat in the interstate market may still pose a multistate, cost-benefit collective-action problem, given the existence of states with many farmers and few poor people even if other states have few farmers and many poor people. Congress gets to decide if it rationally believes that its intervention would be a cost-benefit improvement. Requiring unanimity before Congress can act would mean that Congress could almost never act.

Implied Powers, the Necessary and Proper Clause, and Collective Action

Marshall reads the Necessary and Proper Clause broadly, thereby facilitating the solution of collective-action problems by the federal government in three ways. These ways differ from two unpersuasive interpretations of the Necessary and Proper Clause. A third interpretation is more defensible.

Marshall's Broad Reading of the Necessary and Proper Clause

As noted, after Marshall concludes that the national bank is within Congress's powers, he turns to the last clause of Section 8, which has been called the Elastic Clause, the Sweeping Clause, and—since the twentieth century—the Necessary

---

[63] *See* Chapters 4 and 5.
[64] *See* Chapter 2.

44 THE COLLECTIVE-ACTION CONSTITUTION

and Proper Clause. It authorizes Congress "[t]o make all Laws which shall be necessary and proper for carrying into Execution the foregoing Powers, and all other Powers vested by this Constitution in the Government of the United States, or in any Department or Officer thereof."[65] He invokes this power as confirmation that the Constitution "has not left the right of Congress to employ the necessary means, for the execution of the powers conferred on the government, to general reasoning."[66]

Representing Maryland, Luther Martin follows Jefferson's prior position by interpreting the word "necessary" in the clause in the highly restrictive sense of a necessary condition.[67] Marshall responds that the term "necessary" means different things depending on the context, and it "frequently imports no more than that one thing is convenient, or useful, or essential to another." He notes that Article I, Section 10, uses the phrase "absolutely necessary": states may not tax imports or exports except when absolutely necessary for executing their inspection laws, which means something more restrictive than the word "necessary." He also reads the term "proper" as qualifying any severity that might be attributed to the word "necessary." And he emphasizes that the text places and phrases the clause as an additional power, not (like Article I, Section 9) as limiting powers already granted.

"Let the end be legitimate, let it be within the scope of the constitution," Marshall declares in laying down a rule of law governing to this day, "and all means which are appropriate, which are plainly adapted to the end, which are not prohibited, but consist with the letter and spirit of the constitution, are constitutional."[68] He concludes that the bank easily meets this test. It is simply a means, and only a means, to several ends in Section 8, such as taxing, borrowing money, regulating interstate and foreign commerce, and supporting a military.

Marshall's Reading and the Federal Solution of Collective-Action Problems

In three ways, *McCulloch*'s broad understanding of the Necessary and Proper Clause advances the Constitution's purpose to facilitate collective action by states in Congress. First, Marshall's interpretation implies that Congress can both solve collective-action problems directly by using its enumerated powers and

---

[65] U.S. CONST. art. I, § 8, cl. 18.

[66] *McCulloch*, 17 U.S. (4 Wheat.) at 411.

[67] Thomas Jefferson, Opinion on the Constitutionality of the Bill to Establish a National Bank (Feb. 15, 1791), *in* CONTEXTS OF THE CONSTITUTION, *supra* note 6, at 540, 542 (permitting only "those means without which the [implemented] grant of the power would be nugatory").

[68] *McCulloch*, 17 U.S. (4 Wheat.) at 413, 414–15, 418–19, 419–20, 421.

FOUNDATIONS   45

pass laws that do not themselves solve such problems but help carry into execution congressional powers that do.[69] One example, in *McCulloch*, is the law creating the bank, which made more effective various powers to solve collective-action problems for the states, including by funding the national government, combating state protectionism, responding with one voice to foreign trade aggression, and raising and paying a military.[70]

Second, a Marshallian interpretation of the Necessary and Proper Clause allows Congress to solve certain collective-action problems when other powers are unavailable. An example is *United States v. Comstock* (2010),[71] where the issue was whether the Necessary and Proper Clause authorizes Congress to permit the attorney general to civilly commit mentally ill, sexually dangerous federal prisoners after they complete their federal sentences if no state will accept custody of them. It is well settled that Congress can use the Interstate Commerce Clause to criminalize certain behavior and the Necessary and Proper Clause to create federal prosecutors to prosecute such offenses and federal prisons to hold those convicted. But may Congress also use the Necessary and Proper Clause to prevent individuals scheduled to be released from harming people? The Court said "yes" by a vote of seven to two, partly because the case implicated a Pareto collective-action problem involving any number of states.

The Court and individual justices in *Comstock* emphasized that federal intervention helped to solve a NIMBY (not in my backyard) collective-action problem. After the sentences of sexually dangerous prisoners have expired, the federal government might release them for civil commitment in several possible states, including the state where they had previously lived, or had been tried, or were currently housed. A state government (say, North Carolina) that assumes custody must pay the full financial costs of their indefinite commitment. Meanwhile, other states potentially enjoy all the benefits from North Carolina's decision to commit the individuals, who might otherwise move to (or through) these states upon release because the federal government severed their ties to North Carolina by imprisoning them for a long time. Instead of emphasizing that the federal government had helped create the problem it now sought to solve, the Court cited evidence that states often refuse to assume custody, potentially hoping to free ride on some other state's decision to do so. Both the Court and Justices Kennedy and Alito, who concurred in the judgment, stressed that the federal statute helped solve this cooperation problem.[72]

---

[69] Neil S. Siegel, *Free Riding on Benevolence: Collective Action Federalism and the Minimum Coverage Provision*, 75 LAW & CONTEMP. PROBS. 29, 61–73 (2012) (Issue No. 3).

[70] *See* Chapters 4, 5, and 6.

[71] 560 U.S. 126 (2010).

[72] *Id.* at 143 ("Congress could . . . have reasonably concluded (as detailed in the Judicial Conference's report) that a reasonable number of such individuals would likely *not* be detained by the States if released from federal custody, in part because the Federal Government itself severed

46   THE COLLECTIVE-ACTION CONSTITUTION

Third, Marshall's broad understanding of the Necessary and Proper Clause has implications not only for the "federalism" component of the clause but also for its "separation of powers" component, which permits federal laws that are convenient for executing "all other Powers vested by this Constitution in the Government of the United States, or in any Department or Officers thereof." His interpretation implies that Congress enjoys broad power to structure the executive and judicial branches. As Professor Akhil Amar explains, Congress has done so from the start by deciding "how many cabinet departments would fill the executive branch; how [they] would be shaped and bounded; how many justices would compose the Supreme Court; [and] where and when the Court would sit."[73] Under the Articles of Confederation, there was no real national executive or judiciary, so federal law was largely unenforceable.[74] Under the Constitution, Congress can ensure that federal solutions to collective-action problems are enforced.[75]

Unpersuasive Interpretive Claims and Constitutional Limits

The arguments above about the relationship between the Necessary and Proper Clause and federal solutions to collective-action problems differ from two other claims, neither of which is tenable. First, it might be suggested that, to use the Necessary and Proper Clause, Congress must be solving a collective-action problems facing the states.[76] *McCulloch* is no authority for this proposition, and the clause is broader for at least two reasons. As explained above, there are indirect ways in which the clause supports federal power to solve collective-action problems facing the states, including by enabling Congress to pass laws that do not themselves solve such problems but instead support federal laws or branches

---

their claim to 'legal residence in any State' by incarcerating them in remote federal prisons" (citation omitted)); *id.* at 139 (similar); *id.* at 154 (Kennedy, J., concurring in judgment) (similar); *id.* at 156 (Alito, J., concurring in judgment) (similar); *id.* at 158 (similar).

[73] AKHIL REED AMAR, AMERICA'S CONSTITUTION: A BIOGRAPHY 111 (2005); *see id.* at 110–13.

[74] *See* Chapters 4 and 7.

[75] *See* Chapter 7. Long-standing historical practice based on the separation-of-powers component of the Necessary and Proper Clause strongly suggests that Marshall correctly construes the word "necessary" to mean convenient, not indispensable. Every (re)organization of federal departments throughout history was required to be "necessary" for carrying out the powers granted to the federal government. Rather than being indispensable, each was a convenient way of organizing the executive branch. BALKIN, *supra* note 19, at 179.

[76] *Cf.* Stephen Gardbaum, *Rethinking Constitutional Federalism*, 74 TEXAS L. REV. 795, 812–14, 831–36 (1996) (arguing that the Necessary and Proper Clause should be interpreted in light of a principle like subsidiarity); Vicki C. Jackson, *Subsidiarity, the Judicial Role, and the Warren Court's Contribution to the Revival of State Government, in* NOMOS LV: FEDERALISM AND SUBSIDIARITY 190, 192 (James E. Fleming & Jacob T. Levy eds., 2014) (explaining, but not endorsing, this position).

FOUNDATIONS   47

of government that do. In addition, the federal government does not just solve collective-action problems for the states; it performs other functions, especially protecting rights—and the Necessary and Proper Clause helps the federal government accomplish this function.[77]

Second, it might be suggested that the Necessary and Proper Clause is the exclusive textual basis for federal power to pass laws that address collective-action problems.[78] But this claim misses many other powers that authorize Congress to solve collective-action problems.[79] In short, the Necessary and Proper Clause does more than permit Congress to solve multistate collective-action problems, and it does less than serve as the only power to address such problems.

McCulloch is also inconsistent with the claims of the modern Court, individual justices, and certain commentators that the Necessary and Proper Clause contains separate requirements. On this view, laws passed pursuant to this power must be not just "necessary" but also "proper."[80] As noted above, Marshall writes that the "only possible effect" of the term "proper" is to render the word "necessary" less severe than it otherwise might be.[81] The text can be read as he reads it; for example, it does not provide that federal laws must be "both necessary and proper." Granted, one could say, as some commentators have, that federal laws are not "proper" if they violate rights, the separation of powers, or federalism principles.[82] But one could also directly invoke rights, the separation of powers, or federalism principles. Other than finding a textual home for certain structural principles, it is unclear what turns on whether one views the term "proper" as imposing another limit. In any event, with one exception flagged by Marshall and discussed below, this book follows *McCulloch* in reading the phrase "necessary and proper" as imposing one requirement.[83]

---

[77] *See* Chapter 9.

[78] *See* Steven G. Calabresi & Lucy D. Bickford, *Federalism and Subsidiarity: Perspectives from U.S. Constitutional Law*, *in* NOMOS LV: FEDERALISM AND SUBSIDIARITY 145–46 (James E. Fleming & Jacob T. Levy eds., 2014) (asserting with approval that, "[f]rom 1789 to the present, the Supreme Court has consistently read the Constitution as giving the federal government the power under the Necessary and Proper Clause [to legislate] as if [the Constitution] had enacted the words of the Bedford Resolution rather than a categorical enumeration of powers"). The Bedford Resolution was the amended, final version of Resolution VI, which guided the Philadelphia Convention's eventual enumeration of powers in Section 8. Chapter 4 shows that the language of the Bedford Resolution can persuasively be read as expressing an intent to give Congress the power to solve collective-action problems for the states—although, of course, the Resolution itself never became law.

[79] *See* Chapters 4, 5, and 6.

[80] *See, e.g.*, NFIB v. Sebelius, 567 U.S. 519, 558–61 (2012) (opinion of Roberts, C.J.); Printz v. United States, 521 U.S. 898, 923–24 (1996); *infra* notes 82–84 and 87–88 (citing relevant scholarship).

[81] *McCulloch*, 17 U.S. (4 Wheat.) at 418–19.

[82] *See, e.g.*, BALKIN, *supra* note 19, at 179.

[83] The argument that the term "proper" limits the Necessary and Proper Clause had early skeptics. *See* H. JEFFERSON POWELL, THE CONSTITUTION AND THE ATTORNEYS GENERAL 7 (1999) (quoting Attorney General Edmund Randolph's view that friends and foes of the bank bill should view the term "proper" in the clause "as among the surplusage which as often proceeds from inattention as caution").

48 THE COLLECTIVE-ACTION CONSTITUTION

Finally, Marshall suggests in passing that there are constitutional limits on the Necessary and Proper Clause. "The power of creating a corporation," he writes, "is not, like the power of making war, or levying taxes, or of regulating commerce, a great substantive and independent power, which cannot be implied as incidental to other powers, or used as a means of executing them." "It is never the end for which other powers are exercised," he adds, "but a means by which other objects are accomplished."[84] This distinction between great substantive and independent powers on one hand, and incidental or derivative powers on the other hand, reappeared in 2012 in *NFIB v. Sebelius*, where the Court concluded that a requirement to buy health insurance was a great power.[85] The distinction makes sense in principle. For example, the powers to tax and declare war are too great an exercise of sovereign authority to be viewed as incidental to facilitating interstate commerce. For Congress to possess them, they must be listed separately.

In practice, however, it is difficult to apply the distinction, and neither Marshall nor Chief Justice Roberts in *NFIB* offered much guidance regarding how to distinguish great powers from incidental ones.[86] For instance, it is unclear why a purchase mandate is a great power when a national bank is not, nor is the power to deport people or imprison or execute them for violating federal criminal laws, nor are many mandates that Congress has historically imposed, including mandates to acquire firearms for militia service, register for selective service, aid law enforcement, exchange gold for paper currency, file tax returns, respond to the census, report for jury duty, and surrender property.[87] How many teeth the Court reads into the distinction will determine whether it impedes use of the Necessary and Proper Clause to solve collective-action problems for the states, whether directly or indirectly. Application of the distinction should be informed not only by historical practice,[88] but also by whether the law helps solve a multistate collective-action problem, as in *Comstock*.

---

[84] *McCulloch*, 17 U.S. (4 Wheat.) at 411. For an originalist elaboration of this distinction and a restrictive understanding of the Necessary and Proper Clause more generally, see GARY LAWSON, GEOFFREY P. MILLER, ROBERT G. NATELSON, & GUY I. SEIDMAN, THE ORIGINS OF THE NECESSARY AND PROPER CLAUSE (2010).

[85] *NFIB*, 567 U.S. at 559–61 (opinion of Roberts, C.J.).

[86] Neil S. Siegel, *More Law than Politics: The Chief, the "Mandate," Legality, and Statesmanship, in* THE HEALTH CARE CASE: THE SUPREME COURT'S DECISION AND ITS IMPLICATIONS 192, 203–05 (Nathaniel Persily et al. eds., 2013).

[87] Siegel, *Free Riding on Benevolence, supra* note 69, at 31, 50–54; *see* William Baude, *Rethinking the Federal Eminent Domain Power*, 122 YALE L.J. 1738, 1817–18 (2013) (noting the lack of historical support for the Court's conclusion that purchase mandates are great powers).

[88] Baude, *supra* note 87, at 1738 (arguing that "history can provide some guidance" in distinguishing great powers from incidental ones).

Parsing Marshall's Reference to a Pretextual Purpose

Marshall writes in *McCulloch* that "should congress, under the pretext of executing its powers, pass laws for the accomplishment of objects not intrusted to the government; it would become the painful duty of this tribunal . . . to say, that such an act was not the law of the land."[89] Marshall's suggestion that a pretextual purpose would doom a federal law raises the question of whether Congress lacks the authority to act if it does not intend to solve a multistate collective-action problem, even if the law in question does in fact solve such a problem. If this is what Marshall's reference to pretext means, and if Marshall's meaning accurately captures the meaning of the Constitution, then Congress's powers are significantly limited, given the many situations in which Congress presumably acts with a moral, social, or political purpose, and not with the purpose to solve a collective-action problem facing the states—even though good collective-arguments exist to justify the law in question. One example is the Civil Rights Act of 1964, which (among other things) prohibited racial discrimination in places of public accommodation.[90] Modern constitutional law has dealt with this potential problem by ignoring this part of *McCulloch*; Congress's motive in using the Necessary and Proper Clause has not been thought to matter in assessing the constitutionality of legislation passed under this clause,[91] just as Congress's motive has not been thought to matter when Congress exercises its other powers under Article I, Section 8.[92]

Marshall's language need not be read, however, to mean that Congress must be intending to solve a multistate collective-action problem, as opposed to a moral or other problem. Just because the Constitution has a fundamental purpose to empower Congress to solve multistate collective-action problems does not mean that Congress may not act if its members do not possess this subjective purpose. Instead, Marshall's language can be read as prohibiting Congress from justifying a law on collective-action grounds when the members who voted for the law do not in good faith believe that the law solves a multistate collective-action problem. In other words, Congress does not have to really want to solve a collective-action problem; it is permissible for Congress to regard racism in

---

[89] *McCulloch*, 17 U.S. (4 Wheat.) at 423.

[90] *See* Chapter 5 (discussing cases upholding the Civil Rights Act of 1964 under the Interstate Commerce Clause).

[91] *See, e.g.,* United States v. Comstock, 560 U.S. 126, 134 (2010) ("We have since made clear that, in determining whether the Necessary and Proper Clause grants Congress the legislative authority to enact a particular federal statute, we look to see whether the statute constitutes a means that is rationally related to the implementation of a constitutionally enumerated power." (citing Sabri v. United States, 541 U.S. 600, 605 (2004) and Gonzales v. Raich, 541 U.S. 1, 22 (2005))).

[92] *See* United States v. Darby, 312 U.S. 100, 115 (1941) ("The motive and purpose of a regulation of interstate commerce are matters for the legislative judgment upon the exercise of which the Constitution places no restriction, and over which the courts are given no control.").

50   THE COLLECTIVE-ACTION CONSTITUTION

public accommodations (or child labor in factories) as unconscionable, as long as there is a sufficient collective-action rationale to justify the law. What Congress cannot do is state that it is banning, say, guns in schools because the states cannot handle the problem on their own when Congress does not in fact believe this to be the case, and it is not in fact the case.[93]

Democratic Illegitimacy

After interpreting Congress's power broadly, thereby enabling the federal government to solve multistate collective-action problems, Marshall interprets state power narrowly, thereby preventing states from harming the federal government or causing certain collective-action problems for one another. Marshall holds that states may not tax federal institutions within their borders, even though taxation is a concurrent power and nothing in Article I, Section 10, prohibits states from doing so. "There is no express provision for the case," Marshall acknowledges.[94] But he offers two other arguments. The first is a questionable syllogism, and the second is a promising structural argument.

The three premises of the syllogism are that (1) the power to create is the power to preserve; (2) the power to destroy is incompatible with the power to preserve; and (3) the power to tax is the power to destroy. The conclusion is that state power to tax the bank is incompatible with federal power to create it, which Marshall establishes earlier in the opinion. Moreover, given principles of federal supremacy (and the Supremacy Clause), which he also establishes earlier, his final conclusion is that federal power to create the bank trumps state power to tax its branches.[95]

Marshall's logic is not vulnerable, but one premise is: the power to tax is not necessarily the power to destroy, particularly given judicial review of exercises of the taxing power. Maryland's tax evidenced hostility toward the bank, but the tax did not destroy it, and more than a century later, Justice Oliver Wendel Holmes, Jr., memorably wrote that "[t]he power to tax is not the power to destroy while this Court sits."[96] Granted, Marshall is writing during a period of state hostility to the bank, and so he may want to nip the problem in the bud out of concern that states cannot be trusted to tax nondestructively.[97] But as shown below, this

---

[93] *See* Chapter 5 (discussing a case invalidating a gratuitous federal ban on gun possession in school zones).

[94] *McCulloch*, 17 U.S. (4 Wheat.) at 425–26.

[95] *Id.* at 426–27, 431.

[96] Panhandle Oil Co. v. Mississippi ex rel. Knox, 277 U.S. 218, 223 (1928) (Holmes, J., dissenting).

[97] *McCulloch*, 17 U.S. (4 Wheat.) at 431 ("But is this a case of confidence? Would the people of any one state trust those of another with a power to control the most insignificant operations of their state government? We know they would not. Why, then, should we suppose, that the people of any one

FOUNDATIONS 51

concern is better captured by his structural argument. Marshall also deems inappropriate judicial efforts to determine when uses of the taxing power are excessive. "We are not driven to the perplexing inquiry, so unfit for the judicial department," he writes, "what degree of taxation is the legitimate use, and what degree may amount to the abuse of the power."[98] But the Constitution requires federal courts to conduct such an inquiry regarding uses of *federal* taxing power, as the modern Court did in *NFIB*.[99]

Marshall's structural argument is more persuasive. "The only security against the abuse of [the taxing] power, is found, in the structure of the Government itself," he asserts, for "[i]n imposing a tax, the legislature acts upon its constituents," who can hold their representatives accountable for the taxes they impose. Americans who reside outside a state are not represented in the state's legislature, however, so "the means employed by the Government of the Union have no such security, nor is the right of a State to tax them sustained by the same theory."[100]

Later in his opinion, Marshall insists that each state is only part of the whole, and a part may not tax the whole, even nondestructively.[101] As a matter of democratic principle, he reasons, no legislature in America may target individuals and entities not represented in the political process that elects the legislators who impose the tax. To restate his structural argument as an ethos argument from the Revolution, "no taxation without representation." His "intelligible standard" is that state taxation authority extends only to "[a]ll subjects over which the sovereign power of a State extends."[102] His argument anticipates the process theory of judicial review by well more than a century. The Court proposed this theory in its famous footnote four in *United States v. Carolene Products Company* (1938), and Professor John Hart Ely developed it decades later into a theory of judicial review.[103]

Collective-action reasoning supports Marshall's structural analysis of when state taxation is democratically illegitimate and when it is legitimate. A state internalizes all the benefits of taxing federal institutions because the taxing state obtains all the tax revenue from doing so and reduces potential federal

---

state should be willing to trust those of another with a power to control the operations of a government to which they have confided their most important and most valuable interests?").

[98] *Id.* at 430. This section of the chapter mixes together arguments that Marshall presents as based on the Constitution with arguments that he presents at pages 428–30 as grounded in "just theory," *id.* at 430, even though he brackets his theory arguments at the beginning and end as distinct from the "test of the Constitution," *id.* at 428. It is not clear why he drew this distinction, however, and there is no apparent objection to treating his theory discussion as part of his constitutional analysis.

[99] *NFIB*, 567 U.S. 519 (discussed in Chapter 4).

[100] *McCulloch*, 17 U.S. (4 Wheat.) at 428.

[101] *Id.* at 435–36.

[102] *Id.* at 429–30.

[103] 304 U.S. 144, 152 n.4 (1938) (discussed in Chapter 9); ELY, *supra* note 23 (same).

52 THE COLLECTIVE-ACTION CONSTITUTION

competition with its institutions only, not with those in other states. By contrast, the taxing state externalizes most of the costs—the impaired functioning of the federal institutions—onto sister states because these institutions serve the whole nation. Because the taxing state internalizes all the benefits of taxing federal institutions and externalizes most of the costs, it is incentivized to overtax federal institutions. Further, all states are similarly situated. But if they all externalize costs in this way, most or all of them will end up worse off from their own perspectives than if none of them do so.

A similar logic helps explain other constitutional provisions and principles that constrain state power. For example, even when a state taxes imports and exports because doing so is "absolutely necessary" to executing its inspection laws, the second clause of Article I, Section 10, provides that "the net Produce" of such taxes "shall be for the Use of the Treasury of the United States," thereby preventing the taxing state from making a profit. Moreover, all such state laws "shall be subject to the Revision and Control of the Congress," thereby empowering Congress to further protect against cost externalization by states onto sister states. Similarly, the dormant commerce doctrine usually prevents states from causing collective-action problems by taxing or regulating in ways that discriminate against interstate commerce or that unduly burden it. Likewise, most provisions in Article IV help prevent states from "racing to the bottom," among other potential collective-action problems.[104]

A Cautionary Tale

One last lesson of *McCulloch* requires discussing, and unlike the others, it is sobering. Like all structural accounts, the vision Marshall sketches—and this book develops using the logics of collective action—is no guarantee that federal power will be used in morally defensible ways. As presaged by his ethos argument for manifest destiny, Marshall's justification of robust federal authority to raise revenues and armies would, along with private capital and migration west, enable white Americans to build a continental empire by dispossessing, removing, and slaughtering Native Americans.[105]

For example, the Indian Removal Act of 1830 authorized the president to negotiate with Southern tribes for their removal to federal territory west of the Mississippi River in return for the settlement of their ancestral lands by white

---

[104] *See* Chapters 5, 8, and 9.

[105] CLAUDIO SAUNT, UNWORTHY REPUBLIC: THE DISPOSSESSION OF NATIVE AMERICANS AND THE ROAD TO INDIAN TERRITORY (2021); JEFFREY OSTLER, SURVIVING GENOCIDE: NATIVE AMERICANS AND THE UNITED STATES FROM THE AMERICAN REVOLUTION TO BLEEDING KANSAS (2019).

FOUNDATIONS 53

Americans.[106] This law resulted mainly from the opposition of states to the presence of tribal populations within their borders. Although many Anglo-Native American interactions were complex, the relocation of the tribes to unorganized federal territories could be viewed as a federal solution to a NIMBY collective-action problem for the states. Such a problem did not exist for the tribes, which disputed whose "backyard" it was anyway.

Moreover, a structural, collective-action argument could have been invoked to support the slavery-protective fugitive slave acts passed by Congress in 1793 and 1850 to protect the constitutional rights of slaveowners conferred by the Fugitive Slave Clause.[107] Given the movements of allegedly fugitive enslaved people across state lines, the states would have had to act collectively, not individually, to fully enforce the clause, which the original Constitution appeared to contemplate. Moreover, Northern states like Pennsylvania, which sought to ensure that the return of fugitive enslaved people (the "rendition" process) would be accomplished nonviolently and consistently with procedural protections for Black people accused of being fugitives, were arguably imposing negative externalities on Southern states. Such externalities, if ignored, might have provoked (and eventually did provoke) Southern states to retaliate, causing a collective-action problem for Southern and Northern states alike.

Such structural arguments for federal power and against state power should not necessarily have carried the day. The Court's decision in *Prigg v. Pennsylvania*, which upheld the 1793 act and declared it exclusive of state power to regulate the rendition process, was legally questionable in several ways.[108] But the foregoing structural arguments supported the decision in *Prigg*.

There were other times when exercises of federal power, arguably justified structurally on collective-action grounds, were used to wrong people in ways that Americans today properly understand to have been deeply immoral or otherwise misguided.[109] It is partly for this reason that the constitutional purpose

---

[106] An act to provide for an exchange of lands with the Indians residing in any of the states or territories, and for their removal west of the river Mississippi (Indian Removal Act), ch. 148, 4 Stat. 411 (1830).

[107] U.S. CONST. art. IV, § 2, cl. 2 (discussed in Chapter 8).

[108] 41 U.S. (16 Pet.) 539 (1842) (analyzed in Chapter 8). The Court upheld the 1850 act in *Abelman v. Booth*, 62 U.S. (21 How.) 506 (1859).

[109] In the late nineteenth and early twentieth centuries, Congress used its naturalization, immigration, and deportation powers to enforce white supremacy and other forms of exclusion. For example, the Chinese Exclusion Act of 1882 suspended Chinese immigration for ten years and rendered Chinese immigrants ineligible for naturalization. *See* Act of May 6, 1882 (Chinese Exclusion Act), ch. 126, 22 Stat. 58 (repealed 1943). Congress also used its postal and interstate-commerce powers to enforce conceptions of public morality that most Americans today would deem oppressive. For example, the Comstock Act prohibited as "obscene" any person from selling or distributing in the United States mail articles used "for the prevention of conception" or for "causing unlawful abortion," or from sending information concerning these practices. Comstock Act ch. 258, 17 Stat. 598, 599 (1873). The Mann Act criminalized the transportation of "any women or girl" in interstate commerce not only "for the purpose of prostitution or debauchery" but also "for any other immoral purpose." *See* White-Slave Traffic (Mann) Act, ch. 395, 36 Stat. 825 (1910) (codified as amended at 18 U.S.C. §§ 2421–2424). The Federal Lottery Act prohibited the importation or interstate shipment of lottery

54 THE COLLECTIVE-ACTION CONSTITUTION

to empower Congress to solve multistate collective-action problems does not trump the purpose to protect constitutional rights. It is also partly for this reason that a collective-action account of the Constitution is superior to more nationalist ones, which impose essentially no structural limits on federal power.

It is also not difficult, however, to identify many times when state power was used immorally to enact awful policies, including against Native Americans and African Americans. As noted, the Indian Removal Act largely did the bidding of the states. All states treated Native Americans terribly, so their future might have been as bloody had Maryland won in *McCulloch* and had its victory endured.[110]

Moreover, many states, not the federal government, permitted slavery, passed the Black Codes, enforced Jim Crow, and disenfranchised Black people (as well as a significant percentage of poor white people with whom Black people had formed populist coalitions) for many decades.[111] Southern states had authoritarian political regimes from the late 1800s until passage of the Voting Rights Act of 1965, notwithstanding the Republican Form of Government Clause of Article IV, Section 4, and the Fourteenth and Fifteenth Amendments.[112] The conduct of these states is no less consequential in a "federalism calculus" just because one can also note the racism behind federal actions and inactions along the way, or because one can also find states that were generally more progressive on matters of race than the federal government was at a given time.

No structural account can save Americans, or other people subject to American power, from terrible politics. The most that any structural theory can offer from a moral and policy perspective are reasons to believe that American society will be better off on balance, by its own lights and for its own ends, within a particular time horizon if the theory is adopted instead of a competing structural account.[113] It counts in favor of the Marshallian,

---

tickets. Act of Mar. 2, 1895, ch. 191, 28 Stat. 963. Today, statutes like most of these might violate constitutional rights (including equal protection, travel, free speech, and reproductive autonomy). But they would not generally be problematic from a federalism standpoint, whether under the Court's doctrine or from a collective-action perspective.

[110] *See, e.g.,* LAURENCE M. HAUPTMAN, CONSPIRACY OF INTERESTS: IROQUOIS DISPOSSESSION AND THE RISE OF NEW YORK STATE (2001) (showing how, as early as the 1790s, state politicians conspired with entrepreneurs, Christian missionaries, civic leaders, and federal officials to separate the Six Nations of the Iroquois League from their lands); Nell Jessup Newton, *Federal Power over Indians: Its Sources, Scope, and Limitations,* 132 U. PENN. L. REV. 195, 215 (1984) (observing that "[t]he states," not the federal government, "had proven themselves to be the greatest enemies of the Indian tribes").

[111] C. VANN WOODWARD, THE STRANGE CAREER OF JIM CROW (1955); Richard H. Pildes, *Why the Center Does Not Hold: The Causes of Hyperpolarized Democracy in America,* 99 CAL. L. REV. 273, 288, 290–94 (2011).

[112] *See* Chapter 9.

[113] There is also the question of whether the broader world will be better off. This question cannot be engaged here.

FOUNDATIONS 55

collective-action theory that federal power was used to end the international slave trade as soon as the Constitution permitted;[114] to prohibit slavery in various federal territories (an issue of greater significance to slavery's future than enforcement of the Fugitive Slave Clause); to end slavery in Southern states; and, roughly a century later, to prohibit racial discrimination in public education, places of public accommodation, and voting. Today, it counts in favor of a collective-action account that the United States faces many problems—noted at the start of this book—that can be addressed more effectively by Congress than by the states because the scope of the problems disrespects state borders. The same holds for problems that ignore national borders, such as nuclear proliferation, terrorism, and climate change. Understanding Congress to possess this collective-action role will safeguard its authority to help solve these problems.[115]

Global collective-action problems raise the question of whether world governance institutions should be given the power to address them. The structural questions identified in this chapter include not only whether a particular level of government matches the geographic scope of a problem but also whether this level of government has the democratic legitimacy to settle disagreements over whether and how to solve it. As one moves from nations to supranational institutions, concerns about democratic legitimacy may be more significant than when one moves from US states to Congress. (A large literature examines the "democratic deficit" of supranational institutions.) Federal powers are legitimated not only by the state ratifying conventions that initially approved them but also by the authority of American voters to decide which leaders will temporarily exercise them. A treaty or executive agreement concluded by the United States can be analogized to a national ratifying convention that initially legitimates the powers of the institution created by the treaty or agreement to solve a global collective-action problem.[116] But Americans do not vote on who will control the powers of the institution. The point is not that global governance institutions are illegitimate; most democracies participate in them, and presidents, who *are* elected, can withdraw from them. The point, rather, is that one cannot simply "scale up" the structural theory developed here without determining whether the move can be justified on the same terms.

---

[114] U.S. CONST. art. I, § 9, cl. 1 (prohibiting Congress from banning the importation of enslaved people until 1808); art. V (prohibiting constitutional amendments affecting the previous provision until 1808).

[115] References re Greenhouse Gas Pollution Pricing Act, 2021 CarswellSask 170, para. 12 (Can. S.C.C.) (WL) (upholding a federal carbon tax because "addressing climate change requires collective national and international action").

[116] Treaties and executive agreements are discussed in Chapter 10.

Conclusion

Recall the main claim of this book, which consists of two subclaims: the primary structural purpose of the Constitution is to empower the federal government to solve many kinds of collective-action problems for the states and to prevent state governments from undermining federal solutions or causing such problems. *McCulloch* captures these two subclaims. In addition to identifying the main structural goal of the Constitution and modeling pluralist interpretation, Marshall interprets federal power broadly but not limitlessly—in terms of both ends and means—so that the federal government can solve collective-action problems for the states. Moreover, his theory of the superior democratic legitimacy of the federal government justifies giving Congress the authority to resolve disagreements among states regarding whether there are multistate collective-action problems in need of solving. In addition, a multistate collective-action problem is at the core of Marshall's explanation of why it is democratically illegitimate for states to tax federal instrumentalities.

The chapters to come will substantiate these two subclaims. First, however, it is necessary to be more precise about what collective-action problems are and to identify the different forms they can take.

2

The New "Science of Politics"

Introduction

In rebutting "the advocates of despotism" who characterized "all free government as inconsistent with the order of society," Alexander Hamilton observed in *Federalist 9* that "[t]he science of politics . . . like most other sciences, has received great improvement." As Hamilton saw it, "[t]he efficacy of various principles is now well understood, which were either not known at all, or imperfectly known to the ancients." Hamilton was referring to structural elements of constitutional design like the separation of powers, checks and balances, an independent judiciary, representative democracy, and "the consolidation of several smaller States into one great Confederacy."[1] Political science, like economics, has received further improvement since Hamilton's day. Among many other things, it has developed certain technical concepts and analytical methods that were "imperfectly known"—as opposed to "not known at all"—to Americans who framed and ratified the US Constitution. This chapter describes, in a manner that privileges accessibility over complexity, some of these concepts and methods. Subsequent chapters will use them to illuminate the collective-action logics animating the Constitution and judge-made constitutional law. As will be shown, there are several logics of collective action, not just one.

To help identify and distinguish these logics with precision, this chapter uses simple 2 x 2 matrix game theory, which models the different strategic interactions that can arise between two actors when each must choose between two strategies. Such games provide illuminating models of many strategic interactions, but they do not adequately capture many others. In this book, their primary virtue is not their realism but the parsimony and clarity with which they model the categories of collective-action problems. In addition, when their underlying assumptions are examined and adjusted, they can help point the way to potential solutions.[2]

---

[1] THE FEDERALIST NO. 9, at 72 (Alexander Hamilton) (Clinton Rossiter ed., 1961).

[2] For relatively accessible introductions to game theory, see, for example, ROBERT GIBBONS, GAME THEORY FOR APPLIED ECONOMISTS (1992); JAMES D. MORROW, GAME THEORY FOR POLITICAL SCIENTISTS (1994); and DOUGLAS G. BAIRD, ROBERT H. GERTNER & RANDAL C. PICKER, GAME THEORY AND THE LAW (1994). For more technical treatments, see, for example, ARIEL RUBINSTEIN & MARTIN J. OSBORNE, A COURSE IN GAME THEORY (1994); and DREW FUDENBERG & JEAN TIROLE, GAME THEORY (1991).

The Collective-Action Constitution. Neil S. Siegel, Oxford University Press. © Neil S. Siegel 2024.
DOI: 10.1093/oso/9780197760963.003.0003

58 THE COLLECTIVE-ACTION CONSTITUTION

This chapter first offers a definition of the classic collective-action problems studied by game theorists, which this book calls "Pareto collective-action problems." The chapter then uses game theory to sort such problems into two categories. The chapter next notes potential differences between 2 × 2 matrix models and many kinds of strategic interactions that may arise in life. These complexities do not generally change the number or nature of the collective-action problems that can occur, but the complexities can affect the likelihood that collective action will succeed. The chapter then identifies potential solutions to collective-action problems, some of which are better suited to certain kinds of collective-action problems and strategic environments than others, and each of which may face significant challenges. Regarding the Constitution, the most important such solution was to create a national government empowered to address many collective-action problems for the states and to ordinarily exercise its powers by majority vote. Relatedly, the chapter concludes by distinguishing Pareto collective-action problems from what this book calls "cost-benefit collective-action problems," which typically arise in the US federal system. When this book refers to multistate collective-action problems, it means to include both Pareto and cost-benefit collective-action problems.

As will become obvious, this chapter does not purport to present the "cutting edge" of game theoretic scholarship in economics and political science. On the contrary, the level of sophistication is modest because the primary goals are to identify the different kinds of collective-action problems and to reach an audience of legal scholars and jurists who may be unfamiliar with game theory but whose understanding of the Constitution would be enhanced if they were to self-consciously use the tools and ideas discussed in this chapter. Subsequent chapters will demonstrate that the Supreme Court has used them intuitively in many areas of constitutional law.

Definitions and Behavioral Assumptions

Collective-action problems arise between two or more actors. These actors may be, among other entities, individuals, organizations, businesses, countries, or states within countries. In this book, the relevant actors are the states in the United States.

There is not one universally accepted definition of a collective-action problem in the social sciences. Some theorists have offered a limited definition, focusing only on the so-called free-rider (or cooperation) problems, which are defined below.[3] Others have offered more encompassing definitions, focusing as well on

---

[3] RUSSELL HARDIN, COLLECTIVE ACTION 25 (1982) (writing that "the problem of collective action and the Prisoners' Dilemma are essentially the same").

coordination problems, which are also defined below.[4] This book uses the more inclusive definition because it is both more accurate and more relevant to understanding the Constitution. According to this definition, collective-action problems arise for states when two or more of them have a choice between alternatives and all would be better off by their own estimations if they could cooperate or coordinate their behavior, but there are impediments to their doing so. There are two primary impediments. First, each state may have an incentive to act in ways that produce collectively harmful results. This is what is meant by the above-mentioned free-rider or cooperation problems. Second, states may have difficulty coordinating their actions so that each does (or does not do) what others do. This is what is meant by coordination problems. Regarding both cooperation and coordination problems, the challenge of acting collectively may be exacerbated by the fact that each way of cooperating or coordinating benefits some states more than the other states. This is a cooperation or a coordination problem combined with a distribution (or inequality) problem.[5]

Because all states would be better off from their own perspectives if collective action succeeded, the classic collective-action problems studied by game theorists can be called "Pareto collective-action problems." An outcome is Pareto optimal or efficient if the only way to make one state better off by deviating from the outcome is to make another state worse off.[6] Because all states must be made better off—or at least not worse off—by any deviation from the status quo, Pareto optimality is an extraordinarily demanding conception of efficiency.

Collective-action problems arise only in strategic situations, when one state's best choice from its perspective depends partly on the choices made by other states. An example of a nonstrategic situation is a competitive market, in which the behavior of each buyer and seller has a negligible effect on the price of the goods. As a result, buyers and sellers do not take the behavior of other buyers and sellers into account in deciding what purchases to make or how many goods to sell. Because each buyer and seller is a "price taker," the study of competitive markets is not especially helpful in understanding collective-action problems.

Game theory, by contrast, focuses on interactive situations. Noncooperative game theory, in which the players act independently of one another (meaning that they may not communicate and form binding agreements), is useful in

---

[4] MICHAEL TAYLOR, THE POSSIBILITY OF COOPERATION 18–19 (1987) (deeming too restrictive the limitation of collective-action problems to the Prisoner's Dilemma and writing that "a collective action problem exists where rational individual action can lead to a strictly Pareto-inferior outcome, that is, an outcome which is strictly less preferred by every individual than at least one other outcome").

[5] For a broader conception of the universe of collective-action problems, see Katharina Holzinger, The Problems of Collective Action: A New Approach 9, 13, 15 (2003) (unpublished manuscript), https://perma.cc/757X-KFBB (adding pure distribution, disagreement, and instability problems to the two kinds of collective-action problems discussed in this chapter).

[6] MORROW, *supra* note 2, at 95.

60   THE COLLECTIVE-ACTION CONSTITUTION

illuminating the kinds and causes of collective-action problems, the challenges they pose, and the potential ways of solving them.[7] To model a strategic interaction among states as a noncooperative game, one must specify: (1) the number of states; (2) the strategies available to each state, which combine to produce different possible outcomes; (3) each state's preference ordering regarding these outcomes; and (4) an assumption about how each state behaves. In game theory, the standard assumption is that each state is narrowly self-interested, meaning that it acts to achieve its most preferred outcome subject to constraints that include the anticipated actions of other states.

Most economists and political scientists who use game theory to study collective-action problems would adopt the language of "rationality" in describing this behavioral assumption.[8] They would say, for example, that collective-action problems include situations in which individually rational actions by members of a group produce collectively irrational results for the group as a whole. On this view, it is rational for an actor to seek to benefit from collective action but not contribute to it, even if collective action fails when all actors behave this way and each actor regards itself as worse off as a result. This same view holds that it is irrational to behave otherwise.

To call behavior "rational" or "irrational," however, is to make a normative claim. Moreover, the modern economic understanding of instrumental rationality is not timeless or uncontroversial, whether historically or today. Political theorist Richard Tuck has argued that the now-conventional assertion in economics and political science that it would be irrational to contribute to the solution of a collective-action problem instead of free riding is a product of early-twentieth-century thinking in economics.[9] Notably, during the Critical Period of the 1780s, nationalists such as Madison, Hamilton, and Wilson did not describe such behavior by states as rational. In drafting a memorandum as he prepared for the Constitutional Convention, Madison labeled the narrowly self-interested behavior of states that ignored the general welfare as an "evil," "perverseness," and among the "vices" of the Articles of Confederation, even as he acknowledged the frequency of such behavior.[10] Similarly, in *Federalist 23*, Hamilton wrote that the Articles' requisition scheme was premised on the erroneous belief that the states

---

[7] Cooperative game theory studies the formation and interactions of groups of players ("coalitions"), based on the assumption that players can communicate and make binding agreements before and during the game. In cooperative game theory, players can act as a coalition to achieve a joint payoff that is later divided in some way among the members of the coalition. Cooperative game theory has been criticized for avoiding the question of how agreements are enforced. *See id.* at 75–76. For a brief introduction, see *id.* at 111–19. For an extended treatment, see HERVÉ MOULIN, COOPERATIVE MICROECONOMICS: A GAME-THEORETIC INTRODUCTION (1995).

[8] *See, e.g., supra* note 4 (quoting Professor Michael Taylor).

[9] RICHARD TUCK, FREE RIDING (2008).

[10] JAMES MADISON, *Vices of the Political System of the United States* (April 1787), *in* 2 THE WRITINGS OF JAMES MADISON 361 (Gaillard Hunt ed., 1904).

THE NEW "SCIENCE OF POLITICS"   61

would contribute their fair shares of money and troops to the Confederation treasury and military out of "a sense of their true interests, and a regard to the dictates of good faith."[11] Likewise, many modern scholars would deny that the only rational way for an actor to behave is to free ride off the contributions of other agents to a collective project from which the actor stands to benefit.

Fortunately, to agree with the arguments in this book, one need not accept or reject the main (although not the only[12]) understanding of instrumental rationality in modern economics and formal theory in political science. This is so for three reasons.

First, regarding collective-action problems caused by cooperation difficulties, it does not matter whether one believes that it is rationally self-interested or foolishly short-sighted for, say, North Carolina to free ride off the contributions of other states to the solution of a multistate collective action problem. The critical point is that such free riding happened often enough and raised sufficiently serious concerns, during the 1780s and over the course of American history, that it makes sense to view the Constitution as empowering the federal government to overcome collective-action failures by states and as prohibiting states from undermining federal solutions or causing collective-action problems. Accordingly, one can find value in particular concepts and analytical tools used in economics and political science without accepting a controversial conception of human or institutional rationality.

Second, regarding collective-action problems caused by coordination difficulties, the coordination problem often exists independently of both the assumption that agents behave in a narrowly self-interested fashion and the assertion that such behavior is rational. Many coordination problems remain even if one assumes that each state reasons (and thinks that other states reason) only in terms of collective welfare. One might question what it means for a complex collective entity like a state to "reason." For example, the Constitution separately references state electorates, state legislatures, state executives, and state courts.[13] It suffices for present purposes that states—meaning subunits of states that are empowered to act in certain ways in certain situations—make regulatory

---

[11] THE FEDERALIST NO. 23, at 251 (Alexander Hamilton) (Clinton Rossiter ed., 1961).

[12] For example, economist Amartya Sen famously critiqued this understanding. Amartya K. Sen, *Rational Fools: A Critique of the Behavioral Foundations of Economic Theory*, 6 PHIL. & PUB. AFF. 317 (1977). Moreover, political scientist Elinor Ostrom, whose work is discussed later in this chapter, shared the Nobel Prize in Economics in 2009 for her influential studies of how communities succeed or fail at managing common-pool resources. For an emphasis on "other-regarding preferences" in the context of social norms as an explanation for human cooperation, see SAMUEL BOWLES & HERBERT GINTIS, BEYOND ENLIGHTENED SELF-INTEREST: SOCIAL NORMS, OTHER-REGARDING PREFERENCES, AND COOPERATIVE BEHAVIOR (2009).

[13] *See, e.g.*, U.S. CONST. art. I, § 2, cl. 1 (state electorate); art. II, § 1, cl. 2 (state legislature); art. IV, § 4 (state legislature and state executive); art. VI, § 1, cl. 2 (state judges).

62 THE COLLECTIVE-ACTION CONSTITUTION

decisions and so are "individuals" in the sense of having individual decisions to make.

Third, the analysis that follows will not always be wedded to the game-theoretic assumption of narrowly self-seeking behavior. It will note circumstances in which changing the behavioral assumption can help solve collective-action problems. It will also note situations in which the behavioral assumption did not hold, such as when states contributed some money and troops to the Confederation during the 1780s. When the behavioral assumption does not entirely hold, as it often does not in the real world, certain solutions to collective-action problems become more likely to succeed. As discussed below, these solutions include voluntaristic ones, which are often supported by an internalized obligation to follow cooperative social norms. In the context of intergovernmental relations, however, such motivations cannot routinely be counted on. For example, as will be explained, states during the 1780s did not contribute nearly as much money and soldiers as was requested, and they thereby rendered themselves more vulnerable militarily and economically.

To avoid accepting or rejecting a contested conception of rationality, the definition of a collective-action problem in the paragraphs above self-consciously uses the phrase "narrowly self-interested behavior," not "rational behavior." Describing behavior as "narrowly self-interested" may have problems of its own—it may seem overly judgmental of state motivations. But the purpose of using this alternative phrase is to avoid taking a position in a debate about human and institutional rationality that need not be resolved to show that the logics of collective action can help illuminate the US Constitution and constitutional law.

Categories of Classic Collective-Action Problems

There are two categories of collective-action problems that are classically studied by game theorists. These two categories are distinguished by whether any of their predicted outcomes are efficient in the demanding sense of Pareto optimality. This section discusses each category in turn.

Cooperation Problems

The first category is the most familiar. Made famous by Professor Mancur Olson's *The Logic of Collective Action*,[14] this kind of collective-action problem involves

---

[14] MANCUR OLSON, THE LOGIC OF COLLECTIVE ACTION: PUBLIC GOODS AND THE THEORY OF GROUPS (1965).

THE NEW "SCIENCE OF POLITICS" 63

a situation in which no outcome predicted by game theory is Pareto optimal. A group of actors is predicted to fail to achieve an outcome that each actor values more than the outcome that results, because each actor wants to achieve their most preferred outcome without paying for it—each actor imposes costs on other actors without paying for them.

Externalities refer to unpriced benefits and costs. The conferral of unpaid benefits is called a *positive externality*. For example, an individual who gets vaccinated or wears a mask during a pandemic benefits other people by reducing their risk of exposure to a contagious disease. The recipients of this benefit do not pay for it.[15]

The most famous and important examples of positive externalities are "pure public goods." This term refers to goods that cannot be financed by market prices because they possess two technical characteristics. First, pure public goods are *nonrivalrous*, meaning one person's enjoyment of the good does not detract from another's enjoyment. For example, when a strong military provides security from foreign invasion, one citizen's enjoyment of this security does not detract from another's. By contrast, private goods are *rivalrous*. For instance, when one person buys a small lot of land and builds a home on it, another person cannot build there.

Second, pure public goods are *nonexcludable*, meaning excluding individuals from enjoying the benefits produced by the goods is infeasible or too costly. For example, no resident of a country with a strong national defense can be excluded from enjoying the security provided by this defense short of forcing the individual to leave the country. By contrast, private goods are excludable when a legal system protects property rights. For instance, a landowner has legal means to prevent others from using the land.[16]

Because it is difficult or impossible to exclude people from enjoying a public good, people who enjoy it have an incentive to *free ride* by not paying for the benefits they obtain. This incentive causes a collective-action problem.[17] When beneficiaries do not pay, suppliers of the good cannot earn a profit. As a result, the market undersupplies the good. An unregulated market will undersupply national defense and other public goods.[18]

---

[15] The next several paragraphs draw partly from Robert D. Cooter & Neil S. Siegel, *Collective Action Federalism: A General Theory of Article I, Section 8*, 63 STAN. L. REV. 115, 135–36 (2010).

[16] Although the two characteristics of public goods often appear together, they are distinct. An uncongested bridge is nonrivalrous, but a tollbooth could exclude people. A congested road with many entrances is rivalrous, but it would be expensive to exclude people from using it.

[17] OLSON, *supra* note 14, at 9–16 (arguing that the nonexcludability property of public goods creates a free-rider problem).

[18] Technical characteristics of goods can cause markets to fail. Market failure is the conventional justification in economics for having the government supply and regulate goods. For early uses of the categories of market failure to assess regulations, see STEPHEN BREYER, REGULATION AND ITS REFORM (1982); and CHARLES L. SCHULTZE, THE PUBLIC USE OF PRIVATE INTEREST (1977).

64　THE COLLECTIVE-ACTION CONSTITUTION

		California	
		Cooperate	Don't
North Carolina	Cooperate	3,3	1,4̲
	Don't	4̲,1	**2,2**

Figure 2.1 Prisoners' Dilemma.

Sometimes, an activity confers not unpaid benefits but unpaid costs. The imposition of unpaid costs is called a *negative externality*. For example, burning fuel causes dirty air, and absent legal intervention, the polluters need not pay for the resulting reduction in air quality.

A collective-action problem caused by a negative externality can be modeled using 2 × 2 matrix game theory. Such a collective-action problem may, although need not, take the form of the Prisoners' Dilemma. The one-shot version of the game is represented in the following 2 × 2 matrix, in which there are two players that must decide to either contribute to the achievement of some objective (behave cooperatively) or not contribute (behave uncooperatively). The goal could be staying silent amidst police questioning and so not incriminating the other suspect (hence the name of the game), giving a proportionate share of money to an institution (say, the federal government) that requires funding to survive, or resisting the temptation to attract wealthy businesses and residents to one's jurisdiction by further reducing corporate and individual income tax rates, thereby pressuring other states to do the same.

Figure 2.1 models the interaction between two states, North Carolina and California. The cells in the matrix contain each state's ranking of the four possible outcomes from most preferred (4) to least preferred (1). North Carolina's ranking of each outcome is listed first.

Both states prefer the outcome (Cooperate, Cooperate) to the outcome (Don't Cooperate, Don't Cooperate), but each state has an incentive not to cooperate regardless of whether the other state does. If California cooperates (see column one), North Carolina's *best reply* is not to cooperate because achieving its most preferred outcome (indicated by the number 4) is superior to obtaining its second most preferred outcome (indicated by the number 3).[19] This best reply is noted by underlining the number 4 in the lower left quadrant. If California does not cooperate (see column two), North Carolina's best reply once again is not to cooperate because achieving its third most preferred outcome (indicated by the number 2) is superior to obtaining its least preferred outcome (indicated

---

[19] A best reply is a strategy that is always at least as advantageous as any other strategy for a player against a strategy of the other player. MORROW, *supra* note 2, at 79–80.

THE NEW "SCIENCE OF POLITICS" 65

by the number 1). Because the states are similarly situated (the game is symmetrical), the same holds true for California regardless of what North Carolina does (California prefers a payoff of 4 to 3 and 2 to 1).[20] So, not cooperating *strictly dominates* cooperating for each state.[21]

The outcome of this game is predicted by the primary solution concept in game theory, the *Nash equilibrium*, which is indicated in bold. A Nash equilibrium exists if neither player has an incentive to deviate from their choice of strategy given the other player's choice of strategy.[22] Assuming California chooses not to cooperate (the right column), North Carolina will also choose not to cooperate (the bottom row) because a payoff of 2 is greater than 1. The game is symmetrical, so if North Carolina chooses not to cooperate (the bottom row), California will also choose not to cooperate (the right column), again because 2 is greater than 1. So, this outcome, unlike any other, is stable in that neither state has a narrowly self-interested incentive to deviate from it once it results. The Nash equilibrium need not be the upshot of this game—any outcome is possible—but the Nash equilibrium will result if each state is narrowly self-interested.

A collective-action problem exists because both states prefer the outcome in which they both cooperate (3,3) to the outcome in which they both do not (2,2), but they will end up not cooperating anyway if the behavioral assumption holds. Mutual cooperation is the collective optimum (and so is italicized) because it is Pareto optimal or efficient. Mutual noncooperation is suboptimal because both states are better off moving to mutual cooperation. Cooperation problems are distinguished by the fact that no Nash equilibrium is Pareto efficient.

The Prisoners' Dilemma is a familiar game, but what may be less familiar is the cause of the collective-action problem—each state's externalization of costs onto the other. When California cooperates and North Carolina does not, North Carolina obtains its most preferred outcome (4) instead of its second most preferred (3), but North Carolina also harms California by moving California from its second most preferred outcome (3) to its least preferred (1). North Carolina does not pay for the harm that it imposes on California; instead, North Carolina simply externalizes this harm onto California. The same holds true when the roles are reversed. But when both states internalize the benefits of their behavior and externalize the costs—and when the externalized costs (moving California

---

[20] In a symmetrical game, the payoffs associated with choosing a strategy depend only on the strategies chosen by the other players, not on the identities of the players choosing these strategies. The players are interchangeable in that their identities can be swapped (they can be relabeled) without changing the payoffs produced by their strategy choices, given the strategy choices of the other players. *Id.* at 96–97.

[21] Strategy A strictly (or strongly) dominates strategy B for a player if choosing A is always more advantageous for the player than choosing B no matter what strategy the other player chooses. *Id.* at 77–79.

[22] *Id.* at 80–81, 91–94. A Nash equilibrium is a profile of strategies in which no player has an incentive to change its strategy, given the strategies of the other players.

66 THE COLLECTIVE-ACTION CONSTITUTION

from 3 to 1) exceed the internalized benefits (moving North Carolina from 3 to 4)—a collective-action problem exists and both states will deem the outcome that results from narrowly self-interested behavior inferior to mutual cooperation.[23]

Another example of a cooperation problem is the Tragedy of the Commons, which is a Prisoners' Dilemma extended to more than two players.[24] Actors tend to overuse common-pool resources such as air basins, grazing lands, fish stocks, and oil reserves because they internalize all the benefits of each use but externalize most of the costs of depleting the resource onto other users. Just as an unregulated market will undersupply positive externalities, so an unregulated market or common-pool resource will oversupply negative externalities. This is generally true of the behavior of businesses and individuals, and it is generally true of the behavior of state governments. For example, states may seek to keep or attract businesses by declining to regulate commercial activities that produce interstate pollution, deplete migratory fish stocks, or kill migratory species.

Although externalities often cause collective-action problems, not every externality does so. Thus, to establish a collective-action problem, more must be shown than an externality. Perhaps the imposition of a negative externality by one actor onto another invites retaliation that makes both actors worse off than if neither had externalized costs. This is a "race to the bottom." But if retaliation is impossible, there is no collective-action problem if a state benefits more from sending pollution across its border than it harms its neighbor.

A further clarification is warranted. Although all situations that can be modeled as a Prisoners' Dilemma involve collective-action problems, not all collective-action problems can be modeled as a Prisoners' Dilemma—although an eminent scholar suggested otherwise.[25] This is so for two reasons. First, the Prisoners' Dilemma is not the only game modeling a cooperation problem in which the Pareto optimum deviates from the Nash equilibrium. There are asymmetric dilemma games in which narrowly self-interested behavior externalizes costs and produces an equilibrium that is not Pareto optimal.[26] In Figure 2.2, the

---

[23] The rankings in Figure 2.1 are ordinal, not cardinal. The numbers reflect the order in which each state ranks outcomes; they do not reflect the welfare levels achieved by each state in each outcome, whether measured by dollars or in another way. As a result, outcomes that receive the same ranking in the preference orderings of the states may be associated with different welfare levels for each state. Without some way of making interpersonal (here, interstate) comparisons of utility, it cannot be determined whether external costs exceed internal benefits in the game. The easiest way to manage this difficulty is to assume that given differences in ordinal payoffs reflect equivalent differences in cardinal payoffs. This way, it is certain that North Carolina harms California more than it helps itself when it does not cooperate and California does. Alternatively, one can use cardinal payoffs directly. If they create a Prisoners' Dilemma, externalized costs will exceed internalized benefits for each state.

[24] For the classic statement of this collective-action problem, see Garrett Hardin, *The Tragedy of the Commons*, 162 SCIENCE 1243 (1968).

[25] *See supra* note 3 (quoting Russell Hardin).

[26] *See* Holzinger, *supra* note 5, at 9, 11, 14 (discussing asymmetric dilemma games).

THE NEW "SCIENCE OF POLITICS"   67

California

		Cooperate	Don't
North Carolina	Cooperate	4̲,3	1,4̲
	Don't	3,1	2̲,2̲

Figure 2.2 Asymmetric Dilemma.

Pareto optimum (mutual cooperation) and the Nash equilibrium (mutual non-cooperation) are the same as in the Prisoners' Dilemma.

Although North Carolina most prefers the cooperative outcome, the analysis of this game is the same as that of the Prisoners' Dilemma: mutual noncooperation is the suboptimal Nash equilibrium. In asymmetric dilemma games, however, it may be more difficult to solve the collective-action problem because the payoffs would be unequal if the Pareto optimum were somehow reached (and, in the game above, the payoffs are equal in the Nash equilibrium). There is both a free-rider problem and a distribution (inequality) problem. Even if the standard game-theoretic assumptions were relaxed and the states could communicate and bargain their way to an enforceable agreement, concluding it might be difficult. If the states place a high value on equality, there will be an additional impediment to collective action.[27]

An Asymmetric Dilemma captures a situation in which a state externalizes costs that are greater than the benefits it secures for itself onto another state and a transfer payment between the states is possible. This kind of externality problem, which can be called a net-negative externality, *is* a collective-action problem. For example, suppose that the benefits accruing to the state that externalizes costs are worth $10 and the costs borne by the state being harmed are valued at $15. If so, both states could be made better off by a redistribution of these costs and benefits—for example, no cost externalization and a transfer payment of $12.50. The payoff matrix is reflected in Figure 2.3.

North Carolina's options are to pay $12.50 to South Carolina or not to pay. South Carolina's options are not to act (and so not to externalize costs onto North Carolina) or to act (and so to externalize costs). If South Carolina does not act,

---

[27] As explained *supra* note 23, the payoffs in each matrix are ordinal, not cardinal, so inequality in ordinal payoffs within a cell may not mean inequality in welfare between the two states within the cell. One can manage this problem either by assuming (as in note 23) that given differences in ordinal payoffs reflect equivalent differences in cardinal payoffs or by assuming that the states care about ordinal inequality. Because inequality problems are primarily problems of relative welfare, not relative rankings, the former assumption probably makes more sense. For discussion, see Holzinger, *supra* note 5, at 7–8. As explained *supra* note 23, one can also manage this problem by using cardinal payoffs directly in the matrix.

68   THE COLLECTIVE-ACTION CONSTITUTION

		South Carolina	
		Don't Act	Act
North Carolina	Pay	−12.5,12.5	−27.5,22.5
	Don't Pay	0,0	−15,10

Figure 2.3 Net-Negative Externality as Asymmetric Dilemma[a]

[a] This game is asymmetric, even though each state is better off not cooperating regardless of what the other state does (as in the Prisoners' Dilemma), because the players are not interchangeable: They do not have the same strategy choices, and their payoffs are asymmetric. *See supra* note 20.

North Carolina's best reply is not to pay because it saves itself the $12.50 and receives a payoff of $0. If South Carolina acts, North Carolina's best reply is also not to pay because it obtains a payoff of -$15 (the harm caused by the negative externality), as opposed to -$27.50 (the harm caused by the negative externality plus the $12.50 transfer payment). If North Carolina pays, South Carolina's best reply is to act because it receives a payoff of $22.50 (the $10 benefit to itself from externalizing costs plus the transfer payment of $12.50). If North Carolina does not pay, South Carolina's best reply is also to act because it obtains a payoff of $10 instead of $0. Based on each state's best replies, the Nash equilibrium is produced by the strategies (Don't Pay, Act), where collective welfare is -15 plus 10, or -5. The Pareto optimum is produced by the strategies (Pay, Don't Act), where collective welfare is -12.5 plus 12.5, or 0.

There is a second reason that not all collective-action problems studied by game theorists can be modeled as a Prisoners' Dilemma. Not all such problems involve a discrepancy between the Pareto optimal outcome and the Nash equilibrium. Collective-action problems can also be caused by the failure of actors to coordinate their behavior when each one prefers coordinating to not coordinating. Coordination difficulties are the second category of Pareto collective-action problems.

Coordination Problems

The classic example is the pure coordination problem of deciding which side of the road to drive on in a society in which automobiles have recently been introduced. No one cares much whether everyone drives on the left side or the right, but everyone cares greatly that everyone drive on the same side. Regarding interstate relations, an example of a pure coordination problem might be building an interstate, north-south railroad or highway so that the segment constructed in one state connects to the one built in the adjacent state. Assuming that the

THE NEW "SCIENCE OF POLITICS" 69

South Dakota

West East

North Dakota West *1,1* 0,0

East 0,0 *1,1*

Figure 2.4 Pure Coordination game.

states do not care which of two possible locations is chosen, they face a pure co-ordination problem.

Figure 2.4 captures this problem. The cells include each state's ranking of the four possible outcomes from most preferred (1) to least preferred (0), with North Dakota's ranking listed first.

Although both states prefer to coordinate, they may fail to do so because two ways of coordinating exist—hence the collective-action problem. Both (West, West) and (East, East) are Nash equilibria and Pareto optimal (and so are in-dicated in bold and italics). Assuming South Dakota chooses West (the left column), North Dakota's best reply is to choose West because 1 is greater than 0. Assuming South Dakota chooses East (the right column), North Dakota's best reply is to choose East because 1 is greater than 0. The game is symmetrical, so the same is true if we hold each row constant and ask how South Dakota will respond.

Another coordination game is the Assurance game. It is so named because each player requires assurance that if it chooses the mutually most preferred but riskier strategy, the other player will do the same.[28] For example, in an America without the US Constitution, two groups of states, Northern and Southern, may prefer that both groups embargo goods coming from Great Britain in retaliation for trade restrictions imposed by Britain, but an embargo also imposes economic pain on the states responsible for it, and it can succeed only if both groups im-pose it. (If one group does not embargo foreign goods, they can be imported into these states and moved across state lines and sold throughout the nation—a sce-nario the Founders knew well.) Figure 2.5 models an example of this interaction.

The outcome (Embargo, Embargo) is the Pareto optimum, and both the strategies (Embargo, Embargo) and (No Embargo, No Embargo) are Nash equilibria. But the interests of the two groups outside the two equilibria are not fully aligned. If one group imposes an embargo and the other does not, each

---

[28] This game is also called Stag Hunt (a stag is a male deer) because Rousseau used an example involving hunting a deer (which is most preferred but requires the other hunter also to hunt the deer) and hunting a hare (which is less preferred but also less risky because a hunter can do so alone). *See* JEAN JACQUES ROUSSEAU, THE SOCIAL CONTRACT AND DISCOURSES 238 (C.D.H. Cole trans., E.P. Dutton & Co. 1950) (1755).

70   THE COLLECTIVE-ACTION CONSTITUTION

Southern

Embargo No Embargo

Northern   Embargo   <u>4</u>,<u>4</u>   1,3

No Embargo   3,1   <u>2</u>,<u>2</u>

Figure 2.5 Assurance game.

group would prefer to be the one that does not, because it can then avoid the economic pain and the embargo will not succeed anyway. Figure 2.5 reflects the fact that imposing an embargo is the riskiest strategy. Each group will end up with its least preferred outcome (1) instead of its most preferred (4) if it imposes an embargo and the other group does not. By contrast, not imposing an embargo is the least risky strategy because each group is then guaranteed not to obtain its least-preferred outcome (1) regardless of what the other group does. If the Northern and Southern groups are unable to coordinate, the result may not be the Pareto optimum or the other equilibrium.

One could question the realism of the prior two examples. As explained later, communication can solve many pure coordination difficulties, and state officials could presumably communicate to coordinate their highway-construction efforts or adoption of embargo policies. In more realistic situations, however, it may be impossible to communicate sufficiently, perhaps including when ongoing coordination on numerous decisions is required on a national scale. For example, states may require assurance that sister states not only will formally adopt embargo policies but also will continue to vigorously enforce them. More often, real-world coordination problems are impure; they also involve disagreements over how to coordinate. Communication does not suffice to resolve such disagreements—bargaining often fails—as discussed in the following game.

Just as some cooperation problems are exacerbated by distribution problems (recall the Asymmetric Dilemma of Figure 2.2), so there are coordination problems that include inequality problems. A prominent example is the unfortunately named Battle of the Sexes game, which is also called the Bach or Stravinsky game. It imagines a man and a woman—or, in the nongendered version, two people—who want to spend the evening together but who disagree about what to do. In interstate relations, one can—to coin a term—call this the Bridge or Seaway game. An example, represented in Figure 2.6, imagines that New York and New Jersey want to facilitate transportation across their common border, but they disagree over whether to do it with a bridge or passenger ferryboats.

Both states prefer the two outcomes in which they come together—(Bridge, Bridge) and (Seaway, Seaway)—to the outcomes in which they do not—(Seaway, Bridge) and (Bridge, Seaway). Like in the Pure Coordination game and the

		New Jersey	
		Bridge	Seaway
New York	Bridge	**4,3**	2,1
	Seaway	1,2	**3,4**

Figure 2.6 Bridge or Seaway game.

Assurance game, the states agree on the need to avoid certain outcomes and so face a coordination problem. Unlike in the prior two games, however, the states disagree over which Nash equilibrium is preferable. New York prefers (Bridge, Bridge) and New Jersey prefers (Seaway, Seaway). Accordingly, for collective action to succeed in a Bridge or Seaway game—meaning either equilibrium is chosen, because both are Pareto optimal—the states must overcome both a coordination and an inequality problem. Given the distributive implications of coordinating one way versus the other, it may be more difficult to solve a collective-action problem best modeled as a Bridge or Seaway game than it is to solve one involving just a coordination problem. As discussed in the next two sections, communication may not suffice to solve a Bridge or Seaway problem.[29]

Similar to the Bridge or Seaway game is the Chicken game, so named because it models an interaction where the issue is which player will "blink first" to avoid the worst outcome for both players. (Picture two cars colliding because neither driver was willing to swerve out of the way. Each driver most prefers to be the one who does not blink, but neither player wants to die for this personal cause.) This game, represented in Figure 2.7, imagines that Maryland and Virginia want to settle a dispute over territory between them and so avoid litigating, but each wants to be the one that holds out for a settlement more favorable to itself. Accordingly, each state most prefers that the other state be the only one to give in, followed by mutual giving in and then giving in by itself. Mutual refusing to give

		Virginia	
		Give In	Don't
Maryland	Give In	3,3	**2,4**
	Don't	**4,2**	1,1

Figure 2.7 Chicken game.

---

[29] For a discussion of the relationship between inequality in ordinal payoffs within a cell and inequality in cardinal payoffs, see *supra* notes 23 and 27.

72 THE COLLECTIVE-ACTION CONSTITUTION

in is least preferred by each state, although that will happen if each one aims for its most preferred outcome.

Like in the Bridge or Seaway game, there are two Nash equilibria, both of which are Pareto optimal. Unlike in the Bridge or Seaway game, the two equilibria involve strategy combinations in which each state does the opposite of what the other state does. Also, relative to the Bridge or Seaway game, the inequality problem in a Chicken game is greater. Now the "bad" equilibrium for each state entails its getting its third-most-preferred outcome (2), not its second-most-preferred outcome (3). This fact may make solving the collective-action problem more difficult than in the Bridge or Seaway game. But the Chicken game has a third Pareto optimal outcome (Give In, Give In). It is not an equilibrium, but it exhibits equality. If bargaining is allowed, this outcome may help solve the collective-action problem of avoiding mutual obstinance.

More Complex Strategic Interactions

The 2 × 2 matrix models capture the essence of many strategic interactions in the real world, whether among states or other actors.[30] Two parties—or two groups of parties—may interact once, and they may face a problem of cooperation or coordination, either alone or along with a distribution problem. Moreover, as discussed below, changing the game to a relatively small number of parties that interact a limited number of times may not significantly change the strategic outlook. In addition, the assumption of simultaneous play and no communication may be appropriate when there are many actors and the costs of bargaining are prohibitively high.[31]

That said, 2 × 2 models do not capture many strategic interactions that occur in life. One should therefore be mindful of the assumptions built into these models and the potential effects of changing them. Of greatest relevance in this book are interactions among several or many states, as opposed to two (or two groups). This frequent occurrence helps explain why the constitutional text, mostly for better but occasionally for worse, expresses skepticism that states will solve their own collective-action problems—and expresses optimism that Congress will be more likely to succeed. Also potentially relevant are repeated interactions, as opposed to one; a larger number of strategies, as opposed to two; heterogeneous agents in terms of their payoffs or resources, as opposed to homogeneous agents; and player knowledge of what strategy the other player will choose, whether through communication or sequential play (in which players choose

---

[30] BAIRD, GERTNER & PICKER, *supra* note 2, at 32, 45.
[31] *Id.* at 32.

their strategies one at a time), as opposed to no such knowledge when all players choose their strategies without prior communication and simultaneously. As will be discussed, these complexities do not generally change the number or nature of the collective-action problems that can occur in strategic interactions, but the complexities can affect the likelihood that collective action will succeed and the solutions most likely to help. This section discusses the complexities, leaving the most important one—increasing the number of players—for last.[32]

Increasing the Number of Times an Interaction Occurs

Increasing the number of iterations in a game generally increases the likelihood that collective action will succeed, although success is far from certain. In infinitely (or indefinitely) repeated games involving cooperation problems, each player now has the option of making its own future cooperation tacitly contingent on the past cooperation of the other player. As a result, the additional payoff that a player obtains by not cooperating in a given round may be lower than the longer-term losses it suffers when the other player "punishes" its noncooperation by not cooperating in future rounds. The most famous and important strategy that can potentially sustain mutual cooperation in an infinitely repeated Prisoners' Dilemma is Tit for Tat. According to this strategy, a player initially chooses cooperation and then chooses whatever the other player chose in the previous round.[33] Significantly, however, cooperation is not remotely assured in repeated games; a multitude of equilibria are possible, including the one in which neither player ever cooperates.[34]

The strategic structure of Prisoners' Dilemma–type games is less affected by repeating them a finite number of times, meaning that the players know the interaction will last a specified number of rounds. Game theory predicts that a

---

[32] Additional complications include games of incomplete and possibly asymmetric information, as opposed to games in which each player knows everything but the other player's choice of strategy; the use of mixed strategies by players (which randomize over possible strategies), as opposed to each player's use of a single, pure strategy; and games embedded in larger games. Another complication not considered here is the unsatisfactory nature of Nash equilibria in extensive games, which specify the order of events. Nash equilibria ignore the sequential structure of the decision problems in extensive games and so do not distinguish between equilibria that do and do not depend on noncredible threats. Because Nash equilibria do not account for the credibility of threats supporting equilibria, it is necessary to define an equilibrium that captures this consideration. This solution concept, subgame perfection, eliminates Nash equilibria in which player threats are not credible by requiring that the actions prescribed by each player's equilibrium strategy be optimal, given the strategies of the other players, within each subgame. All these complications are not as important in executing this book's argument as the ones discussed in the text. For explications of these complexities, see the texts referenced *supra* note 2.

[33] The pathmarking work is Robert Axelrod, The Evolution of Cooperation (1984).

[34] Morrow, *supra* note 2, at 262–79 (discussing iterated Prisoners' Dilemmas and "folk theorems," which prove the existence of vast equilibria in infinitely repeated games).

74 THE COLLECTIVE-ACTION CONSTITUTION

finitely repeated Prisoners' Dilemma will produce no cooperation in any round given that the last round is just a one-shot Prisoners' Dilemma and so will generate mutual noncooperation, which will make the penultimate round in effect the last round and so will also generate mutual noncooperation, and so on.[35] This prediction is not entirely accurate regarding both finitely repeated games and one-shot games,[36] but the point remains that the strategic structure is not significantly different when the game is repeated a limited number of times.

Coordination problems are also more likely to be solved through repetition. In pure coordination games, indefinite or finite repetition provides ways for the players to develop common knowledge and so for "focal points" to emerge.[37] In coordination games with distribution problems (such as Bridge or Seaway, or Chicken), indefinite repetition provides a way for the players to make costly threats credible. Because these games have multiple equilibria of different desirability in the one-shot game, a player can enforce one way of coordinating by playing the less preferable Nash equilibrium in subsequent rounds if the other player deviates in the current round. As with cooperation games, however, a vast number of equilibria are possible when a coordination game is indefinitely repeated. In contrast to cooperation games, if coordination games with multiple equilibria of different desirability in the one-shot game are finitely repeated, reciprocal threats can still produce stable, optimal, and equal outcomes. Once again, the players can use the threat of playing the less preferable Nash equilibrium in the last rounds to enforce coordination in earlier rounds.[38]

Increasing the Number of Available Strategies

The 2 × 2 matrix games permit each player to choose between two strategies. In some strategic interactions, players may have more than two strategies available. Whether a larger number of potential strategies changes the strategic structure of an interaction depends on the payoffs associated with the new strategies. In

---

[35] *Id.* at 279–80 (explaining this process of reasoning, called "backward induction," that generates the prediction); Elinor Ostrom, *Collective Action and the Evolution of Social Norms*, 14 J. ECON. PERSP. 137, 139–40 (2000) (same). For more on backward induction, see MORROW, *supra* note 2, at 124–28.

[36] Ostrom, *supra* note 35, at 140 (reporting repeated findings of public-good experiments, including that "[s]ubjects contribute between 40 and 60 percent of their endowments to the public good in a one-shot game as well as in the first round of finitely repeated games"; that "[a]fter the first round, contribution levels tend to decay downward, but remain well above zero"; and that "over 70 percent of subjects contribute nothing in the announced last round of a finitely repeated sequence").

[37] THOMAS C. SCHELLING, THE STRATEGY OF CONFLICT 57 (paperback ed. 1963) (1960). Finding a focal point "may depend on analogy, precedent, accidental arrangement, symmetry, aesthetic or geometric configuration, casuistic reasoning, and who the parties are and what they know about each other." *Id.*

[38] MORROW, *supra* note 2, at 279.

general, however, the same kinds of collective-action problems remain if players have more than two strategies, and whether increasing the number of strategies makes it easier to solve collective-action problems depends on whether communication and bargaining are permitted. A greater number of strategies means a greater number of potential outcomes that the players can negotiate over and jointly select, which can be especially helpful in solving inequality problems.[39]

Introducing Different Kinds of Actors

Almost all the 2×2 matrix games examined in this chapter have symmetrical (or homogeneous) players.[40] Some strategic interactions in life involve asymmetrical (or heterogeneous) actors. Certain kinds of heterogeneities in the actors that face a common problem may make collective action more likely. Such heterogeneities include differences in payoffs and resources. One or a few actors may stand to benefit disproportionately from solving a free-rider problem, perhaps because the actor is especially harmed by it. Or, one (or a few) of these actors may possess greater resources than the others and so may be able to solve the problem without contributions from the others. In either case, the one actor may have an incentive to solve the problem itself and permit others to free ride.[41] Whether this outcome endures in repeated interactions, however, may depend on whether the actor that solves the problem initially comes to resent the free riding and so terminates its efforts later on or tries to exclude free riders from continuing to benefit.

Heterogeneity may, however, make collective action less likely. For example, in the Asymmetric Dilemma game modeled in Figure 2.2, which contains the same free-rider problem as the Prisoners' Dilemma, Player 1 has greater incentive than Player 2 to solve the collective-action problem individually because Player 1 stands to benefit more than Player 2 from collective action. But if Player 1 cannot or will not solve the problem individually, the heterogeneity may (as noted in the previous section) make it more difficult to act collectively if communication and bargaining become possible—a relaxation of another assumption underlying 2×2 matrix games discussed below. This is because Player 2 will not benefit from collective action as much as Player 1, and so agreeing may be more difficult.

---

[39] Holzinger, *supra* note 5, at 17–18.

[40] For the definition of symmetrical games, see *supra* note 20.

[41] CLINT PEINHARDT & TODD SANDLER, *Principles of Collective Action and Game Theory*, in TRANSNATIONAL COOPERATION: AN ISSUE-BASED APPROACH 37 (2015); Aziz Huq, *Does the Logic of Collective Action Explain Federalism Doctrine?*, 66 STAN. L. REV. 217, 244–45 (2014) (discussing the literature demonstrating the potentially positive effects on collective action of a "critical mass" of high-income actors despite free riders).

76 THE COLLECTIVE-ACTION CONSTITUTION

More generally, relative homogeneity between or among agents—for example, in terms of preferences, financial resources, geographic proximity, and perceptions of whether there is a problem in need of a solution—reduces the "transaction costs of cooperation." These costs are a function of the obstacles to collective action that either increase the time and effort needed for cooperation to occur or block it. They include impediments to communication, distrust, asymmetric information, holdouts, and disputes over how to divide the fruits of cooperation. A famous proposition offered by Professor Ronald Coase, which helped him win the Nobel Prize in Economics, is that actors will bargain successfully unless transaction costs prevent them. The point of the Coase Theorem is to isolate the cause of bargaining failure, not to deny the possibility of bargaining failure.[42]

Heterogeneities may make collective action less likely for other reasons. One example is when there are several well-resourced actors that stand to benefit disproportionately from collective action, and it is unclear which one will step up given the existence of the others. Solving the free-rider problem in one game may require solving a separate game of Chicken.[43]

Agent heterogeneity does not help solve pure coordination problems. Having agents of different incomes, for example, does not affect the challenge they face. For the reasons discussed above, player heterogeneity may or may not make it easier to solve the inequality aspect of certain coordination games. On one hand, the player that has the highest income may not care about obtaining a lower benefit than the other player if collective action succeeds. On the other hand, if both agents care about equality of payoffs, inequality in payoffs makes it more challenging to act collectively.

Allowing Communication or Other Forms of Information Sharing

The 2 × 2 matrix games assume simultaneous play (in which all players choose their strategies at the same time), so no player knows what strategy the other players will choose. Accordingly, players cannot communicate even tacitly before they choose. As discussed above, this is sometimes a realistic assumption, but not always. If communication is permitted, pure coordination and assurance problems generally disappear, at least when the number of players is relatively small. (As already noted, and as the next section discusses, it can be harder to use

---

[42] Cooter & Siegel, *supra* note 15, at 139.

[43] Huq, *supra* note 41, at 246–47 (discussing this possibility and situations where there are private substitutes for the collective good that are accessible to only certain wealthier actors or the benefits achieved by collective action decline sharply with one or a few free riders).

THE NEW "SCIENCE OF POLITICS" 77

communication to coordinate with many actors.) Moreover, if information can be revealed about the strategies of players in other ways, like assuming sequential play instead of simultaneous play, coordination problems either do not occur or become much easier to solve. In Pure Coordination, Assurance, Bridge or Seaway, and Chicken games, if Player 2 can observe Player 1's choice of strategy before making its own choice, and, in the latter two games, if Player 2 does not care about inequality of payoffs, coordinating at a Pareto optimal equilibrium will not be challenging.[44]

Communication will not, however, solve the inequality problem in coordination games with a distributive dimension; communication enables bargaining but does not ensure its success. Nor may sequential play, although if the game is played only once, Player 1 has the distributive advantage: If Player 1 chooses the equilibrium that is more desirable for it, Player 2's best reply is to choose the same equilibrium. Finally, communication or sequential play does not change the strategic structure of Prisoners' Dilemma games. The incentive not to cooperate remains after there is communication or Player 1 moves first, regardless of Player 1's strategy. Communication or sequential play may, however, facilitate a bargained-for solution to free-rider problems.

Increasing the Number of Actors

The 2×2 matrix games assume only two actors. In general, increasing the number of actors whose cooperation or coordination is necessary for collective action to succeed does not change the strategic structure of noncooperative games.[45] But increasing the number of actors does make collective action less likely to succeed if cooperative solutions are permitted. This proposition is among the principles of collective action articulated by Professor Olson in *The Logic of Collective Action*.[46] The proposition that larger groups are less likely to act collectively than smaller groups is better thought of as a general tendency than as a social scientific law, given the other determinants (including the ones discussed above) of whether collective action will occur. But for two reasons, the proposition makes intuitive sense.

First, the greater the number of actors required for collective action to succeed, the higher the organizing costs they will face. Given these transaction costs, two or three actors are, in general, substantially more likely than many actors to work together to solve a collective-action problem.[47] For example, with

---

[44] Holzinger, *supra* note 5, at 19.
[45] *Id.* at 18–19. There are complex exceptions, but the statement in the text holds generally. *Id.*
[46] OLSON, *supra* note 14, at 1–2.
[47] *Id.* at 22–36.

78 THE COLLECTIVE-ACTION CONSTITUTION

each additional actor whose participation is required, the more difficult it may be for all actors to use communication to coordinate their behavior or to bargain over a distribution problem, and the greater the likelihood that one or more actors will hold out for a greater share of the fruits of cooperation. (A holdout problem, unlike a free-rider problem or pure coordination problem, can be modeled as a coordination game with a distributive dimension.) Unanimity rule, which governs whether individual agents will voluntarily act collectively, threatens to paralyze organizations as their membership grows.[48] As the next section discusses, alternative decision-making procedures, like majority rule, may be required.

Second, the greater the number of actors that must cooperate, the less likely it is that each one will perceive the net benefits generated by its costly acts of cooperation.[49] With a collective-action problem facing many actors, such as funding a government or reducing the pollution generated by productive activities, the value of each actor's contribution to collective action may be small, and each one may wonder whether the costs it incurs in helping solve the problem will be wasted given free riding. By contrast, two or three actors will generally be better able to calculate the net benefits of doing their part to solve the problem. Their individual contributions may be essential for collective action to succeed, and the universe of possible free riders is limited.[50]

Relevance

In subsequent chapters, the foregoing complexities will occasionally arise, but it will be unnecessary to return to them often. This is because the US Constitution permits Congress to act without first assessing whether collective action by state governments will succeed—although conscientious members of Congress should consider this likelihood before authorizing federal intervention. The Constitution does not require such a congressional assessment for several reasons. First, it is often obvious that the states will not succeed in solving collective-action problems outside Congress, such as by contributing their fair shares to the national treasury or military or by negotiating favorable trade agreements and military alliances. Many collective-action problems are national or nearly national in scope, and it is very difficult for many states to act collectively when they must achieve unanimous agreement—as evidenced

---

[48] Cooter & Siegel, *supra* note 15, at 139–43.

[49] PEINHARDT & SANDLER, *supra* note 41, at 35.

[50] Not only is collective action generally less likely as one increases the number of actors that must act collectively, but noncooperative behavior by individual actors also imposes substantially greater collective costs. *Id.* at 36.

THE NEW "SCIENCE OF POLITICS" 79

in part by the low median number of states that are parties to existing interstate compacts.[51] Second, it may be questionable whether the states should solve their own collective-action problems given the potential for state-based solutions to harm the federal government or states that are not parties to the interstate compact crafting the solution, which is why congressional oversight is specified in the third clause of Article I, Section 10.[52] Third, as discussed at the end of this chapter, requiring Congress to first assess the likelihood of state collective action outside Congress wrongly assumes that Congress may pursue only those objectives that make all states better off.

The above complexities help explain why the Constitution puts substantially more trust in Congress than in the states to identify and solve collective-action problems for the states. As will be discussed, answers include narrowly self-interested behavior by states during the 1780s, coordination difficulties, disagreements among the states, and the number of states whose agreement was needed under the Articles of Confederation before Congress could act (nine or thirteen, depending on the issue).[53] The fact that states could communicate with one another did not reassure nationalist Framers that the states would surmount these obstacles. Nor did the availability of several strategies to each state, substantial heterogeneities among the states, or the possibility that repeated interactions would generate more collective action.[54]

Solutions to Collective-Action Problems

This section discusses three sets of possible solutions to collective-action problems, each of which must confront potentially significant challenges. They do not exhaust the universe of solutions, but they are most relevant in examining how the Constitution helps solve collective-action problems facing the states by authorizing and limiting federal and state power.[55] There is a basic difficulty shared by all these solutions, which is discussed after each solution is considered in turn.

---

[51] *See* Chapter Three.

[52] *See id.*

[53] ARTICLES OF CONFEDERATION of 1781, art. IX (requiring the approval of nine states in the Confederation Congress to take various important actions); art. XIII (requiring unanimity to amend the Articles).

[54] The author is indebted to Professor Huq, *see supra* note 41, for pressing him to consider these complexities.

[55] For example, moral motivations are one possible explanation of why collective action occurs, but they seem less relevant to intergovernmental relations than the considerations analyzed here. For discussion of moral motivations, see Jon Elster, *Rationality, Morality, and Collective Action*, 96 ETHICS 136, 148–54 (1985).

80 THE COLLECTIVE-ACTION CONSTITUTION

Voluntary Solutions, Social Norms, and Compensation

Certain collective-action problems can be solved voluntarily through the cooperative actions of individual agents. For example, political scientist Elinor Ostrom has argued theoretically and empirically that problems involving common-pool resources can potentially be solved by voluntary organizations created and governed by users of the resource. These users clearly define the boundaries of the users and the resource, set their own rules, monitor compliance themselves or through an agent accountable to them, sanction noncompliance in a graduated fashion, and resolve disputes or change rules through mechanisms that the users control.[56] Relevant to the probable success of such efforts are whether actors can communicate with one another, whether there is trust among them, whether they believe they must share a common future, and whether actors who benefit the most from individual action can block collective action.[57]

Voluntary solutions are often most likely to succeed if supported by social norms. Social norms are "the informal rules that govern behavior in groups and societies," and they "are supported by shared expectations about what should or should not be done in different types of social situations."[58] As H.L.A. Hart and Philip Pettit separately explain, people feel obligated to follow social norms insofar as they take the internal point of view toward them, fear social sanctions for noncompliance, or both.[59] Whereas the internalization account of norm compliance changes the behavioral assumption informing game-theoretic analysis, the fear-of-sanctions account is consistent with the behavioral assumption but supplements game-theoretic analysis with rational expectations extrinsic to such analysis.[60]

Cooperative social norms can encourage actors to contribute their fair share to collective action and can discourage actors from free riding on the contributions of others. Notably, people cooperate in Prisoners' Dilemma–type situations more

---

[56] ELINOR OSTROM, GOVERNING THE COMMONS: THE EVOLUTION OF INSTITUTIONS FOR COLLECTIVE ACTION (1990).

[57] *Id.* at 21.

[58] Cristina Bicchieri, Ryan Muldoon & Alessandro Sontuoso, *Social Norms*, THE STANFORD ENCYCLOPEDIA OF PHILOSOPHY (Edward N. Zalta ed., 2018), https://perma.cc/9TTF-GGHJ.

[59] H.L.A. HART, THE CONCEPT OF LAW 57 (1961); PHILIP PETTIT, ON THE PEOPLE'S TERMS: A REPUBLICAN THEORY AND MODEL OF DEMOCRACY 128 (2012). There are also game-theoretic accounts of social norms, according to which a norm is an equilibrium of a strategic interaction. *See, e.g.*, Bicchieri, Muldoon & Sontuoso, *supra* note 58.

[60] Nothing turns on the use of term "norms" instead of "conventions." Philosopher David Lewis conceived of conventions as coordination devices that people comply with out of self-interest. DAVID LEWIS, CONVENTION: A PHILOSOPHICAL STUDY (1969). But norms can be respected out of self-interest, and conventions can be followed because of an internalized obligation to comply. For discussion, see Curtis A. Bradley & Neil S. Siegel, *Historical Gloss, Constitutional Conventions, and the Judicial Separation of Powers*, 105 GEO. L.J. 255, 265–68 (2017).

THE NEW "SCIENCE OF POLITICS"   81

frequently than predicted by the games discussed in this chapter.[61] In addition, social norms can be focal points, encouraging actors to choose one way of coordinating over another.[62] Social norms may also make distributive disagreements less intense if norms address how to allocate the fruits of cooperation.

Still, social norms will often fail to solve free-rider problems. Their informality renders them vulnerable to destruction by actors that do not want to be bound.[63] Even when not destroyed, norms can be degraded: Debates over whether a norm violation has occurred may result in its being distinguished away.[64] In addition, even when a norm has plainly been violated, punishment options (like social opprobrium) may have limited efficacy. Without an effective enforcement mechanism, norms may not endure. Norms are most likely to help solve free-rider problems when the number of actors that stand to benefit from cooperation is relatively small and when the community of which they are a part is relatively small and close-knit.[65]

Norms are more likely to solve pure coordination and assurance problems. Because the interests of the parties are either entirely or mostly aligned, a narrowly self-interested incentive to reject or degrade the norm is unlikely to exist. Regarding coordination problems with distributive elements, certain norms may make initial disagreements less intense, but whether they continually solve the distribution problem depends on whether actors that do not prefer the equilibrium established by the norm deviate from it and whether others follow their lead.

Regarding interstate relations, social norms can likely play at most a modest role in helping states solve collective-action problems. Except perhaps in unusual circumstances that temporarily bind Americans closer together (perhaps an existential threat posed by a foreign power, terrorist organization, or natural disaster), relations between even two states are distinct from interpersonal relations in the small, close-knit communities that scholars have identified as most likely to sustain social norms.

Another voluntary solution is compensation. Recall the earlier discussion of a net-negative externality with the possibility of a transfer payment, which has the strategic structure of the asymmetric dilemma in Figure 2.3. If a state benefits less than the costs it imposes on another state, a collective-action problem exists,

---

[61] *See, e.g.*, Ostrom, *supra* note 35 (discussing evidence from laboratory experiments and field studies).

[62] On focal points as solutions to coordination problems, see SCHELLING, *supra* note 37, at 57.

[63] *See, e.g.*, Elster, *supra* note 55, at 153 ("Social norms are Janus faced. They present themselves as absolute, yet they may be quite extraordinarily corruptible.").

[64] On norm degradation, see Josh Chafetz & David E. Pozen, *How Constitutional Norms Break Down*, 65 UCLA L. REV. 1430 (2018).

[65] A classic study is ROBERT C. ELLICKSON, ORDER WITHOUT LAW: HOW NEIGHBORS SETTLE DISPUTES (1991).

82 THE COLLECTIVE-ACTION CONSTITUTION

and it is possible for the two states to negotiate a solution that makes each state better off than it is when one state externalizes costs onto the other. The realism of such a solution, in which one state essentially agrees to pay the other for not imposing costs on it, likely depends on the circumstances.

Government Creation and Regulation

A second—and, in the constitutional context, more promising—set of ways to potentially solve collective-action problems involves the establishment of a government. Government can coerce or incentivize behaviors in a decentralized fashion or a centralized fashion, and it can be designed in a decentralized fashion or a centralized fashion. One decentralized example of coercion is for the law to confer property rights.[66] With private ownership, it may be possible for owners to exclude would-be free riders from freely accessing a positive externality (like an invention) or from overusing a common-pool resource (like grazing lands). It may also be possible to force actors that impose negative externalities to internalize them. For instance, polluters that damage privately owned land or waters could be forced to pay the owners of the land or waters.

It will often be infeasible, however, to confer property rights. As discussed earlier, it is characteristic of public goods that exclusion is impossible or impractical. Moreover, private ownership of certain resources may raise moral concerns, especially if the prices imposed for access exceed the ability of some actors to pay. For instance, the distributive effects of completely privatizing education would likely be extreme.

Finally, property rights will not help solve coordination problems, because they cannot be solved through exclusion. Nor will property rights help solve coordination problems with a distributive component. Distribution problems entail disagreements over what the collective goal should be. It is only after such disagreements are resolved that legal coercion may help.[67]

Regarding US constitutional federalism, there are times when the federal government effectively gives property rights to a state government by authorizing it to exclude others from accessing the state's resources or facilities. For example, Congress can use an exception to the dormant commerce doctrine—which almost always prohibits states from discriminating against interstate commerce or unduly burdening it—and, as part of a solution to a multistate collective action problem, permit some states (such as those with waste-disposal facilities) to

---

[66] *See, e.g.*, Hardin, *supra* note 24, at 1245 (arguing that "the tragedy of the commons as a food basket is averted by private property, or something formally like it").

[67] Similarly, enforceable contracts exemplify decentralized legal coercion that can better solve free-rider problems than coordination or distribution problems.

THE NEW "SCIENCE OF POLITICS"   83

exclude out-of-state waste.[68] More often, Congress bypasses states and confers property rights on individuals and businesses by using its enumerated powers, such as the Intellectual Property Clause.[69] Congress does not, however, tend to solve collective-action problems for the states by granting property rights.

Groups with many members can be regulated in a decentralized fashion by creating a federal structure within the group.[70] Unlike complete centralization, a federal structure organizes the large number of group members into a smaller number of subgroups. Within each subgroup, individual group members may be more likely to interact with one another. As a result, they may be more likely to contribute to collective action and recognize the contributions of others. They may also be better able to coordinate their behavior. Such ties and recognition may produce a greater degree of collective action than would otherwise be possible. Unions, charities, and militaries may be structured this way. So may nations, including the United States, and so were the states during the Revolution and the 1780s. As difficult as it often was for the several states to act collectively, it would have been substantially more difficult for large numbers of Americans living within these states to cooperate or coordinate with large numbers of Americans living in other states without state governments to serve as intermediaries.

Although it is defensible to view individual Americans as group members and the states as subgroups, it is also defensible to view the states as group members and the federal government as the government of the group as a whole. This book takes the latter approach.[71] Subgroups of states are not usually created in the American federal system. They occasionally are, however, when some states form interstate compacts or informal agreements, including when Congress incentivizes states to form regional compacts.[72]

Centralized legal regulation can also help solve collective-action problems.[73] Law can identify and enforce solutions to coordination problems, such as by requiring group members to build and connect highways and railroads at prescribed locations. Further, a centralized entity can coerce group members to contribute a certain amount to the solution of a public-goods problem.[74] This

---

[68] *See, e.g.*, New York v. United States, 505 U.S. 144 (1992) (discussed in Chapter Five).

[69] U.S. CONST. art. I, § 8, cl. 8 (discussed in Chapter Six).

[70] PEINHARDT & SANDLER, *supra* note 41, at 39.

[71] For an explanation of this choice, see the Postscript on Methodology at the end of this book.

[72] The statute at issue in *New York*, cited *supra* note 68, is an example.

[73] *See, e.g.*, Hardin, *supra* note 24, at 1245 (writing that "the air and waters surrounding us cannot readily be fenced, and so the tragedy of the commons as a cesspool must be prevented by ... coercive laws or taxing devices that make it cheaper for the polluter to treat his pollutants than to discharge them untreated").

[74] *See, e.g.*, *id*. at 1247 (calling for "mutual coercion, mutually agreed upon by the majority of the people affected" to solve commons problems regarding which conferring property rights is infeasible). *But see* OSTROM, *supra* note 56 and accompanying text (showing that common-pool-resource

84 THE COLLECTIVE-ACTION CONSTITUTION

classic solution to a public-goods problem raises questions about the scope of the US Supreme Court's anti-commandeering doctrine, according to which Congress may not require states to enact, administer, or enforce a federal regulatory program.[75] Alternatively, the federal government in the United States is authorized to solve multistate collective-action problems by bypassing group members (states) and coercing individuals and private entities directly. An important part of the US constitutional structure follows the internalization principle, according to which power is assigned to the federal government when it is the smallest unit of government that internalizes the effects of its exercise. By internalizing the effects of interstate externalities, which exist when benefits and costs from activities in one state spill over to another state without being priced, the federal government solves the collective-action problems that they cause.[76]

For example, the internalization principle explains why Congress can condemn land to designate national parks, national historic sites, and national battlefields. If establishing them would attract visitors from all over the nation, the national government, not state governments, represents all the beneficiaries. If most financing must come from taxes and not entrance fees, financing from a national tax puts the burden on the beneficiaries. Federal officials have better incentives than state officials to build and maintain a large park or memorial that would attract visitors nationally. Responsibility for them should thus fall on officials with a national perspective, which is mostly what we observe.

The full internalization of costs and benefits may, however, require attention to considerations beyond usage viewed as a consumption item. In 1896, in explaining why federal condemnation of land to preserve the Gettysburg battlefield was for a public use and should be a federal responsibility, the Supreme Court emphasized the role of such preservation in fostering patriotism, which it deemed essential to national defense. "Such a use seems necessarily not only a public use," it reasoned, "but one so closely connected with the welfare of the republic itself as to be within the powers granted Congress by the Constitution for the purpose of protecting and preserving the whole country." "The greater the love of the citizen for the institutions of his country," the Court continued, "the greater is the dependence properly to be placed upon him for their defence in time of necessity, and it is to such men that the country must look for its safety."[77]

---

problems may be solvable through voluntary organization instead of government coercion or privatization).

[75] *See* Chapter Five (discussing, *inter alia, New York*).
[76] Cooter & Siegel, *supra* note 15, at 137–38. *See* Chapter Five (analyzing the Interstate Commerce Clause).
[77] U.S. v. Gettysburg Electric Railway Co., 168 U.S. 668, 682 (1896). *See id.* at 681–83.

THE NEW "SCIENCE OF POLITICS"   85

Centralized coercion need not, however, be the only way of ensuring collective action. A centralized entity can also create incentive structures to force the internalization of externalities. For example, centralized governance can reward cooperative behavior by group members and punish noncooperative behavior. Congress may condition related federal funds to the states on their agreement to regulate in certain ways, including by raising their drinking ages to a national standard and thereby contributing to the solution of a multistate coordination problem caused by the interstate driving of young people to purchase alcohol in states with lower drinking ages than the states where they live.[78] In addition, although Congress may not tax states under the doctrine of intergovernmental tax immunity first established in *McCulloch*,[79] Congress may bypass the states and tax individuals and entities in ways that incentivize the internalization of interstate externalities that cause collective-action problems for the states. Regulatory taxes that force such internalization include those on pollution that crosses state lines and going without health insurance.[80]

A central authority can also offer certain group members selective incentives that promise private gains in addition to public benefits. For example, educational institutions often incentivize large donations by naming buildings or rooms after donors or by celebrating their generosity. The donation contributes to the production of the public good, whereas the naming and notoriety provide the selective incentive and inducement to personal gain.[81] In the federalism context, an example might be the idea of a race to the top in education policy. The federal funding goes to specific state grantees, while the ideas generated and tested by the proposals may benefit the states generally. Another example might be the siting of military facilities. Only sited states obtain the jobs and other financial benefits associated with the presence of military bases within their borders, but the bases contribute to the security of the states collectively.

In addition, a central government can use taxation or transfer payments to require proportionate cost sharing, meaning that each group member pays a proportionate share of the cost that any group member incurs by contributing to collective action.[82] With cost sharing, the strategic structure of the Prisoners' Dilemma is transformed. Imagine it costs one state $15 to cooperate but such cooperation generates $10 in benefits for both states. The resulting game is a

---

[78] South Dakota v. Dole, 483 U.S. 203 (1987) (discussed in Chapter Four).

[79] *See, e.g.*, Metcalf & Eddy v. Mitchell, 269 U.S. 514, 521 (1926); United States v. Railroad Co., 84 U.S. 322, 327 (1893).

[80] NFIB v. Sebelius, 567 U.S. 519 (2012) (upholding the exaction for noninsurance in the Affordable Care Act as a conditional federal tax). *See* Chapters Four and Five (discussing this case).

[81] *See* OLSON, *supra* note 14, at 132–35 (discussing selective incentives); PEINHARDT & SANDLER, *supra* note 41, at 38–39 (same).

[82] PEINHARDT & SANDLER, *supra* note 41, at 39–41.

86 THE COLLECTIVE-ACTION CONSTITUTION

		California	
		Cooperate	Don't
North Carolina	Cooperate	**$5, $5**	$2.50, $2.50
	Don't	$2.50, **$2.50**	$0, $0

Figure 2.8 Cost sharing.

Prisoners' Dilemma. Now imagine it costs one state $15 to cooperate but that *both* the costs and the benefits of cooperation are shared evenly by the states. This game is represented in Figure 2.8.

Although the payoffs associated with (Cooperate, Cooperate) and (Don't Cooperate, Don't Cooperate) are the same as in the Prisoners' Dilemma version of the game, the payoffs when only one state cooperates are decisively different. Instead of the cooperating state losing $5 and the noncooperating state gaining $10, now both states receive the same payoffs because the cost of cooperation is evenly divided between them, so each pays $7.50. When this cost is subtracted from the benefit of $10 that each state receives, each ends up with $2.50. With the interests of both states perfectly aligned and no cost externalization, the Nash equilibrium is also the Pareto optimum ($5, $5). The Nash equilibrium becomes the Pareto optimum as each state fully internalizes the external costs that it previously imposed on the other.

Again, Congress may not tax states directly, so the above example requires translation. The general approach of the Constitution is to authorize the federal government to bypass the states and regulate private behavior directly, including by taxing it and making transfer payments.[83] Direct federal taxation of individuals and businesses can ensure that the federal tax revenues generated in each state suffice to prevent free riding on the contributions to collective action of individuals and entities in other states.

There are, however, familiar problems with centralized regulation. Frequently, at least some of the information required to solve the collective-action problem is privately held.[84] An example might be knowledge of how much it costs one state in Figure 2.8 to cooperate. If the regulator cannot access this information, it will struggle to use cost sharing to transform the Prisoners' Dilemma into a game in which each state is incentivized to contribute to collective action. More generally, one cannot assume, as reasoning from cooperation and coordination games sometimes does, that there are no costs associated with solving such games through the creation of a government of the group. In addition to

---

[83] *See* Chapter Four.
[84] BAIRD, GERTNER & PICKER, *supra* note 2, at 190–91, 202–03.

information costs, there are the costs of creating bureaucracies and monitoring their behavior, as well as trade-offs with the values of federalism discussed in the next chapter.[85] Prudentially, these costs matter in deciding whether central intervention is justified. The constitutional scope of federal power does not, however, turn on such a benefit-cost analysis.[86]

A final point about government regulation as a solution to multistate collective-action problems concerns the basic difference between cooperation and coordination problems. With cooperation problems, no Nash equilibrium is Pareto optimal. With coordination problems, at least one Nash equilibrium is Pareto optimal. As a result, cooperation problems generally present a more compelling case for government intervention than coordination problems. The US Supreme Court's doctrine reflects this distinction by, for example, subjecting state discrimination against interstate commerce (a potential cooperation problem) to more demanding scrutiny than state burdens on interstate commerce (a potential coordination problem).[87]

Procedural Mechanisms

A third set of solutions includes procedural mechanisms for facilitating collective action. As explained in the previous section, sequential choices or communication between actors, where feasible, can help solve coordination problems and facilitate bargaining over distribution and free-rider problems. Even if bargaining is possible, however, collective-action problems may endure when many actors, including many states, must all agree to act collectively. In this circumstance, switching from unanimity rule to supermajority rule, or from supermajority rule to majority rule, will make collective action more likely.[88] As an institution grows, it may switch from unanimity rule to some form of majority rule to avoid paralysis or extensive delays before actions can be taken. For example, as more countries have joined the European Union, the Council of Ministers has increasingly followed qualified majority rule rather than unanimity rule.[89] Majority rule solves the problem of holdouts and makes collective action possible when unanimous agreement cannot be obtained. But as discussed further in the next section,

---

[85] On the advantages and disadvantages of centralized versus decentralized regulatory systems, see Jonathan B. Wiener & Alberto Alemanno, *The Future of International Regulatory Cooperation: TTIP as a Learning Process toward a Global Policy Laboratory*, 78 L. & CONTEMP. PROBS. 103, 122–31 (2015) (No. 4).

[86] *See* Chapters Four and Five.

[87] *See* Chapter Five (discussing the dormant commerce doctrine).

[88] Cooter & Siegel, *supra* note 15, at 139–43.

[89] *Id.* at 142.

88 THE COLLECTIVE-ACTION CONSTITUTION

majority rule risks exploiting the minority and permits joint action when not all group members will regard themselves as better off.[90]

Constitutional provisions or principles may address concerns about minority exploitation. For example, congressional majorities representing most states and their citizens may not impose taxes on only a minority of states and their citizens. The federal government lacks this power due to both the prohibition on federal taxation of state governments and the command that "all Duties, Imposts and Excises shall be uniform throughout the United States."[91] Such a power, if exercised regularly, might destroy the Union.

Practically, the Articles of Confederation could not be amended to require the agreement of less than all or two-thirds of the states to take various actions. Amending the Articles required the unanimous agreement of all thirteen states, and at least one always refused to consent.[92] To facilitate collective action, and notwithstanding possible concerns about minority exploitation, the Framers wrote in Article VII of the Constitution that it would be established if approved by a two-thirds majority (nine state ratifying conventions), not all thirteen.[93] In addition, Article V does not require unanimity for constitutional amendments. And the Constitution typically permits federal powers to be exercised by majority vote in each chamber of Congress.

A Common Vulnerability

All the potential solutions to collective-action problems discussed above share a vulnerability: They all require a separate collective-action problem to first be solved. To be effective, voluntary solutions (including social norms and compensation) and governmental coercion or incentives require enforcement mechanisms, and these mechanisms function as a public good. Thus, establishing and maintaining them itself poses a free-rider problem.[94] Similarly, changing the voting rules of an institution to facilitate collective action may itself require

---

[90] *Id.* at 142–43. Economists James Buchanan and Gordon Tullock stressed the advantages of unanimity rule in their book reviving contractarianism. JAMES M. BUCHANAN & GORDON TULLOCK, THE CALCULUS OF CONSENT: LOGICAL FOUNDATIONS OF CONSTITUTIONAL DEMOCRACY 88–96 (1962).

[91] U.S. CONST. art. I. § 8, cl. 1 (discussed in Chapter Four).

[92] ARTICLES OF CONFEDERATION of 1781, art. IX (requiring the approval of nine states to take various actions); art. XIII (requiring unanimity to amend the Articles). *See* Chapters Three and Four.

[93] As Chapter Ten explains, states that refused to ratify the Constitution would not have been bound by its terms. Realistically, however, each state was under great pressure not to "go it alone" as a nation if the Constitution were ratified without its support. Thus, concerns about minority exploitation remained real.

[94] PEINHARDT & SANDLER, *supra* note 41, at 26; Huq, *supra* note 41, at 252.

overcoming a holdout problem or a disagreement problem among the members of the institution.

Even so, if these second-order collective-action problems can be overcome more easily than the first-order collective-action problems to which they relate, the foregoing solutions become potentially viable. This is not a heroic assumption given the many instances in which social norms, compensation, government institutions, and new voting procedures are established and maintained. Americans did solve a second-order collective-action problem facing the states by abandoning the Articles of Confederation and ratifying the US Constitution, and in doing so, they created a new federal government with substantially greater powers that can usually be exercised without securing supermajority support, let alone unanimous approval. The burden of Part II of this book is to demonstrate that the federal government was thereby empowered to solve a sobering series of first-order collective-action problems, including funding the national government, effectively conducting foreign relations, combating economic protectionism by state governments, and defending the nation.

Collective-Action Reasoning as a Justification for Federal Power

Recall that the classic collective-action problems canvassed in this chapter can be called Pareto collective-action problems because all states would be better off by their own estimations if collective action succeeded. Congress would almost never be able to act, however, if it could do so only if it satisfied the strict, Pareto-superior analysis of collective-action problems studied by game theorists—if it could intervene only where all states would regard themselves as better off as a result of the federal intervention. If adopted, this position would largely erase federal power because there would almost always be at least one state that opposed any congressional intervention; to reiterate, the requirement of Pareto optimality is extremely demanding. For example, at least one state typically objected under the Articles of Confederation, and today there are fifty states, not thirteen.

On the other hand, Congress would almost always be able to act if it were authorized to do so just because activities in one state had spillover effects in another state. Interstate externalities are pervasive, especially in a modern, integrated economy and society. The position that Congress can intervene just because activities producing extensive benefits in one state also generate minor costs in another state does not have a limiting principle with any practical bite, and the position does not involve collective action by states at all.

This book endorses an intermediate case, which also provides a limiting principle where collective-action reasoning is potentially relevant to whether federal

90 THE COLLECTIVE-ACTION CONSTITUTION

intervention is justified. (Such reasoning will not be relevant when, for example, the constitutional text precludes it.) In contrast to Pareto collective-action problems, "cost-benefit collective-action problems" refer to certain situations in which some states would regard themselves as better off if collective action succeeded, but other states would regard themselves as worse off. Almost all multistate collective-action problems in the history of US federalism fall into this category. Congress, as the government institution in the nation in which all states (and almost all individuals and interests in states) are represented, is authorized to resolve disagreements among states over whether collective action should succeed if, but only if, Congress rationally determines that its intervention would help the one group of states more than it would harm the other. When this book refers to multistate collective-action problems, it means to include not only Pareto collective-action problems but also cost-benefit collective-action problems.

To illustrate the idea of a cost-benefit collective-action problem, imagine that most states regard the use of child labor as triggering a race to the bottom, but that a minority of states (say, the Carolinas in the early twentieth century) view the use of child labor as involving a race to the top—as involving healthy economic competition that rewards the lowest-cost producers. The payoff matrix is captured in Figure 2.9.

The preferences of the majority of states reflect a Prisoners' Dilemma, while the preferences of the minority of states do not. The states in the minority prefer to use child labor regardless of what other states do. Mutual use of child labor is not only the Nash equilibrium; it is also Pareto optimal in part because the minority of states would be made worse off if Congress banned child labor nationally, thereby moving the outcome from mutual use of child labor to mutual nonuse. Even so, most states would be made better off if Congress moved the outcome to mutual nonuse. Because Congress is not limited to solving Pareto collective-action problems, it can move the states from the Pareto optimal Nash equilibrium to another outcome that is a cost-benefit improvement, meaning that the states in the majority would benefit more from the move (their payoff increases from $2 to $4) than the states in the minority would be harmed (their payoff decreases from $3 to $2).

		Minority	
		Don't Use	Use
Majority	Don't Use	$4, $2	$1, $5
	Use	$5, $1	$2, $3

Figure 2.9 Cost-benefit collective-action problem.

THE NEW "SCIENCE OF POLITICS" 91

One might object that a cost-benefit collective-action problem is no collective-action problem at all; rather, it is a contradiction in terms. This would be true if the only relevant conception of efficiency were Pareto optimality. There are other conceptions, however, including cost-benefit (or Kaldor–Hicks) efficiency. An outcome is cost-benefit efficient if it produces more benefits than costs.[95] Cost-benefit efficiencies are also known as instances of potential Pareto optimality because both groups of states can be made better off by achieving a cost-benefit-efficient outcome if the group that is made better off compensates the group that is made worse off, as in the net-negative externality game represented in Figure 2.3. Cost-benefit efficiency does not require, however, that such compensation occur. Accordingly, collective-action problems that harm both groups of states are Pareto inefficiencies, whereas collective-action problems that harm one group more than they benefit the other are cost-benefit inefficiencies. In other words, permitting Congress to solve cost-benefit collective-action problems is analytically equivalent to authorizing Congress to internalize interstate externalities where the costs externalized by a group of states exceed the benefits internalized by the group.[96]

Notably, the very same phenomena that fuel multistate collective-action problems in the strict, Pareto sense also drive such problems in the cost-benefit sense. The mobility of firms, people, species, and pollution across state lines causes both kinds of collective-action problems for the states. Relatedly, inter-state externalities produced by differences in state regulatory regimes also generate both Pareto and cost-benefit collective-action problems.

Where the externalized costs are less than the internalized benefits, federal intervention cannot be justified in the name of solving cost-benefit collective-action problems, let alone Pareto collective-action problems. Put differently, if a group of states benefits itself more than it harms a group of sister states from externalizing costs onto them, and if complications such as retaliation and conflict escalation are not a possibility, it is both Pareto optimal and cost-benefit efficient for the cost externalization to continue. Figure 2.10 captures this scenario.

From both a Pareto and a cost-benefit perspective, Congress has no basis to intervene because moving from mutual use of child labor to mutual nonuse helps most states (by $1) less than it harms the minority of states (by $2).

---

[95] *See, e.g.*, ROBERT D. COOTER, THE STRATEGIC CONSTITUTION 32–35 (2000) (discussing cost-benefit efficiency); *Kaldor-Hicks Efficiency*, A DICTIONARY OF FINANCE AND BANKING (6th ed. 2018) (ebook).

[96] Where such interstate externalities exist, it is possible that cost-externalizing states are also internalizing some costs (e.g., by imposing them on outvoted minorities within their borders) and externalizing some benefits (e.g., by conferring them on people in other states who agree with, or gain from, the conduct of the cost-externalizing states). This possibility can be handled by comparing net externalized costs (i.e., externalized costs minus externalized benefits) with net internalized benefits (i.e., internalized benefits less internalized costs). If net externalized costs exceed net internalized benefits, there is a cost-benefit collective-action problem.

92 THE COLLECTIVE-ACTION CONSTITUTION

		Minority	
		Don't Use	Use
Majority	Don't Use	$3, $2	$1, $5
	Use	$5, $1	$2, $4

Figure 2.10 No collective-action problem.

That said, Congress is the institution in which competing interests from all the states are weighed and balanced, so state representatives in Congress get to decide, within a broad range of reasonableness, what values should be assigned to the relevant costs and benefits. In addition, Congress need not be bound by traditional understandings of cost-benefit analysis, which give the same weight to the well-being of the rich and the poor by assuming that the marginal value of a dollar is the same to everyone. In a multistate cost-benefit calculus, Congress is permitted to care about issues of fair distribution and assign extra weight to Americans who are worse off.[97]

In sum, according to this book's intermediate position, which is especially relevant when Congress wishes to rely on the Interstate Commerce Clause, Congress may act to address both collective-action problems that harm all states (Pareto inefficiencies) and collective-action problems that harm some states a lot and benefit other states a little (cost-benefit inefficiencies). This point is critical. As will be shown, compared with the Articles of Confederation, the Constitution facilitates collective action by states in Congress by generally moving from the Articles' voting rule of unanimous or two-third support (depending on the issue) to simple majority rule in each chamber of Congress. If the states are facing a situation that is either Pareto inefficient or cost-benefit inefficient, Congress can act by simple majority rule to address the situation. The states, whether inside or outside Congress, need not unanimously support the federal intervention.

Conclusion

The 2 × 2 matrix games presented in this chapter are stylized, but they illustrate the two basic kinds of collective-action problems, their causes, and possible solutions when certain assumptions are changed. The following chapters use these games, and the technical concepts they illuminate, to explain the role

---

[97] *See, e.g.*, MATTHEW D. ADLER & OLE F. NORHEIM EDS., PRIORITARIANISM IN PRACTICE (2022) (discussing prioritarianism, an ethical theory that assigns extra weight to the well-being of people who are worse off); *see also* Cass R. Sunstein, *Willingness to Pay vs. Welfare*, 1 HARV. L. & POL'Y REV. 303 (2007).

of the federal government in solving Pareto and cost-benefit collective-action problems for the states. These games also illuminate the role of the Constitution and Congress in prohibiting states from undermining federal solutions to collective-action problems or causing such problems.

State governments need not, however, only cause multistate collective-action problems. It is important to examine when states can help solve them. The next chapter turns to this question.

PART II

A COLLECTIVE-ACTION THEORY OF THE FEDERAL STRUCTURE—AND ITS LIMITS

3

The Roles of the States and the Interstate Compacts Clause

Introduction

Many constitutional provisions make clear that state governments are the default regulators in the American republic. This chapter examines when states are likely to solve multistate collective-action problems on their own by forming interstate compacts or less formal agreements, and when they are likely to require the federal government to step in.[1]

The states are more likely to act effectively when only two or a few of them seek to act collectively. Even then, however, proposed compacts may undermine federal supremacy or harm sister states, and states may disagree about whether a given compact solves or causes a collective-action problem. For these reasons, the Constitution presumptively prohibits states from creating compacts. "No state shall, without the Consent of Congress," the text provides, "enter into any Agreement or Compact with another State."[2] This language reflects concern that states may attempt to solve their own collective-action problems.

Still, in permitting interstate compacts when Congress approves, the text leaves the door open for states to try. The Constitution assigns the question of whether proposed compacts solve or cause collective-action problems to Congress, where, as Chief Justice Marshall explained in *McCulloch v. Maryland* (1819), all the states and all the people are represented. This chapter uses collective-action reasoning to help explain and evaluate the Constitution's qualified skepticism that states can and should solve their own collective-action problems.

---

[1] As Chapter 2 explained, governments are corporate actors: the federal government and each state are a "they" composed of many individuals, interests, and institutions, not an "it." Even so, this book often—although not always—uses the simplifying assumption, common in law and politics, of characterizing each government as an "it" for certain purposes. Regarding collective-action problems, these actors are individuals "in the sense of having one decision to make." Jon Elster, *Rationality, Morality, and Collective Action*, 96 Ethics 136, 136 (1985).

[2] U.S. Const. art. I, § 10, cl. 3.

The Collective-Action Constitution. Neil S. Siegel, Oxford University Press. © Neil S. Siegel 2024.
DOI: 10.1093/oso/9780197760963.003.0004

98 THE COLLECTIVE-ACTION CONSTITUTION

Preliminary Distinctions

The claim that the states are the default regulators in the US system is distinct from two other claims, which are controversial and need not be accepted (or rejected) to find value in the approach taken in this book. First, one need not accept the validity of "states-first" histories of America, according to which the original thirteen states as individual entities preceded the collective entity called the Union, as evidenced by the deeds and words of state governments and individual leaders of the Founding generation.[3] Second, one need not accept "state-compact" accounts of the US Constitution, according to which the Constitution is a compact among the states.[4]

These are complex and contested debates over how best to understand early American political and legal history. But they concern who the sovereign principals are in the American constitutional system; they do not concern the identity of their agents. Even if one believes that the Union preceded the states (or, perhaps more interestingly, that the Union and the states arose together as cocreators[5]), and even if one believes that "the people" (whether as a whole or state by state) ratified the Constitution and divided government power between the federal and state governments, it is still accurate and useful to view state governments as the default regulators in the American republic and to analyze how the Constitution allocates regulatory power between the two levels of

---

[3] For claims by historians and legal scholars that the states came first and created the Union, see AKHIL REED AMAR, AMERICA'S CONSTITUTION: A BIOGRAPHY 21–39 (2005); DAVID C. HENDRICKSON, PEACE PACT: THE LOST WORLD OF THE AMERICAN FOUNDING ix–x (2003); MICHAEL J. KLARMAN, THE FRAMERS' COUP: THE MAKING OF THE UNITED STATES CONSTITUTION 14 (2016); PAULINE MAIER, RATIFICATION: THE PEOPLE DEBATE THE CONSTITUTION, 1787–1788, at 17 (2010); and JACK N. RAKOVE, ORIGINAL MEANINGS: POLITICS AND IDEAS IN THE MAKING OF THE CONSTITUTION 163–64 (1996). *But see* ABRAHAM LINCOLN, MESSAGE TO CONGRESS IN SPECIAL SESSION (Jul. 4, 1861), *reprinted in* 2 ABRAHAM LINCOLN: COMPLETE WORKS COMPRISING HIS SPEECHES, LETTERS, STATE PAPERS, AND MISCELLANEOUS WRITINGS 62 (John G. Nicolay and John Hay eds., 1894) ("The Union is older than any of the States; and, in fact, it created them as States."). For an argument that the Union emerged before the states, see Richard B. Morris, *The Forging of the Union Reconsidered: A Historical Refutation of State Sovereignty over Seabeds*, 74 COLUM. L. REV. 1056 (1974).

[4] According to Chief Justice Marshall, Maryland insisted that, in interpreting the Constitution, it was important "to consider that instrument, not as emanating from the people, but as an act of sovereign and independent states." McCulloch v. Maryland, 17 U.S. (4 Wheat.) 316, 402 (1819). As Chapter 1 explained, Marshall disagreed (and erroneously attributed to Maryland the view that state governments, as opposes to state peoples, created the Constitution). On this issue, President Ronald Reagan sided with the Southern constitutionalists. *See* Ronald Reagan, First Inaugural Address (Jan. 20, 1981), *in* VARIOUS PRESIDENTS OF THE UNITED STATES, INAUGURAL ADDRESSES OF THE PRESIDENTS OF THE UNITED STATES, S. Doc. No. 101-10, at 333 (1989) ("[T]he Federal Government did not create the States; the States created the Federal Government."). Other presidents—most notably Lincoln—sided with Marshall. *See* LINCOLN, *supra* note 3 and accompanying text.

[5] For explication of this unconventional view, see Craig Green, *United/States: A Revolutionary History of American Statehood*, 119 MICH. L. REV. 1 (2020). *Cf.* Jack P. Greene, *The Background of the Articles of Confederation*, 12 PUBLIUS 15, 43 (1982) ("The process by which the American union was formed is . . . too complicated to support either a national or a compact theory of its origins. The Continental Congress gathered to itself broad powers at the same time that the colonies, as old and continuing corporate entities, were changing themselves into states.").

THE ROLES OF THE STATES   99

government.[6] In many places, the constitutional text presupposes or guarantees the regulatory authority, effective functioning, democratic legitimacy, continued existence, key roles, and reserved powers of state governments. For example, the Tenth Amendment, which declares that all powers not given to the federal government or taken from the states are reserved to the states, merely reaffirms what is evident in other parts of the text.[7]

The American constitutional system could not function without state governments performing various roles. This assertion may seem obvious upon reflection, but as Professor John Hart Ely remarked in another context, "[f]amiliarity breeds inattention."[8] The next section considers the roles of state governments, the limits of which help identify the main structural role of the federal government.

Values of Federalism

Many scholars and jurists have illuminated the roles of state governments in the American constitutional system. They have argued textually that the Constitution requires or permits states to perform various roles, and they have argued historically that the politics of the day required the Framers to preserve much state authority. They have also argued functionally that preserving state power helps vindicate various "values of federalism."[9] Federalism values are commonly thought to include the following:

- prevention of federal tyranny, because power is diffused between the federal and state governments, and states can resist federal overreach;[10]

---

[6] For more on this subject, see the Postscript on Methodology at the end of this book.

[7] U.S. CONST. amend. X; see art. I, § 1 (assigning to Congress "[a]ll legislative powers herein granted," implying that federal authority is limited to enumerated powers); art. I, § 8 (enumerating Congress's powers, implying that federal power is limited); art. I, § 10 (disabling states from exercising certain powers, either absolutely or without congressional consent, implying that states could otherwise exercise such powers because state governments are governments of general, plenary powers). In addition, as Chapter 9 analyzes, the federal government must ensure that state governments remain democratic and must protect them from invasion and, upon request, from internal violence. See U.S. CONST. art. IV, § 4. This is partly because the democratic legitimacy of the federal government depends in part on the democratic legitimacy of state governments, which set the qualifications for electors of representatives and senators, see U.S. CONST. art. I, § 1, cl. 1; amend. XVII; and which appoint the electors who cast votes for president in the Electoral College, see U.S. CONST. art. II, § 1, cl. 2. Moreover, as Chapter 10 discusses, state governments typically play a key role in proposing or ratifying constitutional amendments. U.S. CONST. art. V.

[8] JOHN HART ELY, DEMOCRACY AND DISTRUST: A THEORY OF JUDICIAL REVIEW 18 (1980).

[9] In this context, the term "federalism" is typically used to denote state powers or limits on federal powers, not the division of authority between the federal and state governments, which is how this book generally uses the term.

[10] See, e.g., Andrzej Rapaczynski, From Sovereignty to Process: The Jurisprudence of Federalism after Garcia, 1985 S. Ct. REV. 341, 380–95; THE FEDERALIST No. 51 (James Madison) (Clinton Rossiter ed., 1961); Gregory v. Ashcroft, 501 U.S. 452, 458 (1991); FERC v. Mississippi, 456 U.S. 742, 790 (1982) (O'Connor, J., dissenting).

100 THE COLLECTIVE-ACTION CONSTITUTION

- promotion of political participation, because state governments are closer to the people than the federal government;[11]
- enhanced political accountability, because state citizens have greater influence over state elections than federal elections, and because state citizens can more easily inform themselves about state issues and monitor state officials;[12]
- greater degree of political responsiveness (more efficient and less corrupt government) insofar as state residents and businesses are mobile, because they can vote with their feet if they prefer the public goods, taxation levels, and government services offered by another state;[13]
- greater satisfaction of local preferences and greater vindication of local values, because different states or regions can prioritize distinct preferences and values;[14] and
- problem solving through experimentation, because it is less harmful for experiments to fail in individual state "laboratories" than across the nation, and because successful local experiments can be reproduced elsewhere.[15]

Scholars and judges have also looked to custom as a guide to what states are good for, stressing asserted traditional subjects of state regulation such as family law, criminal law, and education.[16] More recently, scholars have defended, or

[11] *See, e.g.*, Rapaczynski, *supra* note 10, at 395–408; *Gregory*, 501 U.S. at 458; FERC v. Mississippi, 456 U.S. at 789 (O'Connor, J., dissenting) (discussing 1 ALEXIS DE TOCQUEVILLE, DEMOCRACY IN AMERICA 181 (H. Reeve trans. 1961)).

[12] *See, e.g.*, *Gregory*, 501 U.S. at 458; Richard A. Epstein, *Exit Rights Under Federalism*, 55 LAW & CONTEMP. PROBS. 149 (1992); Robert P. Inman & Daniel L. Rubinfeld, *The Political Economy of Federalism*, *in* PERSPECTIVES ON PUBLIC CHOICE (Dennis C. Mueller ed., 1997); Charles Tiebout, *A Pure Theory of Local Expenditures*, 64 J. POL. ECON. 416 (1956).

[13] *See, e.g.*, Tiebout, *supra* note 12; ILYA SOMIN, FREE TO MOVE: FOOT VOTING, MIGRATION, AND POLITICAL FREEDOM (2020).

[14] *See, e.g.*, *Gregory*, 501 U.S. at 458; Jenna Bednar, *Subsidiarity and Robustness: Building the Adaptive Efficiency of Federal Systems*, *in* NOMOS LV: FEDERALISM AND SUBSIDIARITY 231, 232 (2014). This claim conflicts with the previous one, because competition requires sameness regarding everything but price (substitutes), not differences in what is being priced. *See* Bednar, *supra*, at 238–39. For discussion of participation, accountability, and preference satisfaction as values of federalism, see DAVID L. SHAPIRO, FEDERALISM: A DIALOGUE 91–92 (1995).

[15] *See, e.g.*, New State Ice Co. v. Liebmann, 285 U.S. 262, 311 (1932) (Brandeis, J., dissenting); *Gregory*, 501 U.S. at 458; *FERC v. Mississippi*, 456 U.S. at 788–89 (O'Connor, J., dissenting). *But see* Rapaczynski, *supra* note 10, at 408–14 (criticizing the experimentation rationale). The purpose of state experiments is to produce information. For the information to be useful, there needs to be a mechanism for comparatively assessing all the information produced through state experiments. The federal government is most likely to play this coordinating role. In other words, the "laboratories of experimentation" rationale for state power is also an argument for federal power.

[16] *See, e.g.*, United States v. Lopez, 514 U.S. 549, 564 (1995); United States v. Morrison, 529 U.S. 598, 615–16 (2000).

sympathetically described, states as empowering dissenters from the exercise of federal power; as staging grounds for partisan competition; and as sources of political identity.[17] Some or all of the foregoing functional or expressive arguments support the view that the states play valuable roles in the constitutional system and are the default regulators in it.

Considered collectively and generally, these arguments have force. They offer good reasons to reject unlimited federal power. For example, same-sex marriage is widely accepted in the United States today in part because some states permitted it before the Supreme Court intervened in 2015.[18] The states that served as laboratories of experimentation (and constitutionalism) demonstrated to the rest of the nation that same-sex marriage would not harm children, or make it less likely that opposite-sex couples would marry, or cause other harmful societal consequences that opponents of marriage equality invoked.[19]

The foregoing arguments for state authority are, however, contested. For example, many Americans today might care more about national politics than about state or local politics, and modern technology makes it easy to satisfy their preference for national news. For these Americans, state governments may not significantly vindicate values of participation and accountability. Further, certain state policies might reflect violations of fundamental rights or interests, not commendable diversity regarding preferences or values. For instance, racial subordination in the United States has historically been defended on federalism grounds.[20] Moreover, arguments that federalism promotes efficient government and preference satisfaction assume free mobility and no interstate spillovers.[21] But many Americans may not be mobile for various reasons, and significant interstate externalities may often be present, creating collective-action problems for the states. So, specific arguments for state power need not be unassailable,

---

[17] See, e.g., Jessica Bulman-Pozen & Heather K. Gerken, Uncooperative Federalism, 118 YALE L.J. 1256 (2009) (empowered dissent); Jessica Bulman-Pozen, Partisan Federalism, 127 HARV. L. REV. 1077 (2014) (partisan competition); Ernest A. Young, The Volk of New Jersey? State Identity, Distinctiveness, and Political Culture in the American Federal System (2015), https://perma.cc/ 2HXY-XTYQ (political identity).

[18] Obergefell v. Hodges, 576 U.S. 644 (2015) (holding that the fundamental constitutional right to marry includes same-sex marriage).

[19] Neil S. Siegel, Federalism as a Way Station: Windsor as Exemplar of Doctrine in Motion, 6 J. LEGAL ANAL. 87, 118–19 (2014).

[20] See, e.g., Declaration of Constitutional Principles (the Southern Manifesto), 102 Cong. Rec. 4515, 4516 (1956) (condemning Brown v. Board of Education, 347 U.S. 483 (1954), as lawlessly "encroach[ing] on rights reserved to the States").

[21] See Tiebout, supra note 12 (conditioning his argument for interjurisdictional competition on free mobility); WALLACE E. OATES, FISCAL FEDERALISM (2011) (originally published 1972) (conditioning his argument for decentralization on no interjurisdictional externalities).

102 THE COLLECTIVE-ACTION CONSTITUTION

or even persuasive on balance, to be part of the conversation about the values of federalism.

Defenders of state power may dispute the frequency and seriousness of multistate collective-action problems, but they do not tend to argue that the states are well situated to address them; they instead concede without analysis that such problems justify the exercise of federal power.[22] Ultimately, this chapter corroborates the widely shared intuition, reflected in the constitutional text, about the limited role of the states in solving their own collective-action problems. But it explains why the intuition is mostly sound (all the reasons are not obvious), and along the way, it explains why the intuition is somewhat overstated. Part of what is missing from most federalism debates is sustained analysis of the potential role of the states in solving collective-action problems that arise for them.

Pre-ratification History

Colonial history partially supports the supposition that, at least when a cooperation or coordination problem exists among few states, they may sometimes be able to solve the problem through negotiation and agreement. Because almost every colonial charter failed to clearly demarcate the borders of the colony in question, some way was required to peacefully settle boundary disputes. This was particularly true of the conflicting claims of the colonies along the Atlantic seaboard, whose expanding populations were coming into increasing contact with one another.[23] Such disputes could be settled nonviolently through negotiation or a mechanism akin to litigation. Negotiation typically entailed joint commissions and difficult discussions that could last years. If negotiation succeeded, the Crown needed to approve. If negotiation failed, or if the disputing colonies sought an alternative to negotiation, they could "litigate" by appealing directly to the Crown, which usually referred the matter to a Royal Commission, whose decision could be appealed to the Privy Council. These two methods of dispute resolution were commonly used for a century before the American Revolution.[24]

By the Revolution, however, many boundary disputes remained unresolved, which concerned the Second Continental Congress when it drafted the Articles

---

[22] *See, e.g.,* Steven G. Calabresi & Lucy D. Bickford, *Federalism and Subsidiarity: Perspectives from U.S. Constitutional Law, in* NOMOS LV: FEDERALISM AND SUBSIDIARITY 123, 132 (James E. Fleming & Jacob T. Levy eds., 2014).

[23] Felix Frankfurter & James M. Landis, *The Compacts Clause of the Constitution: A Study in Interstate Adjustments,* 34 YALE L.J. 685, 692 (1925).

[24] *Id.* at 692–93; *see id.* at 730–32 (describing nine intercolonial boundary agreements).

THE ROLES OF THE STATES   103

of Confederation in 1777.[25] Boundary disputes were the main reason why the Articles did not formally go into effect until 1781, when it was ratified by the thirteenth state, Maryland.[26] It had held out because of Virginia's vast western territorial claims. To overcome the collective-action impasse, the Second Continental Congress proposed in 1780 that the disputed lands "be ceded or relinquished to the United States, . . . be disposed of for the common benefit of the United States, and be settled and formed into distinct republican states, which shall become members of the federal union."[27] New York and Virginia ceded their lands and other states followed suit.[28]

The Articles failed to authorize the Confederation Congress to take territory, but it otherwise generally reflected this history while moving in a less centralizing direction. It authorized two methods that states could use to resolve disputes between them. First, Article VI apparently permitted states to enter into agreements with one another without the consent of Congress. Article VI prohibited states from entering "any treaty, confederation or alliance" with other states without congressional consent but mandated that states obtain congressional consent for "any conference, agreement, alliance or treaty" with another nation. By implication, congressional approval was apparently not required for an "agreement" between states.[29]

Second, to resolve boundary disputes and other disagreements when states failed to reach agreement on their own, Article IX provided that "[t]he united states in congress assembled shall . . . be the last resort on appeal in all disputes and differences now subsisting or that hereafter may arise between two or more states concerning boundary, jurisdiction or any other cause whatever." Article IX then described at length the procedure Congress would use to settle such disputes between states. During the period in which the Articles was in effect (1781–88), the Article IX procedure was employed only to resolve a disagreement between Pennsylvania and Connecticut over land on the banks of the Susquehanna River.[30] By contrast, states made several agreements resolving boundary disputes, none of which Congress approved.[31] Yet, by the Constitutional Convention,

---

[25] *Id.* at 693.

[26] Green, *supra* note 5, at 35–41.

[27] Resolution of Oct. 10, 1780, *in* 18 J. CONT'L. CONG. 1774–1789, at 915 (Gaillard Hunt ed., 1912).

[28] JOSEPH F. ZIMMERMAN, INTERSTATE COOPERATION: COMPACTS AND ADMINISTRATIVE AGREEMENTS 5 (2d ed. 2012).

[29] Abraham C. Weinfeld, *What Did the Framers of the Federal Constitution Mean by "Agreements or Compacts?,"* 3 U. CHI. L. REV. 453, 455–56 (1936) (making this observation).

[30] RICHARD H. FALLON ET AL., HART AND WECHSLER'S THE FEDERAL COURTS AND THE FEDERAL SYSTEM 6 n.34 (7th ed. 2015) (citing HAMPTON L. CARSON, THE SUPREME COURT OF THE UNITED STATES 67–74 (1891)).

[31] Frankfurter & Landis, *supra* note 23, at 732–34 (describing four such agreements).

104   THE COLLECTIVE-ACTION CONSTITUTION

numerous boundary disputes between states remained unresolved, as discussed below.[32]

The states had similarly limited success solving other collective-action problems. They provided some troops to the national military and some money to the national treasury. From 1777 to 1783, political scientist Keith Dougherty finds, states delivered 53 percent of the soldiers requisitioned by the Confederation Congress, and from 1782 to 1789, they paid 40 percent of the funds requisitioned.[33] But overall, the Articles' requisition scheme was deemed a failure by leading nationalists then and most (although not all) subsequent historians and legal scholars. As just noted, states did not provide almost half the requested soldiers and almost 60 percent of the requested funds. Although exact numbers vary, other studies support this conclusion. Professor George Van Cleve reports that "[t]he states paid only 31 percent of the requisitions Congress made to them from 1781 to mid-1787, based on the most generous possible assumptions."[34] And according to Professor Roger Brown, "[t]he money [that states] supplied the federal treasury never came close to the amount Congress requested," even as "the requisition system did not completely fail" and "Congress's six federal requisitions between October 1781 and August 1786 show an overall rate of compliance by the state governments of 37 percent." Professor Brown adds, however, that "by early 1787 they had almost completely ceased."[35] For good reason, the Constitution replaced the requisition scheme with key congressional powers in Article I, Section 8.[36]

The Confederation Congress understood that necessity required the newly self-declared states not only to act together militarily and financially if they were to separate from Great Britain but also to prevent individual states from causing serious collective-action problems. Regarding the latter issue, Felix Frankfurter and James Landis observed, in a *Yale Law Journal* article during the 1920s, that "it was perhaps even more important [than facilitating interstate dispute resolution] to protect the new Union of States established by the Articles of Confederation, from the destructive political combination of two or more States."[37] Thus, as

[32] *See infra* note 52 and accompanying text (noting that eleven boundary disputes were unresolved).

[33] KEITH L. DOUGHERTY, COLLECTIVE ACTION UNDER THE ARTICLES OF CONFEDERATION 13 (2001).

[34] GEORGE WILLIAM VAN CLEVE, WE HAVE NOT A GOVERNMENT: THE ARTICLES OF CONFEDERATION AND THE ROAD TO THE CONSTITUTION 52 (2017).

[35] ROGER H. BROWN, REDEEMING THE REPUBLIC: FEDERALISTS, TAXATION, AND THE ORIGINS OF THE CONSTITUTION 12 (1993).

[36] *See* Chapter 4. According to Professor Huq, "Preratification historical practice demonstrates that states were capable of *some* cooperation even without federal coercion." Aziz Huq, *Does the Logic of Collective Action Explain Federalism Doctrine?*, 66 STAN. L. REV. 217, 259 (2014). True enough, but the data and trendline reveal that "*some* cooperation" is not saying much. Nor does he address the relatively small number of interstate compacts throughout US history. *Id.* at 265–66. The import of this fact is discussed below.

[37] Frankfurter & Landis, *supra* note 23, at 693.

THE ROLES OF THE STATES   105

partially quoted above, Article VI provided that "[n]o state without the Consent of the united states in congress assembled, shall send any embassy to, or receive any embassy from, or enter into any conference, agreement, alliance or treaty with any King, prince or state," and "[n]o two or more states shall enter into any treaty, confederation or alliance whatever between them, without the consent of the united states in congress assembled, specifying accurately the purposes for which the same is to be entered into, and how long it shall continue."

These were striking limitations on state power in a document that mostly created a weak central government, but they tracked Article IX's assignment to Congress of authority to conduct foreign relations and war. The limitations on state power in Article VI provided "insurance against competing political power,"[38] because such arrangements between states and other nations or other states were conducive to political or military conflicts. Such arrangements might benefit the states making them substantially less than they would harm other states, and they would likely be viewed as sufficiently threatening by other states that they would cause these states to make similar arrangements in response, leaving the states collectively worse off.

The Constitution

The Constitution generally tracks the Articles, albeit in a more centralizing direction. It imposes greater categorical and noncategorical limits on state authority to cause certain collective-action problems for the states. The first clause of Article I, Section 10, categorically prohibits states from "enter[ing] into any treaty, alliance, or confederation."[39] In this instance, the Constitution itself prevents the race to the bottom.

Regarding noncategorical limits, the Constitution appears to reflect concern about giving states unsupervised authority to try to solve common problems, including cooperation or coordination problems, but nonetheless permits states to try—with congressional approval. As noted, the Interstate and Foreign Compacts Clauses provide that "[n]o State shall, without the Consent of Congress, . . . enter into any Agreement or Compact with another State, or with a foreign Power."[40] These clauses are framed as a prohibition, but they permit states—at least when Congress approves—to form compacts and less formal agreements with other states or nations (and with the District of Columbia and US territories).[41]

[38] *Id.* at 694.
[39] U.S. CONST. art. I, § 10, cl. 1.
[40] U.S. CONST. art. I, § 10, cl. 3.
[41] "An interstate compact is a formal binding contract, authorized by or enacted as legislation, between two or more states in their capacity as states." MICHAEL L. BUENGER ET AL., THE EVOLVING LAW AND USE OF INTERSTATE COMPACTS xxi (2d ed. 2016); *see id.* at 3 (same).

106   THE COLLECTIVE-ACTION CONSTITUTION

Compacts and agreements are apparently treated the same for constitutional purposes.[42] Interstate compacts, the focus of this chapter, are judicially enforceable contracts under the Contracts Clause,[43] which prohibits states from passing any "law impairing the obligation of contracts."[44] Therefore, states relinquish part of their sovereign authority by forming compacts that regulate behavior or develop projects. Unless they are merely advisory or just study a problem, interstate compacts establish "the equivalent of a uniform law in the territory covered by the compact."[45]

Unfortunately, neither the proceedings of the Constitutional Convention, nor the state ratifying conventions, nor *The Federalist Papers* offer much insight into the original meaning of (or intent behind) the Interstate Compacts Clause.[46] Two commentators tie the clause to the Convention's partial acceptance of Madison's position that Congress should be authorized to closely monitor state legislation. Professor Michael Greve argues that, although the Convention rejected Madison's proposed "negative" on state laws (which Professor Greve questionably asserts would have required congressional approval before any state law could go into effect), "[t]he congressional consent requirement for state agreements and compacts is the Madisonian negative, in a specified range of application."[47] Jacob Finkel speculates that Madison's June 19 speech, in which he assailed state encroachments on federal authority and state compacts without congressional consent (between Virginia and Maryland, and between Pennsylvania and New

---

[42] Virginia v. Tennessee, 148 U.S. 503, 520 (1893) ("Compacts or agreements—and we do not perceive any difference in the meaning, except that the word 'compact' is generally used with reference to more formal and serious engagements than is usually implied in the term 'agreement'—cover all stipulations affecting the conduct or claims of the parties.").

[43] Green v. Biddle, 21 U.S. (8 Wheat.) 1, 13 (1823); Virginia v. West Virginia, 246 U.S. 565 (1918).

[44] U.S. CONST. art. I, § 10, cl. 1.

[45] ZIMMERMAN, *supra* note 28, at 35. Still, "states are not required to enact uniform laws or model acts verbatim," so "uniform and model acts do not constitute a contract between the states even if adopted by all states in the same form." BUENGER ET AL., *supra* note 41, at 37.

[46] Duncan B. Hollis, *Unpacking the Compact Clause*, 88 TEX. L. REV. 741, 761–62 (2010); Frankfurter & Landis, *supra* note 23, at 694.

[47] Michael S. Greve, *Compacts, Cartels, and Congressional Consent*, 68 MO. L. REV. 285, 313 (2003). The conventional (and almost certainly correct) view is that Madison proposed giving Congress a "negative" on select state legislation to prevent it from going into effect when Congress objected, not to require Congress to approve every state law. *See, e.g.*, AMAR, *supra* note 3, at 109 ("As Madison saw it, state governments lacked sufficient ballast, and a general congressional 'negative' over all new state laws would enable continental representatives of greater wisdom and reputation to prevent ill-considered or oppressive state laws from taking effect."). Madison's model was the power exercised by the British king (really the Privy Council) before the Revolution. Legislation passed by colonial assemblies did not await the Council's approval before it went into effect. *See* Letter from James Madison to General Washington (Apr. 16, 1787), *in* 1 LETTERS AND OTHER WRITINGS OF JAMES MADISON, PUBLISHED BY ORDER OF CONGRESS, 1769–1793, at 288 (R. Worthington ed., 1884) (calling for "a negative in *all cases whatsoever* on the Legislative acts of the States, as heretofore exercised by the Kingly prerogative," and calling this negative a "defensive power"). It would be extraordinary, even with only thirteen state legislatures in 1787 (let alone more to come), if Madison meant that no state law on any subject, no matter how local and irrelevant nationally, could go into effect unless both Houses of Congress overcame the various impediments to action and approved it.

Jersey), led South Carolina delegate John Rutledge, as chair of the Committee of Detail, to introduce the phrase "any agreement or compact."[48] Regardless of whether Finkel is right (he confesses uncertainty), the phrase continued to be used by the Committee of Style and was included in Article I, Section 10, all without apparent discussion of its meaning.[49]

Madison himself, in *Federalist 44*, declined to elaborate, either because he did not think he needed to (which is what he wrote) or because he did not want to call attention to the Constitution's nationalistic resolution of the issue of interstate compacts.[50] He quoted the second and third clauses of Section 10; commented on the prohibition on import and export duties by states; and wrote that "[t]he remaining particulars of this clause [including the Interstate Compacts Clause] fall within reasons which are either so obvious, or have been so fully developed, that they may be passed over without remark."[51] The debates in the state ratifying conventions proved no more enlightening.

Fortunately, the foregoing colonial and postcolonial history, which the Framers and Ratifiers knew well, offers greater illumination. "[A]t the adoption of the Constitution," the Court observed in 1838, "there were existing controversies between eleven states respecting their boundaries, which arose under their respective charters and had continued from the first settlement of the Colonies."[52] The Interstate Compacts Clause continued the tradition of resolving disputes between states through negotiation and approval by a higher authority. Moreover, when negotiation failed or was deemed undesirable by at least one disputing state, Article III's grant of original jurisdiction to the Supreme Court in "Controversies between two or more States" continued the tradition of resolving interstate disagreements through litigation.[53]

Collective-action reasoning helps explain why, both originally and today, the Interstate Compacts Clause leaves room for the states to act in concert.[54] Border disputes between states are collective-action problems insofar as both states prefer making concessions and avoiding litigation to not making concessions and requiring litigation, even as each state wants the other to make more concessions. If both states least prefer to litigate, collective-action problems involving boundary disputes and other disagreements between two states can be

---

[48] Jacob Finkel, *Stranger in the Land of Federalism: A Defense of the Compact Clause*, 71 STAN. L. REV. 1575, 1581–83 (2019).

[49] Hollis, *supra* note 46, at 761.

[50] Greve, *supra* note 47, at 313.

[51] THE FEDERALIST NO. 44, at 283 (James Madison) (Clinton Rossiter ed., 1961).

[52] Rhode Island v. Massachusetts, 37 U.S. (12 Pet.) 657, 724 (1838).

[53] U.S. CONST. art. III, § 2, cl. 1. Chapter 7 discusses Article III.

[54] BUENGER ET AL., *supra* note 41, at 24 (describing interstate compacts as "preserving the states' ability to take appropriate collective action in addressing supra-state problems"); *id.* at 26 (explaining that "interstate compacts can broaden parochial focus by allowing states to act collectively and jointly in addressing regional and national problems").

108 THE COLLECTIVE-ACTION CONSTITUTION

		State 2	
		Major	Minor
State 1	Major	3,3	**2,4**
	Minor	**4,2**	1,1

Figure 3.1 Two-state bargaining as Chicken game.

modeled as a one-shot game of Chicken (see Figure 2.7 in Chapter 2) in which communication is permitted.[55] Both states agree on the desirability of avoiding the outcome in which they fail to reach agreement, which will happen if both states make only minor concessions. Each state would prefer, however, not to be the one to make major concessions; each would instead prefer to hold out for the other state to "blink" first. Figure 3.1 captures this interaction, in which "Major" is a strategy that has a state make relatively significant concessions and "Minor" has a state make relatively minor ones.

Before the Constitution was ratified, pairs of states were sometimes able, in effect, to achieve one of the three Pareto optimal outcomes—whether one of the two equilibria characterized by inequality, or the one nonequilibrium characterized by equality—without the intervention of the Confederation Congress acting in a quasi-judicial capacity. As noted, the border disputes that colonies/states resolved themselves during the colonial era and under the Articles of Confederation illustrate the potential for states to sometimes succeed in acting collectively. So do the requisition orders that states honored. Yet, all the border disputes that remained unresolved, like all the requisitions that were disregarded, illustrate the limitations of relying on the states.

Collective-action considerations also justified the Framers' concerns about states' forming political combinations with other states or foreign nations, whether a "treaty, alliance, or confederation."[56] For two reasons, a potentially massive collective-action problem is at the root of such conduct by states. First, a political combination formed by a group of states with one another or with

---

[55] If each state least prefers the outcome in which it makes major concessions and the other state makes minor ones, the interaction is better modeled as a Prisoners' Dilemma. One need only switch the 1s and 2s in Figure 3.1.

[56] U.S. CONST. art. I, § 10, cl. 1. The distinction between treaties and compacts at the Founding was unclear. The Founders tended to use the terms interchangeably, as did the next generation. *See* Greve, *supra* note 47, at 309–10 (citing, inter alia, Barron ex rel. Tiernan v. Mayor & City Council of Baltimore, 32 U.S. (7 Pet.) 243, 249 (1833)). For discussion of the different positions of commentators, see Joseph Blocher, *Selling State Borders*, 162 U. PA. L. REV. 241, 274–77 (2014). Although the Constitution requires a distinction between state treaties, which are categorically barred, and interstate compacts, which are not, "centuries of study show that the distinction is neither textually apparent nor historically evident." Katherine Mims Crocker, *A Prophylactic Approach to Compact Constitutionality*, 98 NOTRE DAME L. REV. 1185 (2023).

another nation might harm the excluded states more than they would benefit the combining states, creating a cost-benefit collective-action problem. For example, a mutual defense treaty between a group of states and another nation might draw all states into war with foreign powers. If the other nation were attacked, the states with the treaty relationship would be obliged to lend military support, which could cause the attacking foreign power to wage war against the United States—the states collectively.

Second, states that form political combinations with other states or nations tend to invite retaliatory behavior by the excluded states. For example, had Southern states formed a confederation with one another, Mid-Atlantic or Northern states would likely have responded in kind, creating a race to the bottom. In *Federalist 6*, Hamilton wrote that "if these States should either be wholly disunited, or only united in partial confederacies, the subdivisions into which they might be thrown would have frequent and violent contests with each other."[57] Or, if one group of states had allied itself with England, another group might have felt compelled to ally itself with France or Spain, again fueling a race to the bottom. In *Federalist 7*, Hamilton expressed this concern:

> America, if not connected at all, or only by the feeble tie of a simple league offensive and defensive, would by the operation of such opposite and jarring alliances [between the different States or confederacies and different foreign nations] be gradually entangled in all the pernicious labyrinths of European politics and wars; and by the destructive contentions of the parts, into which she was divided would be likely to become a prey to the artifices and machinations of powers equally the enemies of them all.[58]

The states were each likely to be better off by their own estimations, particularly as the time horizon was extended, if they avoided political combinations with foreign powers and other states. The same almost certainly remains true today.[59]

---

[57] THE FEDERALIST NO. 6, at 54 (Alexander Hamilton) (Clinton Rossiter ed., 1961).

[58] THE FEDERALIST NO. 7, at 65–66 (Alexander Hamilton) (Clinton Rossiter ed., 1961).

[59] As noted, the Foreign Compacts Clause prohibits states, "without the Consent of Congress," from "enter[ing] into any Agreement or Compact . . . with a foreign Power." U.S. CONST. art. I, § 10, cl. 3. The number of agreements between states and foreign governments ("foreign-state agreements" or "FSAs") has increased substantially over the past several decades. It cannot be addressed here whether certain of them are consistent with the Foreign Compacts Clause when they do not receive congressional approval, or whether certain of them are consistent with the prohibition on states' entering into treaties, confederations, or alliances. For skepticism of FSAs, see Hollis, *supra* note 46. For an effort to unearth hundreds of previously unpublished US state commitments with the national, provincial, and local governments of foreign sovereigns, see Ryan Scoville, *The International Commitments of the Fifty States*, 70 UCLA L. REV. 310 (2023). For discussion of why international agreements by US states do not tend to trigger significant pushback from the federal government (but why "both the lack of transparency and the potential for federal-state conflicts are likely to require attention going forward"), see Curtis A. Bradley, *State International Agreements: The United States, Canada, and Constitutional Evolution*, 60 CANADIAN Y.B. INT'L L. 6, 28 (2023).

110 THE COLLECTIVE-ACTION CONSTITUTION

		Group 2	
		No Alliance	Alliance
Group 1	No Alliance	3,4	1,3
	Alliance	4,1	**2,2**

Figure 3.2 State alliances as Asymmetric Dilemma game.

A race to the bottom involving alliances between two groups of states and foreign powers can be modeled as an asymmetric dilemma like the one in Figure 2.2
in Chapter 2. Imagine that the first group most prefers that only it form an alliance with another nation and the second group most prefers that no group forms
such an alliance. Each group least prefers the outcome in which only the other
group forms an alliance. Both groups prefer the outcome in which neither group
forms an alliance to the outcome in which both groups form an alliance. Each
group also prefers the outcome in which only it forms an alliance to the outcome
in which both groups form an alliance. The game is sequential: the first group of
states moves first and then the second group must decide how to respond. The
strategic structure is the same, however, if the interaction is modeled as the simultaneous game in Figure 3.2.[60]

Even though Group 2 most prefers the outcome in which neither group
forms an alliance, it is predicted to do so in equilibrium (if it behaves in a narrowly self-interested fashion), given the decision of Group 1 to form an alliance. If communication is possible, the groups may solve this collective-action
problem by negotiating their way to the Pareto optimal outcome (in which neither group forms an alliance). But depending on the number of states involved
and the intensity of the disagreement between the two groups, negotiation
may fail. Under the Articles, congressional consent for alliances was required
as a safeguard when states failed to solve this collective-action problem on
their own. Under the Constitution, not even congressional consent can allow
alliances involving states. The Constitution itself solves the collective-action
problem by categorically prohibiting them.[61] Congressional consent does suffice, however, if states want to "engage in War," and such consent is not required
if states are "actually invaded, or in such imminent Danger as will not admit
of delay."[62] It is structurally sensible to let Congress determine whether war
making by states helps solve or cause a collective-action problem for the states,

---

[60] If the game were repeated a limited number of times, the strategic structure would be like the
one-shot game. It is not clear that the game would be repeated indefinitely or that indefinite repetition would produce cooperative behavior (no alliances) in a decentralized fashion.

[61] U.S. CONST. art. I, § 10, cl. 1.

[62] U.S. CONST. art. I, § 10, cl. 3.

THE ROLES OF THE STATES   111

unless the emergency is such that Congress does not have a reasonable opportunity to decide.

Historical Practice

Whereas treaties, alliances, or confederations involving states did not survive the Constitution, interstate compacts did. If one consults later historical practice concerning their use, collective-action justifications for permitting them remain plausible—arguably more so. Although the process had begun before the Civil War, the American economy was rapidly industrializing and nationalizing in the late nineteenth century. With spectacular economic growth producing good and bad consequences and greater interstate travel came federal legislation that increasingly preempted state and local regulations. For example, the Interstate Commerce Act of 1877 (ICA) authorized federal regulation of railroads, and the Sherman Antitrust Act of 1890 authorized federal regulation of monopolies and other restraints on trade.[63] Both laws helped solve collective-action problems for the states. To maintain the successful operation of interstate railroads, states must coordinate and cooperate with one another.[64] For instance, tracks must be laid across state lines in a coordinated fashion, and the financial viability of interstate railroads may be threatened by inconsistent state regulations and prices. There is also a risk that some states will free ride off the contributions of other states to the development of such interstate infrastructure. Similarly, states must act collectively, not individually, to control a monopoly that produces or sells goods in multiple states. Given the limited legislative jurisdiction of each state, no one state can effectively regulate such a monopoly on its own.

During this period, organizations representing state regulatory interests sought to discourage additional federal preemption of state laws. They encouraged state legislatures to pass uniform laws regarding various commercial transactions. They reasoned that if the states were facilitating interstate commerce and travel—including by proactively solving their own collective-action problems—Congress would perceive less need to intervene. In 1889, the American Bar Association resolved to encourage the passage of uniform state laws. In 1892, the National Conference of Commissioners on Uniform State Laws (known today as the Uniform Law Commission) was created.[65] Uniform laws can help states coordinate their activities and solve cooperation problems. For example, depending on how many states adopt them, such laws can help

---

[63] DANIEL A. FARBER & NEIL S. SIEGEL, UNITED STATES CONSTITUTIONAL LAW 127 (2d ed. 2024).
[64] *See* Chapter 5.
[65] ZIMMERMAN, *supra* note 28, at 12; *see* Overview, Uniform Law Commission, https://perma.cc/ME8R-P7BJ.

112   THE COLLECTIVE-ACTION CONSTITUTION

combat races to the bottom by insulating the participating states from competitive pressures to, for example, reduce regulations to dissuade businesses from moving to jurisdictions with less regulation.[66]

During this era, states also enacted reciprocal legislation.[67] Like uniform laws, reciprocal legislation facilitates coordination and cooperation by states in the economic sphere and other areas. The structure of such legislation is that State A grants certain advantages to the businesses or individuals in State B in exchange for State B's granting the same advantages to the corresponding businesses or individuals in State A.

In addition, states increasingly formed compacts to solve common problems, including multistate collective-action problems. In 1921, New York and New Jersey, with congressional approval, created the New York Port Authority, which today is responsible for (among other things) airports and marine ports and terminals in New York City and Newark, New Jersey, as well as bridges and tunnels between the two states.[68] In 1925, Felix Frankfurter and James Landis published the aforementioned *Yale Law Journal* article celebrating the potential for interstate compacts to solve problems whose scope was interstate or regional, but not national.[69] In 1934, Congress consented in advance to state agreements to control crime.[70] The Crime Compact of 1934 provides for the supervision of parolees and probationers.[71]

In the ensuing decades, the number and nature of interstate compacts increased substantially. "No longer simply a tool for dispute settlement," Professor Duncan Hollis explains, "the New Deal saw interstate compacts become mechanisms for states to share information and to jointly study, and even regulate, various collective action or coordination problems."[72] More precisely, interstate compacts were increasingly used to solve collective-action problems caused by either cooperation or coordination difficulties. The subjects of these compacts have included, among other topics, the joint construction and maintenance of bridges and tunnels; crime control and corrections (e.g., the interstate transfer of sentenced prisoners for unrelated trials, and the supervision, as noted above, of individuals on parole or probation); the allocation and conservation of water supplied by interstate bodies of water; the regulation of fishing in inland waters; the conservation of oil and natural gas; environmental protection;

---

[66] *See, e.g.*, Jill Elaine Hasday, *Interstate Compacts in a Democratic Society: The Problem of Permanency*, 49 FLA. L. REV. 1, 7 (1997).

[67] Frankfurter & Landis, *supra* note 23, at 688.

[68] Hollis, *supra* note 46, at 763.

[69] Frankfurter & Landis, *supra* note 23.

[70] Crime Control Consent Act, 48 Stat. 909 (1934); *see* ZIMMERMAN, *supra* note 28, at 54.

[71] FREDERICK L. ZIMMERMAN & MITCHELL WENDELL, THE INTERSTATE COMPACT SINCE 1925, at 91 (1951).

[72] Hollis, *supra* note 46, at 763.

THE ROLES OF THE STATES 113

flood and pollution control; emergency management mutual assistance; motor vehicles; multistate taxation; resource pooling for the provision of expensive professional education; and the disposal of low-level radioactive waste.[73]

Many, if not most, of the interstate compacts formed over the past century address collective-action problems. As with railroad construction, the erection of ports, bridges, and tunnels across state lines requires successful coordination and cooperation by the affected states. Some states may disagree (as in the Bridge or Seaway game in Figure 2.6 in Chapter 2), or hold out (as in the Chicken game in Figure 2.7 in Chapter 2), or attempt to free ride on the efforts of other states to provide and maintain these channels of interstate commerce (as in the Prisoners' Dilemma game in Figure 2.1 in Chapter 2). In addition, as Chapter 2 explained, state overuse of natural resources such as water, fish, and natural gas can create a multistate tragedy of the commons. Similarly, a state that externalizes pollution costs onto other states may invite retaliation by these states or may benefit itself less than it harms them. In either scenario, a collective-action problem would exist. A similar analysis would apply if states declined to help other states with the transfer of alleged criminals or with their supervision upon release from prison,[74] or if states disproportionately taxed American taxpayers who pay taxes in multiple states. Likewise, mutual aid and resource pooling, whether in emergency or nonemergency situations, can make all participating states better off than they would be on their own, but such arrangements also require the policing of efforts to free ride. The disposal of low-level radioactive waste creates a NIMBY (not in my backyard) collective-action problem.[75]

Congressional Consent in Theory

Collective-action reasoning also helps clarify why the constitutional text ostensibly prohibits interstate compacts and agreements unless Congress approves. (The reason for use of the qualifier "ostensibly" will become clear.) The Court and commentators have identified two reasons for this requirement. First, congressional approval protects against compacts that threaten the supremacy of the federal government. Compacts that alter the balance of political power between Congress and the states risk harming the states collectively by undermining Congress's constitutional authority, including its power (and potentially greater ability) to solve multistate collective-action problems.[76] Congressional approval

---

[73] ZIMMERMAN, *supra* note 28, at 62–72; The Law Library of Congress, Interstate Compacts in the United States 10–11 (2018), https://perma.cc/E397-VP6W.
[74] *See* Chapter 8 (analyzing the Extradition Clause).
[75] *See* Chapter 5 (discussing New York v. United States, 505 U.S. 144 (1992)).
[76] *See* Chapters 4–6.

114 THE COLLECTIVE-ACTION CONSTITUTION

serves an anti-backsliding function: it prevents the erosion of federal power and the expansion of state power toward how the Articles of Confederation distributed power. The Constitution empowers Congress to prevent such compacts by prohibiting them or approving them with conditions that address this concern.[77] The Constitution also authorizes Congress to terminate or limit such compacts via preemption by using its enumerated powers.[78]

The Court has long recognized the role of congressional approval in ensuring that states do not use compacts to encroach on federal authority. In *Virginia v. Tennessee* (1893), a suit to establish the correct boundary line between the two states, Justice Field suggested for the Court that congressional consent is required for a compact that "is directed to the formation of any combination tending to the increase of political power in the States, which may encroach upon or interfere with the just supremacy of the United States."[79] Throughout the twentieth century, federal and state courts cited *Virginia v. Tennessee* for this proposition, and the Supreme Court invoked it in *New Hampshire v. Maine* (1976). The Court there stated that a proposed consent decree fell outside the Interstate Compacts Clause because it was "directed simply to locating precisely th[e] already existing boundary" between the two states, not to "adjusting the boundary between them." As a result, "neither State can be viewed as enhancing its power" in any sense that threatens the supremacy of the Federal Government."[80]

As commentators have recognized, the Court's functional test is vague, and the justices have not received much guidance from the legal academy, given the lack of sustained scholarly interest in the Interstate Compacts Clause.[81] But a proposed compact would likely flunk the Court's test and so require congressional approval if, for example, it would seek to alter the boundary line between two states (as opposed to locating the already existing line),[82] or would impose obligations that conflicted with (and so were preempted by) an existing federal statute or program, or would interfere with federal powers that are exclusive. Less clear is whether and when a proposed compact requires congressional

[77] ZIMMERMAN, *supra* note 28, at 55–56.
[78] *Id.* at 58. Preemption is discussed in Chapter 5.
[79] 148 U.S. 503, 519 (1893).
[80] 426 U.S. 363, 369–70 (1976). Two years later, in *U.S. Steel Corporation v. Multistate Tax Commission*, 434 U.S. 452 (1978), the Court described *New Hampshire v. Maine* as having turned the federal-supremacy test from dictum into holding. *Id.* at 459–60. Professor Michael Greve disputes this claim. Greve, *supra* note 47, at 304–05. Given that *U.S. Steel Corporation* embraced the test in its holding, little turns on who is right.
[81] David E. Engdahl, *Characterization of Interstate Arrangements: When Is a Compact Not a Compact?*, 64 MICH. L. REV. 63, 63 (1965) (noting "the relative lack of attention which the subject [of interstate compacts] has received from legal scholars"); Adam Schleifer, *Interstate Agreement for Electoral Reform*, 40 AKRON L. REV. 717, 719 (2007) (noting "a general scholarly disinterest in the law of interstate compacts," and observing that "the jurisprudence of the Interstate Compact Clause has demonstrated a surprising lack of precision").
[82] BUENGER ET AL., *supra* note 41, at 69.

THE ROLES OF THE STATES 115

consent under the Court's test when the compact would regulate in an area of concurrent legislative jurisdiction, but Congress has not acted.[83] Congressional consent would appear not to be required when states act as market participants, as opposed to regulators.[84] This distinction also appears in the Court's anti-commandeering and dormant commerce doctrines.[85]

A second reason for congressional approval concerns the potential effects of compacts on states that are not parties to them. *Northeast Bancorp, Inc. v. Board of Governors of the Federal Reserve System* (1985) involved a dispute over Massachusetts and Connecticut statutes that permitted out-of-state bank holding companies to acquire in-state banks if they were from another state in the region that gave reciprocal privileges to Massachusetts and Connecticut companies. The Court doubted that there was a compact to exclude non–New England banking organizations, but assuming otherwise for the sake of argument, the Court seemed to indicate that congressional approval is required when a compact would "enhance the *political* power of the [compacting] States at the expense of other States."[86] The Court perceived no such threat in the case, but it did not really explain why, and how this could occur is unclear. It might happen, however, if a regulatory problem significantly affected several states, but only some were permitted to join the compact.[87] For example, two or more states might seek to form a compact allocating water access between them that affected the water access of nonparty states. Or two states might seek to form a compact providing for mutual aid during a natural disaster or a flu pandemic affecting a region, and the compact might prohibit other states nearby from joining it.[88] In such situations, the compacting states might externalize greater costs onto other states than the benefits they were creating for themselves (a cost-benefit collective-action problem absent compensation), or they might cause other states to retaliate with exclusionary compacts of their own (a Pareto cooperation problem).

---

[83] *Id.* at 69–75 (offering arguably inconsistent answers to this question).

[84] Blocher, *supra* note 56, at 279 (suggesting this distinction based on the Court's statement in *Virginia v. Tennessee*, 148 U.S. at 518, that Congress need not consent when a state buys "a small parcel of land" within its borders from another state).

[85] *See* Chapter 5.

[86] 472 U.S. 159, 176 (1985) (emphasis in original). *See* Florida v. Georgia, 58 U.S. (17 How.) 478, 494 (1854) (describing the Interstate Compacts Clause as "obviously intended to guard the rights and interests of the other States, and to prevent any compact or agreement between any two States, which might affect injuriously the interests of the others," and adding that "the right and the duty to protect these interests is vested in the general government").

[87] BUENGER ET AL., *supra* note 41, at 69.

[88] In addition, compacts that would otherwise violate the dormant commerce doctrine require congressional consent for reasons explained in Chapter 5. Moreover, compacts that would violate the Privileges and Immunities Clause, U.S. CONST. art. IV, § 2, cl. 1, are conventionally thought to be impermissible even with congressional consent. Chapter 9 questions the conventional understanding.

116 THE COLLECTIVE-ACTION CONSTITUTION

From a collective-action perspective, therefore, the above two rationales for requiring congressional approval make sense. They track Madison's concerns about "the evil of imperia in imperio," or states within a state, which he thought had doomed the Articles of Confederation and prior federal unions. In Madison's view, which he expressed before, during, and after the Constitutional Convention, the prevention of this problem required "a controuling power . . . by which the general authority may be defended against encroachments of the subordinate authorities, and by which the latter may be restrained from encroachments on each other."[89] As later chapters demonstrate, much of the Constitution is concerned with preventing states from harming the federal government and one another—including by undermining federal solutions to multistate collective-action problems or causing such problems.

There is a deeper reason, however, for requiring Congress to approve interstate compacts, one that neither the Court nor commentators have recognized. A group of states that forms a compact to solve a Pareto collective-action problem for its members may simultaneously create a problem, including possibly a cost-benefit collective-action problem, for states that are and are not parties to the compact. When states disagree, the technical task of identifying a multistate collective-action problem is not just a scientific exercise; it also requires contestable value judgments. States may disagree with one another over whether the absence of cooperation or coordination by states is a good thing (e.g., because it prevents a threat to federal power or prevents a price-fixing cartel from forming)[90] or a problem (e.g., because the federal government cannot act or policy competition among states is fueling a race to the bottom regarding environmental protection or income support for vulnerable Americans).[91]

The Constitution does not take sides on such questions. As Justice Holmes memorably wrote, "[A] constitution is not intended to embody a particular economic theory, whether of paternalism and the organic relation of the citizen to the State or of *laissez faire*. It is made for people of fundamentally differing views."[92] The Constitution instead identifies institutions that are authorized to decide these questions in particular contexts. By requiring interstate compacts

---

[89] Letter from James Madison to Thomas Jefferson (Oct. 24, 1787), *in* 5 THE WRITINGS OF JAMES MADISON 23 (Gaillard Hunt ed., 1904); *see* JAMES MADISON, *Vices of the Political System of the United States* (April 1787), *in* 2 THE WRITINGS OF JAMES MADISON 361–62 (Gaillard Hunt ed., 1904) (decrying, inter alia, "Encroachments by the States on the federal authority" and "Trespasses of the States on the rights of each other").

[90] For arguments that certain interstate compacts were price-fixing cartels, see Greve, *supra* note 47, at 325–27, 333–35, 354–55, and Note, *State Collective Action*, 119 HARV. L. REV. 1855, 1861–62 (2006).

[91] For arguments that interstate compacts are justified by their suppression of policy competition among states on certain subjects, see Hasday, *supra* note 66, at 7, and Note, *To Form a More Perfect Union? Federalism and Informal Interstate Cooperation*, 102 HARV. L. REV. 842, 846 (1989).

[92] Lochner v. New York, 198 U.S. 45, 75–76 (1905) (Holmes, J., dissenting).

THE ROLES OF THE STATES   117

to obtain congressional consent, the Interstate Compacts Clause identifies Congress as the institution entitled to make such judgment calls when states seek to form agreements. As discussed below, relying on Congress raises concerns that the Framers did not anticipate. But as Marshall argued in *McCulloch*, no other government institution better represents the interests of all the states and (almost) all the people.

Congressional Consent in Practice

In practice, however, the Supreme Court has not required congressional consent for "any Agreement or Compact with another State." Although a majority of interstate compacts existing today have received congressional consent, 46 percent apparently have not.[93] For example, Congress did not consent to the Multistate Tax Compact, which primarily addresses taxes that affect businesses operating in multiple states. The compact includes a model act, which states may voluntarily adopt; it was drafted in 1957 by the Uniform Law Commission. This act "provides for the attribution of multi state income on a consistent basis among the states."[94] Even though congressional consent was sought and could not be obtained (numerous bills were introduced in Congress, but apparently none were voted on), and even though historical practice indicated that consent was required, the Court held that past practice did not control and consent was unnecessary because the compact did not implicate the doctrine's focus on threats to federal supremacy.[95] The Court has never invalidated a compact for encroaching on federal supremacy or harming state non-parties to the compact. Until 2015, no court in the United States ever had.[96]

More generally, the Court has placed few restrictions on states seeking to form interstate agreements. The Court permits Congress to consent before or after a

---

[93] Of the 178 interstate compacts involving at least two states or US territories in the database created by the National Center for Interstate Compacts, *see infra* note 130, 96 compacts have obtained congressional consent. National Center for Interstate Compacts Database, https://perma.cc/GR9D-T5NU. To use the database, go to https://apps.csg.org/ncic/#:~:text=National%20Center%20for%20Interstate%20Compacts%20Database&text=CSG's%20National%20Center%20for%20Interstate,for%20researching%20interstate%20compacts%20available.

[94] Multistate Tax Commission, *About the Multistate Tax Compact, with Suggested Enabling Act* (2015), https://perma.cc/227X-SWNW.

[95] *See, e.g.,* U.S. Steel Corp. v. Multistate Tax Comm'n, 434 U.S. 452, 458 n.8 (1978). *See id.* at 471 ("[M]ost multilateral compacts have been submitted for congressional approval. But this historical practice, which may simply reflect considerations of caution and convenience on the part of the submitting States, is not controlling.").

[96] In 2015, a state court held that an interstate compact violated the Interstate Compacts Clause because Congress had not consented. Sauer v. Nixon, No. 14AC-CC00477, 2015 WL 4474833, at *1 (Mo. Cir. Ct. Cole Cty. Feb. 24, 2015), *appeal dismissed as moot*, 474 S.W.3d 624, 626 (Mo. Ct. App. 2015).

118   THE COLLECTIVE-ACTION CONSTITUTION

compact is formed.[97] It infers consent from the surrounding context even when Congress has not expressly approved.[98] And the Court concludes that coordinated behavior by states such as model uniform laws and reciprocal legislation are not agreements or compacts because the states did not expressly agree, even though one could plausibly argue that an agreement exists.[99] The reasons for deference may include the perceptions that many multistate disputes are best settled through negotiation, not litigation;[100] that the subjects of compacts are such that Congress can pass preemptive legislation if it wishes; and that it is sufficiently difficult for states to form interstate compacts (see below) that the judiciary should not impose additional impediments. The Court may also believe that states have used compacts overwhelmingly to settle boundary disputes and solve other local collective-action problems, not to threaten federal supremacy or other states. Finally, the doctrine may reflect the ideological commitment of certain justices to states as sovereigns.[101]

From a collective-action standpoint, the doctrine has three primary advantages. First, judicial deference makes it easier for states to solve collective-action problems that arise for them. The existence of a federal system inevitably results in various cooperation and coordination difficulties for the states, whether caused by interstate externalities, disharmonious state regulations, or other state conduct. The states historically have shown that they can play a role in solving them. The states have largely avoided proposing compacts that would be preempted by federal law or arguably interfere with exclusive federal powers. Moreover, the states have generally invited other states to join compacts; they have not excluded them.

Second, judicial deference can avoid the hold-up problem that might result from always requiring congressional approval. Bilateral or regional interactions may render an interstate compact sensible, but the proposed compact may not command majority support in Congress if only because a congressional majority may not care about the subject of the compact. In this situation, the requirement of congressional consent empowers a majority to demand some sort of rent from the states that want to compact. Alternatively, a compact involving a few states might produce major benefits for the compacting states and minor costs for states that are not parties to the compact. Such a compact should be permitted

---

[97] *See, e.g.*, Virginia v. Tennessee, 148 U.S. 503 (1893); *see* ZIMMERMAN, *supra* note 28, at 53–54.

[98] *See, e.g.*, Virginia v. West Virginia, 78 U.S. (11 Wall.) 39 (1871).

[99] *See, e.g.*, *Northeast Bancorp, Inc.*, 472 U.S. at 175 (doubting that two state statutes created a compact even though they required reciprocity); *see* Hollis, *supra* note 46, at 765–66.

[100] BUENGER ET AL., *supra* note 41, at 24 (noting that "the Supreme Court regularly suggests states resolve their differences by compact rather than litigation"); *see* Frankfurter & Landis, *supra* note 23, at 696, 705–07.

[101] On the last point, see, for example, *Northeast Bancorp, Inc.*, 472 U.S. at 178–80 (O'Connor, J., concurring).

THE ROLES OF THE STATES   119

from a cost-benefit perspective, but an unwavering requirement of congressional consent would likely defeat it.

Third, interstate compacts can help solve multistate collective-action problems when Congress is unable or unwilling to do so. It may be especially important for the states to be given leeway during periods of partisan polarization and animosity, including the current era.[102] As Part III discusses, the Framers did not anticipate political parties, let alone ideological parties and constant razor's edge elections, which often make bipartisan cooperation in Congress difficult or impossible depending on the issue and the situation. Yet, given the bicameralism and presentment requirements that must be met before a bill can become a law,[103] and given the emergence of policy-based vetoes of bills during the nineteenth century, cooperation is necessary to pass legislation during divided government, which has been the norm since the 1970s.[104] Moreover, given the Senate filibuster,[105] bipartisanship is typically required to enact most federal laws even during unified government. In such an environment, Congress may be unable or unwilling to solve pressing problems, including collective-action problems for the states.[106] The Court's doctrine concerning the Interstate Compacts Clause effectively creates a workaround that is supported by some practice.

The foregoing considerations likely justify the Court's generosity regarding the forms that congressional consent can take. They also likely justify the Court's refusal to regard uniform laws and reciprocal legislation as agreements or compacts. And perhaps the effects of hyper-polarization and related phenomena on Congress's ability or willingness to legislate should inform the Court's assessment of whether an interstate compact threatens "federal supremacy," a concept that the Court has never satisfactorily defined. Because power tends to flow to where it can be exercised, a polarized Congress has led to greater action by the executive branch and by state governments, including in concert. As Professor Jessica Bulman-Pozen argues, "courts might give states more leeway to enter

---

[102] Jessica Bulman-Pozen, *Executive Federalism Comes to America*, 102 VA. L. REV. 953, 1025–30 (2016) (championing interstate compacts as methods of interstate and federal-state cooperation amid partisan polarization).

[103] U.S. CONST. art. I, § 7, cl. 2.

[104] Dean Lacy et al., *Measuring Preferences for Divided Government: Some Americans Want Divided Government and Vote to Create It*, 41 POL. BEHAVIOR 79, 80 (2019) ("Relatively rare in earlier periods in US history, divided government has become the new normal. The party of the president failed to control at least one house of Congress in eighteen of the twenty-five congresses between 1969 and 2017.").

[105] The filibuster is a Senate rule (not a constitutional requirement) that effectively requires a sixty-vote majority to pass most bills. Under Senate Rule 22.2, a motion to end debate "shall be decided . . . by three-fifths of the Senators duly chosen and sworn—except on a measure or motion to amend the Senate rules, in which case the necessary affirmative vote shall be two-thirds of the Senators duly present and voting." COMM. ON RULES AND ADMIN., SENATE MANUAL, S. Doc. No. 116-1, at 21 (2020).

[106] *See* Chapter 11.

120 THE COLLECTIVE-ACTION CONSTITUTION

into interstate agreements insofar as the federal executive branch is prompting or incorporating such action into federal governance."[107] The idea is that federal supremacy, whatever its exact meaning, seems less likely to be threatened if the executive branch has effectively blessed an agreement.

It is less clear, however, whether such concerns justify dispensing with congressional consent altogether when an interstate agreement or compact plainly exists and would have significant effects outside the compacting states. The text of the Interstate Compacts Clause indicates otherwise, and the historical practice does not appear to support such a result.[108] Structurally, as explained above, there may be a risk that certain compacts will encroach on federal power or threaten sister states. But the more fundamental concern, also discussed above, is that states supporting and opposing a compact may disagree about whether the compact solves a multistate collective-action problem or creates one for the states. The Interstate Compacts Clause, tracking the Marshallian theory of democratic legitimacy, authorizes Congress to resolve such disagreements, and there is a major difference between requiring Congress to approve compacts and requiring it to reject them. Requiring Congress to approve is exceptional under the Constitution. Requiring Congress to disapprove is typical—Congress does it by passing legislation that preempts state law under the Supremacy Clause.[109] Given the difficulty of securing congressional action, the default rule will decide many cases.[110]

The most recent opinion of the Office of Legal Counsel (OLC), issued in 1980, views congressional consent as a real requirement. According to OLC's interpretation of the Court's cases, "[c]onsent is required only when two or more states agree among themselves to impose some legal obligation or disability on state or federal governments or private parties." OLC concludes that interstate compacts interfere with federal supremacy and so require congressional consent if "(1) they involve a subject matter which Congress is competent to regulate ... and (2) they purport to impose some legal obligation or disability." It further concludes that interstate agreements require congressional consent unless "each state is free to accept or reject [any determination made under the agreement] or any of its provisions and has the unfettered right to withdraw from" it.[111] Under OLC's test,

[107] Bulman-Pozen, *supra* note 102, at 1030.

[108] *See supra* note 95 and accompanying text (discussing the Court's refusal to be bound by past practice).

[109] U.S. CONST. art. VI, § 1, cl. 2. Chapter 7 discusses the Supremacy Clause.

[110] Given the extraordinary default rule established in the Interstate Compacts Clause itself, it is unclear that Congress can reverse it via statute, as one scholar has proposed. *See* Crocker, *supra* note 56.

[111] Applicability of Compact Clause to Use of Multiple State Entities Under the Water Resources Planning Act, 4B Op. Off. Legal Counsel 828, 828, 830–31 (1980). *See* Amicus Curiae Brief of Constitutional Law Scholars in Support of the Petition, S&M Brands, Inc. v. Caldwell (No 10-622), 562 U.S. 1270 (Mem) (2011) (brief of Professors Alan Morrison, Richard Epstein, and Kathleen Sullivan endorsing and applying OLC's opinion). These scholars argued that the Master Settlement

THE ROLES OF THE STATES   121

most interstate compacts that impose regulatory solutions to collective-action problems would appear to require congressional consent.

In 2018, Justice Gorsuch, writing for a unanimous Court, emphasized the importance of congressional consent in a case involving an interstate water dispute that did not turn on whether such consent was required:

> Congress's approval serves to "prevent any compact or agreement between any two States, which might affect injuriously the interests of the others." It also ensures that the Legislature can "check any infringement of the rights of the national government." So, for example, if a proposed interstate agreement might lead to friction with a foreign country or injure the interests of another region of our own, Congress may withhold its approval.[112]

Along similar lines, in 2023, Justice Kavanaugh wrote for a unanimous Court that "[u]nder Article I, § 10, of the Constitution, each State possesses the sovereign authority to enter into a compact with another State, subject to Congress's approval," and that "New York and New Jersey obtained Congress's approval of the Compact [in question] in 1953, consistent with the Compact Clause of the Constitution."[113] It remains to be seen whether the Court will require congressional consent more often in the years ahead. Given the textualist and originalist commitments of several members of the Court, such a change would not be surprising.

One implication of the foregoing analysis could help guide the Court. Compacts that have significant, negative effects outside the states wishing to form a compact should require congressional consent so that Congress can determine whether the compact is justified from a cost-benefit perspective. By contrast, compacts that do not have significant, negative effects outside the compacting states should ordinarily not require congressional consent. Although the Court has less institutional competence and democratic legitimacy than Congress to find the relevant facts, in this instance the question is whether the Court should effectively require Congress to weigh in, and the Court can order briefing on this issue and render the best judgment that it can.

Because collective-action concerns illuminate the reasons both for and against making congressional consent a significant barrier to the formation of

---

Agreement (MSA) between forty-six states and the major tobacco companies required congressional approval. The Court denied certiorari. 562 U.S. 1270 (2011).

[112] Texas v. New Mexico, 138 S. Ct. 954, 958 (2018) (quoting Florida v. Georgia, 58 U.S. (17 How.) 478, 494 (1855), and 3 JOSEPH STORY, COMMENTARIES ON THE CONSTITUTION OF THE UNITED STATES § 1397, 272 (1833)).

[113] New York v. New Jersey, 143 S. Ct. 918, 922 (2023) (holding that, notwithstanding New York's opposition, New Jersey may unilaterally withdraw from the 1953 Waterfront Commission Compact).

interstate compacts, collective-action theory cannot fully explain the form of the congressional check that exists in the Constitution—that is, why the form is congressional permission, as opposed to a congressional veto. Indeed, other democratic federal constitutions vary on this question. In some systems, approval by the central government is required (e.g., Germany) and in other systems, it is not (e.g., Switzerland). In some systems, the central government must be notified of the interstate agreement (e.g., Switzerland), and in other systems, it need not be notified (e.g., Nigeria).[114] Other factors likely explain the precise form of the check in a particular constitution, such as specific national histories and experiences and different degrees of trust in different government institutions. Regarding the US Constitution, the text of the Interstate Compacts Clause seems to reflect distrust of what groups of states may do on their own absent congressional oversight, which is unsurprising given the concerns raised by nationalist Framers and Founders during the 1780s.

The Practical Difficulties of Relying on the States

Collective-action reasoning helps explain why relying primarily on the states would make it very challenging to solve multistate collective-action problems. In general, it is difficult for states to form compacts because of all the actors and institutions that must approve. First, negotiators from every potentially interested state must reach agreement on a proposed compact. Second, each house of each state legislature must pass the same bill enacting the compact. Third, each state governor must sign the bill into law and execute it. Fourth, for compacts requiring congressional consent, both houses of Congress and the president must approve.[115] Political scientist Joseph Zimmerman, a student and supporter of interstate compacts, has written that "for even the relatively simple compacts established or proposed in the past, each step has proved to be a significant, sometimes insurmountable obstacle." It does not help that "[n]umerous proposed compacts relate to extremely divisive problems, such as apportionment of waters of a major river basin, and usually involve extended negotiations." Nor does it help that "negotiators often have to address important administrative,

---

[114] JOHANNE POIRIER ET AL. EDS., INTERGOVERNMENTAL RELATIONS IN FEDERAL SYSTEMS: COMPARATIVE STRUCTURES AND DYNAMICS 225, 293, 394 (2015).

[115] It is uncertain whether the congressional-consent requirement originally required presidential approval. But historical practice and scholarly commentary suggest an affirmative answer, meaning the president must approve or Congress must override a veto. For example, President Franklin Delano Roosevelt vetoed two resolutions of congressional consent to proposed interstate compacts because he thought that they interfered with federal authority, and Congress acquiesced. For examples of scholarly agreement with such practice, see ZIMMERMAN & WENDELL, *supra* note 71, at 94; Bulman-Pozen, *supra* note 102, at 1026–27; and Greve, *supra* note 47, at 319 n.38.

THE ROLES OF THE STATES   123

financial, substantive, and technical issues relating to a major proposed compact, and agreements must be reached on resolving each issue—an extremely difficult task, before the compact can be submitted to the concerned state legislatures."[116]

Part of the problem described above concerns the number of parties within each state that have veto power over the proposed compact. Another part is that compacts require unanimous agreement among the compacting states. There have been numerous instances, from the Founding to the present, in which two or more states failed to solve collective-action problems on their own. The long-enduring border disputes discussed above are an example, as is the general failure of the requisition scheme of the Articles of Confederation. Today, even "[a] bilateral interstate compact may prove to be exceptionally difficult to negotiate."[117] Two other scholars and supporters of interstate compacts agree that "the most obvious difficulty [with compacts] is the necessity for securing agreement among several jurisdictions."[118] Another group of scholars notes that "the ratification of a compact change by two or more state legislatures is likely to be a lengthy process at best; at worst it may constitute an impossible obstacle."[119]

The numbers appear consistent with these observations. Although research has not revealed how many interstate compacts have been attempted throughout American history, states approved only thirty-six of them between 1783 and 1920, mostly to settle border disputes.[120] To be sure, there was less need for interstate compacts when the country was mostly agricultural, and the numbers rose significantly during the twentieth century, especially after World War II. But assuming the accuracy of the information provided by the Council of State Governments' National Center for Interstate Compacts, today there are fewer than two hundred interstate compacts.[121]

---

[116] ZIMMERMAN, *supra* note 28, at 45. *See* Blocher, *supra* note 56, at 266–77 (noting the difficulty of negotiating interstate compacts and suggesting side payments to help lubricate the bargaining process).

[117] ZIMMERMAN, *supra* note 28, at 46.

[118] FREDERICK L. ZIMMERMAN & MITCHELL WENDELL, THE LAW AND USE OF INTERSTATE COMPACTS 54 (1976).

[119] ROSCOE C. MARTIN ET AL., RIVER BASIN ADMINISTRATION AND THE DELAWARE 131 (1960).

[120] National Center for Interstate Compacts, Council of State Governments, *When Are Interstate Compacts Used?*, https://web.archive.org/web/20210310081539/https:/www.csg.org/knowledgecenter/docs/ncic/FactSheet.pdf.

[121] *Compare* National Center for Interstate Compacts, Council of State Governments, *National Center for Interstate Compacts Summary*, https://web.archive.org/web/20210310081539/https:/www.csg.org/knowledgecenter/docs/ncic/FactSheet.pdf (stating that more than 200 interstate compacts are in effect), *with* National Center for Interstate Compacts Database, *supra* note 93 (listing 192 compacts in use). *See* Ann O'M Bowman, *Trends and Issues in Interstate Cooperation, in* THE BOOK OF STATUTES 35 (2004) (finding that, of the 192 interstate compacts in a 2003 Council of State Governments directory, 155 were in effect). There are actually 191 separate interstate compacts in the database. *See infra* note 129 (explaining the discrepancy). "[T]he council of state governments for many decades has played a major role in drafting and promoting the adoption of compacts, and currently operates the national center for interstate compacts [which] assists in the development of new compacts and modifications, if needed, of existing compacts." ZIMMERMAN, *supra* note 28, at 219.

124   THE COLLECTIVE-ACTION CONSTITUTION

That is a much higher number than in early American history, and it does not include less formal kinds of interstate cooperation. In addition, one cannot know how many more interstate compacts would exist if preemptive federal statutes did not constrain the kinds of compacts that states could form.[122] But preemptive federal legislation results partially from the refusal or inability of states to form compacts and otherwise cooperate: "The failure of state legislatures in the mid-1960s to act cooperatively in an effective manner to solve critical regional and national regulatory problems acted as a centripetal political force pressuring Congress to preempt regulatory authority of the states."[123] Moreover, the numbers in the database are arguably inflated because it apparently includes compacts that are advisory or study an issue; the database is not limited to regulatory and developmental compacts. Further, if there were two thousand total instances of significant interstate cooperation today instead of two hundred, the number would still pale in comparison to the number of federal statutes in the fifty-one titles of the US Code that address multistate collective-action problems in numerous areas of federal law, let alone the multitude of federal regulations addressing such problems.

Not only may two or three states find it impossible to form an interstate compact, but as Chapter 2 explained, the likelihood that states acting on their own will solve collective-action problems also declines as one increases the number of states that must cooperate or coordinate. Unanimity rule threatens to paralyze groups with many members. This is not just a prediction of game theory; it helps explain why the Articles of Confederation were effectively impossible to amend,[124] and why the Framers of the Constitution, who understood the logics of collective action from experience, provided that ratification by nine of the thirteen states would suffice to establish the Constitution.[125] Similar collective-action concerns explain why, as the European Union grows, it has switched from unanimity rule to majority rule to avoid paralysis.[126]

---

[122] Ann O'M. Bowman & Neal D. Woods, *Expanding the Scope of Conflict: Interest Groups and Interstate Compacts*, 91 Soc. Sci. Q. 669, 676–82 (2010) (finding that states use compacts as "[s]ubstitutes for national policy making"); Ann O'M. Bowman & Neal D. Woods, *Strength in Numbers: Why States Join Interstate Compacts*, 7 St. Pol. & Pol'y Q. 347, 364 (2007) (finding that states "join fewer new compacts during periods of national policy centralization").

[123] Zimmerman, *supra* note 28, at 231; *see id.* at 233 ("The relative failure of state legislatures to promote interstate cooperation in the form of interstate compacts, interstate administrative agreements, reciprocity agreements, and uniform state laws encourages a number of interest groups and citizens to continue to pressure Congress to enact additional partial and complete preemption statutes—removing regulatory powers from the states to solve the interstate problems.").

[124] Articles of Confederation of 1781, art. XIII (requiring the unanimous agreement of all thirteen states to amend the Articles).

[125] U.S. Const. art. VII (discussed in Chapter 10).

[126] Robert D. Cooter & Neil S. Siegel, *Collective Action Federalism: A General Theory of Article I, Section 8*, 63 Stan. L. Rev. 115, 142 (2010) (discussing the European Union).

THE ROLES OF THE STATES   125

State experience with interstate compacts reflects the difficulties of acting collectively under unanimity rule as the number of compacting states expands. "The degree of difficulty in reaching unanimity among negotiators on a proposed compact," writes Professor Joseph Zimmerman, "often is related directly to the number of involved states with a small number of states often able to reach an agreement in a shorter period of time than a large number of states."[127] In practice, numerosity has appeared to matter more than the possibility of repeated, related interactions between the states, although repetition is important when compacts require continued performance by each compacting state (unlike border disputes). Numerosity has also appeared to matter more than heterogeneities in the states that are potential parties to the compact. Such heterogeneities have no generally predictable impact on the likelihood of concluding an agreement. It seems likely that the prospects for some compacts were enhanced by the fact that certain states had more resources or stood to benefit disproportionately from concluding an agreement and so were incentivized to play a leadership role. It also seems likely that the prospects for other compacts suffered from the fact that certain states did not stand to benefit as much as other states from concluding an agreement, because a distribution problem was added to a bargaining problem—and a potential free-rider problem.[128]

Again, the numbers appear consistent with these observations. There are 191 separate interstate compacts listed in the database created by the National Center for Interstate Compacts.[129] According to this author's calculations, the average number of states per compact in the database is 9.43, and the median number of states per compact is 3.[130] Similarly, Ballotpedia's chart of interstate compacts formed between 1785 and 2014 includes a total of 207 compacts.[131] The average

---

[127] ZIMMERMAN, *supra* note 28, at 45–46.

[128] State experience with interstate compacts undermines Professor Huq's objection that, in predicting whether state collective action will succeed, special importance should not be placed on the number or states that must act collectively. *See* Huq, *supra* note 36, at 299.

[129] There are actually 192 interstate compacts listed in the database, *see supra* note 121, but the Texas Low Level Radioactive Waste Disposal Compact is listed twice.

[130] The database provided by National Center for Interstate Compacts, *see supra* note 93, does not provide information on the number of states that have joined each listed compact. To generate this information and calculate the mean and median number of states per compact, the author secured the assistance of Donald G. Hopkins, assistant director for empirical research and data services at the Goodson Law Library of Duke Law School. He used R, an open-source programming language designed specifically for statistical computing and data analysis. To download data for the 192 listed compacts, he used a web scraping program (or web scraper), a software tool used to extract data from a website. He excluded the duplicate entry for the Texas Low Level Radioactive Waste Disposal Compact, which reduced the number of compacts to 191. For each compact, he removed the few listed members that were not US states or territories (specifically, Congress, Canada, or parts of Canada). He then counted the number of members remaining for each compact and excluded the thirteen compacts that have only one US state or territory as a member, which reduced the number of compacts to 178. Finally, he calculated the mean and median number of members, which are 9.427 and 3, respectively.

[131] *Chart of Interstate Compacts*, BALLOTPEDIA, https://perma.cc/7EZU-3M6U.

126   THE COLLECTIVE-ACTION CONSTITUTION

number of states per compact is 9, and the median number is again 3.[132] Some compacts have attracted all or almost all states, but not many have done so.

To be sure, there are problems with such calculations. It is not evident what the originally desired number of states was for each listed compact; border disputes necessarily involve only two states, and many problems are regional, not national. But the data are at least consistent with Professor Zimmerman's general observation that the number of states involved in compact negotiations significantly affects the likelihood that a compact will form. The National Center for Interstate Compacts proudly reports that 22 active interstate compacts "are national in scope, including several with 35 or more member states and an independent commission to administer the agreement," and "[m]ore than 30 compacts are regional, with eight or more member states."[133] In truth, these numbers are relatively modest.[134] They give little cause for confidence that states can regularly succeed in using interstate compacts and other agreements to solve collective-action problems that arise for more than a few of them—even if, as some commentators speculate, their use increases in the years ahead, given permissive doctrine, partisan polarization, and congressional dysfunction.[135]

Indeed, the states have not shown sustained interest in trying. According to Professor Zimmerman, there has been a "general neglect of interstate relations by national- and state-elected officers unless there is a major multistate problem demanding a solution or the threat of congressional preemption of state regulatory powers."[136] From his perspective, "[t]he subject of interstate cooperation clearly needs to be placed much higher on the agendas of governors, state legislators, and Congress."[137] It is worth asking why, in the third decade of the twenty-first century, interstate cooperation and coordination are not higher on the agendas of elected state officials, and why "few people have studied compacts."[138] The general lack of interest among state politicians may relate to their perceptions of (1) what is in the self-interest of their states and (2) the difficulty and efficacy of creating voluntary state solutions to multistate collective-action problems.[139]

---

[132] The number of states per interstate compact is listed on the website. The mean and median number of states per compact was calculated by transferring these numbers to an Excel spreadsheet and using the Excel mean and median functions.

[133] National Center for Interstate Compacts, Council of State Governments, *Compact Fact Sheet*, https://web.archive.org/web/20210310081539/https://www.csg.org/knowledgecenter/docs/ncic/FactSheet.pdf.

[134] *Accord* Hasday, *supra* note 66, at 4 (writing as of 1997 that "[t]hus far, there have been few compacts—about 175 in all of United States history").

[135] Finkel, *supra* note 48, at 1579–80.

[136] ZIMMERMAN, *supra* note 28, at 230–31.

[137] *Id.* at 231.

[138] BUENGER ET AL., *supra* note 41, at xxiv.

[139] *Id.* at 27 (observing that "it is difficult to get state legislatures to adopt compacts because of the strict requirement of substantive sameness between all member states and the tendency of parochial political interest to trump consideration for interstate cooperation").

One could posit that state officials are not generally incentivized to act in the best interests of their states.[140] But to whatever extent a principal-agent problem exists, there is no reason to think that it is going away, so it further counsels against strong reliance on interstate compacts and agreements to solve multistate collective-action problems. Moreover, a principal-agent problem does not seem like the only explanation. State officials likely appreciate how arduous the compacting process can be.

True, it is easier for certain state officials to cooperate and coordinate less formally, especially because the political parties and ideological advocacy groups on the left and right encourage the officials they target to individually pass certain legislation (e.g., environmental protections or abortion restrictions) or to jointly pursue certain litigation (e.g., against the policies of a Republican or a Democratic administration). Not all this activity is partisan or ideological—for example, litigation against tobacco companies and opioid manufacturers was not—although much of it is. Such activity can be thought of as a constitutional workaround, given how difficult it is for states to form interstate compacts. But this activity, some of which may seek to solve multistate collective-action problems, seems unlikely to serve as an adequate substitute for regulatory compacts, and the activity does not generally avoid the normative concerns discussed above that the state officials who act in some sort of concert (1) may harm the federal government or sister states and (2) lack the democratic warrant to decide for themselves that collective-action problems for their states should be addressed at the expense of state nonparties to the joint activity. Indeed, partisan or ideological organizations seem especially likely to encourage the states with which they are aligned to externalize costs onto states controlled by their partisan or ideological adversaries. Such conduct can be cost-benefit inefficient or trigger a retaliatory race to the bottom.

Conclusion

Collective-action reasoning cannot fully account for the expanse and limits of the Interstate Compacts Clause or the Court's doctrine applying it, let alone the other clauses in Article I, Section 10, discussed in this chapter. For example, more

---

[140] *Cf.* Steven G. Calabresi, *"A Government of Limited and Enumerated Powers": In Defense of United States v. Lopez*, 94 MICH. L. REV. 752, 797 (1995) ("[I]t is sometimes in the interest of state and local officials for them to pass the buck on the hardest problems of government by deferring to the folks in Washington, D.C."); Daryl J. Levinson, *Empire-Building Government in Constitutional Law*, 118 HARV. L. REV. 915, 941 (2005) ("Federal regulation and spending obviously can, and often does, benefit state-level constituencies. Consequently, state officials who are primarily interested in maximizing political support will have no reliable interest in decreasing federal power (or, the equivalent, in increasing state power" (footnotes omitted).).

than the logics of collective action are needed to determine whether and when congressional consent is or should be required. Even so, this chapter has shown that collective-action reasoning can illuminate the tradeoffs involved. More generally, such reasoning can help explain and evaluate the qualified concerns reflected in the Interstate Compacts Clause about state attempts to solve their own collective-action problems. The text presumptively prohibits interstate compacts and agreements, and it ostensibly requires congressional consent to overcome the presumption. Still, the Constitution does not categorically prohibit interstate compacts—the language resides in the third clause of Section 10, not the first, where the categorical ban on state treaties and the like is placed. So, the Constitution leaves the door open for states to try to form interstate compacts.

On one hand, it is plausible to argue that one role of the states in the US constitutional system—one value of federalism—is to solve collective-action problems that arise for them, whether through forming interstate compacts or by cooperating or coordinating their actions less formally. There are important examples, historically and today, of states acting collectively. There are also current instances of most or even all states acting collectively. Such examples support the Constitution's refusal to categorically ban interstate compacts and agreements. The examples also support the Court's refusal to strictly enforce the textual requirement of congressional consent, particularly given the frequent inability or unwillingness of Congress to act due to partisan polarization and related phenomena.

On the other hand, collective-action logics support the general skepticism revealed in the constitutional text. Proposed compacts may undermine federal supremacy or harm sister states. In addition, a group of states may cause a cost-benefit collective-action problem for the states generally while solving a Pareto collective-action problem for the group, and states may disagree over whether a compact helps or harms on balance. Given the possibility of disagreements among states, an interstate umpire is required. The Constitution assigns this role to Congress, where the interests of all states are represented. In this way, the Interstate Compacts Clause is deeply connected to the Interstate Commerce Clause.[141] Both clauses concern regulatory power to address certain multistate collective-action problems, and both clauses give Congress primary responsibility to determine whether such problems exist and are sufficiently serious to warrant government intervention.

In addition, compacts are difficult to form given all the parties within a state that must approve, and compacts require unanimous agreement among the compacting states, which makes cooperation or coordination even harder to achieve. Making matters worse, impediments to collective action tend to

---

[141] U.S. Const. art. I, § 8, cl. 3 (discussed in Chapter 5).

increase sharply with the number of states that must act together, which is why in practice compacts tend to involve a relatively small number of states. In general, if the proposed compact must encompass many states to accomplish its goals, free rider, holdout, and disagreement problems are likely to paralyze it—or substantially increase the time required to form it.

A national government substantially more powerful than the Confederation Congress was and remains required to solve most multistate collective-action problems. The next chapter explains the most serious flaws of the Articles of Confederation and the primary ways in which the Constitution sought to empower the federal government to solve collective-action problems for the states.

4

The Necessity of Federal Power

Taxing, Spending, and Borrowing

Introduction

The Articles of Confederation were more nationalist and collective-action-forcing than anything that came before it. But the Articles created a structure of governance that, combined with state parochialism, frequently resulted in most or all states not acting collectively to pursue common interests. States were unable to act collectively outside the Confederation Congress, and Congress itself was either unable to exercise the powers it was granted or denied the powers it needed. Specifically, Congress was unable to raise sufficient revenue to run the government and repay the Revolutionary War debts, which was required to restore the nation's credit and preserve its ability to borrow to fund future wars.[1] In addition, Congress lacked the power to regulate interstate commerce. States were engaging in trade wars with one another and, if they had prominent ports, were imposing tariff barriers that raised the cost of imported goods in sister states. Congress also lacked the authority to regulate foreign commerce, which meant that the states were unable to act collectively, and so effectively, to combat foreign trade aggression. Moreover, Congress was unable to raise and support an adequate military, which was needed to protect the states collectively from military attack by more powerful European nations and Native American tribes—and to initiate attacks against tribes. The Constitutional Convention was called mainly to solve these collective-action problems.

The design of the Articles prevented the central government from significantly interfering with state authority and individual (negative) liberty. From this perspective, the foregoing congressional incapacities were features, not bugs, as the Anti-Federalists emphasized in opposing the proposed constitution that emerged from the Philadelphia Convention in 1787. From the perspective of facilitating collective action by states, however, the constitutional limits imposed

---

[1] As noted at the start of Chapter 2, scholars dispute whether there was an American "nation" before ratification of the Constitution. The term is used here for ease of exposition, not to take sides in this debate. It is a linguistically efficient way of describing the states collectively during the early and mid-1780s.

The Collective-Action Constitution. Neil S. Siegel, Oxford University Press. © Neil S. Siegel 2024.
DOI: 10.1093/oso/9780197760963.003.0005

132   THE COLLECTIVE-ACTION CONSTITUTION

on the Confederation Congress too often left it nearly impotent notwithstanding serious problems, as the Federalists underscored in advocating ratification of the Constitution. Although this claim about the existence and severity of collective-action failures during the 1780s does not reflect the conclusions of all historians, legal scholars, and political scientists, it does generally capture the conclusions of most of them.[2]

This chapter begins by detailing the Articles' main structural problems. It then turns to the ways in which nationalist Framers sought to eliminate them. As will be shown, Article I, Section 8, which houses most of Congress's legislative authority, contains many of the federal powers to solve multistate collective-action problems proposed by the Framers. Foremost among them is Congress's taxing authority—and, relatedly, its powers to spend and borrow. This chapter focuses on these powers.

Structural Problems with the Articles

Historians, legal scholars, and political scientists have mostly criticized the Articles of Confederation, but the Articles did have strengths. The Articles created the legal categories of both statehood and the United States under a new system of national law.[3] In calling for independence from Great Britain on June 7, 1776, the Virginia delegation to the Continental Congress moved in part that "a Confederation be formed to bind the colonies more closely together."[4] The

---

[2] *See* AKHIL REED AMAR, AMERICA'S CONSTITUTION: A BIOGRAPHY 5–53 (2005); MAX M. EDLING, A REVOLUTION IN FAVOR OF GOVERNMENT: ORIGINS OF THE U.S. CONSTITUTION AND THE MAKING OF THE AMERICAN STATE (2003); DAVID C. HENDRICKSON, PEACE PACT: THE LOST WORLD OF THE AMERICAN FOUNDING (2003); CALVIN H. JOHNSON, RIGHTEOUS ANGER AT THE WICKED STATES: THE MEANING OF THE FOUNDERS' CONSTITUTION (2005); JACK N. RAKOVE, ORIGINAL MEANINGS: POLITICS AND IDEAS IN THE MAKING OF THE CONSTITUTION 23–34 (1996); GEORGE WILLIAM VAN CLEVE, WE HAVE NOT A GOVERNMENT: THE ARTICLES OF CONFEDERATION AND THE ROAD TO THE CONSTITUTION (2017). For dissenting positions that view the Constitution primarily as a conservative counterrevolution by an economic elite determined to preserve its wealth and political power, see MERRILL JENSEN, THE NEW NATION: A HISTORY OF THE UNITED STATES DURING THE CONFEDERATION 1781–89 (1950); and CHARLES A. BEARD, AN ECONOMIC INTERPRETATION OF THE CONSTITUTION OF THE UNITED STATES (1935). For discussion of Jensen's and Beard's views and an explanation of why the late Confederation period was indeed one of "extraordinary economic and political stresses," see VAN CLEVE, *supra*, at 7–8. For a cogent discussion of the historiography, *see id.* at 311–12. Scholars who are persuaded by class-based or other egalitarian critiques of the Constitution may nonetheless agree with this book's claim that the Articles had serious structural problems that needed to be addressed. For a position along these lines, see MICHAEL J. KLARMAN, THE FRAMERS' COUP: THE MAKING OF THE UNITED STATES CONSTITUTION 14 (2016).

[3] Craig Green, *United/States: A Revolutionary History of American Statehood*, 119 MICH. L. REV. 1, at 8–9, 15–41 (2020) (arguing that the Articles of Confederation simultaneously created the legal categories of statehood and the United States, producing the framework for what Americans ever since have called "federalism").

[4] 5 JOURNAL OF THE CONTINENTAL CONGRESS, 1774–1789, at 1087 (Worthington Chauncey Ford ed., 1906).

THE NECESSITY OF FEDERAL POWER   133

Articles did just that by bringing to bear a different kind of law—call it "constitutional"—to support the efforts of the colonies-turned-states to act collectively, not individually, often enough to get the young nation through the Revolution and achieve independence from a great European power. These accomplishments are not nothing. Viewed as a waystation on the path to a more effective national government, the Articles were an impressive achievement.

The structural difficulties with the Articles were, however, apparent to political leaders with a nationalist vision, including Alexander Hamilton, James Madison, James Wilson, George Washington, Benjamin Franklin, and John Adams, all of whom (along with other nationalists) pushed for reforms during the 1780s. In 1783, Hamilton asked the Confederation Congress to call "a General Convention for the purpose of revising and amending the federal Government." Madison did not then support Hamilton's request, but Madison changed his mind as events unfolded, and nationalists increasingly concluded that the Articles were failing.[5] From their perspective, the Articles' general flaw was that it reflected Revolutionary America's extraordinary distrust of centralized power and discounted the importance of a national government that could effectively solve collective-action problems facing the states, whether Pareto collective-action problems (in which all states would be better off by their own estimations if collective-action succeeded), or cost-benefit collective-action problems (in which some states would regard themselves as worse off). The Articles declared in Article II that "[e]ach State retains its sovereignty, freedom, and independence, and every power, jurisdiction, and right, which is not by this Confederation expressly delegated to the United States in Congress assembled." Article III added that the States were "enter[ing] into a firm league of friendship with each other," not forming one nation with a central government powerful enough to protect the states from other countries and from one another.[6]

There were at least four more specific problems with the Articles, each of which is illuminated by the logics of collective action. First, the Articles established no real national executive and no real national judiciary; it instead gave all central powers to the Confederation Congress.[7] Without executive or judicial branches, Congress could not protect its own authority from encroachments by states and enforce federal commitments against states, including peace treaties and trade treaties. States that violated such treaties encouraged noncompliance

---

[5] JAMES MADISON, *Notes on Debates* (April 1, 1783), *in* 1 THE WRITINGS OF JAMES MADISON 439 (Gaillard Hunt ed., 1904).

[6] ARTICLES OF CONFEDERATION of 1781, arts. II & III.

[7] The only semblance of an executive was found in Article IX, which gave the Confederation Congress authority to appoint such "committees and civil officers as may be necessary for managing the general affairs of the united states under their direction" and "to appoint one of their number to preside; provided that no person be allowed to serve in the office of president more than one year in any term of three years." Chapter 7 describes the miniscule national judiciary under the Articles.

134   THE COLLECTIVE-ACTION CONSTITUTION

by European powers, increased the likelihood of wars, and impeded future treaty negotiations, causing the states collectively to suffer. For example, states violated the country's two primary obligations under the 1783 Treaty of Paris with Great Britain (the peace treaty ending the Revolutionary War and recognizing American independence), which were to repay all prewar debts owed to British creditors and limit confiscation of property from British subjects and American loyalists. Britain retaliated by refusing to comply with its obligation under the treaty to evacuate its western forts, which were strategically significant.[8]

Second, the Confederation Congress had great difficulty exercising the powers given to it. Each state had one vote in Congress, and under Article IX most significant actions required nine states to agree (a two-thirds majority). This supermajority requirement effectively gave each section of the confederation veto power over any decision supported by most states to requisition the states for taxes or troops, conclude treaties, or engage in war—among other things.[9] The Articles were increasingly regarded as a failure in part because Congress was unable to exercise the powers it theoretically possessed.

Third, Congress's powers were sharply circumscribed in terms of both the ends it could achieve and the means it could use to achieve them. Regarding ends, Congress lacked the powers to regulate foreign and interstate commerce. As a result, it was powerless to retaliate effectively against the punishing trade restrictions imposed by Great Britain and other European powers and to stop states from engaging in trade wars with one another, which hampered economic development and made the states collectively worse off. As Madison wrote in his *Vices Memo*, which he drafted while preparing for the Constitutional Convention, "[t]he practice of many States in restricting the commercial intercourse with other States, and putting their productions and manufactures on the same footing with those of foreign nations, though not contrary to the federal articles, is certainly adverse to the spirit of the Union, and tends to beget retaliating regulations, not less expensive & vexatious in themselves, than they are destructive of the general harmony."[10] In addition, states with significant

---

[8] VAN CLEVE, *supra* note 2, at 33–35, 69–72. On trade treaties, see *id.* at 105–06. *See* AKHIL REED AMAR, THE WORDS THAT MADE US: AMERICA'S CONSTITUTIONAL CONVERSATION, 1760–1840, at 171 (2021) ("[S]trictly honoring American treaties was not always in each state's short-term interest, even if it was in the union's long-term interest.").

[9] ARTICLES OF CONFEDERATION of 1781, art. IX ("The united states, in congress assembled, shall never engage in a war, nor grant letters of marque and reprisal in time of peace, nor enter into any treaties or alliances, nor coin money, nor regulate the value thereof, nor ascertain the sums and expenses necessary for the defence and welfare of the united states, or any of them, nor emit bills, nor borrow money on the credit of the united states, nor appropriate money, nor agree upon the number of vessels of war to be built or purchased, or the number of land or sea forces to be raised, nor appoint a commander in chief of the army or navy, unless nine states assent to the same . . . .").

[10] JAMES MADISON, *Vices of the Political System of the United States* (April 1787), *in* 2 THE WRITINGS OF JAMES MADISON 363 (Gaillard Hunt ed., 1904). As Chapter 5 explains, scholars dispute the frequency and severity of interstate trade restrictions, but there is substantial evidence that many states imposed them.

THE NECESSITY OF FEDERAL POWER   135

ports had a potential trading advantage relative to states without them, and the states with ports exploited this advantage by imposing tariffs on goods entering through their ports, which increased the prices paid for such goods by inhabitants of neighboring states. State disagreements over whether to authorize Congress to tax imports, discussed below, turned significantly on whether a state was benefiting from, or being harmed by, the state import taxes then in effect.[11]

Regarding the means available to Congress, most troubling was its lack of authority to raise revenue directly through taxation of individuals and to raise a military directly through conscription of individuals. Congress was limited to borrowing money and "requisitioning" the states to contribute their share of taxes to the national treasury and troops to the national military. For example, Congress was permitted to apportion taxes among the states, but levying and collection were left to state governments. By the late 1780s, states had ignored requisitions to such an extent that Congress had little money and the states collectively were vulnerable to attack by European powers and Native nations. A well-funded Congress and a strong military were public goods, and states were—to a significant but not complete extent—free riding on the contributions of other states, leaving the states collectively worse off.[12] The Confederation Congress was thus unable to address the most pressing national-security problem facing the states collectively after the war—repayment of the Revolutionary War debts—which, to reiterate, was essential to restoring the nation's credit and so enabling it to borrow money from other countries to finance future wars.[13] "States will contribute or not according to their circumstances and interests," Hamilton said at the New York ratifying convention. "They will all be inclined to throw off their burdens of government upon their neighbors."[14]

The establishment of the Bank of North America, which the Continental Congress chartered in 1781, illustrated Congress's lack of necessary powers. As Madison underscored at the time, the bank was beyond Congress's authority to create.[15] The Articles nowhere authorized a bank, and, as noted above, Article II made plain that Congress possessed only those powers that were "expressly delegated" by the state governments. The justification for the bank was existential, not constitutional: given the need to finance the war with Great Britain,

---

[11] VAN CLEVE, *supra* note 2, at 88, 96; *see* DANIEL A. FARBER & NEIL S. SIEGEL, UNITED STATES CONSTITUTIONAL LAW 87–88 (2d ed. 2024).

[12] VAN CLEVE, *supra* note 2, at 48–69.

[13] W. ELLIOT BROWNLEE, FEDERAL TAXATION IN AMERICA 16 (2d ed. 2004) ("Among the most pressing [practical problems] were how to finance the Revolutionary War debts, and how to establish the credit of the nation in a way that would win respect in international financial markets."); VAN CLEVE, *supra* note 2, at 48–52; JOHNSON, *supra* note 2, at 15–26.

[14] *See* KLARMAN, *supra* note 2, at 326 (quoting Hamilton).

[15] 6 THE WRITINGS OF JAMES MADISON 40 (Gaillard Hunt ed., 1906) ("The Bank of North America he had opposed, as he considered the institution as a violation of the Confederation.").

136   THE COLLECTIVE-ACTION CONSTITUTION

Congress deemed the bank indispensable.[16] One could also ask how, exactly, Congress had the authority to take federal territories: nothing in the Articles granted Congress such authority. Yet, Congress passed the Northwest Ordinance of 1787, which provided for the establishment of a territorial government that would eventually become several states in the vast expanse of land east of the Mississippi River and to the north and west of the Ohio River.[17] From almost the moment the Articles went into effect, Congress was pushed to attempt constitutionally dubious expedients to do what it believed needed doing.

Fourth, the foregoing problems could not be addressed within the legal regime created by the Articles because the Articles were effectively impossible to amend. Under Article XIII, amendments required unanimous agreement among the states. Amendments that would have increased Congress's power were routinely rejected by individual states. For example, in the early 1780s, Rhode Island, Virginia, and New York each blocked proposals that would have given Congress the power to raise critically needed revenue for the federal government by taxing imports. All three states had major ports, and they sought to preserve their own powers to tax imports at the expense of other states. Such narrowly self-interested actions by individual states were producing collectively harmful results.[18]

Madison detailed the above problems in his *Vices Memo*. Among other difficulties, he identified the "Failure of the States to comply with the Constitutional requisitions," "Encroachments by the States on the federal authority," state "Violations of the law of nations and of treaties," "Trespasses of the States on the rights of each other," "want of concert" by states "in matters where common interest requires it," and Congress's lack of coercive power, which Madison called "want of sanction to the laws, and of coercion in the Government of the Confederacy." He characterized "want of concert in matters where common interest requires it" as a "defect . . . strongly illustrated in the state of our commercial affairs" and rhetorically asked "[h]ow much has the national dignity, interest, and revenue, suffered from this cause?" He also decried "the want of uniformity in the laws concerning naturalization & literary property; of provision for national seminaries, for grants of incorporation for national purposes, for canals and other works of general utility, [which] may at present be defeated by the perverseness of particular States whose concurrence is necessary."[19]

---

[16]   *Id.* ("The Bank of North America was . . . the child of necessity; as soon as the war was over, it ceased to operate as to Continental purposes.").

[17]   Ordinance of Jul. 13, 1787, 32 JOURNALS OF THE CONTINENTAL CONGRESS 1774–1789, at 334–43 (Roscoe R. Hill ed., 1936); *see* Ordinance of 1787: The Northwest Territorial Government, *reprinted in* 1 U.S.C. LVII (2018).

[18]   The 1781 impost proposals were vetoed first by Rhode Island and then by Virginia. The 1783 impost proposal was vetoed by New York. *See* JOHNSON, *supra* note 2, at 26–28; VAN CLEVE, *supra* note 2, at 84–101.

[19]   Madison, *Vices Memo, supra* note 10, at 361–64.

THE NECESSITY OF FEDERAL POWER   137

In sum, the Confederation Congress could not reliably enforce federal law or exercise the powers it possessed; it lacked the authority—either absolutely or effectively—to protect the states from commercial and military warfare waged by foreign powers and from commercial warfare and other troubling behavior waged by one another; and it was practically impossible to address these problems from within the Articles' own legal regime. Further, states were largely unable to solve these difficulties on their own. For the most part, they acted individually when they needed to act collectively. The problems of collective action confronting America, Larry Kramer observes, "necessitated a government with many more powers than were possessed by Congress under the Articles—including the great powers to tax, to raise and support armies, and to regulate commerce." Facing these problems also "necessitated conferring authority to exercise these powers by acting directly on individual citizens rather than through the agency of the states, both in legislating and in enforcing federal rules or standards."[20] Finally, the new Congress would ordinarily need to be able to act by majority vote in each chamber—not by unanimity rule or supermajority rule—so that it could solve not only Pareto collective-action problems but also cost-benefit collective-action problems. No longer would one or a few states be able to defeat collective action.

The Constitutional Convention

Reflecting the increasingly perceived need for reform, the Virginia General Assembly, with Madison's support, called for a limited conference among the states "to take into consideration the trade of the United States; to examine the relative situations and trade of said States; [and] to consider how far a uniform system in their commercial regulations may be necessary to their common interest and their permanent harmony."[21] The resulting Annapolis Conference, in September 1786, attracted only a dozen delegates from five states. They recommended another, broader convening "to take into consideration the situation of the United States" and "to devise such further provisions as shall appear to them necessary to render the constitution of the Foederal Government adequate to the exigencies of the Union."[22]

[20] Larry Kramer, *Madison's Audience*, 112 HARV. L. REV. 611, 619–20 (1999).

[21] Resolution of the General Assembly of Virginia, Jan. 21, 1786, proposing a Joint Meeting of Commissioners from the States to consider and recommend a Federal Plan for regulating Commerce, *in* THE DEBATES IN THE FEDERAL CONVENTION OF 1787 WHICH FRAMED THE CONSTITUTION OF THE UNITED STATES OF AMERICA xlvii (Gaillard Hunt & James Brown Scott eds., 1920).

[22] NATIONAL ARCHIVES, THE FORMATION OF THE UNION 50 (1970) (Publication no. 70–13).

138   THE COLLECTIVE-ACTION CONSTITUTION

Rendering a vote of no confidence in itself, the Confederation Congress in February 1787 acknowledged that "experience hath evinced that there are defects in the present Confederation," and it recognized the necessity of "establishing in these states a firm national government." It therefore approved a convention "for the sole and express purpose of revising the Articles of Confederation and reporting to Congress and the several legislatures such alterations and provisions therein as shall when agreed to in Congress and confirmed by the States render the federal constitution adequate to the exigencies of Government & the preservation of the Union."[23] The delegates to this Constitutional Convention began meeting in Philadelphia in May, and they quickly decided that remedying the collective-action failures of the Articles would require a new constitution, not amendments to the current one.

As Professor Akhil Amar explains, "Federal power over genuinely interstate and international affairs lay at the heart of the plan approved by the Philadelphia delegates."[24] This was apparent in the delegates' deliberations over congressional power, which would eventually produce Article I, Section 8, of the Constitution. Their deliberations originated with the Virginia Plan, so named because it was drafted by the Virginia delegation (especially Madison) before the Convention was ready to proceed. The Virginia Plan incorporated most of Madison's assessment of what ailed America. Introduced by Edmund Randolph in Convention on May 29, it formed the basis of the Convention's first two weeks of debate.[25]

Resolution VI of the Virginia Plan announced a structural principle that would guide the Convention's approach to congressional power. It provided that Congress would "enjoy the Legislative Rights vested in Congress by the Confederation & moreover [be authorized] to legislate in all cases to which the separate States are incompetent, or in which the harmony of the United States may be interrupted by the exercise of individual Legislation."[26] On May 31, the Convention approved Resolution VI by a vote of nine states in favor, zero against, and one state delegation divided.[27] On June 19, the Convention approved this language again and the Virginia Plan more generally, at the same time rejecting William Patterson's New Jersey Plan, which would have created a substantially less powerful national government. This time, the vote was seven states in favor of the Virginia Plan, three against, and one state delegation divided.[28]

---

[23] *Id.*
[24] AMAR, *supra* note 2, at 108.
[25] RAKOVE, *supra* note 2, at 59.
[26] 1 THE RECORDS OF THE FEDERAL CONVENTION OF 1787, at 21 (Max Farrand ed., rev. ed. 1966).
[27] *Id.* at 47, 53–54.
[28] *Id.* at 322.

THE NECESSITY OF FEDERAL POWER   139

On July 17, the Convention again considered Resolution VI. Roger Sherman of Connecticut, who had cast the only initial vote against it, moved to amend it in a way that he construed as protecting state power from federal interference:

> To make laws binding on the People of the United States in all cases which may concern the common interests of the Union: but not to interfere with the government of the individual States in any matters of internal police which respect the government of such States only, and wherein the general welfare of the United States is not concerned.[29]

Wilson had initially seconded the amendment because he viewed it as "better expressing the general principle," but he ultimately voted against it—as did the Convention by a margin of eight to two—when Sherman revealed that he intended for it to deny Congress the power to tax individuals directly.[30]

Gunning Bedford of Delaware then offered his own amendment to Resolution VI to clarify its meaning. He slightly altered Sherman's reference to "the common interests of the Union," proposing that Congress be authorized to advance "the general interests of the Union":

> That the national Legislature ought to possess the Legislative Rights vested in Congress by the Confederation; and moreover to legislate in all cases for the general interests of the Union, and also in those to which the States are separately incompetent, or in which the harmony of the United States may be interrupted by the exercise of individual Legislation.[31]

The delegates approved Bedford's motion to amend Resolution VI by a vote of six to four, and they approved Resolution VI as amended by a vote of eight to two.[32]

It is not clear how Bedford's three proffered justifications for federal power fit with one another; Bedford himself perceived redundancy, and he was not alone. As Professor Donald Regan explains, "The Framers themselves were unclear about the precise reach and interrelations of the various clauses."[33] The three clauses appeared to be different ways of expressing the need to empower Congress to solve the collective-action problems facing the states that the states had proven unable to solve on their own. On this interpretation, an "interest" is "general" when the states are "separately incompetent" to advance the interest,

---

[29] 2 THE RECORDS OF THE FEDERAL CONVENTION OF 1787, *supra* note 26, at 21, 25.

[30] *Id.* at 26.

[31] *Id.* at 14, 21, 26; *see* 131–32 (substantively equivalent version of the Committee of Detail).

[32] *Id.* 21, 27.

[33] Donald H. Regan, *How to Think about the Federal Commerce Power and Incidentally Rewrite United States v. Lopez*, 94 MICH. L. REV. 554, 570 n.70 (1995).

140   THE COLLECTIVE-ACTION CONSTITUTION

whether because "individual legislation" interrupts national "harmony" or for some other reason—when the states must act collectively to accomplish an objective. More speculatively, perhaps the reference to separate state incompetence refers primarily to cooperation problems; the reference to national harmony being disrupted by individual legislation refers principally to coordination problems; and Bedford's addition of "general Interests" refers to cost-benefit collective-action problems.

On July 23, the Convention charged its Committee of Detail with drafting constitutional text reflective of the decisions of the delegates, including Resolution VI.[34] On August 6, this Committee, which included Wilson and Randolph, shared its work with the Convention. Notably, as Robert Stern observes, when the Committee of Detail made its report, "[i]t had changed the indefinite language of Resolution VI into an enumeration of the powers of Congress closely resembling Article I, Section 8 of the Constitution as it was finally adopted."[35] This "radical change" wrought by the Committee of Detail was uncontroversial among the delegates; the Convention "accepted *without discussion* the enumeration of powers made by a committee which had been directed . . . that the Federal Government was 'to legislate in all cases for the general interests of the Union . . . and in those to which the states are separately incompetent.' "[36]

Because the Committee's enumeration went unchallenged, historian Jack Rakove concludes that it "was only complying with the general expectations of the Convention," meaning that the Committee was attempting "to identify particular areas of governance where there were 'general interests of the Union,' where the states were 'separately incompetent,' or where state legislation could disrupt the national 'Harmony.' "[37] The enumeration appeared directed at satisfying concerns expressed earlier by some delegates that Resolution VI was too vague.[38] As Stern writes, "If the Convention had thought that the committee's enumeration was a departure from the general standard for the division of powers to which it had thrice agreed, there can be little doubt that the subject would have been thoroughly debated on the Convention floor."[39] Professor Regan agrees that

[34] 2 THE RECORDS OF THE FEDERAL CONVENTION OF 1787, *supra* note 26, at 95–96. The five committee members were Oliver Ellsworth of Connecticut, Nathaniel Gorham of Massachusetts, Randolph, John Rutledge of South Carolina, and Wilson. *Id.* at 97.

[35] Robert L. Stern, *That Commerce Which Concerns More States Than One*, 47 HARV. L. REV. 1335, 1340 (1934).

[36] *Id. See* Robert L. Stern, *The Commerce Clause and the National Economy, 1933–1946 (Part Two)*, 59 HARV. L. REV. 883, 947 (1946) (referencing "the language of the Constitution as understood by those who wrote it, and . . . the spirit in which it was written, as manifested by the thrice-approved [Resolution VI]").

[37] RAKOVE, *supra* note 2, at 178.

[38] 1 THE RECORDS OF THE FEDERAL CONVENTION OF 1787, *supra* note 26, at 53 (noting May 31 objections of South Carolina delegates Charles Pinckney, John Rutledge, and Pierce Butler); 2 THE RECORDS OF THE FEDERAL CONVENTION OF 1787, *supra* note 26, at 17 (noting July 16 objections of Butler and Rutledge).

[39] Stern, *supra* note 35, at 1340.

THE NECESSITY OF FEDERAL POWER 141

"there is no reason to think the Committee of Detail was rejecting the spirit of the Resolution when they replaced it with an enumeration."[40] The delegates apparently perceived a connection between the general statements in Resolution VI and the specific powers conferred in Section 8.

During the ratification battle in Pennsylvania, Wilson discussed the challenge posed by dividing government power vertically—the "[difficulty] of drawing a proper line between the national government and the governments of the several states." Consistent with the understanding of other Convention delegates, he insisted that "[w]hatever object of government is confined, in its operation and effects, within the bounds of a particular state, should be considered as belonging to the government of that state; whatever object of government extends, in its operation and effects, beyond the bounds of a particular state, should be considered as belonging to the United States."[41] Two years earlier, Wilson had reasoned similarly (and more questionably, given the Articles' text) in defending the legality of the Bank of North America. "Whenever an object occurs, to the direction of which no particular state is competent," he wrote, "the management of it must, of necessity, belong to the United States in congress assembled." "For many purposes," he continued, "the United States are to be considered as one undivided, independent nation; and as possessed of all the rights, and powers, and properties, by the law of nations incident to such."[42]

In his statements during the Pennsylvania ratifying convention, Wilson might have been more precise and less robustly nationalist: effects are not the same thing as external effects, and not all external effects cause collective-action problems, whether of the Pareto or of the cost-benefit variety. But like Resolution VI of the Virginia Plan and the Convention's instructions to the Committee of Detail, Wilson generalized in a way that linked Congress's enumerated powers to the structural principle or purpose underlying them:

> But though this principle be sound and satisfactory, its application to particular cases would be accompanied with much difficulty, because, in its application, room must be allowed for great discretionary latitude of construction of the principle. In order to lessen or remove the difficulty arising from discretionary construction on this subject, an enumeration of particular instances, in which

---

[40] Regan, *supra* note 33, at 556.

[41] James Wilson, *quoted in* 2 THE DEBATES IN THE SEVERAL STATE CONVENTIONS ON THE ADOPTION OF THE FEDERAL CONSTITUTION AS RECOMMENDED BY THE GENERAL CONVENTION AT PHILADELPHIA 424 (John Elliot ed., 2d ed. 1836). Professor Jack Balkin has emphasized the importance of Wilson's statement. *See* JACK M. BALKIN, LIVING ORIGINALISM 143 (2011).

[42] James Wilson, *Consideration of the Bank of North America (1785)*, *in* CONTEXTS OF THE CONSTITUTION: A DOCUMENTARY COLLECTION ON PRINCIPLES OF AMERICAN CONSTITUTIONAL LAW 368 (Neil H. Cogan ed., 1999).

142 THE COLLECTIVE-ACTION CONSTITUTION

the application of the principle ought to take place, has been attempted with much industry and care.[43]

Section 8 was the "enumeration of particular instances." Wilson's generalization, like Resolution VI originally and as amended, captured the primary purpose of granting Congress the Section 8 powers: solving multistate collective-action problems. This is the structural principle underlying these powers.[44]

The Constitution

Understanding Resolution VI in this way has important implications. Critics of collective-action approaches emphasize that the Constitution does not include Resolution VI or expressly reference multistate collective-action problems.[45] This is obviously correct. The Constitution does not contain Resolution VI, nor should Section 8 be interpreted as if it is Resolution VI, nor should it be construed as if it provides that "Congress shall have the power to solve collective-action problems facing the states." The Framers reduced the general principle in Resolution VI to more specific powers to provide better guidance and limit discretion, even at the cost of being under- and overinclusive with respect to Section 8's purpose. This is a common move in American law.[46]

Even so, recognizing Resolution VI as the main justification for conferring the Section 8 powers enhances understanding in at least three ways. First, the

[43] Wilson, *supra* note 41, at 424–25.

[44] Professor Kurt Lash speculates that Wilson was not referencing Resolution VI, but Roger Sherman's proposed replacement. Kurt T. Lash, *Resolution VI: The Virginia Plan and Authority to Resolve Collective Action Problems under Article I, Section 8*, 87 NOTRE DAME L. REV. 2123, 2156–58 (2013). According to Professor Lash, Wilson's language is closer to Sherman's than to Resolution VI. It seems unlikely, however, that Wilson had Sherman's amendment in mind when he had voted against it once Sherman clarified his intent. *See supra* notes 29–30 and accompanying text. Moreover, even assuming Wilson was referring to Sherman's amendment, Wilson likely had his own understanding in mind, not Sherman's. Contrary to what Professor Lash asserts, *see id.* at 2157–58, Sherman's amendment was not much different from Resolution VI, which explains why Wilson initially seconded Sherman's proposal. One can read Sherman's amendment as making explicit what was implicit in Resolution VI: states would retain their powers on matters regarding which they were not separately incompetent. The Framers understood Resolution VI to be both a grant of power and a limitation. Professor Lash has not shown that Wilson was referencing Sherman's statement of a structural principle (as opposed to Resolution VI or Wilson's own articulation) for the same reason that it would not matter if Professor Lash had: each formulation distinguishes between problems that require collective action by states and those that do not. Sherman distinguished "the *common* interests of the Union" and "the *general* welfare of the United States" (emphases added) from "matters of internal police which respect the government of such States only." *See supra* note 29 and accompanying text.

[45] Lash, *supra* note 44; Randy E. Barnett, *Jack Balkin's Interaction Theory of "Commerce,"* 2012 U. ILL. L. REV. 623 (2012).

[46] FREDERICK SCHAUER, PLAYING BY THE RULES: A PHILOSOPHICAL EXAMINATION OF RULE-BASED DECISION-MAKING IN LAW AND IN LIFE 135–66 (1991).

THE NECESSITY OF FEDERAL POWER   143

structural principle captured by Resolution VI illuminates Americans' primary accomplishment in ratifying the Constitution: helping solve the preexisting collective-action problems facing the states by giving the national government certain new powers or making it easier for Congress to use preexisting ones, instead of relying on states to act collectively outside the federal government. Recall from Chapter 2 that "solving" a collective-action problem facing group members by positing a government to regulate the members simply replaces one collective-action problem with another—the problem of creating the government. Ratification accomplished this feat, which was facilitated by Article VII's declaration that "Ratification of the Conventions of nine States," not all thirteen, "shall be sufficient for the Establishment of this Constitution between the States so ratifying the Same."[47] Instead of permitting holdout states to veto ratification, as individual states had vetoed proposed amendments to the Articles, the ratifying states forced the holdouts to confront the prospect of going it alone. Rather than suffer this precarious fate, North Carolina ratified on November 21, 1789, and Rhode Island ratified on May 29, 1790.

Second, Resolution VI helps in the interpretation of certain parts of certain clauses in Section 8. Where language in Section 8 is fully determinate, it is inappropriate to draw inferences from the constitutional structure embodied in Resolution VI. But where language is under-determinate and relates to concepts and distinctions articulated in Resolution VI, the structural principle it announces can aid in interpretation.[48] Interpretation of the Interstate Commerce Clause requires a distinction between commerce that is "among the several States" and commerce that is internal to a state.[49] The Taxing and Spending Clause announces two purposes of spending federal tax revenue (in addition to paying national debts), which also appear in the Preamble: providing for the "common" defense and "general" welfare.[50] Even if this purposive language does not empower courts to restrict Congress's spending power (an issue analyzed below), Resolution VI still bears on what these words mean, and collective-action reasoning can account for most federal spending. Moreover, as Chapter 1 explained, Resolution VI can partially explain when legislation enacted under

---

[47] U.S. CONST. art. VII. Chapter 10 discusses the collective-action dimensions of this provision.

[48] Because this book offers a methodologically pluralist account of the Constitution, not an originalist one (*see* Chapter 1), it uses the term "interpretation" in an informal sense, which covers both what many contemporary originalists mean by constitutional "interpretation" (i.e., original semantic meaning) and what they mean by constitutional "construction" (i.e., other kinds of arguments to which resort must be made when original meaning runs out). For discussions of this distinction, see, for example, BALKIN, *supra* note 41, at 3–6, 341 n.2; KEITH E. WHITTINGTON, CONSTITUTIONAL CONSTRUCTION: DIVIDED POWERS AND CONSTITUTIONAL MEANING 5–9 (1999); Randy E. Barnett, *Interpretation and Construction*, 34 HARV. J.L. & PUB. POL'Y 65 (2011); and Lawrence B. Solum, *Originalism and Constitutional Construction*, 82 FORDHAM L. REV. 453 (2013).

[49] U.S. CONST. art. I, § 8, cl. 3.

[50] U.S. CONST. art. I, § 8, cl. 1.

144   THE COLLECTIVE-ACTION CONSTITUTION

the Necessary and Proper Clause is "necessary and proper."[51] Just as it is untenable to treat Resolution VI like constitutional text, so also it is untenable to dismiss Resolution VI as a mere "placeholder"[52] in the strong sense that its content is irrelevant, which is how it is characterized by strict originalists who seem anxious about its implications.[53]

Third, Resolution VI helps explain what the eighteen clauses of Section 8 have in common—what binds them together and so accounts for their placement in the same section. Reflecting the structural vision of Resolution VI, these eighteen clauses mostly concern Pareto and cost-benefit collective-action problems. Figure 4.1 assigns numbers to these clauses. The Taxing and Spending Clause, which comes first, authorizes Congress to "lay and collect Taxes . . . to pay the Debts and provide for the common Defence and general Welfare of the United States." Sixteen powers follow. The final clause authorizes Congress to use means "necessary and proper" to achieve authorized ends—the Necessary and Proper Clause discussed in Chapter 1.

The rest of this chapter analyzes the collective-action dimensions of Congress's powers to tax, spend, and borrow. Chapter 5 examines congressional authority to regulate interstate and foreign commerce. Chapter 6 discusses the other Section 8 powers. Collectively, these chapters establish the usefulness of collective-action

---

[51] U.S. CONST. art. I, § 8, cl. 18.

[52] Professor Lash repeatedly characterizes Resolution VI this way. Lash, *supra* note 44, at 2140, 2148, 2152, 2155.

[53] Professor Lash argues that Resolution VI can at most inform claims about the original intent of the Framers—claims he thinks incorrect because he concludes that the Convention rejected Resolution VI. He contends that Resolution VI cannot inform claims about the original meaning of any Section 8 powers, because he concludes that Resolution VI did not become part of the constitutional text and it played no role in the ratification debates. Lash, *supra* note 44, at 2145–63. As noted, *see supra* note 44, Professor Lash believes that Wilson was not referring to Resolution VI in the version of his speech quoted above. He further argues that the version of Wilson's speech quoted above was at best heard by the delegates at the Pennsylvania ratifying convention in November 1787 and was at worst heard by no one, given uncertainty about which of two differently transcribed versions of the speech he delivered. According to Professor Lash, the version initially published and widely distributed around the nation used the phrase "nature and operation," not "operation and effects." *Id.* at 2158–63.

The fact that Pennsylvania Federalists quickly objected to the version of the speech initially published suggests that it was not the correct version. But even assuming Professor Lash is correct about the impossibility of knowing which version Wilson delivered, it does not matter for the account of the Constitution offered in this book: collective-action problems are the kinds of problems that by their "nature and operation extend beyond a particular State." In addition, Professor Lash's other claims—and Professor Randy Barnett's similar claims about the irrelevance of Resolution VI to the original meaning of the Interstate Commerce Clause, *see* Barnett, *supra* note 45, at 644–49— are overstated, given the frequent use by originalists of original intentions as evidence of original meaning. In any event, this book offers a pluralist account, not an exclusively originalist one. As Chapter 1 explains, the book is interested in these historical materials primarily because of what they can potentially tell us about the main original structural purpose of the Constitution, not because of what the materials potentially indicate about the original semantic meaning of particular words or clauses in Section 8.

THE NECESSITY OF FEDERAL POWER   145

The Congress shall have Power

1. To lay and collect Taxes, Duties, Imposts and Excises, to pay the Debts and provide for the common Defence and general Welfare of the United States; but all Duties, Imposts and Excises shall be uniform throughout the United States;

2. To borrow Money on the credit of the United States;

3. To regulate Commerce with foreign Nations, and among the several States, and with the Indian Tribes;

4. To establish a uniform Rule of Naturalization, and uniform Laws on the subject of Bankruptcies throughout the United States;

5. To coin Money, regulate the Value thereof, and of foreign Coin, and fix the Standard of Weights and Measures;

6. To provide for the Punishment of counterfeiting the Securities and current Coin of the United States;

7. To establish Post Offices and post Roads;

8. To promote the Progress of Science and useful Arts, by securing for limited Times to Authors and Inventors the exclusive Right to their respective Writings and Discoveries;

9. To constitute Tribunals inferior to the supreme Court;

10. To define and punish Piracies and Felonies committed on the high Seas, and Offenses against the Law of Nations;

11. To declare War, grant Letters of Marque and Reprisal, and make Rules concerning Captures on Land and Water;

12. To raise and support Armies, but no Appropriation of Money to that Use shall be for a longer Term than two Years;

13. To provide and maintain a Navy;

14. To make Rules for the Government and Regulation of the land and naval Forces;

15. To provide for calling forth the Militia to execute the Laws of the Union, suppress Insurrections, and repel Invasions;

16. To provide for organizing, arming, and disciplining, the Militia, and for governing such Part of them as may be employed in the Service of the United States, reserving to the States respectively, the Appointment of the Officers, and the Authority of training the Militia according to the discipline prescribed by Congress;

17. To exercise exclusive Legislation in all cases whatsoever, over such District (not exceeding ten Miles square) as may, by Cession of particular States, and the Acceptance of Congress, become the Seat of the Government of the United States, and to exercise like Authority over all Places purchased by the Consent of the Legislature of the State in which the same shall be, for the Erection of Forts, Magazines, Arsenals, dock-Yards, and other needful Buildings;—And

18. To make all Laws which shall be necessary and proper for carrying into Execution the foregoing Powers, and all other Powers vested by this Constitution in the Government of the United States or in any Department or officer thereof.

Figure 4.1 The eighteen clauses in Article I, Section 8.

146 THE COLLECTIVE-ACTION CONSTITUTION

logics in understanding the origins of these enumerated powers, their enduring rationales, and, in vitally important instances, their scopes.

Taxing

"A nation cannot long exist without revenue," Hamilton wrote in *Federalist 12*.[54] Federal power "[t]o lay and collect Taxes, Duties, Imposts and Excises" comes first in Section 8 for a reason.[55] This clause, called the Taxing Clause (or the Taxing and Spending Clause, or the General Welfare Clause), empowers Congress to tax individuals and entities, thereby overcoming the preexisting, existential collective-action problem of funding the national government. As discussed, the requisition system of the Articles forced Congress to finance the federal government by requisitioning funds from the states, with the amount per state set "in proportion to the value of all land within each State."[56] The scheme largely failed because states free rode with impunity off the contributions of sister states. The predictable consequence was grossly insufficient revenue. For example, the "Requisition of 1786, the last before the Constitution, 'mandated' payments by the states of $3.8 million, but collected only $663."[57] Robert Livingston, a prominent Federalist delegate to the New York ratifying convention, colorfully described this system as "pompous petitions for public charity, which have made so much noise and brought so little cash into the treasury."[58] Madison, drawing upon "reason" and "our own experience" in defending the Constitution's taxation regime, wrote of requisition schemes like the Articles' that states "who furnish most will complain of those who furnish least," and "[f]rom complaints on one side will spring ill will on both sides; from ill will, quarrels; from quarrels, wars; and from wars a long catalogue of evils including the dreadful evils of disunion and a general confusion."[59]

Robust Power to Tax

The text of the Taxing Clause underscores the robustness of Congress's taxing power. It compiles a duplicative list of the federal exactions that Congress can

[54] THE FEDERALIST NO. 12, at 96 (Alexander Hamilton) (Clinton Rossiter ed., 1961).
[55] U.S. CONST. art. I, § 8, cl. 1.
[56] ARTICLES OF CONFEDERATION of 1781, art. VIII.
[57] JOHNSON, *supra* note 2, at 1.
[58] KLARMAN, *supra* note 2, at 326 (quoting Livingston's speech to the New York ratifying convention on June 27, 1788).
[59] Letter from James Madison to George Thompson (Jan. 29, 1789), *in* 2 THE PAPERS OF JAMES MADISON 433–34 (Robert A. Rutland & Charles F. Hobson eds., 1977).

impose. The distinctions among "Duties, Imposts and Excises" are not entirely clear, and all are kinds of "Taxes"—mainly on consumption items. This overlapping list indicates that if Congress complies with other constitutional limits on federal taxation, it can impose almost any exaction that it wants.[60] Congressional power to tax imports ("Imposts" or tariffs) might have met the revenue needs of the federal government at the time, but the Taxing Clause confers substantially more authority.

The broad scope of congressional taxing authority is also evident from the limits on federal taxation set forth in the constitutional text: all but one do not significantly restrain Congress. The command in the Taxing Clause that "all Duties, Imposts and Excises shall be uniform throughout the United States" is important: it prevents use of federal taxing power to exploit the inhabitants of a minority of states by the representatives of a majority of states. But this requirement also does not significantly constrain Congress's ability to raise revenue; it simply means that Congress must impose taxes subject to the requirement on the same things and at the same rates in every state. Likewise, the directive in the Origination Clause that "[a]ll bills for raising Revenue shall originate in the House of Representatives"[61] does not seriously limit Congress because both houses must approve revenue bills anyway—and the Senate has long felt entitled to strip out the language in a House bill and insert its own. Similarly, the edict that "[n]o Tax or Duty shall be laid on Articles exported from any State"[62] has an interesting original history (southern economies relied on exports) and raises interesting interpretive issues (like what is a "Tax or Duty"), but the Export Clause has bite only in limited circumstances, and Congress can tax many other items.[63] Nor is federal taxing authority much constrained by the prohibitions on giving preferential treatment to certain ports and imposing duties on interstate vessels.[64] The modesty of such limits reflects the Framers' insight, gained through experience, that taxation with representation was as essential as taxation without representation was illegitimate.[65]

---

[60] Erik M. Jensen, *The Power to Tax, in* THE POWERS OF CONGRESS: WHERE CONSTITUTIONAL AUTHORITY BEGINS AND ENDS 1–2 (Brien Hallett ed., 2016).

[61] U.S. CONST. art. I, § 7, cl. 1.

[62] U.S. CONST. art. I, § 9, cl. 5.

[63] Jensen, *supra* note 60, at 7.

[64] U.S. CONST. art. I, § 9, cl. 6.

[65] Another restriction on federal taxing power, mooted by the Thirteenth Amendment, was the $10 limitation on taxing each imported enslaved individual. Art. I, § 9, cl. 1. In addition, Congress must respect individual rights when it taxes, but rights protections constrain Congress generally.

148 THE COLLECTIVE-ACTION CONSTITUTION

Direct versus Indirect Taxes

One textual limitation on the taxing power does greatly constrain Congress, and tellingly it has been construed very narrowly almost without exception from its inception. The second of the two Direct Tax Clauses provides that "[n]o Capitation, or other direct, Tax shall be laid, unless in Proportion to the Census or Enumeration herein before directed to be taken."[66] Elaborating the earlier provision requiring apportionment for both direct taxes and Representatives in the House,[67] this clause requires the financial burden of any "direct" tax imposed by Congress to fall equally on each state in terms of its population. For example, if two states have the same population, the citizens of each state collectively must pay the same amount of direct tax to the US Treasury. Apportionment renders the imposition of direct taxes untenable because it requires Congress to privilege regressivity over progressivity: citizens of relatively wealthy states must pay at lower rates than citizens of relatively poor states to make the total payment for states of equal population come out the same.

At the Founding, it was not entirely clear which kinds of taxes were "direct." During the Philadelphia Convention, on August 20, Massachusetts delegate Rufus King "asked what was the precise meaning of *direct* taxation?" According to Madison's notes, "No one answd."[68] It is clear that "Duties, Imposts and Excises" are not direct taxes because they are expressly subject to the uniformity requirement and so cannot satisfy the apportionment requirement. (The only way that an exaction could satisfy both requirements would be if each state's share of the tax base equaled its percentage of the national population, an extraordinarily unlikely scenario.) The text of Article I, Section 9, contemplates that "capitation" taxes, also called "head" or "poll" taxes, qualify as direct taxes. Capitations are taxes on people just because they exist. The Framers required apportionment for capitations primarily to protect Southerners from high head taxes on the people they enslaved—and, in the extreme, to disable Congress from taxing slavery out of existence. The constitutional text, by referencing "other direct[] Tax," may imply that at least one other kind of tax is direct. For many Founders, taxes on land were also likely direct because they were connected to capitations. When the Confederation Congress, following Article VIII of the Articles, sought to apportion taxes among the states based on land values and ran into valuation problems, it counted heads as a proxy, with enslaved individuals

---

[66] U.S. CONST. art. I, § 9, cl. 4.

[67] U.S. CONST. art. I, § 2, cl. 3 ("Representatives and direct Taxes shall be apportioned among the several States which may be included within this Union, according to their respective Numbers, which shall be determined by adding to the whole Number of free Persons, including those bound to Service for a Term of Years, and excluding Indians not taxes, three-fifths of all other Persons."). The tainted origins of the Direct Tax Clauses are discussed *infra* notes 69–70 and accompanying text.

[68] 2 THE RECORDS OF THE FEDERAL CONVENTION OF 1787, *supra* note 26, at 350.

THE NECESSITY OF FEDERAL POWER   149

counting at three-fifths—presaging how the Constitution would count them.[69] Categorizing land taxes as direct was another boon to Southern states because they possessed disproportionately more land than the North, which had a higher overall population.[70]

The Supreme Court has always understood only very few taxes to be direct. In *Hylton v. United States* (1796), the Court's first case considering the issue, the justices unanimously held that an unapportioned federal luxury tax on carriages was not direct, reasoning in part that apportionment should be required only where practicable, and it would be nonsensical for the rate paid by carriage owners to vary radically depending on the number of carriages in their state.[71] The three justices who wrote—all prominent Framers or Founders—each suggested, without definitively declaring, that only capitations and land taxes are direct.[72] Over the nineteenth century, the Court upheld unapportioned federal taxes on insurance premiums, state bank notes, inheritances, and income.[73]

In 1895, however, the Court changed course by invalidating the progressive federal income-tax statute. Fracturing five-to-four, the Court held in *Pollock v. Farmers' Loan & Trust Company* that federal taxation of income derived from real or personal property—in *Pollock*, rental or dividend income—was direct and so subject to apportionment, unlike income taxes on wages (among other things), which were not.[74] The Court implausibly reasoned that certain income taxes could qualify as direct taxes on the underlying property from which the income was derived. The Court's holding and reasoning were rejected in 1913 upon ratification of the Sixteenth Amendment, which authorizes Congress to

[69] *See supra* note 67 (quoting the first Direct Tax Clause).

[70] AMAR, *supra* note 2, at 613–14 (explaining the link between head taxes and land taxes); Bruce Ackerman, *Taxation and the Constitution*, 99 COLUM. L. REV. 1, 7–13 (1999) (detailing the compromises over slavery at the Constitutional Convention that produced the Direct Tax Clauses); Hylton v. United States, 3 U.S. (3 Dall.) 171, 177 (1796) (opinion of Patterson, J.) ("The provision was made in favor of the southern States. They possessed a large number of slaves; they had extensive tracts of territory, thinly settled, and not very productive. A majority of the states had but few slaves, and several of them a limited territory, well settled, and in a high state of cultivation. The southern states, if no provision had been introduced in the Constitution, would have been wholly at the mercy of the other states. Congress in such case, might tax slaves, at discretion or arbitrarily, and land in every part of the Union after the same rate or measure: so much a head in the first instance, and so much an acre in the second."); Pollock v. Farmers' Loan & Trust Co., 158 U.S. 601, 684 (1895) (Harlan, J., dissenting) (describing the Constitution's direct tax provisions as "originally designed to protect the slave property against oppressive taxation").

[71] *Hylton*, 3 U.S. (3 Dall.) at 174 (opinion of Chase, J.).

[72] *Id.* at 175 ("I am inclined to think, but of this I do not give a judicial opinion, that the direct taxes contemplated by the Constitution, are only two, to wit, a capitation, or pell tax, simply, without regard to property, profession, or any other circumstances; and a tax on LAND."); *id.* at 177 (opinion of Patterson, J.); *id.* at 183 (opinion of Iredell, J.).

[73] Ackerman, *supra* note 70, at 25 & n.90. *See, e.g.*, Springer v. United States, 102 U.S. 586, 602 (1881) (upholding an unapportioned Civil War tax falling mainly on earned income as "within the category of an excise or duty" and declaring that "*direct* taxes, within the meaning of the Constitution, are only capitation taxes, as expressed in that instrument, and taxes on real estate").

[74] 158 U.S. 601 (1895).

150   THE COLLECTIVE-ACTION CONSTITUTION

tax "incomes, from whatever source derived, without apportionment among the several States." Tracking the previous, long-standing rule on direct taxes, the amendment clarifies that income, not ownership, is being taxed, so there is no apportionment requirement. The Court continued to hold, however, that taxes on personal property require apportionment.[75] Today, the Direct Tax Clause renders impracticable only federal capitations, taxes on land ownership, and taxes on personal property.[76]

A narrow definition of direct taxes is structurally sound for at least two reasons, each of which is illuminated by collective-action reasoning. First, the Constitution vests federal taxing authority in Congress, not state intermediaries, so that it can overcome free riding by states on the tax contributions of other states. It makes scant sense to render the exercise of much federal taxing authority effectively impossible—or absurd in the eyes of most Americans—by requiring the imposition of higher rates on poorer taxpayers. Unless the text requires it, the Constitution should not be read to give Congress a broad sovereign power with one hand while senselessly eviscerating it with the other. Granted, there would be no contradiction in doing so, and collective-action reasoning alone cannot distinguish direct from indirect taxes. The distinction's morally odious origins are also relevant, as are historical practice and judicial precedent. But the logic of cooperation problems supports the Court's historically dominant approach of strictly limiting the category of direct taxes. Just imagine the implications for congressional power today if Congress had to apportion federal income taxes. To quote the first Justice Harlan's dissent in *Pollock*, "[s]uch a result [would be] one to be deeply deplored. It [could not] be regarded otherwise than as a disaster to the country."[77]

Second, whether to impose a progressive tax system is a policy question that the Constitution does not decide. It assigns this decision to popular majorities, who choose elected officials. The Court in *Pollock* did not appreciate this point. Insofar as Americans support higher taxes on wealthy Americans, a key question is whether the federal government or each state is best positioned structurally to sustain them. Although both levels of government may try, the answer is the federal government. A state that imposes high taxes on wealthy residents risks losing such residents to states that tax the wealthy at low rates. As a result, states are under competitive pressure not to impose taxes as progressive as their

---

[75] Eisner v. Macomber, 252 U.S. 189 (1920) (holding that stock dividends are not income before they are sold or converted and so federal taxation of them requires apportionment).

[76] *See, e.g.*, NFIB v. Sebelius, 567 U.S. 519, 570–71 (2012) (limiting direct taxes to these three categories in holding that a tax for lacking health insurance was indirect). For a more sympathetic account of *Pollock* (and a critique of *Hylton*), see Eric M. Jensen, *The Apportionment of "Direct Taxes": Are Consumption Taxes Constitutional?*, 97 COLUM. L. REV. 2334 (1997). For a refutation, see Ackerman, *supra* note 70, at 52–56.

[77] Pollock v. Farmers' Loan & Trust Co., 158 U.S. 601, 684 (1895) (Harlan, J., dissenting).

residents may want. Congress, by contrast, has nationwide legislative jurisdiction and so is not vulnerable to competitive pressure from the states. It can impose a uniform national tax policy as progressive as Americans want without triggering a race to laissez-faire.[78] Whether Congress may be under competitive pressure from other nations regarding corporate taxation is another matter, but the states are worse situated than Congress in this domain too because they must contend with both interstate and international pressures.

Coercive versus Uncoercive Exactions: An Effects Theory of the Taxing Power

The apportionment requirement for direct taxes, like the other modest restrictions discussed above, are external limits on Congress's taxing power. Although efforts to broaden the category of direct taxes are misguided, they are likely animated by understandable concerns about preserving state regulatory authority and individual liberty, given both the breadth of federal taxing authority and the difficulty of avoiding many federal taxes. It is therefore worth considering whether there are internal constitutional limits on Congress's taxing power—limits that courts should enforce.

In *McCulloch v. Maryland* (1819), Chief Justice Marshall thought not. As Chapter 1 explained, he focused there on whether states could tax federal instrumentalities, but he wrote broadly that the power to tax, where it exists, "involves the power to destroy."[79] On this view, redress for misuse of federal taxing power lies with the political process, where citizens who feel overtaxed can express their sentiments at the polls.[80] By contrast, Justice Oliver Wendell Holmes famously wrote that the power to tax, while broad, "is not the power to destroy while this Court sits."[81] Holmes was more persuasive. The Taxing Clause,

---

[78] Amar, *supra* note 2, at 408. As Chapter 2 explained, a race to the bottom is a Pareto cooperation problem. It is also possible that disagreements among states over the progressivity of their income-tax policies create a cost-benefit collective-action problem, with states opposed to progressivity externalizing costs (in the form of competitive pressure) onto progressivity-oriented states that are greater than the benefits they internalize from regressivity.

[79] 17 U.S. (4 Wheat.) 316, 431 (1819).

[80] *See id.* at 428 ("The only security against the abuse of this power, is found, in the structure of the government itself. In imposing a tax, the legislature acts upon its constituents. This is, in general, a sufficient security against erroneous and oppressive taxation."); *id.* at 430 ("We are not driven to the perplexing inquiry, so unfit for the judicial department, what degree of taxation is the legitimate use and what degree may amount to the abuse of the power.").

[81] Panhandle Oil Co. v. Mississippi ex rel. Knox, 277 U.S. 218, 223 (1928) (Holmes, J., dissenting). *See id.* ("The power to fix rates is the power to destroy if unlimited, but this Court while it endeavors to prevent confiscation does not prevent the fixing of rates. A tax is not an unconstitutional regulation in every case where an absolute prohibition of sales would be one." (citing Hatch v. Reardon, 204 U.S. 152, 162 (1907))).

152   THE COLLECTIVE-ACTION CONSTITUTION

unlike regulations passed under the Interstate Commerce Clause and other federal powers, does not justify coercive exactions. This means that exercises of the taxing power ordinarily must be consistent with revenue-raising. A federal exaction is consistent with revenue-raising if it dampens the conduct subject to the exaction but does not prevent it. Taxes, unlike penalties, raise revenues just because they dampen conduct, as opposed to destroying it.[82]

The effect of a penalty is largely to prevent conduct, thereby raising little or no revenue, whereas the effect of a tax is to dampen conduct, thereby raising revenue. Three material characteristics of a mandatory payment create incentives that either prevent or dampen conduct. These characteristics provide criteria for distinguishing between penalties and taxes. First, a pure penalty condemns actors for wrongdoing. Second, they must pay more than the usual gain from the forbidden conduct. And third, they must pay at an increasing rate with intentional or repeated violations. Thus, a penalty expressively coerces people by condemning their conduct, and it materially coerces with relatively high rates and enhancements for repeated violations. By contrast, a pure tax permits actors to engage in the taxed conduct. In addition, they must pay an amount less than the usual gain from the taxed conduct. And finally, intentional or repeated conduct does not enhance the rate. Thus, a tax does not coerce expressively because it signals that individuals can permissibly engage in the taxed conduct, and it does not coerce materially because relatively low rates without enhancements leave people with a reasonable financial choice to engage in the taxed conduct.[83]

Historically, the Court has sometimes, although not always, focused on the coerciveness of federal exactions in Taxing Clause cases.[84] In *NFIB v. Sebelius*

---

[82] *See* Robert D. Cooter & Neil S. Siegel, *Not the Power to Destroy: An Effects Theory of the Tax Power*, 98 Va. L. Rev. 1195 (2012). Exactions can be noncoercive without raising revenues when they are reduced to $0. A $0 exaction raises no revenue because it is entirely uncoercive. Is such an exaction a tax for purposes of Congress's tax power? This may seem like an absurd hypothetical—Congress does not require an enumerated power to require no one to do anything—but a constitutional challenge to such an exaction made it to the Supreme Court. *See* California v. Texas, 141 S. Ct. 2104 (2021) (not reaching this question by holding that the plaintiffs lacked standing to challenge the minimum coverage provision of the Affordable Care Act).

[83] Cooter & Siegel, *supra* note 82, at 1222–36.

[84] The Court invalidated federal taxes as coercive in *Bailey v. Drexel Furniture Company (The Child Labor Tax Case)*, 259 U.S. 20 (1922) (invalidating a 10-percent exaction on the annual net profits of firms employing child labor); *Hill v. Wallace*, 259 U.S. 44, 68 (1922) (invalidating a twenty-cent-per-bushel exaction on sales of certain grain future contracts in addition to the two-cent tax on every hundred dollars in value of such sales); *United States v. Constantine*, 296 U.S. 287 (1935) (invalidating a $1,000 exaction on certain liquor dealers in addition to the $25 tax required of all such dealers); and, in the context of the Double Jeopardy Clause, *Department of Revenue of Montana v. Kurth Ranch*, 511 U.S. 767 (1994) (invalidating a high state exaction on dangerous drugs in addition to an already imposed criminal penalty). The Court was unconcerned about potential coercion in *Veazie Bank v. Fenno*, 75 U.S. (8 Wall.) 533 (1869) (upholding an increase in the federal tax on state bank notes from 1 to 10 percent); *McCrary v. United States*, 195 U.S. 27 (1904) (upholding an increase in the federal tax on yellow oleomargarine from two to ten cents, while the tax on white oleomargarine remained one-quarter of a cent per pound); and *United States v. Sanchez*, 340 U.S. 42 (1950)

THE NECESSITY OF FEDERAL POWER   153

(2012), the Court confronted past decisions that were arguably inconsistent with one another.[85] The Court there considered whether certain provisions of the Patient Protection and Affordable Care Act (popularly known as the ACA or Obamacare) imposed a penalty or a tax by requiring most individuals either to obtain health insurance or make a payment to the Internal Revenue Service. Writing for the Court, Chief Justice Roberts concluded that this "shared responsibility payment" for going without insurance was a tax for purposes of the Taxing Clause, even though Congress called it a penalty, primarily because it was not coercive.[86]

The foregoing effects theory of the federal taxing power, which this author developed with Professor Robert Cooter, provides the best theoretical justification for the Court's holding, and the Court's reasoning, rhetoric, and citations largely tracked it.[87] The ACA's required payment for being uninsured likely expressed a penalty because that is what the statute called the payment (although the ACA placed the exaction in the Internal Revenue Code and required "taxpayers" to

---

(upholding a $100-per-ounce federal tax on certain transferors of marijuana). For discussion, see Cooter & Siegel, *supra* note 82, at 1210–22.

[85] Professor Barry Cushman argues that the Court's taxing-power decisions before *NFIB* consistently held that "a nominal tax is in fact a regulatory penalty where it imposes an exaction triggered by departure from a detailed and specified course of conduct, and the exaction is sufficiently onerous to induce those engaged in the targeted conduct generally to alter their behavior." Barry Cushman, NFIB v. Sebelius *and the Transformation of the Taxing Power*, 89 NOTRE DAME L. REV. 134, 137 (2013); *see id.* at 181–84 (emphasizing that the first criterion was most central to the Court). On this view, in determining whether an exaction is a tax or a penalty, it is critical whether the regulatory scheme with which individuals or entities must comply to avoid paying the exaction is reasonably related to a fiscal purpose. *Id.* at 184–85. Professor Cushman offers an impressive analysis that rationalizes cases spanning more than a century. It seems unlikely, however, that the Court's taxing-power jurisprudence remained entirely stable throughout this period amid dramatic changes in American society and constitutional law, including with respect to the Court's view of the Interstate Commerce Clause (*see* Chapter 5) and its willingness to police legislative purpose in some areas of constitutional law. *See* Caleb Nelson, *Judicial Review of Legislative Purpose*, 83 N.Y.U. L. REV. 1784 (2008). No Justice in *NFIB* saw the Court's taxing-power cases as Professor Cushman does, and it seems unlikely that contemporary judicial conservatives would permit Congress to "tax" carrying a firearm in a school zone at a rate of $25,000 per instance, even absent a detailed regulatory scheme. *Cf.* United States v. Lopez, 514 U.S. 549 (1995) (discussed in Chapter 5); *infra* note 98.

Whether there is a detailed regulatory scheme unrelated to a fiscal need seems a manipulable inquiry, as may be suggested by Professor Cushman's characterization of the ACA exaction for noninsurance as contingent on departure from a detailed and specified course of conduct, as opposed to the consequence of simply failing to obtain qualifying health insurance. Cushman, *supra*, at 191–94. In addition, it is not clear why, if fiscal purpose matters when there is a detailed regulatory scheme, it does not matter when there is not. A draconian exaction for doing what Congress does not want one to do (or not doing what Congress wants) is entirely regulatory; there is no ambiguity regarding whether Congress had a fiscal object, and courts today (unlike in times past) are willing to examine legislative purpose in many areas of constitutional law. Finally, a draconian exaction by itself may interfere with the states' police powers and individual liberty as much as such an exaction when it is attached to a detailed course of conduct. It depends on how much states and individuals care about the conduct that Congress is regulating with its taxing power.

[86] NFIB v. Sebelius, 567 U.S. 519, 564–68 (2012).

[87] Neal Kumar Katyal, *Foreword: Academic Influence on the Court*, 98 VA. L. REV. 1149 (2012).

154   THE COLLECTIVE-ACTION CONSTITUTION

pay it as part of their income tax returns[88]). But the exaction had the material characteristics of a tax—Roberts called them "practical characteristics"[89]— because the amount of the exaction was less than the cost of insurance for most Americans and could never be more for anyone, giving people a reasonable financial choice to pay the tax instead of buying insurance. Moreover, there was no scienter requirement or recidivism enhancement. The constitutional identity of the exaction for purposes of the Taxing Clause depended on the reasonable expectations of the enacting Congress concerning its effect. If Congress could have reasonably concluded that the exaction would dampen—but not prevent—the general class of conduct subject to it (people going without health insurance) and thereby raise revenue, it was a tax regardless of what the statute called it. If Congress could have reasonably concluded only that the exaction would prevent the conduct of all or nearly all people subject to it and thereby raise little or no revenue, it was a penalty. The nonpartisan Congressional Budget Office predicted that the required payment for noninsurance would dampen uninsured behavior but not prevent it, thereby raising several billion dollars in revenue each year.[90] Accordingly, the payment was a tax for purposes of the Taxing Clause.

It is irrelevant whether Congress primarily intended to raise revenues or instead primarily intended to regulate behavior when it assessed people for lacking health insurance or for any other acts or omissions.[91] The Court has at times suggested otherwise, including in *The Child Labor Tax Case* (1922), where it struck down a 10 percent exaction on the annual net profits of businesses employing children as laborers.[92] But the Taxing Clause, unlike the Origination Clause, does not require Congress's primary purpose to be "for raising Revenue."[93] And turning from text to practice, many federal taxes historically have had regulatory purposes in addition to revenue-raising purposes—for example, the eighteenth-century imposts that raised revenues from imports and suppressed foreign competition with American industry.[94] In his *Commentaries*

[88]   Cooter & Siegel, *supra* note 82, at 1241. The amount of the exaction was also calculated in part as a percentage of the taxpayer's household income for the tax year at issue. *Id.*

[89]   *NFIB*, 567 U.S. at 565, 573.

[90]   *Id.* at 564; *see* Cooter & Siegel, *supra* note 82, at 1242–43.

[91]   As evidenced by the Constitution's grant of power to enact capitations, U.S. CONST. art. I, § 9, cl. 4, there is no plausible argument that Congress may not tax "inactivity." The Court in *NFIB* endorsed such a limit on the Interstate Commerce Clause, as Chapter 5 discusses.

[92]   *Drexel Furniture Co.*, 259 U.S. at 38 ("Taxes are occasionally imposed in the discretion of the legislature on proper subjects with the primary motive of obtaining revenue from them and with the incidental motive of discouraging them by making their continuance onerous.").

[93]   U.S. CONST. art. I, § 7, cl. 1 ("All Bills for raising Revenue shall originate in the House of Representatives . . . .").

[94]   BROWNLEE, *supra* note 13, at 22 (describing Hamilton's 1791 proposal for "tariffs to protect new industries and exemptions from tariffs for raw materials needed for industrial development," which he justified not only on revenue-raising grounds but also on the regulatory ground that they would "encourage Americans to spend their money and energy to advance industrial technology"). Although Congress rejected most of Hamilton's program for industrialization, in 1792 it enacted

on the Constitution, Joseph Story observed that "the taxing power is often, very often, applied for other purposes, than revenue."[95] Similarly, the tax historian W. Elliot Brownlee concludes a history of federal taxation in America by observing that "[h]istorically, the introduction of new tax regimes that enhance confidence in American government has required," among other things, "regulation of behavior in ways that were widely regarded as improving national well-being."[96]

The constitutional text does not expressly state the requirement of noncoercion for federal taxes, but it is fairly implied by the language of the Taxing and Spending Clause, which gives Congress taxing authority "to pay the Debts and provide for the Common Defence and general Welfare of the United States."[97] Congress can neither pay debts nor provide for the nation's defense or general welfare without generating revenue. And to repeat, coercive federal exactions do not raise much or any revenue. The noncoercion requirement responds to concerns about preserving state regulatory power and individual liberty that likely have animated efforts to expand the category of direct taxes. Unlike such efforts, however, the noncoercion requirement does not risk disabling Congress from solving the collective-action problem that the grant empowers it to overcome.[98]

---

most of the tariff program he had recommended: higher tariffs on manufactured goods and lower tariffs on raw materials. *Id.* For many examples of federal taxes with regulatory purposes during different historical eras, see BROWNLEE, *supra* note 13; Ruth Mason, *Federalism and the Taxing Power*, 99 CAL. L. REV. 975, 984–92 (2011); and Cooter & Siegel, *supra* note 82, at 1204–10.

[95] 2 JOSEPH STORY, COMMENTARIES ON THE CONSTITUTION OF THE UNITED STATES § 962, p. 434 (1833); *see id.* ("It is often applied, as a regulation of commerce.").

[96] BROWNLEE, *supra* note 13, at 245. For responses to other objections to the effects theory, including that Congress's choice of label for an exaction should be dispositive and, relatedly, that the federal government should not be able to evade political accountability by calling an exaction one thing in the political arena and another in litigation, see Cooter & Siegel, *supra* note 82, at 1211–13, 1220–21, 1243–45.

[97] U.S. CONST. art. I, § 8, cl. 1. For this reason and those offered in the previous five paragraphs, it is unfair to conclude that the effects theory "is not firmly grounded in [the Taxing] Clause's text, history, and precedent," although it is correct that the theory is not mainly originalist. Robert J. Pushaw, Jr., *The Paradox of the Obamacare Decision: How Can the Federal Government Have Limited Unlimited Power?*, 65 FLA. L. REV. 1993, 2031, 2033 (2003). It is also true that the theory does not rationalize cases that may resist rationalization. *See supra* note 85.

[98] Moreover, without a noncoercion limit on the Taxing Clause, Congress could circumvent even modest limits on the Interstate Commerce Clause. As Chapter 5 discusses, the Court has held since 1995 that this clause empowers Congress to use penalties to regulate economic conduct, but not noneconomic conduct. What prevents Congress from penalizing noneconomic conduct by calling a penalty a tax and invoking the Taxing Clause? It is the distinction between a penalty and a tax. This point holds if one replaces the Court's distinction between economic and noneconomic conduct with the distinction between individual and collective action by states, as Chapter 5 also discusses. The Court has been most concerned to police limits on the Taxing Clause when it has been most concerned to police limits on the Interstate Commerce Clause. *See, e.g., Drexel Furniture Co.*, 259 U.S. 20 (1922).

156 THE COLLECTIVE-ACTION CONSTITUTION

Spending

The Constitution does not expressly grant Congress the power to spend federal tax revenue. Instead, its spending power is conventionally viewed as implied in the opening clause of Section 8, which is quoted immediately above. This clause thus gives Congress the power to spend federal tax revenue for three purposes: paying debts, providing for national defense, and promoting the general welfare. (It is worth underscoring that textually these purposes relate to how Congress can spend federal tax revenue, not to how it can exercise its taxing power.) The Articles of Confederation also referenced "the common defence or general welfare" to describe problems that the central government can solve better than the states, even as its requisition system for troops and taxes rendered the Confederation Congress incapable of reliably doing so.[99] The Constitution deems federal provision of the common defense and general welfare to be so important that it scraps the requisition system and introduces these twin objectives in the document's Preamble, just as the term "general" ultimately appeared in Resolution VI.

General versus Local Welfare: Historical Practice

There are several historical and doctrinal questions surrounding the expanse and limits of the spending power. From a collective-action perspective, the most important one is the extent to which collective-action reasoning can both illuminate the requirement that federal spending be for "common" or "general" purposes and account for the extraordinarily broad modern scope of Congress's spending authority. Reasoning from the logics of collective action, defense is "common" and welfare is "general" when the federal government can obtain them and the states cannot—when the states face Pareto or cost-benefit collective-action problems.[100] The modern Court does not, however, distinguish between general and local welfare. Deferring to Congress's judgment that federal spending promotes the general welfare, the Court instead imposes other restrictions on federal spending when Congress conditions federal funds to the state on their agreement to comply with requirements that Congress may not constitutionally impose on them directly.[101] Importantly, however, the distinction between

---

[99] ARTICLES OF CONFEDERATION of 1781, art. VIII ("All charges of war, and all other expenses that shall be incurred for the common defence or general welfare, and allowed by the united states in congress assembled, shall be defrayed out of a common treasury, which shall be supplied by the several states....").

[100] Robert D. Cooter & Neil S. Siegel, *Collective Action Federalism: A General Theory of Article I, Section 8*, 63 STAN. L. REV. 115, 119 (2010).

[101] South Dakota v. Dole, 483 U.S. 203, 218 n.2 (1987) (deferring to Congress). The *Dole* Court wrote that all spending must be for the general welfare; conditions must be clearly stated; conditions

general and local welfare has an historical pedigree in early American constitutional politics (albeit not an entirely consistent one), and collective-action reasoning appears in several of the Court's most significant conditional-spending decisions.

Hamilton and Madison famously disagreed about the spending power. Hamilton believed that Congress could spend for the general welfare regardless of whether the expenditure could plausibly be viewed as carrying out another enumerated power. Madison, by contrast, argued that Congress possessed no independent power to spend for the general welfare; rather, the phrase "general Welfare" was defined and limited by the grants of authority in clauses 2 through 17 of Section 8.[102] But notably (and ironically), in justifying his otherwise nationalist position, Hamilton insisted that Congress "cannot rightfully apply the money they raise to any purpose merely or purely local"; in his view, "[t]he constitutional *test* of a right application must always be, whether it be for a purpose of *general* or *local* nature."[103] By contrast, in justifying his relatively narrow view of Congress's spending authority, Madison insisted that "the terms 'common defense and general welfare' embrac[e] every object and act within the purview of a legislative trust."[104] Similarly, in his *Commentaries*, Joseph Story referenced "the generality of the words to 'provide for the common defence and general welfare,'" doubting that they could independently limit federal power.[105]

A major antebellum controversy concerned whether the General Welfare Clause authorized Congress to spend money on "internal improvements" such as canals and roads. Numerous Democratic-Republican presidents and, later, Democratic presidents vetoed internal-improvements bills on constitutional

---

must be related to the purpose of the spending program; and conditions must not violate independent constitutional limits. *Id.* at 207–08. In addition, at the end of its opinion, the Court mentioned that a "financial inducement offered by Congress might be so coercive as to pass the point at which 'pressure turns into compulsion.'" *Id.* at 211 (quoting Steward Mach. Co. v. Davis, 301 U.S. 548, 590 (1937)). But the Court upheld the challenged condition because Congress was offering only "relatively mild encouragement to the States." *Id.* As discussed below, the Court held a condition coercive for the first time in *NFIB v. Sebelius*, 567 U.S. 519 (2012).

[102] *Compare* ALEXANDER HAMILTON, *Report on the Subject of Manufactures* (1791), *reprinted in* 10 THE PAPERS OF ALEXANDER HAMILTON 230, 302–04 (Harold C. Syrett ed., 1966), *with* THE FEDERALIST NO. 41, at 262–64 (James Madison) (Clinton Rossiter ed., 1961). *See* United States v. Butler, 297 U.S. 1, 65–66 (1936) (discussing Hamilton's expansive view of the General Welfare Clause and Madison's restrictive view).

[103] Alexander Hamilton, *Opinion as to the Constitutionality of the Bank of the United States* (Feb. 23, 1791), *reprinted in* 3 THE WORKS OF ALEXANDER HAMILTON 445, 485 (Henry Cabot Lodge ed., 1904) (emphases in original).

[104] James Madison, *Veto Message on Internal Improvement Bill*, 30 ANNALS OF CONG. 211, 212 (Mar. 3, 1817).

[105] 1 STORY, *supra* note 95, at § 904, p. 367. Story, like Madison, mainly wanted to reject the view that Congress possesses freestanding regulatory (as opposed to spending) power to provide for the common defense and the general welfare, but his skepticism about the constraining power of the words applies to the spending power.

158 THE COLLECTIVE-ACTION CONSTITUTION

grounds or otherwise articulated narrow views of federal spending authority. Some of them agreed with Madison that Congress lacked independent power to spend for the general welfare.[106] Others concluded, as President James Monroe put it, that Congress lacks authority to "apply money in aid of State administrations, for purposes strictly local, in which the nation at large has no interest, although the State would desire it."[107] After President Andrew Jackson voiced constitutional objections in vetoing the Maysville Road Bill in 1830, subsequent Democratic presidents—Tyler, Polk, Pierce, and Buchanan—articulated increasingly narrow conceptions of congressional authority over internal improvements. "And thus on the eve of the Civil War," Professor David Currie writes, "Congress found itself unable even to remove obstructions to naturally navigable waters, which Andrew Jackson himself had conceded it not only could but ought to do."[108]

Similarly, before and after the war, some presidents or members of Congress raised concerns about whether spending on disaster relief (for victims of fires, floods, and droughts) was for the "general Welfare" or the particular welfare of those benefiting from the spending.[109] Much practice supported expenditures to help disaster victims, but qualms endured.[110]

General versus Local Welfare: Judicial Precedent

The Supreme Court did not weigh in until 1936, likely in part because of past vetoes. The issue in *United States v. Butler* was the constitutionality of the Agricultural Adjustment Act of 1933, which granted subsidies to farmers willing to limit their crop production. The Court agreed with Hamilton that Congress possesses independent authority to spend for the general welfare, and it endorsed his distinction between general and local welfare for purposes of the Spending Clause. The Court did not clarify the distinction, however, because it invalidated the law at issue on the distinct ground (soon overruled) that the regulation of

---

[106] *See, e.g.*, Thomas Jefferson, *Sixth Annual Message to the Senate and House of Representatives of the United States in Congress* (Dec. 2, 1806), *in* 10 THE WORKS OF THOMAS JEFFERSON 302, 317–18 (Paul Leicester Ford ed., 1905); Madison, Veto Message, *supra* note 104, at 312.

[107] James Monroe, *Views of the President of the United States on the Subject of Internal Improvements*, 39 ANNALS OF CONG. 1809, 1841 (May 4, 1822).

[108] DAVID P. CURRIE, THE CONSTITUTION IN CONGRESS: DEMOCRATS AND WHIGS, 1829–1861, at 25 (2005).

[109] An example is the fascinating House debates in 1796 over whether it was consistent with the general welfare to appropriate funds for Savannah, Georgia, following a devastating fire. 6 ANNALS OF CONG. 1711–27 (1796).

[110] MICHELLE DAUBER LANDIS, THE SYMPATHETIC STATE: DISASTER RELIEF AND THE ORIGINS OF THE AMERICAN WELFARE STATE 5–6, 17–34 (2013).

THE NECESSITY OF FEDERAL POWER 159

production was left to the states.[111] Nor have subsequent decisions elucidated this distinction, and congressional spending authority is extraordinarily broad as a result.

Even so, since the constitutional crisis of 1937, collective-action rationales for conditional spending have appeared in historic spending-power decisions, and these rationales are more limited than the Court's application of deferential, rational-basis review.[112] In 1937, in *Steward Machine Company v. Davis*, the Court upheld the federal unemployment-compensation system created by the Social Security Act (SSA).[113] In *Helvering v. Davis*, decided the same day, the Court upheld the SSA's old-age pension program, which had been funded exclusively by federal taxes.[114] In both cases, the Court based its decision partly on a collective-action problem facing the states, which can potentially be modeled as a Prisoners' Dilemma with multiple players. Writing for the Court in *Steward Machine*, Justice Benjamin Cardozo emphasized economic competition among states that many states deemed unfair, which had resulted in a first-mover problem:

> [I]f states had been holding back before the passage of the federal law, inaction was not owing, for the most part, to the lack of sympathetic interest. Many held back through alarm lest, in laying such a toll upon their industries, they would place themselves in a position of economic disadvantage as compared with neighbors or competitors. Two consequences ensued. One was that the freedom of a state to contribute its fair share to the solution of a national problem was paralyzed by fear. The other was that in so far as there was failure by the states to contribute relief according to the measure of their capacity, a disproportionate burden, and a mountainous one, was laid upon the resources of the Government of the nation.[115]

As evidence for the collective-action problem, Cardozo noted a Massachusetts bill that would remain inoperative unless the federal bill became law or eleven states from a list of twenty-one "impose[d] on their employers burdens substantially equivalent."[116] States like Massachusetts feared harming in-state businesses and possibly causing them to leave.

---

[111] United States v. Butler, 297 U.S. 1, 65–67 (1936). As Chapter 5 discusses, subsequent Courts have rejected the *Butler* Court's conclusion that Congress may not regulate production.

[112] Rational-basis review is the most deferential form of judicial review known to US constitutional law. Such review places the burden on the challenger to show that the law in question is not rationally related to a conceivable (even if not an actual), legitimate government interest. It is nearly impossible for a law to flunk rational-basis review.

[113] 301 U.S. 548 (1937).

[114] 301 U.S. 619 (1937).

[115] *Steward Machine*, 301 U.S. at 588 (citations and footnote omitted).

[116] *Id.* at 588 n.9.

160   THE COLLECTIVE-ACTION CONSTITUTION

Cardozo also wrote for the Court in *Helvering*, and again he underscored a collective-action problem involving unfair competition from the perspective of many states:

> [S]tates and local governments are at times reluctant to increase so heavily the burden of taxation to be borne by their residents for fear of placing themselves in a position of economic disadvantage as compared with neighbors or competitors. We have seen this in our study of the problem of unemployment compensation. *Steward Machine Co. v. Davis.* A system of old age pensions has special dangers of its own, if put in force in one state and rejected in another. The existence of such a system is a bait to the needy and dependent elsewhere, encouraging them to migrate and seek a haven of repose. Only a power that is national can serve the interests of all.[117]

Given the interstate movements that deterred states from establishing their own pension programs—the movement of taxpayers out of state and the movement of needy and elderly people into the state—the Court thought it made structural sense for Congress to have the authority to intervene.[118]

Alternatively, to the extent there were states that rejected unemployment-compensation and old-age pension programs on policy grounds, the strategic environment is best modeled as a cost-benefit collective-action problem, not a Pareto cooperation problem. On the cost-benefit view, Congress rationally determined that a minority of states should not be able to put competitive pressure on the majority of states, which did support unemployment-compensation and pension programs, because the benefits to the minority of states of vindicating their policy preferences were outweighed by the costs they were imposing on the rest of the nation.

True, the Court in these cases did not hold that Congress may spend only to solve multistate collective-action problems. Instead, Cardozo emphasized that the Court would defer to Congress's determination that spending advances the general welfare "unless the choice is clearly wrong, a display of arbitrary power, not an exercise of judgment."[119] But the logics of collective action were present,

---

[117] *Helvering*, 301 U.S. at 644 (citation omitted).

[118] The interactions among states in *Steward Machine* and *Helvering* seem better modeled as a Prisoners' Dilemma or Asymmetric Dilemma than as an Assurance game for reasons explained in Chapter 2. Assurance problems can be solved when one player moves first and chooses the strategy that forms part of the Pareto optimal Nash equilibrium. Having received assurance, the other player chooses the same strategy. By contrast, permitting one player to move first does not solve a Prisoners' Dilemma because the second player's incentive not to cooperate remains regardless of what the first one does. It is possible, however, that states may require (re)assurance not only about whether other states will pass certain laws but also about whether they will vigorously enforce them. Even with sequential play, therefore, an Assurance game may not be easy for states to solve within a certain time horizon.

[119] *Id.* at 640.

THE NECESSITY OF FEDERAL POWER   161

including perhaps in his statement that "the concept of the general welfare" is not "static" and that "[n]eeds that were narrow or parochial a century ago may be interwoven in our day with the well-being of the Nation."[120]

A similar pattern was evident decades later in *South Dakota v. Dole* (1987), where the Court held that Congress could deny 5 percent of federal highway funds to states that did not establish a twenty-one-year-old drinking age, even assuming that Congress could not impose a drinking age directly.[121] Writing for the Court, Chief Justice William Rehnquist stressed that "[i]n considering whether a particular expenditure is intended to serve general purposes, courts should defer substantially to the judgment of Congress," adding that "[t]he level of deference to the congressional decision is such that the Court has more recently questioned whether 'general welfare' is a judicially enforceable restriction at all."[122] Yet, he explained why a multistate collective-action problem justified the federal age restriction, observing that the federal goal of safe interstate travel "had been frustrated by varying drinking ages among the States." "A Presidential commission appointed to study alcohol-related accidents and fatalities on the Nation's highways," he wrote, "concluded that the lack of uniformity in the States' drinking ages created 'an incentive to drink and drive' because 'young persons commut[e] to border States where the drinking age is lower.'"[123]

Although the interstate movements were apparently significant in *Dole*, it is not clear that there was a cooperation problem. Rather, as suggested by Rehnquist's reference to a "lack of uniformity," the problem appeared to have been a lack of coordination by the states amid disagreements over what the drinking age should be. States that imposed a twenty-one-year-old drinking age could not make their regulation fully effective without the same regulation being in effect in adjacent states. And states that preferred an eighteen-year-old drinking age presumably dispreferred attracting out-of-state young people between eighteen and twenty-one years of age who were inclined to drink and drive within their borders. Possibly facing a Bridge or Seaway game involving different groups of states, Congress used the spending power to end the disagreement and solve the coordination problem.[124] In sum, in several of the Court's pivotal

---

[120] *Id.* at 641. Justice Cardozo's use of the word "interwoven" echoes Chief Justice Marshall's use of the term "intermingled" in Gibbons v. Ogden, 22 U.S. (9 Wheat.) 1, 194 (1824), discussed in the next chapter.

[121] 483 U.S. 203 (1987). Whether Congress can use the Interstate Commerce Clause to establish a twenty-one-year-old drinking age directly is a difficult question because of Section 2 of the Twenty-First Amendment, which gives states special authority to regulate alcohol.

[122] *Id.* at 207 & n.2 (citing Buckley v. Valeo, 424 U.S. 1, 90–91 (1976) (per curiam)).

[123] *Id.* at 209 (alteration in original) (quoting PRESIDENTIAL COMMISSION ON DRUNK DRIVING, FINAL REPORT 11 (1983)).

[124] If the states with different drinking ages simply disagreed with one another and did not prefer coordination to noncoordination, there was no Pareto collective-action problem. In this scenario, whether Congress's intervention was justified by a cost-benefit collective-action problem turned on

162   THE COLLECTIVE-ACTION CONSTITUTION

spending-power cases, the Court itself effectively recognized that a collective-action understanding of the "general Welfare" justified the challenged programs.

In previous conditional-spending cases, the Court had mentioned the possibility that a condition attached to federal funds might put so much financial pressure on states as to be coercive and so unconstitutional, but the Court did not invalidate a condition on this ground until *NFIB v. Sebelius* (2012).[125] Writing the controlling opinion for three justices, Chief Justice Roberts reasoned that the ACA's expansion of the federal Medicaid program was coercive because Congress had conditioned the continued receipt of a huge amount of money (roughly 10 percent of the average state's budget) in an entrenched program (the pre-ACA Medicaid program) on the agreement by states to participate in a separate and independent program (the ACA's Medicaid expansion).[126] Collective-action reasoning cannot illuminate the conceptually difficult question of whether and when conditions attached to a gratuitous benefit are capable of coercing.[127] But collective-action theory can explain why, even putting deference logic aside, both the pre- and post-ACA Medicaid programs advanced general, not merely local, welfare. As in *Steward Machine* and *Helvering*, states that finance health care for the poor through an income tax put themselves at a competitive disadvantage in attracting residents and businesses relative to states that do not provide health care to the poor. States may also attempt to free ride on the superior health-care systems of bordering states by encouraging poor residents to move interstate permanently to obtain health insurance or temporarily to obtain emergency care. Medicaid helps avoid this race to the bottom, which would likely be far more noticeable absent the program.[128]

Another collective-action justification for federal spending is economies of scale.[129] Economies of scale exist when the cost per unit of output decreases as one increases the scale of the operation producing the outputs. Although

whether the benefits to states with drinking ages below twenty-one years of age were less than the costs they were externalizing onto states with twenty-one-year-old drinking ages.

[125] 567 U.S. 519 (2012).

[126] *Id.* at 581–85 (opinion of Roberts, C.J.). For explication of this part of Roberts' opinion and the other opinions on this issue, see Samuel Bagenstos, *The Anti-Leveraging Principle and the Spending Clause after NFIB*, 101 Geo. L.J. 861 (2013).

[127] This question has long perplexed scholars in several areas of constitutional law. *See, e.g., id.;* Mitchell N. Berman, *Coercion, Compulsion, and the Medicaid Expansion: A Study in the Doctrine of Unconstitutional Conditions*, 91 Tex. L. Rev. 1283 (2013).

[128] For discussion and examples, see Neil S. Siegel, *Free Riding on Benevolence: Collective Action Federalism and the Minimum Coverage Provision*, 75 Law & Contemp. Probs. 29, 56–69 (2012) (Issue No. 3).

[129] *See, e.g.*, Steven G. Calabresi & Lucy D. Bickford, *Federalism and Subsidiarity: Perspectives from U.S. Constitutional Law*, *in* NOMOS LV: Federalism and Subsidiarity 131–132 (James E. Fleming & Jacob T. Levy eds., 2014) (justifying federal power based partly on economies of scale in funding a program).

economies of scale are often invoked as justification for the use of federal power, it is not often recognized that economies of scale are not distinct from collective-action reasoning. Generally, economies of scale generate positive externalities that cause collective-action problems for the states, which would have to coordinate to internalize such externalities.[130] Examples include spending on networks of transportation like the interstate-highway system and spending on agencies that respond to emergencies or that protect health and safety—for instance, the Federal Emergency Management Agency (FEMA), the Centers for Disease Control and Prevention (CDC), the Food and Drug Administration (FDA), and the Occupational Safety and Health Administration (OSHA). It would waste scarce resources for each state to fund their own substitutes for what these federal agencies do. There also might not exist sufficient expertise to populate all of them.

Still another collective-action rationale for federal expenditures is interstate redistribution. Money has declining marginal value. For example, a millionaire values an additional dollar of income less than an impoverished individual. Accordingly, an effective wealth transfer from a relatively rich state to a relatively poor one is a cost-benefit improvement if the costs and benefits are measured in terms of relative welfare levels. Accomplishing such wealth transfers requires, however, an allocative mechanism to ensure that funds actually flow to residents of states with higher marginal utilities of income. Whatever one's views concerning the choice between command-and-control redistribution and market allocation in other contexts, the federal government has extensive informational resources at its disposal to distinguish between richer and poorer states and individuals, and it can use its taxing and spending authority to achieve interstate redistribution.

Interstate Psychological Externalities

Beyond the Court's cases, economies of scale, and interstate redistribution, the number of federal spending programs for which collective-action reasoning can account may depend partly on whether interstate psychological externalities, in addition to material externalities, are deemed relevant to whether a multistate collective-action problem exists. Potential examples of psychological externalities include the concerns of people in one state for the health, education, environment, and physical and financial security of people in another state. Psychological externalities can be especially large after a natural disaster, as illustrated by certain spending controversies in the early Republic discussed above

---

[130] Cooter & Siegel, *Collective Action Federalism, supra* note 100, at 140.

164 THE COLLECTIVE-ACTION CONSTITUTION

and by the responses of governments, charities, and individuals to hurricanes and earthquakes in modern America. Most Americans care whether other Americans live or die during a pandemic, have clean air and water, have access to food and shelter, and are receiving a basic education.[131]

But if weak feelings that people in one state have for people in another count as interstate externalities that can cause collective-action problems, collective action is a pervasive problem and a collective-action understanding of the general welfare seems unilluminating.[132] Professor Amartya Sen has explained that negative psychological externalities—preferences about other people's preferences—threaten individualism in economic theory by making it impossible to make everyone better off (to make Pareto improvements). Amid such externalities, every deviation from the status quo that would make one party better off would necessarily make another party worse off.[133] Similarly, psychological externalities pose a threat to state regulatory autonomy in constitutional theory by potentially justifying unlimited federal power. Every move by a state to, say, prefer tax cuts to the provision of poverty relief or other humanitarian aid would make another state worse off.[134]

Significantly, however, unlike when Congress accomplishes regulatory objectives through its interstate-commerce power, Congress's achievement of regulatory objectives through its conditional-spending power is not cost free; Congress must literally pay to vindicate its regulatory concerns.[135] Reasoning by analogy, the tradition of cost-benefit analysis neither excludes nor includes psychological externalities categorically; they are credited only if there is a demonstrated willingness to pay to vindicate one's expressions of sympathy for others. Cheap talk does not suffice. Similarly, the concerns of people in one state

---

[131] See, e.g., Daniel C. Esty, Revitalizing Environmental Federalism, 95 MICH. L. REV. 570, 638–48 (1996) (discussing different externalities, including psychological externalities). Professor Amartya Sen refers to this externality as "sympathy." Amartya K. Sen, Rational Fools: A Critique of the Behavioral Foundations of Economic Theory, 6 PHIL. & PUB. AFF. 317, 326–29 (1977).

[132] Cf., e.g., Esty, supra note 131, at 595 n.73 ("[W]ithout a 'willingness to pay' mechanism to check the reality and depth of [psychological] harms, there exists a moral hazard problem of potentially significant proportions because those claiming injury have little reason to report accurately on their welfare losses and much reason to exaggerate.").

[133] Amartya Sen, The Impossibility of a Paretian Liberal, 78 J. POL. ECON. 152 (1970) (explaining why meddlesome preferences undermine the usefulness of Pareto efficiency as a normative criterion); see id. at 157 n.6 ("The difficulties of achieving Pareto optimality in the presence of externalities are well known. What is at issue here is the acceptability of Pareto optimality as an objective in the context of liberal values, given certain types of externalities" (emphases in original).).

[134] Constitutional law has struggled with psychological harm in the context of standing doctrine. See Friends of the Earth, Inc. v. Laidlaw Envtl. Servs. (TOC), Inc., 528 U.S. 167 (2000); Lujan v. Defenders of Wildlife, 504 U.S. 555 (1992); Sierra Club v. Morton, 405 U.S. 727, 760 (1972) (Blackman, J., dissenting) (invoking John Donne's Devotions XVII).

[135] Brian Galle, Federal Grants, State Decisions, 88 B.U. L. REV. 875, 883 n.34 (2008) (noting that spending "might allow Congress to enact legislation that would go beyond the limits of its other main sources of authority," but "Congress must literally pay a price, both in treasury dollars and political capital, for such expansions").

THE NECESSITY OF FEDERAL POWER   165

for people in another might count as interstate externalities insofar as they are willing to pay to vindicate them.[136]

Congress's willingness to pay now may also help justify permitting it to operate within a more extended time horizon when spending than when regulating interstate commerce. Sometimes, the issue is the period within which a collective-action problem is likely to occur. For example, given the years required for children to grow and become part of the labor force, and given labor mobility in a modern, integrated, national economy, the collective consequences of state underinvestments in public education (and races to the bottom) likely become greater the further one looks into the future. While it may be too attenuated to conclude that a regulation of interstate commerce is justified now because of effects on national productivity in two decades, Congress's willingness to devote funds now to its long-term concerns may change the result.[137]

Granted, willingness to pay has problems of its own, and the analogy to it is imperfect.[138] Congress, after all, spends other people's money. Congress can also raise taxes to support more spending without putting itself at a competitive disadvantage relative to the states, and it can deficit spend. In addition, Congress may overstate the amount of future welfare that its current spending will secure. Even so, Congress's ability to keep spending is limited both financially and politically; it is not cost free for Congress to work its will through the spending power. Congress's need to pay in conditional-spending cases may justify a broader conception of collective-action problems than when Congress can simply regulate. Congress's need to pay is one way to understand long-standing judicial deference to congressional determinations that federal spending provides for the general welfare.

Still, Congress spends so much on so many programs in contemporary America that it may be impossible to justify some of it even on capacious collective-action grounds without sapping the idea of a collective-action problem of its distinguishing content. This conclusion seems especially sound because some federal spending to promote local welfare appears motivated by a desire to increase the reelection chances of congressional incumbents, which is an agency problem.[139] Thus, collective-action theory likely cannot account for the full scope of modern federal spending.

---

[136] For discussion of the claims in this paragraph and the two prior, see Cooter & Siegel, *supra* note 100, at 152–54; and Neil S. Siegel, *Collective Action Federalism and Its Discontents*, 92 Tex. L. Rev. 1937, 1961–64 (2013).

[137] *Cf.* United States v. Lopez, 514 U.S. 549, 563–65 (1995) (denying that the eventual link between guns in schools and national productivity permits use of the Interstate Commerce Clause to ban gun possession in schools).

[138] For discussion of the limitations of using willingness to pay as a proxy for welfare, see Cass R. Sunstein, *Willingness to Pay vs. Welfare*, 1 Harv. L. & Pol'y Rev. 303 (2007).

[139] For the canonical work that predicts the behavior of members of Congress based on the assumption that they are "single-minded seekers of reelection," see David R. Mayhew, Congress: The Electoral Connection (1974).

166   THE COLLECTIVE-ACTION CONSTITUTION

Different commentators may draw different lessons from this conclusion. Advocates of states' rights, who believe in assertive judicial review in federalism cases,[140] may let the chips fall where they may.[141] Nationalists, who believe in little or no judicial review in federalism cases, may insist that the general-welfare limitation should remain effectively nonjusticiable.[142] This author concludes that federal spending must find its justification elsewhere if it cannot be supported on collective-action grounds even broadly conceived. There may be room for agreement, however, that constitutionally conscientious members of Congress should use a collective-action lens to help guide their spending decisions and that a collective-action justification suffices to satisfy the general-welfare requirement regardless of whether it is necessary. Structural concerns inform whether it is necessary, but so do the constitutional text, originalism, practice, and precedent.

Congress as Cause of a Multistate Collective-Action Problem?

Finally, because the national treasury can be thought of as a common-pool resource, one might reason that federal spending to promote local welfare can cause collective-action problems for the states in the form of a tragedy of the commons (or a cost-benefit collective-action problem).[143] Whether pork-barrel spending constitutes a collective-action problem facing the states depends, however, on who speaks for the states, particularly when they disagree. As Chapter 1 explained, the answer is majorities in Congress, where all the states are represented. And majorities in Congress sign off on all federal spending. Because the states act collectively primarily through Congress, the Constitution does not have the structural purpose of preventing Congress from causing collective-action problems for the states. Congressional majorities can, however, cause other problems, including agency problems and exploitation of minorities.

---

[140] Calling advocates of states' rights "federalists," as is common today, invites confusion because the original Federalists were nationalists. The Anti-Federalists were defenders of states' rights.

[141] *See, e.g.*, John C. Eastman, *Restoring the "General" to the General Welfare Clause*, 4 CHAP. L. REV. 63 (2001).

[142] *See, e.g.*, Erwin Chemerinsky, *Protecting the Spending Power*, 4 CHAP. L. REV. 89 (2001).

[143] The idea that legislators may use spending (or regulations) to direct concentrated benefits to their districts (or interest groups) at the diffuse cost to the general public has the same structure as classic works in public choice theory on rent-seeking and pork-barrel politics, which emphasize the logic of concentrated benefits and diffuse costs (and diffuse benefits and concentrated costs). *See, e.g.*, MANCUR OLSON, THE LOGIC OF COLLECTIVE ACTION: PUBLIC GOODS AND THE THEORY OF GROUPS (1965); James Q. Wilson, *The Politics of Regulation, in* THE POLITICS OF REGULATION 370–71 (James Q. Wilson ed., 1984); *see also* William N. Eskridge, Jr., *Politics without Romance: Implications of Public Choice Theory for Statutory Interpretation*, 74 VA. L. REV. 275, 285–89 (1988). There are many debates about, and critiques of, the hypotheses of public choice theory.

Borrowing

With the ability to reliably raise tax revenue once the Constitution was ratified, Congress could regain sufficient credibility in European capital markets to "borrow money on the Credit of the United States,"[144] as the Borrowing Clause of Section 8 empowers it to do. Article IX of the Articles of Confederation had given the Confederation Congress borrowing authority, which was essential because the nation needed to borrow large amounts of money, mostly from the French government and Dutch bankers, to finance the Revolutionary War. On New Year's Day in 1783, the public debt of the United States was a hefty $43,000,000. The ability to borrow would also be necessary in the wars to come, which is why repayment of the Revolutionary War debts was not only a matter of fiscally sound governance but also a national-security problem.[145]

During the war, the states were able to meet Article IX's nine-state requirement to borrow money. After the war, however, obtaining the approval of nine states proved difficult. The Borrowing Clause of the Constitution addresses this collective-action problem by giving Congress the power to borrow by simple majority vote in each chamber, and it does so in sweeping language that places no limits on how Congress may exercise this authority. The clause "does not limit what debt instruments may be used, does not state how the government should finance its debt, makes no mention of repudiating debt, and does not state how credit should be maintained."[146]

Whether the federal government has the constitutional authority to assume state debts is an issue that has arisen at different times in American history, including in recent years given the increasing financial distress of state and local governments, as well as Puerto Rico. Congress assumed state Revolutionary War debts during the Washington Administration in accordance with Hamilton's proposal to finance the combined debt of the national and state governments,

---

[144] U.S. CONST. art. I, § 8, cl. 2.

[145] AMAR, *supra* note 2, at 107 ("Without the ability first to borrow money from abroad when war threatened and then to pay back the loans on time . . . America would become a tempting target for European empires lusting after dominion."); BROWNLEE, *supra* note 13, at 16–17 ("A central goal was to fund the foreign debts that the Confederation had inherited from the Revolutionary War, and to do so in a way that would win the confidence of the international financial markets to which the new nation would have to turn for capital."); *see supra* notes 1, 13, and accompanying text (discussing the existential dimension of debt repayment).

[146] Jacob Holt, *The Power to Borrow Money, in* THE POWERS OF CONGRESS, *supra* note 60, at 19. The Fourteenth Amendment limits Congress's borrowing power by prohibiting Congress from repudiating US debt ("The validity of the public debt of the United States . . . shall not be questioned."), and by barring Congress or the states from assuming or paying any debts "incurred in aid of insurrection or rebellion against the United States, or any claim for the loss or emancipation of any slaves." U.S. CONST. amend. XIV, § 4. The import of some of this language has been debated in recent decades as some members of Congress have threatened not to raise the statutory debt ceiling, causing the United States to default.

168   THE COLLECTIVE-ACTION CONSTITUTION

which amounted to $54,000,000 in 1790.[147] So, early historical practice favors congressional authority. In 1840, however, constitutional and policy objections prevented federal assumption of state debts following the Panic of 1837.[148] Moreover, "the national government has resisted outright bailouts of the states since the 1840s," although in recent decades it has provided significant financial assistance to states in economic duress.[149]

Today, there may be plausible constitutional objections to certain conditions that Congress attaches to an assumption of state debts, especially because a federal bailout gives Congress greater control over state taxing and spending decisions.[150] For various reasons, however, it seems a stretch at this late date to argue generally that Congress lacks authority to assume state debts no matter what the financial circumstances. These reasons include the aforementioned early practice and the decades-long practice of substantial federal aid to the states during recessions. These reasons also include the enormous expanse of the federal government's resources and activities today relative to the 1840s; the modern role of the states in implementing most federal programs; and the great extent to which federal law incentivizes state spending. As suggested by financing attorney Emily Johnson and Professor Ernest Young, "These developments both increase the pressure on Congress to bail out state governments and give rise to a plausible argument that it is only fair for Congress to do so."[151]

Still, difficult questions of constitutional policy endure, and a collective-action perspective can help illuminate them. On one hand, the existence of a federal "backstop" could perversely incentivize a state to make irresponsible financial decisions, given its confidence on the front end that the rest of the nation would come to its rescue should it be unable to pay its debts on the back end. Every state would have an incentive to behave this way, because each of them would internalize more benefits than costs of its own under-taxing and overspending. This is a moral-hazard problem and a collective-action problem.[152]

On the other hand, it makes structural sense for Congress to have the option of assuming state debts for reasons that became evident after the 1837 panic: all states found it challenging to borrow money after several states defaulted or repudiated their debts. If this occurred today, other states might default not due

---

[147] Holt, *supra* note 146, at 19–21. Southern Congressmen accepted federal assumption of state debts in exchange for a commitment to locate the capital on the banks of the Potomac River. DAVID P. CURRIE, THE CONSTITUTION IN CONGRESS: THE FEDERALIST PERIOD, 1789–1801, at 76–78 (1997).

[148] Holt, *supra* note 146, at 21.

[149] Emily D. Johnson & Ernest A. Young, *The Constitutional Law of State Debt*, 7 DUKE J. CONST. L. & PUB. POL'Y 117, 137–38 (2012).

[150] *Id.* at 138–46.

[151] *Id.* at 148; *see id.* at 147–48.

[152] JONATHAN A. RODDEN, HAMILTON'S PARADOX: THE PROMISE AND PERIL OF FISCAL FEDERALISM 124, 131–33 (2006). For similar advocacy of a credible commitment by Congress not to bail out states, see Paul E. Peterson & Daniel Nadler, *Freedom to Fail: The Keystone of American Federalism*, 79 U. CHI. L. REV. 253 (2012).

THE NECESSITY OF FEDERAL POWER   169

mainly to their own fiscal irresponsibility, but because they would no longer be able to borrow new money.[153] Defaults by some states can impose massive external costs onto sister states, which implies that the states must also act collectively, not just individually, to avoid defaults. When states internalize all the benefits of spending beyond their means but externalize much of the costs, the result is likely to make all or most states worse off by their own estimations than they would be if none of them overspent—meaning that there is either a Pareto or a cost-benefit collective-action problem. In an extreme case, the federal government's own international credit rating could be affected.[154] Analogizing to the Guarantee Clause of Article IV, sister states and the federal government have an abiding interest in ensuring that each state is guaranteed not just "a Republican Form of Government"[155] but also a fiscally sound one. Relative to other government institutions, Congress is best positioned to assess whether the costs associated with leaving this collective-action problem unaddressed outweigh the benefits of sticking with a "no bailout" policy and thereby avoiding the other collective-action problem.

Conclusion

This chapter has discussed the structural problems with the Articles of Confederation from the perspective of nationalist Founders who sought to facilitate collective action by states. It has also identified the primary ways in which the Framers sought to address these problems. Most notably, they approved Resolution VI of the Virginia Plan and used it as a structural guide in drafting the clauses of Article I, Section 8, which confer many powers to ameliorate multistate collective-action problems. Foremost among them is Congress's taxing power, which gives it the cash and credibility to spend and borrow, as the first two clauses of Section 8 also permit it to do.

Nationalist Founders had additional concerns, however, including the Confederation Congress's lack of authority to regulate interstate and foreign commerce. The next chapter turns to the collective-action problems that these powers have enabled Congress to solve.

---

[153] Holt, *supra* note 146, at 27.

[154] *Cf.* RODDEN, *supra* note 152, at 78–79; Peterson & Nadler, *supra* note 152, at 270. One might argue that today only a truly massive default and bailout could potentially impair the credit rating of US Treasury notes and bonds because standing behind them are the US taxpayer and a virtually limitless depth of pocket. But this may not have been true in the past, and it may not be true in the future. "This provision is made in a constitution, intended to endure for ages to come, and consequently, to be adapted to the various *crises* of human affairs." McCulloch v. Maryland, 17 U.S. (4 Wheat.) 316, 415 (1819).

[155] U.S. CONST. art. IV, § 4 (analyzed in Chapter 9).

5
Interstate Commerce, Foreign Commerce, and Related Principles

Introduction

The Articles of Confederation made it impossible for the Confederation Congress to regulate interstate and foreign commerce. Congress simply lacked these powers, and the Articles could not be amended to confer them to even a modest extent because the states had to all agree to amendments, and they never did. Moreover, the states could not act collectively outside Congress to protect themselves from trade restrictions imposed by one another and, especially, by other countries. The Constitution empowered Congress to solve these collective-action problems in the third clause of Article I, Section 8. It authorizes Congress "[t]o regulate commerce with foreign nations, and among the several States, and with the Indian tribes."

This chapter uses collective-action reasoning to explain the origins of the Interstate Commerce Clause, to critique the Supreme Court's formal distinctions in many cases interpreting this clause, and to identify a more functional replacement for the Court's approach: the distinction between collective and individual action by states. To act in the commercial sphere, this chapter argues, Congress must rationally believe that the states face a Pareto or cost-benefit collective-action problem caused by interstate spillovers with economic effects and that its intervention will help address the problem. Under this approach, *Gibbons v. Ogden* (1824)[1] is correctly decided, as are all the most important decisions from 1937 to the 1990s, including *Heart of Atlanta Motel, Inc. v. United States* (1964) and *Katzenbach v. McClung* (1964), both of which upheld the Civil Rights Act of 1964 (CRA).[2] A collective-action approach also explains why the contemporary Court has so far decided most, although not all, of its interstate-commerce cases correctly, albeit for reasons other than what its doctrine expressly states.

This chapter next questions the categorical nature of the Court's anti-commandeering principle, which prohibits Congress from requiring states to

---

[1] 22 U.S. (9 Wheat.) 1 (1824).
[2] Heart of Atlanta Motel, Inc. v. United States, 379 U.S. 241 (1964); Katzenbach v. McClung, 379 U.S. 294 (1964).

The Collective-Action Constitution. Neil S. Siegel, Oxford University Press. © Neil S. Siegel 2024.
DOI: 10.1093/oso/9780197760963.003.0006

172   THE COLLECTIVE-ACTION CONSTITUTION

enact, administer, or enforce a federal regulatory program. Collective-action reasoning is more consistent with the availability of commandeering where the states face Pareto collective-action problems because government coercion is a classic solution to such problems and all states would regard themselves as better off if collective action succeeded. Collective-action theory is also more consistent with a presumption against commandeering where the states face a cost-benefit collective-action problem because some states would view themselves as worse off if collective action succeeded and commandeering is especially coercive. But this presumption should be rebuttable because equally efficacious regulatory alternatives may not be reasonably available to Congress. By contrast, collective-action theory helps justify the Court's dormant commerce doctrine, which almost always prohibits state laws that discriminate against interstate commerce or that unduly burden it. Collective-action reasoning also explains and justifies the congressional-approval exception to the doctrine and, partially, the market-participant exception.

This chapter then uses collective-action logics to illuminate the Founding history and substantive scope of the Foreign and Indian Commerce Clauses. The states must act collectively, not individually, to act effectively in their commercial relations with other countries and Native peoples. Moreover, although originalists disagree about the meaning of the word "Commerce" in these two clauses, it makes sense to interpret this term in the way that it is structurally best understood in the Interstate Commerce Clause: to include interactions and affairs outside markets in addition to trade and other economic activities.

Finally, this chapter discusses preemption doctrine, which enforces the constitutional principle that valid federal law supersedes conflicting state law. Although aspects of the doctrine are controversial, the general principle of preemption is not, and it follows straightforwardly from a collective-action account of the Constitution.

The Interstate Commerce Clause

Under the Articles of Confederation, Hamilton diplomatically observed in *Federalist* 7, some states were "less favorably circumstanced" economically than others. For example, as Chapter 4 discussed, states with prominent ports taxed imports, raising revenue for their citizens while increasing the prices paid for imported goods by citizens in neighboring states. Hamilton feared future "[c]ompetitions of commerce" with disunion, warning that "Connecticut and New Jersey [would not] long submit to be taxed by New York for her exclusive benefit."[3]

---

[3] THE FEDERALIST NO. 7, at 62–63 (Alexander Hamilton) (Clinton Rossiter ed., 1961).

Another problem during the 1780s was trade wars between states, although historians and legal scholars disagree about the frequency and seriousness of such disputes.[4] Interstate-trade conflicts were apparently not as worrisome as the insolvency of the Confederation Congress, but Professor Van Cleve observes that "various states' trade laws favoring their citizens over noncitizens, suggest that some states thought that they could harm noncitizens with impunity."[5] Moreover, prominent nationalists seemed genuinely concerned that if Congress were not given the power to regulate interstate commerce, protectionism would proliferate. "The interfering and unneighborly regulations of some States, contrary to the true spirt of the Union, have, in different instances, given just cause of umbrage and complaint to others," Hamilton wrote in *Federalist 22*, "and it is to be feared that examples of this nature, if not restrained by a national control, would be multiplied and extended till they became . . . serious sources of animosity and discord." Madison made similar arguments. Here as elsewhere, one can dismiss such statements in *The Federalist Papers* as polemical, but Madison also expressed such concerns to himself in his *Vices Memo*.[6]

The Distinctiveness of the Interstate Commerce Clause

The third clause of Section 8 authorizes Congress to remedy and prevent state practices of economic protectionism by "regulat[ing] Commerce . . . among the several States."[7] The Interstate Commerce Clause thereby enables Congress

---

[4] *Compare generally, e.g.*, Brannon P. Denning, *Confederation-Era Discrimination against Interstate Commerce and the Legitimacy of the Dormant Commerce Clause Doctrine*, 94 Ky. L.J. 37 (2005) (defending the conventional view and identifying examples of state discrimination against interstate commerce during the 1780s), *with, e.g.*, Calvin H. Johnson, Righteous Anger at the Wicked States: The Meaning of the Founders' Constitution 189–201 (2005) (rejecting the conventional position and minimizing the role played by concerns over interstate commerce in leading to the Constitution). Denning, *supra* at 40–43, summarizes the views of prominent scholars in the debate, including John Fiske, Charles Beard, Merrill Jensen, and William Zornow.

[5] George William Van Cleve, We Have Not a Government: The Articles of Confederation and the Road to the Constitution 283 (2017).

[6] The Federalist No. 22, at 144 (Alexander Hamilton) (Clinton Rossiter ed., 1961); *see* The Federalist No. 42, at 267–68 (James Madison) (Clinton Rossiter ed., 1961) (discussing "[t]he defect of power in the existing Confederacy to regulate the commerce between its several members," and writing that without the Interstate Commerce Clause, "[w]e may be assured by past experience" that the states' practice of imposing import and export duties on articles from other states "would be introduced by future contrivances; and both by that and a common knowledge of human affairs, that it would nourish unceasing animosities, and not improbably terminate in serious interruptions of the public tranquility"); James Madison, *Vices of the Political System of the United States* (April 1787), *in* 2 The Writings of James Madison 363 (Gaillard Hunt ed., 1904) ("The practice of many States in restricting the commercial intercourse with other States, and putting their productions and manufactures on the same footing with those of foreign nations, though not contrary to the federal articles, is certainly adverse to the spirit of the Union, and tends to beget retaliating regulations, not less expensive & vexatious in themselves, than they are destructive of the general harmony.").

[7] U.S. Const. art. I, § 8, cl. 3.

174 THE COLLECTIVE-ACTION CONSTITUTION

to overcome failures by the states to act collectively to protect the commercial interests of all or most of them. Economic balkanization threatens to make all or most states in a multistate trade war worse off than they would be with free trade across state lines, as in the Prisoners' Dilemma and Asymmetric Dilemma games or the cost-benefit collective-action problems discussed in Chapter 2. By replacing state collective inaction with the capacity for congressional action, the interstate-commerce power is like Congress's other Section 8 powers.

The language of the Interstate Commerce Clause raises, however, a question that distinguishes it from Congress's other powers (except perhaps the spending power given its "general Welfare" language): whether Congress can use its interstate-commerce authority only when it legislates to solve a multistate collective-action problem. More precisely, the issue is whether commerce is interstate—"among the several States"—and so regulable by Congress only when, from Congress's perspective, there is a collective-action problem of a commercial nature facing the states. Conversely, the issue is whether commerce is intrastate—internal to a state—and so unreachable by Congress using this power when there is no collective-action problem involving commerce for it to address.

This question matters. Since 1937, the Interstate Commerce Clause has authorized Congress to target many problems that the states cannot solve on their own and that are unreachable through other enumerated powers. This clause has also empowered Congress to combat private racial discrimination and other subordination when precedent precluded use of Section Five of the Fourteenth Amendment, which authorizes Congress to remedy or prevent violations of the Equal Protection Clause.[8] Fortunately, a collective-action approach can account for the expanse and limits of the Interstate Commerce Clause in a way that tracks early and modern historical practice, most judicial precedent, and certain prominent originalist accounts.[9] One need not embrace the current Court's "economic activity" test or the utterly deferential "substantial effects" test that held sway from the 1930s to 1995. Nor need one permit Congress to internalize interstate externalities absent a link to multistate collective-action problems.

[8] The Civil Rights Cases, 109 U.S. 3 (1883) (holding that Section Five permits Congress to target only state action, not private action). The Court reaffirmed this decision in *United States v. Morrison*, 529 U.S. 598 (2000). Chapter 9 discusses congressional power to enforce the Reconstruction Amendments.

[9] For such originalist accounts, see AKHIL REED AMAR, AMERICA'S CONSTITUTION: A BIOGRAPHY 107–08 (2005); and JACK M. BALKIN, LIVING ORIGINALISM 138–59 (2011).

Collective-Action Theory and Foundational Doctrine

The Court has long struggled to distinguish between "what is truly national and what is truly local" in interstate-commerce cases, as the Court characterized its core concern in 1995 and 2000.[10] In the early nineteenth century, the Court articulated functional reasoning that appeared sensitive to collective-action logics. Writing for the Court in *Gibbons v. Ogden* (1824), Chief Justice Marshall theorized that "[t]he genius and character of the whole government seems to be, that its action is to be applied to all the external concerns of the nation, and to those internal concerns which affect the States generally."[11] Marshall defined "Commerce" as "intercourse," not just "buying and selling," and he wrote, "The word 'among' means intermingled with. A thing which is among others, is intermingled with them. Commerce among the States, cannot stop at the external boundary line of each State, but may be introduced into the interior." Yet, Marshall also explained, "[c]omprehensive as the word 'among' is, it may very properly be restricted to that commerce which concerns more States than one ... The completely internal commerce of a State, then, may be considered as reserved for the State itself."[12] Reading the Interstate Commerce Clause broadly but not limitlessly, he held that Congress could regulate navigation.

Marshall can be understood as using collective-action reasoning to achieve a sensible mean between extremes. If commerce from different states "intermingle[s]," large collective advantages accrue when states cooperate and coordinate in maintaining the channels and instrumentalities of interstate commerce, including by ensuring access and uniformity. Business firms may seek the opposite from state governments to protect themselves from competition, as happened in *Gibbons* itself, where the recipient of a state-granted navigation monopoly between parts of New York and New Jersey asserted interference by a federal licensee operating in the same waters. Like exclusionary tariffs, such policies may invite retaliation, making all states worse off from their own perspectives. For example, New Jersey would likely not long tolerate New York's grant of a monopoly on navigation between the states. Alternatively, such policies create modest individual advantages for the state imposing them and large collective costs for the rest of the states. Federal regulation of navigation, potentially including intrastate navigation (as discussed below), solves these Pareto or cost-benefit collective-action problems for the states regarding the channels and instrumentalities of interstate commerce.[13]

---

[10] United States v. Lopez, 549 U.S. 514, 567–68 (1995); United States v. Morrison, 529 U.S. 598, 617–18 (2000).

[11] 22 U.S. (9 Wheat.) 1, 195 (1824).

[12] *Id.* at 189–90, 194–95.

[13] Robert D. Cooter & Neil S. Siegel, *Collective Action Federalism: A General Theory of Article I, Section 8*, 63 STAN. L. REV. 115, 159–60 (2010).

176 THE COLLECTIVE-ACTION CONSTITUTION

Another example is the coordination problems that would likely result if the states were solely responsible for interstate infrastructure, such as the creation of the interstate-highway system. North Dakota and South Dakota might have no preference between one of two locations along their shared border for connecting the portions of the highway in their respective states, but each would obviously care whether it chose the same location as the other state. This would be a pure coordination problem. Alternatively, the two states might disagree about where the connection should occur, but they would likely still prefer coordinating to not coordinating. This situation would be best modeled as a Bridge or Seaway game. Either way, coordinating their plans so the roads meet in the same place involves a collective-action problem. So does coordinating their plans with other states. Without successful coordination, the point of an interstate-highway system is defeated. The federal government solved this problem, thereby facilitating national defense and interstate commerce, by working with the states to create a coherent interstate-highway system that linked routes in adjoining states. By ensuring coordination and providing funds, the federal government enabled a system that far surpassed what the states could have accomplished on their own.[14]

In the decades after *Gibbons*, Congress passed few laws regulating interstate commerce. Congress became active in the late nineteenth century, legislating to ameliorate perceived negative consequences of industrialization, including firms wielding monopoly power or using child labor. During the Republican Era, which lasted until 1937, a Court ideologically committed to a relatively unregulated American economy pushed back.[15] But the economic crisis of the Great Depression exploded the Court's categorical differentiations between "production" and "commerce," between "direct" and "indirect" effects on interstate

---

[14] The Public Roads Administration (PRA) "requested the States to propose routes for inclusion in the National System of Interstate Highways." After the states did so, PRA "eliminat[ed] all routes that were not justified . . . and add[ed] a small mileage at the request of the War Department." In March 1946, "a map showing this tentatively integrated system was transmitted to the States with the request that they concur in the routes as shown or propose alternates," and the states were informed that routes to which they agreed "might be regarded as tentatively established, *provided there was no reason to believe that disagreement on the part of adjacent States might jeopardize their final designation.*" By the end of the fiscal year, "acceptances had been received from 37 states and the District of Columbia," while "[s]even States had not replied officially and *four still proposed alternate routes that did not meet the routes proposed by adjoining States.*" 1942 BUREAU OF PUB. RDS., FED. WORKS AGENCY ANN. REP., WORK OF THE PUB. RDS. ADMIN. 1942, at 11 (1941–1950) (emphases added). *See* 1961 BUREAU OF PUB. RDS, DEP'T. OF COMM. ANN. REP., HIGHWAY PROGRESS 1961, at 35 (Nov. 1961) (explaining that the Bureau of Public Roads reviewed states' selection of routes); David R. Levin, *Federal Aspects of the Interstate Highway Program*, 38 NEB. L. REV. 377, 400 (1959) ("Carefully derived standards governed the selection of the routes of the National System of Interstate and Defense Highways by the State highway departments and the Bureau of Public Roads.").

[15] *See, e.g.*, BARRY FRIEDMAN, THE WILL OF THE PEOPLE: HOW PUBLIC OPINION HAS INFLUENCED THE SUPREME COURT AND SHAPED THE MEANING OF THE CONSTITUTION 150–212 (2009); DANIEL A. FARBER & NEIL S. SIEGEL, UNITED STATES CONSTITUTIONAL LAW 126–36 (2d ed. 2024).

INTERSTATE COMMERCE AND RELATED PRINCIPLES   177

commerce, between goods in and out of the "flow" of interstate commerce, and between "harmful" and "harmless" goods in interstate commerce.[16] These formal distinctions achieved the Court's objective of limiting federal power to regulate the economy, but they did so at the enormous costs of disabling the federal government from addressing serious collective-action problems for the states in the commercial realm—including during an economic catastrophe— and of imperiling the Court's legitimacy.[17]

In *Hammer v. Dagenhart (The Child Labor Case)* (1918), the Court invalidated a federal ban on the shipment in interstate commerce of goods produced by child labor, deeming irrelevant the fact that labor progressivism was causing capital flight as textile looms moved southwards. "There is no power vested in Congress to require the States to exercise their police power so as to prevent possible unfair competition," the Court insisted.[18] Moreover, as late as 1936, the year before President Franklin Delano Roosevelt (FDR) introduced his Court-packing proposal,[19] the Court in *Carter v. Carter Coal Company* dismissed the "proposition,

---

[16] On production versus commerce, see, for example, *United States v. E.C. Knight Company*, 156 U.S. 1, 12–13 (1895) (preventing the Sherman Antitrust Act from being used to thwart a monopoly in the sugar-refining industry because Congress could not regulate manufacturing, which was antecedent to commerce), and *Carter v. Carter Coal Company*, 298 U.S. 238, 303–04 (1936) (invalidating the Bituminous Coal Conservation Act of 1935 because federal regulation of wages and hours concerned production, not commerce). On direct versus indirect effects, compare, for example, *Houston, East & West Texas Railway Company v. United States (The Shreveport Rate Cases)*, 234 U.S. 342, 353 (1914) (permitting federal regulation of intrastate railroad rates because of their direct effects on interstate commerce), with, for example, *A.L.A. Schechter Poultry Corporation v. United States*, 295 U.S. 495, 523–25, 527–28, 542–51 (1935) (invalidating the Federal Live Poultry Code for New York City, which regulated the sale of diseased chickens and included wage, hour, and child-labor provisions, based on an "indirect" relationship to interstate commerce). On goods in the flow versus out, compare, for example, *Swift & Company v. United States*, 196 U.S. 375, 398–99 (1905) (upholding application of the Sherman Act to price fixing by stockyard owners), with, for example, *Schechter Poultry*, 295 U.S. at 543 (reasoning that "[s]o far as the poultry here in question is concerned, the flow in interstate commerce had ceased" because "[t]he poultry had come to a permanent rest within the state"). On harmful versus harmless goods, see, for example, *Hammer v. Dagenhart (The Child Labor Case)*, 247 U.S. 251, 268–72, 276–77 (1918) (invalidating a federal ban on the shipment in interstate commerce of goods produced by child labor because "[t]he goods shipped [were] of themselves harmless," and distinguishing decisions in which the Court upheld federal regulation as cases in which "the use of interstate transportation was necessary to the accomplishment of harmful results").

[17] The Court's distinctions were also criticized as difficult to justify (because, e.g., businesses seek monopolies over production to charge monopoly prices in commerce); difficult to apply consistently (especially the distinction between direct and indirect effects); and easy to view as ideologically biased in favor of laissez faire.

[18] *Dagenhart*, 247 U.S. at 273. *See* HUGH D. HINDMAN, CHILD LABOR: AN AMERICAN HISTORY 59 (2002); STEPHEN B. WOOD, CONSTITUTIONAL POLITICS IN THE PROGRESSIVE ERA: CHILD LABOR AND THE LAW 9 (1968); Edward Porritt, *The Cotton Mills in the South*, 18 NEW ENG. MAG. 575 (1896); Neil S. Siegel, *Free Riding on Benevolence: Collective Action Federalism and the Minimum Coverage Provision*, 75 LAW & CONTEMP. PROBS. 29, 64–65 (2012) (Issue No. 3).

[19] President of the United States, Recommendation to Reorganize Judicial Branch, H.R. Doc. No. 75–142 (1937); *see* MARIAN C. MCKENNA, FRANKLIN ROOSEVELT AND THE GREAT CONSTITUTIONAL WAR: THE COURT-PACKING CRISIS OF 1937 (2002); FRIEDMAN, *supra* note 15, at 212–36; Curtis A. Bradley & Neil S. Siegel, *Historical Gloss, Constitutional Conventions, and the Judicial Separation of Powers*, 105 GEO. L.J. 255, 269–87 (2017).

178   THE COLLECTIVE-ACTION CONSTITUTION

often advanced and as often discredited, that the power of the federal government inherently extends to purposes affecting the nation as a whole with which the states severally cannot deal or cannot adequately deal."[20] The Court in this case invalidated the Bituminous Coal Conservation Act of 1935, including its regulation of wages and hours. FDR disagreed, reasoning more persuasively that "if forty states go along with adequate legislation and eight do not . . . we get nowhere."[21]

Roosevelt lost the battle over Court-packing but fortunately defeated the Court's narrow interpretation of the Interstate Commerce Clause. By 1942, he had appointed eight justices, all committed New Dealers. The result—an unfortunate one because "[t]he enumeration" of congressional powers in Section 8 "presupposes something not enumerated"[22]—was more than a half-century of effectively unlimited federal authority. From 1937 to 1995, a nationalist Court asked only whether Congress could have rationally concluded that the regulated conduct at issue, considered cumulatively, substantially affected interstate commerce. (The aggregation principle focuses on the cumulative effects on interstate commerce of the conduct of all similarly situated people or entities, not just of the regulated party in the case.) In a modern, integrated economy and society, it is extraordinarily difficult for a federal statute to fail this test.

Notably, however, a collective-action rationale more demanding than the Court's test can account for the Court's foundational decisions during this period, some of which emphasized a multistate collective-action problem. Consider first *Wickard v. Filburn* (1942), where the Court correctly upheld federal regulation of wheat grown by farmers for home consumption. *Wickard* is controversial because home production of wheat seems local to many people, even if Congress could have rationally concluded that all such production substantially affected interstate commerce.[23] The decision looks different, however, from a collective-action perspective. Congress perceived a national problem of low wheat prices caused by the overproduction of wheat, which was harming farmers. It sought to fight deflation by limiting wheat production, thereby driving up prices. A state that imposed limits on wheat production would have disadvantaged its farmers relative to unregulated farmers in other states and likely would not have significantly raised the price in the interstate market, given all the wheat produced

---

[20]   298 U.S. at 291.

[21]   FRIEDMAN, *supra* note 15, at 208 (quoting Letter from President Franklin D. Roosevelt to David Grey (Jun. 17, 1935)); *see E.C. Knight Co.*, 156 U.S. at 45 (Harlan, J., dissenting) (insisting that a monopoly operating in multiple states "cannot be adequately controlled by any one State" and "[t]he common government of all the people is the only one that can adequately deal with a matter which directly and injuriously affects the entire commerce of the country, [and] which concerns equally all the people of the Union").

[22]   Gibbons v. Ogden, 22 U.S. (9 Wheat.) 1, 195 (1824).

[23]   *See, e.g.*, United States v. Lopez, 514 U.S. 549, 560 (1995) (describing *Wickard* as "perhaps the most far reaching example of Commerce Clause authority over intrastate activity").

INTERSTATE COMMERCE AND RELATED PRINCIPLES 179

by farmers in other states. As a result, wheat-producing states likely would have faced serious problems acting collectively to raise the price of wheat, whether due to a cooperation problem or a coordination problem.

Wheat-producing states may have failed to cooperate because, regardless of what other states did, each state may have had an incentive not to limit wheat production in its own jurisdiction, thereby externalizing the costs of its inaction onto sister states whose farmers produced wheat. In this scenario, the strategic interaction is best modeled as a Prisoner's Dilemma with numerous players. Alternatively, the wheat-producing states may have failed to coordinate because each one could not be assured that others would limit production if it did, and each would prefer not to limit production if others did not. In this situation, the best model is an Assurance Game with numerous players. Which kind of game was being played depended on whether each wheat-producing state most preferred the outcome in which only it declined to limit production or the outcome in which all such states limited production. As Chapter 2 explained, this is the only difference between the two games.

A Prisoners' Dilemma seems more probable because the incentive not to limit production remains even if states decide sequentially, whereas an Assurance Game can be solved by sequential play: the first state acts and then the second state, having received assurance, chooses the strategy corresponding to the Pareto optimal Nash equilibrium. States may require assurance, however, not only about whether other states will pass legislation limiting production but also about whether they will vigorously enforce such legislation. It may therefore be difficult to solve an Assurance Game within the time horizon of concern to state governments. Moreover, states may not know exactly what kind of game they are playing, in which case no state may be willing to move first. Regardless of the exact kind of collective-action problem, however, national regulation can effectively reduce the production of wheat.

The above analysis focused on the Pareto collective-action problem facing states that wanted to raise the price of wheat. It is the correct analysis if all states favored raising the price of wheat. But what if some states did not? What, then, about the relationship between states that supported government regulation of the wheat market and states that opposed it, perhaps because their residents— including poor residents—would have to pay more for food containing wheat if the price rose? In this scenario, for the federal law at issue in *Wickard* to have been justified under the Interstate Commerce Clause, the law had to have helped solve a cost-benefit collective-action problem for the two groups of states. Specifically, Congress had to have had a sufficient basis to conclude that states in favor of a wheat-production quota were harmed more by the absence of such a quota in each state than the other group of states were benefited. From a collective-action perspective, *Wickard* is conceptually a straightforward case. The primary

180 THE COLLECTIVE-ACTION CONSTITUTION

questions are how much basis Congress had for concluding that externalized costs exceeded internalized benefits in the states opposed to a wheat-production quota, and how deferential the Court should be to Congress's determination. As discussed further below, judges owe substantial deference to a decision by the national legislature, in which all states and interests within states are represented, that it is more important to help farmers by raising the price of wheat than it is to keep the price low for the benefit of others.

During the post-1937 period, the Court often decided interstate-commerce cases involving allegedly unfair competition. Again, collective-action reasoning best explains why they were rightly decided. As in the 1937 spending-power decisions in *Steward Machine* and *Helvering*, which were discussed in Chapter 4, a key contention in these cases was that a business practice in one state that other states deemed unfair gave businesses within this state a competitive advantage over out-of-state businesses that were prohibited from engaging in the practice. In national markets, competition advantages the lowest-cost producers. Accordingly, without federal regulation, economic pressure will cause businesses to choose practices that lower costs, such as using child labor, paying low wages, requiring employees to work many hours a week, failing to maintain a safe workplace, allowing discrimination in the workplace, and degrading the environment during the production process. Even when state governments view such practices as unfair and as reflecting huge differences in bargaining power between employers and employees, states may resist regulating because they fear putting in-state businesses at a competitive disadvantage or causing them to move to a state without such regulations.[24]

If all states are of this view, then the likely consequence is a race to the bottom or an assurance problem.[25] If, as seems more probable, most states are of this view while a minority of states favor unrestrained interstate competition for businesses, then the strategic environment is best modeled as a cost-benefit collective-action problem, not a Pareto collective-action problem. On the cost-benefit view, Chapter 4 explained, a minority of states should not be able to put

---

[24] For a history of industrial relocation from the 1930s to the 1990s chronicling one major corporation's migrations from the Northeast to the Midwest, then to the South, and finally to Mexico in search of stable, cheap, and pliable labor, see JEFFERSON COWIE, CAPITAL MOVES: RCA'S SEVENTY-YEAR QUEST FOR CHEAP LABOR (1999).

[25] For contributions to debates on races to the bottom (or top), see Kirsten H. Engel, *State Environmental Standard-Setting: Is There a "Race" and Is It "to the Bottom"?*, 48 HASTINGS L.J. 271 (1997); Daniel C. Esty, *Revitalizing Environmental Federalism*, 95 MICH. L. REV. 570 (1996); Richard L. Revesz, *The Race to the Bottom and Environmental Regulation: A Response to Critics*, 82 MINN. L. REV. 535 (1997); Richard L. Revesz, *Rehabilitating Interstate Competition: Rethinking the "Race-to-the-Bottom" Rationale for Federal Environmental Regulation*, 67 N.Y.U. L. REV. 1210 (1992); Joshua D. Sarnoff, *The Continuing Imperative (but Only from a National Perspective) for Federal Environmental Protection*, 7 DUKE ENVTL. L. & POL'Y F. 225, 278–85 (1997); and Peter P. Swire, *The Race to Laxity and the Race to Undesirability: Explaining Failures in Competition Among Jurisdictions in Environmental Law*, 14 YALE L. & POL'Y REV. 67 (1996).

competitive pressure on the majority of states because the benefits to the minority of vindicating their policy preferences are outweighed by the costs that they externalize onto the rest of the nation. (In principle, it is possible that most states prefer unrestrained competition, but in practice it is unlikely that a bill restraining competition will survive the demanding federal law-making process while reflecting the preferences of a minority of states.)

In *NLRB v. Jones & Laughlin Steel Corporation* (1937), the Court upheld the National Labor Relations Act (NLRA or Wagner Act), which protected the right of workers to unionize and bargain collectively (among other things), and which created the National Labor Relations Board to enforce the law. The Court emphasized the magnitude (not the direct or indirect nature) of the effects on interstate commerce of "the stoppage of [the steel company's] operations by industrial strife," a rationale for federal power that is potentially quite broad, given the pervasive presence of activities with substantial effects on interstate commerce. The Court might, however, have observed more narrowly that even states sympathetic to unionization might not protect unions out of fear that businesses like the steel company would leave the state rather than be subjected to higher labor costs attributable to the enhanced bargaining power of their employees.[26] Four years later, the Court invoked this "unfair competition" argument in *United States v. Darby* (1941), which concerned a constitutional challenge to the Fair Labor Standards Act of 1938 (FLSA). The FLSA prohibited, among other things, the shipment in interstate commerce of goods produced in violation of the law's minimum-wage and maximum-hour regulations. In upholding the law, the Court overruled *The Child Labor Case*.[27] Four decades later, in *Hodel v. Virginia Surface Mining & Reclamation Association* (1981), the Court articulated the same unfair-competition rationale in upholding federal regulation of environmentally destructive business practices.[28]

The Court's decision in *Perez v. United States* (1971), which upheld a federal criminal prohibition on "loan-sharking" activities (e.g., charging excessive interest and using violence or threats to collect debts), may seem difficult to justify from a collective-action perspective, and it *is* difficult to justify as applied to individual loan sharks.[29] Organized crime often engages in loan-sharking

---

[26] 301 U.S. 1, 41 (1937). In addition, as Professor Donald Regan has noted, businesses and unions may be organized on a national scale, so no one state can regulate them effectively. Donald H. Regan, *How to Think about the Federal Commerce Power and Incidentally Rewrite* United States v. Lopez, 94 MICH. L. REV. 554, 603–604 (1995). Rather, to succeed, regulation requires multistate coordination.

[27] 312 U.S. 100, 115, 122 (1941). The Court also used collective-action reasoning in upholding the 1961 amendments to the FLSA. *See* Maryland v. Wirtz, 392 U.S. 183, 190–93 (1968), *overruled by* Nat'l League of Cities v. Usery, 426 U.S. 833 (1976), *overruled by* Garcia v. San Antonio Metropolitan Transit Authority, 469 U.S. 528 (1985).

[28] 452 U.S. 264, 281–82 (1981). Note that an unfair-competition argument is potentially sound when firms responsible for environmentally destructive practices are mobile. A mine cannot, however, be moved from one state to another.

[29] 402 U.S. 146 (1971).

182 THE COLLECTIVE-ACTION CONSTITUTION

activities, however, and it characteristically operates in multiple states. In passing the Consumer Credit Protection Act, the Court noted, Congress had found that organized crime operates across state (and national) borders and generates much of its income from "extortionate credit transactions."[30] As a result, state law-enforcement officials would need to act collectively, not individually, to effectively police loan-sharking activities by interstate criminal organizations. Officials in multiple states would need to coordinate their efforts to combat criminal behavior that disrespects state boundaries; otherwise, for example, members of criminal enterprises could commit their crimes in one state and flee to another, whether temporarily or permanently. Article IV's Extradition Clause helps facilitate coordination by states in criminal law enforcement.[31] The Interstate Commerce Clause more powerfully enables coordination.

The Role of Judicial Review

The above discussion illustrates an important characteristic of collective-action reasoning when states disagree, a characteristic also evident in Chapter 3's analysis of the Interstate Compacts Clause. The situation in *Wickard*, which Congress and presumably states with many farmers regarded as a cost-benefit collective-action problem, was presumably viewed by states with few farmers and many consumers (including poor ones) as no problem at all; absent federal regulation, their residents would pay less for food containing wheat. From their perspective, federal regulation created the problem—a cartel that limited production to charge higher prices than could be obtained in a competitive market.[32] Similarly, what some states regarded as unfair competition caused by other states' permitting businesses to pay low wages and demand long hours was likely regarded by the latter states as fair competition reflecting the different interests and values of different states or regions. There is no avoiding this difficulty when states disagree about whether government regulation is warranted.

Neither the Constitution generally nor the Interstate Commerce Clause specifically chooses sides between advocates of regulation and laissez faire. Moreover, state unanimity has never been thought required for collective-action concerns to justify the creation or exercise of federal power—consider, for example, Rhode Island's and New York's opposition to change during the 1780s.

---

[30] *Id.* at 147 n.1. Typically, federal prosecutors use the Racketeer Influenced and Corrupt Organizations (RICO) statute to prosecute interstate criminal organizations. *See* Racketeer Influenced and Corrupt Organizations Act (RICO), 18 U.S.C. §§ 1961–1968.

[31] U.S. CONST. art. IV, § 2, cl. 2 (discussed in Chapter 8).

[32] Ilya Somin, *Federalism and Collective Action*, JOTWELL (Jun. 20, 2011), https://perma.cc/2WUL-PAKY.

The question, then, is which government institution is empowered to resolve disagreements. As with the Interstate Compacts Clause, the Constitution primarily assigns this power to majorities in Congress, the only legislature where all states and individuals are represented. In Congress, representatives of the states can determine whether there is a cost-benefit collective-action problem facing the states.

Framed precisely, for purposes of determining whether the Interstate Commerce Clause supports federal legislation when states disagree, the question is whether Congress rationally believes that the states face a cost-benefit collective-action problem in the commercial realm. If Congress rationally believes that a regulatory problem possesses this structure, Congress may act in a way that it rationally believes will help ameliorate the problem. The question is not whether enough states want to act collectively when Congress intervenes; there is no need to "count states" to determine whether there is a certain level of threshold support for Congress's objective. The counting takes place in Congress, where: (1) states and residents of states are represented by US Senators and Representatives, who are elected by all or some of each state's electorate and who have ties to state political parties and politicians; and (2) at least majority support is required in each chamber before bills can pass. Constitutional provisions concerning the election of members of Congress and the president, as well as pro-democratic norms that have grown around them, are important partly because they help bestow democratic legitimacy on such decisions by the federal government.[33]

As Justice Brennan wrote in his dissent in *National League of Cities v. Usery* (1976), a case in which the Court invalidated application of the FLSA to state governments on federalism grounds that did not last long,[34] "Congress is constituted of representatives in both the Senate and House *elected from the States.* . . .* Decisions upon the extent of federal intervention under the Commerce Clause into the affairs of the States are in that sense decisions of the States themselves."[35] Justice Brennan likely overclaimed to some extent, but the interests

---

[33] U.S. Const. art. I, § 2 (House elections); amend. XVII (Senate elections); art. II, § 1 (presidential elections); amend. XII (same). Presidential approval is ordinarily required to pass legislation, and democratic norms—not constitutional provisions—have enabled citizens to vote for electors and electors to respect the will of their states' voters. These norms are under pressure in the current era. *See* Neil S. Siegel, *The Trump Presidency, Racial Realignment, and the Future of Constitutional Norms, in* Amending America's Unwritten Constitution (Richard Albert et al. eds., 2022).

[34] Nine years later, in *Garcia v. San Antonio Metropolitan Transit Authority*, 469 U.S. 528 (1985), the Court rejected the *Usery* Court's position that Congress cannot use the Interstate Commerce Clause "to displace the States' freedom to structure integral operations in areas of traditional governmental functions." National League of Cities v. Usery, 426 U.S. 833, 852 (1976). The Rehnquist and Roberts Courts rejected, however, the *Garcia* Court's broader conclusion that federalism cases are nonjusticiable.

[35] *Usery*, 426 U.S. at 876–77 (Brennan, J., dissenting).

184   THE COLLECTIVE-ACTION CONSTITUTION

of states are represented in Congress. As Madison wrote in *Federalist 45*, "The State governments may be regarded as constituent and essential parts of the federal government."[36] This point is recognized even by advocates of significantly limited federal power. The scholarly debate is over the extent to which states are represented, including after the Seventeenth Amendment provided for direct election of senators, and over whether judicial safeguards are needed to protect state regulatory autonomy in addition to political safeguards.[37] As Professor Aziz Huq reports, "In the last century, states have developed an 'intergovernmental lobby,' including the Council of State Legislators and the National Governors Association, to represent their interests in the national legislative process," and "[e]mpirical studies find that this intergovernmental lobby chalks up many successes."[38]

The claim that states are represented in Congress is even more defensible once one stops anthropomorphizing states or equating states only with state governments. A "state" is a fictional person; it acts through real people who hold elective office in the state's government or in Congress, and it represents people—the people of the state. States are represented in Congress to a significant extent in the sense that the interests of both state governments and state political communities are represented there.

The Constitution does not authorize the Court to decide de novo whether there is a cost-benefit collective-action problem facing the states. The interests of all states and individuals are not represented in the Court, and it lacks the democratic warrant of even one state legislature. Thus, the Court's role is limited to determining the rationality of Congress's judgments that (1) a cost-benefit collective-action problem exists and (2) its intervention will help solve the problem. Such an approach "cues" Congress to focus on problems that have a certain structure, but it does not license courts to invalidate many laws and overturn much precedent. A properly deferential approach also substantially addresses the objection that collective-action theory tasks judges with making determinations that they are ill-suited to make.[39]

---

[36] THE FEDERALIST NO. 45, at 291 (James Madison) (Clinton Rossiter ed., 1961)).

[37] *See* Bradford R. Clark, *Separation of Powers as a Safeguard of Federalism*, 79 TEX. L. REV. 1321, 1323–25, 1342–46, 1367–72 (2001); Ernest A. Young, *Two Cheers for Process Federalism*, 46 VILL. L. REV. 1349, 1357–58 (2001). For major contributions to the literature on the political safeguards of federalism, see JESSE H. CHOPER, JUDICIAL REVIEW AND THE NATIONAL POLITICAL PROCESS 171–259 (1980); Larry D. Kramer, *Putting the Politics Back into the Political Safeguards of Federalism*, 100 COLUM. L. REV. 215 (2000); Larry Kramer, *Understanding Federalism*, 47 VAND. L. REV. 1485 (1994); Andrzej Rapaczynski, *From Sovereignty to Process: The Jurisprudence of Federalism after Garcia*, 1985 SUP. CT. REV. 341; and Herbert Wechsler, *The Political Safeguards of Federalism: The Role of the States in the Composition and Selection of the National Government*, 54 COLUM. L. REV. 543 (1954).

[38] Aziz Huq, *Does the Logic of Collective Action Explain Federalism Doctrine?*, 66 STAN. L. REV. 217, 290 (2014) (citation omitted).

[39] Neil S. Siegel, *Collective Action Federalism and Its Discontents*, 92 TEX. L. REV. 1937, 1964–66 (2013); Cooter & Siegel, *supra* note 13, at 180–83. On the cuing function of courts in federalism cases, see Jenna Bednar & William N. Eskridge, Jr., Ste*adying the Court's "Unsteady Path": A Theory*

INTERSTATE COMMERCE AND RELATED PRINCIPLES   185

Under a collective-action approach, however, basically deferential judicial review is no euphemism for nonjusticiability. When the question was whether Congress could rationally believe that the regulated activity substantially affected interstate commerce in the aggregate, the answer was always going to be "yes." Were the question to become whether Congress could rationally believe that the states face a Pareto or a cost-benefit collective-action problem, the answer would not always be "yes." For example, as will become clear in the discussion below of decisions since the 1990s, state officials do not ordinarily need to cooperate or coordinate their behavior to prevent gun possession in schools or many other crimes, nor do states typically externalize significant costs onto other states in deciding whether and how to regulate potentially criminal behavior. A collective-action analysis of federal power and intergovernmental relationships rests on realities rather than formalisms. To argue that Congress can act just because one can articulate a collective-action rationale, no matter how far-fetched, would be to treat the idea of collective action formalistically. Congress should have to offer a plausible theoretical rationale that a multistate collective-action problem exists, as well as some empirical evidence to support the rationale. The stronger the theoretical rationale, the less the evidence that should be required. And the less plausible the theoretical rationale, the more the evidence that should be required. One might call this approach reasonableness review, as opposed to toothless rational-basis review, and the references to "rational" congressional beliefs in this book are not intended to indicate otherwise.[40]

Discrimination (and Other Forms of Pollution)

In *Heart of Atlanta Motel, Inc. v. United States* (1964) and *Katzenbach v. McClung* (1964), the Court issued landmark decisions upholding the Civil Rights Act of 1964 (CRA).[41] One of the most important laws ever passed by Congress, the CRA broadly prohibits private racial (and other) discrimination in much of public life, including in employment and places of public accommodation. Because the CRA aimed to end brutal practices of racial (and other) subordination, it is

---

of Judicial Enforcement of Federalism, 68 S. CAL. L. REV. 1447, 1484 (1995); Daniel J. Meltzer, *The Seminole Decision and State Sovereign Immunity*, 1996 SUP. CT. REV. 1, 63; and Ernest A. Young, *State Sovereign Immunity and the Future of Federalism*, 1999 SUP. CT. REV. 1, 51. For an argument that collective-action reasoning in federalism cases contravenes the judicial role, see Ernest A. Young, *Protecting Member State Autonomy in the European Union: Some Cautionary Tales from American Federalism*, 77 N.Y.U. L. REV. 1612, 1647–48, 1677–82 (2002).

[40] Siegel, *supra* note 39, at 1965.
[41] Heart of Atlanta Motel, Inc. v. United States, 379 U.S. 241 (1964) (upholding application of the CRA to a motel); Katzenbach v. McClung, 379 U.S. 294 (1964) (upholding application of the CRA to a Birmingham restaurant).

186 THE COLLECTIVE-ACTION CONSTITUTION

unfortunate that both the political branches and the Court felt the need to justify the statute under the Interstate Commerce Clause and not Section Five of the Fourteenth Amendment, which empowers Congress to enforce (among other things) the Amendment's Equal Protection Clause. The interstate-commerce power was deemed the path of least constitutional resistance to upholding the CRA because the Court had held broadly in *The Civil Rights Cases* (1883) that Congress may not target private discrimination when using its Section Five power, and the CRA did just that.[42]

Even so, from a collective-action perspective, the Court correctly held that the CRA was valid commerce-power legislation. This is (of course) not because collective-action problems impeded the ability of all states, Southern ones included, to champion racial equality and facilitate the interstate mobility of African Americans. Given Southern (and other) opposition to the CRA, there was no Pareto collective-action problem.

Turning to potential cost-benefit collective-action rationales, one might be inclined to argue that unfair-competition arguments justified the CRA. Antidiscrimination provisions that cover the workplace may increase the costs of doing business by, for example, requiring firms to offer equal pay for equal work, educate employees about discrimination, accommodate employees requiring accommodation, police problematic behavior, keep records, and defend against lawsuits. Thus, states may be disinclined to impose such costs on employers operating within their jurisdictions unless a certain number of other states do the same. In other words, competitive pressures can impede a state from trying to end discrimination in the workplace.

An important question, however, is whether an unfair-competition argument described reality in the 1960s, given how strongly held were the convictions of many people who opposed or defended racial discrimination. If states (and their representatives in Congress) on both sides of the issue did not care enough about differential competitiveness effects to change their views on the propriety of banning racial discrimination in places of public accommodation, an unfair-competition argument must be stretched too far to cover the CRA and related statutes. Today, it may be implausible to justify federal antidiscrimination protections primarily on such grounds. For example, whether states ban discrimination based on sexual orientation or gender identity may not be greatly affected by concerns about potentially putting in-state businesses at a competitive disadvantage. Although businesses do not like being sued, the business community tends to pressure conservative states to be less discriminatory on such matters.[43] The reasons are likely related to the success of federal law in protecting

---

[42] 109 U.S. 3 (1883) (discussed in Chapter 9).

[43] Susan S. Kuo & Benjamin Means, *The Political Economy of Corporate Exit*, 71 VAND. L. REV. 1293, 1295–96, 1320–25 (2018) (documenting the role of corporations in defeating proposed or

INTERSTATE COMMERCE AND RELATED PRINCIPLES   187

the nationalized market. Because big business plays to the national market for profit reasons, it tends to resist market balkanization and to appeal to the national market even if the opposite view is strongly held in some states.[44]

This observation suggests that, even absent competitiveness concerns that dissuade most states from prohibiting discrimination, another cost-benefit collective-action problem justifies use of the Interstate Commerce Clause to combat discrimination. The Court's 1964 decisions were lawful because Southern racism impeded the ability of most other states to protect interstate travel by African Americans, and the Interstate Commerce Clause lets Congress settle disagreements among states about whether collective action is warranted in the commercial sphere—and to pursue this objective when achieving it would benefit the rest of the states in the Union more than it would harm popular majorities in Southern states.

Most states in 1964 wanted to create a national free-trade zone in which their own labor forces could move freely throughout the zone; businesses within their jurisdictions could efficiently distribute labor and capital within the zone; and their residents could travel for business and leisure throughout the zone.[45] All these goals were and remain important to most states in a modern, national economy and society: the unrestricted mobility of goods, services, capital, labor, and leisure around a very large land area goes far toward explaining the nation's remarkable economic performance for more than 150 years and related increases in the quality of life of most Americans over this period.[46]

Accomplishment of these ends requires access to, and safe passage through, national transportation networks. These goals are undermined by discrimination in certain states or regions because state governments, businesses, individuals, and families must account for the discrimination in determining whether, when, and how potential victims of discrimination will move interstate.[47] The *Green*

enacted laws in Georgia, Indiana, and North Carolina that prohibited transgender individuals from using bathrooms corresponding to their gender identity or allowed businesses to deny service to people based on their sexual orientation or gender identity).

[44] For an argument that the Civil Rights Act of 1964 is constitutional on coordination grounds, see Maxwell L. Stearns, *The New Commerce Clause Doctrine in Game Theoretical Perspective*, 60 VAND. L. REV. 1, 66–69 (2007); and Leslie Meltzer Henry & Maxwell L. Stearns, *Commerce Games and the Individual Mandate*, 100 GEO. L.J. 1117, 1148–50, 1157–58 (2012).

[45] For example, in *Heart of Atlanta*, California argued that its "industry is a prime recipient of government contracts, which can necessitate travel to the nation's capital or defense installations in other states"; that "Californians serve in the armed forces of our nation, which frequently requires them to travel through and reside in sister states"; that Californians, "in the course of their business and employment, must utilize places of public accommodation throughout the United States"; and that Californians engage in "interstate travel for educational and recreational purposes." Brief of the State of California as Amicus Curiae at 5–6, Heart of Atlanta Motel, Inc. v. United States, 379 U.S. 241 (1964) (No. 515), 1964 WL 81384, at *5–6 (footnotes omitted).

[46] Siegel, *supra* note 39, at 1946–47; Cooter & Siegel, *supra* note 13, at 149–50, 161 n.60.

[47] In addition, rampant discrimination can cause mass migrations from one region to another— and led to the Great Migration of African Americans to Northern cities. Such migrations can bring

188   THE COLLECTIVE-ACTION CONSTITUTION

Book, which helped African Americans find accommodations on the road in the Jim Crow South, underscores the impediments to travel that Southern states imposed.[48] Congress's intervention to combat Southern interference with safe access to, and the effective functioning of, national transportation networks exemplifies a broader trend: many interstate-commerce cases have involved congressional efforts to regulate the channels and instrumentalities of interstate commerce or activities affecting them.[49]

A focus on cost externalization by Southern states obviates the need to tie certain acts of discrimination to specific channels of, or effects on, interstate commerce. The Court in *McClung* stressed the dollar value of the food sold by the restaurant that had moved interstate.[50] This approach was more awkward when the Court upheld the CRA's application to a snack bar in a club,[51] and the approach was constitutionally unnecessary, given the Court's emphasis in *Heart of Atlanta* and *McClung* on the difficulties that African Americans had experienced traveling interstate.[52]

Professor Donald Regan, who endorses the result in *McClung* based on congressional power to enforce the Reconstruction Amendments, deems "strained at best" the argument that discrimination by Ollie's Barbecue in *McClung* burdened interstate travel by African Americans. He emphasizes the lack of evidence that the restaurant served interstate travelers and the lack of reason to think that it did, given its location many blocks from an interstate highway.[53] It would seem difficult, however, to confidently say whether a particular restaurant has served interstate travelers; restaurants cannot reasonably be required to ask customers for such information, and customers may not answer anyway.

---

with them not just benefits to the receiving states but also lower wages, housing shortages, and greater discrimination. BALKIN, *supra* note 9, at 167–68. These negative interstate externalities further contributed to the cost-benefit collective-action problem.

[48] *See, e.g.*, Celia McGee, *The Open Road Wasn't Quite Open to All*, N.Y. TIMES (Aug. 22, 2010), http://www.nytimes.com/2010/08/23/books/23green.html, on file with author at https://perma.cc/TW3N-8U4C.

[49] In addition to *Heart of Atlanta* and *McClung*, examples include *Gibbons v. Ogden*, 22 U.S. (9 Wheat.) 1 (1824), and *Houston, East & West Texas Railway Company v. United States* (*The Shreveport Rate Cases*), 234 U.S. 342 (1914).

[50] *McClung*, 379 U.S. at 296–305.

[51] Daniel v. Paul, 395 U.S. 298 (1969).

[52] *Heart of Atlanta Motel, Inc.*, 379 U.S. at 252–53; *McClung*, 379 U.S. at 300. Congress wrote the hotel and restaurant provisions differently. Hotels, motels, and inns were deemed to "affect commerce" if they "provide[d] lodging to transient guests." Restaurants were deemed to "affect commerce" only if they served or offered to serve interstate travelers, or if a substantial portion of the food they served or the products they sold moved in interstate commerce. *Heart of Atlanta Motel, Inc.*, 379 U.S. at 247–48. It is therefore unsurprising that the Court made the interstate movement of the food a key part of its analysis in *McClung* but did not feature the proximity of the motel to an interstate highway in *Heart of Atlanta*. Instead, the Court began its opinion in *Heart of Atlanta* by noting the close proximity, *id.* at 243, likely for rhetorical reasons.

[53] Regan, *supra* note 26, at 601.

Nor is it reasonable to assume that interstate travelers will always hew closely to the interstate highway when they want to eat, particularly when they stay overnight. Further, they may be deterred from traveling interstate by the knowledge that rampant discrimination exists once one moves a certain distance from the highway. Moreover, they could reasonably expect a hostile reception in such states even at restaurants formally open to them. Congress, at least, could rationally draw such conclusions, and it likely could gather evidence supporting them.

To be sure, governing racial groups in Southern states during the 1960s did not share the goals described above to the point of being willing to compromise their racism, and the same may be true of some states or regions today regarding other discrimination. But neither did all states share the objective of abandoning the Articles of Confederation, raising the price of wheat, or preventing employers from paying low wages, demanding long hours, or harming the environment. Again, the Interstate Commerce Clause empowers Congress to solve not only Pareto collective-action problems but also cost-benefit collective-action problems.

Similarly, economically productive activity in one state generates pollution that often crosses state lines.[54] When this happens, the state producing the pollution and the state being polluted may not both want to reduce pollution. Only one state is being harmed by it, and the other state is benefiting from the activity that generates it.[55] Further, the states may disagree on how to balance economic development and environmental protection. Even so, because the pollution migrates across state borders, Congress may combat it if it rationally concludes that the externalized costs exceed the internalized benefits. As with racial discrimination, this rationale for much federal environmental regulation supplements concerns about unfair competition.[56]

A key lesson of the discussion in this section is that use of the Interstate Commerce Clause to combat discrimination is not pretextual just because Congress also has moral motivations for its interventions. Regardless of whether Congress has authority under the Reconstruction Amendments to protect people from private discrimination, the Interstate Commerce Clause is available when the states face a collective-action problem in the commercial sphere.[57]

---

[54] JAMES SALZMAN & BARTON H. THOMPSON, JR., ENVIRONMENTAL LAW AND POLICY 25 (5th ed. 2019) ("Air pollution, water pollution, and wildlife certainly pay no heed to state (or national) borders, with the result that often the generator of the pollution is politically distinct from those harmed.").

[55] *Id.* (discussing the difficulty of controlling acid rain in the 1970s–1980s and the pollution of lakes and forests in the Northeast and Canada by midwestern power plants).

[56] For an argument that spillover effects justify federal regulation, see Richard Revesz, *Federalism and Interstate Environmental Externalities*, 144 U. PA. L. REV. 2341 (1996).

[57] Chapter 9 discusses congressional power under the enforcement clauses of the Reconstruction Amendments.

190 THE COLLECTIVE-ACTION CONSTITUTION

Contemporary Doctrine: Economic versus Interstate

Just as certain changes in constitutional politics produced nationalist Courts in the decades after 1937, so also different changes during the 1980s and early 1990s produced a five-justice majority that, for the first time since 1936, imposed some limits on the Interstate Commerce Clause. In *United States v. Lopez* (1995), the Court invalidated a federal criminal ban on gun possession in school zones.[58] In *United States v. Morrison* (2000), the Court held that Congress could not empower victims of gender-motivated violence to sue their assailants for damages in federal court.[59] In both cases, the Court essentially grafted onto prior decisions—none of which it overruled—a requirement that the regulated activity in question (in these cases, gun possession in schools and gender-motivated violence) be "commercial" or "economic" in nature, or (as in *Wickard*) be "an essential part of a larger regulation of economic activity, in which the regulatory scheme could be undercut unless the intrastate activity were regulated."[60] In *Gonzales v. Raich* (2005), the Court permitted Congress to prohibit the local cultivation and use of marijuana in compliance with state law permitting such use for medicinal purposes. The Court relied upon *Wickard*, which it read as "establish[ing] that Congress can regulate purely intrastate activity that is not itself 'commercial,' in that it is not produced for sale, if it concludes that failure to regulate that class of activity would undercut the regulation of the interstate market in that commodity." The Court saw "striking" similarities between *Raich* and *Wickard*: Congress could have rationally concluded that leaving home-consumed wheat or marijuana outside the regulatory scheme would affect interstate price and market conditions, particularly through unlawful diversion of the commodity into the market.[61]

Since 1995, then, the Court has purported to distinguish between general classes of "economic" activity, which Congress may regulate using its interstate-commerce power, and general classes of "noneconomic" activity, which Congress may not reach using this power. Unless the Court first concludes that the general class of regulated activity is economic, it will deem irrelevant whether Congress could have rationally concluded that the effects of this activity on interstate commerce are substantial. Judging only from what the Court has said,

---

[58] 514 U.S. 549 (1995).

[59] 529 U.S. 598 (2000). The Court also held the provision beyond Section Five of the Fourteenth Amendment. Chapter 9 critiques this part of *Morrison*.

[60] *Lopez*, 514 U.S. at 561. More precisely, the Court permitted use of the aggregation principle only when the regulated conduct was economic. *Morrison*, 529 U.S. at 613. But because Congress can almost always rationally conclude that the regulated activity substantially affects interstate commerce once the effects of the intrastate activity are aggregated, the result was to make the characterization of the regulated activity dispositive.

[61] 545 U.S. 1, 18–19 (2005).

the doctrine provides that if the Court thinks the regulated activity (or the general class of which it is a part) is economic and so "Commerce," it is also "among the several States" (given rational basis review of this question) and so within this enumerated power. The formal issue of categorization ostensibly answers the functional question of substantial effects on interstate commerce.

The Court's economic-activity test has worrisome vulnerabilities, but before identifying them, it is important to appreciate its strengths. The test respects two fundamental principles of the Constitution, both of which draw support from *Gibbons*. First, Congress enjoys broad power to regulate using this clause, including to regulate the national economy. Second, this power is not unlimited; in Chief Justice Marshall's canonical formulation, "[t]he enumeration presupposes something not enumerated."[62] Fidelity to both principles requires the Court to find a judicially administrable and substantively defensible way to separate what is and is not within Congress's interstate-commercial power. The Court's test accomplishes these tasks to a nontrivial extent. It crafts a relatively formal rule that judges can apply without needing to make difficult judgment calls in most cases (unlike the pre-1937 distinction between direct and indirect effects). It also identifies a reasonable domain of "usually beyond Congress" matters, especially ordinary crime.[63] Moreover, in further contrast to the often meaningless pattern of pre-1937 doctrine, excluding ordinary criminal-law enforcement from congressional power serves an identifiable constitutional goal. Decentralizing such enforcement takes a serious tool of potential tyranny away from the federal government.

There is a basic problem with the distinction between economic and noneconomic activity, however, and it becomes evident once one appreciates what primarily motivates the distinction: the Court has repeatedly said it must distinguish the "truly national" from the "truly local."[64] Economic conduct does not generally cause collective-action problems for the states, and noneconomic conduct is not generally free from collective-action problems. Consequently, Congress is not generally better at regulating economic conduct, and the states are not generally better at regulating noneconomic conduct. The distinction between economic and noneconomic conduct is both over- and underinclusive with respect to whether commerce is "national" or "local"—whether it is among the several states or within each state. A better way to distinguish the "national" from the "local" is to consult collective-action logics, which draw this

---

[62] *Gibbons v. Ogden*, 22 U.S. (9 Wheat.) 1, 195 (1824).

[63] Examples of ordinary crime include theft, assault, and gun possession by students in a school, as in *Lopez*.

[64] *Morrison*, 529 U.S. at 617–18; *Lopez*, 514 U.S. at 567–68; *see id.* at 564 (emphasizing that if Congress can regulate gun possession in schools, then Congress can regulate anything).

192 THE COLLECTIVE-ACTION CONSTITUTION

distinction by contrasting problems whose solution would require collective action by states with problems regarding which individual action by states would suffice.[65]

Even so, perhaps the fact that the economic-activity test sorts some similar activities into different categories, and some different activities into the same category, is a price worth paying to prevent the Interstate Commerce Clause from collapsing into its underlying justifications and so licensing nearly unlimited congressional power. As Chapter 4 explained, Article I, Section 8, replaced Resolution VI to avoid this problem. There are, however, two difficulties with this defense of the doctrine.

First, the overinclusiveness and especially the underinclusiveness of the Court's economic-activity test can really matter. Regarding overinclusiveness, the outcome in *Lopez* should not change just because Congress subsequently adds a jurisdictional element to the statute providing that it applies only when the gun "has moved in or . . . otherwise affects interstate or foreign commerce."[66] This requirement will always, or nearly always, be satisfied, and as explained below, the states can handle gun possession in school zones regardless of whether a jurisdictional element is satisfied.[67] The same is ordinarily true of many other crimes.

Regarding underinclusiveness, troubling questions arise. For example, can Congress protect the environment from degradation not caused by economic actors, such as the contamination of drinking water by naturally occurring arsenic that flows to other states, or the pollution of non-navigable interstate waters by private landowners located in one state, or the killing by private individuals of endangered species that migrate?[68] Can Congress prohibit arsons that spark forest fires across state borders?[69] Can Congress reach the many noneconomic uses of interstate networks of transportation and communication? Can Congress require mask-wearing during a pandemic given a mobile population and demilitarized state borders? Can Congress, where no market exists and no money changes hands, criminalize behavior often preceded by the interstate transport of victims—like the practice of female genital mutilation

[65] Cooter & Siegel, *supra* note 13, at 116, 118, 164, 184.

[66] Act of Sept. 30, 1996, Pub. L. No. 104-208, § 657, 110 Stat. 3009-369 (Gun Free School Zones Act of 1996).

[67] Much federal criminal-law enforcement depends on the use of jurisdictional elements, and the suggestion here is not to demolish such use. But in a circumstance where a jurisdictional element can be satisfied by the happenstance that something moved at some point in interstate commerce, and that happenstance has no relationship to the matter Congress seeks to address that is not otherwise within its interstate-commerce power (like firearms in schools), it is not clear why the jurisdictional element renders the statute constitutional.

[68] Cooter & Siegel, *supra* note 13, at 172–73.

[69] *Cf.* Jones v. United States, 529 U.S. 848 (2000) (practicing constitutional avoidance by construing a federal law criminalizing the arson of "any building . . . used in interstate or foreign commerce or in any activity affecting interstate or foreign commerce" not to apply to the arson of a private residence).

(FGM)?[70] Can Congress prohibit the "mere" possession of deadly pathogens? Can Congress ban the unleashing of communicable diseases?

The answer to some of these questions under the Court's doctrine may be "yes." The Court has permitted use of jurisdictional elements, and it might accept certain prohibitions on possession as a necessary and proper way to enforce prohibitions on sale. Moreover, the Court might permit Congress to reach certain kinds of noneconomic activity (e.g., mask-wearing during recreation) to make effective its regulations of economic activity (e.g., mask-wearing while working or shopping).[71] The Court also permits Congress to protect the channels and instrumentalities of interstate commerce. But it is uncertain whether such arguments, where potentially available, would succeed regarding some of the above problems, and these arguments will not be even potentially available regarding all these problems and other structurally similar ones. Just as importantly, the doctrine imparts seriousness and gravity to these questions, and so provides the opportunity for judicial and political mischief that threatens to leave no level of government capable of addressing a pressing problem effectively. In 2018, for example, a federal district court held that a federal statute criminalizing FGM was unsupported by the Interstate Commerce Clause, and the Trump administration declined to appeal because it thought no reasonable argument could be made for the law's constitutionality.[72] Moreover, if one wants to find a way to answer these questions affirmatively, it is likely due to the sense that Congress can better address the problems than the states can, not that the conduct really is economic.

The second difficulty with the administrability defense of the doctrine is that it exaggerates how much more determinate the Court's test is than collective-action reasoning. As discussed below, it is much easier to describe certain problems than others as having the objective structure of a cooperation game, a coordination game, or a cost-benefit collective-action problem, particularly if one imposes reasonable limits on Congress's discretion to extend the time horizon within which it reasons about collective-action problems. Moreover, difficult questions can arise regarding how to apply the Court's test. One problem is determining what the regulated activity is. Why, for example, was it not regulation of firearms in certain sensitive workplaces in *Lopez*, given all the teachers,

---

[70] The text expresses uncertainty because FGM "often occur[s] under a shroud of secrecy." Daniel Rice, *Female Genital Mutilation and the Treaty Power: What Congress Can Do*, JUST SECURITY (Oct. 29, 2019), https://perma.cc/BDG7-LYPD.

[71] The argument would be that Congress can require mask-wearing by the vast swath of people who will engage in some sort of economic activity while out in public and that to make this mask-wearing requirement effective, Congress can sweep in everyone out in public regardless of their individual intentions or actions.

[72] United States v. Nagarwala, 350 F. Supp. 3d 613 (E.D. Mich. 2018). On the Trump administration's position, see Rice, *supra* note 70.

194 THE COLLECTIVE-ACTION CONSTITUTION

counselors, administrators, administrative assistants, cafeteria staff, janitors, coaches, and so on who work in schools and who can die in school shootings? Another difficulty is determining whether the regulated activity is economic. Why, for example, is marriage, the general regulation of which the Court would not let Congress take from the states, not an economic activity, given the financial considerations that inform whether, when, and for how long people marry and the tax and other financial consequences that an individual's marital status can have? Still another challenge is deciding upon the level of abstraction at which to define the relevant market—the level of generality at which to determine whether the class of regulated activity is economic. The Court in *Wickard* and *Raich* handled this problem by deferring to Congress's reasonable understanding of the general class of activity at issue (the interstate wheat and marijuana markets, respectively). As explained below, however, the Court did not defer in *NFIB v. Sebelius* (2012), where Congress sought to ensure access to the health-care market and the Court focused on the health-insurance market.[73]

Notwithstanding these concerns, if the Court's distinction between economic and noneconomic activity is still somewhat easier to apply than the distinction between collective and individual action by states, the best defense of the doctrine is that it is an imperfect but relatively administrable proxy for a collective-action approach. This understanding can help courts decide cases where it is uncertain whether the (general class of) regulated activity should be described as economic. To date, the Court has tended to use its economic-activity test this way.[74] For example, enforcing a ban on firearms within school zones, unlike suppressing an interstate market for firearms, does not require cooperation or coordination among law enforcement in different states.[75] Nor is it plausible to assert that states externalize significant costs onto sister states by failing to regulate guns in schools to the same extent as the federal law invalidated in *Lopez*. The Court correctly deemed the conduct local. Only by extending the time horizon decades into the future could one plausibly contend that federal regulation of firearms in schools is justified on collective-action grounds. The argument would be that states that do not effectively address violence in schools will produce less-well-educated students, and such states will eventually externalize significant costs onto sister states because some of these students will move to other

---

[73] 567 U.S. 519 (2012). *See* Siegel, *supra* note 18, at 55–56 (explaining how opponents and defenders of the federal health-care law defined the market differently).

[74] There is another context in which the Court uses the issue of whether something is "economic" as a questionable proxy. The doctrinal test for determining the level of scrutiny applicable to vagueness challenges requires courts to decide, inter alia, whether a challenged regulation is "economic." Vill. of Hoffman Ests. v. Flipside, Hoffman Ests., Inc., 455 U.S. 489 (1982). This inquiry seems a poor proxy for what the Court cares about, which is whether the regulated parties are sophisticated actors who can fairly be held to a higher standard of notice. For a doctrinal critique and reconstruction, see Daniel B. Rice, *Reforming Variable Vagueness*, 23 J. CONST. L. 1, 13–20 (2021).

[75] Cooter & Siegel, *supra* note 13, at 164.

states later in life and be less productive members of the labor force than they otherwise would have been. A reasonable collective-action test will reject this argument for federal regulation under the Interstate Commerce Clause.

Raich, by contrast, involved a potential spillover problem in the present and not-too-distant future, given the inability to differentiate medical marijuana from recreational marijuana and the marijuana market's disrespect for state borders. Just as Congress gets to decide whether production is too high or competition is unfair if it rationally concludes that externalized costs exceed internalized benefits, so it gets to decide that an interstate drug market should be suppressed without medicinal exceptions if it rationally makes the same determination. States that permit marijuana use likely undermine the efforts of neighboring states to enforce their bans on marijuana use.[76] Accordingly, a collective-action test would authorize Congress both to suppress an interstate drug market and to reach intrastate conduct that Congress rationally believes will undermine its suppression of this market if left out of the regulatory scheme.

The Court in *Raich* seemed to sense the interstate nature of the problem, but the doctrine required it to describe the cultivation or use of marijuana not produced for sale as part of a larger regulation of economic activity. The Court could have said that such marijuana was part of a larger regulation of *interstate* activity.[77] The distinction between collective and individual action by states seemed to be doing the analytical work in *Lopez* and *Raich*. Justice Anthony Kennedy may have also been reasoning from a collective-action perspective when he wrote in *Lopez* that "the reserved powers of the States are *sufficient* to enact" laws prohibiting firearm possession in schools.[78] Their reserved powers suffice because the states need not act collectively to regulate guns in schools.

Morrison is intermediate between *Lopez* and *Raich*. In *Morrison*, Congress found that gender-motivated violence "deter[s] potential victims from traveling interstate."[79] The Court moved quickly past this finding, apparently because it understood it to be just another reason offered by Congress to explain why gender-motivated violence substantially affects interstate commerce—which is how Congress presented it—an argument that the Court deemed irrelevant.[80]

---

[76] *See, e.g.*, Nebraska v. Colorado, 577 U.S. 1211, 1214 (2016) (Thomas, J., dissenting from the denial of motion for leave to file complaint) (noting Nebraska's and Oklahoma's allegations that a Colorado constitutional amendment facilitating recreational use of marijuana "has 'increased trafficking and transportation of Colorado-sourced marijuana' into their territories, requiring them to expend significant 'law enforcement, judicial system, and penal system resources' to combat the increased trafficking and transportation of marijuana" (citation omitted)).

[77] SANFORD LEVINSON ET AL., PROCESSES OF CONSTITUTIONAL DECISIONMAKING: CASES AND MATERIALS 698 (8th ed. 2022) (suggesting this substitution).

[78] *Lopez*, 514 U.S. at 581 (Kennedy, J., concurring) (emphasis added). *See* Regan, *supra* note 26, at 566 (suggesting this reading of Justice Kennedy's statement).

[79] *Morrison*, 529 U.S. at 615; *see id.* at 634 (Souter, J., dissenting).

[80] *Id.* at 615 (majority opinion) (quoting the House Report's findings that gender-motivated violence substantially affects interstate commerce "by deterring potential victims from traveling

196 THE COLLECTIVE-ACTION CONSTITUTION

The Court's reaction can be contrasted with its response in *Heart of Atlanta* and *McClung* to Congress's deterrence-of-interstate-travel finding in support of the CRA. Had the Court in *Morrison* registered that this congressional finding was different from, and more limited than, the others (and had it found this finding plausible), it would have been unlikely to write that "if Congress may regulate gender-motivated violence, it would be able to regulate murder or any other type of violence."[81] Crimes do not ordinarily deter interstate travel, and so murder and other violence are, at least in general, potentially distinguishable from gender-motivated violence. Like in *Lopez*, the Court seemed to care most that the problem was "intrastate,"[82] not noneconomic, although if it may have erred regarding the geographic scope of the problem.

Whether *Morrison*'s interstate-commerce holding is correct depends on: (1) whether Congress could have rationally concluded that gender-motivated violence deters interstate travel; and, if so, (2) whether the states that were failing to take such violence seriously were externalizing significant costs onto other states, which were trying to facilitate safe interstate travel by women. These are questions regarding the geographic scope and intensity of the problem of gender-motivated violence, not a question of characterization regarding the economic or noneconomic nature of gender-motivated violence. The interstate-commerce issue in *Morrison* might have been decided differently had the Court considered whether it found reasonable Congress's finding that gender-motivated violence deterred women from traveling interstate.

Overall, should a collective-action approach replace the Court's distinction between economic and noneconomic activity? Although such an assessment requires balancing incommensurable considerations, the answer is likely "yes". Like the economic-activity test, understanding the phrase "among the several States" to mean "a collective-action problem facing the states" avoids the interpretive extreme of dramatically limiting interstate-commerce power, as would some conservative originalist accounts notwithstanding long-standing doctrine, contrary practice, and the widely perceived needs of modern American governance. Also like the economic-activity test, such an understanding avoids the opposite extreme of effectively licensing unlimited interstate-commerce

---

interstate, from engaging in employment in interstate business, and from transacting with business, and in places involved in interstate commerce; . . . by diminishing national productivity, increasing medical and other costs, and decreasing the supply of and the demand for interstate products") (citation omitted); *id.* (rejecting these findings because they reflect "reasoning" that "seeks to follow the but-for causal chain from the initial occurrence of violent crime (the suppression of which has always been the prime object of the States' police power) to every attenuated effect upon interstate commerce").

[81] *Id.*
[82] *Id.* at 618.

INTERSTATE COMMERCE AND RELATED PRINCIPLES   197

power, as would some liberal nationalist accounts notwithstanding more recent decades of doctrine and the widely shared view that the Interstate Commerce Clause does not confer a general police power.[83] As between the two tests, it bears repeating that a collective-action inquiry best reflects the structural principle in Resolution VI of the Virginia Plan—the regulatory goals that Congress is structurally better situated to accomplish than the states. Moreover, because the Court's application of the economic-activity test seems more functionally focused on the geographic scope of the problem than the Court admits, a collective-action approach is more transparent; it thus provides better guidance to governments, lower courts, and litigants. These advantages probably outweigh the possibility that the economic-activity test is more administrable than a collective-action approach.

But what about the word "Commerce" in the Interstate Commerce Clause? Perhaps, relative to a collective-action approach, the economic-activity test better respects the core economic meaning of this term and so the authority of the constitutional text more broadly. Note, however, that the Court's doctrine effectively ignores the phrase "among the several States" in the text, and so it can lay no claim to greater textual fidelity. As for fidelity to the meaning of the term "Commerce" specifically, there is a long-standing debate among scholars and jurists—from *Gibbons* to the present—over whether the original meaning of this word is (1) limited to trade (the most restrictive view); or (2) also includes all economic conduct (the Court's view); or (3) also includes the interaction or exchange of people and ideas outside markets, which encompasses commercial intercourse in all its branches as well as networks of transportation and communication (the most expansive view). Serious arguments and impressive evidence have been compiled by proponents of each theory.[84] The first view, as discussed at the outset of this chapter, reflects the primary concerns of nationalist Framers and other Founders: interstate-trade restrictions. Advocates of the other two theories insist, however, that the original meaning of the word "Commerce" was not limited to the primary concerns animating its inclusion in

---

[83] Determining what is an interpretive virtue or vice becomes more complex if the Court has interpreted another power too narrowly, increasing pressure on the Interstate Commerce Clause to do more work. If the Court has defined congressional power under Section Five of the Fourteenth Amendment too narrowly, which Chapter 9 argues, then the test for the Interstate Commerce Clause should potentially be more permissive than it otherwise should be. This chapter does not consider such doctrinal path dependence.

[84] For defenses of the trade theory, see *Lopez*, 514 U.S. at 584–86 (Thomas, J., concurring); and RANDY E. BARNETT, RESTORING THE LOST CONSTITUTION: THE PRESUMPTION OF LIBERTY 291–93 (2004). For a defense of the economic theory, see Grant S. Nelson & Robert J. Pushaw Jr., *Rethinking the Commerce Clause: Applying First Principles to Uphold Federal Commercial Regulations but Preserve State Control over Social Issues*, 85 IOWA L. REV. 1 (1999). For defenses of the interaction or exchange theory, see BALKIN, *supra* note 9, at 138–59; and AMAR, *supra* note 9, at 107–08.

198 THE COLLECTIVE-ACTION CONSTITUTION

the constitutional text.[85] The economic-activity test aligns with the second position, and a collective-action approach is most compatible with the third.

This book, unlike strictly originalist accounts, does not choose among these alternatives based only on originalist considerations. If one supplements originalist reasoning with structural analysis, there is much to be said for Professor Amar's and Professor Balkin's broad interpretation of "Commerce" as including exchanges of people and ideas outside of markets—as including interactions and affairs—in addition to trade and other economic activity. This approach makes it least likely that Congress will be powerless to address what it views as serious collective-action problems facing the states. Moreover, as explained below, this approach avoids difficulties in interpreting the Foreign and Indian Commerce Clauses if the term "Commerce" means the same thing in all three clauses.

In addition, there is a link between the third approach and the economic component of "Commerce." It would be sensible to understand the "Commerce" requirement to be satisfied where the spillovers that create collective-action problems produce economic effects. Such spillovers can be called material externalities, in contrast to the psychological externalities discussed in Chapter 4 as possibly justifying certain federal spending as advancing the "general Welfare."[86] The Rehnquist Court changed the interstate-commerce inquiry from whether the regulated activity has economic effects to whether it is economic activity. The suggestion here is to ask whether the states face a collective-action problem caused by spillovers that produce economic effects. "Welfare" is a more general category than "Commerce," and so federal spending arguably need not be constrained by an inquiry into the materiality of the interstate externalities at issue.

Finally, a collective-action approach to the Interstate Commerce Clause does not render the rest of Article I, Section 8, superfluous. This is so for two reasons. First, this clause authorizes Congress to regulate—to pass laws imposing duties on individuals and entities. Many other Section 8 powers authorize Congress to solve collective-action problems for the states by nonregulatory interventions, such as spending federal tax revenue, coining money, providing for the national defense, and conferring intellectual-property rights.

Second, regarding regulatory interventions, it bears repeating that a collective-action approach limits use of the Interstate Commerce Clause. For example, if Congress wants to regulate activities absent multistate collective-action problems, it must use another power (like the Taxing Clause), which may

---

[85] *See, e.g.,* BALKIN, *supra* note 9, at 153; Robert J. Pushaw, Jr. & Grant S. Nelson, *A Critique of the Narrow Interpretation of the Commerce Clause,* 96 NW. U. L. REV. 695, 700 (2002).

[86] U.S. CONST. art. I, § 8, cl. 1.

INTERSTATE COMMERCE AND RELATED PRINCIPLES   199

be an imperfect substitute. As Chapter 4 explained, federal taxing authority is both broader than the interstate-commerce power because it permits taxation absent multistate collective-action problems and narrower because it prohibits coercion.

Contemporary Doctrine: Regulating versus Requiring Commerce

In *NFIB v. Sebelius* (2012), the Court added to its economic/noneconomic distinction an additional limitation on the Interstate Commerce Clause. The Court distinguished between the regulation of activity and inactivity—between *regulating* interstate commerce, which the Court permits, and *requiring* interstate commerce, which it forbids. Fearful of virtually unlimited federal power if Congress could require individuals allegedly doing nothing to purchase a product such as health insurance from a third party, the Court read the word "regulate" in the Interstate Commerce Clause as including prohibitions and permissions on behavior but excluding requirements.[87] Applying this distinction, the Court concluded that the clause did not support the minimum coverage provision in the Affordable Care Act (ACA). As Chapter 4 discussed, this provision required individuals to purchase health insurance (the so-called individual mandate) or pay for not doing so (the shared responsibility payment).[88]

The ACA sought to achieve near-universal health-insurance coverage in the United States. None of the litigants disputed that the Interstate Commerce Clause supports the ACA provisions that prohibit insurance companies from denying coverage based on preexisting conditions, canceling insurance absent fraud, charging higher premiums based on medical history, and imposing lifetime limits on benefits.[89] Congress added the individual mandate and shared responsibility payment ("mandate" for short) to reduce the incentive that these other provisions give financially able individuals without insurance to free ride on healthy people with insurance by entering the market only when they require

---

[87] *NFIB*, 567 U.S. at 552 (opinion of Roberts, C.J.) (worrying that permitting congressional regulation of inactivity "would open a new and potentially vast domain of congressional authority").

[88] *Id*. at 551–52 (opinion of Roberts, C.J.). Chief Justice Roberts wrote alone on this point, but the four dissenters agreed with him (and so were not dissenters regarding the point). *See* 567 U.S. at 649–50 (Scalia, Kennedy, Thomas, & Alito, JJ., dissenting).

[89] United States v. South-Eastern Underwriters Ass'n, 322 U.S. 533, 540–41 (1944) (permitting use of the Interstate Commerce Clause to regulate insurance markets); *see* Siegel, *supra* note 18, at 33, 61–62. As explained below, these ACA provisions solve multistate collective-action problems by discouraging the flight of insurance companies from states that guarantee access to states that do not; discouraging older and sicker people from moving in the opposite direction; disincentivizing states from free riding on the more generous health-care systems of sister states; and facilitating labor mobility. *Id*. at 61–66.

200 THE COLLECTIVE-ACTION CONSTITUTION

expensive care. Health economists call such market-timing behavior "adverse selection" in insurance markets.[90]

In considering whether the mandate was supported by the Interstate Commerce Clause or the Necessary and Proper Clause, the Court seemed unconcerned that Congress could rationally believe that cost-benefit collective-action problems would impair the ability of states to maintain near-universal health-insurance coverage within their jurisdictions. If some states tried to do so (call them "mini-ACA" states) while others did not, older and sicker people would move to mini-ACA states to obtain coverage, and (more speculatively) some number of younger and healthier people might move out of mini-ACA states to avoid having to buy insurance. Given the effects of such movements on the composition of the risk pool in mini-ACA states—and like arguments about unfair competition in prior cases— some number of insurance companies would likely move from mini-ACA states to states that did not prohibit them from controlling their costs in traditional ways. All these movements in both directions would likely raise the costs of health insurance (through higher premiums) for everyone in the mini-ACA states and lower the costs in the other states, undermining the objective of the mini-ACA states to expand access to affordable health insurance and so health care. Moreover, to combat rising premiums by covering part of the higher costs of providing health-care services, mini-ACA states would likely need to cut services or raise taxes, further incentivizing healthier, younger residents and businesses to leave the state. Even states that wanted to become mini-ACA states would likely face economic pressure to hold back and externalize costs onto other states that sought to become mini-ACA states.[91]

Congress could have rationally believed that there were other negative interstate externalities being imposed on mini-ACA states. Just as the CRA has facilitated the interstate mobility of African Americans and others, so prohibiting insurance companies from controlling their costs in traditional ways facilitates labor mobility by ensuring that people will not lose affordable health-insurance coverage if they move interstate to pursue job opportunities.[92] Health economists call insurance-based impediments to labor mobility "job lock."[93]

Given the likelihood of the foregoing spillover effects, it is unsurprising that, before Congress intervened, only Massachusetts had instituted what the ACA accomplished nationally. When Massachusetts passed health-care reform, it had a relatively low number of uninsured residents, a relatively healthy economy, and ample financial resources.[94] It therefore had sufficient market power to prevent

[90] CHARLES E. PHELPS, HEALTH ECONOMICS 271–72 (6th ed. 2018).
[91] Siegel, *supra* note 18, at 61–66.
[92] BALKIN, *supra* note 9, at 177.
[93] PHELPS, *supra* note 90, at 277–78.
[94] Siegel, *supra* note 18, at 66–68.

both insurers and younger, healthier residents from leaving the state, notwithstanding its imposition of an individual mandate. Most states were not so fortunate. The regulatory environment was different from the one in *Lopez*, where Justice Kennedy underscored that "over forty states already have criminal laws outlawing the possession of firearms on or near school grounds."[95] In *NFIB*, Justice Ginsburg seemed correct in her dissent on this issue that the "[s]tates cannot resolve the problem of the uninsured on their own," and "Congress's intervention was needed to overcome this collective-action impasse."[96]

A collective-action account of the Interstate Commerce Clause can accommodate *NFIB* by viewing it as imposing an independent limit on congressional power akin to other such limits. But the theory can also be used to critique the activity-inactivity distinction for making it harder for Congress to address serious problems that the states are likely incompetent to address effectively on their own. Even if, in retrospect, the individual mandate was not needed to accomplish health-care reform, Congress still rationally imposed it, given the previous exodus of insurance companies from states that banned coverage denials based on preexisting conditions without imposing a mandate.[97] More generally, national mandates—like mandatory vaccination during a pandemic—may be needed to solve certain multistate collective-action problems, given the relative ease with which many Americans can cross state (or national) lines, and so the likelihood that states with deregulatory policies will externalize high costs onto other states. True, the Court did ultimately uphold the mandate under the Taxing Clause, but for reasons already discussed, the two powers are not perfect substitutes. The Taxing Clause may not be used to coerce and thereby ensure that people obtain insurance (or get vaccinated).

A collective-action account cannot refute the argument that the activity/inactivity distinction is simply required by the Constitution, but other arguments can. For example, it is questionable whether there is an activity/inactivity distinction in the context of Congress's Section 8 powers. As Chapter 1 explained, Congress possesses long-standing authority to impose various mandates to secure collective action. It is also questionable whether the uninsured are generally inactive, given the tens of billions of dollars' worth of health-care services they receive each year without paying for them, thereby significantly raising

---

[95] *Lopez*, 514 U.S. at 581 (Kennedy, J., concurring).

[96] *NFIB*, 567 U.S. at 594, 595 (Ginsburg, J., concurring in part, concurring in judgment in part, and dissenting in part). Justice Ginsburg quoted amicus briefs reporting that emergency rooms in Massachusetts were serving thousands of uninsured, out-of-state residents, imposing millions of dollars in costs each year. *Id.* at 595. *See* Siegel, *supra* note 18, at 59–61 (offering examples of cross-state hospital use).

[97] Siegel, *supra* note 18, at 65–66. In 2017, Congress reduced the payment for noninsurance to $0, leaving the rest of the ACA intact. Dire consequences for insurance companies have apparently not ensued. *See* California v. Texas, 141 S. Ct. 2104 (2021) (holding after this legislative change that the plaintiffs lacked standing to challenge the minimum coverage provision).

insurance premiums for households.[98] As noted, whether the uninsured are inactive depends partly on whether one focuses on their relation to the health-insurance market or the health-care market.[99] The question also turns on the time horizon within which one asks it. These distinctions are famously manipulable in many areas of law if courts do not defer to reasonable legislative judgments. Because the activity/inactivity distinction turns on a manipulable verbal characterization, it risks reproducing the pointlessness of most of the pre-1937 case law, unlike the constitutional goal served by decentralizing ordinary criminal law enforcement.

Abortion Regulation and the Interstate Commerce Clause

In *Dobbs v. Jackson Women's Health Organization* (2022), the Court overruled *Roe v. Wade*, the 1973 decision that initially protected the right of pregnant women to abort a nonviable fetus; *Planned Parenthood of Southeastern Pennsylvania v. Casey*, the 1992 decision that reaffirmed the core of this right; and many other decisions that vindicated the right for decades.[100] Because the Court no longer regards the right as protected under Section One of the Fourteenth Amendment, its doctrine would not permit Congress to protect abortion access under Section Five—or, for that matter, to ban abortion using Section Five.[101] This sea change in constitutional law raises the question of whether Congress can use the Interstate Commerce Clause to protect—or deny—abortion access nationally.

One might be tempted to argue that national legislation regulating access to abortion would combat a destructive race to the bottom—that is, a Pareto cooperation problem. In the wake of the Court's decision, conservative states have increasingly passed significant restrictions on abortion access; liberal states have increasingly moved to protect such access; and pregnant women have increasingly traveled from conservative states to liberal ones to obtain abortions. Not since before the Civil War have the states been so divided over a moral question that involves the movement of individuals across state lines. In such an environment, one can expect a cycle of state legislative responses and counterresponses, including attempts by states to regulate abortion beyond their borders and efforts by other states to thwart such regulation. For example, the Center for

---

[98] *See* Siegel, *supra* note 18, at 55–56.

[99] *See supra* note 73 and accompanying text.

[100] Dobbs v. Jackson Women's Health Org., 142 S. Ct. 2228 (2022) (overruling, *inter alia*, Roe v. Wade, 410 U.S. 113 (1973), and Planned Parenthood of Se. Pa. v. Casey, 505 U.S. 833 (1992)).

[101] City of Boerne v. Flores, 521 U.S. 507 (1997) (holding that statutory rights provided by Congress under Section Five of the Fourteenth Amendment must be "congruent and proportional" to violations of constitutional rights protected under Section One as the Court understands Section One).

Reproductive Rights reports that "[i]nterstate shield laws protect abortion providers and helpers in states where abortion is protected and accessible from civil and criminal consequences stemming from abortion care provided to an out-of-state resident."[102] Congressional intervention could put a stop to interstate conflict escalation.[103]

Given the intensity of the disagreements among states over access to abortion, however, it seems implausible to suggest that there is a Pareto collective-action problem. Instead, the issue seems to be whether, given the fundamental right of Americans to travel interstate,[104] there is a cost-benefit collective-action problem. The existence of significant negative interstate externalities could authorize Congress to protect or prohibit access to abortion.

Regarding a federal law protecting abortion rights nationwide, states that ban abortion incentivize pregnant women who live within their borders to travel interstate (if they have the resources) to obtain a lawful, safe abortion. Such interstate travel, by increasing the demand for reproductive health-care services in other jurisdictions, threatens to undermine the efforts of sister states to ensure effective, timely access to abortion. The demand for such services may outstrip the supply or result in long wait times before women can obtain abortion services. Accordingly, antiabortion states might impose significant negative externalities on states that seek to protect access to abortion.[105] The only way to achieve a truly secure pro-choice regime in "blue" states, especially those that border "red" states, might be to do it nationally.

Note, however, that this collective-action argument for a federal law protecting abortion rights depends on out-of-state demand for abortion putting pressure on in-state supply on more than a very temporary basis. The mere fact that there

---

[102] Center for Reproductive Rights, *After* Roe *Fell: Abortion Laws by State* (Glossary), https://perma.cc/P6H7-MXMR.

[103] One might argue that states that ban (protect) abortion in effect free ride on the public goods provided by states that protect (ban) abortion, such as less economic vulnerability and so less need for public assistance (or a higher population and so a larger eventual workforce). These cooperation rationales seem more speculative, however, than the cooperation rationale developed in the text.

[104] Chapter 9 discusses the three components of the right to travel. For an overview of the interjurisdictional conflicts that will likely arise in a nation without constitutionally protected abortion rights, see David S. Cohen, Greer Donley, & Rachel Rebouché, *The New Abortion Battleground*, 123 Colum. L. Rev. 1 (2023).

[105] *Dobbs*, 142 S. Ct. at 2345 n.25 (Breyer, Sotomayor, & Kagan, JJ., dissenting) ("[I]ncreased out-of-state demand [for abortion] will lead to longer wait times and decreased availability of services in States still providing abortions. This is what happened in Oklahoma, Kansas, Colorado, New Mexico, and Nevada last fall after Texas effectively banned abortions past six weeks of gestation" (citation to an amicus brief omitted).); *see* Margot Sanger-Katz et al., *Interstate Abortion Travel Is Already Straining Parts of the System*, N.Y. Times (Jul. 23, 2022), https://www.nytimes.com/2022/07/23/ups hot/abortion-interstate-travel-appointments.html, on file with author at https://perma.cc/3NEH-BGN5; Angie Leventis Lourgos, *Abortions in Illinois for Out-of-State Patients Have Skyrocketed: And Some Wait Times Are Exceeding Three Weeks*, Chicago Tribune (Aug. 2, 2022), https://www.chicago tribune.com/news/breaking/ct-illinois-abortion-increase-post-roe-20220802-eottdwcfnjfjxdvbfgd 4kwefwu-story.html, on file with author at https://perma.cc/L852-7JHH.

204   THE COLLECTIVE-ACTION CONSTITUTION

is regulatory disuniformity, such that some states offer a good or service while others do not, does not suffice to create a cost-benefit collective-action problem.

Regarding a federal prohibition on abortion nationwide, pregnant women who have the financial means can (as noted) thwart their home state's ban on abortion by traveling interstate to obtain an abortion. Accordingly, pro-choice states might impose significant negative externalities on states that seek to ban abortion. The only way to enact a truly secure antiabortion regime in "red" states, especially those that are near "blue" states, might be to do it nationally.[106]

There is no value-neutral way for Congress or a court to assess whether the benefits to states that protect (or ban) abortion exceed the costs that such states externalize onto other states with the opposite view of the issue. This is not just a question of fact, although facts (such as the amount of pressure on "blue"-state supply of abortion services or the amount of avoidance of "red"-state prohibitions on abortion services) are relevant in any rational cost-benefit calculus. In a prior century, enslaved people in Maryland could thwart their state's laws protecting slavery by escaping to Pennsylvania to be free. Today, defenders and opponents of abortion rights debate whether banning abortion is more akin to allowing slavery or prohibiting it. Under the Interstate Commerce Clause, majorities in Congress get to decide this moral question, including by crafting a compromise formation, and to assign values to the internalized benefits and externalized costs of different state regulatory regimes based in part upon this moral judgment. In constitutional litigation, a court should defer to whatever rational cost-benefit judgment Congress makes. Again, Congress is where all states, and all interests within states, are represented.

The Court's economic-activity test also allows both nationwide protection of abortion access and a national ban because obtaining an abortion is presumably considered economic activity; it typically involves the provision of health-care services in exchange for money.[107] Further, the liberal nationalist view of the Interstate Commerce Clause would allow national protection or a national ban because Congress could rationally believe that the provision of abortion services substantially affects interstate commerce in the aggregate. There may be no doctrinal test that would prevent national pro-choice or antiabortion legislation without also devastating many other important federal laws enacted under the interstate-commerce power.

---

[106] *Cf. Dobbs*, 142 S. Ct. at 2309 (Kavanaugh, J., concurring) ("[M]ay a State bar a resident of that State from traveling to another State to obtain an abortion? In my view, the answer is no based on the constitutional right to interstate travel.").

[107] For example, Congress used its interstate-commerce power to pass the Partial-Birth Abortion Ban Act of 2003, which was at issue in *Gonzales v. Carhart*, 550 U.S. 124 (2007) (rejecting a facial individual-rights challenge).

The Anti-commandeering Principle

The Court's anti-commandeering doctrine categorically prohibits Congress from requiring states to enact, administer, or enforce a federal regulatory program.[108] Under a collective-action approach to the Interstate Commerce Clause, the uncompromising nature of the doctrine is problematic. Congress should be able to commandeer state legislatures and executives to solve Pareto collective-action problems, and there should be a presumption against commandeering when Congress seeks to solve cost-benefit collective-action problems. The presumption should be rebuttable where Congress lacks a regulatory alternative that would be about as efficacious.

The constitutional text imposes no commandeering limitation on Congress. Scholars and jurists dispute how much originalist support the doctrine enjoys, including whether the Constitution only expanded congressional power or also withdrew the authority to commandeer states, and whether there is a constitutional difference between commandeering state legislatures and state executives. Commentators and judges also dispute whether the Court is correct that the doctrine does and should maintain clear lines of accountability between the federal government and the states, and whether the Court enforces accountability values selectively.[109]

The collective-action theory developed in this book reflects the conviction that the Constitution substantially expanded federal power. Because it is a nonoriginalist account, however, it will not canvas all the nuanced originalist arguments on both sides, including the potential significance of the point that the Articles of Confederation permitted the commandeering of state legislatures (requisitions), but only regarding taxes and troops.[110] It seems problematic for all originalist argumentation that few leaders at the Founding likely imagined that commandeering could succeed absent the use of military force against the states. The situation is different today.

The political-accountability rationale for the doctrine is questionable. Either reasonable accountability concerns can be addressed by telling citizens which government is responsible for which regulations, or it is difficult to understand why federal preemption (discussed at the end of this chapter) and

---

[108] New York v. United States, 505 U.S. 144 (1992); Printz v. United States, 521 U.S. 898 (1997); Murphy v. National Collegiate Athletic Ass'n, 138 S. Ct. 1461 (2018).

[109] For treatments on both sides of these and other issues, see the cases cited *supra* note 108 and, for example, Evan H. Caminker, *State Sovereignty and Subordinacy: May Congress Commandeer State Officers to Implement Federal Law?*, 95 COLUM. L. REV. 1001 (1995); Vicki C. Jackson, *Federalism and the Uses and Limits of Law: Printz and Principle*, 111 HARV. L. REV. 2180 (1998); H. Jefferson Powell, *The Oldest Question of Constitutional Law*, 79 VA. L. REV. 633 (1993); Saikrishna Prakash, *Field Office Federalism*, 79 VA. L. REV. 1957 (1993); and Neil S. Siegel, *Commandeering and Its Alternatives: A Federalism Perspective*, 59 VAND. L. REV. 1629 (2006).

[110] Prakash, *supra* note 109, at 1974–88.

206   THE COLLECTIVE-ACTION CONSTITUTION

conditional spending (discussed in the previous one) do not also raise accountability concerns of similar significance, a proposition that the Court has never
embraced.[111] Nor do the vertical and horizontal constitutional structures seem
designed to preserve accountability; the Constitution's several diffusions of
power seem more likely to encourage blame-shifting for the passage and enforcement of unpopular regulations.

Although the accountability rationale is unpersuasive, the anti-
commandeering principle makes structural sense insofar as it helps preserve
the states' regulatory autonomy, which collective-action limits on the Interstate
Commerce Clause also seek to protect.[112] (Whether the anti-commandeering
doctrine succeeds in this regard depends partly on whether not being
commandeered frees the states up to regulate as they wish, and partly on whether
Congress passes preemptive legislation when it cannot commandeer.[113]) The
categorical bar on commandeering is less structurally sound when it impairs
Congress's ability to solve what it rationally believes are multistate collective-
action problems, especially Pareto collective-action problems, in which all states
would be better off by their own estimations if collective action succeeded.

New York v. United States (1992) involved a Pareto collective-action problem
facing the states. "Radioactive material is present in luminous watch dials, smoke
alarms, measurement devices, medical fluids, research materials, and the protective gear and construction materials used by workers at nuclear power plants,"
Justice O'Connor explained for the Court in this case. "Low level radioactive
waste is generated by the Government, by hospitals, by research institutions,
and by various industries." Because "[t]he waste must be isolated from humans
for long periods of time, often for hundreds of years," it must be disposed of in
special facilities.[114] In *New York*, the three states with disposal facilities opposed
continuing to receive waste from the rest of the country. Instead of building their
own regional disposal facilities, forty-seven states were free riding on the disposal efforts of these three states. Because all states wanted to continue to attract
the businesses and institutions that produced the waste, the states faced a Pareto
collective-action problem—a NIMBY ("not in my backyard") problem. As
Chapter 2 explained, government coercion of group members is a classic solution
to Pareto collective-action problems, even if Congress had not commandeered
much before *New York*. The Court nonetheless held that Congress could not
require the states to arrange for the safe disposal of low-level radioactive waste
produced within their borders.[115] Such coercion was justified in *New York*,

---

[111] Siegel, *supra* note 109, at 1631–33.
[112] Powell, *supra* note 109, at 681–88.
[113] *See generally* Siegel, *supra* note 109.
[114] 505 U.S. 144, 149–50 (1992).
[115] The Court did identify permissible alternatives to commandeering: giving funds to the
states conditional on their agreement to be commandeered; making states choose between being

however, because all states would have been better off by their own estimations if collective action succeeded. As Justice White wrote in dissent, the federal law at issue in *New York* "resulted from the efforts of state leaders to achieve a state-based set of remedies to the waste problem. They sought not federal pre-emption or intervention, but rather congressional sanction of interstate compromises they had reached."[116]

By contrast, *Printz v. United States* (1997) likely involved a possible cost-benefit collective-action problem. The question presented, which the Court answered in the negative, was whether Congress could require state and local law-enforcement officials to conduct background checks on would-be handgun buyers until a federal computer database was operational.[117] Given the controversiality of gun-control measures, states were presumably divided over government background checks for individuals who wanted to purchase firearms. Because many individuals can travel interstate to buy firearms and return home, states that did not conduct background checks, such as at gun shows, were externalizing costs onto neighboring states. If these external costs exceeded the internal benefits to the states that declined to conduct background checks, there was a cost-benefit collective-action problem. Because some states would regard themselves as worse off if collective action succeeded, commandeering, which is especially coercive of states, should have been presumptively unavailable to Congress. The issue in *Printz* should have been whether regulatory alternatives were reasonably available to Congress, and the answer was no: preemption was impossible until the federal database was online, and noncoercive conditional spending would likely not have been as effective as commandeering, given state discretion to decline the funds. So *Printz*, like *New York*, was wrongly decided, albeit for different reasons.

In *Murphy v. National Collegiate Athletic Association* (2018), the Court invalidated a federal law prohibiting states from allowing sports gambling.[118] Given disagreements among states regarding the permissibility of sports gambling, there was at most a cost-benefit collective-action problem, not a Pareto collective-action problem. Moreover, a regulatory alternative was reasonably available: Congress could have itself prohibited sports gambling instead of barring states from permitting it. Accordingly, *Murphy* was correctly decided.

---

commandeered and being preempted; and preempting state law. But the Court did not examine their likely efficacy in solving the collective-action problem. *Id.* at 166–68.

[116] *Id.* at 189–90 (White, J., dissenting). *See* Vicki C. Jackson, Seminole Tribe, *The Eleventh Amendment, and the Potential Evisceration of* Ex Parte Young, 72 N.Y.U. L. Rev. 495, 541–42 (1997) (In *New York* . . . , the record of state participation in resolving an ongoing problem at a national level through legislation to which states as such significantly contributed is clear.").

[117] 521 U.S. 898 (1997).

[118] 138 S. Ct. 1461 (2018).

208   THE COLLECTIVE-ACTION CONSTITUTION

Collective-action reasoning, which has a strong structural, textual, historical, and doctrinal pedigree, suggests that the Court should permit commandeering to solve Pareto collective-action problems and should impose a presumption against commandeering, not a flat ban, when Congress seeks to solve cost-benefit collective-action problems. This presumption can be overcome when Congress rationally believes that there is a cost-benefit collective-action problem and regulatory alternatives are unlikely to be about as effective. Possible situations in which commandeering may be needed to address multistate collective-action problems, in addition to the facts of *New York* and *Printz*, include a deadly flu pandemic, a natural disaster in a region, or a terrorist attack in multiple states. In these scenarios, time is of the essence, and federal officials may require the help of state officials to successfully execute their responsibilities: the states have the most "boots on the ground" because the overwhelming majority of law-enforcement officials in the nation work for state and local governments.[119] Thus, adequate alternatives to commandeering may be unavailable.

Even when commandeering is justified, however, Congress should have to pay the states what it costs them to be commandeered. Just as the Takings Clause requires just compensation when government takes private property,[120] so also the Constitution requires just compensation when Congress "takes" state regulatory authority. Requiring Congress to internalize the costs of commandeering helps ensure that Congress does not over-commandeer.[121] Granted, if the costs of regulatory compliance are high, being preempted can cost states more than being commandeered. But there is no structural presumption against the states' being preempted, as discussed at the end of this chapter.

The Dormant Commerce Principle

Collective-action theory illuminates the Court's doctrine under the Dormant (or Negative) Commerce Clause. In *New York*, the three states with waste-disposal facilities could not have embargoed out-of-state waste because of the constitutional constraints on state laws imposed by the dormant commerce doctrine. Since the Marshall Court, the Court has developed, reimagined, and applied its dormant commerce doctrine to limit state and local power to affect interstate commerce when Congress's interstate-commerce power is "in its dormant state."[122]

---

[119] Siegel, *supra* note 109, at 1630, 1655, 1684–88; *see* FARBER & SIEGEL, *supra* note 15, at 170–71.
[120] U.S. CONST. amend. V.
[121] Siegel, *supra* note 109, at 1644–45; *see Printz, supra* note 108, at 975–76 (Souter, J., dissenting) (reading *Federalist 36* as requiring Congress to pay for commandeering).
[122] The term originates in Chief Justice Marshall's opinion in Willson v. Black Bird Creek Marsh Company, 27 U.S. (2 Pet.) 245 (1829), which held that a Delaware law permitting a dam that blocked

Today, the doctrine almost always prohibits state and local laws that discriminate against out-of-state producers or unduly burden interstate commerce. Dormant commerce cases usually involve state regulations or taxes that have the purpose or effect of giving a competitive advantage to in-state economic actors over their out-of-state counterparts. Courts are virtually certain to invalidate state laws that discriminate against interstate commerce.[123] State laws that instead burden interstate commerce are substantially more likely to survive judicial review; courts apply relatively deferential scrutiny and will strike down such laws only if they conclude that the burdens on interstate commerce exceed the public-regarding benefits of the law—primarily public health, safety, road conservation, or environmental protection.[124] As discussed below, however, collective-action concerns explain why the Court has invalidated state laws that burden the use of national transportation networks by trucks and railroads. Collective-action concerns also explain why the Court should review nondiscriminatory state laws that effectively seek to impose the states' moral or policy views on the rest of the nation by leveraging their market share.

Text, History, Structure, and Democratic Legitimacy

The dormant commerce doctrine had greater textual support during the Marshall Court, when prominent jurists thought there was "great force" to the argument that Congress had exclusive power to regulate interstate commerce.[125] This view has long been rejected, so the textual argument for the doctrine is relatively weak

---

a small navigable stream was a valid exercise of the state's police power and so was not "repugnant to the power to regulate commerce in its dormant state." *Id.* at 252. The Marshall Court distinguished between Congress's commerce power and the states' police power. This distinction did not endure. Nor did the distinction in *Cooley v. Board of Wardens*, 53 U.S. (12 How.) 299 (1852), between subjects requiring uniform national regulation, meaning Congress's commerce power is exclusive, and subjects demanding diverse local regulation, meaning states have concurrent authority.

[123] Nat'l Pork Producers Council v. Ross, 143 S. Ct. 1142, 1153 (2023) ("Today, this antidiscrimination principle lies as the 'very core' of our dormant Commerce Clause jurisprudence.") (quoting Camps Newfound/Owatonna, Inc. v. Town of Harrison, 520 U.S. 564, 581 (1997)).

[124] *Compare, e.g.*, Philadelphia v. New Jersey, 437 U.S. 617 (1978) (invalidating a state law that facially discriminated against interstate commerce by prohibiting the importation of certain waste originating outside the state), *with, e.g.*, South Carolina State Highway Dept. v. Barnwell Brothers, 303 U.S. 177 (1938) (upholding a nondiscriminatory state law limiting truck size to improve safety and road conservation).

[125] *Gibbons v. Ogden*, 22 U.S. (9 Wheat.) 1, 209 (1824). *See* City of New York v. Miln, 36 U.S. (11 Pet.) 102 (1837) 102, 158–61 (1837) (Story, J., dissenting) (embracing the exclusive-power theory after Marshall's death and contending that it had been Marshall's view); Barry Friedman & Daniel T. Deacon, *A Course Unbroken: The Constitutional Legitimacy of the Dormant Commerce Clause*, 97 VA. L. REV. 1877, 1882 (2011) (finding "plain textualist and originalist support for the dormant Commerce Clause," given the early understanding of the Interstate Commerce Clause as exclusive).

210 THE COLLECTIVE-ACTION CONSTITUTION

today, as Justice Thomas has emphasized.[126] But the originalist case for the doctrine is strong. The concerns expressed by Hamilton and Madison about state economic warfare (or worse) if the Constitution were not ratified partially justifies the doctrine, as the Court has repeatedly underscored.[127]

Structural concerns also support the doctrine and connect it to the Interstate Commerce Clause. A cost-benefit collective-action problem caused by negative interstate externalities is at the core of any state regulation that benefits in-staters less than it harms out-of-staters. A Pareto cooperation problem is also at the core of any state regulation that provokes sister states to retaliate, resulting in conflict escalation and making the states as a whole worse off. "If New York, in order to promote the economic welfare of her farmers, may guard them against competition with the cheaper prices of Vermont," the Court wrote in *Baldwin v. G.AF. Seelig, Inc.* (1935), "the door has been opened to rivalries and reprisals that were meant to be averted by subjecting commerce between the states to the power of the nation."[128] Further, as explained below, solutions to coordination problems involving networks of transportation can be impeded when a state imposes regulations incompatible with the related regulations of sister states.

For these reasons, the Court's dormant commerce doctrine is best viewed today as enforcing a structural principle of constitutional law—a collective-action principle for the most part. It should be called the "dormant commerce principle," not the Dormant Commerce Clause or the Negative Commerce Clause. According to this principle, the constitutional structure authorizes the federal courts to act as Congress's agent when its declines to exercise its interstate-commerce power to solve collective-action problems for the states. Until Congress intervenes, the federal courts prevent states from causing collective-action problems for one another through protectionism or the imposition of certain burdens on interstate commerce.

The strongest argument against the dormant commerce doctrine is not a lack of textual warrant, but a potential lack of democratic warrant. The federal courts lack the democratic legitimacy of Congress and so one might ask why they get to resolve disagreements among states when there are potential cost-benefit collective-action problems. On the other hand, it would likely be impossible for Congress to police state protectionism nearly as well as the courts can, given that

---

[126] *See, e.g.*, South Dakota v. Wayfair, 138 S. Ct. 2080, 2100 (2018) (Thomas, J., concurring) (again rejecting the Court's "entire negative Commerce Clause jurisprudence").

[127] *See supra* note 6 and accompanying text (quoting Hamilton and Madison); *see, e.g.*, Granholm v. Heald, 544 U.S. 460, 472 (2005) (emphasizing the "tendencies toward economic Balkanization that had plagued relations among . . . the States under the Articles of Confederation" (quoting Hughes v. Oklahoma, 441 U.S. 322, 325–26 (1979))); H.P. Hood & Sons, Inc. v. Du Mond, 336 U.S. 525, 533 (1949) (same). As explained, the Court may have overstated matters: scholars debate how much protectionist legislation states passed during the 1780s. There were at least some such instances, however, and serious people warned about future protectionism if the Constitution were rejected.

[128] 294 U.S. 511, 522 (1935).

they can act more quickly and contextually, focusing on the nuances of particular cases. Moreover, the dormant commerce principle has existed for centuries with the knowledge and apparent approval of Congress. Congress could pass a general framework statute authorizing the courts to do what they do under modern dormant commerce doctrine, so the democratic objection may be a quibble at this point in US constitutional development. Finally, and perhaps most importantly, the federal courts act as Congress's agent in dormant commerce cases. However they decide such matters, Congress can overrule them by statute, in which case its interstate-commerce power no longer lies dormant. From a collective-action perspective, ultimate control by Congress is most important.

Three Theories of the Dormant Commerce Principle

The Court's dormant commerce doctrine is complex, controversial, and internally inconsistent. A collective-action account cannot rationalize the Court's overall approach or offer an alternative that can decide every case well. A collective-action lens does, however, offer illumination. The logics of collective action help identify the strengths and limitations of the three main competing theories of the dormant commerce principle, which have both overlapping and partially diverging implications for what the doctrine should look like. Collective-action theory explains what these theories have in common—what binds them together—and what divides them. Relatedly, the theory helps explain why the Court has tended to treat transportation cases differently from others involving burdens on interstate commerce.

Some commentators, most prominently Professor Donald Regan, argue that the dormant commerce principle exists to help preserve the United States as a political union. "Protectionist legislation is the economic equivalent of war," Regan writes. "It is hostile in its essence."[129] Professor Regan identifies tariffs, embargos, quotas, and similar measures as the core regulations known to the Framers that sought to protect local producers from foreign competition. He argues that the Court should use the dormant commerce doctrine to police only "purposeful economic protectionism," which he defines as measures "adopted for the purpose of improving the competitive position of local (in-state) economic actors, just because they are local, vis-à-vis their . . . out-of-state competitors."[130] In many cases, the Court has railed against state laws with a protectionist purpose. For example, in *Granholm v. Heald* (2004), Michigan and New York permitted

---

[129] Donald H. Regan, *The Supreme Court and State Protectionism: Making Sense of the Dormant Commerce Clause*, 84 MICH. L. REV. 1091, 1113 (1986); *see* Brannon P. Denning, *Reconstructing the Dormant Commerce Clause Doctrine*, 50 WM. & MARY L. REV. 417 (2008).

[130] REGAN, *supra* note 129, at 1092, 1094–95.

212 THE COLLECTIVE-ACTION CONSTITUTION

in-state wineries, but not out-of-state wineries, to ship directly to consumers. The Court struck down the state laws at issue, reiterating that "States may not enact laws that burden out-of-state producers or shippers simply to give a competitive advantage to in-state businesses," describing "[t]his rule [a]s essential to the foundations of the Union."[131] The political theory of the dormant commerce principle tasks courts with preventing states from causing cost-benefit collective-action problems or Pareto cooperation problems, but not Pareto coordination problems.

Other commentators, most prominently Professor Earl Maltz, argue that the doctrine exists mainly to promote free trade among the states and so to maintain an economic union.[132] On this view, state laws that facially discriminate or have a discriminatory purpose impede economic progress and the development of a national free-trade zone by permitting higher-cost in-state producers to compete with lower-cost out-of-state producers, harming consumers and national economic performance. "The material success that has come to inhabitants of the states which make up this federal free trade unit has been the most impressive in the history of commerce," the Court wrote in *H.P. Hood & Sons, Inc. v. Du Mond* (1949), "but the established interdependence of the states only emphasizes the necessity of protecting interstate movement of goods against local burdens and repressions."[133] In this case, the Court struck down a New York statute that prevented a company from building another depot for receiving milk. The law had the consequence of retaining more milk for consumption in New York at the expense of consumers in Massachusetts. The economic theory of the dormant commerce principle analogizes to international trade, where tariffs favor domestic producers over foreign producers and domestic consumers. Tariff agreements restrict tariffs, and these restrictions are accompanied by bans on regulations or taxes that discriminate against foreign goods.[134] Like the theory of political union, the theory of economic union focuses on the harms produced when states cause cost-benefit collective-action problems or Pareto cooperation problems.

Still other commentators, most prominently Professor John Hart Ely, argue that protectionist or unduly burdensome state legislation reflects a failure of the democratic process. On this account, which is an intellectual heir to Chief Justice Marshall's process argument against state taxation of the national bank in *McCulloch v. Maryland* (1819), protectionist or unduly burdensome laws reflect the power of groups possessing representation in the state's political

---

[131] *Granholm*, 544 U.S. at 472.
[132] Earl M. Maltz, *How Much Regulation Is Too Much: An Examination of Commerce Clause Jurisprudence*, 50 GEO. WASH. L. REV. 47 (1981).
[133] *H.P. Hood & Sons*, 336 U.S. at 538.
[134] FARBER & SIEGEL, *supra* note 15, at 172; Cooter & Siegel, *supra* note 13, at 167.

process to externalize costs onto groups lacking representation in the state's political process. This democratic defect lets legislatures impose regulations and taxes whose social costs exceed their social benefits. The dormant commerce principle, by insisting that out-of-staters not be treated worse than in-staters, functions as an "equality provisio[n], guaranteeing virtual representation to the politically powerless" by "constitutionally binding the interests of out-of-state manufacturers to those of local manufacturers represented in the legislature."[135] "Underlying the stated rule," Justice Harlan Fiske Stone wrote for the Court in *South Carolina State Highway Department v. Barnwell Brothers* (1938), "has been the thought, often expressed in judicial opinion, that when the regulation is of such a character that its burden falls principally upon those without the state, legislative action is not likely to be subjected to those political restraints which are normally exerted on legislation where it affects adversely some interests within the state."[136] Those attracted to the democratic-process theory of the dormant commerce principle target not only laws that facially discriminate or have a discriminatory purpose but also laws that burden out-of-staters in certain ways.[137] Accordingly, this theory justifies the intervention of the federal courts to prevent states from causing cost-benefit collective-action problems, Pareto cooperation problems, or Pareto coordination problems.

Animating each of these three accounts is at least two categories of multistate collective-action problems that, depending on the account, threaten political union, economic union, or political equality. Structurally, that is how to understand "the thought" referenced by Justice Stone in *Barnwell Brothers*. When commentators and jurists disagree over whether the Court should police only protectionist laws or also nondiscriminatory laws that burden interstate commerce, they are disagreeing primarily about which kinds of collective-action problems in the commercial sphere the Court should review.

The logics of cost-benefit collective-action problems or coordination difficulties help explain why the Court has been willing to invalidate state laws that burden instrumentalities of interstate commerce, particularly trucks and railroads. (If all states prefer coordination to noncoordination but disagree about how to coordinate, it is a coordination problem. If fewer than all states agree on the need to coordinate, it is a cost-benefit collective-action problem.) As noted, the Court generally applies a fairly deferential balancing inquiry, not the strict scrutiny reserved for discriminatory laws, to state regulations that merely burden interstate commerce, including in transportation cases where

---

[135] JOHN HART ELY, DEMOCRACY AND DISTRUST: A THEORY OF JUDICIAL REVIEW 83–84, 90–91 (1980).

[136] 303 U.S. 177, 184 n.2 (1938).

[137] Regan, *supra* note 129, at 1093 n.3 (noting the tendency of process theorists to support balancing).

214 THE COLLECTIVE-ACTION CONSTITUTION

there is a reasonable safety interest.[138] But regulation of a national transportation network requires uniformity—and, therefore, multistate coordination—to accomplish the purpose of the network to produce positive network externalities.[139] Such externalities "arise when later entrants follow an early leader respecting the choice of technology, thus increasing marginal benefits for those who now enjoy the common approach."[140] The Court has invalidated regulations, including nonconforming regulations of train or truck size or of truck mudflaps, when the safety or other state interest is questionable and "national uniformity in the regulation adopted, such as only Congress can prescribe, is practically indispensable to the operation of an efficient and economical national railway system."[141] As explained in discussing the Interstate Commerce Clause, the federal government is structurally better situated than the states to overcome cost-benefit or coordination problems facing the states and to create national transportation networks, including the national railway system, the interstate highway system, and the airspace throughout the nation. Just as creating these networks requires collective-action problems to be solved, so also maintaining them requires such problems to be prevented. The Court has prevented these problems in transportation cases by invalidating state laws whose harm to the network likely exceeds the noneconomic benefits obtained by the regulating states.[142]

Even where instrumentalities of interstate commerce are not burdened, the balancing inquiry that applies to nondiscriminatory state laws can help prevent collective-action problems. For example, *National Pork Producers Council v. Ross* (2023) involved a dormant commerce challenge to a nondiscriminatory California law that required all pork products sold in the state—whether

[138] South Carolina State Highway Dept. v. Barnwell Brothers, 303 U.S. 177 (1938) (upholding a nondiscriminatory state law limiting truck size to improve safety and road conservation).

[139] Nat'l Pork Producers Council v. Ross, 143 S. Ct. 1142, 1170 (2023) (Roberts, C.J., concurring in part and dissenting in part) (correctly observing that "we have applied [balancing] to state laws that neither concerned transportation nor discriminated against commerce," while acknowledging that the "balance may well come out differently when it comes to interstate transportation, an area presenting a strong interest in 'national uniformity'") (quoting General Motors Corp. v. Tracy, 519 U.S. 278, 298 n.12 (1997)).

[140] Henry & Stearns, *supra* note 44, at 1143 n.142. As Chapter 6 explains, the post office also generates positive network externalities.

[141] Southern Pacific Co. v. Arizona, 325 U.S. 761 (1945) (invalidating a state law regulating train size where the safety interest was dubious and the burden on interstate commerce was significant); *see* Bibb v. Navajo Freight Lines, Inc., 359 U.S. 520 (1959) (invalidating a state statute regulating mudflaps on trucks that conflicted with regulations in other states); Raymond Motor Transp., Inc. v. Rice, 434 U.S. 429 (1978) (invalidating a state law limiting truck size where the safety justification was speculative and the burden on interstate commerce was significant); Kassel v. Consolidated Freightways Corp., 450 U.S. 662 (1981) (similar).

[142] REGAN, *supra* note 129, at 1182–85 (acknowledging that the Court goes beyond suppressing protectionism in transportation cases to protect national transportation networks).

produced in California or elsewhere—to come from pigs that were not confined in a manner that the state deemed cruel. The Court, in a fractured decision, upheld the law on the narrow ground that the complaint failed to allege a substantial burden on interstate commerce.[143] But six justices reaffirmed the general principle of *Pike v. Bruce Church, Inc.* (1970) that where a state law "regulates even-handedly to effectuate a legitimate local public interest, and its effects on interstate commerce are only incidental, it will be upheld unless the burden imposed on such commerce is clearly excessive in relation to the putative local benefits."[144]

From a collective-action perspective, it is a good thing that the Court preserved the *Pike* balancing test. When externalized costs exceed internalized benefits, it is troubling that individual states can effectively impose their regulatory policies on the rest of the country by leveraging their significant share of a specific market. If California can seek to vindicate its conception of humane treatment of animals in this way, then other states can potentially prohibit the sale of goods produced by workers who are unlawfully present in the United States, or who are not—or who are—paid a certain minimum wage, or who are denied—or who are granted—insurance coverage of contraception or abortion by their employers.[145] Such state laws seem likely to externalize significant costs onto sister states, potentially creating a cost-benefit collective-action problem. Such laws also seem likely to provoke retaliation and so interstate conflict escalation, potentially resulting in a Pareto cooperation problem. On the other hand, states often pass laws that have extraterritorial effects, whether it be giving tax breaks to certain businesses or individuals, which can incentivize them to move, or banning a carcinogen in certain foods, which can affect production of the food in other states. Many state regulations create an incentive for out-of-state firms to comply in order to enter the market. The undue burden test, for all its under-determinacy, is better able to balance these competing considerations than either a categorical refusal to review nondiscriminatory state laws, which would leave many multistate collective-action problems unaddressed, or a constitutional ban on state laws with extraterritorial effects, which would severely compromise the capacity of states to regulate within their borders.

---

[143] 143 S. Ct. 1142, 1161–63 (2023) (plurality op. of Gorsuch, J., joined by Thomas, Sotomayor, & Kagan, JJ.); *id.* at 1166 (Sotomayor, J., joined by Kagan, J., concurring in part).

[144] 397 U.S. 137, 142 (1970). *See Nat'l Pork Producers Council*, 143 S. Ct. at 1165 (Sotomayor, J., joined by Kagan, J., concurring in part); *id.* at 1167 (Roberts, C.J., joined by Alito, Kavanaugh, & Jackson, JJ., concurring in part and dissenting in part).

[145] *Id.* at 1174 (Kavanaugh, J., concurring in part and dissenting in part) (positing similar potential state laws).

216 THE COLLECTIVE-ACTION CONSTITUTION

Exceptions to the Dormant Commerce Principle

The foregoing collective-action account can explain and justify one of the two doctrinal exceptions to the dormant commerce principle. State regulations that would otherwise violate the principle are permissible if Congress approves them, in which case the interstate-commerce power no longer lies dormant.[146] This exception has been criticized for reasons that justify the existence of the principle.[147] Yet, congressional approval may be part of a larger regulatory program that aims to solve what Congress deems a multistate cooperation problem. For example, to address the NIMBY problem in *New York*, Congress authorized states with disposal facilities to eventually deny other states access to their disposal sites.[148] "[W]hen Congress acts," the Court wrote in 1984, "all segments of the country are represented, and there is significantly less danger that one State will be in a position to exploit others." More fundamentally, the congressional-approval exception reflects the Constitution's conferral on Congress of power to determine, amid disagreements among states, whether there is a cost-benefit collective-action problem to be solved. "Furthermore," the Court added in the 1984 decision, "if a State is in such a position [to exploit other states], the decision to allow it is a collective one."[149] The congressional-approval exception is thus linked to the Interstate Commerce Clause and the Interstate Compacts Clause.

A collective-action account can also help explain and justify the other exception to the dormant commerce principle, which partially compromises collective-action concerns to vindicate other values, including state regulatory autonomy. The market-participant exception permits states to discriminate against out-of-state economic interests when states act as market participants as opposed to market regulators.[150] Examples include state preferences for in-state businesses or residents as beneficiaries of state contracts, product sales, hiring practices, and lower public-university admissions requirements or tuition. Professor Laurence Tribe argues that this exception reflects "[t]he sense of

---

[146] Prudential Ins. Co. v. Benjamin, 328 U.S. 408 (1946) (upholding a South Carolina law taxing only out-of-state insurance companies because federal law authorized it).

[147] Norman R. Williams, *Why Congress May Not "Overrule" the Dormant Commerce Clause*, 53 UCLA L. REV. 153 (2005).

[148] *New York*, 505 U.S. at 152–53.

[149] South-Central Timber Dev., Inc. v. Wunnicke, 467 U.S. 82, 92 (1984).

[150] Hughes v. Alexandra Scrap Corp., 426 U.S. 794 (1976) (introducing the market-participant exception in upholding a Maryland program that favored in-state scrap processors over out-of-state processors); Reeves, Inc. v. Stake, 447 U.S. 429 (1980) (permitting a state to restrict to state residents the sale of cement produced by a state-owned plant); White v. Mass. Council of Constr. Employers, Inc., 460 U.S. 204 (1983) (allowing a local-worker hiring preference under the market-participant exception).

fairness in allowing a community to retain the public benefits created by its own public investment."[151] This is not a collective-action rationale.

Certain public benefits would not, however, be produced without the market-participant exception. For example, if state universities had to charge the same tuition to in-staters and out-of-staters, numerous states might forego having universities, instead free riding on the public investments of neighboring states to maintain them. The result might be to defeat the raison d'être of many public universities: making higher education affordable to state residents. A similar rationale guides application of the Privileges and Immunities Clause.[152]

Foreign and Indian Commerce

During the 1780s, nationalist Americans realized that the Confederation Congress required the authority to regulate foreign commerce, and not just so that it could raise revenue by taxing imports. European powers—Great Britain especially, but also France, Spain, and others—sought to thwart the trade development of the United States by imposing significant commerce restrictions. For example, two months before the Treaty of Paris was signed in 1783, Britain closed its West Indies colonies to American ships, sailors, and many major exports. These actions significantly damaged American exporters, shipbuilders, and shippers, particularly (but not only) in New England.[153] Yet, Britain continued exporting inexpensive goods to the states and did not fear American retaliation because, as James Madison summarized the views of the Earl of Sheffield, "the interests of the States are so opposite in matters of Commerce, & the authority of Congs. so feeble that no defensive precautions need be feared on the part of the U.S."[154] In 1784, France imposed new, consequential trade restrictions on Americans, and Spain announced that it exclusively controlled navigation on the Mississippi River and would exclude American exporters from it absent successful negotiation of a treaty between the two nations.[155] "By early 1785," Professor Michael Klarman writes, "Spain was regularly seizing American vessels that were engaging in 'illicit' trade on the river."[156]

---

[151] LAURENCE H. TRIBE, CONSTITUTIONAL CHOICES 145 (1985).

[152] U.S. CONST. art. IV, § 2, cl. 1 (discussed in Chapter 9).

[153] VAN CLEVE, *supra* note 5, at 102–10; MICHAEL D. RAMSEY, THE CONSTITUTION'S TEXT IN FOREIGN AFFAIRS 35–37, 40 (2007).

[154] Letter from James Madison to Edmund Randolph (Aug. 30, 1783), *in* 2 THE WRITINGS OF JAMES MADISON 12 (Gaillard Hunt ed., 1904) (discussing JOHN LORD SHEFFIELD, OBSERVATIONS ON THE COMMERCE OF THE AMERICAN STATES (2d ed. 1784) (1783)); *see id.* at 11 ("A Pamphlet has lately come over from G. Britain which appears to be well adapted to retard if not prevent a commercial Treaty, & which is said to be much attended to.").

[155] VAN CLEVE, *supra* note 5, at 113–14.

[156] MICHAEL J. KLARMAN, THE FRAMERS' COUP: THE MAKING OF THE UNITED STATES CONSTITUTION 49 (2016).

218 THE COLLECTIVE-ACTION CONSTITUTION

As the Earl of Sheffield recognized, Congress could not retaliate against countries that barred Americans from their markets because the Articles of Confederation did not grant it power to regulate commerce with other countries. In 1784, Congress observed that "[a]lready has Great Britain adopted regulations destructive of our commerce with her West India islands," and Congress proposed that the states give it modest retaliatory powers. "Unless the United States in Congress assembled shall be vested with powers competent to the protection of commerce," Congress contended, "they can never command reciprocal advantages in trade; and without these, our foreign commerce must decline, and eventually be annihilated."[157] Adopting the proposal would have required amending the Articles, which meant that all states had to agree. For various reasons, including conflicting state economic interests and fear of increasing federal power, unanimity proved as unattainable here as elsewhere. The following year, Congress rejected a proposal to give it robust authority to regulate and tax foreign and interstate commerce.[158]

With Congress unable to exercise trade-retaliation powers, the only alternative was retaliation by the states, which individually did tax and regulate foreign commerce during the 1780s. But no one state's retaliatory tariffs and regulations were sufficiently effective to change the behavior of European powers. Collective action by the states would have proven more promising, but collective action would have required them to want to coordinate their behavior and to agree on how to do so, and some states did not want to coordinate while others disagreed on what form a coordinated response should take. Collective action would have also required the states to resist the temptation to invite foreign commerce to their ports, thereby undermining or free riding on the foreign-trade restrictions imposed by other states.

For example, in 1785, Massachusetts prohibited all foreign ships from exporting goods from the state and imposed discriminatory duties on numerous foreign goods and ships, many of which were prohibitively high and applied only to nations that imposed trade restrictions on the United States. Massachusetts also initiated a nationwide campaign to persuade other states to impose similar restrictions. Only two states, both in New England, did so. Others benefited when foreign ships avoided the Massachusetts restrictions by entering their ports instead. A few states, including Connecticut, tried to undermine the Massachusetts regulations. A year later, Massachusetts suspended its retaliatory regime until all

---

[157] Minutes of Apr. 30, 1784, in 26 J. CONT'L. CONG. 1774–1789, at 321–22 (Gaillard Hunt ed., 1928); *see id.* at 322 ("Hence it is necessary that the states should be explicit, and fix on some effectual mode by which foreign commerce, not founded on principles of equality, may be restrained.").

[158] VAN CLEVE, *supra* note 5, at 115–17.

INTERSTATE COMMERCE AND RELATED PRINCIPLES   219

other states adopted similar ones, which would never happen. The states individually lacked leverage over powerful nations, and the states collectively could not or would not act.[159]

Similar stories could be told regarding tariffs and embargos. The Articles did not grant Congress power to impose either, and the states proved unable or unwilling to coordinate so that they could use them effectively to improve the trade situation of the United States. States with ports, including New York, Rhode Island, Virginia, Massachusetts, and Pennsylvania, did tax imports to raise revenue, protect their industries, or retaliate against foreign trade restrictions, but these imposts gained the taxing states no leverage vis-à-vis other nations. Instead, as discussed, the tariffs generated significant hostility in other states, which earned no revenue from them but whose citizens had to pay more for the taxed goods.[160]

In contrast to the Articles' denial of congressional authority to regulate foreign commerce and impose tariffs and embargos, Article IX did give Congress the power of "entering into treaties" with the proviso that it not conclude commercial treaties barring the states "from imposing such imposts and duties on foreigners, as their own people are subjected to," or "from prohibiting the exportation or importation of any species of goods or commodities whatsoever." Moreover, Article VI prohibited states from entering into treaties without the consent of Congress and precluded them from taxing imports in a manner "which may interfere with any stipulations in treaties." Congress lacked power, however, to make and enforce laws preventing states from violating US treaty obligations, including the 1783 peace treaty with Great Britain. In 1785, Washington opined in private correspondence that without significant changes to the Articles that gave Congress commerce powers, the Union would stand "in a ridiculous point of view in the eyes of the Nations of the Earth; with whom we are attempting to enter into Commercial Treaties without means of carrying them into effect and who must see, & feel, that the Union, or the States individually, are Sovereigns, as it best suits their purposes." Bitterly observing that "we are one Nation today, & thirteen tomorrow," he asked, "Who will treat with us on such terms?"[161] With no power to enforce treaties domestically and states individually in control of tariffs, Congress could not persuade other nations to lower their imposts on American exports or loosen other trade restrictions, because it could not credibly promise reciprocity.

---

[159] *Id.* at 112–13, 117–18; RAMSEY, *supra* note 153, at 36, 42.
[160] VAN CLEVE, *supra* note 5, at 112–13; RAMSEY, *supra* note 153, at 42–44.
[161] Letter from George Washington to James McHenry (Aug. 22, 1785), *in* 3 PAPERS OF GEORGE WASHINGTON: CONFEDERATION SERIES 198–99 (W. W. Abbot ed., 1994).

220 THE COLLECTIVE-ACTION CONSTITUTION

The Constitution and Collective Action

The Framers were well-acquainted with these events, and they sought to replace the impotence of the Confederation Congress with federal powers sufficient to overcome the collective-action failures of the states. The Constitution gave Congress authority to tax imports (as Chapter 4 discussed) and comprehensive control over the nation's commercial relations with the world. The Foreign Commerce Clause, located in the third clause of Article I, Section 8, authorizes Congress to "regulate commerce with foreign nations."[162] In *The Federalist Papers*, Hamilton defended these federal powers as necessary not only to raise much-needed revenue by taxing imports[163] but also to achieve a bargaining advantage in trade negotiations. According to Hamilton, the imposition of "prohibitory regulations" on other nations was key to securing reciprocity. "Suppose," he asked, "we had a government in America, capable of excluding Great Britain (with whom we have at present no treaty of commerce) from all our ports; what would be the probable operation of this step upon her politics?" He answered that it would "enable us to negotiate, with the fairest prospect of success, for commercial privileges of the most valuable and extensive kind in the dominions of that kingdom."[164] Hamilton predicted that imposing trade restrictions on Britain "would produce a relaxation in her present system."[165]

When Congress regulates foreign commerce, it enables the states to speak with one voice in international commercial affairs. Congress thereby overcomes coordination problems facing the states by ending disagreements among them. Moreover, Congress prevents states from externalizing costs onto other states—as Connecticut did to Massachusetts in the episode discussed above. Such negative externalities are often higher than the benefits received by the externalizing state, which creates a cost-benefit collective-action problem. And the externalities risk triggering a multistate cooperation problem, as might have occurred had Massachusetts retaliated against Connecticut for undermining its retaliation against Great Britain. In the short run, Massachusetts might have retaliated economically. Over time, such retaliation might have turned violent.

The imposition of international-trade restrictions exemplifies a situation in which the states must act collectively to act effectively. The states must also act collectively, not individually, to act effectively in their noneconomic interactions with "foreign Nations" and "Indian tribes"—to invoke the language of the

---

[162] U.S. CONST. art. I, § 8, cl. 3.
[163] THE FEDERALIST No. 12, at 93–96 (Alexander Hamilton) (Clinton Rossiter ed., 1961).
[164] THE FEDERALIST No. 11, at 85–86 (Alexander Hamilton) (Clinton Rossiter ed., 1961).
[165] *Id.* at 86.

Foreign and Indian Commerce Clauses.[166] At least regarding relations with other countries and tribes, the word "Commerce" has a broader meaning than trade, navigation, or economic activity.[167] As Professors Akhil Amar and Jack Balkin have separately observed, before the Committee of Detail compressed the three components of the third clause of Section 8 ("foreign Nations," "several States," and "Indian Tribes") into one clause, the Framers had used the term "affairs" instead of "Commerce" in empowering Congress to regulate relations with Indian tribes, and the first Congress regulated both economic and noneconomic dimensions of the nation's interactions with tribes.[168] The modern Court, too, insists that "Congress's power under the Indian Commerce Clause encompasses not only trade but also 'Indian affairs.'"[169] Moreover, a similar reading of the Foreign Commerce Clause better justifies congressional power to regulate immigration than does the Court's plenary power doctrine,[170] which has no basis in the constitutional text.[171] In *Chy Lung v. Freeman* (1875), the Court invalidated a California law that reflected hostility to Chinese immigration. The justices grounded federal immigration power in the Foreign Commerce Clause and emphasized its exclusivity for the collective-action reason that "otherwise, a single State can, at her pleasure, embroil us in disastrous quarrels with other nations."[172]

---

[166] U.S. CONST. art. I, § 8, cl. 3.

[167] Textually, it is not evident how the word "Commerce," which appears once in the third clause of Section 8, could have a different meaning depending on which of the three categories of commerce is at issue. As discussed earlier, Professors Amar and Balkin emphasize this textualist point in advocating for a broad meaning of the word "Commerce" in the Interstate Commerce Clause. *See supra* note 84 and accompanying text. But regardless of whether they are correct about the meaning of this clause, one could argue based on Section 8's drafting history that the Framers made a stylistic choice of linguistic compression, so the meaning of the word "Commerce" in the Interstate Commerce Clause should not determine its meaning in the Foreign and Indian Commerce Clauses, particularly when the Framers likely did not think through the full interpretive implications of the compression. Strict textualists will, however, reject this argument, which is unnecessary anyway insofar as one credits Professor Amar's and Professor Balkin's understanding of commerce as the exchange of people and ideas in addition to goods and services and other economic activity. Most originalists, however, reject their argument. *See id.*

[168] 2 THE RECORDS OF THE FEDERAL CONVENTION OF 1787, at 321 (Max Farrand ed., rev. ed. 1966) (Aug. 18, 1787); *id.* at 493 (Sept. 4, 1787); AMAR, *supra* note 9, at 107–08 (noting that in 1790, Congress "regulat[ed] noneconomic interactions and altercations—'intercourse'—with Indians," including crimes committed by Americans on tribal lands); BALKIN, *supra* note 9, at 156–57 (discussing the noneconomic nature of the interactions with tribes that federal Trade and Intercourse Acts regulated beginning in 1790).

[169] Haaland v. Brackeen, 143 S. Ct. 1609, 1630 (2023) (quoting Cotton Petroleum Corp. v. New Mexico, 490 U.S. 163, 192 (1989)).

[170] United States v. Curtiss-Wright Export Corp., 299 U.S. 304 (1936).

[171] BALKIN, *supra* note 9, at 157–59. The text references immigration obliquely in imposing citizenship requirements for federal elective offices, U.S. CONST. art. I, § 2, cl. 2; art. I, § 3, cl. 3; art. II, § 1, cl. 5, and in temporarily restricting federal power (presumably under the Foreign Commerce Clause) to prohibit the importation of enslaved people, art. I, § 9, cl. 1. For criticism of inherent foreign-affairs powers, see RAMSEY, *supra* note 153.

[172] 92 U.S. 275, 280 (1875).

222 THE COLLECTIVE-ACTION CONSTITUTION

True, the history canvassed above indicates that the Founders were primarily focused on international trade in debating whether the Confederation Congress and then the US Congress should be empowered to regulate foreign commerce. This does not mean, however, that federal power under the Foreign Commerce Clause is limited to the imposition of trade regulations, particularly given the historic relation between trade restrictions and military conflict between nations. Founding discussions of the treaty power also tended to focus on trade relations, as Washington illustrated in expressing his exasperation about concluding trade treaties absent changes to the Articles. Even so, few would argue that the United States may conclude treaties only on subjects related to trade (or war and peace, another topic of treaties at the Founding).[173]

In sum, the Foreign and Indian Commerce Clauses, like the power to tax imports, authorize Congress to solve what it rationally deems collective-action problems facing the states in their relations with other countries or Native American tribes. Additional provisions of the Constitution facilitate the ability of the nation to speak with one voice by preventing the states from causing collective-action problems. For example, recall the examples from Chapter 3 in which independent action by US states, such as the formation of military alliances or treaties with other states or countries, or the violation of treaty obligations to other nations, is likely to result in states' externalizing costs onto other states in ways that cause collective-action problems. The tenth section of Article I contains specific prohibitions on state behavior in the international arena, including an absolute bar on "enter[ing] into any treaty, alliance, or confederation."[174] Further, states require congressional consent to "lay any Imposts or Duties on Imports or Exports." The only exception is when such taxes are "absolutely necessary for executing [their] inspection Laws," and even then "the net Produce of [such] Duties and Imposts . . . shall be for the Use of the Treasury of the United States; and all such Laws shall be subject to the Revision and Control of the Congress."[175] As Chapter 1 explained, these provisions strictly limit state authority to tax imports or exports; prevent states from making a profit in the rare circumstance in which they may do so; and empower Congress to provide additional protection against cost externalization by states onto sister states. States also require congressional approval to "enter into any Agreement or Compact . . . with a foreign Power."[176]

[173] Chapter 10 discusses the Treaty Power.
[174] U.S. CONST. art. I, § 10, cl. 1.
[175] U.S. CONST. art. I, § 10, cl. 2.
[176] U.S. CONST. art. I, § 10, cl. 3.

Preemption

The Supremacy Clause of Article VI declares that federal law is "the supreme Law of the Land." This clause provides the textual foundation for preemption, the fundamental constitutional principle that constitutionally valid federal law trumps conflicting state law. As Chief Justice Marshall wrote in *Gibbons*, "[A]cts of the State Legislatures [that] interfere with, or are contrary to the laws of Congress, made in pursuance of the constitution, or some treaty made under the authority of the United States [are invalid because] [i]n every such case, the act of Congress, or the treaty, is supreme; and the law of the State, though enacted in the exercise of powers not controverted, must yield to it."[177] Although discussion of the Supremacy Clause will be postponed until Chapter 7, preemption is discussed here because many preemption issues arise when Congress exercises its powers under the Interstate and Foreign Commerce Clauses, and because certain forms of preemption implicate tradeoffs that arise in debates over the dormant commerce principle.

The Court's preemption doctrine is complex. There are two main categories of preemption: express preemption and implied preemption. Federal law may expressly preempt state law when a federal statute includes explicit preemptive language. Federal law may impliedly preempt state law when Congress's preemptive intent is implicit in the "structure and purpose" of the federal statute. There are two subcategories of implied preemption: field preemption, "where the scheme of federal regulation is so pervasive as to make reasonable the inference that Congress left no room for the States to supplement it," and conflict preemption, "where compliance with both federal and state regulations is a physical impossibility, or where state law stands as an obstacle to the accomplishment and execution of the full purposes and objectives of Congress."[178] These various categories and subcategories are not entirely distinct, however, and regardless of the (sub) category at issue, the Court has made clear that "[t]he question whether a certain state action is pre-empted by federal law is one of congressional intent."[179] Accordingly, preemption cases are statutory interpretation cases, and the modern Court hears numerous difficult ones because there are many federal and state laws in existence that potentially conflict with each other, and Congress's intent is often not entirely clear.

The general principle of preemption follows from a collective-action account of the Constitution. If valid federal law did not supersede conflicting state law, federal law could not succeed in solving or preventing collective-action problems

---

[177] Gibbons v. Ogden, 22 U.S. (9 Wheat.) 1, 211 (1824).

[178] *See, e.g.,* Gade v. National Solid Wastes Management Assn., 505 U.S. 88, 98 (1992) (internal quotation marks and citations omitted).

[179] *Id.* at 96 (internal quotation marks omitted).

224 THE COLLECTIVE-ACTION CONSTITUTION

for the states. For example, state governments could simply violate with impunity any of the valid federal statutes discussed in this chapter—from the federal navigation license at issue in *Gibbons*, which was in part a preemption case; to the CRA; to the federal Controlled Substances Act as applied to the plaintiffs in *Raich*—and follow conflicting state law instead.

From a collective-action perspective, preemption cases are in principle straightforward where a federal statute contains an express preemption provision or there is a direct conflict between federal law and state law, such that it is impossible to comply with both. In such cases, Congress has actually or effectively spoken to the issue of preemption, so one can be relatively confident that there is an adequate democratic warrant for a judicial finding that a federal solution to a multistate collective-action problem must prevail over conflicting state law. By contrast, preemption cases are less straightforward in principle where field preemption and obstacle preemption are at issue.

Field preemption is the strongest form of preemption. Even where a federal statutory scheme contains no express preemption clause (so that the case falls within the category of implied preemption), and even where there is no conflict between federal law and state law (so that the case falls outside the category of implied conflict preemption), the Court has held that it will find state law impliedly preempted if Congress has made clear its intent that federal law should exclusively occupy an entire field of regulation. Notably, two main fields that the Court has identified as under exclusive federal control, even absent an express declaration of exclusivity from Congress, involve obvious multistate collective-action problems: immigration law and foreign affairs.[180] At the same time, field preemption is less closely tied to actual congressional intent than express preemption and impossibility preemption. In field preemption cases, Congress could intervene and expressly preempt; there is no impediment to its doing so. But it has not done so. So, the subject of field preemption implicates a tradeoff between broadly solving multistate collective-action problems on one hand and ensuring an adequate democratic warrant for such solutions on the other— especially where different states are likely to disagree on the subject in question, meaning that a cost-benefit collective-action problem is at issue.

A similar tradeoff is evident in cases of obstacle preemption. For example, in *American Insurance Association v. Garamendi* (2003), the Court held preempted a California law requiring insurers in business in the state to disclose certain information about policies they sold in Europe during the Holocaust.[181] And in *Crosby v. National Foreign Trade Council* (2000), the Court held that a

---

[180] *See, e.g., Arizona v. United States*, 567 U.S. 387 (2012) (alien registration); *Hines v. Davidowitz*, 312 U.S. 52 (1941) (same).
[181] 539 U.S. 396 (2003).

INTERSTATE COMMERCE AND RELATED PRINCIPLES   225

federal sanctions law against the country of Burma (Myanmar) preempted a Massachusetts law prohibiting the state from buying goods or services from companies in business with Burma.[182] Concerns about the collective consequences of state interventions in international commercial affairs may support the Court's holdings in these cases that federal law broadly preempts state law because of foreign policy concerns, even where no federal statute or executive agreement expresses an intent to preempt, and even where federal and state law are not inconsistent with each other. In *Crosby*, for example, the Court reasoned in part that "the differences between the state and federal Acts in scope and type of sanctions . . . compromise the very capacity of the President to speak for the Nation with one voice in dealing with other governments."[183] On the other hand, it can be asked of both *Garamendi* and *Crosby* why Congress should not have to decide the preemption question—giving states a say—and satisfy the collective-action threshold of majority rule, particularly when foreign-relations problems will likely be brought to Congress's attention.

In considering how to resolve this tradeoff, aforementioned debates over the dormant commerce doctrine are relevant. A key question in both areas of law is whether the federal courts are better positioned than Congress to intervene more frequently and nimbly. Courts can act more quickly than Congress and can address relatively modest collective-action problems before they become relatively major ones. Moreover, courts can consider cases retrospectively and contextually, whereas Congress must legislate prospectively and generally. On the other hand, courts lack the democratic legitimacy of Congress, and their rulings in favor of federal power and against state power flip the burden of inertia in Congress. Although reasonable minds can differ on how to resolve this tradeoff, the most important point from a collective-action standpoint is that courts must act as Congress's faithful agent in both dormant commerce and preemption cases. If courts do so, the democratic objection to judicial review is substantially weakened. Relatedly, the longer a doctrine has existed without objection from Congress, the more likely it is that judicial application of the doctrine is consistent with congressional will.

The basic point that the Court is Congress's agent, not its own principal, calls into question the Court's presumption against preemption. In preemption cases, the Court has sometimes, but not consistently, applied this substantive canon of statutory construction. Substantive (or normative) canons, unlike textual (or semantic) canons, do not aim to discern actual legislative intent; rather, they put thumbs on the scale in favor of particular substantive values that the Court deems important. To help preserve the regulatory authority of the states,

---

[182] 530 U.S. 363 (2000).
[183] *Id.* at 381.

226 THE COLLECTIVE-ACTION CONSTITUTION

the presumption against preemption instructs courts not to hold that federal law preempts state law "unless that was the clear and manifest purpose of Congress."[184] An increasingly textualist Court no longer applies the presumption in express preemption cases, where by definition Congress has expressed its intention to preempt state law in the language of the statute.[185] Moreover, the Court does not consistently apply the presumption in implied preemption cases, especially where they involve subjects that the states have not traditionally regulated or areas in which the federal government has traditionally engaged in significant regulation.[186] The Court appears most likely to apply the presumption against preemption in implied preemption cases where Congress intervenes in areas that the Court regards as traditional subjects of state regulation, including criminal law, domestic relations (or family) law, regulations of wages and hours, insurance law, consumer protection, and advertising.[187]

In addition to looking to historical practice for guidance in determining whether to apply the presumption against federal preemption of state law, the Court should reason structurally. Application of this presumption should be informed by whether (1) the federal law at issue appears to address a multistate collective-action problem and (2) the state law in question is thwarting a federal solution to such a problem or causing one. When the states face collective-action problems, judicial efforts to preserve the regulatory authority of individual states are misplaced, and the vindication of validly exercised federal authority should be the primary constitutional objective. In such situations, therefore, the Court would be well advised to put the presumption against preemption aside and instead seek to discern actual congressional intent.[188]

---

[184] Rice v. Santa Fe Elevator Corp., 331 U.S. 218, 230 (1947).

[185] Puerto Rico v. Franklin Cal. Tax-Free Trust, 579 U.S. 115, 125 (2016) ("[B]ecause the statute contains an express pre-emption clause, we do not invoke any presumption against pre-emption but instead focus on the plain wording of the clause, which necessarily contains the best evidence of Congress' preemptive intent.") (internal quotation marks omitted).

[186] JAY B. SYKES & NICOLE VANATKO, CONG. RSCH. SERV., R45825, FEDERAL PREEMPTION: A LEGAL PRIMER, at 5 (Jul. 23, 2019).

[187] 81A C.J.S. *States* § 48 (2023). *See, e.g., Rice*, 331 U.S. at 230 ("Congress legislated here in a field which the States have traditionally occupied. So we start with the assumption that the historic police powers of the States were not to be superseded by the Federal Act unless that was the clear and manifest purpose of Congress" (citations omitted).).

[188] In *Garamendi*, the Court suggested a blending of historical practice and structural considerations:

> If a State were simply to take a position on a matter of foreign policy with no serious claim to be addressing a traditional state responsibility, field preemption might be the appropriate doctrine, whether the National Government had acted and, if it had, without reference to the degree of any conflict, the principle having been established that the Constitution entrusts foreign policy exclusively to the National Government. Where, however, a State has acted within what Justice Harlan called its "traditional competence," but in a way that affects foreign relations, it might make good sense to require a conflict, of a clarity or substantiality that would vary with the strength or the traditional importance of the state concern asserted. Whether the strength of the federal foreign policy interest should itself be weighed is, of course, a further question.

Garamendi, 539 U.S. at 419 n.11 (citations omitted).

Conclusion

This chapter has added to the catalogue of federal powers that are largely explicable in collective-action terms. Like the authorities to tax, spend, and borrow, the powers to regulate interstate, foreign, and Indian commerce were conferred so that Congress could exercise national legislative jurisdiction by majority vote to solve collective-action problems for the states, whether cooperation problems that form a multistate Prisoners' Dilemma; coordination problems that are pure or involve disagreements; or, as is most common, cost-benefit collective-action problems. The Interstate Commerce Clause is special because a collective-action approach can be used to identify the scope of this power—to distinguish between interstate and intrastate commerce. Collective-action theory also helps explain and justify the Court's long-standing dormant commerce doctrine, a constitutional principle that prevents states from causing collective-action problems, as well as preemption doctrine, a general principle that flows directly from a collective-action account of the Constitution.

In addition, this chapter has demonstrated the critical acuity of a collective-action account. The theory suggests that the Court should stop distinguishing between economic and noneconomic activity in defining the scope of the interstate-commerce power and should instead distinguish between collective and individual action by states—between problems whose solution would require the states to act collectively and problems whose solution would not. Alternatively, the Court should register that the economic/noneconomic distinction is a proxy for the distinction between collective and individual action by states; such knowledge can help guide application of the economic-activity test in close cases. A collective-action approach also suggests that the Court should reconsider its distinction between regulating and requiring commerce, as well as the categorical nature of the anti-commandeering doctrine.

This chapter and the previous one have considered many, but not all, of the congressional powers in Article I, Section 8. The next chapter considers those that remain. They too are substantially illuminated by the logics of collective action.

6

National Security, Positive Externalities, and National Uniformity

Introduction

When scholars and judges identify the failures of the Articles of Confederation, they focus on taxation, interstate commerce, and foreign commerce. They also emphasize national (in)security, a topic analyzed in this chapter. Most Founders featured these subjects, too. This is unsurprising and illuminating. The problems of funding the national government, regulating commerce, and defending the nation posed the greatest existential threats to the states individually and collectively during the 1780s.

Still, concentrating on roughly half of Article I, Section 8, misses something important about the other clauses and Section 8 as a whole. Section 8 is not a heterogeneous compilation of unrelated powers, or a combination of collective-action powers and unrelated powers. The Section 8 clauses that are often overlooked also authorize Congress to address multistate collective-action problems. This chapter shows how they do so.

The chapter begins with the collective-action rationales for authorizing Congress to define and punish certain offenses with national-security implications and to provide for the nation's defense. It then examines the postal and intellectual-property powers, both of which—like the military-defense clauses—enable Congress to internalize positive interstate externalities. The chapter next explains why Congress is authorized to insist on national uniformity in regulating naturalization and bankruptcy, after which it considers standards, currency, and counterfeiting, which also implicate concerns about the collective costs of divergent state regulations. The chapter concludes with the congressional powers to create lower federal tribunals and govern federal enclaves. These powers exist not only to facilitate federal administration but also to help solve collective-action problems for the states.

The Collective-Action Constitution. Neil S. Siegel, Oxford University Press. © Neil S. Siegel 2024.
DOI: 10.1093/oso/9780197760963.003.0007

230   THE COLLECTIVE-ACTION CONSTITUTION

Positive Interstate Externalities: National Security

The military clauses of Section 8 (Clauses 11 through 16) obviously concern national defense and are discussed below. First, however, note the clause that precedes them. It empowers Congress to define three crimes and punish those who commit them.

Offenses and Collective Action

The tenth clause is the Define and Punish Clause. It authorizes Congress to criminalize piracy, maritime felonies, and violations of the law of nations.[1] These are three of the five crimes that the Constitution expressly gives Congress the power to punish. (The other two are counterfeiting, initially part of this clause and discussed below,[2] and treason, defined in Article III.[3]) The three offenses in the Define and Punish Clause implicate national defense, foreign commerce, and foreign relations, as exemplified by the state-sponsored pirates operating along the Barbary Coast of North Africa during the 1780s. By the end of 1783, they were attacking American ships trading in the Mediterranean Sea, seizing them, enslaving their sailors, and demanding ransoms or selling them. These actions severely damaged New England exports (especially from Massachusetts), but neither the states individually nor the Confederation Congress could stop the attacks. Congress would have required the funds to build a strong Navy; the power to regulate foreign commerce; and sufficient economic and military might to be taken seriously in European diplomatic circles, where American efforts to persuade European nations to fight piracy fell on deaf ears.[4] The states would have needed to overcome collective-action problems to act effectively against the pirates—to avoid free riding on the tax and troop contributions of other states, and to coordinate their diplomatic or military responses.

Article IX of the Articles of Confederation authorized the Confederation Congress to "appoint[] courts for the trials of piracies and felonies committed on the high seas," but this clause referred to the appointment of state courts, and Congress lacked power to punish other violations of the law of nations. As a

[1] U.S. Const. art. I, § 8, cl. 10.
[2] 2 The Records of the Federal Convention of 1787, at 181–82 (Max Farrand ed., 1911) (Aug. 6).
[3] U.S. Const. art. III, § 3 ("Treason against the United States, shall consist only in levying War against them, or in adhering to their Enemies, giving them Aid and Comfort."). The Constitution mentions only five offenses, but Congress enjoys broad Necessary and Proper Clause authority to define and punish many other crimes.
[4] George William Van Cleve, We Have Not a Government: The Articles of Confederation and the Road to the Constitution 107–08, 114 (2017).

result, when countries appealed to Congress during the 1780s to protect rights secured by the law of nations, Congress could only refer these countries to the relevant state governments. States defined and punished such crimes differently, however, which raised concerns that states, if they did not appropriately enforce international law, would harm the young nation's relations with other countries. Such cost externalization by individual states would generate a cost-benefit collective-action problem.

Most infamously, in 1784, a French citizen named Charles de Longchamps assaulted France's Consul General Marbois in Philadelphia. France demanded that Congress surrender de Longchamps to French authorities, but Congress lacked the authority to do so and sheepishly advised the French to ask Pennsylvania. Although the states mostly responded responsibly to such incidents—for example, Pennsylvania punished de Longchamps even as it declined to extradite him—Congress's weakness was displayed to foreign powers. Moreover, leaving serious international matters to individual states was viewed as perilous at a time when nations went to war over asserted violations of their rights.[5] Madison had such concerns in mind when, in his *Vices* Memo, he decried state "[v]iolations of the law of nations and of treaties."[6]

To avoid having to rely on the states individually, the Constitution gives Congress the power to criminalize violations of the law of nations, which today includes customary international law and possibly treaty law as well.[7] Congress has long used this power, along with the Treaty and Necessary and Proper Clauses, to make the international law of war part of domestic US law and to prohibit various other criminal or civil offenses against the law of nations. Examples include offenses involving torture, human trafficking, hostage taking on aircraft, terrorism, the use of chemical weapons and other weapons of mass destruction, alien torts, and foreign sovereign immunities.[8] Given the

---

[5] MICHAEL D. RAMSEY, THE CONSTITUTION'S TEXT IN FOREIGN AFFAIRS 38–39 (2007).

[6] JAMES MADISON, *Vices of the Political System of the United States* (April 1787), *in* 2 THE WRITINGS OF JAMES MADISON 362 (Gaillard Hunt ed., 1904).

[7] Whether the law of nations also includes treaty law is disputed. On one hand, the Constitution lists the treaty power separately and the Alien Tort Statute, enacted in 1789, refers separately to treaties and the law of nations. On the other hand, Professors Sarah Cleveland and William Dodge argue that the Framers understood the law of nations to include both custom and treaties. *See* Sarah H. Cleveland & William S. Dodge, *Defining and Punishing Offenses Under Treaties*, 124 YALE L.J. 2202 (2015). More generally, scholars dispute the scope of Congress's power under the Define and Punish Clause. For different perspectives, see, in addition to Cleveland & Dodge, *supra*, Eugene Kontorovich, *The "Define and Punish" Clause and the Limits of Universal Jurisdiction*, 103 Nw. U.L. REV. 149 (2009); and Beth Stephens, *Federalism and Foreign Affairs: Congress's Power to "Define and Punish . . . Offenses against the Law of Nations,"* 42 WM. & MARY L. REV. 447 (2000).

[8] Cindy Galway Buys, *The Power to Punish Piracies and Other Offenses against the Law of Nations*, *in* THE POWERS OF CONGRESS: WHERE CONSTITUTIONAL AUTHORITY BEGINS AND ENDS 123–33 (Brien Hallett ed., 2016). Congress has also punished the counterfeiting of foreign bank notes in the United States, which the Court upheld in *United States v. Arjona*, 120 U.S. 479 (1887), under several powers, including the Define and Punish Clause.

232 THE COLLECTIVE-ACTION CONSTITUTION

national-security, commercial, or foreign-policy implications of these issues and the typical locations of many of the offenses, authorizing Congress to handle them empowers it to solve multiple potential collective-action problems for the states. Congressional action frees states of the need to coordinate their separate enforcement activities and avoids possible free riding by some states. Most importantly, congressional action prevents individual states from antagonizing other nations, thereby externalizing potentially massive costs onto sister states and generating a major cost-benefit collective-action problem.

Notably, however, federal power in this area need not be exclusive. States, too, can define and punish violations of the law of nations if state law is neither preempted by federal law nor prohibited by federal due-process limits on extraterritoriality.[9] For example, states can criminalize torture within their jurisdictions. As evidenced by the historical episodes above, the idea then and now has not been to disable the states but to enable Congress to select issues that require national law (like a statute prohibiting piracy or assault of a foreign diplomat), rather than leaving the matter just to state-law definitions and enforcement efforts that might cause foreign-relations problems for the nation.

National Defense

The opening clause of Article I, Section 8, like the Preamble, references "the common Defence."[10] Defense is "common" when the states must act collectively, not individually, to secure it—when the states are separately incompetent. Recall that Resolution VI of the Virginia Plan ultimately proposed giving Congress the power "to legislate in all Cases for the general Interests of the Union, and also in those Cases to which the States are separately incompetent, or in which the Harmony of the United States may be interrupted by the Exercise of individual Legislation." Military defense is a standard example of a good with positive interstate externalities that affect an entire nation. As Chapter 2 explained, such externalities exist when an activity in one state benefits people in another who do not pay for it. Given the technical characteristics of the activity, the provider in one state—whether the state itself or another entity—has no practical way to collect fees from the beneficiaries in another state.

Without a national military, each state would have to provide for its own defense. The benefits of defense in one state would spill over to people in another state. It would be infeasible for each state to collect money from out-of-state

---

[9] *Cf.* American Insurance Ass'n v. Garamendi, 539 U.S. 396 (2003). For discussion, see Curtis A. Bradley et al., Foreign Relations Law: Cases and Materials 122–23 (7th ed. 2020).
[10] U.S. Const. art. I, § 8, cl. 1.

beneficiaries to pay for the costs of the defense it provides. As a result, each state would have an incentive to free ride on the security provided by other states, leaving all states insecure. It would also be challenging to coordinate the defense forces of the (now fifty) states when the nation was at war. Moreover, an individual state might make military decisions that harmed other states more than it helped itself, such as by keeping its troops at home to defend its borders when the troops were needed more in the parts of the Union (or the world) where war was being waged.[11]

A central government does not suffer from these disadvantages because of the national scope of its taxing, spending, and regulatory jurisdiction. Such a government can internalize the positive interstate externalities and thereby avoid cooperation problems, which would result in underproduction of national defense. A national government with one military force can also overcome coordination difficulties facing the states, and it can make military decisions that are cost-justified from the perspective of the nation as a whole, not of one state. So, a central government can, in principle, provide for the common defense more effectively than the separate states. Presumably reflecting this understanding, Article IX of the Articles of Confederation gave the Confederation Congress military-defense powers, including to engage in war; to grant letters of marque and reprisal (which are commissions to privately owned ships to capture enemy vessels); to determine the money needed for national defense; to decide the number of warships to be built or bought; to identify the number of land and sea forces to be raised; and to appoint a commander in chief of the army and navy.

There were, however, two significant problems with the Articles in this domain. First, for the Confederation Congress to exercise these military powers, nine states had to agree. As Chapter 4 discussed, supermajority requirements can severely impede collective action. Second, Congress was powerless to raise land and naval forces directly. As with taxation, Congress could only requisition the states for their proportionate share of troops. During the Revolutionary War, this scheme had harmed the states, which (as Chapter 4 also discussed) often ignored the requisition orders for troops and taxes.[12] General Washington captured the situation on March 4, 1783. In his prior letter to Washington, Hamilton had expressed concern that the soldiers in the Continental Army were growing increasingly upset because the states had not contributed sufficient funds to pay them. Broadly sharing Hamilton's view, Washington responded that "[t]he

---

[11] There is also the danger—partially addressed by the third clause of Article I, Section 10, *see* Chapter 3—that states with their own militaries might use them against sister states, triggering retaliation and an arms race.

[12] AKHIL REED AMAR, AMERICA'S CONSTITUTION: A BIOGRAPHY 114 (2005).

234   THE COLLECTIVE-ACTION CONSTITUTION

sufferings of a complaining army on one hand, and the inability of congress and tardiness of the states on the other, are the forebodings of evil."[13]

The situation hardly improved once the war ended. Fear of military vulnerability in a war—whether with Britain, Spain, or Native nations, or among the states or sections themselves—was a main reason why the Constitution was ratified despite strong opposition in some state ratifying conventions. Not coincidentally, the argument that national security demanded ratification dominates the seven essays in *The Federalist Papers* immediately after Hamilton's introduction in *Federalist 1*. The Founders distrusted military power (especially standing armies), but collective action trumped this concern amid existential threats.[14]

In three primary ways, the Constitution authorizes Congress to solve the collective-action problems that must be overcome to provide for the common defense not just in theory but also in practice. First, as Chapter 4 discussed, the opening clause of Section 8 gives Congress plenary authority to tax individuals directly, not through the states. Congress can thereby raise the funds it deems necessary to spend on national defense.

Second, Clauses 11 through 16 give Congress direct powers of national defense. They include the authority to "declare War";[15] to "raise and support Armies" subject to a temporal restriction on appropriations for this purpose (again, because standing armies were distrusted);[16] to "provide and maintain a Navy"[17] with no temporal restriction on appropriations (because navies were not viewed as threatening liberty); to "make Rules for the Government and Regulation" of the nation's military forces;[18] to "provide for calling forth the Militia" for certain purposes;[19] and to "provide for organizing, arming, and disciplining, the Militia," as well as "for governing such Part of them as may be employed in the Service of the United States."[20] Collectively, these clauses empower Congress to solve the collective-action problems of defending the nation by raising, supporting, governing, regulating, and authorizing the president to use a national military force.

---

[13] Letter from George Washington to Alexander Hamilton (Mar. 4, 1783), *reprinted in* II HISTORY OF THE REPUBLIC OF THE UNITED STATES OF AMERICA, AS TRACED IN THE WRITINGS OF ALEXANDER HAMILTON AND OF HIS CONTEMPORARIES 380 (John C. Hamilton ed., 1868).

[14] AMAR, *supra* note 12, at 46–47.

[15] U.S. CONST. art. I, § 8, cl. 11. This clause also authorizes Congress to "grant Letters of Marque and Reprisal" and "make Rules concerning Captures on Land and Water." *Id.*

[16] U.S. CONST. art. I, § 8, cl. 12 (granting the power "[t]o raise and support Armies," but providing that "no Appropriation of Money to that Use shall be for a longer Term than two Years").

[17] U.S. CONST. art. I, § 8, cl. 13.

[18] U.S. CONST. art. I, § 8, cl. 14.

[19] U.S. CONST. art. I, § 8, cl. 15. These purposes are "to execute the Laws of the Union, suppress insurrections and repel Invasions." *Id.*

[20] U.S. CONST. art. I, § 8, cl. 16. This clause "reserv[es] to the States respectively, the Appointment of the Officers, and the Authority of training the Militia according to the discipline prescribed by Congress." *Id.*

NATIONAL SECURITY AND NATIONAL UNIFORMITY   235

Third, as with other Section 8 powers, Congress can wield these military powers by majority vote in each chamber, not by the two-thirds requirement of the Articles. Just as supermajority rule impedes collective action, majority rule animates it. Majority rule makes it more likely that Congress will be able to solve not just Pareto collective-action problems for the states, but cost-benefit collective-action problems as well.

Positive Interstate Externalities: The Postal and Intellectual-Property Powers

Congressional authority to create and run a national postal system and confer intellectual-property rights are not often discussed together. Nor are they typically linked to Section 8's military-defense clauses. All three, however, empower Congress to solve collective-action problems by internalizing positive interstate externalities.

The Postal Network

Article IX of the Articles of Confederation assigned to Congress the exclusive power to "establish[] or regulat[e] post offices from one State to another, throughout all the United States, and exacting such postage on the papers passing through the same as may be requisite to defray the expenses of the said office." In giving Congress this power, the states generally followed the practice of the Second Continental Congress, which largely looked to the British imperial postal system. As Professor Robert Natelson explains, both the Continental Congress and the Confederation Congress generally "saw the purposes of the post office in much the same way the British did," which was to serve as "a medium for official government intercourse, as a source of government intelligence and revenue, and as an aid for commerce."[21]

The Framers of the Constitution were also influenced by British practice. Benjamin Franklin was most responsible for establishing the US post office. He had gained roughly a half-century of experience serving as postmaster at Philadelphia (in 1737), deputy postmaster general for the American Colonies

---

[21] Robert G. Natelson, *Founding-Era Socialism: The Original Meaning of the Constitution's Postal Clause*, 7 Brit. J. Am. Legal Stud. 1, 8, 33 (2018). *See* United States Postal Service v. Council of Greenburgh Civic Assns., 453 U.S. 114, 121 (1981) ("By the early 18th century, the posts were made a sovereign function in almost all nations because they were considered a sovereign necessity. Government without communication is impossible, and until the invention of the telephone and telegraph, the mails were the principal means of communication.").

236 THE COLLECTIVE-ACTION CONSTITUTION

(1753), and the first postmaster general named by the Continental Congress (1775).[22] He hewed to the British model, as did the Framers. Consistency with tradition helps explain why the inclusion in Section 8 of the power "[t]o establish Post Offices and post Roads"[23]—language from a British postal statute[24]—provoked relatively little controversy during the Convention and ratification debates.

The Founders did not, however, simply follow tradition. The Postal Clause extends congressional power to intrastate postal operations and post roads and so is broader than the Articles' grant. During the 1780s, there was substantial uncertainty regarding whether the Confederation Congress could establish intrastate postal routes, and in any event intrastate federal service was unreliable. To obtain service on certain routes, several states had to pay some or all the expenses or salaries of government riders, and New Hampshire, Maryland, and the district of Vermont even resorted to establishing their own internal postal systems.[25] The reference in Resolution VI of the Virginia Plan to separate state incompetence likely referred partly to the need for a comprehensive federal postal power: Franklin's early draft of the Articles of Confederation had included similar language regarding state incompetence and named the post office as one example.[26] The impediments to expanding the postal network during the 1780s likely helped produce the consensus that the federal government should establish a national postal system that ignored state borders.

Given everything else they disagreed about, however, nationalists and advocates of states' rights likely did not agree on all the purposes to which the postal power should be put. For example, Madison offered the disarming reassurance in *Federalist 42* that "[t]he power of establishing post roads must, in every view, be a harmless power."[27] Yet, in the ensuing decades, controversies arose over whether this power limited Congress to designating existing roads as postal routes or instead authorized Congress to (1) build such roads; (2) build post roads without the consent of the states in which the roads would reside; (3) operate its own system of mail transports; and (4) monopolize mail

[22] *Council of Greenburgh Civic Assns.*, 453 U.S. at 121.

[23] U.S. CONST. art. I, § 8, cl. 7.

[24] Natelson, *supra* note 21, at 8.

[25] RICHARD R. JOHN, SPREADING THE NEWS: THE AMERICAN POSTAL SYSTEM FROM FRANKLIN TO MORSE 45 (1995); George L. Priest, *The History of the Postal Monopoly in the United States*, 18 J.L. & ECON. 33, 50 (1975).

[26] Natelson, *supra* note 21, at 8, 32–33, 42–52. For Franklin's reference, see Franklin's Articles of Confederation, art. V, *in* 2 J. CONT'L. CONG. 1774–1789, at 195, 196 (Jul. 21, 1775) (Worthington Chauncey Ford ed., 1905) ("The Congress shall also make such general Ordinances as tho' necessary to the General Welfare, particular Assemblies cannot be competent to; viz. Those that may relate . . . to the Establishment of Posts.").

[27] THE FEDERALIST No. 42, at 271 (James Madison) (Clinton Rossiter ed., 1961).

carriage.[28] Framers who sought to limit federal power and then Anti-federalists generally favored the post office as a revenue source. By partial contrast, nationalist Framers and then Federalists sought "to strengthen the federal government, and those in control of the federal government."[29] They believed that, in addition to raising revenue, the postal power would facilitate communication between the federal government and the public and would work with other Section 8 powers authorizing Congress to overcome preexisting collective-action failures by the states. A federal postal system would, for example, help military and civilian leaders convey orders and intelligence and pay the troops on time. The development of commerce, too, required the ability to convey information and payments across state and national lines without interference from inconsistent or parochial state regulations. Although the Framers generally opposed monopolies, they deemed these objectives sufficiently important that they gave Congress "a single sweeping power: erecting and operating a national transportation, freight, and communication monopoly."[30]

Over time, the nationalist understanding of the postal power would prevail, even as some of the perceived purposes of the postal system would change. Reflecting the view that the dissemination of political information was essential not just to amplifying the voices of federal officials but also to preserving free government in America, the Post Office Act of 1792 transformed federal postal policy by guaranteeing all newspapers the right to use the mails at heavily subsidized rates and by prohibiting postal agents from surveilling the contents of the mail.[31] The Act's creation of a legal norm against government surveillance of the mail was regarded as a significant development (particularly given the surveillance practices of Great Britain, France, the German states, and Russia), even

---

[28] Richard B. Kielbowicz, *The Power to Establish Post Offices and Post Roads*, *in* THE POWERS OF CONGRESS, *supra* note 8, at 83.

[29] Natelson, *supra* note 21, at 7.

[30] *Id.* at 6, 7; *see id.* at 55 ("The system was a network designed primarily to (1) facilitate information flow between the central government and the public at large (including government intelligence and propaganda), (2) raise revenue, and (3) facilitate trade and commerce."). *See also Council of Greenburgh Civic Assns.*, 453 U.S. at 121 ("The Post Office played a vital yet largely unappreciated role in the development of our new Nation. Stagecoach trails which were improved by the Government to become post roads quickly became arteries of commerce. Mail contracts were of great assistance to the early development of new means of transportation such as canals, railroads, and eventually airlines."); *see also id.* ("[B]ecause of the trend toward war [in the 1770s], the Continental Congress undertook its first serious effort to establish a secure mail delivery organization in order to maintain communication between the States and to supply revenue for the Army.").

[31] Geneveive Lakier, *The Non-First Amendment Law of Freedom of Speech*, 134 HARV. L. REV. 2299, 2309–11 (2021). Other speakers, particularly merchants, had to pay more for using the mails, thereby subsidizing newspapers. *Id.* at 2313–14; *see* JOHN, *supra* note 25, at 39–40 ("To reduce the cost of securing political information for citizen-farmers, many of whom lived in the South and West, Congress increased the cost of doing business for merchants, most of whom lived in the North and East. In the broadest sense, then, this policy was . . . regulatory or, more precisely, redistributive."). On the uses of the post office as a political tool of federal officials in the years after ratification of the Constitution, see Priest, *supra* note 25, at 51–55.

238   THE COLLECTIVE-ACTION CONSTITUTION

though the Act's prohibition on surveillance was violated with some frequency, and judicially enforced First Amendment limits on surveillance did not come until the twentieth century.[32] As for revenue-raising, today's US Postal Service tends to lose more money than it generates.[33]

Even as certain purposes have come into prominence and others have receded, there continue to be collective-action rationales for giving the postal power to the federal government, as opposed to the states individually.[34] Like the powers to maintain a national transportation network (which the previous chapter discussed), provide for the common defense (which, as noted, the Postal Clause facilitates), and confer intellectual-property rights (which is discussed below), the postal power enables Congress to internalize positive interstate externalities. The post office is a network that becomes more valuable for each user as it acquires more pick-up and delivery points. In this regard, the post office in the eighteenth century resembles the railroad and the telegraph in the nineteenth century, the telephone in the nineteenth and twentieth centuries, the interstate-highway system in the twentieth century, and the internet in the late twentieth and twenty-first centuries. Legal scholars who observed positive externalities on the internet called them "network effects."[35]

The status of the post office as a network helps structurally justify the Supreme Court's broad and dynamic view of the Postal Clause. So does Congress's ability to use this power to overcome collective-action problems and establish a national free-trade zone. In *Pensacola Telegraph Company v. Western Union Telegraph Company* (1877), the Court described the breadth of federal postal power and its link to the Interstate Commerce Clause:

> The [interstate commerce and postal] powers . . . are not confined to the instrumentalities of commerce, or the postal service known or in use when the Constitution was adopted, but they keep pace with the progress of the country,

---

[32] JOHN, *supra* note 25, at 41–44. On judicial review, see *Lamont v. Postmaster General*, 381 U.S. 301 (1965) (invalidating a federal law on First Amendment grounds for the first time). The statute empowered the Post Office to detain mail that it deemed "communist political propaganda" and to forward it only if the addressee notified the Post Office of her desire to receive it.

[33] Kielbowicz, *supra* note 28, at 92–93. In 1971, Congress converted the Post Office Department into an independent government corporation, the US Postal Service (USPS), ceding much of its power over postal affairs. *Id.* at 82.

[34] A question not addressed here is whether any level of government should run a postal system today, given the efficiency of private businesses that deliver mail and packages. In addition to efficiency concerns, it is relevant that postal subsidies remain an important government benefit that newspapers and magazines receive.

[35] *See, e.g.*, Brett M. Frischmann & Barbara van Schewick, *Network Neutrality and the Economics of an Information Superhighway: A Reply to Professor Yoo*, 47 JURIMETRICS J. 383, 402 n.62 (2007) ("A network effect exists if consumers' valuation of the good increases with the number of users of the good; this leads to an externality because a user who considers joining the network does not consider the positive impact of his adoption decision on other users.") (citing Michael L. Katz & Carl Shapiro, *Network Externalities, Competition, and Compatibility*, 75 AM. ECON. REV. 424 (1985)).

NATIONAL SECURITY AND NATIONAL UNIFORMITY 239

and adapt themselves to the new developments of time and circumstances. They extend from the horse with its rider to the stage coach, from the sailing vessel to the steamboat, from the coach and the steamboat to the railroad, and from the railroad to the telegraph, as these new agencies are successively brought into use to meet the demands of increasing population and wealth. They were intended for the government of the business to which they relate, at all times and under all circumstances. As they were entrusted to the general government for the good of the nation, it is not only the right but the duty of Congress to see to it that intercourse among the states and the transmission of intelligence are not obstructed or unnecessarily encumbered by state legislation.[36]

The Court in this case held that a state law granting a telegraph monopoly was preempted by a federal law prohibiting states from granting such monopolies.[37] A year later, the Court again emphasized the breadth of the postal power, writing that it "has been practically construed, since the foundation of the government, to authorize not merely the designation of the routes over which the mail shall be carried, and the offices where letters and other documents shall be received to be distributed or forwarded, but the carriage of the mail, and all measures necessary to secure its safe and speedy transit, and the prompt delivery of its contents."[38]

Given their limited territorial jurisdiction, states acting individually could not maintain a nationwide postal network. Moreover, the fifty states, or more than a few private firms, that tried to expand the network absent congressional oversight would likely face significant cost-benefit collective-action problems, cooperation problems, or coordination-plus-disagreement problems. For example, states would have to resist temptations to favor in-staters over out-of-staters in various ways and to free ride off the contributions of other states to the maintenance and use of interstate routes. States would also need to coordinate their approaches along many dimensions, including interconnectivity, universal service, and the locations of post offices and post roads. A single state with divergent regulations could significantly undermine the efficacy of the network. And states would have to overcome disagreements about the purposes of the network

---

[36] 96 U.S. 1 (1877).

[37] The Court deemed the federal statute supported by the Interstate Commerce and Postal Clauses combined with the Necessary and Proper Clause. The Court did not view the telegraph as part of the postal system; rather, it reasoned that the state law interfered with the erection of telegraph lines on post roads by corporations not granted the monopoly, in contravention of the federal law. *Id.* at 11; *see id.* at 10 ("It is not necessary now to inquire whether Congress may assume the telegraph as part of the postal service, and exclude all others from its use. The present case is satisfied, if we find that Congress has power, by appropriate legislation, to prevent the States from placing obstructions in the way of its usefulness.").

[38] Ex parte Jackson, 96 U.S. 727, 732 (1878). From a First Amendment standpoint, *Ex parte Jackson* is troubling. It upheld congressional power to close the postal system to literature concerning lotteries.

240   THE COLLECTIVE-ACTION CONSTITUTION

and how to accomplish them. For all that has changed over time regarding views of the post office, there have not been serious proposals to return the power to the states, and collective-action reasoning explains why.

True, as with other enumerated powers, collective-action logics do not comprehensively explain the Postal Clause. For example, collective-action theory cannot determine whether the postal network should be used primarily to raise revenue, to defend the nation, to facilitate interstate commerce, to enhance federal officials' influence on public opinion, to protect democratic self-government, or to accomplish some combination of these purposes or others. Moreover, collective-action reasoning cannot explain why the federal government long monopolized mail delivery itself and did not instead regulate how corporations delivered the mail—as with the rail, telegraph, and phone networks.[39] Even so, once it is determined that the postal network will be used to accomplish certain purposes and that government, not private entities, will achieve them, collective-action rationales explain why the federal government, not the states, has controlled the network, both historically and today.[40]

Intellectual Property

The Intellectual Property Clauses authorizes Congress "[t]o promote the Progress of Science and useful Arts, by securing for limited Times to Authors and Inventors the exclusive Right to their respective Writings and Discoveries."[41] This power to make uniform intellectual-property law appropriately follows the Postal Clause; the two have much in common, even if the similarities are not obvious. First, the subject of both clauses is partly communication—the transmission of information—through the mails or certain creative works. Congress can thus use both powers to facilitate knowledge acquisition and intellectual life in the nation.

Second, notwithstanding the general hostility of the Founders to monopolies after bitter experience with them in England, both clauses grant Congress the power to establish monopolies: government-run in the case of the post office and government-sanctioned in the case of patents and copyrights. The English system of monopolies invisibly taxed citizens by granting exclusive patents for items (like salt) that citizens already possessed to raise revenue for the Crown

---

[39] For discussion of the reasons for this difference in treatment, see Kielbowicz, *supra* note 28.

[40] *See* Priest, *supra* note 25, at 51 ("The founders understood . . . that, like the commerce power, Congress's postal power is essential to give the federal government authority to restrain actions of individual states that might impede or interfere with intercourse national in scope. The authority to designate routes and to establish offices is necessary to this objective. The power to provide service and to monopolize it is not" (footnote omitted).).

[41] U.S. CONST. art. I, § 8, cl. 7.

and to reward its supporters.[42] In several ways, the Intellectual Property Clause seems constructed to prevent the reproduction of such corruption. The clause opens by declaring that the power—or, depending on one's interpretive position, the purpose of the grant—is "[t]o promote the Progress of Science and useful Arts," not some other power or purpose, such as raising revenue for the government, rewarding political allies or donors, or protecting the moral or natural rights of creators.[43] The clause then restricts the duration of the grant of monopoly power ("for limited Times"), and finally limits the beneficiaries of the grant to "Authors" who produce "Writings" and "Inventors" who make "Discoveries," thereby implying requirements of originality in the case of copyright and both novelty and nonobviousness in the case of patent. No longer could the government tax citizens for items they already had (due to the requirements of originality and novelty) or would inevitably obtain (due to the requirement of nonobviousness).[44]

Third, both the postal and intellectual-property powers, like the military clauses, are instances of federal power to internalize positive externalities. Whereas the post office is a network, an author without a copyright cannot prevent someone else from reprinting their book, and an inventor without a patent cannot prevent someone else from copying their invention. Moreover, if the book and invention can be reproduced cheaply, one person's use of them does not prevent another person from using them. Thomas Jefferson recognized these public-good qualities in 1813, writing in a letter to Isaac McPherson that "the moment [an idea] is divulged, it forces itself into the possession of every one, and the receiver cannot dispossess himself of it." Put differently, ideas are non-excludable. Jefferson added that "no one possess the less, because every other possess the whole of it." In other words, ideas are non-rivalrous.[45] Effective intellectual-property law, which permits not the ownership of ideas but temporary ownership of their expression or application, combats the underproduction

---

[42] Colin D. Moore, *The Power to Regulate Patents and Copyright*, in THE POWERS OF CONGRESS, *supra* note 8, at 96.

[43] *See* Wheaton v. Peters, 33 U.S. (8 Pet.) 591 (1834) (reaffirming that copyright is a congressional grant of monopoly power, not a natural right). Congress had expressed the same view in the Copyright Act of 1790. Moore, *supra* note 42, at 100.

[44] In 1952, Congress codified the nonobviousness requirement to obtain a patent. In *Graham v. John Deer Company*, 383 U.S. 1 (1966), the Court justified it based on the Founders' utilitarian reasons for authorizing Congress to issue patents (as evidenced by the opening language of the Intellectual Property Clause), not based on a moral or natural rights view. Contrary to the dominant understanding today, the Court viewed this power as limited by its opening language. *Id.* at 5–6.

[45] Letter from Thomas Jefferson to Isaac McPherson (Aug. 13, 1813), *in* XIII THE WRITINGS OF THOMAS JEFFERSON 326, 333–34 (Albert Ellery Bergh ed., 1907). For a reading of this letter emphasizing both Jefferson's skepticism about intellectual property rights given the monopolistic dangers they pose and his acknowledgment that society may want to confer them anyway for temporary periods for society's benefit (not to respect natural rights), see JAMES BOYLE, THE PUBLIC DOMAIN: ENCLOSING THE COMMONS OF THE MIND 17–41 (2008).

242 THE COLLECTIVE-ACTION CONSTITUTION

of creations due to their generation of positive externalities by enabling creators to collect fees from users, which provides added incentive for creativity.[46] More accurately, effective intellectual-property law balances the social utility of providing externality-internalizing incentives to creators against the social utility of promoting and preserving the public domain so that the public, including future creators, can benefit from prior creations.[47]

Fourth, and most importantly here, the positive externalities generated by the activities that the Postal and Intellectual Property Clauses empower Congress to encourage are interstate in scope. Regarding intellectual-property rights, the problem of unauthorized use extends across state lines, so states acting individually cannot solve it. The problem is national, so Congress, with its national legislative jurisdiction, is structurally best situated to solve it. Federal intellectual-property law enables creators to collect fees from users across the nation, which creates a unified national market for creative works. Intellectual property, like the postal service and military defense, affects the "general" welfare because of positive interstate externalities.[48]

The Intellectual Property Clause is unique among these three powers, however, because the Articles of Confederation denied Congress the authority to regulate any aspect of the problem. The issue was left to the states, but the states had divergent regulatory schemes.[49] Unsurprisingly, therefore, Madison in his *Vices* Memo decried "want of uniformity in the laws concerning . . . literary property."[50] Although Madison was more nationalist than many Framers and Founders, his views on granting a federal intellectual-property power were widely shared; the

---

[46] Robert D. Cooter & Neil S. Siegel, *Collective Action Federalism: A General Theory of Article I, Section 8*, 63 STAN. L. REV. 115, 148–49 (2010). *See* 3 JOSEPH STORY, COMMENTARIES ON THE CONSTITUTION OF THE UNITED STATES § 1147, p. 49 (1833) ("[T]he only boon, which could be offered to inventors to disclose the secrets of their discoveries, would be the exclusive right and profit of them, as a monopoly for a limited period. And authors would have little inducement to prepare elaborate works for the public, if their publication was to be at a large expense, and, as soon as they were published, there would be an unlimited right of depredation and piracy of their copyright.").

[47] Jefferson is typically read as having been hostile to intellectual-property rights, in contrast to Madison. *See, e.g.*, EDWARD C. WALTERSCHEID, THE NATURE OF THE INTELLECTUAL PROPERTY CLAUSE: A STUDY IN HISTORICAL PERSPECTIVE 4–9 (2002). At least in this letter, however, Jefferson seemed to emphasize the need to balance incentives for creativity and public access. BOYLE, *supra* note 45, at 20–21. This need is also a point of Professor Boyle's book. *See also* Lawrence Lessig, Commentary, *The Creative Commons*, 65 MONT. L. REV. 1, 11 (2004) ("The idea here is that we need to build a layer of reasonable copyright law, by showing the world a layer of reasonable copyright law resting on top of the extremes. Take this world that is increasingly a world by default regulating all and change it into a world where once again we can see the mix between all, none, and some, using the technology of the Creative Commons."). *But see* William M. Landes & Richard A. Posner, *Indefinitely Renewable Copyright*, 70 U. CHI. L. REV. 471, 471–75 (2003) ("rais[ing] questions concerning the widely accepted proposition that economic efficiency requires that copyright protection should be limited in its duration").

[48] Cooter & Siegel, *supra* note 46, at 149.

[49] *See infra* note 55 and accompanying text.

[50] Madison, *Vices Memo*, *supra* note 6, at 363.

NATIONAL SECURITY AND NATIONAL UNIFORMITY   243

Framers adopted the clause without recorded debate or dissent, and it was uncontroversial at the ratifying conventions and among the public.[51]

"The utility of this power will scarcely be questioned," Madison observed in *Federalist 43*. He reasoned that "[t]he public good fully coincides in both cases [patent and copyright] with the claims of individuals," and "[t]he States cannot separately make effectual provision for either of the cases, and most of them have anticipated the decision of this point by laws passed at the instance of Congress."[52] Madison was making two points. First, individual creators would benefit financially from exclusive ownership of their creations for a time, and society would benefit from the creations incentivized by the temporary grants of monopoly power. Second, the interstate scope of the problem of unauthorized use meant that, in the language of Resolution VI, the states were separately incompetent to handle it and the national harmony would be interrupted by individual state legislation. The general interests of the Union required federal control.

More precisely, to adequately address—but not over-address—the problem of unauthorized use, the states would potentially have to solve coordination problems, cooperation problems, or cost-benefit collective-action problems. States would have an incentive to coordinate their intellectual-property regimes because the problem of unauthorized use spills across state borders, so no state can adequately enforce its regime of rights protection without help from sister states. As Edward Walterscheid observes, "the states in their individual capacities had sought to provide some form of limited-term exclusive rights in their writings and discoveries to inventors and authors," but "by early in 1787 the defects in the state copyright and patent custom were obvious." The greatest "defect was that states could only legislate with respect to their own territory," so "state patents and copyrights could be infringed with impunity in adjoining

---

[51] 2 THE RECORDS OF THE FEDERAL CONVENTION OF 1787, *supra* note 2, at 505 (Sept. 5). *See* WALTERSCHEID, *supra* note 47, at 2, 10–11 (noting the lack of dispute over the Intellectual Property Clause during the Philadelphia Convention and the state ratifying conventions); Edward C. Walterscheid, *Originalism and the IP Clause: A Commentary on Professor Oliar's "New Reading"*, 58 UCLA DISCOURSE 113, 115 n.11 (2010) (noting the lack of debate at the Philadelphia Convention); Moore, *supra* note 42, at 97–98 (same); EDWARD C. WALTERSCHEID, TO PROMOTE THE PROGRESS OF USEFUL ARTS 58–59 (1998) (noting the lack of debate during the state ratifying conventions and among the public). For an effort to discern the original intent behind the Intellectual Property Clause through examination of its drafting history, see Dotan Oliar, *The (Constitutional) Convention on IP: A New Reading*, 57 UCLA L. REV. 421 (2009); Dotan Oliar, *Making Sense of the Intellectual Property Clause: Promotion of Progress as a Limitation on Congress's Intellectual Property Power*, 94 GEO. L.J. 1771 (2006). For a critique of this effort, see Walterscheid, *Originalism and the IP Clause*, *supra*. Walterscheid's essay draws partly from his history of the Intellectual Property Clause. *See* WALTERSCHEID, *supra* note 47.

[52] THE FEDERALIST NO. 43, at 271–72 (James Madison) (Clinton Rossiter ed., 1961). *See* 3 STORY, *supra* note 46, at § 1147, p. 49 ("The states could not separately make effectual provision for either of the cases, and most of them, at the time of the adoption of the constitution, had anticipated the propriety of such a grant of power, by passing laws on the subject at the instance of the continental congress.").

244 THE COLLECTIVE-ACTION CONSTITUTION

states." Further, obtaining "multiple state patents or copyrights was time consuming, expensive, and frequently frustrating."[53]

Insofar as states wanted to coordinate, they would have to overcome disagreements over which regulatory regime to adopt, as in the Bridge or Seaway game. Walterscheid notes that "there was no certainty or consistency in terms and conditions from state to state."[54] At the Founding, state regimes differed along several dimensions, including the term and renewability of the grant of exclusivity; the number and nature of exceptions to the grant; the conditions, if any, attached the grant; the possible reservation of an option to revoke the grant in exchange for a monetary payment; and the issuance of compulsory licenses notwithstanding the grant if the public was denied access to the creation at a reasonable price.[55] The Intellectual Property Clause empowers Congress to solve this coordination-plus-disagreement problem by choosing one regime among reasonable alternatives. Without this power, Joseph Story wrote in his *Commentaries*, "authors and inventors . . . would have been subjected to the varying laws and systems of the different states on this subject, which would impair, and might even destroy the value of their rights."[56]

For either of two reasons, states might face a cooperation problem, with a multistate Prisoners' Dilemma being the model. First, if one state's grant of intellectual-property rights was disrespected in another, the first state would be incentivized to respond in kind, potentially making both states worse off. "Some of the state copyright statutes" in the 1780s, Walterscheid reports, "declared that they would not come into force until all states had enacted similar laws, while the majority of them extended protection to residents of other states only on the basis of reciprocity."[57] Second, states might be tempted to compete for businesses or luminaries by granting intellectual-property rights when doing so was unnecessary to properly incentivize the production of creations. Such state behavior would risk triggering a race to the bottom among them as they offered monopoly rents in exchange for no social benefit from the perspective of the states collectively. Leaving the regulation of intellectual property to the states would risk reproducing the corrupt English system of monopolies.[58]

Turning from Pareto collective-action problems to cost-benefit collective-action problems, individual states might grant intellectual-property rights to in-state individuals or businesses in ways that harmed out-of-state individuals or

---

[53] WALTERSCHEID, *supra* note 47, at 76.

[54] *Id.*

[55] BRUCE W. BUGBEE, GENESIS OF AMERICAN PATENT AND COPYRIGHT LAW 84–103 (1967) (state patent laws); *id.* at 104–24 (state copyright laws); COPYRIGHT OFFICE, LIBRARY OF CONGRESS, COPYRIGHT ENACTMENTS 1783–1900, at 9–29 (1900) (state copyright laws).

[56] 3 STORY, *supra* note 46, at § 1147, pp. 48–49.

[57] WALTERSCHEID, *supra* note 47, at 77.

[58] *See supra* note 42 and accompanying text (discussing the English system).

NATIONAL SECURITY AND NATIONAL UNIFORMITY   245

businesses more than they helped the in-state holders of the state patents and copyrights. This would happen, for example, if a state permitted certain in-staters to own facts and ideas. Such state regimes would render impossible the creation of a unified national market for creative works, and they would war with the goal of creating a national free-trade zone.[59] Relatedly, such state regimes appear constitutionally problematic under the dormant commerce principle, which raises the fascinating question of how much work the Interstate Commerce Clause, amplified by the Necessary and Proper Clause, can do regarding intellectual-property rights.

Relative to the states acting individually, Congress can better solve the foregoing collective-action problems by creating a uniform regime of limited protection for intellectual property. And over the course of American history, Congress has mostly done so, facilitating the many successes of creative expression, industrialization, and science in the United States.[60] Moreover, given (dis)agreements with other countries over (dis)respect for intellectual property rights, federal control enables the states to speak with one voice in international negotiations and prevents individual states from drawing the nation into conflict with other nations.

Today, the problem of unauthorized use is often addressed through public funding, especially in science. It makes substantially more sense for the federal government, not the states, to provide the money, given the incentive of states to underfund research. A state that funds research internalizes all the costs of doing so and externalizes most of the benefits. Because all states are similarly situated, there is a multistate collective-action problem.[61]

The insight that Congress can grant intellectual-property rights to solve certain collective-action problems for the states bears on the debate over whether congressional power is limited by the "[t]o promote" language that opens the clause. The modern interpretation of the clause views the "by securing" language as the grant of power and the "[t]o promote" language as the purpose of the grant.[62] The prevailing understanding also views the opening language as

---

[59] Preemption analysis in copyright cases can reproduce these collective-action concerns because the Copyright Act, read literally, implies that it does not preempt state laws that would allow the ownership of ideas or facts, a result that courts have deemed unacceptable. For discussion, see James Boyle & Jennifer Jenkins, INTELLECTUAL PROPERTY: LAW AND THE INFORMATION SOCIETY, CASES AND MATERIALS 605–08 (4th ed. 2018).

[60] Moore, *supra* note 42, at 102–03, 105–06.

[61] The Philadelphia Convention rejected proposals by Madison and Charles Cotesworth Pinckney of South Carolina to give Congress the power to grant encouragements (bounties), which would have paid creators for their works. For discussion, see Oliar, *supra* note 51, at 1797–1803. The First Congress declined an inventor's request for funding due to concerns about the cost of doing so and the poor state of the federal purse. For discussion, see Edward C. Walterscheid, *To Promote the Progress of Science and Useful Arts: The Background and Origin of the Intellectual Property Clause of the United States Constitution*, 2 J. INTEL. PROP. L. 1, 34–35 (1994).

[62] Walterscheid, *supra* note 51, at 117–18.

246   THE COLLECTIVE-ACTION CONSTITUTION

a nonbinding, purposive preamble, although the leading treatise on the subject expresses this view (perhaps tellingly) with multiple qualifications.[63] These interpretations of the clause avoid the potentially enormous and unintended structural implications of rendering the "by securing" language superfluous. For example, Congress might then be able to use this enumerated power to federalize all education in the United States, because doing so could reasonably be viewed as promoting the progress of science and useful arts.[64]

Notably, however, the Intellectual Property Clause is alone among Congress's powers in declaring its purpose as the grant of the power.[65] Moreover, the "by securing" language can still serve as a limitation if the "[t]o promote" language is viewed as the grant. Professor Lawrence Solum reads the Intellectual Property Clause in light of Congress's other Section 8 powers and concludes that the opening phrase is a grant of power while the "by securing" phrase is a limitation.[66] And recent scholarship questions the dominant view that the language opening the clause has no operative force.[67]

A collective-action understanding of the Intellectual Property Clause cannot settle this debate, given the several interpretive modalities that are relevant to its resolution. But a collective-action perspective lends support to scholars who question the prevailing wisdom. Putting aside the issue of what qualifies as "progress"—for example, is it just incentives to create or is it the dissemination of ideas as well?—it is difficult to see why Congress would have been given this power if it were unconstrained by some reasonable understanding of progress, which would exclude rewarding the rent-seeking behavior of political allies or donors.

---

[63]   1 MELVILLE B. NIMMER & DAVID NIMMER, NIMMER ON COPYRIGHT § 1.03 (2020) ("This introductory phrase is, *in the main*, explanatory of the purpose of copyright without, in itself, constituting a *rigid* standard against which any copyright act must be measured" (emphases added).); *id.* § 1.03[B][1] ("[T]he constitutional reference to '[t]o promote the Progress of Science' is best read as *largely* in the nature of a preamble, indicating the purpose of the power, but not in limitation, of its exercise. In fact, the introductory phrase, rather than constituting a limitation on Congressional authority, has *for the most part tended* to expand such authority" (footnotes omitted) (emphases added).).

[64]   At the Philadelphia Convention, Pinckney and Madison proposed not only federal copyright and patent powers but also a federal education power. Madison would have authorized Congress to establish a national university, and Pinckney would have authorized Congress to create seminaries for the promotion of literature and the arts and sciences. The Convention rejected their proposals. For discussions, *see* Oliar, *The (Constitutional) Convention on IP, supra* note 51, at 447, and Oliar, *Making Sense of the Intellectual Property Clause, supra* note 51, at 1815.

[65]   WALTERSCHEID, *supra* note 47, at 3–4 (arguing that the opening language is the grant of power); *see* Walterscheid, *Originalism and the IP Clause, supra* note 51, at 118.

[66]   Lawrence B. Solum, *Congress's Power to Promote the Progress of Science:* Eldred v. Ashcroft, 36 LOY. L.A. L. REV. 1, 10–25 (2002).

[67]   Professor Oliar, whose works are cited *supra* note 51, argues that the opening phrase limits congressional power. Commentators and the justices dispute whether the modern Congress and Court have adequately minded the language opening the Intellectual Property Clause. *See* Eldred v. Ashcroft, 537 U.S. 186 (2003) (permitting Congress to extend by twenty years the term of existing copyrights); Golan v. Holder, 565 U.S. 302 (2012) (permitting Congress to extend copyright protection to works previously in the public domain).

As explained above, part of the collective-action justification for this power is the concern that states may otherwise race to the bottom by reproducing the corrupt English system of monopolies. Without some limiting idea of progress, however, Congress would be free to impose such a corrupt system nationally. This use of the power would likely be a cure worse than the disease of state failures to act collectively.

Courts should approach the question of progress deferentially. Judges are less likely than elected officials to identify progress in the area of intellectual property, and the issue implicates value judgments that Congress possesses the strongest democratic warrant to make. But from a collective-action perspective, the possibility of judicial review in extreme cases would be salutary.

The Virtues of Uniformity: Naturalization and Bankruptcy

As shown, several Section 8 powers, including the Interstate Commerce Clause, the Postal Clause, and the Intellectual Property Clause, authorize Congress to achieve regulatory uniformity. But the phrases "uniform Rule" and "uniform Laws" appear only in the text of the Naturalization and Bankruptcy Clauses, respectively. These word choices reflect the special importance that the Framers placed on national legislative uniformity in these two domains.

Naturalization

The Naturalization Clause gives Congress power "[t]o establish a uniform Rule of Naturalization" in the United States.[68] At the Founding, this clause let Congress effectively determine the Republic's immigration policy. As Professor James Pfander and attorney Theresa Wardon explain, the voyage to the United States from Europe was so arduous and expensive that "those sailing to the new world were (almost invariably) making a permanent decision to relocate." Moreover, "[a]t common law, in England and in the colonies, and newly independent states of North America, aliens could not obtain a fee simple title to real property," so "those contemplating a one-way trip to the United States would have paid close attention to naturalization rules in making their decision."[69]

Letting Congress set naturalization requirements for the nation helped solve collective-action problems for the states in two ways. The first concerns the

---

[68] U.S. Const. art. I, § 8, cl. 4.

[69] James E. Pfander & Theresa R. Wardon, *Reclaiming the Immigration Constitution of the Early Republic: Prospectivity, Uniformity, and Transparency*, 96 Va. L. Rev. 359, 366 (2010).

248   THE COLLECTIVE-ACTION CONSTITUTION

Naturalization Clause itself, and the second concerns its relationship to other powers. First, the Naturalization Clause solved the preexisting collective-action problems that arose when the colonies, and later the states, had their own naturalization policies. The colonies/states perceived no need to embrace restrictive policies; they believed that immigration increased national wealth by expanding the supply of, and the demand for, consumer goods.[70] As a result, the colonies "competed with one another to recruit émigrés from the British Isles and the continent."[71] Great Britain shared the colonists' view of the benefits of population gains and the costs of population losses. Its strenuous efforts to reduce emigration to the colonies eventually earned the colonists' rebuke in the Declaration of Independence that King George III "has endeavoured to prevent the population of these States; for that purpose obstructing the Laws for Naturalization of Foreigners; refusing to pass others to encourage their migrations hither, and raising the conditions of new Appropriations of Lands."[72]

After the war, the states set their own naturalization policies, and "they responded with a profusion of approaches meant to attract new immigrants from Europe."[73] A race to liberalism in naturalization policies may have resulted in some states. These states may have been under pressure to further liberalize their policies regardless of whether they preferred to do so, making them collectively worse off from their own perspectives. The strategic environment was more complex than a simple race to liberalism, however, because South Carolina and some other states resisted liberal policies.[74]

It is less speculative to infer the existence of a coordination or cost-benefit collective-action problem facing states that wanted to enforce restrictions in their naturalization policies. The problem was caused by interstate mobility combined with Article IV of the Articles of Confederation. Article IV's privileges and immunities clause, the precursor to the one in Article IV of the Constitution, provided that "the free inhabitants of each of these States . . . shall be entitled to all privileges and immunities of free citizens in the several States; and the

---

[70] Naturalization policy became more restrictive in the 1790s, in response to European crises set off by the French Revolution and perceived threats to national security both externally and internally. *See* JAMES H. KETTNER, THE DEVELOPMENT OF AMERICAN CITIZENSHIP, 1608–1870, at 232–47 (1978). Generally, however, naturalization and immigration were inclusive (and tended to be viewed as different matters to be dealt with by the federal and state governments, respectively) relative to the restrictions imposed beginning in the 1870s and 1880s, when Congress first effectively claimed that its power over naturalization implied power over immigration. For discussion of how, "[a]t each historical moment, the immigrant body has been constructed in ways that mirror the prevailing political, social, and economic issues of the day—and Congress's response to the political-electoral risks and opportunities these issues presented," see Joanna Mosser, *The Power to Regulate Immigration, in* THE POWERS OF CONGRESS, *supra* note 8, at 51, 43–56.

[71] Pfander & Wardon, *supra* note 69, at 372.

[72] DECLARATION OF INDEPENDENCE (1776).

[73] Pfander & Wardon, supra note 69, at 383; *see* KETTNER, *supra* note 70, at 213–19.

[74] Pfander & Wardon, *supra* note 69, at 383–85.

NATIONAL SECURITY AND NATIONAL UNIFORMITY   249

people of each State shall have free ingress and regress to and from any other State." This provision, Pfander and Wardon explain, "effectively permitted an alien to seek naturalization in a state with permissive naturalization practices and then move to a state with tighter restrictions, and still be entitled to all the incumbent rights of naturalized citizens in the second state."[75] For example, an alien could be naturalized in Pennsylvania and move to South Carolina, evading South Carolina's tougher requirements.[76] For this reason, Madison in *Federalist 42* would later call this provision a "very improper power."[77] The states with relatively restrictive policies needed the help of sister states to enforce their naturalization policies, even as they disagreed about which naturalization policy to adopt. If states preferred coordination to noncoordination, this situation is appropriately modeled as a Bridge or Seaway game involving multiple states. If states did not prefer coordination to noncoordination, the situation involved cost externalization by states with more liberal policies onto states with more restrictive ones, potentially creating a cost-benefit collective-action problem.

Given these potential collective-action problems, it is unsurprising that, as early as 1782, Madison called for the establishment of a uniform rule of naturalization that would bind all states. Broad agreement with this position "made the transfer of naturalization power to the new federal government one of the least controversial features of the new Constitution," Pfander and Wardon write. A uniform national rule "would limit state competition for new immigrants"— the possible cooperation problem—"and would prevent immigrants from seeking citizenship under one state's regime and then transferring their newly acquired citizenship to another state under the privileges and immunities clause"—the potential coordination or cost-benefit collective-action problem.[78]

Madison and Edmund Randolph understood naturalization to fall within Resolution VI. Recall that Randolph had introduced the Virginia Plan on May 29. On June 16, he expressed to the Convention his view that a "provision for harmony among the States, as in trade, naturalization . . . must be made."[79] By conferring power to create a national rule, the Constitution authorized Congress to solve the previous collective-action problems that harmed many or most colonies during the colonial era and many or most states during the 1780s. Hamilton thus emphasized in *Federalist 32* that federal naturalization power "must necessarily be exclusive; because if each State had power to prescribe a DISTINCT RULE, there could not be a UNIFORM RULE."[80] Today, the Naturalization

---

[75] *Id.* at 384.
[76] KETTNER, *supra* note 70, at 221.
[77] THE FEDERALIST No. 42, at 270 (James Madison) (Clinton Rossiter ed., 1961).
[78] Pfander & Wardon, *supra* note 69, at 385, 388.
[79] 1 THE RECORDS OF THE FEDERAL CONVENTION OF 1787, *supra* note 2, at 256.
[80] THE FEDERALIST No. 32, at 199 (Alexander Hamilton) (Clinton Rossiter ed., 1961).

250   THE COLLECTIVE-ACTION CONSTITUTION

Clause prevents the collective-action problems that would result if states could establish their own naturalization policies, whether they be races to liberalism or severity, coordination-plus-disagreement problems, or cost-benefit collective-action problems.

Letting Congress set naturalization requirements for the nation helps solve collective-action problems in a second way. Such authority enhances the efficacy of congressional power under the Interstate Commerce Clause to create a national free-trade zone. Labor mobility increases when people need not fear the citizenship (and other immigration) implications of their moving interstate for employment purposes.[81] Further, granting Congress the naturalization power amplifies the states' ability to speak with one voice in international affairs, including under the Foreign Commerce Clause. The nation's naturalization and immigration policies have implications for its interactions with other countries. Today, for example, such policies at the nation's Southern border impact diplomatic relations with Latin American countries.

Bankruptcy

The Bankruptcy Clause, housed with the Naturalization Clause, authorizes Congress to "establish . . . uniform Laws on the subject of Bankruptcies throughout the United States."[82] The clause occasioned little debate at the Constitutional Convention. On August 29, 1787, Professor Kurt Nadelmann explains, Charles Pinckney of South Carolina moved for a federal bankruptcy power "in consequence of a discussion of interstate conflicts problems in the field of insolvency"[83]—a suggestion by Wilson and William Johnson of Connecticut that "acts of the Legislature should be included" within the Full Faith and Credit Clause "for the sake of Acts of insolvency."[84] On September 1, the Committee of Detail recommended adding the authority "[t]o establish uniform laws on the subject of Bankruptcies" to the Naturalization Clause.[85] On September 3, this clause was adopted "with practically no debate."[86]

---

[81]   Cooter & Siegel, *supra* note 46, at 150.

[82]   U.S. CONST. art. I, § 8, cl. 4.

[83]   Kurt H. Nadelmann, *On the Origin of the Bankruptcy Clause*, 1 AM. J. LEGAL HIST. 215, 216–19, 227 (1957).

[84]   2 THE RECORDS OF THE FEDERAL CONVENTION OF 1787, *supra* note 2, at 447. Chapter 8 discusses the Full Faith and Credit Clause of Article IV, Section 1, which concerns interstate-conflicts problems.

[85]   2 THE RECORDS OF THE FEDERAL CONVENTION OF 1787, *supra* note 2, at 484; *see* Thomas E. Plank, *The Constitutional Limits of Bankruptcy*, 63 TENN. L. REV. 487, 527 (1996).

[86]   Nadelmann, *supra* note 83, at 216. Only Connecticut voted no, apparently because Roger Sherman voiced concerns about empowering Congress to execute bankrupts, which English law allowed in certain situations. *Id.* at 216–17; *see* BRUCE H. MANN, REPUBLIC OF DEBTORS: BANKRUPTCY

The delegates thus agreed that the Constitution, unlike the Articles of Confederation (which had no provision regarding bankruptcies), should confer federal power to create a uniform bankruptcy regime. As Professor Bruce Mann writes, "[t]he idea that bankruptcy raised issues that were better addressed on a national level rather than through the mechanisms of interstate comity seems to have taken at least tentative root during the convention." Key delegates "clearly recognized the problems inherent in applying state insolvency and bankruptcy rules to debtors and creditors who lived in different states. Credit, like commerce, could not be contained within state boundaries."[87] As developed below, one advantage of federal power over bankruptcy was that it would amplify congressional authority under the Interstate Commerce Clause to solve the collective-action problems that inhibited free trade among the states. A second advantage was that the Bankruptcy Clause would empower Congress to address two separate collective-action problems, one caused by the failure of the states to coordinate their divergent bankruptcy regimes, and the other by their potential failure to cooperate or internalize full costs in this arena.

First, the Bankruptcy Clause, like the Naturalization Clause, enhanced congressional power to facilitate the development of interstate commerce and thereby create a national free trade zone. As Professor Mann observes, uniform federal bankruptcy laws, "which subjected debtors and creditors to the same rules and procedures regardless of where they lived, would be more in keeping with the interstate nature of commerce and the credit relations on which commerce rested."[88] Madison, in the sole reference to the Bankruptcy Clause in *The Federalist Papers*, recognized the link between bankruptcy and commerce. In *Federalist 42*, he wrote that "[t]he power of establishing uniform laws of bankruptcy is so intimately connected with the regulation of commerce, and will prevent so many frauds where the parties or their property may lie or be removed into different States, that the expediency of it seems not likely to be drawn into question."[89] Here as elsewhere, Madison focused on the interests of creditors, but Professor Mann explains that "the purpose behind empowering Congress to establish uniform laws on bankruptcy was to protect debtors—albeit not all debtors—as well as creditors."[90] Congress

---

IN THE AGE OF AMERICAN INDEPENDENCE 169 (2002). For the vote, see 2 THE RECORDS OF THE FEDERAL CONVENTION OF 1787, *supra* note 2, at 489.

[87] MANN, *supra* note 86, at 185.
[88] *Id.* at 186.
[89] THE FEDERALIST NO. 42, at 271 (James Madison) (Clinton Rossiter ed., 1961).
[90] MANN, *supra* note 86, at 186. The first federal bankruptcy statute, passed in 1800, was limited to relatively wealthy merchants because these debtors were most likely to have out-of-state creditors and so their bankruptcies were most likely to affect interstate commerce. Randolph J. Haines, *The Uniformity Power: Why Bankruptcy Is Different*, 77 AM. BANKR. L.J. 129, 156–57 (2003).

252   THE COLLECTIVE-ACTION CONSTITUTION

eventually passed uniform bankruptcy laws, increasing stability and trust in capital markets.[91]

Second, as the quotation above from Madison implies, the Bankruptcy Clause gave Congress power to solve a potential coordination problem facing the states. Uniformity in state bankruptcy legislation was lacking before ratification of the Constitution, and this disuniformity was problematic not just for the creditors Madison championed but also for debtors. As the Supreme Court explained in 2006, "the American Colonies, and later the several States, had wildly divergent schemes for discharging debtors [from prison] and their debts."[92] A result of this divergence was that debtors released from prison in one state could, if they traveled to another state, be imprisoned in that state for nonpayment of a debt owed to a creditor there.[93] Unlike in England, where a discharge fully protected the debtor from both imprisonment and creditors, "the uncoordinated actions of multiple sovereigns, each laying claim to the debtor's body and effects according to different rules, rendered impossible so neat a solution."[94] With individual action by states instead of coordinated collective action, no state could effectively enforce its discharge of a debtor and their debts when the debtor traveled interstate.

Professor Nadelmann explains the magnitude of the problem. "Imprisonment for debt, an institution inherited from the mother country, had become one of the great plagues of the time," he writes. "Insolvent debtors, victims of the consequences of the war and, in particular, of the monetary disorders, filled the prisons to capacity. Legislation, different in each state, was inadequate to cope with the situation." Professor Nadelmann identifies as "[t]he great question" during this period "whether action in one state could protect the debtor if he ventured into another state."[95] This was as much a concern for creditors as

---

[91] Cooter & Siegel, *supra* note 46, at 150. "Despite repeated efforts, Congress failed to enact even a temporary bankruptcy law until 1800, and a permanent one not until 1898." MANN, *supra* note 86, at 187. "The apparent ease of including the bankruptcy clause in the constitution was misleading" because of moral opprobrium directed at debtors, which softened during the late eighteenth century but remained present. *Id.* Also, the politics of bankruptcy implicated more than interstate relations: "the debate over bankruptcy relief in the 1790s was conducted in the language and imagery of dependence and independence, slavery and freedom, commerce and agriculture, vice and virtue, nationalism and federalism." *Id.* at 169.

[92] Central Va. Community College v. Katz, 546 U.S. 356, 365 (2006); *see* Plank, *supra* note 85, at 528–29 (discussing the different approaches of different states).

[93] Nadelmann, *supra*, note 83, at 224–25 (discussing *James v. Allen*, 1 Dall. 188 (C. P. Phila. Cty. 1786), and *Millar v. Hall*, 1 Dall. 229 (Pa. 1788)); *Katz*, 546 U.S. at 366–68 (same). One of the attorneys who litigated these cases was Jared Ingersoll of Pennsylvania, a delegate to the Constitutional Convention. While the delegates were meeting in Philadelphia, he was preparing to argue, or had recently argued (the timing is unclear), the *Millar* case, which presented the question of what legal effect a bankruptcy discharge in one state had in another state. MANN, *supra* note 86, at 183–85. Accordingly, such issues were plainly on the minds of at least some delegates.

[94] *Katz*, 546 U.S. at 366.

[95] Nadelmann, *supra* note 83, at 223–24.

NATIONAL SECURITY AND NATIONAL UNIFORMITY 253

debtors, because in-state creditors could not obtain their pro rata share of the assets of an in-state debtor if the debtor refused to agree due to the presence of out-of-state creditors, who themselves might not be notified of the bankruptcy and so receive their pro rata share. "This was a problem no individual state could solve," US bankruptcy judge Randolph Haines observes, "because no state could enact an insolvency law that would affect out of state creditors."[96] The states had good reason to coordinate on a common regime with uniform rules for handling the interstate movements of debtors, but they had to overcome disagreements as to which regime to adopt.

The Bankruptcy Clause also authorized Congress to solve a potential cooperation or cost-benefit collective-action problem. Different states had different policies that partially reflected their views about whether creditors or debtors—and which creditors or debtors—were most deserving of statutory protection.[97] Revealing again his sympathy for creditors over debtors, Madison wrote in his *Vices Memo* that "[a]s the Citizens of every State aggregately taken stand more or less in the relation of Creditors or debtors, to the Citizens of every other State, Acts of the debtor State in favor of debtors, affect the Creditor State, in the same manner, as they do its own citizens who are relatively creditors towards other citizens."[98] If "creditor states" retaliated by favoring creditors over debtors to a greater extent than they otherwise would, a potential cooperation problem would exist. Even if "creditor states" did not retaliate, the policies of "debtor states" were externalizing costs onto "creditor states," potentially creating a cost-benefit collective-action problem.

In his *Commentaries*, Joseph Story described a different cooperation problem. He criticized state bankruptcy and insolvency statutes that "best suit[] [their] own local interests, and pursuits," including by "prefer[ring] creditors living within the state to all living without; securing to the former an entire priority of payment out of the assets," which "may work gross injustice and inequality, and nourish feuds and discontents in neighbouring states." According to Story, "[t]here will always be found in every state a large mass of politicians, who will deem it more safe to consult their own temporary interests and popularity, by a narrow system of preferences, than to enlarge the boundaries, so as to give to distant creditors a fair share of the fortune of a ruined debtor."[99] Story was effectively describing a race to the bottom fueled by state preferences for in-state creditors over out-of-state creditors. This rationale also applies to foreign creditors.

---

[96] Haines, *supra* note 90, at 155; *see id.* at 155–56.

[97] State regimes varied during the late 1700s, and the debate pitted both creditors against debtors and certain debtors against others. Also, many merchants were both creditors and debtors. *See* MANN, *supra* note 86, at 166–220.

[98] Madison, *Vices Memo, supra* note 6, at 362.

[99] 3 STORY, *supra* note 46, at § 1102, p. 7.

254 THE COLLECTIVE-ACTION CONSTITUTION

"Unless the general government were invested with authority to pass suitable laws, which should give reciprocity and equality in cases of bankruptcies here," Story wrote, "there would be danger, that the state legislation might, by undue domestic preferences and favours, compel foreign countries to retaliate."[100]

The same collective-action concerns apply to preferences for in-state debtors over out-of-state debtors. The Bankruptcy Clause does not just let Congress preempt state preferences; its uniformity requirement bars Congress from arbitrarily imposing its own. This requirement, the Court held in *Siegel v. Fitzgerald* (2022), "prohibits Congress from arbitrarily burdening only one set of debtors with a more onerous funding mechanism than that which applies to debtors in other States."[101] The Court in this case unanimously held that the uniformity requirement was violated by a federal statute imposing higher administrative fees on businesses filing for bankruptcy in forty-eight states than in Alabama and North Carolina.

More Uniformity: Standards, Currency, and Counterfeiting

The fifth clause in Section 8 authorizes Congress "[t]o coin Money, regulate the Value thereof, and of foreign Coin, and fix the Standard of Weights and Measures."[102] The sixth clause empowers Congress "[t]o provide for the Punishment of counterfeiting the Securities and current Coin of the United States"[103] This section considers these clauses and other provisions that limit state power in this area. Given the connection between the powers to provide a national currency and to punish counterfeiting it, the discussion will consider them successively after analyzing Congress's authority to set standards.

Standards of Weights and Measures

The Framers approved congressional power to ensure national uniformity in weights and measures without much controversy for reasons of both custom and collective action. As Madison explained in *Federalist 42*, "the regulation of weights and measures is transferred from the Articles of Confederation,"[104] which

---

[100] *Id.* at § 1104.

[101] 142 S. Ct. 1770, 1782–83 (2022); *id.* at 1781 ("[T]he Bankruptcy Clause offers Congress flexibility, but does not permit the arbitrary, disparate treatment of similarly situated debtors based on geography.").

[102] U.S. CONST. art. I, § 8, cl. 5.

[103] U.S. CONST. art. I, § 8, cl. 6.

[104] THE FEDERALIST No. 42, at 269 (James Madison) (Clinton Rossiter ed., 1961).

itself reflected traditional understandings of the Crown's prerogatives.[105] In addition, national standards were deemed useful for regulating trade, participating in trade, defending the nation, advancing scientific progress, and engaging in other activities. Arthur Frazier reports, however, that because of "local political rivalries," the states would have been unlikely to achieve uniformity any time soon. "All of the original thirteen states had been operating with standards of their own choosing and to which they had long since become accustomed, but no two sets were exactly alike." Indeed, "a few of them differed quite drastically from those of the others, and changing them would have entailed serious local hardships."[106] If the states preferred coordination to noncoordination, there was a coordination problem combined with a disagreement problem, as in the Bridge or Seaway game.

Notably, however, and notwithstanding calls for congressional action by Jefferson and Madison, Congress did not use this power for many years. Instead, in the early 1830s, the Department of the Treasury adopted its own standards for the yard, pound, gallon, and bushel (the traditional English weights and measures) for use by the Customs Service, and then in 1836 Congress ordered that copies of them be sent to the states "to the end that an uniform standard of weights and measures may be established throughout the United States."[107] The states adopted them shortly thereafter. Congress has never coerced the adoption of national standards. In 1866 and 1975, it encouraged use of the metric system (the international standard), but it has not required such use.[108] A prudential lesson here is that Congress should not act just because a multistate collective-action problem exists. It must determine how serious the problem is, how soon it must be resolved, how much resistance there would be to a coercive solution upsetting local habits and usage, and whether persuasion is preferable.

Currency

Madison and Wilson opined that Congress should have the coinage power because the states were "wholly incompetent" (in Wilson's words) to exercise it.[109] Experience under the Articles of Confederation helps explain why they deemed

[105] David R. Smith & Robert Jefferson Dillard, *The Powers to Regulate Money, Weights, and Measures and to Punish Counterfeiting, in* THE POWERS OF CONGRESS, *supra* note 8, at 69.

[106] Arthur H. Frazier, *United States Standards of Weights and Measures: Their Creation and Creators*, SMITHSONIAN STUD. HIST. & TECH., No. 40, at 1 (1978).

[107] David P. Currie, *Weights and Measures*, 2 GREEN BAG 2d 261, 266 (1999) (quoting 5 Stat. 133 (Jun. 14, 1836)).

[108] *Id.* at 266; *see* Smith & Dillard, *supra* note 105, at 69–70.

[109] 1 THE RECORDS OF THE FEDERAL CONVENTION OF 1787, *supra* note 2, at 331 (Jun. 19); *see id.* at 446 (Jun. 28) (Madison recording his view that states should not be permitted, *inter alia*, to "determine the value of coin").

256 THE COLLECTIVE-ACTION CONSTITUTION

coinage an area of separate state incompetence according to the structural principle of Resolution VI. Article IX of the Articles had given Congress exclusive power to "regulat[e] the alloy and value of coin struck by their own authority, or by that of the respective States," which reflected the fact that states coined money and issued paper currency. Although some states that issued paper money avoided severe depreciation and inflation, others did not, and concerns arose about retaliatory trade wars.

For example, after Rhode Island issued paper money in 1786 at least partly to help protect in-state debtors from out-of-state creditors, out-of-state debtors sought to use Rhode Island paper currency to pay in-state creditors. Infuriated, the Rhode Island legislature barred state judges from recognizing the use of state paper money by out-of-state debtors. Connecticut countered by barring Rhode Island creditors from collecting debts in Connecticut until Rhode Island abandoned its laws discriminating against out-of-state debtors.[110] In *Federalist 44*, Madison described this race to the bottom, as well as other potential collective-action problems facing the states:

> Had every State a right to regulate the value of its coin, there might be as many different currencies as States, and thus the intercourse among them would be impeded; retrospective alterations in its value might be made, and thus the citizens of other States be injured, and animosities be kindled among the States themselves. The subjects of foreign powers might suffer from the same cause, and hence the Union be discredited and embroiled by the indiscretion of a single member. No one of these mischiefs is less incident to a power in the States to emit paper money than to coin gold or silver.[111]

Structurally, Congress is more competent than the states to overcome the various possible collective-action problems associated with state control over the currency used within its borders. Congress has less incentive than individual states to manipulate its currency to favor interests in one state over interests in other states, which (assuming retaliation) causes a cooperation problem. Moreover, federal control obviates the need for states that want to coordinate to overcome disagreements in choosing a common currency; note Madison's reference to "intercourse" among the states being "impeded." Finally, as Madison also observed, federal control prevents individual states from causing foreign-policy problems for the states collectively. This is almost certainly a cost-benefit collective-action

---

[110] Robert G. Natelson, *Paper Money and the Original Understanding of the Coinage Clause*, 31 HARV. J.L. & PUB. POL'Y 1017, 1050–52 (2008).

[111] THE FEDERALIST NO. 44, at 282 (James Madison) (Clinton Rossiter ed., 1961).

NATIONAL SECURITY AND NATIONAL UNIFORMITY   257

problem caused by the decision of individual states to externalize costs onto the rest of the states.

To facilitate the solution of these collective-action problems, several constitutional provisions give Congress exclusive power to provide a national currency and extensive power to protect it. First, the initial clause of Article I, Section 10, deviates from the Articles by providing that states may not "coin Money; emit Bills of Credit; [or] make any Thing but gold and silver Coin a Tender in Payment of Debts." Second, by authorizing Congress "[t]o coin Money, regulate the Value thereof, *and of foreign Coin*,"[112] the Coinage Clause gives Congress powers more comprehensive than those conferred by the Articles, which had not let Congress regulate the value of foreign Coin. This was "a material omission in the Articles of Confederation," Madison opined, because "the proposed uniformity in the *value* of the current coin might be destroyed by subjecting that of foreign coin to the different regulations of the different States."[113]

Third, and in further contrast to the Articles, the Constitution gives Congress broad implied powers under the Necessary and Proper Clause, and, as Chapter 1 explained, the Court has generously construed this power to carry into execution Congress's enumerated powers, many of which are facilitated by congressional provision and protection of a national currency.[114] In *McCulloch v. Maryland* (1819), the Court held that Congress can charter banks and permit them to circulate bank notes.[115] In *Veazie Bank v. Fenno* (1869), the Court upheld Congress's authority to prohibitively tax state bank notes under its powers to tax (see Chapter 4) and to provide a national currency.[116]

In the *Legal Tender Cases* (1870),[117] the Court overruled *Hepburn v. Griswold* (1869) from the prior term and held that Congress enjoys broad authority to provide a national currency not only with coins but also with paper money. Scholars debate whether this expansive view is consistent with the original intent, meaning, or understanding of the Constitution—whether of the Coinage Clause or Congress's fiscal and war powers amplified by the Necessary and Proper Clause.[118] The Court in *The Legal Tender Cases*, mindful of the prominent view that the Coinage Clause authorizes Congress to issue only metallic tokens, declined to rest on it and instead relied on the latter sources of power.[119]

---

[112] U.S. CONST. art. I, § 8, cl. 5 (emphasis added).

[113] THE FEDERALIST NO. 42, at 269 (James Madison) (Clinton Rossiter ed., 1961).

[114] LIBR. OF CONG., *Fiscal and Monetary Powers of Congress*, *in* THE CONSTITUTION OF THE UNITED STATES OF AMERICA, ANALYSIS AND INTERPRETATION, S. Doc. No. 88-39, at 310–11 (1964).

[115] 17 U.S. (4 Wheat.) 316 (1819).

[116] 75 U.S. (8 Wall.) 533 (1869). In so holding, the Court relied partly on historical practice. *Id.* at 548.

[117] The Legal Tender Cases (Knox v. Lee, Parker v. Davis), 79 U.S. (12 Wall.) 457 (1870) (overruling Hepburn v. Griswold, 75 U.S. (8 Wall.) 603 (1869)); *see* Julliard v. Greenman, 110 U.S. 421 (1884) (upholding congressional power to issue Greenbacks as legal tender in peacetime).

[118] For discussion of the debate and a contribution to it, see Natelson, *supra* note 110.

[119] *The Legal Tender Cases*, 79 U.S. (12 Wall.) at 531–47.

258 THE COLLECTIVE-ACTION CONSTITUTION

However one resolves this question, the decision is, for reasons explained, structurally sound: it solves multistate collective-action problems. Also structurally defensible is the Court's 1935 decision in *Nortz v. United States*, which continued this interpretive tradition by upholding congressional power to individually mandate the surrender of gold coin in exchange for currency not redeemable in gold.[120] As broad as federal power is, however, Congress largely lacks the ability to "regulate the Value" of the national currency in today's world economy. The foreign exchange market mostly determines its value.[121]

Notably, the Court in *The Legal Tender Cases* rejected the argument that it should draw, from Congress's power to "coin Money," the negative inference that Congress lacks power to issue paper money. The Court responded that "power over a particular subject may be exercised as auxiliary to an express power, though there is another express power relating to the same subject, less comprehensive." Instead of reasoning by negative implication, the Court emphasized that providing a national paper currency is a permissible way of carrying into execution several express powers. Like the Collective-Action Constitution, the Court viewed these powers as bound together by a structural purpose:

> [T]he powers conferred upon Congress must be regarded as related to each other, and all means for a common end. Each is but part of a system, a constituent of one whole. No single power is the ultimate end for which the Constitution was adopted. It may, in a very proper sense, be treated as a means for the accomplishment of a subordinate object, but that object is itself a means designed for an ulterior purpose. Thus the power to levy and collect taxes, to coin money and regulate its value, to raise and support armies, or to provide for and maintain a navy, are instruments for the paramount object, which was to establish a government, sovereign within its sphere, with capability of self-preservation, thereby forming a union more perfect than that which existed under the old Confederacy.[122]

Self-preservation required then, as it requires now, a Congress empowered to solve the kinds of collective-action problems that the "old Confederacy" was largely impotent to address, including the production and maintenance of a single national currency.

Because the objective of the Section 8 powers is to enable Congress to solve various problems that the states would need to act collectively to address, a "belt and suspenders" approach to constitutional design makes structural sense. The

---

[120] 249 U.S. 317 (1935). Chapter 5 discussed where the Court permits Congress to issue mandates using its Section 8 powers.

[121] Smith & Dillard, *supra* note 105, at 78–79.

[122] *The Legal Tender Cases*, 79 U.S. (12 Wall.) at 544–45.

NATIONAL SECURITY AND NATIONAL UNIFORMITY 259

fact that certain enumerated powers overlap (as demonstrated repeatedly over the past several chapters) provides insurance that Congress will have the authority it needs to solve collective-action problems facing the states. Interpreting the powers narrowly to avoid overlap is not just effectively impossible: try, for example, disentangling the taxing and interstate-commerce powers. Narrow construction also serves no good purpose. Narrow construction does not accomplish the purpose of the enumeration, because the primary purpose is found in Resolution VI. Granted, part of this purpose is to constrain federal authority. But each Section 8 power is limited in other ways.

Counterfeiting

Congress's power "[t]o provide for the Punishment of counterfeiting the Securities and current Coin of the United States"[123] occasioned little debate at the Constitutional Convention.[124] It serves some of the same purposes as the powers to regulate interstate and foreign commerce, which are facilitated by currency that governments and businesses can trust as legitimate in concluding commercial agreements and transactions. Unsurprisingly, therefore, the Court held in *United States v. Marigold* (1850) that Congress has authority under the Interstate and Foreign Commerce Clauses, plus the Coinage and Necessary and Proper Clauses, to prohibit the importation and circulation of counterfeit coins. The Court reasoned that protection of the nation's currency is a "subject of commerce."[125]

Less obvious, perhaps, is that letting Congress punish counterfeiting helps provide for the common defense. Governments have historically used counterfeiting as a weapon of war, including against the United States. During the American Revolution, the Continental Congress issued paper currency to help finance the war. In response, the British produced and distributed counterfeit currency, which contributed to rendering the currency worthless—hence the complaint that something was "not worth a Continental." During the Civil War, public confidence in the federal government was significantly undermined by counterfeit state bank notes, which constituted roughly one-third of all circulating currency in 1863. Congress responded that year by issuing a single national currency that was difficult to counterfeit (called the "Greenback"). Two years later, Congress established the Secret Service within the Treasury Department and charged it

[123] U.S. CONST. art. I, § 8, cl. 6.
[124] 2 THE RECORDS OF THE FEDERAL CONVENTION OF 1787, *supra* note 2, at 312, 315–16 (Aug. 17).
[125] 50 U.S. (9 How.) 560, 567 (1850). The Court did not rely on the Counterfeiting Clause, which it deemed limited to barring counterfeiting under *Fox v. Ohio*, 46 U.S. (5 How.) 410 (1847). *See Marigold*, 50 U.S. (9 How.) at 568.

260 · THE COLLECTIVE-ACTION CONSTITUTION

with combating counterfeiting. Today, widespread counterfeiting of US currency could harm the US economy and threaten national security.[126] The power to deter counterfeiting is thus crucial to solving the collective-action problems that Congress's commerce and war powers authorize it to address.

States may punish activities related to counterfeiting if their laws are not preempted, but Congress has exclusive power to punish counterfeiting itself.[127] From a collective-action perspective, this vertical allocation of authority makes sense. Congress has primary regulatory control so that it can address the national and international dimensions of counterfeiting and linked activities—both economic and security-related. As Federalist (and future Supreme Court Justice) James Iredell said at the North Carolina ratifying convention, counterfeiting, treason, and the three crimes listed in the Define and Punish Clause "are offenses immediately affecting the security, the honor or the interest of the United States at large."[128] Today, counterfeiting "is recognized as an international crime because it strains relations between nations and threatens mutual interests, namely the stability of national and international economic systems and the value of the currencies which operate in those systems."[129] Still, states can ordinarily protect their residents from fraud, which concerns the uses to which counterfeit currency is put.

The Counterfeiting Clause is superfluous.[130] Congress's power to provide a national currency implies the authority to protect its purity, so the Necessary and Proper Clause permits Congress to punish the acts covered by the Counterfeiting Clause and other acts that undermine the integrity of the national currency, including (as noted) the importation or circulation of counterfeit currency.[131] As the Court wrote in *Marigold*, Congress's authority to coin money implies "the correspondent and necessary power and obligation to protect and to preserve in its purity this constitutional currency for the benefit of the nation."[132] The superfluity of the Counterfeiting Clause illustrates once again that interpreting one clause of Section 8 broadly (but consistently with its language) so that it can accomplish its purposes is not suspect just because it means that other clauses do less work or even no independent work. As in *Marigold* and *The Legal Tender Cases* (which cited *Marigold* for this proposition),[133] the Court has expressly

---

[126] Nathan K. Cummings, *The Counterfeit Buck Stops Here: National Security Issues in the Redesign of U.S. Currency*, 8 S. CAL. INTERDISC. L.J. 539, 539, 542–43 (1999).

[127] *Id.* at 563. *See* Fox v. Ohio, 46 U.S. (5 How.) 410 (1847) (upholding a state law barring the passing of counterfeit U.S. coins).

[128] PAUL LEICESTER FORD, PAMPHLETS ON THE CONSTITUTION OF THE UNITED STATES 359 (1888).

[129] Cummings, *supra* note 126, at 563.

[130] *Id.* at 561–62; LIBR. OF CONG., *supra* note 114, at 311–12.

[131] *Marigold*, 50 U.S. (9 How.) 560 (1850) (holding that the Interstate Commerce, Foreign Commerce, Coinage, and Necessary and Proper Clauses permit Congress to criminalize the importation and circulation of counterfeit coins).

[132] *Id.* at 568.

[133] The Legal Tender Cases (Knox v. Lee, Parker v. Davis), 79 U.S. (12 Wall.) 457, 536, 544–45 (1870).

NATIONAL SECURITY AND NATIONAL UNIFORMITY 261

rejected efforts to draw, from the existence of one power, the negative inference that there are greater limitations than there otherwise would be on other powers.

Not Just Administration: Lower Federal Courts and Federal Enclaves

The ninth and seventeenth clauses of Section 8 respectively authorize Congress to create lower federal tribunals and to govern federal enclaves. These powers facilitate federal administration, but they also empower Congress to solve collective-action problems for the states.

Lower Federal Courts

The ninth clause of Section 8 authorizes Congress "[t]o constitute tribunals inferior to the Supreme Court," and the first section of Article III vests federal judicial power "in such inferior Courts as the Congress may from time to time ordain and establish."[134] Chapter 7 analyzes Article III, including the collective-action dimensions of Section 1's grant to Congress of discretion to decide whether to create lower federal courts. For now, it will only be observed that Article I's reference to "tribunals" is broader than Article III's reference to "Courts." Tribunals include not only Article III courts but also so-called non-Article III courts such as bankruptcy courts,[135] which lack the tenure and salary protections of Article III and Article III's jurisdictional limitations.[136] Congress can create non-Article III courts, within constitutional limits, using its Section 8 and other powers. Such tribunals can facilitate solution of the collective-action problems that Congress addresses in exercising its enumerated powers.

Federal Enclaves

The penultimate clause of Section 8 authorizes Congress

[t]o exercise exclusive Legislation in all Cases whatsoever, over such District (not exceeding ten Miles square) as may, by Cession of particular States,

---

[134] U.S. Const. art. III, § 1.

[135] The Court has permitted Congress to create non-Article III bankruptcy tribunals, but it has also imposed constitutional limits on them. *See* Stern v. Marshall, 564 U.S. 462, 494 (2011); N. Pipeline Constr. Co. v. Marathon Pipe Line Co., 458 U.S. 50, 63–64 (1982).

[136] U.S. Const. art. III, § 1 (tenure and salary protections); art. III, § 2, cl. 1 (jurisdictional limitations).

262 THE COLLECTIVE-ACTION CONSTITUTION

and the Acceptance of Congress, become the Seat of the Government of the United States, and to exercise like Authority over all Places purchased by the Consent of the Legislature of the State in which the Same shall be, for the Erection of Forts, Magazines, Arsenals, dock-Yards, and other needful Buildings.[137]

Such regulatory authority includes exercising the "police power" that states wield to secure the health, welfare, safety, and morals of their residents. Federal enclaves include both the district that became the seat of the federal government (Washington, DC) and all lands within the states purchased by Congress—with the consent of the ceding states—to erect federal buildings, military installations, dockyards, and similar facilities.

This power was uncontroversial at the Constitutional Convention. In 1783, the Confederation Congress, sitting in Philadelphia, was forced to negotiate an escape from Independence Hall when a group of former Continental Army soldiers, seeking back pay and debt relief, threatened them and prevented them from leaving the building. Fearing for their safety, the members asked Pennsylvania for protection, but the state did nothing, and they adjourned to Princeton, New Jersey, where the residents promised to protect them.[138] At the North Carolina ratifying convention, James Iredell recalled the episode:

What would be the consequence if the seat of government of the United States, with all the archives of America, was in the power of any one particular state? Would not this be most unsafe and humiliating? Do we not all remember that, in the year 1783, a band of soldiers went and insulted the Congress? The sovereignty of the United States was treated with indignity. They applied for protection to the state they resided in, but could obtain none. It is to be hoped such a disgraceful scene will never happen again; but that, for the future, the national government will be able to protect itself.[139]

Iredell's concerns were both expressive and material. To be effective, the federal government had to be viewed as possessing sovereign dignity, and it had to be able to protect itself and its property. Similarly, Joseph Story justified congressional power to situate the US government within a federal enclave based on

---

[137] U.S. CONST. art. I, § 8, cl. 17.

[138] Mary M. Cheh, *The Power to Exercise Authority over the District of Columbia and Federal Property*, *in* THE POWERS OF CONGRESS, *supra* note 8, at 187.

[139] IV THE DEBATES IN THE SEVERAL STATE CONVENTIONS ON THE ADOPTION OF THE FEDERAL CONSTITUTION AS RECOMMENDED BY THE GENERAL CONVENTION AT PHILADELPHIA IN 1787, at 219–20 (Jonathan Elliot ed., 1941).

NATIONAL SECURITY AND NATIONAL UNIFORMITY   263

"[t]he general dissatisfaction with the proceedings of Pennsylvania, and the degrading spectacle of a fugitive congress."[140]

From a collective-action perspective, this clause responds to a cost-benefit collective-action problem or a cooperation problem facing the states. An individual state like Pennsylvania, if it housed the US government, would internalize all the benefits of undermining or failing to protect the federal government and would externalize most of the costs onto sister states, and these costs would likely exceed the benefits. Moreover, sister states might respond similarly regarding military installations and federal buildings situated within their borders. Once again, this situation involves either cost-externalization that is greater than internalized benefits or a race to the bottom. In either case, there is a democratic-process failure identified in *McCulloch*: the part lacks the power to harm the whole in ways that the whole would not choose to harm itself because the whole is not represented in the part. The collective-action problem is solved when the federal government need not depend on a state for its safety and operations.

In addition, exclusive federal control over the seat of government and other federal facilities prevents the race to the bottom that would likely ensue from the appearance or reality of undue influence by individual states over the federal government or parts of it. Federalization thwarts the emergence of destructive jealousies among the states. During the ratification debates, Federalists made such arguments.[141]

Also noteworthy are the consent requirements built into this clause. The requirement of congressional consent ("the Acceptance of Congress") to land sessions makes it more difficult for one state or a minority of states to harm most states, causing a cost-benefit collective-action problem. The requirement of state consent ("the Consent of the Legislature of the State") to land cessions helps ensure that Congress's facilitation of collective action by most states will not exploit a minority of states, both regarding the initial cessions for the nation's capital (by Maryland and Virginia, as it turned out) and regarding later land purchases. Article IV's Admissions Clause imposes requirements of congressional and state consent when new states are formed out of the territory of existing states, and these requirements are also animated by concerns about the exploitation of a majority or a minority of states.[142]

The primary cost of this arrangement is exploitation of another minority: the residents of Washington, DC. There were few such residents when the Constitution was ratified, but today they number more than seven hundred thousand.[143] They are taxed without being represented in Congress. In this instance,

---

[140] 3 STORY, *supra* note 46, at § 1214, p. 98.
[141] Cheh, *supra* note 138, at 187–88.
[142] U.S. CONST. art. IV, § 3, cl. 1 (discussed in Chapter 8).
[143] U.S. Census Bureau, *Quick Facts: District of Columbia*, https://perma.cc/JZ3C-7EGY.

264 THE COLLECTIVE-ACTION CONSTITUTION

the whole controls the part without the part being represented in the whole. The Twenty-Third Amendment, which effectively awards the District three electoral votes, only partially addresses this democratic deficit by permitting District participation in presidential elections. The long-standing debate over statehood for the District should partly be a debate over whether the collective benefits of denying it statehood are worth the concentrated costs.[144]

Necessary and Proper, Again

As Chapter 1 discussed, the final clause of Section 8 gives Congress implied powers to "make all Laws which shall be necessary and proper for carrying into Execution" other powers granted to the federal government by the Constitution.[145] Moreover, the Tenth Amendment, in reminding the interpreter that "[t]he powers not delegated to the United States" nor prohibited to the states are reserved to the states or the people, self-consciously omits the qualifier "expressly," which Article II of the Articles of Confederation had placed before the phrase "delegated to the United States."[146] The language of the Necessary and Proper Clause and the Tenth Amendment indicates the existence of implied legislative powers, which advance the Constitution's vision of successful state collective action in several ways. To recap, the Necessary and Proper Clause empowers Congress to solve some multistate collective-action problems when other powers are unavailable and permits laws that do not themselves help solve such problems but enhance the efficacy of laws that do. The clause also lets Congress build out the executive and judicial branches, which the Articles lacked and the Constitution requires if federal laws—including solutions to collective-action problems—will be enforced against states and individuals.[147]

Conclusion

Putting aside national defense, this chapter has analyzed Section 8 powers that are less likely than others to be understood in terms of collective-action logics. The chapter has shown that these powers, too, empower Congress to solve multistate

[144] Another question is whether awarding statehood to DC would make the Senate less unreflective of majoritarian sentiment in the national population, and, if so, whether this should be welcomed or condemned. The partisan stakes are high during the current era of American politics.

[145] U.S. CONST. art. I, § 8, cl. 18.

[146] ARTICLES OF CONFEDERATION OF 1781, art. II ("Each State retains its sovereignty, freedom, and independence, and every power, jurisdiction, and right, which is not by this Confederation expressly delegated to the United States in Congress assembled.").

[147] See Chapter 7.

Pareto or cost-benefit collective-action problems, whether generated by positive interstate externalities, divergent state regulations, cost externalizations that exceed internalized benefits, or other causes. The next chapter considers Articles II, III, and VI, which also facilitate federal power to solve problems that the states would need to act collectively to address.

7

Executive Energy, Judicial Authority, and Federal Supremacy

Introduction

Congressional solutions to multistate collective-action problems require executive and judicial enforcement of federal law against states and private parties that violate or otherwise undermine it. Likewise, constitutional or congressional prohibitions on state legislation that causes collective-action problems for the states require executive and judicial enforcement of these prohibitions to ensure the supremacy of federal law. Articles II and III of the Constitution confer powers on the executive and the federal judiciary that enable them to help Congress solve collective-action problems for the states and stop the states from interfering with congressional solutions or causing such problems. Under a collective-action account of the Constitution, this is the primary structural role of the president and the Supreme Court.

The executive has the additional duty of energetically conducting diplomacy and national-security operations—responsibilities that the states would need to act collectively to meet, and that Congress cannot execute due to collective-action problems within Congress. The federal judiciary has its own duties in the areas of foreign relations and national security, and it is also charged with helping ensure domestic peace: by umpiring disputes with international or interstate dimensions, the federal courts solve or prevent collective-action problems for the states. Both the executive and the judiciary play roles in checking Congress so that its solutions to collective-action problems remain within constitutional bounds, and Congress, for its part, has oversight responsibilities regarding the executive and the judiciary.

These functions animate Articles II, III, and VI of the Constitution. This chapter examines each article in turn. Article IV, which concerns interstate relations, is analyzed in Chapters 8 and 9. Article V, which covers constitutional amendments, is discussed in Chapter 10. The current chapter shows how a collective-action account of the Constitution illuminates key provisions of Article II and most provisions of Articles III and VI.

The Collective-Action Constitution. Neil S. Siegel, Oxford University Press. © Neil S. Siegel 2024.
DOI: 10.1093/oso/9780197760963.003.0008

268 THE COLLECTIVE-ACTION CONSTITUTION

Article II

Recall that the Articles of Confederation emerged from the repudiation of the British king and Parliament. The Articles reflected a deep distrust of centralized power and a robust commitment to state sovereignty. As Chapter 4 explained, the Articles lacked a real executive branch.[1] It was therefore impossible to enforce requisition orders and treaty obligations against the states. Also recall from prior chapters that the states needed to act collectively to act effectively in the spheres of foreign affairs and national defense and that they largely failed to do so. Both inside and outside the Confederation Congress, state governments were, among other failings, unable to deter foreign trade aggression and build an adequate national military.

The Constitution addresses these collective-action problems not just by licensing legislation on the subjects examined in the three prior chapters but also by empowering and obliging a single president to do what Congress cannot: enforce federal law, conduct diplomacy, and protect the nation from attack. In addition, by designing the executive to enjoy a high degree of independence from Congress, Article II equips the president to resist congressional abuses of power, thereby increasing the likelihood that federal solutions to collective-action problems will respect the separation of powers, constitutional protections for state autonomy, and individual rights. Given the powers wielded by Congress, it is substantially more important to check congressional abuses of power than it was to check abuses by the Confederation Congress.

Enforcing federal law, relating effectively to the rest of the world, and checking Congress are the three general ways in which Article II helps accomplish the Constitution's structural purposes of empowering the federal government to solve multistate collective-action problems and preventing states from undermining federal solutions or causing such problems, all while remaining within constitutional bounds. In examining these three functions of the executive branch, this section will reference both the relatively sparse, under-determinate text of Article II and initial actions self-consciously taken by President Washington to answer questions that the text does not expressly resolve. His conduct set precedents that subsequent presidents have followed and other branches have mostly respected. As Chapter 1 explained, historical practice helps organize and resolve disagreements about structural questions when the text is unclear and little or no judicial precedent is available. The discussion

---

[1] Article IX gave Congress authority to appoint such "committees and civil officers as may be necessary for managing the general affairs of the united states under their direction" and "to appoint one of their number to preside; provided that no person be allowed to serve in the office of president more than one year in any term of three years."

EXECUTIVE ENERGY AND FEDERAL SUPREMACY   269

below shows, however, that modern Supreme Court decisions and academic commentary have also influenced debates over executive power.

The enormous growth of executive power since the beginning of the twentieth century raises concerns about its abuse, including concerns about contravening or substituting for congressional solutions to multistate collective-action problems. Congress is the institution with primary responsibility to hold the president accountable, but it is often unable or unwilling to do so.[2] When Congress does legislate, however, it almost always has the final say in determining the permissibility of presidential conduct. A collective-action account of the Constitution helps explain why.

Federal Enforcement

The Supremacy Clause identifies the Constitution, federal statutes, and treaties as "the supreme Law of the Land."[3] Many legal provisions falling within these three categories of federal law either solve multistate collective-action problems or prevent them.[4] Article II creates an executive branch with the authority and responsibility to enforce such provisions.

The Take Care Clause provides that the president "shall take Care that the Laws be faithfully executed."[5] By making the president the nation's chief law implementer and enforcer, this clause enables the executive branch to administer federal programs and deter states and individuals from violating federal law (or punish them when they do). The creation of an executive with strong enforcement powers helps secure the efficacy and supremacy of federal law, including by ensuring that the solutions to collective-action problems embodied in federal law are actually implemented and respected.[6] In the enforcement realm, so long as the president lacks good-faith constitutional objections to statutes or treaties, the president is charged with acting as the agent of these statutes or treaties, which helps explain why the word "faithful" appears in the Take Care Clause. The

---

[2] *See* Chapter 10.

[3] U.S. CONST. art. VI, § 1, cl. 2.

[4] Recall from earlier chapters that federal laws or treaties may solve collective-action problems in one of two ways. First, giving Congress or the treaty makers their respective powers may solve the collective-action problems that would arise if the states themselves had to act collectively to exercise the powers in question. Examples include laws passed under most of Congress's enumerated powers in Article I, Section 8. Second, the content of the law or treaty at issue may itself solve a multistate collective-action problem. Examples include legislation passed under the Interstate Commerce Clause and the migratory-bird treaty upheld in *Missouri v. Holland*, 252 U.S. 416 (1920) (discussed in Chapter 10).

[5] U.S. CONST. art. II, § 3.

[6] Moreover, as the next section discusses, the president vindicates the efficacy and supremacy of federal law by enforcing federal judicial decisions and nominating federal judges. U.S. CONST. art. II, § 2, cl. 2.

270　THE COLLECTIVE-ACTION CONSTITUTION

president is not invariably the agent of statutes or treaties when the president sincerely believes that provisions in them are unconstitutional. The Constitution is the supreme law to which the president must be faithful.

The scope of presidential authority to refuse to enforce federal law on constitutional grounds is contested, and a collective-action account cannot help resolve this debate. Nor can the theory speak to disagreements over the distinction in the Appointments Clause between principal and inferior officers;[7] over the proper scope of the president's removal authority; or over the constitutional bounds of the president's exercise of enforcement discretion. These limitations of the Collective-Action Constitution reflect the primary focus of the theory on the Constitution's federal structure, not on its separation and mixing of powers among the branches of the federal government. But at a higher level of generality, presidential power and responsibility to faithfully enforce federal law is a basic theme of the Constitution reflected in many textual provisions, presidential practices, and judicial opinions, and a collective-action account substantially illuminates why the president possesses this power.

Diplomacy and Defense

There is a second way in which Article II helps accomplish the Constitution's structural purposes of empowering the federal government to solve multistate collective-action problems and deterring states from undercutting federal solutions or generating such problems. Article II assigns to the president powers and obligations in the realms of foreign affairs and national security that Congress would be unable to exercise or meet.

As discussed earlier in the book, it makes the most structural sense to vest foreign affairs and military powers in the federal government, as opposed to the states. For example, in *United States v. Pink* (1942), the Court required New York to comply with an executive agreement, the Litvinov Agreement, according to which the United States recognized the Soviet Union and the Soviet Union assigned to the United States its interests in a Russian insurance company in New York.[8] The Court there described foreign affairs as "an exclusive federal function," reasoning that "[i]f state laws and policies did not yield before the exercise of the external powers of the United States, then our foreign policy might be thwarted" and "[t]he nation as a whole would be held to answer if a State created difficulties with a foreign power."[9] Restated, foreign affairs

---

[7] U.S. CONST. art. II, § 2, cl. 2.
[8] Executive agreements are discussed in Chapter 10.
[9] 315 U.S. 203, 232 (1942).

EXECUTIVE ENERGY AND FEDERAL SUPREMACY   271

is an exclusive federal function because (1) giving the federal government authority in this sphere solves collective-action problems for the states by enabling them to speak with one voice and (2) individual state governments would otherwise interfere with these solutions or cause collective-action problems. The same reasoning applies in the national-security context. Thus, as Chapters 5 and 6 explained, Congress has significant authority in both spheres, including the powers to tax and spend; to regulate foreign commerce; to punish offenses committed at sea or against the law of nations; to declare war; and to raise, support, and regulate a national military.[10] Relatedly, as Chapter 3 discussed, Article I, Section 10, categorically bars states from "enter[ing] into any Treaty, Alliance, or Confederation" and presumptively prohibits them from "enter[ing] into any Agreement or Compact . . . with a foreign Power" or "engag[ing] in War, unless actually invaded, or in such imminent Danger as will not admit of delay."

But success in foreign affairs and national defense requires more than federal legislation and prohibitions on state conduct. As Hamilton argued in *Federalist 70*, success requires "energy," including "[d]ecision, activity, secrecy, and dispatch." These qualities, he continued, "will generally characterize the proceedings of one man in a much more eminent degree than the proceedings of any greater number; and in proportion as the number is increased, these qualities will be diminished." Hamilton was justifying Article II's creation of a single president, as opposed to a multiperson executive.[11] His reasoning applies with greater force in comparing the president with Congress.

Certain aspects of Hamilton's argument are straightforward. For example, it is easier for one person to act secretly than it is for several or many, because public disclosure of an activity is less likely when fewer people know of it. Such disclosure could occur inadvertently or intentionally via a public airing of internal disagreements. "Whenever two or more persons are engaged in any common enterprise or pursuit," Hamilton observed, "there is always danger of difference of opinion."[12] Less obvious, perhaps, is that disagreements among two or more individuals can make it more difficult for them to coordinate their behavior, as in the Bridge or Seaway game discussed in Chapter 2. A single executive can avoid the coordination-plus-disagreement problems that would beset the members of a plural executive.

For example, members of a three-person executive might need to coordinate their decision-making in formulating battle plans for the armies they each controlled. Disagreements among them about how to prosecute a war could make coordination difficult. As Hamilton wrote, "in the conduct of war, in which

---

[10] U.S. CONST. art. I, § 8.
[11] THE FEDERALIST No. 70, at 423–24 (Alexander Hamilton) (Clinton Rossiter ed., 1961).
[12] *Id.* at 425–26.

the energy of the executive is the bulwark of the national security, everything would be to be apprehended from its plurality."[13] Along similar lines, Elbridge Gerry remarked at the Constitutional Convention that he "was at a loss to discover the policy of three members of the Executive" because "[i]t wd. be extremely inconvenient in many instances, particular in military matters," where "[i]t would be a general with three heads."[14] This was no hypothetical concern. As Professor Akhil Amar observes, "the absence of a strongly unified military-command structure had indeed compromised America's military effectiveness in the fight against Britain."[15] Coordination difficulties driven by disagreements would also arise if one member of the executive oversaw the military, another controlled diplomacy, and the third managed domestic affairs. Moreover, given the overlap among these three domains, the public would struggle to know who to hold responsible for various decisions amid potential blame-shifting among them, which was another of Hamilton's points.[16]

Another kind of collective-action problem might beset the members of a plural executive. Some members might focus more on campaigning for reelection or other self-interested pursuits and less on governing. In doing so, they would be free riding off the efforts of other members of the executive to perform the responsibilities of the office. If other members of the executive responded in kind, the result would be a race to the bottom. If they did not, there would be a cost-benefit collective-action problem.

Compared with a plural executive (let alone a unitary one), it is much harder to imagine how Congress could command an army in battle or negotiate with representatives of another country—in secret and with dispatch—to conclude a treaty or avoid a war. Congress is constituted by many members who would face serious collective-action problems. These problems might be reduced by the authority of each chamber to operate according to majority rule as opposed to unanimity rule, but they would hardly be eliminated. Thus, the president's key roles in foreign affairs and national defense not only help solve and prevent collective-action problems for the states but also ameliorate collective-action problems facing members of Congress, who are far less able than the president to act collectively to conduct diplomacy and defend the nation. This argument also explains why the president can enforce federal law more effectively than

---

[13] *Id.* at 427.

[14] 1 THE RECORDS OF THE FEDERAL CONVENTION OF 1787, at 97 (Max Farrand ed., rev. ed. 1966) (Jun. 4).

[15] AKHIL REED AMAR, AMERICA'S CONSTITUTION: A BIOGRAPHY 142 (2005); *see* AKHIL REED AMAR, THE WORDS THAT MADE US: AMERICA'S CONSTITUTIONAL CONVERSATION, 1760–1840, at 190 (2021) ("[T]he Confederation Congress had tried to run the Revolutionary War, but administration by committee had not worked well.").

[16] THE FEDERALIST No. 70, at 427–30 (Alexander Hamilton) (Clinton Rossiter ed., 1961).

EXECUTIVE ENERGY AND FEDERAL SUPREMACY   273

Congress. Indeed, in *Federalist 70*, Hamilton defended executive energy partly to ensure "the steady administration of the laws."[17]

Reflecting the foregoing collective-action rationale, Article II empowers the president to lead in foreign affairs—to represent the nation in its interactions with the world. The president can conclude treaties with the consent of two-thirds of the Senate.[18] Washington also established the practice of communicating (including in secret) with foreign governments; negotiating treaties without the Senate's knowledge; seeking Senatorial consent but not advice in the treaty-making process (despite the constitutional text); making the ultimate decision, after Senate approval, to ratify treaties in the name of the nation; and officially declaring American neutrality between countries at war.[19] Moreover, the difficulty of meeting the strict supermajority requirement for treaties has resulted in broad presidential authority to form other international agreements, either alone (sole executive agreements) or with majorities in each house of Congress (congressional-executive agreements).[20] The president can also nominate—and, with Senate consent, appoint—"Ambassadors" and "other public Ministers and Consuls."[21] Further, the president "shall receive Ambassadors and other public Ministers," which by potential implication (and another practice set by Washington) authorizes the president to recognize or not recognize foreign governments.[22]

Turning to national security, Article II gives the president power and responsibility to protect the nation from attack, both during crises and more generally. Article II makes the president the head of the nation's military, declaring that the president "shall be Commander in Chief of the Army and Navy of the United States, and of the Militia of the several States, when called into the actual Service of the United States."[23] In addition, the Presidential Oath Clause requires presidents to swear or affirm to do their best to "preserve, protect and defend the Constitution of the United States."[24] This clause may imply presidential responsibilities in the realm of national security, including surprise military or terrorist attacks. The Commander in Chief Clause may also help ground presidential authority to act in emergencies. In *The Prize Cases* (1863), the Court confirmed that the president, as commander in chief, can respond to attacks on the

---

[17] *Id.* at 423.

[18] U.S. Const. art. II, § 2, cl. 2.

[19] Akhil Reed Amar, America's Unwritten Constitution: The Precedents and Principles We Live By 316–19, 328–29 (2012).

[20] *See* Chapter 10.

[21] U.S. Const. art. II, § 2, cl. 2.

[22] U.S. Const. art. II, § 3. On the practice set by Washington, see Amar, *supra* note 19, at 314–16. Centuries later, in *Zivotofsky v. Kerry* (*Zivotofsky II*), 576 U.S. 1059 (2015), the Court held that the power to recognize foreign governments belongs exclusively to the president.

[23] U.S. Const. art. II, § 2, cl. 1.

[24] U.S. Const. art. II, § 1, cl. 8.

274 THE COLLECTIVE-ACTION CONSTITUTION

nation without awaiting congressional authorization to use military force. The Court there upheld President Lincoln's imposition of a blockade on Southern states even though Congress had not declared war.[25] True, the Court reasoned in part that any possible requirement of congressional authorization had been satisfied by Congress's approval of Lincoln's actions after the fact. But it has been assumed from the beginning that presidents have some authority to use force to defend against attack, in part because in the early years Congress would often be out of session and it would take time for members to gather.

Presidential responsibility during national-security (and other) crises may be presupposed by two additional provisions of Article II. One specifies succession to the presidency in case of removal, death, resignation, or inability to execute the powers and responsibilities of the office.[26] The other authorizes the president, "on extraordinary Occasions, [to] convene both Houses, or either of them."[27] Unlike Congress, the presidency never sleeps. This difference is also evidenced by presidential power to make temporary appointments during Senate recesses.[28]

Even provisions not viewed today as implicating the common defense were originally understood at least partly in these terms. In *Federalist 74*, Hamilton defended the pardon power partially on national-security grounds, writing that timely pardons held the potential to defuse armed conflict "in seasons of insurrection or rebellion."[29] Similarly, limiting presidential eligibility to "a natural born Citizen, or a Citizen of the United States, at the time of the Adoption of the Constitution,"[30] may seem paranoid and xenophobic today. Then, however, it alleviated fears that a European aristocrat would win the presidency and turn it into a monarchy, or, relatedly, that foreign governments would corrupt American democracy by funding the presidential campaign of one of their own hand-picked citizens. For example, Joseph Story wrote in his *Commentaries* that the natural-born-citizen requirement "cuts off all chances for ambitious foreigners, who might otherwise be intriguing for the office; and interposes a

---

[25] 67 U.S. (2 Black) 635 (1863).

[26] U.S. Const. art. II, § 1, cl. 6.

[27] U.S. Const. art. II, § 3.

[28] U.S. Const. art. II, § 2, cl. 3 ("The President shall have Power to fill up all Vacancies that may happen during the Recess of the Senate, by granting Commissions which shall expire at the End of their next session."). The Court has mostly interpreted presidential authority under this clause broadly. In *NLRB v. Noel Canning*, 573 U.S. 513 (2014), the Court held that the Senate is in session when it says it is so long as Senate rules allow it to transact business, but that the Recess Appointments Clause authorizes the president to fill any existing vacancy during any recess of sufficient length regardless of when the vacancy arose and regardless of whether the recess occurs during or between sessions of Congress. For analysis of the relationship between historical practice and the text of this clause in *Noel Canning*, see Curtis A. Bradley & Neil S. Siegel, *After Recess: Historical Practice, Textual Ambiguity, and Constitutional Adverse Possession*, 2014 Sup. Ct. Rev. 1 (2015).

[29] The Federalist No. 74, at 449 (Alexander Hamilton) (Clinton Rossiter ed., 1961); *see* U.S. Const. art. II, § 2, cl. 1 ("[H]e shall have Power to grant Reprieves and Pardons for Offenses against the United States, except in cases of Impeachment."). Chapter 10 discusses impeachment.

[30] U.S. Const. art. II, § 1, cl. 5.

EXECUTIVE ENERGY AND FEDERAL SUPREMACY   275

barrier against those corrupt interferences of foreign governments in executive elections."[31] Requiring presidents to have been US residents for fourteen years also seems directed, at least partially, at protecting the nation and Constitution from being undermined from abroad.[32]

Checking Congress

Article II creates a presidency with the authority and independence to protect its office from congressional encroachments and to oppose proposed legislation on constitutional grounds. For example, the Founders gave presidents the power to veto legislation primarily to prevent Congress from encroaching on their office or acting unconstitutionally, not to routinely express policy disagreements with Congress.[33] Moreover, as noted, presidents have at least some authority not to enforce provisions of federal law that they sincerely deem unconstitutional. When presidents use executive power for these purposes, congressional solutions to collective-action problems are more likely to be constitutional. Limitations on congressional power to solve collective-action problems are sometimes a good thing, because such limitations can check abuses of authority.

Presidents would be far less inclined to use their powers to check Congress if it could select them, fire them, cut or eliminate their salary, or decide not to reselect them after their term has expired. Presidents are chosen via the Electoral College method, not by Congress, and they serve for a term of substantial length (four years) with eligibility to run for reelection.[34] Moreover, Congress may not raise or reduce presidential salaries during the term for which they have been elected, and neither Congress nor individual states can give presidents any other emolument during this same period.[35] (Extending the ban to states disables them from tempting presidents to play favorites among them and thereby generate interstate hostility, which can cause collective-action problems.) Finally,

---

[31] 3 Joseph Story, Commentaries on the Constitution of the United States § 1473, p. 333 (1833).

[32] U.S. Const. art. II, § 1, cl. 5. For discussion of these presidential eligibility requirements in historical context, see Michael Nelson, *Constitutional Qualifications for President*, 17 Pres. Stud. Q. 383, 394–96 (1987).

[33] U.S. Const. art. I, § 7, cl. 2 (discussed in Chapters 10 and 11).

[34] U.S. Const. art. II, § 1, cl. 2 (Electoral College method); amend. 12 (same); U.S. Const. art. II, § 1, cl. 1 (four-year term). Originally, the president could run for reelection without constitutional limit, although there was an apparent constitutional norm—initiated by Washington—prohibiting presidents from serving for longer than two terms. The Constitution did not change until 1951, upon ratification of the Twenty-Second Amendment, which was added after President Franklin Delano Roosevelt successfully ran for a third and then a fourth term. This amendment prohibits anyone from being elected president more than twice, and it prohibits anyone who has acted as president for more than two years of another elected president's term from being elected president more than once.

[35] U.S. Const. art. II, § 1, cl. 7.

276 THE COLLECTIVE-ACTION CONSTITUTION

presidents cannot be removed from office by Congress except via the (likely too) demanding process of impeachment and conviction.[36]

Checking the President

This section has not captured the sheer scope of modern presidential powers and responsibilities, which expanded greatly during the twentieth century. Domestically, presidents provide significant input into federal budget decisions. They set policies and priorities for their administrations by vetting potential appointees using criteria that include support for their policies. They impact the legislative process not just by wielding the veto power, delivering the State of the Union address, and proposing new legislation (powers in the text), but more broadly by setting national reform agendas.[37] They choose federal judges.[38] The office of the president, which has several thousand employees, sits atop an enormous bureaucracy administering federal laws on many subjects. Executive-branch officials and employees collect taxes; pay government benefits such as Social Security and Medicare; disburse other funds; manage federal lands and other property; litigate on behalf of the United States; investigate and prose-cute misconduct; issue regulations; coordinate activities with states; and react to natural disasters, financial crises, and pandemics. Internationally, presidents exert extensive control over ambassadors, the State Department, the Central Intelligence Agency, the National Security Agency, and other agencies respon-sible for diplomacy, espionage, or national security. Presidents are commanders in chief of the world's most formidable military. They personify the nation to the rest of the world.[39]

In short, presidential power has grown considerably since the beginning of the twentieth century.[40] This development raises concerns about the abuse of executive power, including presidential actions that violate or seek to substitute for statutory solutions to multistate collective-action problems. If one individual can do good things more effectively than many people, the same individual

---

[36] U.S. Const. art. II, § 4 (discussed in Chapter 10).

[37] U.S. Const. art. I, § 7, cl. 2 (veto power); art. II, § 3 ("He shall from time to time give to the Congress Information of the State of the Union, and recommend to their Consideration such Measures as he shall judge necessary and expedient.").

[38] U.S. Const. art. II, § 2, cl. 2.

[39] For discussions of the presidential powers and activities included in this paragraph, see Amar, *supra* note 19, at 312; and Daniel A. Farber & Neil S. Siegel, United States Constitutional Law 201–02, 215 (2d ed. 2024).

[40] *Cf.* Richard H. Pildes, *Law and the President*, 125 Harv. L. Rev. 1381, 1381 (2012) (reviewing Eric A. Posner & Adrian Vermeule, The Executive Unbound: After the Madisonian Republic (2010)) ("It is widely recognized that expansion of presidential power from the start of the twentieth century onward has been among the central features of American political development.").

EXECUTIVE ENERGY AND FEDERAL SUPREMACY   277

can do bad things more effectively than many people. Thus, the modern presidency is generally more to be feared than Congress, whose many members must agree on how to exercise power. Moreover, the representation of all states and individuals in Congress justifies giving it the authority to decide, when states disagree, whether there are multistate collective-action problems and how to solve them. Presidential power can lay no equal claim to democratic legitimacy, which is why the Constitution places the executive article after the legislative one and does not permit the president to routinely act in defiance of Congress (as discussed below) or to legislate by executive order. Congress does not consist of one person—no matter how effectively this individual could legislate to address what the individual rationally determines to be multistate collective-action problems—because a one-person Congress would possess too much power and would wield it with too little democratic legitimacy.

Although the federal courts and state governments have some power and responsibility to check abuses of executive power, Congress is the institution with primary responsibility for doing so.[41] Congress must, however, meet two-thirds supermajority requirements both to legislate against executive encroachments on other branches or state governments (assuming vetoes) and to convict a president of impeachable offenses. These requirements, plus other causes of congressional gridlock examined in Part III, have significantly limited Congress's ability and will to combat abuses of executive power. These two supermajority rules likely make collective action by members of Congress—which helps protect collective action by states in Congress—too difficult to accomplish in modern America.[42]

When Congress does legislate, however, the principle of congressional priority provides that Congress, the lawmaker, almost always gets to control the president, the law enforcer—and the Collective-Action Constitution helps explain why. Justice Jackson captured this principle in his canonical analysis of congressional-executive relations in the *Youngstown* steel seizure case, which concerned the constitutionality of President Truman's order directing his secretary of commerce to seize and operate most of the nation's steel mills to prevent a strike that might undermine the US war effort in Korea. Jackson identified three zones into which presidential action may fall—congressional approval of the president's conduct, congressional silence, or congressional disapproval—and he described executive "power [a]s at its lowest ebb" when the president contravenes a congressional bar.[43] Exclusive executive power grounded in Article II—such as the power to recognize foreign governments, the pardon power, and the

---

[41] *See* Chapter 10 (discussing the limited ability of state governments to check presidential abuses of power).

[42] *See id.*

[43] Youngstown Sheet & Tube Co. v. Sawyer, 343 U.S. 579, 635–38 (1952) (Jackson, J., concurring).

278   THE COLLECTIVE-ACTION CONSTITUTION

commander-in-chief power to decide battlefield strategy—is exceptional. The fundamental asymmetry between congressional and executive power is justified not only by the breadth of Congress's powers to solve collective-action problems for the states but also by the lower likelihood that Congress will abuse these powers and its superior democratic warrant to use them.

Article III

Viewed through a collective-action lens, Article III performs several similar purposes to Article II. This functional link between the two branches helps explain why the Appointments Clause groups executive and judicial appointments together, and why Hamilton also did so in defending the Constitution's arrangement of appointment by the president subject to consent by the Senate.[44] Just as the Articles of Confederation lacked a real executive to enforce federal commitments against the states, so also it lacked a real national judiciary to do the same. And just as the Constitution creates an independent executive with the president at the top, so also it establishes an independent judiciary with the Supreme Court at its apex. Like the president, the Court is responsible for ensuring the effective enforcement and supremacy of federal law. In addition, like the president, the Court plays a role in checking Congress so that statutes solving collective-action problems for the states remain within constitutional bounds. As discussed below, Madison and Wilson had sought at the Philadelphia Convention to merge the executive and the judiciary for purposes of reviewing congressional legislation.

Still, differences between Articles II and III reflect the differing capacities of presidents and justices to advance the Constitution's collective-action goals. Presidents are much better situated than justices to conduct diplomacy and protect the nation. The Court is better situated than the presidency to ensure that federal law is interpreted uniformly and to resolve individual disputes that, if not handled properly, could undermine the nation's relations with the rest of the world or generate hostility among states. Finally, both presidents and the Court play roles in keeping each other within constitutional bounds.

There are compelling collective-action rationales for each of the four purposes of federal judicial power discussed in this section. Collective-action reasoning also helps justify the nine heads of jurisdiction in Article III, which can be sorted

---

[44] U.S. CONST. art. II, § 2, cl. 2. *See* THE FEDERALIST NOS. 76 & 77, at 454–64 (Alexander Hamilton) (Clinton Rossiter ed., 1961); *see also* THE FEDERALIST NO. 78, at 464 (Alexander Hamilton) ("As to the mode of appointing the judges: this is the same with that of appointing the officers of the Union in general and has been so fully discussed in the two last numbers that nothing can be said here which would not be useless repetition.").

into four groups according to these purposes. Moreover, collective-action logics call into question two "vesting" theories of Article III and likely support granting Congress discretion to determine federal jurisdiction outside the context of individual-rights cases. Further, collective-action theory, along with a scarcity rationale, justifies Article III's grant of original jurisdiction to the Court in cases falling under two of the nine heads of federal jurisdiction. Finally, a collective-action account helps justify Article III's grant of discretion to Congress to decide whether to create lower federal courts.[45]

Throughout American history, Congress has exercised this discretion to create lower federal courts of different types and jurisdictions. Their work has greatly enhanced the Court's ability to accomplish the primary purposes of federal judicial power. Achieving these purposes requires a significant degree of judicial independence and the power of judicial review. But the leverage that the constitutional text and structure give the political branches—not the states—to ensure judicial accountability suggests that judicial review of federal laws was intended to be less muscular than judicial review of state laws when both were challenged on federalism grounds. Antebellum historical practice reflected this understanding. Thus, the text, original structure, original intent, and early historical practice corroborate the structural reasoning developed in earlier chapters: the Court possesses less democratic legitimacy than Congress, and so it should deferentially review congressional determinations about the existence and seriousness of collective-action problems facing the states. By contrast, the Court is better situated structurally than individual states to determine whether they are causing multistate collective-action problems.

Article III includes some important rights protections. Collective-action reasoning does not provide the main explanation for these rights, but it does play a secondary role in clarifying aspects of them.

The Articles of Confederation

There were some limited gestures in the direction of a national judiciary under the Articles of Confederation. Article IX authorized Congress to appoint state courts "for the trial of piracies and felonies committed on the high seas" and to establish national courts "for receiving and determining finally appeals in all cases of captures." Moreover, as Chapter 3 explained, to nonviolently end boundary disputes and other disagreements when states failed to reach agreement, Article IX provided that "[t]he united states in congress assembled shall . . . be the last resort on appeal in all disputes and differences now subsisting or that hereafter

---

[45] U.S. Const. art. III, § 1; *see* art. I, § 8, cl. 9.

may arise between two or more states concerning boundary, jurisdiction or any other cause whatever." Article IX then described at length the unwieldy procedure Congress would use to settle such disputes between states. The state parties to the disagreement would jointly choose judges unless they could not agree. If they disagreed, Congress would select three individuals from each state; each party would alternately strike names until thirteen remained; and seven or nine of them (whichever number Congress directed) would be drawn by lot to serve as the judges, with five constituting a quorum. There was no appeal from the court's judgment.

Congress used these powers to some extent. In 1781, it designated state judges to try piracies and felonies committed at sea, and it charged Congress or its appointees with handling some appeals. After appointing committees to do so, Congress in 1780 established a national Court of Appeals. It was denied needed powers to ensure compliance with its decisions; Congress meddled in its cases; and its docket shrank. By the Constitutional Convention, the court was no longer operating. In addition, the awkward Article IX procedure for resolving interstate disputes was used only once: to resolve a disagreement between Pennsylvania and Connecticut over land on the banks of the Susquehanna River. Connecticut accepted the unanimous judgment against it, but settlers from the state refused to relinquish their lands.[46]

A national judiciary consists of much more than congressional committees and then one specialized court with very limited authority to decide appeals from state-court judgments falling within one category of maritime disputes. Likewise, a national judiciary consists of much more than one ad hoc tribunal to partially settle one interstate dispute. When state governments during the 1780s ignored treaty obligations and requisition orders, there was no national judiciary to which Congress could turn. It had to rely on state courts to enforce federal commitments against state governments, but state courts "often show[ed] little interest in stopping the violations."[47] State judges could not be counted on to be less parochial than state legislators. And parochialism aside, "[t]he mere necessity of uniformity in the interpretation of the national laws decides the question," Hamilton insisted in *Federalist 80*. "Thirteen independent courts of final jurisdiction over the same causes, arising upon the same laws, is a hydra in government from which nothing but contradiction and confusion can proceed."[48] It is thus unsurprising that the Framers quickly, unanimously, and without discussion "[r]esolved that a national Judiciary be established" alongside a national legislature

---

[46] RICHARD H. FALLON ET AL., HART AND WECHSLER'S THE FEDERAL COURTS AND THE FEDERAL SYSTEM 6 nn.34–36 (7th ed. 2015) (citing HAMPTON L. CARSON, THE SUPREME COURT OF THE UNITED STATES 41–64, 67–74 (1891)).

[47] AMAR, AMERICA'S CONSTITUTION, *supra* note 15, at 301.

[48] THE FEDERALIST No. 80, at 476 (Alexander Hamilton) (Clinton Rossiter ed., 1961).

and executive. There was no dispute at the Convention regarding whether the Constitution should create a supreme court.[49]

Heads of Federal Jurisdiction

The first clause of Article III, Section 2, provides that federal "judicial Power shall extend" to nine categories of cases or controversies, which are numbered below:

[1] to all Cases, in Law and Equity, arising under this Constitution, the Laws of the United States, and Treaties made, or which shall be made, under their Authority; [2] to all Cases affecting Ambassadors, other public Ministers and Consuls; [3] to all Cases of admiralty and maritime Jurisdiction; [4] to Controversies to which the United States shall be a Party; [5] to Controversies between two or more States; [6] between a State and Citizens of another State; [7] between Citizens of different States; [8] between Citizens of the same State claiming Lands under Grants of different States, and [9] between a State, or the Citizens thereof, and foreign States, Citizens or Subjects.[50]

These nine heads of federal jurisdiction can be sorted into four groups according to the roles they enable the federal courts to play in advancing the Constitution's collective-action goals.[51]

The link between the heads of federal jurisdiction and the solution of collective-action problems first appeared in Resolution IX of the Virginia Plan, which proposed to extend "the jurisdiction of the National Judiciary . . . to cases, which respect the collection of the national revenue, impeachments of any national officers, and questions which involve the national peace and harmony." The reference to "national peace and harmony" echoes part of Resolution VI, which (as explained in earlier chapters) originally provided in part that Congress would have the authority "to legislate in all cases to which the separate States are incompetent, or in which the harmony of the United States may be interrupted by the exercise of individual Legislation."[52]

The first group into which the nine heads of jurisdiction can be sorted concerns the enforcement, supremacy, and uniform interpretation of federal law. Like executive enforcement, judicial enforcement is necessary to ensure that federal solutions to collective-action problems are not flouted. As noted, state

---

[49] 1 THE RECORDS OF THE FEDERAL CONVENTION OF 1787, *supra* note 14, at 104–05 (Jun. 4).

[50] U.S. CONST. art. III, § 2, cl. 1.

[51] The four groups discussed in this subsection largely, although not entirely, track the "four central purposes" of federal judicial power identified in FALLON ET AL., *supra* note 46, at 13.

[52] 1 THE RECORDS OF THE FEDERAL CONVENTION OF 1787, *supra* note 14, at 21 (May 29).

282   THE COLLECTIVE-ACTION CONSTITUTION

courts during the 1780s did not reliably enforce federal law and protect federal authority. The first head of federal jurisdiction—federal-question jurisdiction—was uncontroversial during the Constitutional Convention. Federal-question jurisdiction covers many cases in which the United States is a party, but when the federal government is sued under state law (e.g., for breach of contract or trespass on privately owned land), the fourth head of federal jurisdiction permits such cases to be heard in federal court. The fourth head protects federal institutions, interests, and resources from being undermined by litigation before state judges and juries that might be hostile to the federal government.

Hamilton referenced the second and third groups in *Federalist 80*, where he wrote that federal judicial power should extend "to all those [cases] which involve the PEACE of the CONFEDERACY, whether they relate to the intercourse between the United States and foreign nations or to that between the States themselves."[53] The second group gives the federal courts jurisdiction to decide cases implicating foreign affairs and national security. The goal of this grant is to deter states or private parties from undermining federal solutions to collective-action problems (embodied in federal regulations of foreign commerce and treaties) or causing collective-action problems by drawing the states collectively into diplomatic or military conflict with a foreign power. Multiple heads of federal jurisdiction fall within this group: the first head, which partially concerns litigation involving treaties and federal questions implicating national security; the second head, which concerns litigation affecting foreign officials (as discussed below); the ninth head, which concerns certain suits involving foreign nations or their citizens; and the third head, which concerns admiralty cases.

Admiralty jurisdiction encompasses both potentially serious public matters (e.g., prize cases, which involve the wartime capture at sea of ships and their cargo) and many private law disputes (e.g., those relating to maritime commerce). During the Convention, Wilson argued that "the admiralty jurisdiction ought to be given wholly to the national Government, as it related to cases not within the jurisdiction of particular states, & to a scene in which controversies with foreigners would be most likely to happen."[54] Partly for this structural reason, and partly because the colonies-turned-states had not generally exercised jurisdiction over these cases, the inclusion of this head was uncontroversial during the Convention and ratification debates. Hamilton wrote in *Federalist 80* that "[t]he most bigoted idolizers of State authority have not thus far shown a disposition to deny the national judiciary the cognizance of maritime causes."

[53] THE FEDERALIST No. 80, at 476 (Alexander Hamilton) (Clinton Rossiter ed., 1961).

[54] 1 THE RECORDS OF THE FEDERAL CONVENTION OF 1787, *supra* note 14, at 124 (Jun. 5); *see* FALLON ET AL., *supra* note 46, at 872 ("The Founders were particularly concerned with the relationship of maritime matters to international affairs—for example, prize cases required adjudication of the rights and status of foreign claimants and nations, both neutral and belligerent.").

His explanation was grounded in both collective-action reasoning and historical practice. First, these cases "so generally depend on the laws of nations and so commonly affect the rights of foreigners that they fall within the considerations which are relative to the public peace." Second, "[t]he most important part of them are, by the present Confederation, submitted to federal jurisdiction."[55] Hamilton might have added that federal admiralty jurisdiction facilitates establishment of a uniform federal law of admiralty, which solves the coordination or cost-benefit collective-action problems that would result if states had their own partially conflicting laws of admiralty. This national interest in uniformity, and in promoting maritime commerce, helps explain the extension of admiralty jurisdiction to "a large area of private law."[56]

Both the federal courts and Congress develop this body of federal law. In passing admiralty legislation, Congress uses its powers under the Interstate and Foreign Commerce Clauses, as well as under the constitutional structure or the Necessary and Proper Clause. As Chapter 1 explained, the separation-of-powers component of the Necessary and Proper Clause permits congressional legislation that carries into execution the powers of the other branches of the federal government.[57] The separation-of-powers aspect of this clause enables Congress to carry the Article III grant of admiralty jurisdiction into execution. As the Court observed in *Crowell v. Benson* (1932), a case in which it approved the use of non-Article III courts to adjudicate private disputes arising out of maritime accidents, the power to "amend[] and revis[e] the maritime law . . . is distinct from the authority to regulate interstate or foreign commerce and is not limited to cases arising in that commerce."[58] Moreover, in *Romero v. International Terminal Operating Company* (1959), another case involving a maritime injury, the Court stated that Article III "impliedly" "empowered Congress to revise and supplement the maritime law within the limits of the Constitution."[59] As the term "impliedly" suggests, the Court was either grounding congressional power in a structural inference from the Admiralty Clause or in the Necessary and Proper Clause.

The third group into which the heads of jurisdiction can be sorted concerns disputes between or among states, whether because the states themselves are the disputants (the fifth head) or because citizens of one state dispute ownership of land based on grants from different states (the eighth head). Recall the colonial and postcolonial history discussed in Chapter 3. The Interstate Compacts Clause permits compacts between states to settle boundary and other disagreements if,

---

[55] THE FEDERALIST NO. 80, at 478 (Alexander Hamilton) (Clinton Rossiter ed., 1961).
[56] FALLON ET AL., *supra* note 46, at 873.
[57] U.S. CONST. art. I, § 8, cl. 18.
[58] 285 U.S. 22, 55 & n.18 (1932).
[59] 358 U.S. 354, 361 (1959).

284   THE COLLECTIVE-ACTION CONSTITUTION

but only if, Congress approves.[60] In doing so, this clause continues the tradition of peacefully resolving disputes between states through agreement and approval by a higher authority: first the Crown, then the Confederation Congress, and now the US Congress. When negotiation fails or is deemed undesirable by at least one disputing state, Article III's grant of original jurisdiction to the Court in "Controversies between two or more States" continues the colonial and postcolonial tradition of resolving disagreements between states through litigation: first before the Crown, then the Confederation Congress, and now the Court.

The Court's role as interstate umpire might seem secondary today. The Court decides very few cases each term involving disputes between states—typically over land or water.[61] There is little reason to fear violence, let alone war, depending on how these cases are resolved, even though disputes over water in the western part of the country can involve high stakes (especially as climate change increasingly dries up the region).[62] At the Convention, however, several Framers worried about wars breaking out between or among states without a federal government to serve as umpire and thereby ensure peaceful conflict resolution. For example, early in the Convention's proceedings, Edmund Randolph asked, "Look at the public countenance from New Hampshire to Georgia. Are we not on the eve of war, which is only prevented by the hopes from the convention?" Later, when the delegates were at an impasse, Elbridge Gerry encouraged his colleagues to consider "the State we should be thrown into by the failure of the Union. We should be without an Umpire to decide controversies and must be at the mercy of events."[63] Moreover, even today, escalating interstate violence is not feared partly because umpiring by the federal government has proven effective. The Interstate Compacts and Commerce Clauses make Congress the umpire of first resort, and the fifth and eighth heads of jurisdiction make the Court the umpire of last resort.

---

[60] U.S. CONST. art. I, § 10, cl. 3.

[61] Of the sixty-nine cases decided during the October 2020 Term by formal opinions, only two (3 percent) arose under the Court's original jurisdiction. See Stat Pack for the Supreme Court's 2020–21 Term, SCOTUSBLOG (Jul. 2, 2021), at 24, https://perma.cc/5U9A-JGYY. Both cases were disputes over water. See Texas v. New Mexico, 141 S. Ct. 509 (2021) (denying Texas's motion to review the Pecos River Master's determination that New Mexico was entitled to a delivery credit for evaporated water stored at Texas's request under the Pecos River Compact); Florida v. Georgia, 141 S. Ct. 1175 (2021) (holding that Florida failed to establish that Georgia's overconsumption of interstate waters was either a substantial factor contributing to, or the sole cause of, Florida's injuries). The Court decided only one original-jurisdiction case during the October 2021 Term. See Stat Pack for the Supreme Court's 2021–22 Term, SCOTUSBLOG (Jul. 1, 2022), at 24, https://perma.cc/H477-HGT9. It was another water dispute. See Mississippi v. Tennessee, 142 S. Ct. 31 (2021) (holding that the waters of the Middle Claiborne Aquifer are subject to the judicial remedy of equitable apportionment, and Mississippi's complaint is dismissed without leave to amend).

[62] Cf. Arizona v. Navajo Nation, 143 S. Ct. 1804, 1814 (2023) ("Allocating water in the arid regions of the American West is often a zero-sum situation.").

[63] 1 THE RECORDS OF THE FEDERAL CONVENTION OF 1787, supra note 14, at 26 (statement of Randolph) (May 29); id. at 515 (statement of Gerry) (Jul. 2).

In addition, the fifth-through-seventh heads, combined with the separation-of-powers component of the Necessary and Proper Clause or a structural inference from these heads (as with admiralty legislation), empower Congress to be the umpire of first resort when the disputants are from different states.[64] Given that federal jurisdiction extends to disagreements that cross state lines—to conflicts "between" diverse disputants—substantive legislation that prevents, reduces, or resolves such disputes can be a rational way of carrying this portion of federal judicial power into execution. Although potentially surprising even to some specialists, Congress need not rely on the Interstate Commerce Clause to reach such interstate disputes, and so it need not be bound by the Court's distinctions (see Chapter 5) between economic and noneconomic activity or between activity and inactivity.

The fourth group reflects the Framers' worries that state courts might be biased against out-of-state litigants. Such bias raises concerns not only about justice and fairness but also about collective action. As discussed throughout this book, discrimination against out of-staters constitutes a negative interstate externality. Federal jurisdiction in such cases was intended to provide a neutral forum, thereby avoiding either a cost-benefit collective-action problem or the race to the bottom that might ensue if bias in one state court system was met with bias in others. Falling within this group are the sixth head of jurisdiction, which concerns litigation involving a state and a citizen of another state; the seventh head, which concerns litigation involving citizens of different states; and the ninth head, which partially concerns litigation involving an alien. When litigation involving an alien does not implicate foreign-policy or national-security concerns, the case seems best placed here.

In sum, the groups into which the nine heads of federal jurisdiction can be placed reflect a perceived need for federal courts to accomplish four purposes. The first is enforcing federal law and protecting federal authority, thereby ensuring the supremacy and uniformity of federal law. The second is preventing states or private litigants from undermining US foreign relations or national security. The third is neutrally and nonviolently resolving interstate disputes when negotiation fails or Congress fails to approve proposed interstate compacts. The fourth is avoiding parochialism by state courts in litigation involving in-staters and out-of-staters.

Because Article III is non-self-executing except as to the original jurisdiction of the Supreme Court, Congress has always defined federal-court jurisdiction within constitutional limits. At different times, Congress has placed relatively greater emphasis on certain of these four purposes than others. For example (and to oversimplify somewhat), in the decades before the Civil War, Congress

---

[64] The author thanks Professor Paul Mishkin for teaching him this point.

286 THE COLLECTIVE-ACTION CONSTITUTION

placed greater emphasis on providing neutral fora for the resolution of disputes (the third and fourth purposes) and lesser emphasis on ensuring the supremacy and uniformity of federal law (the first purpose). From Reconstruction onward, Congress has placed greater emphasis on the first purpose than on the third and fourth ones.[65] Considerations informing congressional judgments have included the amount of federal law in existence; the degree of political and economic integration of the country; and, relatedly, the resolution of debates over assertions of increasing federal authority over the states.[66]

Two Vesting Theories

Article III describes federal jurisdiction over cases within the first three heads using language that differs from its description of cases within the final six heads. For cases involving federal questions, affecting foreign officials, or concerning admiralty disputes, the first clause of Section 2 states that federal judicial power shall extend to "all Cases." By contrast, for cases falling with the next six heads, the text drops the term "all" and extends federal judicial power to "Controversies," not "Cases." This difference potentially matters because of a debate among federal courts scholars concerning whether Congress is required to vest in the federal courts some or all the judicial power listed in the nine heads of jurisdiction.

Because the opening section of Article III uses mandatory language in providing that the federal judicial power "shall be vested" in the Supreme Court and any lower courts that Congress establishes, Justice Story famously argued that Congress was constitutionally required to vest in the federal courts "the whole judicial power ... either in an original or in appellate form."[67] Story's "vesting theory" has never gained significant traction, largely because it is deeply contrary to historical practice: Congress has never vested all federal judicial power in the federal courts. Professor Amar has, however, amended the theory. He interprets Article III as obliging Congress to vest the three heads of jurisdiction that describe federal judicial power as extending to "all Cases," but not the six heads that

---

[65] For a cogent discussion of the evolution of federal jurisdiction, see FALLON ET AL., *supra* note 46, at 20–47.

[66] It is more difficult to generalize about the evolution of congressional concern regarding the second purpose (foreign policy and national security), at least partly because it contains several heads of federal jurisdiction that have not all followed the same path. For example, "[t]he admiralty jurisdiction has remained unchanged in substance" since the Judiciary Act of 1789. *Id.* at 873. By contrast, this first Judiciary Act made only one limited reference to cases arising under treaties, but the scope of federal jurisdiction over such cases expanded significantly over time, including upon passage of the Judiciary Act of 1875, which gave the federal courts jurisdiction over all civil cases arising under federal law that met an amount-in-controversy requirement. *Id.* at 22, 28.

[67] Martin v. Hunter's Lessee, 14 U.S. (1 Wheat.) 304, 331 (1816).

EXECUTIVE ENERGY AND FEDERAL SUPREMACY   287

describe this power as extending to "Controversies."[68] Most commentators have rejected Professor Amar's theory too as, among other things, inconsistent with the more limited jurisdiction Congress has granted to the federal courts beginning with the Judiciary Act of 1789.[69] Professor Amar's theory is, however, much more consistent with modern practice than Story's. Since 1914, the federal courts have had power to review effectively all cases included in the first three heads.[70]

A structural account by itself cannot resolve this dispute any more than historical practice can. But a collective-action approach sheds some light by calling into question Professor Amar's privileging of the first three heads of federal jurisdiction. More generally, the theory developed in this book would—with the important exception of individual-rights cases—likely leave the vesting of federal jurisdiction to the discretion of Congress.

As was just demonstrated, all nine heads of federal jurisdiction empower the federal courts to solve collective-action problems for the states. It is therefore difficult to see why, from a collective-action perspective, Congress should be required to vest the full judicial power regarding the first three heads but not the final six. True, the first three heads concern federal enforcement, federal supremacy, foreign relations, and national security. Regarding the solution or prevention of collective-action problems facing the states, one might argue that these are the most significant subjects covered by the nine heads of jurisdiction. Thus, if the Constitution should tie Congress's hands and require the full vesting of federal jurisdiction regarding any of the heads, perhaps it should be these.

A serious difficulty with this defense of Professor Amar's theory is that it also applies to several of the heads outside the first three. The fourth head concerns suits in which the federal government is a party. Although federal-question jurisdiction covers many cases in which the United States is a party, it does not cover all of them. To repeat, under a collective-action approach, it is important to protect federal institutions, interests, and resources from hostile litigation before state judges and juries.

The fifth head concerns controversies between states. As explained, there was reason to fear interstate wars at the Founding if disagreements among them could not be resolved peacefully, and such fears are much less warranted today partly because the federal government settles them. Perhaps giving Congress the

---

[68] *See* Akhil Reed Amar, *A Neo-Federalist View of Article III: Separating the Two Tiers of Federal Jurisdiction*, 65 B.U. L. REV. 205, 208–09 (1985); Akhil Reed Amar, *Reports of My Death Are Greatly Exaggerated: A Reply*, 138 U. PA. L. REV. 1651, 1652 (1990); Akhil Reed Amar, *The Two-Tiered Structure of the Judiciary Act of 1789*, 138 U. PA. L. REV. 1499, 1503–05 (1990).

[69] *See, e.g.*, Daniel J. Meltzer, *The History and Structure of Article III*, 138 U. PA. L. REV. 1569, 1585 (1990).

[70] Curtis A. Bradley & Neil S. Siegel, *Historical Gloss, Constitutional Conventions, and the Judicial Separation of Powers*, 105 GEO. L.J. 255, 321 (2017). In 1914, for the first time, Congress extended the Court's appellate jurisdiction to cases in which state courts ruled in favor of federal claims. *See* FALLON ET AL., *supra* note 46, at 30.

288 THE COLLECTIVE-ACTION CONSTITUTION

discretion to decide the scope of federal jurisdiction in controversies between states makes some structural sense because the Constitution makes Congress the umpire of first resort (as approver of interstate compacts) and the Court the umpire of last resort (when the disputing states cannot come to agreement). But this argument does not explain why Congress is empowered to make itself the umpire of only resort in this instance but not with respect to the first three heads.

The ninth head lets federal courts hear suits between states and foreign nations, and there was concern at the Founding that individual states would draw the nation into conflict with European powers. Granted, sovereign immunity generally barred suits against foreign nations, which were usually more provocative than suits by them.[71] But if the rationale for privileging the first three heads of federal jurisdiction includes concerns about foreign relations and national security, it is not obvious why suits by foreign nations against states should not also need to be vested in the federal courts.

From a collective-action standpoint, therefore, Justice Story's vesting theory makes more institutional sense than Professor Amar's. But the more important point is that neither vesting theory makes great institutional sense from a collective-action perspective. Congress is better situated than the federal courts to resolve collective-action problems for the states, and Congress possesses substantially more democratic legitimacy to do so because all the states and (almost) all interests within them are represented in Congress. Accordingly, a collective-action approach is likely more compatible with a plenary view of congressional control over federal jurisdiction, which would let Congress determine the extent to which federal courts should be used to solve multistate collective-action problems.

This issue is nuanced, and one can imagine arguments to the contrary. For example, this book endorses judicial review in federalism cases because it recognizes that Congress is capable of exceeding its enumerated powers, including by using the Interstate Commerce Clause where it cannot reasonably believe that the states face a collective-action problem. But the book endorses deferential judicial review because Congress possesses superior institutional capacity and democratic legitimacy to render the required constitutional judgments regarding the existence, seriousness, and scope of multistate collective-action problems, especially when states disagree—as they routinely do. On balance, it seems difficult to argue on collective-action grounds that Congress must vest some or all federal jurisdiction in cases involving federal-state relations.

There is a vitally important qualification built into this conclusion. The Collective-Action Constitution focuses on the constitutional structure, not

---

[71] The Schooner Exchange v. McFadden & Others, 11 U.S. (7 Cranch) 116 (1812) (holding in effect that foreign nations have sovereign immunity in US courts).

constitutional rights for the most part.[72] A collective-action approach, therefore, does not suggest that Congress should have complete power to determine federal jurisdiction over most individual-rights claims. A collective-action account does not point to one particular resolution of the complex debate over congressional control of federal jurisdiction in individual-rights cases.[73]

Original versus Appellate Jurisdiction

The second clause of Article III, Section 2, gives the Court appellate jurisdiction (subject to congressionally enacted "Exceptions") in almost all cases falling under the nine heads of jurisdiction. It gives the Court original jurisdiction in disputes falling under just two of them: "[i]n all Cases affecting Ambassadors, other public Ministers and Consuls, and those in which a State shall be a Party." Collective-action reasoning helps illuminate the grant of original jurisdiction in these two categories, although a complete explanation also requires a scarcity rationale.

At the Founding, the potential costs of an unredressed affront to a foreign ambassador or other official of a foreign government, as opposed to a foreign citizen, were especially high and could even be a basis for war. As Hamilton wrote in *Federalist 80*, "the denial or perversion of justice by the sentences of courts, as well as in any other manner, is with reason classed among the just causes of war."[74] Although Hamilton was there justifying federal jurisdiction over all cases involving foreign citizens, then as now there is a huge difference between one nation's imprisonment of a citizen of another country and its imprisonment of the country's ambassador.

For diplomatic and national-security reasons, it is structurally sound for the most sensitive disputes to be heard not just by a federal court instead of a state court but by the nation's highest court. Because it will probably take a national perspective, the Supreme Court seems more likely to be knowledgeable about, and sensitive to, the foreign-policy and national-security stakes of the litigation than at least some federal trial courts. Original jurisdiction in the Court may also help remedy the perceived dignitary harm and thereby defuse the situation. "Public ministers of every class are the immediate representatives of their sovereigns," Hamilton observed in *Federalist 81*. "All questions in which they are

---

[72] Chapter 9 discusses the subject of constitutional rights.

[73] There are numerous important contributions to this debate, and they cannot all be cited here. One seminal contribution argues that review by either the Supreme Court or a lower federal court is required for constitutional (and perhaps other federal) claims. *See* Lawrence Sager, *Foreword: Constitutional Limitations on Congress's Authority to Regulate the Jurisdiction of the Federal Courts*, 95 HARV. L. REV. 17 (1981).

[74] THE FEDERALIST No. 80, at 476 (Alexander Hamilton) (Clinton Rossiter ed., 1961).

290   THE COLLECTIVE-ACTION CONSTITUTION

concerned are so directly connected with the public peace," he continued, "that, as well for the preservation of this as out of respect to the sovereignties they represent, it is both expedient and proper that such questions should be submitted in the first instance to the highest judicatory of the nation."[75]

Two considerations make it appropriate to initially litigate cases involving a state party before the Court. First, as explained, disagreements between states were and remain potentially significant; they could cause serious collective-action problems if they turned violent or caused other retaliation. Second, in *Federalist 81*, Hamilton justified original jurisdiction "[i]n cases in which a State might happen to be a party" because "it would ill suit its dignity to be turned over to an inferior tribunal."[76] This expressive concern helps justify extending the Court's original jurisdiction to suits involving one state as a party, as opposed to limiting it to suits involving only states as parties. When voluntary solutions to interstate disputes cannot be obtained through agreement, or when Congress disapproves of proposed agreements because it concludes that they would harm federal supremacy or other states (see Chapter 3), the Court may be the best interstate umpire available. It is the tribunal most likely to command the respect of the disputing states and to express the most respect for them.

Given these rationales, one could ask whether the grant of original jurisdiction to the Court only in these two categories is under-inclusive. For example, suits between a state citizen and a foreign citizen might also generate diplomatic problems for the United States, and suits between citizens of the same state asserting ownership of land under grants of different states might also be sources of interstate hostility. Moreover, federal-question jurisdiction has been important for roughly 150 years now. From a collective-action perspective, Article III does not perfectly sort cases falling within federal judicial power into the Court's original and appellate jurisdictions. Cases involving foreign officials or a US state are, however, among the most sensitive from a collective-action standpoint.

Because capacity limits preclude the Court from serving as a trial court in many cases, certain sensitive cases must be prioritized over others based on their relative frequency. As Hamilton noted in *Federalist 81*, the "two classes of cases" falling within the Court's original jurisdiction are "those of a nature rarely to occur."[77] Reflecting capacity constraints, the Court's current jurisdictional statute, 28 U.S.C. § 1251, assigns only disputes between states exclusively to the Court; it assigns other original-jurisdiction cases nonexclusively to the Court. So, a collective-action perspective offers illumination but not a complete explanation.

---

[75] THE FEDERALIST No. 81, at 487 (Alexander Hamilton) (Clinton Rossiter ed., 1961).
[76] *Id.*
[77] *Id.* at 488.

The Madisonian Compromise

The Framers disagreed about whether the Constitution should require, permit, or prohibit the establishment of lower federal courts in addition to the Supreme Court. John Rutledge, Roger Sherman, and Pierce Butler objected that lower federal courts would encroach on the jurisdiction of the state courts, would be expensive to maintain, and would arouse great opposition. They also emphasized that state-court decisions on federal questions could be appealed to the US Supreme Court, thereby ensuring uniformity in judicial interpretations of federal law and its supremacy over state law.[78] Other delegates disagreed. Wilson, as noted above, emphasized the necessity of federal admiralty jurisdiction because those cases were most likely to involve conflicts with foreigners. Madison, Wilson, and John Dickinson worried about a flood of appeals from state courts to the Supreme Court, and they argued that lower federal courts were needed to avoid the potential bias and parochialism of state judges and juries.[79] Madison asked this question:

> What was to be done after improper Verdicts in State tribunals obtained under the biassed directions of a dependent Judge, or the local prejudices of an undirected jury? To remand the cause for a new trial would answer no purpose. To order a new trial at the supreme bar would oblige the parties to bring up their witnesses, tho' ever so distant from the seat of the Court. An effective Judiciary establishment commensurate to the legislative authority, was essential.[80]

The compromise, which became known as the "Madisonian Compromise" even though Dickinson suggested it and both Wilson and Madison moved it, was to give Congress discretion to decide whether to create lower federal courts. On June 5, the Convention approved the compromise by a vote of eight to two, with one delegation divided.[81] Article III thus opens by stating that "[t]he judicial Power of the United States, shall be vested in one supreme Court, and in such inferior Courts as the Congress may from time to time ordain and establish."[82]

From a collective-action perspective, what is most striking about the Madisonian Compromise is its connection both to the Marshallian theory of the superior democratic legitimacy of Congress and to the other constitutional

---

[78] 1 THE RECORDS OF THE FEDERAL CONVENTION OF 1787, *supra* note 14, at 124–25 (Jun. 5).

[79] *Id.* Rufus King added that "the establishment of inferior tribunals wd. cost infinitely less than the appeals that would be prevented by them." *Id.* at 125.

[80] *Id.* at 124.

[81] *Id.* at 125.

[82] U.S. CONST. art. III, § 1. As Chapter 6 discussed, the compromise also appears in the ninth clause of Article I, Section 8, which authorizes Congress "[t]o constitute tribunals inferior to the Supreme Court."

292 THE COLLECTIVE-ACTION CONSTITUTION

provisions and principles that give Congress the authority to decide whether there are multistate collective-action problems in need of solving. The best justification for calling the compromise Madisonian is that Madison voiced the strongest argument for lower federal courts: potential parochialism by state judges and juries. As discussed above, if such parochialism is directed against federal claims, it can undermine federal solutions to collective-action problems. Such disfavoring of federal claims can be analogized to the structural argument in *McCulloch v. Maryland* (1819) that part of the Union may not tax the whole Union because the whole is not represented in the part.[83] If state-court parochialism is directed at other states or countries (or their citizens), it can create a cost-benefit collective-action problem or a race to the bottom by causing these other states or foreign governments to retaliate.[84]

Yet, the extent to which such concerns are warranted was disputed then, and it remains disputed today in the long-standing debate over whether there is "parity" between federal and state courts along a number of dimensions, including their relative ability to avoid local bias against federal claims and out-of-staters.[85] Hamilton wrote in *Federalist 81* that "the most discerning cannot foresee how far the prevalency of a local spirit may be found to disqualify the local tribunals for the jurisdiction of national causes."[86] Again, Congress, where all states and individuals are represented, is the institution that the Constitution charges with settling disagreements over whether states are undermining federal solutions to collective-action problems or causing such problems. If Congress believes that concerns about state parochialism are weighty enough to warrant a response, it can provide a more comprehensive solution than the Constitution's baseline solution of creating the Supreme Court. The establishment of lower federal courts is the primary solution that the Constitution authorizes Congress to craft. These courts help enforce federal law, ensure its supremacy over state law, and protect out-of-state governments and individuals.[87]

---

[83] 17 U.S. (4 Wheat.) 316, 428, 435–36 (1819).

[84] Retaliation by a foreign government can cause a collective-action problem not only for the United States and the other nation but also for the states within the United States. As explained earlier in this chapter, the state that provokes foreign retaliation often helps itself less than it harms other states, in which case there is a cost-benefit collective-action problem.

[85] For discussion, see FALLON, JR. ET AL., *supra* note 46, at 299–303, 422, and 1415–19. Judge Henry Friendly famously questioned the "sincerity" of Madison's concerns given his failure to provide examples of state judicial bias. Henry J. Friendly, *The Historic Basis of Diversity Jurisdiction*, 41 HARV. L. REV. 483 (1928). For challenges to Friendly's historical research and conclusions, see FALLON, JR. ET AL., *supra* note 46, at 1415–16.

[86] THE FEDERALIST No. 81, at 486 (Alexander Hamilton) (Clinton Rossiter ed., 1961).

[87] This chapter does not examine whether subsequent expansions of federal jurisdiction or the creation of certiorari jurisdiction for the Supreme Court can be understood in collective-action terms. For scholars interested in such questions, a point to bear in mind is that Congress need not have consciously intended to solve a multistate collective problem for a collective-action approach to have potential explanatory power. The effects of congressional action are also relevant to a descriptive account.

EXECUTIVE ENERGY AND FEDERAL SUPREMACY   293

Lower federal courts also play a major role in ensuring that federal law is interpreted more uniformly by judges than would be possible without these courts. This claim might seem counterintuitive, because the existence of lower federal courts means the existence of a greater number of federal judges and so a greater potential for conflicting interpretations of federal law. But given the legal and practical narrowness of the Court's original jurisdiction, there needs to be original jurisdiction to hear federal claims in courts of some kind. Thus, the question is whether the bulk of federal claims should be heard initially in a limited number of lower federal courts or a multitude of state courts; the question is not whether most federal claims should be heard initially in lower federal courts or no courts besides the Supreme Court. Today, the federal courts of appeals, by resolving inconsistencies in federal district-court decisions within their circuits, help the Supreme Court guarantee that important provisions of federal law are construed the same way by federal courts in different parts of the nation, leaving to the Court the task of resolving inconsistencies in circuit-court decisions and, to a much lesser extent, the decisions of state high courts on questions of federal law.[88] Like uniform federal laws, uniform judicial interpretations of them can help solve collective-action problems for the states.[89]

Judicial Independence, Judicial Accountability, and Judicial Review in Two Dimensions

As explained, the federal judiciary performs the vital function of deterring states from thwarting federal solutions to collective-action problems or causing such problems. In addition, the federal courts play a modest role in ensuring that federal solutions to collective-action problems stay within constitutional bounds. Finally, federal judges require sufficient means to protect their lawful authority from encroachments by the political branches.

To execute these responsibilities and protect themselves, federal judges require significant independence from the political branches—independence not enjoyed by the one national court established by the Confederation Congress.[90] Relatedly, federal judges likely require the power of judicial review, which is

---

[88] *See* SUP. CT. R. 10 (setting forth reasons for granting a petition for a writ of certiorari, including a split of authority between federal courts of appeals and/or state courts of last resort). The Court today grants certiorari in relatively few cases coming from state courts. Of the sixty-nine cases decided during the October 2020 Term by formal opinions, only four cases (6 percent) came from state courts. *See* Stat Pack for the Supreme Court's 2020–21 Term, *supra* note 61, at 24. Of the sixty-six cases decided during the October 2021 Term, only five cases (8 percent) came from state courts. *See* Stat Pack for the Supreme Court's 2021–22 Term, *supra* note 61, at 24.

[89] For a classic discussion of the role of the federal courts in ensuring uniformity, see *Martin v. Hunter's Lessee*, 14 U.S. (1 Wheat.) 304, 347–48 (1816).

[90] For discussion of this appellate court, see the paragraph preceding note 46.

294   THE COLLECTIVE-ACTION CONSTITUTION

the authority of courts to decide the constitutionality of government action in cases properly before them. Regarding how the federal judiciary should exercise this power, much textual, originalist, and structural evidence (discussed below) indicates that the Framers intended for federal courts to proceed with caution in reviewing the constitutionality of federal statutes and executive actions, and to act more assertively in ensuring that state governments comply with federal law. These modalities of interpretation, along with antebellum historical practice and the structural logics of collective action, also offer good reasons for modern federal courts to generally do the same when federal laws are challenged on federalism grounds.

Because the Framers learned from experience, the text of Article III evidences a significant, albeit not complete, commitment to judicial independence—especially for the Supreme Court. So does much of the practice that has glossed the meaning of Article III over the centuries. First, as noted, Article III requires the existence of "one supreme Court"; it does not leave the matter to Congress's discretion, as it does for other federal courts.[91] Second, the text offers job security—guaranteed service during "good Behaviour."[92] Hamilton wrote in *Federalist 78* that "nothing can contribute so much to [the federal judiciary's] firmness and independence as permanency in office."[93] Article III's "good Behaviour" language has also been glossed by historical practice to mean life tenure absent impeachment and conviction, which cannot be used just because of disagreement with a judge's decisions.[94] No justice has ever been impeached and convicted, and no federal judge has ever been impeached and convicted based on substantive disagreements with their decisions.

Third, the text provides salary protection for federal judges: Congress may not reduce their salaries for as long as they serve.[95] True, Article III, in contrast to Article II, does permit pay raises—and carrots, like sticks, can compromise independence. But as Hamilton explained in *Federalist 79*, federal judges characteristically serve for longer periods than presidents and so are in greater need of cost-of-living increases.[96] Fourth, although Article III permits Congress to

[91]   U.S. CONST. art. III, § 1.

[92]   U.S. CONST. art. III, § 1 ("The Judges, both of the supreme and inferior Courts, shall hold their Offices during good Behaviour, and shall, at stated Times, receive for their Services, a Compensation, which shall not be diminished during their Continuance in Office.").

[93]   THE FEDERALIST No. 78, at 466 (Alexander Hamilton) (Clinton Rossiter ed., 1961); *see id.* at 469 (writing that "nothing will contribute so much as [the permanent tenure of judicial offices] to that independent spirit in the judges"). *But see* Saikrishna Prakash & Steven D. Smith, *How to Remove a Federal Judge*, 116 YALE L.J. 72, 76 (2006) (arguing that the Constitution's mandate that federal judges hold their offices during "good Behaviour" reflects an original understanding that impeachment was not the only basis for removing them).

[94]   For discussion of the role of historical practice in informing beliefs about the proper bases for removing federal judges, see Bradley & Siegel, *supra* note 70, at 319–20.

[95]   *See supra* note 92 (quoting the provision of Article III providing salary protection).

[96]   THE FEDERALIST No. 79, at 473 (Alexander Hamilton) (Clinton Rossiter ed., 1961) ("What might be extravagant today might in half a century become penurious and inadequate.").

make "Exceptions" to the Supreme Court's appellate jurisdiction, Congress has almost never stripped the Court's appellate jurisdiction.[97] Fifth, although political considerations (among others) did inform occasional changes in the Court's size up until 1869, Congress has not since altered the size of the Court, notwithstanding vehement disagreements with many of its decisions and a strenuous attempt to pack the Court by a powerful, popular president in 1937.[98]

Judicial independence likely requires that federal courts possess the power of judicial review, which enables the federal judiciary to perform its functions. Federal courts that lacked the power of judicial review could never push back against perceived violations of the Constitution by the political branches, even when Congress or the president encroached on the lawful authority of the federal courts, and even when federal solutions to collective-action problems were clearly unconstitutional. Judicial review enables federal judges both to protect their institution and to play a role in ensuring that statutes or treaties addressing collective-action problems remain within constitutional bounds.

Judicial review also empowers federal courts to deter states from undermining federal solutions to collective-action problems or causing such problems by externalizing costs onto other states. The Supremacy Clause of Article VI, discussed below, clearly contemplates judicial review of state laws (vertical judicial review). As will be shown, this is the most important form of judicial review under a collective-action account of the Constitution.

The Framers never debated judicial review during the Constitutional Convention, but the subject arose during other debates. Almost every Framer who took a position on judicial review while participating in these debates spoke in favor of such a power, and those who did not speak declined to object. The views of the Framers on vertical judicial review were most revealed in the debate over the proposal to give Congress the power to veto (or "negative") state laws on constitutional grounds. Resolution VI of the Virginia Plan provided in relevant part that "the National Legislature ought to be impowered . . . to negative all laws passed by the several States, contravening in the opinion of the National Legislature the articles of Union."[99] Both sides in this debate agreed that the federal (and state) courts could invalidate state laws on federal constitutional grounds; they disagreed over whether vertical judicial review would suffice.

---

[97] The main exception is *Ex parte McCardle*, 74 U.S. (7 Wall.) 506 (1868), where the Court upheld a provision of federal law stripping its appellate jurisdiction in certain habeas cases even though Congress had sought to remove the case from the Court's docket to disable it from invalidating the Military Reconstruction Act. But *McCardle* can be read narrowly, *see id.* at 515 (emphasizing that it still had jurisdiction in habeas cases under a different statute), especially given the Court's assumption of jurisdiction a few months later in *Ex parte Yerger*, 75 U.S. 85 (8 Wall.) (1868).

[98] For discussion of the historical practice concerning changes to the Court's composition until 1869, FDR's Court-packing plan of 1937, and the subsequent failure of a proposed Court-protecting amendment to the Constitution, see Bradley & Siegel, *supra* note 70, at 269–87.

[99] 1 THE RECORDS OF THE FEDERAL CONVENTION OF 1787, *supra* note 14, at 21 (May 29).

296 THE COLLECTIVE-ACTION CONSTITUTION

For example, on July 17, Robert Sherman deemed the congressional negative "unnecessary, as the Courts of the States would not consider as valid any law contravening the Authority of the Union, and which the legislature would wish to be negatived."[100] In other words, Sherman thought it unnecessary to give Congress a power of judicial review because it would already exist in the state courts. Madison disagreed, explaining in collective-action terms that "[t]he necessity of a general Govt. proceeds from the propensity of the States to pursue their particular interests in opposition to the general interest." In Madison's view, states "can pass laws which will accomplish their injurious objects before they can be repealed by the General Legislre. or be set aside by the National Tribunals." Moreover, "[c]onfidence can <not> be put in the State Tribunals as guardians of the National authority and interests," he insisted, because "[i]n all the States these are more or less dependt. on the Legislatures."[101] Madison thus supported the idea that both the state and national judiciaries should exercise the power of judicial review, but he did not think either sufficed to invalidate unconstitutional laws issued by state legislatures. Gouverneur Morris opposed the negative but agreed with Madison on vertical judicial review. "A law that ought to be negatived will be set aside in the Judiciary departmt.," he reasoned, "and if that security should fail; may be repealed by a National law."[102]

The proposed negative was voted down by a vote of seven states to three.[103] After the vote, Luther Martin immediately proposed an initial version of the Supremacy Clause, which was unanimously approved.[104] Also unanimously approved was John Rutledge's August 23 proposal to add the words "This Constitution" to the Supremacy Clause.[105] This addition made clear that state judges would be obliged to invalidate state laws that violated the US Constitution. Moreover, the Supremacy Clause implies that federal courts have the same power and duty, given the strength of the structural inference that the Supreme Court is authorized to review state-court decisions on questions of federal law. As noted above, both sides in the debate that culminated in the Madisonian Compromise drew this inference.[106]

Also on August 23, Charles Pinckney asked that the issue of the congressional negative be reconsidered. Wilson, who spoke in favor of the proposal, insisted that "[t]he firmness of Judges is not of itself sufficient" and "[s]omething further is requisite," because "[i]t will be better to prevent the passage of an improper law,

---

[100] 2 *id.* at 27 (Jul. 17).
[101] *Id.* at 27–28.
[102] *Id.* at 28.
[103] *Id.*
[104] *Id.* at 28–29.
[105] *Id.* at 389.
[106] For relevant statements made during this debate, see *supra* text preceding and accompanying notes 78–80.

EXECUTIVE ENERGY AND FEDERAL SUPREMACY 297

than to declare it void when passed."[107] Like the other delegates on both sides of this debate, Wilson was voicing support for vertical judicial review. And like those of other nationalists, his arguments for the congressional negative proved unavailing.[108] In this debate, no Framer voiced opposition to vertical judicial review.[109]

Regarding judicial review of federal laws (horizontal judicial review), there was again broad (although not unanimous) agreement about its propriety on both sides of the debate over the proposed council of revision, which appeared in Resolution VIII of the Virginia Plan. This council, which would have been composed of "the Executive and a convenient number of the National Judiciary," would have been empowered "to examine every act of the National Legislature before it shall operate" and to reject bills on either constitutional or nonconstitutional grounds.[110] Madison and Wilson advocated for the inclusion of federal judges in the council of revision, while opponents disagreed partly for reasons revealing the common ground they largely shared regarding judicial review.[111]

---

[107] 2 *Id.* at 391.

[108] Pinckney withdrew his proposal after a motion to commit the issue failed by a vote of six states to five. *Id.* at 391–92.

[109] The account offered here is consistent with Professor Alison LaCroix's argument that judicial review supplanted the failed negative on state laws and partly reflected long-standing debates over the idea of federalism. *See* ALISON L. LACROIX, THE IDEOLOGICAL ORIGINS OF AMERICAN FEDERALISM (2010).

[110] 1 THE RECORDS OF THE FEDERAL CONVENTION OF 1787, *supra* note 14, at 21. The full language of Resolution VIII read as follows:

> Resolved that the Executive and a convenient number of the National Judiciary, ought to compose a council of revision with authority to examine every act of the National Legislature before it shall operate, and every act of a particular Legislature before a Negative thereon shall be final; and that the dissent of the said Council shall amount to a rejection, unless the Act of the National Legislature be again passed, or that of a particular Legislature be again negatived by of the members of each branch.

Id. The council of revision would thus have had the authority to "veto" not only congressional bills, but also congressional negatives on state laws. The blank space in the above quotation, which left room for a potential veto override by Congress, makes clearer the connection between the council of revision and the president's qualified veto authority, which ultimately emerged from the debate over the council. Part of the debate, which will not be canvassed here, concerned whether the council's revisionary power should be absolute or qualified.

[111] Professor Sylvia Snowiss explains that there were "a variety" of objections to the inclusion of judges in the council of revision:

> [I]t was said that policy judgments inherent in the veto were foreign to judicial expertise; that uniting the executive and judiciary against the legislature would overwhelm the latter; and that as judges would eventually have to expound the laws, they should have no hand in their original passage. In addition, several delegates argued that specific inclusion of the judiciary in the veto power was unnecessary, as judges would have a check on legislation in their capacity to pass on constitutionality.

SYLVIA SNOWISS, JUDICIAL REVIEW AND THE LAW OF THE CONSTITUTION 39 (1990).

298   THE COLLECTIVE-ACTION CONSTITUTION

On June 4, Elbridge Gerry opened the debate by objecting to the participation of judges in the council of revision mostly by emphasizing that they would already possess the power of horizontal judicial review:

> [He] doubts whether the Judiciary ought to form a part of it, as they will have a sufficient check agst. encroachments on their own department by their exposition of the laws, which involved a power of deciding on their Constitutionality. In some States the Judges had <actually> set aside laws as being agst. the Constitution. This was done too with general approbation. It was quite foreign from the nature of ye. office to make them judges of the policy of public measures.[112]

Gerry thus added an argument stressing judges' lack of policy expertise to his primary contention that judges would exercise the power of judicial review on the back end and so need not be involved in any revisionary authority on the front end. Rufus King agreed with Gerry, asserting that "the Judges ought to be able to expound the law as it should come before them, free from the bias of having participated in its formation."[113]

Gunning Bedford also opposed the council of revision, but his opposition also implied opposition to horizontal judicial review. In his view, "it would be sufficient to mark out in the Constitution the boundaries of the Legislative Authority, which would give all the requisite security to the rights of the other departments." He thought that "[t]he Representatives of the People were the best judges of what was for their interest, and ought to be under no external control whatever," adding that "[t]he two branches would produce a sufficient control within <the Legislature itself.>"[114] The Convention voted eight to two to exclude members of the judiciary from the proposed council.[115]

Wilson then moved to reconsider the matter and did so again on June 6. Both times, Madison seconded the motion. On June 6, it was again voted down, this time by a margin of eight to three.[116] On July 21, Wilson tried again:

> The Judiciary ought to have an opportunity of remonstrating agst projected encroachments on the people as well as on themselves. It had been said that the Judges, as expositors of the Laws would have an opportunity of defending their constitutional rights. There was weight in this observation; but this power of the Judges did not go far enough. Laws may be unjust, may be unwise, may

---

[112] 1 THE RECORDS OF THE FEDERAL CONVENTION OF 1787, *supra* note 14, at 97–98 (Jun. 4).
[113] *Id.* at 98.
[114] *Id.* at 100–01.
[115] *Id.* at 104.
[116] *Id.* at 104, 138, 140 (Jun. 6).

be dangerous, may be destructive; and yet may not be so unconstitutional as to justify the Judges in refusing to give them effect.[117]

Wilson was saying that, in their judicial capacity, judges may permissibly invalidate laws only because they are unconstitutional, not because they are bad or even terrible. Thus, Wilson supported both the council of revision and horizontal judicial review.

Luther Martin disagreed with Wilson on the council of revision but agreed on horizontal judicial review. "A knowledge of mankind, and of Legislative affairs cannot be presumed to belong in a higher deger [*sic*] degree to the Judges than to the Legislature," he contended. "As to the Constitutionality of laws," he continued, "that point will come before the Judges in their proper official character," in which capacity "they have a negative on the laws." But, he insisted, "[j]oin them with the Executive in the Revision and they will have a double negative."[118] George Mason responded to Martin by reemphasizing Wilson's distinction between constitutional and nonconstitutional grounds for rejecting bills. Judges "could declare an unconstitutional law void," Mason said, "[b]ut with regard to every law however unjust oppressive or pernicious, which did not come plainly under this description, they would be under the necessity as Judges to give it a free course."[119] Wilson's motion to join the judiciary with the executive in exercising a revisionary power failed for the third time, this one by a margin of four to three with two state delegations divided.[120]

The council of revision was debated for the last time on August 15, when Madison (seconded by Wilson) moved yet again to join the judiciary with the executive in exercising revisionary authority over Congress. John Mercer supported the motion but "disapproved of the Doctrine that the Judges as expositors of the Constitution should have authority to declare a law void," because "laws ought to be well and cautiously made, and then to be uncontroulable." Madison's motion was voted down for the fourth and final time by a margin of eight to three, after which Dickinson said he "was strongly impressed with the remark of Mr. Mercer as to the power of the Judges to set aside the law" and "thought no such power ought to exist," but "[h]e was at the same time at a loss what expedient to substitute." Gouverneur Morris responded that he "could not agree that the Judiciary which was part of the Executive, should be bound to say that a direct violation of the Constitution was law." The power that instead found a home in the Constitution was qualified presidential veto authority over legislation.[121]

---

[117] 2 *Id.* at 73 (Jul. 21).
[118] *Id.* at 76.
[119] *Id.* at 78.
[120] *Id.* at 80.
[121] *Id.* at 298–99 (Aug. 15). For the veto power, see U.S. Const. art. I, § 7, cl. 2.

In the debate over the council of revision, Framers who opined on the legitimacy of horizontal judicial review expressed support by a margin of about three to one (not counting Dickinson, who expressed ambivalence). Delegates on both sides of the debate leveraged the perceived legitimacy of judicial review to bolster their arguments. Delegates who opposed the inclusion of the judiciary in a council of revision won the debate not because they opposed judicial review but partly because they mostly supported it. They believed that judges should concern themselves only with issues of constitutionality and the interpretation of legal texts, not with the fairness or policy wisdom of legislation.

Considering together the debates over the negative on state laws and the council of revision, it is noteworthy that the opposition to, or misgivings about, judicial review that three Framers expressed (Bedford, Mercer, and Dickinson) all occurred during discussions of horizontal judicial review, not vertical judicial review. When vertical judicial review was at issue, the Framers who opined on its legitimacy unanimously supported it. This observation tends to support the conclusion that the Framers intended the federal judiciary to be more assertive in exercising vertical judicial review than horizontal judicial review.

In writing about these debates, Professor Sylvia Snowiss has observed that "[i]t was not always clear . . . whether speakers endorsing judicial review were supporting a general power over legislation or one limited to defense of the courts' constitutional sphere."[122] Notably, the evidence for this observation is limited to the statements about horizontal judicial review that some Framers made during the debate over the council of revision. In endorsing horizontal judicial review, both Gerry and Wilson described it as entailing judicial invocation of the Constitution as a shield, not a sword. Gerry, to repeat, said that federal judges "will have a sufficient check agst. encroachments on their own department by their exposition of the laws, which involved a power of deciding on their Constitutionality." Wilson, to reiterate, agreed that "the Judges, as expositors of the Laws would have an opportunity of defending their constitutional rights," but he did not think judicial review sufficed because "[t]he Judiciary ought to have an opportunity of remonstrating agst projected encroachments on the people as well as on themselves."

Even opponents of judicial review viewed its legitimacy in terms of judicial self-protection. Recall that Bedford believed "it would be sufficient to mark out in the Constitution the boundaries of the Legislative Authority, which would give all the requisite security to the rights of the other departments." And Mercer, just before expressing his "disapprov[al] of the Doctrine that the Judges as expositors of the Constitution should have the authority to declare a law void," said that "[t]he true policy of the axiom [that the judiciary should be not just

---

[122] SNOWISS, *supra* note 111, at 39–40.

EXECUTIVE ENERGY AND FEDERAL SUPREMACY   301

separate from the legislature but independent of it] is that legislative usurpation and oppression may be obviated."[123] Further, the Framers gave presidents the veto power (the chosen alternative to the council of revision) mainly so that they could defend their office against congressional encroachments.[124] This evidence, too, indicates an original intent that the federal courts were to be less aggressive in reviewing the constitutionality of federal laws than state laws.

In *Federalist 78*, however, Hamilton seemed to endorse judicial review of federal laws more generally. For example, he wrote broadly that "the courts of justice are to be considered as the bulwarks of a limited Constitution against legislative encroachments."[125] Some textual support for horizontal judicial review lies in the grant of jurisdiction to hear "all Cases, in Law and Equity, arising under this Constitution," but this language does not answer the question of whether judicial review was intended to be as vigorous horizontally as vertically.[126]

Other textual and structural evidence suggests that the Framers likely intended for the federal courts to play a more modest role in policing the political branches and a more aggressive role in enforcing federal law, including by ensuring its supremacy over state law. As noted, the recognition of judicial review in the Supremacy Clause contemplates vertical judicial review. Also, the judiciary article comes after both the legislative and the executive articles. This order tracks the truth that the judiciary enjoys less democratic legitimacy than the political branches, including to decide whether there are multistate collective-action problems in need of solving.[127]

Further, the several mechanisms for ensuring judicial accountability laid out in the constitutional text empower the political branches, not the states. The Appointments Clause authorizes the president to nominate federal judges and empowers the Senate to grant or deny them confirmation.[128] Article III permits Congress to decide whether to create lower federal courts and gives Congress broad authority to determine their jurisdiction, while the Necessary and Proper Clause or the constitutional structure authorizes Congress to set the size of the Supreme Court and determine many of its procedural rules (among many other things that affect judicial authority, such as today's courthouses, support staff, and law clerks).[129] Congress is also empowered by the aforementioned Exceptions

---

[123] 2 THE RECORDS OF THE FEDERAL CONVENTION OF 1787, *supra* note 14, at 298 (Aug. 15).

[124] *See* Chapters 10 and 11.

[125] THE FEDERALIST NO. 78, at 469 (Alexander Hamilton) (Clinton Rossiter ed., 1961).

[126] U.S. CONST. art. III, § 2, cl. 1.

[127] *Cf.* AMAR, AMERICA'S CONSTITUTION, *supra* note 15, at 208 ("Democratically, Congress ranked first among equals, and the life-tenured judiciary—furthest removed from the people and the states—came last.").

[128] U.S. CONST. art. II, § 2, cl. 2.

[129] U.S. CONST. art. III, § 1 (Madisonian Compromise); art. I, § 8, cl. 18 (Necessary & Proper Clause). As with congressional power to pass admiralty legislation, *see supra* notes 57–59 and accompanying text, it is not clear that Congress must rely on the Necessary and Power Clause to set the Court's size. The first section of Article III mandates the existence of "one supreme Court." If the

302 THE COLLECTIVE-ACTION CONSTITUTION

Clause[130] and by the clause subjecting "all civil Officers," which includes federal judges, to removal via impeachment and conviction.[131] The states possess no such powers to affect the federal judiciary.[132]

This strategy of selective institutional empowerment was likely intended to produce federal courts that would exercise the power of judicial review vertically more frequently and assertively than they would horizontally. As Professor Amar writes, the structure of the Constitution "emboldened the Court to vindicate national values against obstreperous states even as it cautioned the justices to avoid undue provocation of Congress."[133] Consistent with this interpretation is Hamilton's statement in *Federalist 78* that "the judiciary is beyond comparison the weakest of the three departments of power" and that "it can never attack with success either of the other two." On the contrary, he insisted, "it is in continual jeopardy of being overpowered, awed, or influenced by its co-ordinate branches."[134]

This is what happened early on. The Court first exercised the power of judicial review to invalidate a law in *Ware v. Hylton* (1796), where it struck down a Virginia statute as inconsistent with the 1783 Treaty of Peace with Great Britain (and thus with the Supremacy Clause).[135] Until *Dred Scott* in 1857,[136] the Court

---

Necessary and Proper Clause had been left out of the Constitution, Congress would still be obliged to establish the Court. Moreover, Congress has, for good reason (see below), apparently never believed that it can establish the Court without setting the number of justices to serve on it. And having set the number of justices initially, it is not clear why a distinct source of power is required to change the Court's size later on. Again, if there were no Necessary and Proper Clause, it would be implausible to argue that the size of the Court was set in constitutional stone in 1789—when Congress passed the first Judiciary Act—no matter how sensible on good-government grounds it might later become to change the Court's size given profound changes in the country or the organization of the federal-courts system.

Perhaps Congress could establish the Court without setting the number of justices. If Congress did not fix the Court's size, perhaps presidents could nominate as many justices as they wanted, and perhaps the Senate could confirm as many nominees as the Senate wanted. *Cf.* James Durling & E. Garrett West, *Appointments Without Law*, 105 VA. L. REV. 1281 (2019) (arguing that the president can lawfully appoint both diplomats and justices without congressional authorization). The historical practice is, however, uniformly to the contrary. This is fortunate: a Court with a floating size would risk becoming the plaything of the political parties when the same party controlled the presidency and the Senate.

[130] U.S. CONST. art. III, § 2, cl. 2.

[131] U.S. CONST. art. II, § 4.

[132] AMAR, AMERICA'S CONSTITUTION, *supra* note 15, at 213 ("[S]tate governments would have no formal say in determining the Court's general contours or in making the specific decisions about whom to put on it or pull off it.").

[133] *Id.*

[134] THE FEDERALIST No. 78, at 465–66 (Alexander Hamilton) (Clinton Rossiter ed., 1961); *see* THE FEDERALIST No. 81, at 484 (Alexander Hamilton) (Clinton Rossiter ed., 1961) ("[T]he supposed danger of judiciary encroachments on the legislative authority which has been upon many occasions reiterated is in reality a phantom.").

[135] 3 U.S. (3 Dall.) 199 (1796).

[136] Scott v. Sandford, 60 U.S. (19 How.) 393 (1857) (implausibly concluding that Congress could not regulate slavery in the territories).

EXECUTIVE ENERGY AND FEDERAL SUPREMACY 303

invalidated only one provision of federal law (in *Marbury v. Madison* (1803)),[137] and most commentators (including this one) think the Court misread the provision at issue in a way that invited the constitutional question.[138] Meanwhile, up to 1869, Congress altered the Court's size numerous times partly for political reasons. President Franklin Delano Roosevelt's 1937 plan to pack the Court was defeated for a combination of political, conventional, and legal reasons, so it is uncertain what to make of the episode.[139] Putting aside whether and when Court-packing would have destructive effects, it is a highly potent method of ensuring judicial accountability—an instrument that contradicts nothing in the constitutional text and arguably should be available, at least in emergencies, depending on what life-tenured justices do with the great power they have exercised since the Civil War.[140] Similarly, although the executive branch is obliged to enforce and comply with federal-court decisions, one can imagine judicial decisions so extreme—perhaps invalidating Social Security, paper money, or the administrative state, or declaring a war unconstitutional—that the executive would not enforce or comply with the decisions.[141] Again, the states lack such leverage over the federal courts.

Judicial review still tends to be more aggressive vertically today; the formal doctrine presumes the constitutionality of federal laws to a greater extent than it presumes the constitutionality of state laws.[142] As Chapters 4 and 5 detailed, however, the Court can also exercise judicial review aggressively when it considers the constitutionality of federal laws challenged on federalism

---

[137] 5 U.S. (1 Cranch) 137 (1803).

[138] For discussion, see FARBER & SIEGEL, *supra* note 39, at 24–25.

[139] *See* Bradley & Siegel, *supra* note 70, at 271–73, 283.

[140] For an argument that Court-packing is almost always a bad idea and it not entirely free from constitutional difficulty but is probably constitutional and should be available in exceptional circumstances, see Neil S. Siegel, *The Trouble with Court-Packing*, 72 DUKE L.J. 71 (2022).

[141] *See* Richard H. Fallon, Jr., *Judicial Supremacy, Departmentalism, and the Rule of Law in a Populist Age*, 96 TEXAS L. REV. 487 (2018):

> [A] decision holding paper money or Social Security unconstitutional would unleash havoc—if it were implemented. But in the most improbable event that the Supreme Court were to issue such a decision, I doubt very much that Congress and the President would allow it to take effect, at least immediately. I would anticipate either emergency legislation or an executive order effectively staying if not countermanding the Court's decision, at least until other provisions could be made to avert economic chaos and the obliteration of settled financial expectations. Whom then would relevant officials and the citizenry accept as having spoken authoritatively, the Judiciary or Congress and the President? I would anticipate the latter.

Id. at 506–07.

[142] *See, e.g.*, NFIB v. Sebelius, 567 U.S. 519, 537–38 (2012) ("Our permissive reading of [Congress's enumerated] powers is explained in part by a general reticence to invalidate the acts of the Nation's elected leaders. 'Proper respect for a co-ordinate branch of the government' requires that we strike down an Act of Congress only if 'the lack of constitutional authority to pass [the] act in question is clearly demonstrated.'") (quoting United States v. Harris, 106 U.S. 629, 635 (1883)). On the presumption of constitutionality that applies to state laws, see, for example, *McDonald v. Board of Election Commissioners of Chicago*, 394 U.S. 802, 806 (1964).

grounds.[143] Further, the Court's composition has recently changed in a way that is likely to make it more aggressive.[144] Such assertiveness, at least generally, runs contrary to the more restrained conception of horizontal judicial review in such cases reflected in the constitutional text, the original structure, the Framers' probable intentions, and the early practice. This divergence should matter to jurists and scholars who deem arguments from the text, originalism, structure, and early practice relevant to the Constitution's meaning. Even original-meaning originalists tend to regard original intentions or expected applications as evidence of original meaning.[145] To vigorously review the constitutionality of federal laws challenged on federalism grounds in the name of textualism, structuralism, originalism, and "liquidation" of constitutional meaning by practice risks missing the bigger methodological picture, which concerns the proper exercise of horizontal judicial review itself.[146]

Non-originalists tend to argue that the foregoing evidence is pertinent but should not be decisive, because the federal judiciary has changed dramatically since the Founding. It has changed regarding the number of federal judges; the number of courts; the kinds of courts; the scope of their jurisdiction; the nature of the appointments process; and the explosion of constitutional rights since *Brown v. Board of Education* (1954),[147] which may reflect a modern practice and public expectation that the Court plays a prominent role in protecting rights, even as Americans can vigorously disagree about which rights the Court should protect.[148] Regarding constitutional limits on Congress's enumerated powers, however, this book offers a structural argument that many non-originalists can potentially accept: the federal government is empowered to solve many

---

[143] For example, as Chapter 5 discussed, five justices concluded in *NFIB* that neither the Interstate Commerce Clause nor the Necessary and Proper Clause supported the "individual mandate" in the Affordable Care Act, and four justices would have invalidated the entire statute.

[144] Justices Gorsuch, Kavanaugh, and Barrett seem more inclined to invalidate federal laws on federalism grounds than were their predecessors—Justices Scalia, Kennedy, and Ginsburg, respectively.

[145] *See, e.g.,* Jack M. Balkin, Living Originalism 104 (2011) ("[T]oday's original meaning originalists often view original expected applications as very strong evidence of original meaning . . . Hence, even though conservative originalists may distinguish between the ideas of original meaning and original expected applications in theory, they often conflate them in practice.").

[146] For different theories of "liquidation" by prominent originalists, see Caleb Nelson, *Originalism and Interpretive Conventions*, 70 U. Chi. L. Rev. 519, 525–53 (2003); Caleb Nelson, *Stare Decisis and Demonstrably Erroneous Precedents*, 87 Va. L. Rev. 1, 10–21 (2001); and William Baude, *Constitutional Liquidation*, 71 Stan. L. Rev. 1 (2019). For a critique of the liquidation idea as inferior to the historical-gloss approach to historical practice, see Curtis A. Bradley & Neil S. Siegel, *Historical Gloss, Madisonian Liquidation, and the Originalism Debate*, 106 Va. L. Rev. 1 (2020) (arguing that a narrow theory of liquidation, which focuses mainly on early practice and bars "re-liquidation" of constitutional meaning once settled by practice, most clearly distinguishes liquidation from gloss but does so in ways that are normatively problematic, and that a broader account of liquidation (as Professor Baude offers) responds to these normative concerns by reducing the distinction between liquidation and gloss, but that significant differences remain that raise problems for liquidation).

[147] 347 U.S. 483 (1954).

[148] Bradley & Siegel, *supra* note 70, at 313–14.

EXECUTIVE ENERGY AND FEDERAL SUPREMACY 305

collective-action problems for the states, and the modern Court possesses far less democratic legitimacy than Congress to make judgments about the existence and severity of multistate collective-action problems. By contrast, the Court is structurally better situated than an individual state to determine whether it is causing a collective-action problem by violating, for example, the dormant commerce principle. A state can have incentive to impose costs on those lacking representation in the state's legislature.

Rights: An Initial Discussion

The final parts of Article III are not well explained mainly on collective-action grounds. They are rights provisions that aim to prevent the abuse of government power. The third clause of Article III, Section 2, protects the right to a jury trial in criminal cases. It provides that "[t]he Trial of all Crimes . . . shall be by Jury; and such Trial shall be held in the State where the said Crimes shall have been committed." The first clause of Section 3 defines the crime of treason narrowly and imposes strict proof requirements. It specifies that "[t]reason against the United States, shall consist only in levying War against them, or in adhering to their Enemies, giving them Aid and Comfort," adding that "[n]o person shall be convicted of Treason unless on the Testimony of two Witnesses to the same overt Act, or on Confession in open Court." The second clause of Section 3 grants Congress the "Power to declare the Punishment of Treason" but limits the punishments Congress can impose by mandating that "no Attainder of Treason shall work Corruption of Blood, or Forfeiture except during the Life of the Person attainted." These protections were responding to past abuses by the English Crown.[149]

Even regarding these rights provisions, however, collective-action reasoning has some descriptive and normative power. First, the third clause of Article III, Section 2, also states that when crimes are "not committed within any State, the Trial shall be at such Place or Places as the Congress may by Law have directed." Granting Congress this power avoids disputes that states might otherwise have—and avoids conflict escalation among them—over where such trials should

---

[149] 3 STORY, *supra* note 31, at § 1791, p. 668 (describing "[t]he history of England" as "full of melancholy instruction on th[e] subject" of treason because, during times governed by "the ancient common law," the judges, "holding office at the pleasure of the crown" would, "[a]t the instance of tyrannical princes," create "constructive treasons"—i.e., "by forced and arbitrary constructions, [they would] raise offences into the guilt and punishment of treason, which were not suspected to be such"—and "[t]he grievance of these constructive treasons was so enormous, and so often weighed down the innocent, and the patriotic, that it was found necessary, as early as the reign of Edward the Third, for parliament to interfere, and arrest it, by declaring and defining all the different branches of treason" (footnotes omitted)).

306 THE COLLECTIVE-ACTION CONSTITUTION

occur. Second, the phrasing of the Treason Clause makes clear that Americans will be deemed traitors and punished as such by the federal government not only if they fight for nations with which the United States is at war but also if they fight for states that make war against the United States.[150] The clause thereby deters war-making by states against the Union and avoids the massive collective-action problems that such war-making would cause. Section 3's focus on treason partially reflects the concerns about domestic peace and security that animate other parts of Article III.

Article VI

The three clauses of Article VI reflect several major functions of the Constitution that have already been discussed. This section discusses each clause in turn. It begins with the clause assuring creditors and other countries that ratification of the Constitution will not cancel preexisting debts or treaties, turns next to the Supremacy Clause, and concludes with the clause specifying the oath of office that federal and state officials alike must take.

National Defense and Economic Development

Recall from Chapter 4 that, at the Founding, debt repayment was a matter of national security. The first clause of Article VI reassured creditors that the new federal government under the Constitution would assume all the "Debts" incurred by the Confederation Congress.[151] Repaying the massive debts that the old Congress had incurred during the Revolution would enable the young, vulnerable nation to have good credit. And good credit would permit it to borrow money in European capital markets and thereby finance future wars, just as it had been necessary to finance the Revolution.[152] Because the states needed to act collectively, not individually, to adequately protect themselves by repaying debts, it made structural sense for the federal government to assume prior debts. If the Constitution had distributed responsibility for repaying the debts among the states, delinquent states would have externalized most of the national-security costs onto sister states (a free-rider or cost-benefit collective-action problem).

---

[150] AMAR, AMERICA'S CONSTITUTION, *supra* note 15, at 242 (reading the Treason Clause the same way).

[151] U.S. CONST. art. VI, § 1, cl. 1 ("All Debts contracted and Engagements entered into, before the Adoption of the Constitution, shall be as valid against the United States under this Constitution, as under the Confederation.").

[152] Enhanced borrowing capacity might also enable the nation to pursue other diplomatic or domestic goals.

The opening clause of Article VI is thus closely tied to the two opening clauses of Article I, Section 8, which authorize Congress to tax and borrow partly "to pay the Debts and provide for the common Defense."[153]

The initial clause of Article VI also reassured other nations that the new federal government would meet all preexisting treaty obligations—"Engagements entered into" by the Confederation Congress.[154] Recall that complying with treaty obligations was essential both to avoiding wars with European nations and to securing commercial treaties, which the nation desperately needed for its economic development. Violating treaties, as states did during the 1780s, was (and remains) a good way to trigger diplomatic or military conflicts with other nations and to dissuade them from concluding treaties with the United States in the future. The states had to act collectively, not individually, to act effectively in the international arena, which is why the Constitution required the federal government to honor preexisting treaty obligations.

The Supremacy, Enforcement, and Superior Legitimacy of Federal Law

The second clause of Article VI contains the Supremacy Clause, which sets forth the hierarchy of legal authority that the Constitution establishes:

> This Constitution, and the Laws of the United States which shall be made in Pursuance thereof; and all Treaties made, or which shall be made, under the Authority of the United States, shall be the supreme Law of the Land; and the Judges in every State shall be bound thereby, any Thing in the Constitution or Laws of any State to the Contrary notwithstanding.[155]

This language encompasses four themes, some of which may be more apparent than others: (1) the supremacy of federal law over state law; (2) the obligation of state courts to enforce federal law; (3) the status of the Constitution as law, and so the responsibility of state courts—and, by structural implication, federal courts—to exercise the power of judicial review; and (4) the increasing democratic legitimacy—and thus the increasing legal authority—of different kinds of law as one moves from state law to federal statutes and treaties. Each theme is vital to the collective-action theory of the Constitution offered in this book.

---

[153] U.S. CONST. art. I, § 8, cl. 1 (federal power to tax); *see* U.S. CONST. art. I, § 8, cl. 2 (federal power to borrow money on credit).

[154] *See supra* note 151 (quoting the relevant language from Article VI).

[155] U.S. CONST. art. VI, § 1, cl. 2.

308   THE COLLECTIVE-ACTION CONSTITUTION

First, the Supremacy Clause declares that constitutionally valid federal law trumps state law when they conflict. This is what it means, for example, to announce that federal statutes "which shall be made in Pursuance" of the Constitution are "the supreme Law of the Land." The hierarchical relationship between federal law and state law follows straightforwardly from a collective-action account of authorizations of federal power and restrictions on state power. The Constitution, federal statutes, and treaties could not solve or prevent multistate collective-action problems if state governments could violate federal law with impunity and follow conflicting state law.

Second, the Supremacy Clause asserts that state courts, in adjudicating cases, "shall be bound" by federal law regardless of any conflicting state constitutional provision or statute. The collective-action rationale stated above applies here as well. It is not enough that federal law trump state law in principle; it must do so in practice, which requires state judges to enforce federal law, not defer to state law, as they had done under the Articles of Confederation. True, federal courts could still enforce federal law if state courts did not. But as discussed, the constitutional text does not require any federal court other than the Supreme Court, and there were (and are) many more state courts than federal courts. It would likely be impossible to ensure the supremacy of federal law over state law if state courts could privilege state law over federal law, even if federal courts did the opposite. Plaintiffs seeking to avoid federal law would often be able to sue in state court. Further, although the Supreme Court would have the authority (for reasons explained below) to review all state-court decisions contravening federal law, it would likely lack the capacity. Such state-court decisions might also foster a culture of ignoring federal law.

Third, the Supremacy Clause identifies "[t]his Constitution" as "Law," implying that the Constitution is part of the federal law to which state courts "shall be bound" in deciding cases. By providing that state judges are bound by the Constitution, Professor Herbert Wechsler observed, the Supremacy Clause contemplates that state courts must practice some form of judicial review—which partially entails examination of state law to determine its consistency with the Constitution.[156] Moreover, given the rock-solid structural inference that the Supreme Court can review state-court decisions on questions of federal law (an inference that was, to repeat, widely held in the debate culminating in the Madisonian Compromise), there is also a good argument for judicial review by the Supreme Court.[157] This textual and structural argument for vertical

---

[156] Herbert Wechsler, *Toward Neutral Principles of Constitutional Law*, 73 HARV. L. REV. 1 (1959).

[157] *Id.* at 2–5. In *Martin v. Hunter's Lessee*, 14 U.S. (1 Wheat.) 304 (1816), and *Cohens v. Virginia*, 19 U.S. (6 Wheat.) 264 (1821), the Court held that it possesses the power to review the decisions of state high courts on questions of federal law, whether civil or criminal. Note that Professor Wechsler's

EXECUTIVE ENERGY AND FEDERAL SUPREMACY   309

judicial review reflects its essential role in preventing state governments from undermining federal solutions to collective-action problems or generating such problems.

Notably, the Constitution envisions vertical judicial review, not horizontal, in the one clause where it expressly anticipates the practice. This does not mean that horizontal judicial review is illegitimate; this book has defended several horizontal limits and decisions that have enforced them. Taken together, however, the arguments supporting judicial review presented in this chapter suggest that it should be less vigorous horizontally than vertically in federalism cases.

Fourth, the Supremacy Clause lays out a hierarchy of American law with the Constitution at the top, federal statutes and treaties in the middle, and state constitutions and laws at the bottom. This ordering tracks Chief Justice Marshall's theory in *McCulloch* of the superior democratic legitimacy of federal law over state law. As discussed throughout this book, a collective-action theory of the Constitution accounts for—indeed, leverages—this hierarchy of democratic legitimacy and American law. Where the Constitution itself does not resolve the issue, the theory assigns to Congress or the treaty makers the authority to decide, amid disagreements among states, whether there are cost-benefit collective-action problems in need of solving or preventing. In this way, the Collective-Action Constitution reveals connections between the Supremacy Clause and many other constitutional provisions or principles, including the Interstate Compacts Clause, the Interstate Commerce Clause, the congressional-approval exception to the dormant commerce principle, and Article III's opening clause, which instantiates the Madisonian Compromise.[158]

---

argument does not justify all forms of judicial review because it does not explain whether and why state courts can decide the constitutionality of federal statutes, treaties, and presidential actions. If state courts lack this power, then other arguments, whether formal or functional, are needed to explain why the Supreme Court and other federal courts possess it. For discussion, see Sanford Levinson et al., Processes of Constitutional Decisionmaking: Cases and Materials 124–25 (8th ed. 2022). Professor Wechsler's argument does, however, suggest that lower federal courts also possess the power of judicial review. Should Congress choose to create them, they are similarly situated to state courts in the judicial hierarchy, and there is every reason to think that they would have the same obligation to regard the Constitution as the supreme law of the land.

[158] According to Professor Amar, "The Constitution trumped all other laws because it derived more directly and emphatically from the highest lawmaker: the entire American people, whose ordainment would set the whole system in motion." Amar, America's Constitution, *supra* note 15, at 300. In a hierarchy of democratic legitimacy, however, it is unclear that the Constitution wins. By the standards of the time, ratification of the original document was remarkably popular. But that time was long ago, its standards were not ours, and even back then the assertion that "the people made the Constitution" rested on legal fictions and notions of virtual representation. The Constitution ranks first for reasons other than its contemporary democratic pedigree.

310   THE COLLECTIVE-ACTION CONSTITUTION

Oaths of Office

The final clause of Article VI requires not just federal officials to swear or affirm that they will "support this Constitution" but state legislative, executive, and judicial officers as well. Fidelity to the Constitution, not the ability to pass a "religious Test," is mandated to hold "any Office or public Trust under the United States."[159] Requiring state officials to take such an oath reflects and reinforces the commitments to federal supremacy, federal enforcement, judicial review, and democratic legitimacy expressed in the Supremacy Clause.

Conclusion

Article I of the Constitution comes first for a reason. Congress is the only branch that possesses legislative power to solve collective-action problems for the states and, relative to the other branches, it possesses the most democratic legitimacy to use this power. This is by design, given the inevitability of state disagreements over whether they face collective-action problems that should be solved.

Yet, subsequent articles bring federal statutes—and the Constitution generally—to life. As Madison told his colleagues at the Convention, "[a] Government without a proper Executive & Judiciary would be the mere trunk of a body without arms or legs to act or move."[160] Several major functions of the Constitution animate Articles II, III, and VI. These articles aim to secure the effective enforcement of federal law; the energetic conduct of diplomacy and national-security operations; the peaceful resolution of disputes with interstate or international dimensions by judicial umpires who take a national, nonparochial perspective; the supremacy of federal law over state law; and the status of the Constitution as supreme, enforceable law—and so the legitimacy of judicial review, especially vertically. Some of these functions partially bind the three Articles together, and others are more distinct to the executive branch or the federal judiciary.

This chapter has shown that a collective-action theory of the Constitution can significantly illuminate these functions and account for key provisions of Article II and most provisions of Articles III and VI. Collective-action reasoning rarely provides a complete descriptive and normative explanation by itself, but it does offer substantial insight that helps bind seemingly distinct parts of the

---

[159] U.S. CONST. art. VI, § 1, cl. 3.
[160] 1 THE RECORDS OF THE FEDERAL CONVENTION OF 1787, *supra* note 14, at 124 (Jun. 5).

Constitution together. In short, the different parts of the Constitution work in concert to empower the federal government to solve collective-action problems for the states and to disempower state governments from weakening federal law or federal union. The Collective-Action Constitution explains how these parts work together.

8

Races to the Bottom, Interstate Coordination, and Territorial Empire

Introduction

An underappreciated role of the Constitution is to help define the constitutional relationship among the states themselves. The first two sections of Article IV contain several provisions that concern interstate relations. They either limit what states may do or empower Congress to act, whether explicitly or implicitly. The Full Faith and Credit Clause requires each state to give "Full Faith and Credit" to "the public Acts, Records, and judicial Proceedings of every other State," and the Effects Clause provides that "Congress may by general Laws prescribe the Manner in which such Acts, Records and Proceedings shall be proved, and the Effect thereof."[1] The Privileges and Immunities Clause, whose coverage overlaps significantly with the dormant commerce principle, requires each state to extend to the citizens of sister states the same civil rights that their own citizens enjoy.[2] The Extradition Clause, whose enforcement has always been thought to require federal legislation, requires each state, upon request by a sister state, to extradite individuals charged with a crime in the sister state if the individual fled from justice in the sister state and was found in the state receiving the extradition request.[3]

These provisions aim to build and preserve political and economic union by solving or preventing several kinds of collective-action problems for the states. For example, state courts that do not respect the judgments of sister-state courts, or state governments that do not extradite individuals charged with crimes in other states, will almost certainly invite responses in kind from these states, resulting in a race to the bottom. Tragically, the same can be said of the Fugitive Slave Clause, which (until ratification of the Thirteenth Amendment in 1865) required the return of enslaved human beings who had escaped their captivity and fled to sister states.[4] The collective-action justification for exclusive federal power

---

[1] U.S. CONST. art. IV, § 1.
[2] U.S. CONST. art. IV, § 2, cl. 1.
[3] U.S. CONST. art. IV, § 2, cl. 2.
[4] U.S. CONST. art. IV, § 2, cl. 3, *superseded by* amend. XIII.

The Collective-Action Constitution. Neil S. Siegel, Oxford University Press. © Neil S. Siegel 2024.
DOI: 10.1093/oso/9780197760963.003.0009

314   THE COLLECTIVE-ACTION CONSTITUTION

to enforce this clause underscores the significance of constitutional rights as a firm limit on what the federal government can be permitted to do—and state governments can be prevented from doing—to solve or prevent collective-action problems for the states.

The third section of Article IV turns from the interstate movement of persons to the control over territory. It includes two clauses that are notably placed together. The Territory Clause gives Congress exclusive power to dispose of and regulate federal lands and other property,[5] and the Admissions Clause gives Congress exclusive power to admit new states into the Union.[6] These two clauses both empower the federal government to solve collective-action problems for the states and prevent the states from causing them. Their placement together in the same section may reflect an original expectation that federal territories would eventually become states. This has not always been the case, however, which raises questions about the democratic legitimacy of contemporary American empire.

This chapter begins by analyzing three of the four Article IV provisions that seek (or sought) to solve or prevent collective-action problems: the Full Faith and Credit Clause and the Effects Clause; the Extradition Clause; and the Fugitive Slave Clause. The chapter then turns to the Territory and Admissions Clauses. Discussion of the Privileges and Immunities Clause and the Guarantee Clause, which concludes Article IV,[7] will be delayed until the next chapter because both clauses implicate—and illustrate—the collective-action dimensions of the Constitution's protection of individual rights.

Giving Full Faith and Credit

If a New Yorker obtains a judgment against a Texan in a New York court with jurisdiction to hear the case, can the New Yorker enforce the judgment in a Texas court? If a car accident occurs in North Carolina between a North Carolina resident and a Virginia resident, and if suit is brought in Virginia, are Virginia courts free to apply Virginia law, or must they apply North Carolina law? Questions like these arise in a federal union of states, and they are partially addressed by Article IV's first section, which houses two clauses.

The first is the Full Faith and Credit Clause, and the second is the Effects Clause:

---

[5] U.S. CONST. art. IV, § 3, cl. 2.
[6] U.S. CONST. art. IV, § 3, cl. 1.
[7] U.S. CONST. art. IV, § 4.

RACES TO THE BOTTOM AND TERRITORIAL EMPIRE   315

Full Faith and Credit shall be given in each State to the public Acts, Records, and judicial Proceedings of every other State. And the Congress may by general Laws prescribe the Manner in which such Acts, Records and Proceedings shall be proved, and the Effect thereof.[8]

The Full Faith and Credit Clause, which is self-executing, largely tracks part of Article IV of the Articles of Confederation. It contained a clause providing that "[f]ull faith and credit shall be given in each of these states to the records, acts and judicial proceedings of the courts and magistrates of every other state." The Constitution thus made two main changes: it includes state statutes ("public acts") within the ambit of the Full Faith and Credit Clause, and the Constitution adds an Effects Clause, which authorizes Congress to set rules regarding how to prove the authenticity of a state's documents and what legal force they will have in other states.

The Constitutional Convention and Ratification Debates

The Convention delegates disputed whether the requirement of full faith and credit should extend only to court judgments or also include state laws. They also debated the relative roles of the Constitution and Congress in requiring states to give full faith and credit. The Virginia Plan did not propose a full faith and credit clause. Instead, on August 6, the Committee of Detail proposed that "[f]ull faith and credit be given in each State to the acts of the Legislatures, and to the records and judicial proceedings of the Courts and Magistrates of every other State."[9]

On August 29, the Convention considered this proposal. As noted in Chapter 6's discussion of the bankruptcy power, Wilson and William Johnson suggested in part that "acts of the Legislatures should be included" within the Full Faith and Credit Clause "for the sake of Acts of insolvency."[10] This suggestion prompted Charles Pinckney to move for a federal bankruptcy power. Recall that the Founders discussed full faith and credit alongside bankruptcy because interstate problems were created by divergences in state bankruptcy regimes and the mobility of debtors and their assets across state lines.

Madison proposed that "the Legislature . . . be authorized to provide for the *execution* of Judgments in other States, under such regulations as might be expedient." In his view, "this might be safely done and was justified by the nature

[8] U.S. CONST. art. IV, § 1.
[9] 2 THE RECORDS OF THE FEDERAL CONVENTION OF 1787, at 188 (Max Farrand ed., 1911) (Aug. 6).
[10] *Id.* at 447 (Aug. 29).

316   THE COLLECTIVE-ACTION CONSTITUTION

of the Union."[11] Only Edmund Randolph voiced disagreement; he insisted that "there was no instance of one nation executing judgments of the Courts of another nation," and he offered a full faith and credit clause that eliminated any role for Congress but clearly imposed great responsibilities on the states: they would have to both admit sister-state documents into evidence and give them substantive effect.[12] Gouverneur Morris responded by suggesting that fewer responsibilities be imposed on the states and greater ones be placed on Congress; most significantly, his proposal would have required Congress to "determine the proof and effect" of a state's legislative acts, records, and judicial proceedings in other states.[13]

A committee (consisting of John Rutledge, Randolph, Nathaniel Gorham, Wilson, and Johnson) was appointed to consider these proposals, and the draft that emerged from it used discretionary, "ought to" language in the Full Faith and Credit Clause and mandatory, "shall" language in the Effects Clause. The draft also limited Congress's role regarding sister-state effect to legislating the effect of judgments:

> Full faith and credit ought to be given in each State to the public acts, records, and Judicial proceedings of every other State, and the Legislature shall by general laws prescribe the manner in which such acts, Records, & proceedings shall be proved, and the effect which Judgments obtained in one State, shall have in another.[14]

In the ensuing debate on September 3, the Convention voted six to three for an amendment by Morris, who (again) would have required Congress to determine the effect of legislative acts and records in addition to judicial proceedings.[15] Madison then successfully moved (without the need for a vote) to make the language of the Full Faith and Credit Clause mandatory and the language of the Effects Clause discretionary. Madison's intervention apparently ameliorated the concerns of opponents: also without having to vote, the Convention approved

---

[11] *Id.* at 448 (Aug. 29).

[12] *Id.* ("Whenever the Act of any State, whether Legislative Executive or Judiciary shall be attested & exemplified under the seal thereof, such attestation and exemplification, shall be deemed in other States as full proof of the existence of that act—and its operation shall be binding in every other State, in all cases to which it may relate, and which are within the cognizance and jurisdiction of the State, wherein the said act was done.").

[13] *Id.* ("Full faith ought to be given in each State to the public acts, records, and judicial proceedings of every other State; and the Legislature shall by general laws, determine the proof and effect of such acts, records, and proceedings.").

[14] *Id.* at 485 (Sept. 1).

[15] *Id.* at 488 (Sept. 3) (moving to amend by "striking out 'judgments obtained in one State shall have in another' and to insert the word 'thereof' after the word 'effect' ").

the resulting language, which was substantively identical to the final constitutional text.[16]

Neither the Full Faith and Credit Clause nor the Effects Clause provoked much comment or controversy during the ratification debates, which is somewhat surprising given the novelty and potentially broad implications of the Effects Clause. In *Federalist 42*, however, Madison wrote that "[t]he power of prescribing by general laws the manner in which the public acts, records, and judicial proceedings of each State shall be proved, and the effect they shall have in other States, is an evident and valuable improvement on the clause relating to this subject in the Articles of Confederation," which he deemed "extremely indeterminate" and "of little importance under any interpretation which it will bear." By contrast, he argued, the legislative "power here established may be rendered a very convenient instrument of justice, and be particularly beneficial on the borders of contiguous States, where the effects liable to justice may be suddenly and secretly translated in any stage of the process within a foreign jurisdiction."[17] Madison meant that Congress could provide for enforcement of sister-state judicial orders "against judgment debtors absconding with goods."[18]

Theories of the Two Clauses

There has long been disagreement about the Full Faith and Credit and Effects Clauses. Scholars and jurists agree that the Full Faith and Credit Clause requires each state to accord a certain kind of respect to "the public Acts, Records, and judicial Proceedings" of sister states.[19] They also generally agree that the Effects Clause empowers Congress to make at least some statutory rules regarding how the authoritative status of these statutes, records, and proceedings are to be proven in a judicial proceeding and what legal effect they shall possess in the proceeding. From there, positions diverge.[20]

---

[16] *Id.* at 489 (Sept. 3) ("Full faith & credit shall be given in each State to the public acts, records & judicial proceedings of every other State, and the Legislature may by general laws prescribe the manner in which such acts records & proceedings shall be proved, and the effect thereof.").

[17] THE FEDERALIST No. 42, at 271 (James Madison) (Clinton Rossiter ed., 1961).

[18] David E. Engdahl, *The Classic Rule of Faith and Credit*, 118 YALE L.J. 1584, 1587 (2009).

[19] U.S. CONST. art. IV, § 1. There is broad agreement that "public Acts" means statutes, but there is some disagreement regarding whether case law is better understood as "judicial Proceedings" or "Records." For discussion, see Douglas Laycock, *Equal Citizens of Equal and Territorial States: The Constitutional Foundations of Choice of Law*, 92 COLUM. L. REV. 249, 290–95 (1992).

[20] For earlier scholarship, see George P. Costigan, Jr., *The History of the Adoption of Section I of Article IV of the United States Constitution and a Consideration of the Effect on Judgments of that Section and of Federal Legislation*, 4 COLUM. L. REV. 470 (1904); Walter Wheeler Cook, *The Powers of Congress Under the Full Faith and Credit Clause*, 28 YALE L.J. 421 (1919); Edward S. Corwin, *The "Full Faith and Credit" Clause*, 81 U. PA. L. REV. 371 (1933); G. W. C. Ross, *"Full Faith and Credit" in a Federal System*, 20 MINN. L. REV. 140 (1936); Max Radin, *The Authenticated Full Faith and Credit Clause: Its History*, 39 ILL. L. REV. 1 (1944); Robert H. Jackson, *Full Faith and Credit—The Lawyer's*

318 THE COLLECTIVE-ACTION CONSTITUTION

There are two principal modern understandings of the Full Faith and Credit Clause. The first is the broad, "legal-effect" view, which is the majority view in the scholarly literature. The second is the narrow, "authentication" view, which is held by a minority of scholars. If adopted, the two theories would produce very different structural and substantive results.

According to the legal-effect interpretation, the Full Faith and Credit Clause should be read broadly as requiring the states to give legal effect to a sister state's "public Acts, Records, and judicial Proceedings." For example, Professor Douglas Laycock argues that the clause reflects and reinforces the constitutional principle that "[s]tates must treat sister states as equal in authority to themselves."[21] According to Laycock, it follows from this structural principle—and the text of the clause, the original intent behind it, and the sensible outcomes resulting from this interpretation—that the clause includes "all sources of state law." It also follows, he argues, that the clause "is most plausibly read as requiring each state to give the law of every other state the same faith and credit that it gives its own law—to treat the law of sister states as equal in authority to its own."[22]

Moreover, Laycock writes, because the command that each state apply the same law makes sense only on the assumption that sister-state law applies sometimes but not always or never, the Full Faith and Credit Clause "assumes the existence of choice-of-law rules, but it does not specify what those rules are."[23] In his view, Congress may specify these rules under the Effects Clause, but when it does not, the federal courts should do so and the states must follow them. He insists, however, that even if neither Congress nor the federal courts act, states must treat the law of sister states as equal in authority to their own. Because all states are equal, Laycock submits, the states may not prefer their own law or their own view of which state's law is "better" in some sense.[24]

By contrast, scholars who embrace the "authentication" view of the Full Faith and Credit Clause read the clause narrowly. In their view, scholars like Laycock overread the evidence regarding what the Framers prescribed in the Full Faith and Clause, and so such scholars underestimate how much power the Effects Clause gives Congress.[25] For example, Professor Stephen Sachs, who follows in

---

Clause of the Constitution, 45 COLUM. L. REV. 1 (1945); and James D. Sumner, Jr., *The Full-Faith-and-Credit Clause—Its History and Purpose*, 34 OR. L. REV. 224 (1955).

[21] Laycock, *supra* note 19, at 250.

[22] *Id.* at 290, 296.

[23] *Id.* at 297. Choice-of-law rules explain "which jurisdiction's law should apply in a given case." *Choice of Law*, BLACK'S LAW DICTIONARY (11th ed. 2019).

[24] Laycock, *supra* note 19, at 310–15.

[25] In contrast to Sachs, Larry Kramer reads the Full Faith and Credit Clause broadly and the Effects Clause narrowly:

> Given its language, it is more credible to read the Full Faith and Credit Clause as imposing a mandatory requirement of faith and credit (defined by the Supreme Court), with the

RACES TO THE BOTTOM AND TERRITORIAL EMPIRE   319

the footsteps of Professors Ralph Whitten and Kurt Nadelmann and whose interpretation overlaps substantially with that of Professor David Engdahl,[26] views the Full Faith and Credit Clause as providing only a rule of evidence. "On an authentication reading," Professor Sachs writes, the clause "requires state courts to treat the public records of sister states (once properly authenticated) as full evidence of their own existence and contents: there can be no dispute before the jury over whether a court in State *A* really gave judgment for Creditor." Crucially, this is all that Professor Sachs believes the Full Faith and Credit Clause did originally: it "obliged states to admit sister-state records into evidence but did not mandate the substantive effect those records would have." "The real significance of the Clause," he continues, "was the power it granted to Congress to specify that effect later."[27]

Much originalist evidence supports the authentication view. For example, in 1781, a committee consisting of Edmund Randolph, Oliver Ellsworth, and James M. Varnum was "charged with preparing 'supplemental articles'" to the Articles of Confederation. Among other things, the committee suggested "'declaring the method of exemplifying records & the operation of the Acts [and] Judicial Proceedings of the Courts of one State[], contravening thos[e] of the States in which they are asserted.'"[28] If the Articles' full-faith-and-credit provision had already been more than a rule of evidence, this proposal would have likely been unnecessary. Further, the Constitutional Convention rejected Randolph's proposed language discussed above, which would have clearly stated that the Full Faith and Credit Clause covered both the admission of authenticated evidence and its legal

> Effects Clause authorizing Congress to enact whatever national legislation is needed to refine and implement it. Refine and implement, not undermine or abolish—which means that even federal legislation must be tested against, and shown to be consistent with, the core requirements of full faith and credit.
>
> Larry Kramer, *Same-Sex Marriage, Conflict of Laws, and the Unconstitutional Public Policy Exception*, 106 YALE L.J. 1965, 2003 (1997). Kramer concludes that section 2(a) of the Defense of Marriage Act (DOMA) exceeded congressional power (as he defines it above) by permitting states not to recognize (1) marriages lawfully celebrated in sister states and (2) sister-state judgments determining the marital rights or status of same-sex couples. Section 2(a) of DOMA is discussed below.

[26] Engdahl, *supra* note 18; Kurt H. Nadelmann, *Full Faith and Credit to Judgments and Public Acts: A Historical-Analytical Reappraisal*, 56 MICH. L. REV. 33 (1957); Ralph U. Whitten, *The Constitutional Limitations on State Choice of Law: Full Faith and Credit*, 12 MEM. ST. U. L. REV. 1 (1981); Ralph U. Whitten, *The Constitutional Limitations on State-Court Jurisdiction: A Historical-Interpretive Reexamination of the Full Faith and Credit and Due Process Clauses (Part One)*, 14 CREIGHTON L. REV. 499 (1981); Ralph U. Whitten, *The Original Understanding of the Full Faith and Credit Clause and the Defense of Marriage Act*, 32 CREIGHTON L. REV. 255 (1998).

[27] Stephen E. Sachs, *Full Faith and Credit in the Early Congress*, 95 VA. L. REV. 1201, 1230, 1206 (2009).

[28] *Id.* at 1224 & n.94 (citing Committee Report on Carrying the Confederation into Effect and on Additional Powers Needed by Congress (Aug. 22, 1781), *in* 1 THE DOCUMENTARY HISTORY OF THE RATIFICATION OF THE CONSTITUTION 143, 144 (Merrill Jensen ed., 1976)).

320   THE COLLECTIVE-ACTION CONSTITUTION

effect in sister states.[29] Also recall *Federalist 42*, where Madison deemed the Full Faith and Credit Clause unimportant and the Effects Clause significant.

Regarding what happened in Congress, Professor Sachs notes that a 1790 federal statute "avoided the difficult questions, addressing the authentication of state judgments while leaving their substantive effect unchanged."[30] Further, "[o]ver the course of the early nineteenth century, Congress repeatedly returned to the issue, never quite reaching agreement on how and when one state's judgments should bind the others."[31] And "[i]n the absence of congressional leadership, the Supreme Court acted sporadically but failed to develop any comprehensive framework."[32] Regarding modern practice, Congress has almost never legislated choice-of-law rules for states.[33] This vacuum has left choice-of-law issues to the Court, which has embraced neither the authentication view nor the legal-effect view and which has avoided developing choice-of-law rules for the states.

Judicial Interpretation

The Supreme Court has repeatedly stated that the purpose of the Full Faith and Credit Clause is to help constitute the states as a federal union. For example, in 1935, the Court wrote that the "very purpose of the full faith and credit clause was to alter the status of the several states as independent foreign sovereignties, each free to ignore obligations created under the laws or by the judicial proceedings of the others, and to make them integral parts of a single nation throughout which a remedy upon a just obligation might be demanded as of right, irrespective of the state of its origin."[34] Such statements, which describe the clause as fundamentally

[29] *See supra* note 12 and accompanying text (quoting Randolph's proposed language and his reasons for offering it).

[30] Sachs, *supra* note 27, at 1206–07. After specifying the authentication process, the statute declared that "records and judicial proceedings [not statutes] authenticated as aforesaid, shall have such faith and credit given to them in every court within the United States, as they have by law or usage in the courts of the state from whence the said records are or shall be taken." Act of May 26, 1790, ch. 11, 1 Stat. 122 (codified as amended at 28 U.S.C. § 1738 (2018)).

[31] Sachs, *supra* note 27, at 1207.

[32] AKHIL REED AMAR, AMERICA'S CONSTITUTION: A BIOGRAPHY 256 (2005).

[33] For a rare instance, see 28 U.S.C. § 1738B(h) (2018) (specifying choice-of-law rules for child-support orders). Congress also legislated the absence of a choice-of-law rule for the states. *See* Defense of Marriage Act (DOMA), Pub. L. No. 104-199, § 2(a), 110 Stat. 2419 (1996) (permitting states not "to give effect to any public act, record, or judicial proceeding of any other State . . . respecting a relationship between persons of the same sex that is treated as a marriage under the laws of such other State . . . or a right or claim arising from such relationship"). DOMA thereby announced that states could use their own choice-of-law rule instead of a federally required effect for same-sex marriages lawfully celebrated in a sister state.

[34] Milwaukee County v. M.E. White Co., 296 U.S. 268, 276–77 (1935); *see also, e.g.,* Estin v. Estin, 334 U.S. 541, 546 (1948) ("[The Full Faith and Credit Clause] substituted a command for the earlier principles of comity and thus basically altered the status of the States as independent sovereigns. It ordered submission by one State even to hostile policies reflected in the judgment of another State,

altering the constitutional relationship of the states to one another, reflect the legal-effect understanding.

To reiterate, however, the Court has not embraced the legal-effect view. Instead, it has adopted a hybrid approach by distinguishing sister-state judgments from sister-state laws. The Court has come to understand its decision in *Mills v. Duryee* (1813) as holding that the Full Faith and Credit Clause and its implementing statute require states to recognize the court judgments of sister states as conclusive.[35] The Court has been clear that once the deciding court issues its judgment, sister-state courts must view the judgment as determining the rights of the parties. By contrast, courts apparently never suggested that the Full Faith and Credit Clause or its implementing statute required one state to apply another state's laws until the Court's 1887 decision in *Chicago & Alton Railroad Company v. Wiggins Ferry Company.*[36]

The Court has been deferential to state courts that prefer their own state's laws to those of a sister state. In *Alaska Packers Association v. Industrial Accident Commission* (1935), the Court indicated that state courts could apply their own state's laws if they determined that their state had a sufficient interest in doing so.[37] And the Court seemed to end significant judicial review in *Allstate Insurance Company v. Hague* (1981). The plurality there stated that "for a State's substantive law to be selected in a constitutionally permissible manner, that State must have a significant contact or significant aggregation of contacts, creating state interests, such that choice of its law is neither arbitrary nor fundamentally unfair."[38] This is not a difficult test to meet, especially because such contacts often exist in multiple states. As a result, the law that applies will typically turn on where the suit is filed.[39] But the Court does not always allow each state to apply its own law. For example, in *Franchise Tax Board of California v. Hyatt* (2016), the Court held

---

because the practical operation of the federal system, which the Constitution designed, demanded it" (citations omitted).).

[35] *See, e.g.,* Durfee v. Duke, 375 U.S. 106, 107 n.2 (1963) (citing *Mills v. Duryee,* 11 U.S. (7 Cranch) 481, 485 (1813), for the proposition that "[t]he [1790] Act extended the rule of the Constitution to all courts, federal as well as state" (internal quotation marks omitted)). Although there is arguably some ambiguity in the text of the Court's opinion in *Mills, see* 11 U.S. (7 Cranch) at 485, it seems best read as resting on the text of the 1790 statute, not the Full Faith and Credit Clause. Justice Story wrote the Court's opinion in *Mills,* but he later changed his view of the ultimate source of the binding effect of sister-state judgments, and the Court eventually followed the position expressed in his treatises and other writings by emphasizing the Full Faith and Credit Clause itself in addition to the implementing statute. *See* Engdahl, *supra* note 18, at 1584–91, 1652–54.

[36] 119 U.S. 615, 622 (1887); *see* Engdahl, *supra* note 18, at 1589 (discussing the statement in this opinion).

[37] 294 U.S. 532 (1935).

[38] 449 U.S. 302, 312–13 (1981) (plurality opinion).

[39] *See, e.g.,* Sun Oil Co. v. Wortman, 486 U.S. 717, 727 (1988) (observing that "since the legislative jurisdictions of the States overlap, it is frequently the case under the Full Faith and Credit Clause that a court can lawfully apply either the law of one State or the contrary law of another").

322 THE COLLECTIVE-ACTION CONSTITUTION

that the Full Faith and Credit Clause prohibits Nevada from applying a Nevada rule that awards damages against California greater than it could award against Nevada in similar circumstances.[40]

A Collective-Action Account of the Two Clauses

Whether the correct understanding of the Full Faith and Credit and Effects Clauses is the legal-effect interpretation, the authentication view, or the Court's hybrid approach, the two clauses help prevent races to the bottom among all the states or cost-benefit collective-action problems. For example, a state legislature that instructed its courts not to admit the authenticated documents of sister states into evidence, or not to respect the judgments of sister-state courts, would almost certainly provoke retaliation. Eventually, all or most states would likely be worse off from their own perspectives than if all state courts respected all authenticated evidence and court judgments of sister states, even those they found objectionable. Or, to take another example, if state courts always refused to apply any laws but those of their own state, forum shopping would become a serious problem, and states would be disabled from enforcing their laws when parties elected to litigate in another state.[41] It is difficult to see how one group of states (call them A) would tolerate the refusal by another group of states to enforce the laws of A's states without responding in kind, and it is difficult to see how, at least generally, members of both groups would be better off by their own estimations as a result.

Preferences or values might diverge so substantially from one group of states to the other that one or both groups might view themselves as better off in the retaliation scenario. (State regulations of abortion, discussed in Chapter 5 and in the next section, come to mind.) But such a value divergence is more likely internationally than domestically, notwithstanding partisan polarization. For example, no modern American state government will sponsor terrorism against sister states, permit female genital mutilation, behead or poison political adversaries, or violate fundamental rights of speech and conscience—at least not with functioning federal and state courts. The structural function of the Full Faith and Credit and Effects Clauses is to ensure that states do not regard one another as foreign nations regarding certain matters, because states that did so might eventually become foreign nations. Moreover, if members of one group of states viewed themselves as better off in the retaliation scenario, this group

---

[40] 578 U.S. 171 (2016).

[41] *See* Kramer, *supra* note 25, at 1987 (predicting forum shopping in "a world in which courts could not apply any law but their own").

might still be externalizing costs onto the other group that were greater than the benefits it was securing for its members, producing a cost-benefit collective-action problem.

In addition to a cooperation or cost-benefit rationale, there is a coordination logic for the two clauses. States that want to coordinate their conduct but disagree about how to do so stand to benefit from constitutional rules or federal statutes that choose one equilibrium outcome among two or more—and that eliminate equilibrium outcomes in which one state or group of states gets to prefer its own court judgments and laws. The comparison with federal bankruptcy power is again illuminating. As Chapter 6 explained, part of the reason for giving Congress authority to pass uniform bankruptcy statutes is to prevent conflict escalation among states or cost-benefit collective-action problems. But another rationale is the virtue of uniformity given interstate mobility and nationwide commerce—and the need to coordinate individual state bankruptcy regimes to secure uniformity. The Framers empowered Congress through the Effects Clause substantially because states had had disagreements about which rules already applied, such as regarding the effect in sister states of a bankruptcy discharge in one state.

Considering each theory of the two clauses in turn, the legal-effect interpretation of the Full Faith and Credit Clause is attractive from a collective-action perspective. This perspective, like the legal-effect view, regards the states as basically equal in authority and status. (Some qualifications to the idea of state equality are discussed below in analyzing the Admissions Clause.) A collective-action perspective, also like the legal-effect understanding, is broad, structural, and purposive, and it regards the Constitution as seeking to build an integrated political and economic union by imposing significant limits on state authority to externalize costs onto sister states. As just explained, a broad reading of the Full Faith and Credit Clause robustly prevents the races to the bottom or cost-benefit collective-action problems that may result from the states' bias in favor of their own court judgments and laws. A broad interpretation also facilitates uniformity through coordination; on the legal-effect view, the Full Faith and Credit Clause rules out biased equilibria in games like Bridge or Seaway from Chapter 2, and the Effects Clause empowers Congress to articulate choice-of-law rules that produce less biased equilibria—and so equilibria that are likely to prove more stable.

The authentication interpretation of the Full Faith and Credit Clause views it as a narrow, technical "lawyer's clause," but this interpretation too is substantially elucidated by a collective-action account. As noted, if a state was not required to admit into evidence the properly authenticated documents of sister states, a race to the bottom would likely ensue. More importantly, the authentication view empowers Congress to ensure robust cooperation or coordination regarding court judgments and state laws, thereby preventing races to the bottom

324   THE COLLECTIVE-ACTION CONSTITUTION

or cost-benefit collective-action problems and promoting uniformity when Congress deems it desirable. Madison, in endorsing the authentication view in *Federalist 42*, emphasized the power that the Effects Clause gives Congress to internalize the interstate externalities that underlie a race to the bottom. Recall his insistence that congressional power would "be particularly beneficial on the borders of contiguous States, where the effects liable to justice may be suddenly and secretly translated in any stage of the process within a foreign jurisdiction."[42] This was not just a matter of justice; it was also a matter of collective action. If receiving states permitted such circumventions, the states whose creditors were harmed would likely respond in kind.

The Court has split the difference between the legal-effect and authentication positions, albeit not equally. As explained, the Court has required states always to give conclusive effect to the court judgments of sister states but usually has not made them do the same for sister-state laws. This difference is attributable less to collective-action logics and more to historical practice and the difficulty of crafting choice-of-law rules. Historically, Congress did not use its Effects Clause power for state statutes in 1790; courts did not suggest that the Full Faith and Credit Clause applied to state statutes until the Court did in 1887; and when Congress rewrote the full-faith-and-credit statute in 1948 to include "acts" in the final clause, it did not seem to realize that it was making a major change, which helps explain why the Court has not read the words textually.[43]

Giving effect to state laws would require federal choice-of-law rules: because states almost always have some law on the subject at issue, it would be impossible to give conclusive effect to the laws of all fifty states at once. Even a simple car accident would require a federal rule on, for example, whether the scope of automobile insurance is determined by the state in which the accident occurred, the state in which the insurance was issued, or the state in which the parties were domiciled. Neither Congress nor the Court has wanted to develop federal choice-of-law rules. By contrast, judgments binding the parties are relatively rare and can be sorted using the last-in-time rule, so it is easier to give effect to judgments.[44]

---

[42] THE FEDERALIST NO. 42, at 271 (James Madison) (Clinton Rossiter ed., 1961).

[43] Engdahl, *supra* note 18, at 1656–57 ("Absurd consequences from that 1948 drafting fiasco have been avoided only because, in effect, the Supreme Court increasingly has declined to take the 1948 Code's nominal prescription to replicate the effect of sister-state legislative acts seriously" (footnotes omitted).).

[44] On the last-in-time rule, see RESTATEMENT (SECOND) OF JUDGMENTS § 15 (AM. L. INST. 1982) ("When in two actions inconsistent final judgments are rendered, it is the later, not the earlier, judgment that is accorded conclusive effect in a third action under the rules of res judicata."). For the rationale behind the rule, see Ruth Bader Ginsburg, *Judgments in Search of Full Faith and Credit: The Last-in-Time Rule for Conflicting Judgments*, 82 HARV. L. REV. 798, 798–99 (1969) (explaining that the rule is "consistent with the function of res judicata as a normal, but not specially-prized, affirmative defense," whereas a "first-in-time" rule "would assign to res judicata unique importance: despite the opportunity foregone in the second action, the defense would be spared for another day").

Thus, the Full Faith and Credit Clause offers an instance in which, whether read broadly, narrowly, or in between, the Constitution itself solves collective-action problems facing the states. Read broadly, the clause solves collective-action problems by barring states from refusing to give legal effect to the court judgments and laws of sister states. Read narrowly, the clause merely disables states from refusing to admit into evidence the properly authenticated legal documents of sister states, while the Effects Clause empowers Congress to determine the manner of their authentication and their substantive effect. With congressional power lying largely dormant from the beginning (and so historical practice not offering much guidance), and with practicality in mind, the Court has, over time, effectively constructed a compromise formation.

As for adjudicating among the authentication, legal-effect, and hybrid interpretations of the two clauses, more than a collective-action approach is required; one must also determine the original semantic meaning of the clauses, the original intent of the Framers, and the content and weight that should be given to judicial precedent and contemporary circumstances and values. Thus, collective-action rationales cannot determine whether the Constitution or a government institution should decide whether and when states must give effect to the judgments or laws of sister states. Insofar as the answer is a government institution, however, a structural, collective-action approach suggests that the states collectively in Congress—not the (unelected) Court, let alone the (parochial) states individually—should decide whether there are collective-action problems in need of solving regarding the recognition by state courts of sister-state judgments or laws. Because states may disagree regarding whether there is a race to the bottom or whether uniformity is desirable, the institution with the most democratic legitimacy—and thus the lowest likelihood of bias—should make the judgment calls.

Unfortunately, Congress has shown little interest in exercising this power, and the Court has largely let states favor their own residents and laws. Developing federal choice-of-law rules would no doubt prove demanding for the reasons noted above. But the alternative has been a long-standing regime in which local decision-makers have been empowered to make relatively biased local decisions.

A Collective-Action Theory of the Effects Clause

The collective-action perspective leveraged above supports greater use of Congress's Effects Clause power to "by general Laws prescribe the Manner in which such Acts, Records and Proceedings shall be proved, and the Effect thereof." A collective-action perspective can also help determine the scope of this power: perhaps Congress must be acting to solve a multistate collective-action

326 THE COLLECTIVE-ACTION CONSTITUTION

problem, whether a race to the bottom, a cost-benefit collective-action problem, or a coordination difficulty. Notably, in the rare instances in which Congress has used the Effects Clause to legislate the effect of state judgments or laws in sister states, it has acted to facilitate multistate collective action by requiring state courts to give full faith and credit to protection orders,[45] child custody and support decrees,[46] and child support orders issued by sister-state courts.[47]

One might object that the Effects Clause says no such thing—it gives Congress sweeping power to decide matters of authentication and effect. The clause specifies, however, that Congress may pass only "general Laws." A few commentators have read this language "as preventing measures targeting a specific state's laws and judgments," while some other scholars have construed it "as preventing measures targeting a narrow category of laws and judgments for special treatment."[48] The first view risks draining the generality requirement of content given the ease with which Congress can target a particular state's laws and judgments without saying so in the statute. Congress did this in passing the Defense of Marriage Act (DOMA), which reflected Congress's fear that Hawaii would legalize same-sex marriage and other states would have to recognize same-sex marriages celebrated in Hawaii.[49] The second view creates serious baseline problems: in determining whether the generality requirement has been satisfied, there would seem to be no good way to determine whether the proper level of

[45] Full faith and credit given to protection orders, 18 U.S.C. § 2265 (2018). This section is part of the Violent Crime Control and Law Enforcement Act of 1994, Pub. L. No. 103-322, 108 Stat. 1796 (codified as amended in scattered titles of the U.S.C.).

[46] Full faith and credit given to child custody determinations, 28 U.S.C. § 1738A (2018). This section is part of the Parental Kidnapping Prevention Act of 1980, Pub. L. No. 96-611, 95 Stat. 3566 (codified as amended in scattered titles of the U.S.C.).

[47] Full faith and credit for child support orders, 28 U.S.C. § 1738B (2018). This section is part of the Full Faith and Credit for Child Support Orders Act, Pub. L. No. 103-383, 108 Stat. 4063 (codified as amended, 28 U.S.C. § 1738 (1994)).

[48] Gillian E. Metzger, *Congress, Article IV, and Interstate Relations*, 120 HARV. L. REV. 1468, 1494 & n.91 (2007) (collecting sources). *Compare, e.g.*, Engdahl, *supra* note 18, at 1627 n.24 ("To construe this 'general laws' requirement as precluding subject-matter specificity, rather than as contemplating nationwide applicability, would serve no purpose identifiable with concerns aired at the Convention and would severely curtail the discretion the surviving records indicate the delegates intended to ensure."), *with, e.g.*, Julie L. B. Johnson, *The Meaning of "General Laws": The Extent of Congress's Power under the Full Faith and Credit Clause and the Constitutionality of the Defense of Marriage Act*, 145 U. PA. L. REV. 1611 (1997) ("Although the drafters appear to have debated how far Congress's power to decide the 'effects' of acts, records, and proceedings should extend, both sides of the debate incorporated this 'general Laws' language in their proposals. From this, and from the absence of a generality requirement in any of Congress's other powers, one can reasonably infer that the drafters intended Congress's power under the Clause to be exercised only in broad strokes, and not narrowly to determine the effect of particular acts, records, and proceedings.").

[49] *See, e.g.*, 142 CONG. REC. 16,796 (1996) (statement of Rep. Scott McInnis) ("This country is demanding that the tradition of marriage be upheld. What this country does not want is for one State out of 50 States, that is, specifically the State of Hawaii, to be able to mandate its wishes upon every other State in the Union."); *see also* 142 CONG. REC. 17,070 (1996) (statement of Rep. Robert (Bob) Barr) (similar); 142 CONG. REC. 22,437–38 (1996) (statement of Sen. Trent Lott) (similar).

abstraction is, for example, same-sex marriage, marriage, intimate relationships, human relationships, and so on.[50]

The third possible interpretation of the phrase "general Laws" introduced above has not been proposed elsewhere; it is guided by a collective-action account of the Constitution. This approach observes that the term "general" appears in only two other places in the constitutional text: in the General Welfare Clauses of both the Preamble and the first clause of Article I, Section 8. In addition to discussing these clauses, Chapter 4 explained that the term "general" appeared in Resolution VI of the Virginia Plan, which provided in part that Congress would be empowered "to legislate in all Cases for the general Interests of the Union." Later on, Chief Justice Marshall would explain in *Gibbons v. Ogden* (1824) that "[t]he genius and character of the whole government seems to be, that its action is to be applied . . . to those internal concerns which affect the States generally."[51] As Chapter 4 argued, welfare or interests are general, as opposed to particular, when the states would need to act collectively to secure them. Internal concerns of a state affect the states generally when the states would need to act collectively to address them. Reasoning intratextually, perhaps "general Laws" for purposes of the Effects Clause are statutes that Congress could rationally believe will solve general problems—collective-action problems facing the states—regarding either the authentication of official documents or the determination of their effect in sister states.[52]

One objection to this proposal is that the word "general" modifies the term "Laws" in the Effects Clause, not the word "Welfare" or "Interests." It does not seem textually inadmissible, however, to define a "Law" as "general" if (and only if) it addresses a general problem. A general problem, to repeat the theory from earlier chapters, is a problem that the states acting individually cannot solve. To solve such a problem, they must act collectively. In the eyes of the Constitution, they are more likely to do so by majority rule in Congress than by unanimity rule outside it.

To illustrate this interpretation of the Effects Clause, consider, for example, Section 2 of DOMA. It provided in part that "[n]o State . . . shall be required to give effect to any public act, record, or judicial proceeding of any other State . . . respecting a relationship between persons of the same sex that is treated as a marriage under the laws of such other State . . . or a right or claim arising from such relationship."[53] Section 2 was superseded by the Court's holding in

---

[50] Metzger, *supra* note 48, at 1494 (noting the difficulty of knowing whether Congress could "establish choice of law rules governing product liability actions alone" or whether it must "legislate regarding all tort actions").

[51] 22 U.S. (9 Wheat.) 1, 195 (1824).

[52] "Intratextualism" interprets language in the Constitution partly in light of its meaning elsewhere in the text. *See* Akhil Reed Amar, *Intratextualism*, 112 HARV. L. REV. 747 (1999).

[53] Defense of Marriage Act, Pub. L. No. 104-199, § 2(a), 110 Stat. 2419 (1996).

328   THE COLLECTIVE-ACTION CONSTITUTION

Obergefell v. Hodges (2015) that the fundamental right to marry includes same-sex marriage.[54] From an Article IV perspective, however, Section 2 of DOMA was within Congress's power to enact insofar as two things were true: (1) Section 2 did not violate the Full Faith and Credit Clause, a question whose answer depends on which theory of the clause one adopts and whether the clause applies to Congress; and (2) Section 2 was valid Effects Clause legislation, a question whose answer (under the above analysis) depends on whether DOMA solved a multistate collective-action problem by permitting states not to recognize sister-state judgments involving the marital rights or status of same-sex couples and not to recognize sister-state laws permitting same-sex marriage.

Regarding sister-state judgments, the second issue arises only if states are constitutionally required to give full faith and credit to sister-state judgments unless Congress permissibly frees them of this responsibility. If states are not required, then Section 2 lacked a rational basis as applied to sister-state judgments; if states are required and the Full Faith and Credit Clause applies to Congress, then Section 2 violated this clause. So, the assumption for purposes of analysis is that, by default, the states had to give full faith and credit to sister-state judgments determining the marital rights or status of same-sex couples (and that the clause does not apply to Congress). This assumption is valid under both the legal-effect view of the Full Faith and Credit Clause and Supreme Court precedent. So assuming, given that all states were not on the same page—they did not all prefer cooperation to noncooperation or coordination to noncoordination—there was no Pareto collective-action problem. The issue, rather, is whether Congress could have rationally concluded that there was a cost-benefit collective-action problem. Congress, where all states and people are represented, was entitled to conclude that Hawaii, by adopting a minority view on same-sex marriage and thereby requiring all other states to recognize its judgments resolving the marital rights or status of same-sex couples, was externalizing costs onto the rest of the states that were greater than the benefits it was securing for itself.[55] A similar structural analysis would apply if one state were refusing to recognize sister-state judgments resolving the marital rights or status of same-sex couples, it was

---

[54] 576 U.S. 644 (2015). In *United States v. Windsor*, 570 U.S. 744 (2013), the Court held that the Fifth Amendment's Due Process Clause was violated by Section 3 of DOMA, which defined the word "marriage" for all federal-law purposes as meaning "only a legal union between one man and one woman as husband and wife," and which defined the word "spouse" as referring "only to a person of the opposite sex who is a husband or a wife." Defense of Marriage Act, Pub. L. No. 104-199, § 3(a), 110 Stat. 2419 (1996).

[55] When framing the negative externality is morally fraught, the risk exists that federal legislation justified on collective-action grounds will deter the emergence of new understandings of federal constitutional rights. As a prudential matter, there is reason for Congress to proceed with caution. At the same time, social-movement contestation over potential constitutional rights—including over same-sex marriage—mostly unfolds outside Congress. Rather than deter rights recognition, DOMA came to be a statute that a later Congress regretted. *See infra* note 57 and accompanying text.

not otherwise required to do so, and the rest of the states were committed to safeguarding the interstate mobility of married same-sex couples.

By contrast, Section 2 of DOMA also freed states of the "obligation" to recognize same-sex marriages lawfully performed in other states. But under both the authentication view of the Full Faith and Credit Clause and Supreme Court precedent, states were not required to recognize such marriages; the *Hague* test of contacts and state interests is undemanding, and same-sex couples who were married in Hawaii would be living in states that refused to recognize their marriages.[56] As a result, unless one adopts the legal-effect view of the Full Faith and Credit Clause, other states would not be burdened if Hawaii recognized same-sex marriage. Under a collective-action analysis based on the doctrine (or the authentication view), this part of Section 2 was beyond the Effects Clause.

In 2022, Congress repealed DOMA by passing the Respect for Marriage Act (RFMA). This statute requires the federal government and all the states to recognize marriages that are lawful under the law of the state where the marriages were celebrated regardless of the sex, race, ethnicity, or national origin of the parties to the marriage.[57] A collective-action interpretation of the Effects Clause justifies the part of RFMA requiring states to recognize same-sex and interracial marriages that are lawfully celebrated out-of-state. As Chapter 5 explained, a cost-benefit collective-action problem almost certainly exists when a minority of states undermines the ability of the rest of the states to establish a national free trade zone, which requires the facilitation of labor mobility across state lines. Unless they were financially desperate, most employees would be unwilling to move interstate if their new states of residence would refuse to recognize their marriages. By contrast, federalizing the granting of marriage licenses would be both disconnected from the language of the Effects Clause and beyond the scope of the Interstate Commerce Clause: the Court does not regard marriage as economic activity, and complete federalization would be wildly disproportionate to the goal of facilitating labor mobility or solving some other multistate collective-action problem.

The foregoing collective-action account of the "general Laws" requirement is novel. But there is not much of a pedigree for the other two interpretations either, and Congress has exercised its Effects Clause power so rarely that judicial

---

[56] *See supra* notes 38–39 and accompanying text (discussing the *Hague* test). Moreover, states that refused to recognize Hawaiian same-sex marriages would likely not have had to follow their choice-of-law rules that generally require them to recognize marriages lawfully celebrated in other states. As Justice Benjamin Cardozo explained in *Loucks v. Standard Oil Company*, 120 N.E. 198 (N.Y. 1918), the public-policy exception to a state conflicts rule applies when a sister state's law contravenes "some fundamental principle of justice, some prevalent conception of good morals, some deep-rooted tradition of the common weal." *Id.* at 202. Under the legal-effect view of the Full Faith and Credit Clause, however, the public-policy exception is constitutionally problematic.

[57] Pub. L. No. 117-228, 136 Stat. 2305 (2022).

330 THE COLLECTIVE-ACTION CONSTITUTION

precedent is no guide. Moreover, the interpretation offered here accounts for the sparse historical practice, and structurally it connects the Effects Clause to Article IV and the Constitution's federal structure more generally.

Extraditing Alleged Criminals

Article IV of the Articles of Confederation contained an extradition clause, which was situated between its Privileges and Immunities Clause and its Full Faith and Credit Clause: "If any Person guilty of, or charged with, treason, felony, or other high misdemeanor in any state, shall flee from Justice, and be found in any of the united states, he shall upon demand of the Governor or executive power of the state from which he fled, be delivered up, and removed to the state having jurisdiction of his offence." The Constitution's Extradition Clause largely tracks the Articles:

> A Person charged in any State with Treason, Felony, or other Crime, who shall flee from Justice, and be found in another State, shall on Demand of the executive Authority of the State from which he fled, be delivered up to be removed to the State having Jurisdiction of the Crime.[58]

The Framers, therefore, merely replaced "high misdemeanor" with "crime" and limited the Extradition Clause to individuals charged with crimes, as opposed to those already adjudicated guilty.[59]

From the start, the Extradition Clause was deemed non-self-executing, meaning that it was unenforceable until Congress passed legislation carrying it into effect.[60] In the Fugitive Slave Act of 1793, Congress included an extradition clause that tracked the language of the constitutional clause and also pronounced that "it shall be the duty of the Executive authority of the State or Territory to which [a fugitive from justice] shall have fled to cause him or her to be arrested and secured . . . and to cause the fugitive to be delivered."[61] This law responded to Virginia's refusal to extradite to Pennsylvania three fugitives from justice who

---

[58] U.S. CONST. art. IV, § 2, cl. 2.

[59] For an explanation of these changes, see AMAR, *supra* note 32, at 255 (arguing that "crime" was used instead of "high misdemeanor" due to the noncriminal usage of "high . . . Misdemeanor" in the Impeachment Clause, and that those convicted of crimes were covered by the Full Faith and Credit Clause). Whether the second claim is correct depends partly on whether the Full Faith and Credit Clause encompasses the enforcement of judicial judgments generally and penal judgments specifically. Under the doctrine, "the Full Faith and Credit Clause does not require that sister States enforce a foreign penal judgment." Nelson v. George, 399 U.S. 224, 229 (1970).

[60] *See, e.g.*, Kentucky v. Dennison, 65 U.S. (24 How.) 66, 104 (1861) (requiring congressional authorization of extradition).

[61] *See* Act of Feb. 12, 1793, ch. 7, 1 Stat. 302.

had allegedly kidnapped a free Black man named John Davis and sold him into slavery.[62] The incident illustrates a broader pattern: in antebellum America, there were many more disputes over the Fugitive Slave Clause than over the Extradition Clause, but the debates that did arise concerned slavery.[63] For example, the Court's 1861 case of *Kentucky v. Dennison* involved the lawfulness of the Ohio governor's refusal to extradite a fugitive from Kentucky charged with helping a girl escape from slavery. The Court held that the governor was obliged to return the fugitive but could not be required to do so by a writ of mandamus. This holding would not be overruled for more than a century—long after the Thirteenth Amendment ended slavery and rendered the modern interpretation of the Extradition Clause largely uncontroversial.[64]

The Court has been consistent in identifying the purpose of the Extradition Clause. According to the Court in *Dennison*, which was the Court's first occasion to interpret the clause, "the statesmen who framed the Constitution were fully sensible, that from the complex character of the Government, it must fail unless the States mutually supported each other and the General Government." In addition, the Court insisted, the Framers understood that "nothing would be more likely to disturb its peace, and end in discord, than permitting an offender against the laws of a State, by passing over a mathematical line which divides it from another, to defy its process, and stand ready, under the protection of the State, to repeat the offense as soon as another opportunity offered."[65] More recently, the Court has noted more concisely "[t]he obvious objective of the Extradition Clause," which is that "no state should become a safe haven for the fugitives from a sister State's criminal justice system."[66]

These judicial statements reflect the role of the Extradition Clause and the federal Extradition Act[67] in solving certain cooperation problems for the states. Given the importance to states of effectively enforcing their criminal laws, states that refused to honor the extradition requests of sister states would almost certainly elicit retaliation. Such retaliation would likely include having their own

---

[62] California v. Superior Court, 482 U.S. 400, 406 (1987) (describing this incident); *Dennison*, 65 U.S. at 104–05 (same).

[63] Ariela Gross & David P. Upham, *Article IV, Section 2: Movement of Persons Throughout the Union*, NATIONAL CONSTITUTION CENTER: INTERACTIVE CONSTITUTION, https://perma.cc/J3QB-MJYA.

[64] Kentucky v. Dennison, 65 U.S. (24 How.) 66, 107 (1861) (holding that "the Federal Government . . . has no power to impose on a State officer, as such, any duty whatever, and compel him to perform it"), *overruled by* Puerto Rico v. Branstad, 483 U.S. 219, 227–30 (1987) (declaring judicially enforceable the obligations imposed by the Extradition Clause and the federal Extradition Act). *See id.* at 230 ("*Kentucky v. Dennison* is the product of another time. The conception of the relation between the States and the Federal Government there announced is fundamentally incompatible with more than a century of constitutional development.").

[65] *Dennison*, 65 U.S. at 100.

[66] *California*, 482 U.S. at 406.

[67] The current version is at 18 U.S.C. § 3182.

332 THE COLLECTIVE-ACTION CONSTITUTION

extradition requests rejected, and they might include measures more destructive of federal Union, such as giving refuge to alleged criminals from sister states. The resulting race to the bottom would "disturb its peace, and end in discord."

These judicial statements also reflect the role of the Extradition Clause and the federal statute in solving coordination problems for the states. Absent militarized borders, the states need one another to effectively enforce their criminal laws; they must "mutually support[] each other" by coordinating their law-enforcement efforts and resources. As Chapter 5 explained in discussing *Perez v. United States* (1971),[68] states sometimes must coordinate to combat criminal organizations and activities that disrespect state borders. Otherwise, as the *Dennison* Court noted, individuals could commit crimes in one state and move (perhaps temporarily) to a sister state to evade capture and the criminal process. (A cost-benefit collective-action problem is also possible in particular situations, but in general all states likely prefer cooperation to noncooperation and coordination to noncoordination.) For these reasons of collective action, the Court interprets the Extradition Clause—and congressional power to enforce it—very broadly.[69] Further, Congress's power to regulate under the Extradition Clause has survived the Court's anti-commandeering decisions.[70]

Textually, it is curious that the Extradition Clause was deemed non-self-executing from the start. Unlike the Full Faith and Credit Clause, the Extradition Clause contains no provision empowering Congress to legislate. In this regard, it seems more like its self-executing neighbor, the Privileges and Immunities Clause. Early and enduring historical practice favors the Court's doctrine, however, as the Court has long insisted.[71] Practice aside, the Court has reasoned that the Extradition Clause "has never been considered to be self-executing" because it "does not specifically establish a procedure by which interstate extradition is to take place."[72]

This explanation does not, however, answer whether Congress should be empowered to establish such a procedure, or whether the matter must be left

---

[68] 402 U.S. 146 (1971) (upholding a federal criminal prohibition on "loan sharking" activities under the Interstate Commerce Clause).

[69] For example, the Court held in *Michigan v. Doran*, 439 U.S. 282 (1978), that the federal statute permits consideration of only four issues before the fugitive is handed over: "(a) whether the extradition documents on their face are in order; (b) whether the petitioner has been charged with a crime in the demanding state; (c) whether the petitioner is the person named in the request for extradition; and (d) whether the petitioner is a fugitive." *Id.* at 289.

[70] *See* Printz v. United States, 521 U.S. 898, 908–09 & n.3 (1997) (distinguishing extradition requests from impermissible commandeering).

[71] For an example of the Court's invocation of historical practice, see *Roberts v. Reilly*, 116 U.S. 80, 94 (1885) ("There is no express grant to Congress of legislative power to execute this provision, and it is not, in its nature, self-executing, but a contemporary construction contained in the act of 1793, ever since continued in force . . . has established the validity of its legislation on the subject" (citation omitted).).

[72] *California*, 482 U.S. at 406.

to the states. The structural logics of collective action help answer this question: because the states need to act collectively, not individually, for interstate extradition to function well, Congress should be permitted to act. Congressional intervention ended the impasse between Virginia and Pennsylvania in the early 1790s. As the Court in *Dennison* underscored, "[t]his duty of providing by law the regulations necessary to carry [the Extradition Clause] into execution, from the nature of the duty and the object in view, was manifestly devolved upon Congress, for if it was left to the States, each State might require different proof to authenticate the judicial proceeding upon which the demand was founded."[73] Congress is empowered to impose a uniform national solution because the states might fail to do so on their own due to the cooperation or coordination problem noted above.

More technically, a well-functioning system of interstate extradition is important to the preservation of the Union. The states must act collectively, not individually, to flesh out the constitutional requirement and establish such a system. The Constitution reflects the view that Congress acting by majority rule in each chamber is structurally better situated to achieve national uniformity than the states acting by unanimity rule. This collective-action account helps explain why Congress can implement the Extradition Clause even absent an enumerated power.

If one nonetheless seeks an enumerated power, a collective-action understanding of the Interstate Commerce Clause supports congressional authority to implement the Extradition Clause.[74] As Chapter 5 explained, under such an account, the key question is whether the states face a collective-action problem involving economic or noneconomic interactions that have economic (as opposed to the psychological) effects. This test encompasses many crimes that the modern doctrine would categorize as "noneconomic," as well as extradition to hold people accountable for committing them. By contrast, under the Court's doctrine, Congress can target only crimes that the Court would categorize as "economic." Moreover, the Court has deemed noneconomic most criminal conduct, including carrying a firearm to a school and gender-motivated violence.[75] It is thus unclear why Congress could mandate extradition for noneconomic crimes, although its control over the channels and instrumentalities of interstate

[73] *Dennison*, 65 U.S. at 104.

[74] One might also look to the Effects Clause. *See Dennison*, 65 U.S. at 105 (stating that "[a]ll difficulty as to the mode of authenticating the judicial proceeding [supporting the extradition request] was removed by the [Full Faith and Credit and Effects Clauses]"). The Effects Clause likely authorizes Congress to identify the method that states must use to authenticate the judicial proceedings upon which the extradition request relies. It is not clear, however, how the Effects Clause authorizes Congress to compel states to transfer accused individuals interstate.

[75] United States v. Lopez, 514 U.S. 549 (1995) (invalidating a federal law prohibiting firearms possession in school zones); United States v. Morrison, 529 U.S. 598 (2000) (invalidating a private damages remedy for victims of gender-motivated violence).

334   THE COLLECTIVE-ACTION CONSTITUTION

commerce might give it leverage regarding the parts of the extradition process that use them.[76]

One might still question whether federal power really is necessary given that almost all states have acted collectively outside Congress to regulate interstate extradition. To supplement the bare Extradition Clause and the somewhat less bare federal statute, forty-eight states plus Puerto Rico and the Virgin Islands have adopted the Uniform Criminal Extradition Act (UCEA). This uniform law provides procedural guidelines for states to follow in transferring an individual against whom criminal charges are pending.[77] The UCEA offers some procedural protections, including "a right to a pretransfer 'hearing' at which he is informed of the receiving State's request for custody, his right to counsel, and his right to apply for a writ of habeas corpus challenging the custody request."[78] This uniform law was first drafted in 1926 and revised in 1936. Mississippi, South Carolina, and Washington, DC, have declined to pass it. Criticisms of the UCEA and a proposed uniform law to replace it have not gained traction for decades.[79]

Taking the objection that federal power is unnecessary on its own consequentialist terms, the lesson to draw from this example of state collective action outside Congress is unclear. The uniformity achieved by the federal statute is not easily compared with the near-but-not-complete uniformity achieved by the UCEA because the UCEA supplements the federal law and covers somewhat different subject matter. For this reason, the UCEA neither shows that federal power is unnecessary nor that it is necessary.

The UCEA objection should not, however, be taken on its own terms. Regarding the structural logics of collective action, the constitutional test is not whether a particular use of congressional power "really is necessary." This was Maryland's losing position in *McCulloch*, and it has never been the law. The issue, rather, is whether congressional power is justified because the states face a collective-action problem. The fact that most, nearly all, or all states might be able to act collectively outside Congress does not defeat congressional authority to act. Nor does the fact that states have managed to act collectively render an existing federal law unconstitutional.

The Extradition Clause, as well as the Full Faith and Credit Clause and the Effects Clause, may be implicated in future litigation over access to abortion. As

---

[76] Metzger, *supra* note 48, at 1489 n.73.

[77] UNIFORM CRIM. EXTRADITION ACT (UNIF. L. COMM'N 1936). *See* 31A AM. JUR. 2d *Extradition* § 11 (2012) (stating that the UCEA "has codified the procedural features relating to extradition and served to expedite the execution of both the Extradition Clause of the United States Constitution and federal law" and should "be interpreted [to] effectuate its purpose to make consistent the laws of the states enacting it").

[78] Cuyler v. Adams, 449 U.S. 433, 443 (1981).

[79] *See, e.g.*, John J. Murphy, *Revising Domestic Extradition Law*, 131 U. PA. L. REV. 1063, 1063–64 (1983).

Chapter 5 explained, the Supreme Court ended federal constitutional protection for abortion rights in *Dobbs v. Jackson Women's Health Organization* (2022).[80] Since *Dobbs* was decided, conservative states have increasingly restricted access to abortion; liberal states have increasingly protected such access; and pregnant women have increasingly traveled from conservative states to liberal ones to obtain abortions. One should expect an escalating cycle of state legislative responses and counterresponses, including attempts by some states to regulate abortion beyond their borders and attempts by other states to prevent them from doing so effectively.[81] The collective-action rationales developed above and in Chapter 5 would help justify federal regulation of interstate access to abortion—either to expand or to contract it—under the Effects Clause, the Extradition Clause, and the Interstate Commerce Clause, although such regulation would likely require unified control of the political branches by one political party and a willingness to terminate the Senate filibuster as to legislation.[82]

Enforcing the Fugitive Slave Clause

The Fugitive Slave Clause was one of several provisions in the original Constitution that concerned slavery but did not use the word.[83] The clause gave slaveowners a constitutional right to the return of the human beings they claimed as property who had escaped into another state. The clause was superseded by the Thirteenth Amendment, which in 1865 ended the institution of chattel slavery in the United States. Even so, the clause warrants examination because past debates over its interpretation illustrate an important point about collective-action reasoning. Like structural reasoning generally, there is no guarantee that collective-action rationales will be used in morally acceptable ways. Thus, debates over the Fugitive Slave Clause illustrate the need for robust individual-rights protections

---

[80] 142 S. Ct. 2228 (2022) (overruling, *inter alia*, Roe v. Wade, 410 U.S. 113 (1973), and Planned Parenthood of Se. Pa. v. Casey, 505 U.S. 833 (1992)).

[81] Note, however, that the Extradition Clause requires states to extradite only accused criminals who flee to their states; thus, states would have no constitutional obligation to extradite doctors who provided abortions to individuals who came from other states. For the Extradition Clause to be implicated, the doctors themselves would need to travel interstate to perform abortions in states where abortion was unlawful and then return to their home states. True, some states have extradition statutes that are broader than the constitutional clause, but states that pass shield laws exempt from extradition in-state abortion providers who treat out-of-state patients. *See* David S. Cohen, Greer Donley, & Rachel Rebouché, *The New Abortion Battleground*, 123 COLUM. L. REV. 1, 47–48 (2023).

[82] *See* Chapter 11 (discussing the Senate filibuster).

[83] U.S. CONST. art. IV, § 2, cl. 3 (Fugitive Slave Clause), *superseded by* amend. XIII; *see* art. I, § 2, cl. 3 (apportioning Representatives and direct taxes according to a state's total population of free persons plus three-fifths of their population of enslaved people); art. I, § 9, cl. 1 (disabling Congress from prohibiting the importation of enslaved people until 1808); amend. V (prohibiting amendments affecting the importation provision until 1808).

336 THE COLLECTIVE-ACTION CONSTITUTION

as independent limits on collective-action justifications for the use of federal power or the disabling of state power.

The Fugitive Slave Clause immediately followed the Extradition Clause and used the same "shall be delivered" passive-voice language as the Extradition Clause:

> No Person held to Service or Labour in one State, under the Laws thereof, escaping into another, shall, in Consequence of any Law or Regulation therein, be discharged from such Service or Labour, but shall be delivered upon Claim of the Party to whom such Service or Labour may be due.[84]

The intended beneficiary of this clause was unnamed, but it was clearly slaveowners. Because of the use of the passive voice, the party with the constitutional obligation to capture and "deliver[]" escaped enslaved individuals ("fugitives" for short) was also unnamed and arguably unclear: was it the federal government or the government of the state into which a fugitive fled?

It did not take long for Congress to regulate "rendition"—the process by which fugitives were identified, captured, and returned. It passed the Fugitive Slave Act of 1793 "with almost no opposition or debate."[85] The Act permitted slaveowners (and the private slave catchers they hired) to seize (kidnap) alleged fugitives in a sister state and, after a nominal hearing before a federal or local judge, to deliver the individuals to their owners.[86] "From the 1830s until 1850," legal historian Ariela Gross reports, "many Northeastern states tried to protect Northern free blacks from kidnapping by slave catchers and to provide some legal protections for escaped slaves who faced recapture in the North." Northern legislatures prohibited state officials from participating in the capture of alleged fugitives, forbade the use of state property for this purpose, and gave alleged fugitives procedural rights in judicial proceedings so that they could prove they were free.[87]

Abolitionists argued that Congress lacked power to pass the 1793 Act. Slaveholders contended that Northern state laws were preempted by the Act and violated their rights under the Fugitive Slave Clause. In *Prigg v. Pennsylvania*

---

[84] U.S. CONST. art. IV, § 2, cl. 3, *superseded by* amend. XIII.

[85] Gross & Upham, *supra* note 63.

[86] Fugitive Slave Act of 1793, ch. 7, §§ 3–4, 1 Stat. 302. This statute permitted slaveowners (or private slave catchers acting as their agents), on affidavit sworn before their home county justice of the peace, to enter another state, seize an alleged fugitive, bring the individual before a federal or local judge, and obtain a certificate of removal entitling them to transport the individual back to the slaveowner, so long as the affidavit included sufficient detail to constitute "proof to the satisfaction" of the federal or local judge. The seized individual had no right to a jury trial, protection against self-incrimination, or right to testify. There was no statute of limitations.

[87] Ariela Gross, *Slavery, Anti-Slavery, and the Coming of the Civil War, in* II CAMBRIDGE HISTORY OF LAW IN AMERICA: THE LONG NINETEENTH CENTURY (1789–1920) 280, 304–05 (Michael Grossberg & Christopher Tomlins eds., 2008).

RACES TO THE BOTTOM AND TERRITORIAL EMPIRE   337

(1842), the Court mostly vindicated the interests of slaveowners. The Court reversed the conviction under Pennsylvania law of a slave catcher who had kidnapped and sold into slavery Margaret Morgan and her two children. Justice Joseph Story held for the Court that the obligation imposed by the Fugitive Slave Clause was directed at Congress, not the states, and that federal power under the Necessary and Proper Clause to meet this obligation was exclusive of state regulation.[88] Such regulation included Pennsylvania's attempt to prevent slave catchers from using self-help (violence against alleged fugitives) instead of the state's civil process. *Prigg* meant that all such Northern state laws were unconstitutional. Congress passed an even more slavery-protective (and absurdly biased) Fugitive Slave Act in 1850,[89] and the Court upheld it in *Ableman v. Booth* (1859).[90]

The Court's decision in *Prigg* was textually questionable, although textual objections to the Court's reasoning were not unassailable. The text of the Fugitive Slave Clause references only states, not the federal government. This fact seemed to suggest that the obligation to return fugitives was imposed on government officials in sister states, just as the obligation to return charged individuals under the Extradition Clause is imposed on government officials in sister states— although the prior section explained that Congress has always legislated to implement the Extradition Clause. Moreover, unlike the Effects Clause, which empowers Congress to enforce the Full Faith and Credit Clause, there was no clause in Article IV empowering Congress to enforce the Fugitive Slave Clause— although, again, the same is true of the Extradition Clause. In addition, the Fugitive Slave Clause was housed in Article IV, not in Article I, where most of Congress's enumerated powers are located—although the Effects Clause and the Territory Clause[91] are found in Article IV, and they are both enumerated powers. Most importantly, even if Congress could enforce the Fugitive Slave Clause, it is unclear that this power was exclusive of reasonable state procedural regulations. The text did not indicate federal exclusivity, and several provisions (including

---

[88] 41 U.S. (16 Pet.) 536, 614–19 (1842).

[89] The 1850 Act authorized federal commissioners to capture fugitives; authorized federal marshals to order "bystanders" to assist in their capture; criminalized helping fugitives; empowered slaveowners to obtain from their local judge a certificate for a fugitive through a one-sided proceeding; and compelled courts in other states to accept the certificate as conclusive proof of fugitive status. The Act even provided for the payment of $10 to officials who found that the Black person in question was enslaved but only $5 if they found that the individual was free. Fugitive Slave Act of 1850, ch. 60, 9 Stat. 462, 462–65. Once this law was passed, Black people "in any state, whether free or not, were in danger of being accused of fleeing from bondage," and "[g]angs of bounty hunters began kidnapping African Americans to sell southward." Gross, *supra* note 87, at 306.

[90] 62 U.S. (21 How.) 506 (1859).

[91] U.S. Const. art. IV, § 3, cl. 2.

338 THE COLLECTIVE-ACTION CONSTITUTION

the Tenth Amendment) underscore that the states enjoy reserved powers.[92] As discussed, federal power to implement the Extradition Clause is not exclusive.

Nor is *Prigg* a model of sound originalist reasoning. According to Justice Story, "it cannot be doubted that [the Fugitive Slave Clause] constituted a fundamental article, without the adoption of which the Union could not have been formed."[93] Story cited nothing for this proposition, and it is questionable. The absence of a fugitive slave clause in the Articles of Confederation did not bring about the Constitutional Convention, and the Fugitive Slave Clause was not much debated during the Convention.[94] In supporting ratification, Charles Cotesworth Pinckney accurately told fellow South Carolinians that "[w]e have obtained a right to recover our slaves in whatever part of America they may take refuge, which is a right we had not before."[95]

Nor was *Prigg* compelled by judicial precedent; the case was the Court's first occasion for deciding the issue. Further, historical practice supported federal power to regulate rendition, given that Congress had done so as early as 1793. But practice likely did not support the *Prigg* Court's assertion of federal exclusivity, given extensive state regulation of alleged fugitives. For example, states diverged over whether to provide them with procedural protections.[96]

It remains to consider arguments from the constitutional structure. Unfortunately, *Prigg* was most defensible structurally: collective-action reasoning supported the Court's holding that Congress had exclusive power to regulate rendition. The logics of both coordination and cooperation problems shored up the Court's position.

First, absent federal intervention, the states would have had to overcome a coordination problem to enforce the Fugitive Slave Clause. The Constitution required the return of fugitives. Their movement across state lines meant that the states would have needed to coordinate their behavior to identify, capture, and return them to their owners. Different ways of coordinating were possible. Northern states might have had to respect the lax procedures of Southern states for purposes of establishing the enslaved status of individuals, or the Southern states might have had to respect the demanding procedures of Northern states.

---

[92] See also Article I, Section 1, which references "[a]ll legislative Powers herein granted," and Article I, Section 8, which enumerates legislative powers and so "presupposes something not enumerated." Gibbons v. Ogden, 22 U.S. (9 Wheat.) 1, 195 (1824).

[93] *Prigg*, 41 U.S. at 611.

[94] DON FEHRENBACHER, THE DRED SCOTT CASE 25 (1978) (explaining that the Fugitive Slave Clause "was not a significant issue in the Convention" and "aroused little debate and received unanimous approval").

[95] SPEECH OF CHARLES COTESWORTH PINCKNEY AT THE SOUTH CAROLINA RATIFYING CONVENTION (Jan. 17, 1788), *reprinted in* 4 THE DEBATES IN THE SEVERAL STATE CONVENTIONS ON THE ADOPTION OF THE FEDERAL CONSTITUTION, AS RECOMMENDED BY THE GENERAL CONVENTION AT PHILADELPHIA IN 1787, at 277, 286 (Jonathan Elliot ed., 2d ed. 1836).

[96] Gross, *supra* note 87, at 304–05.

RACES TO THE BOTTOM AND TERRITORIAL EMPIRE   339

Exclusive federal power to regulate rendition solved coordination problems like this. As Story wrote in *Prigg*, "the nature of the provision and the objects to be attained by it, require that it should be controlled by one and the same will, and act uniformly by the same system of regulations throughout the Union."[97]

Second, absent federal regulation, the refusal of Northern states to return fugitives likely would have caused a cooperation problem. Northern states might have declared fugitives free just because they had moved within their borders. Story so reasoned in *Prigg*:

> [I]f the Constitution had not contained this clause, every non-slaveholding state in the Union would have been at liberty to have declared free all run- away slaves coming within its limits, and to have given them entire immunity and protection against the claims of their masters; a course which would have created the most bitter animosities, and engendered perpetual strife between the different states.[98]

Alternatively, Northern states might have imposed procedural requirements that were difficult or impossible to satisfy. Either way, Southern states would have retaliated in various ways, likely resulting in an escalating cycle of hostility be- tween the two sections.

Even with federal regulation of rendition, interstate comity dissolved as sec- tional conflict over slavery increased. Northern and Southern courts alike "became increasingly aggressive."[99] In *Scott v. Emerson* (1852), the Missouri Supreme Court rejected earlier precedent holding that enslaved people were freed when their masters took them to live in a free jurisdiction, as opposed to merely sojourning there. The court adverted to sectional conflict in explaining why, in Dred Scott's suit for emancipation, he remained enslaved:

> Times are not as they were when the former decisions on this subject were made. Since then not only individuals but States have been possessed of a dark and fell spirit in relation to slavery, whose gratification is sought in the pursuit of measures, whose inevitable consequences must be the overthrow and de- struction of our government. Under such circumstances it does not behoove the State of Missouri to show the least countenance to any measure which might gratify this spirit.[100]

---

[97]   *Prigg*, 41 U.S. at 623.
[98]   *Id.* at 612.
[99]   Gross, *supra* note 87, at 306–07.
[100]   15 Mo. 576, 586 (1852).

340 THE COLLECTIVE-ACTION CONSTITUTION

Whether or not Justice Story was right in *Prigg* that vigorous enforcement of the Fugitive Slave Clause was essential to the preservation of the Union,[101] exclusive federal power to regulate the rendition process was arguably justified structurally based on concerns about a race to the bottom resulting between the two sections. Such structural reasoning may help explain why Story deemed it a "natural inference" that "the national government is clothed with the appropriate authority and functions to enforce" the right given to slaveowners by the Fugitive Slave Clause.[102]

Perhaps, however, the states were too divided over enforcement of the Fugitive Slave Clause for Pareto collective-action problems to provide appropriate models of the strategic interactions that existed among the states. From a cost-benefit perspective, the question is whether states like Pennsylvania were imposing negative externalities on Southern states that were not cost-justified from the perspective of the states collectively. Given how biased the Fugitive Slave Acts of 1793 and 1850 were in favor of slave states, the states collectively in Congress seemed to answer this question in the affirmative.

The foregoing structural defense of *Prigg* is disturbing. As Professor Jamal Greene writes, "[t]he human tragedy of the decision is breathtaking"; it "abided the constant threat of enslavement experienced by free brown-skinned Americans in both the North and the South." "By constitutionally forbidding states from preventing private violence against blacks," Professor Greene continues, "*Prigg* worked a simultaneous assault on due process and on equal protection, the twin pillars of the modern Fourteenth Amendment."[103]

True, the foregoing structural arguments should not necessarily have prevailed given the other modalities discussed above, and *Prigg* was not entirely pro-slavery anyway. Its declaration of federal exclusivity also rendered unconstitutional slave-state laws that sought to fortify the 1793 federal act by authorizing the seizure and detention of Black people suspected of being fugitives until their alleged owners could be found. Moreover, *Prigg* approved of decisions by free state governments to prohibit their employees, including sheriffs and judges, from cooperating in executing the federal act.[104] Because many states had only one or two federal judges, this part of the decision rendered the act largely unenforceable in states hostile to slavery, a result decried in the dissents by Chief Justice Roger Taney and Justice Peter Daniel in *Prigg*.[105]

---

[101] *Prigg*, 41 U.S. at 610–12.

[102] *Id.* at 615.

[103] *See* Jamal Greene, *The Anticanon*, 125 HARV. L. REV. 379, 428 (2011).

[104] *Prigg*, 41 U.S. at 622 ("As to the authority so conferred upon state magistrates, while a difference of opinion has existed, and may exist still on the point, in different states, whether state magistrates are bound to act under it; none is entertained by this Court that state magistrates may, if they choose, exercise that authority, *unless prohibited by state legislation*" (emphasis added).)

[105] *Id.* at 630–32 (Taney, C.J., dissenting); *id.* at 656–58 (Daniel, J., dissenting); *see* Leslie Friedman Goldstein, *A "Triumph of Freedom" After All? Prigg v. Pennsylvania Re-examined*, 29 LAW & HIST.

Even so, *Prigg* offers a cautionary tale. Its moral is that individual-rights guarantees—including, but not limited to, the Reconstruction Amendments—are required to prevent a collective-action account of the Constitution from being used to justify morally indefensible exercises of government power. In this regard, a collective-action account is like other structural theories. This moral explains why Chapter 1 argued that constitutional rights trump constitutional structure when they conflict.

The Court's decision in *Prigg* did not, of course, prevent disputes over slavery from eventually being settled by force. These disputes were partially over enforcement of this clause, but they were primarily over whether Congress could prohibit slavery in the territories.

Regulating Federal Territory

The third section of Article IV turns from the movement of persons across state lines to the control over territory belonging to the United States but not part of any state. The first clause of Section 3, the Admissions Clause, authorizes Congress to pass laws admitting into the Union new states formed from such territory. The second clause of Section 3, the Territory Clause, empowers Congress to enact laws regulating the territory or property owned by the United States. Unlike the Full Faith and Credit Clause, the Privileges and Immunities Clause, the Extradition Clause, and the Fugitive Slave Clause, the Admissions and Territory Clauses expressly empower Congress to legislate; they do not restrict how states may treat one another. The Admissions and Territory Clauses are nonetheless appropriately housed in Article IV because they were also designed in part to prevent states from racing to the bottom, like congressional enforcement of the Full Faith and Credit Clause, the Extradition Clause, and the Fugitive

---

REV. 763, 763–64, 777–81 (2011) (discussing the antislavery aspects of *Prigg* noted in the text and these dissents). Scholars have long disagreed regarding the extent to which *Prigg* was pro- or antislavery. *See, e.g.*, II CHARLES WARREN, THE SUPREME COURT IN U.S. HISTORY 358 (1923) ("The decision was equally unsatisfactory to both pro-slavery and anti-slavery men."); Barbara Holden-Smith, *Lords of Lash, Loom, and Law: Justice Story, Slavery, and* Prigg v. Pennsylvania, 78 CORNELL L. REV. 1086, 1091 (1993) ("Story's antislavery reputation is seriously overblown," and he "cared far more about the protection of property rights and the expansion of federal power than he did about the injustices being done to black people by the fugitive slave law."); Paul Finkelman, *Story Telling on the Supreme Court:* Prigg v. Pennsylvania *and Justice Joseph Story's Judicial Nationalism*, 1994 SUP. CT. REV. 247, 251 ("Story favored national power over any other value, even if it meant strengthening slavery."); Goldstein, *supra*, at 768 ("[A]ttention to the Cherokee cases helps the modern reader see why a need for federal habeas control of persons wrongfully held in state custody—including free black seamen and wrongly accused fugitives—would be salient for Justice Story at the time of the *Prigg* decision, and therefore why antislavery Northerners such as Story and [Charles] Sumner would have looked to a federal remodeling of the Fugitive Slave Act that could provide procedural protections for all such persons.").

342 THE COLLECTIVE-ACTION CONSTITUTION

Slave Clause. This section considers the Territory Clause, and the next one turns to the Admissions Clause.

The Taney Court considered the politically explosive question of congressional authority to regulate slavery in the territories in *Scott v. Sandford* (1857), Dred Scott's federal-court suit for his freedom. The Court there delivered the remarkable conclusion that Congress lacked power to ban slavery in the territories.[106] Textually, this conclusion is implausible. The Territory Clause provides in relevant part that "[t]he Congress shall have Power to dispose of and make all needful Rules and Regulations respecting the Territory or other Property belonging to the United States."[107] The word "all" would seem to mean, well, all, and the term "needful" would seem to give Congress broad discretion. Moreover, contrary to the Taney Court's suggestion, the phrase "the Territory," as opposed to "*any* territory" or "*Territories*,"[108] is not persuasively limited to lands owned by the federal government when the Constitution was written. Just as "the steam engine," "the automobile," or (closer to the constitutional text) "the Recess of the Senate"[109] can refer to one thing or numerous things within one category, so can "the Territory." The text makes no distinction between territory owned by the federal government in 1787 and territory later acquired, even though it would have been easy to do so if that had been the intent: just add the words "in 1787" after the phrase "belonging to the United States."

Putting aside the failure to add such language, it is highly improbable that the Territory Clause originally meant, or was intended to mean, that the federal government could regulate only federal territory that existed in 1787. The Confederation Congress had regulated slavery in the territories in the Northwest Ordinance of 1787, which banned the introduction of slavery from the large expanse of land east of the Mississippi River and to the north and west of the Ohio River, and which provided for the establishment of a territorial government that would eventually become several states.[110] As Chapter 4 explained, Congress did so out of perceived necessity and "without the least color of constitutional authority," as Madison put it in *Federalist 38*. The Articles of Confederation had not

---

[106] 60 U.S. (19 How.) 394, 432–42 (1857). The case is conventionally called *Dred Scott v. Sandford*, even though cases are not typically titled according to the first names of the parties. Because the use of Scott's full name appears attributable to his status as an enslaved person at some point, this book does not follow the convention.

[107] U.S. CONST. art. IV, § 3, cl. 2.

[108] *Scott*, 60 U.S. (19 How.) at 436.

[109] U.S. CONST. art. II, § 2, cl. 3 ("The President shall have Power to fill up all Vacancies that may happen during the Recess of the Senate, by granting Commissions which shall expire at the End of their next session."). As noted in Chapter 7, the Court has, for the most part, broadly interpreted presidential authority under this clause. *See* NLRB v. Noel Canning, 573 U.S. 513 (2014).

[110] Ordinance of Jul. 13, 1787, 32 JOURNALS OF THE CONTINENTAL CONGRESS 1774–1789, at 334–43 (Roscoe R. Hill ed., 1936); *see* Ordinance of 1787: The Northwest Territorial Government, *reprinted in* 1 U.S.C. LVII (2018).

RACES TO THE BOTTOM AND TERRITORIAL EMPIRE 343

given Congress power to regulate federal territories. This was a well-known defect; for example, Madison quickly added that he "mean[t] not . . . to throw censure on the measures which have been pursued by Congress." He thought that "they could not have done otherwise," because "[t]he public interest, the necessity of the case, imposed upon them the task of overleaping their constitutional limits."[111] Given this recent experience against which Article IV was drafted, debated, and ratified, it was implausible to think that the national government would again have to behave lawlessly to regulate new territory, just as it was implausible to think that the country would never acquire any. The Founders understood that the country was surrounded by enemies and that future diplomacy or military conflicts might produce more federal territory. A decade earlier, the Articles had contemplated the possibility of Canada's joining the Union.[112]

The proceedings of the Constitutional Convention suggest as much. On August 18, Madison proposed that Congress be empowered "[t]o dispose of the unappropriated lands of the U. States" and "[t]o institute temporary Governments for New States arising therein."[113] Although not directly taken up by the Convention, Gouverneur Morris successfully moved on August 30 to add language substantively equivalent to the Territory Clause as drafted by the Committee of Style and approved by the Convention.[114] This language "was evidently adapted from the proposals which Madison made on August 18."[115] Notably, however, Morris's language was much broader than Madison's, and Professors David Currie and Gillian Metzger separately conclude that the Convention's "choice of Morris's more general and empowering phrasing 'seems to suggest the propriety of a broad construction.'"[116]

Nor could the Taney Court find support in past practice. When the Constitution was ratified, the first Congress passed a law embracing the Northwest Ordinance, including its ban on the introduction of slavery.[117] Thirty-plus years later, the Missouri Compromise of 1820, which sought to maintain a

---

[111] THE FEDERALIST NO. 38, at 239–40 (James Madison) (Clinton Rossiter ed., 1961).

[112] See ARTICLES OF CONFEDERATION OF 1781, art. XI ("Canada acceding to this confederation, and joining in the measures of the united states, shall be admitted into, and entitled to all the advantages of this union . . . ."). The Continental Congress had adopted the Articles on November 15, 1777; as Chapter 3 explained, Maryland did not ratify them until March 1, 1781, because it objected to Virginia's vast western land claims.

[113] 2 THE RECORDS OF THE FEDERAL CONVENTION OF 1787, supra note 9, at 324.

[114] Id. at 466.

[115] WILLIAM M. MIEGS, THE GROWTH OF THE CONSTITUTION IN THE FEDERAL CONVENTION OF 1787: AN EFFORT TO TRACE THE ORIGIN AND DEVELOPMENT OF EACH SEPARATE CLAUSE FROM ITS FIRST SUGGESTION IN THAT BODY TO THE FORM FINALLY APPROVED 268 (1900).

[116] Metzger, supra note 48, at 1519 (quoting David P. Currie, The Constitution in the Supreme Court: Article IV and Federal Powers, 1836-64, 1983 DUKE L.J. 695, 734 n.251).

[117] Act of Aug. 7, 1789, ch. 8, 1 Stat. 50. This statute "tweaked the old [Northwest] ordinance to 'adapt' its territorial governance system to the Constitution's apparatus of presidential appointment and removal but left the ordinance's free-soil rules untouched." AMAR, supra note 32, at 264–65.

344 THE COLLECTIVE-ACTION CONSTITUTION

permanent balance between slave and free states, regulated slavery in the territories acquired in the Louisiana Purchase (the Midwest Purchase, really). The Missouri Compromise permitted slavery in these territories south of the 36°30' latitude line (the southern border of Missouri) and banned slavery in these territories north of that line (other than in Missouri).[118] Pro-slavery President James Monroe of Virginia signed the bill into law. The Missouri Compromise governed in the 1830s and 1840s, and it was not repealed until passage of the Kansas-Nebraska Act in 1854, three years before the Court's decision in *Scott*.[119]

The structural theory developed in this book also indicates that the decision was unsound. Federal control over the territories, and sensible management of the lands by the federal government, helped solve several related collective-action problems for the states that were examined in earlier chapters. They include funding the national government, encouraging immigration, defending the nation, and expanding the national free-trade zone.

Madison wrote in *Federalist 38* that "the Western territory is a mine of vast wealth to the United States."[120] Federal land sales would raise money for the national treasury. The promise of cheap land would draw (armed) settlers from the original thirteen states and Europe. With an increasing population and a vast stretch of territory forming the nation's western border, the states would be better protected from military attack by European powers and Native American tribes, and the land would fund and otherwise facilitate military attacks by Americans aimed at building an American empire. Finally, the land was rich in economic potential and resources—including agricultural products, animal products, minerals, and timber—and the Mississippi River offered a highway to the ocean on which these items of interstate and foreign commerce could travel. Other waterways and roads could be constructed to expand the national free-trade zone, thereby facilitating the economic development of the nation.[121]

Given the structural stakes from a collective-action perspective, it was untenable for the Taney Court to conclude that federal regulation of slavery in the territories was beyond the Territory Clause. (Tellingly, the Court was mindful of collective-action logics in *Prigg* but mindless of them in *Scott*.) After the Civil War, a structurally sounder view of the Territory Clause would emerge: "In the territories of the United States, Congress has the entire dominion and sovereignty, national and local, and has full legislative power over all subjects upon which the legislature of a State might legislate within the State."[122] This view remains the law today.

---

[118] Act of Mar. 6, 1820, ch. 22, § 8, 3 Stat. 545, 548.
[119] Kansas-Nebraska Act, ch. 59, 10 Stat. 277 (1854).
[120] THE FEDERALIST NO. 38, at 239 (James Madison) (Clinton Rossiter ed., 1961).
[121] This account largely tracks that of AMAR, *supra* note 32, at 271–73.
[122] Simms v. Simms, 175 U.S. 162, 168 (1899).

In addition to solving collective-action problems for the states, the Territory Clause was designed to prevent states from causing collective-action problems. By assigning control over federal territories to the states collectively in Congress and not to the states individually (which would continue to make conflicting land claims), the hope was to avoid conflict escalation and a race to the bottom. Before ratification of the Constitution, disputes over Western land claims caused tension and hostility among states. Recall from Chapter 3 that Maryland refused to ratify the Articles of Confederation until 1781 because it feared Virginia's future wealth and power if it did not cede its vast western territorial claims to the Union. Less than a decade later, Hamilton warned in *Federalist 7* that if the Constitution were not ratified and Congress were not given control of federal territories, the states would go to war with one another. "In the wide field of Western territory," he wrote, "we perceive an ample theater for hostile pretensions, without any umpire or common judge to interpose between the contending [state] parties." Hamilton thought there was "good ground to apprehend that the sword would sometimes be appealed to as the arbiter of their differences."[123] In this regard, the antebellum Constitution failed. Slave and free states had explosive fights in Congress and the territories over slavery, especially when Congress (e.g., in the Kansas-Nebraska Act) permitted settlers of certain territories to decide for themselves whether to permit slavery.

Today, in a world without American territorial expansion, there remains a collective-action rationale for the Territory Clause. Relative to the states acting by unanimity rule, Congress acting by majority rule can more effectively govern US territories, which most prominently include American Samoa, Guam, the Northern Mariana Islands, Puerto Rico, and the US Virgin Islands. As the next section explains, however, there is a serious democratic deficit associated with such governance.

Admitting (or Not Admitting) New States

The Admissions Clause gives Congress, by passing statutes, exclusive power to admit new states into the Union, subject to certain constraints:

> New states may be admitted by the Congress into this Union; but no new State shall be formed or erected within the Jurisdiction of any other State; nor any State be formed by the Junction of two or more States, or Parts of States,

---

[123] THE FEDERALIST NO. 7, at 61 (Alexander Hamilton) (Clinton Rossiter ed., 1961).

346   THE COLLECTIVE-ACTION CONSTITUTION

without the Consent of the Legislatures of the States concerned as well as of the Congress.[124]

The clause thus gives Congress an enumerated power and limits its exercise. Thirty-seven states were admitted using this clause, from Vermont in 1791 to Alaska and Hawaii in 1959. It thus confers significant power, and in four ways, it is illuminated by the logics of collective action. After discussing these ways, this section considers the meaning and democratic implications of the Framers' decision to house the Admissions Clause with the Territory Clause.

The Admissions Clause and Collective Action

First, the Admissions Clause authorizes Congress to admit new states by passing statutes, a major improvement over the Articles of Confederation in terms of facilitating collective action that possesses democratic legitimacy. Article XI of the Articles, in addition to providing for the admission of Canada into the Confederation should it wish to join, provided that "no other colony shall be admitted into the same, unless such admission be agreed to by nine states." Unlike this initial two-thirds supermajority rule, the Constitution's Admissions Clause provides for the admission of new states presumptively by majority rule in Congress.[125] Moreover, absent amendment of the Articles, its nine-state admissions rule could have unintentionally become minority rule over time as admissions grew in number.[126] The Constitution's majority voting rule on admissions decisions animates collective action relative to supermajority rule while avoiding the democratic illegitimacy of minority rule.

Second, by requiring the states concerned and Congress to consent to the admission of new states formed within an existing state or by the fusion of part or all of existing states, the Admissions Clause ensures both that collective action in Congress will not exploit a minority of states and that individual action by a minority of states will not cause multistate collective-action problems.[127] For example, if Southern states in the antebellum years had sought to increase

---

[124] U.S. Const. art. IV, § 3, cl. 1. For analysis of whether the second semicolon in the Admissions Clause means that states may never be created from territory within an existing state, see Vasan Kesavan & Michael Stokes Paulsen, *Is West Virginia Unconstitutional?*, 90 Calif. L. Rev. 291, 332–95 (2002). The authors conclude that, although the text is ambiguous, the original understanding supports the constitutionality of forming new states in this scenario. *Id.* at 395.

[125] Part III discusses the potential complication of the president's veto power. *See* U.S. Const. art. I, § 7, cl. 2.

[126] Amar, *supra* note 32, at 273 (recording this observation).

[127] For discussion of how the Admissions Clause was interpreted to justify the creation of West Virginia during the Civil War, see Curtis A. Bradley & Neil S. Siegel, *Constructed Constraint and the Constitutional Text,* 64 Duke L.J. 1213, 1259–62 (2015).

their voting power in the Senate by ceding territory to create more slave states, Northern states would likely have responded in kind (and vice versa). Because Congress had to approve, such a race to the bottom was less likely.[128] Today, it would require both an aggressive Congress and a compliant state legislature to subdivide, say, California or Texas into multiple states to secure partisan advantage.

Third, when Congress has decided whether and when to admit new states into the Union, it has been more concerned to ensure that the states remain able to act collectively in Congress and less concerned that states be able to differ individually, which can cause collective-action problems. True, the Court held in *Coyle v. Smith* (1911) that Congress may not impose conditions on admission that would otherwise be beyond its powers to legislate for other states. The Court in *Coyle* rejected Congress's attempt to require Oklahoma, as a condition of its admission into the Union, to designate the city of Guthrie as its state capital for seven years.[129] The historical practice has, however, been different. Professor Eric Biber has examined the conditions imposed by Congress on all states that it admitted to the Union and on the eleven Southern states that it readmitted to Congress after the Civil War. He has discerned "a significant pattern":

> Congress has imposed conditions on the admission of states where it has concerns about whether the citizenry of the new state can be assimilated as a loyal, democratic unit of government within the United States, sometimes because that citizenry has been perceived as fundamentally different from mainstream American politics and society.

Examples include Louisiana, which was primarily French when it was admitted in the early 1800s; the Southern states during Reconstruction, which had been disloyal; Utah, which was populated by Mormons viewed as disloyal and different from other Americans; and New Mexico, which had a substantial Mexican population. Moreover, in imposing conditions on admission, Congress has regulated "in a wide range of fields, ranging from family law, to criminal procedure, to suffrage, to official language." Accordingly, in making admissions decisions, Congress has legislated beyond its Section 8 powers.[130]

---

[128] Recall from Chapter 6 that the penultimate clause of Article I, Section 8, which gives Congress the power to govern federal enclaves, also contains requirements of state and congressional consent, which seek to prevent the exploitation of either a minority or a majority of states.

[129] 221 U.S. 559 (1911).

[130] Eric Biber, *The Price of Admission: Causes, Effects, and Patterns of Conditions Imposed on States Entering the Union*, 46 AM. J. LEGAL HIST. 119, 120 (2004). Southern states were not formally readmitted under the Admissions Clause, because the prevailing (although not unanimous) view was that they had never left the Union and so did not assume the status of federal territories after the war. *See generally* R. Craig Green, *Beyond States: A Constitutional History of Territory, Statehood,*

348   THE COLLECTIVE-ACTION CONSTITUTION

This historical practice can be understood in collective-action terms. By insisting on loyalty and assimilation (for better and worse in terms of political morality),[131] Congress has sought to accomplish two constitutional goals. The first is to reduce the frequency and magnitude of disagreements between states, thereby making it easier for collective action by states in Congress to succeed and, relatedly, to lower the stakes of losing when collective action succeeds. Recall from Chapter 2 that disagreement problems are one primary reason why collective action may fail, whether the problem sounds in coordination (the Bridge or Seaway game), or cooperation (an Asymmetric Prisoners' Dilemma), or a cost-benefit collective-action problem. The second goal is to reduce the likelihood that states will cause races to the bottom. Conflict escalation between states and sections ultimately produced the Civil War.

Put differently, increasing the number of states in the Union makes it harder for collective action to succeed when the voting rules in the political branches remain the same. Unlike the European Union, the United States did not adjust its voting rules (such as by terminating the President's veto power) as it added more member states.[132] Adding more states also increases opportunities for interstate conflicts. Congress has historically been attuned to such collective-action concerns in exercising its power under the Admissions Clause. As Professor Biber explains, "The historical context of admission conditions reveals a federal system in which state sovereignty at the very moment of its creation is subsidiary to the unity and stability of the federal government as a whole even before the Civil War." Specifically, "Congress has always been concerned with the potential loyalty of the new state, and was willing and able to take steps to provide at least symbolic, and sometimes quite effective, measures to ensure that the state would be thoroughly Americanized and made part of a harmonious Union of states."[133]

Fourth, understood in collective-action terms, the Admissions Clause—alone and with other parts of the Constitution—has implications for the long-standing debate over whether the states are all equal in sovereign status. The best answer is probably that they are presumptively equal and that the constitutional text makes this presumption irrebuttable regarding some matters and rebuttable by

---

and Nation-Building, 90 U. Chi. L. Rev. 813 (2023). But Congress did impose conditions on the ex-Confederate states that they needed to satisfy before they could send representatives to Congress.

[131] The dark side of American territorial expansion predates specific admission decisions. For a history of how the federal government leveraged its control over federal land policy to help produce settlements and removals that realized national aspirations for an empire dominated by white settlers, see Paul Frymer, Building an American Empire: The Era of Territorial and Political Expansion (2017).

[132] Chapter 2 discussed the movement of the European Union to qualified majority rule as it increased its membership.

[133] Biber, *supra* note 130, at 123.

Congress regarding others. This nuanced answer follows from considering together the original intent, constitutional text, historical practice, and constitutional structure.

During the Philadelphia Convention, Gouverneur Morris successfully moved to excise, from the draft constitution produced by the Committee of Detail, an explicit textual guarantee that "the new States shall be admitted on the same terms with the original States." He did not want to require Congress "to admit Western States on the terms here stated." Madison objected that "the Western States neither would nor ought to submit to a Union which degraded them from an equal rank with the other States," but the Convention approved Morris's motion by a vote of nine states to two.[134] The Convention thus left state equality upon admission to congressional discretion. Textually, the Admissions Clause gives Congress an independent power and does not bar it from imposing conditions; this point is missed by the argument that allowing conditions would let Congress circumvent limits on its enumerated powers.[135] Further, as explained, Congress has long imposed different conditions on different states at different times to promote national loyalty and social cohesion.

In addition, after states have been admitted, Congress has continued to treat some states differently when using the Interstate Commerce Clause.[136] It has also done so under the enforcement clauses of the Reconstruction Amendments, most notably by passing and repeatedly reauthorizing the Voting Rights Act of 1965, one of the most politically transformative statutes ever enacted by Congress.[137] The Reconstruction Amendments changed the constitutional order by giving individuals new constitutional rights against their state governments and empowering Congress to enforce these rights "by appropriate legislation."[138]

---

[134] 2 THE RECORDS OF THE FEDERAL CONVENTION OF 1787, *supra* note 9, at 454.

[135] *See* DAVID P. CURRIE, THE CONSTITUTION IN CONGRESS: THE JEFFERSONIANS, 1801–1829, at 244–45 (2001) (calling the equal-footing doctrine "historically dubious" because the Framers rejected the idea of state equality, but regarding "the notion that Congress can effectively regulate all the affairs of new states by imposing conditions on their admission" as "very difficult to square with the enumeration and its underlying premise of a federal Government of limited powers").

[136] *See* Metzger, *supra* note 48, at 1519 (observing that "the text of the Commerce Clause does not impose . . . a uniformity requirement on Congress, and the Court has stated that Congress can subject the states to distinct regulatory regimes") (citing Ry. Labor Executives' Ass'n v. Gibbons, 455 U.S. 457, 468 (1982); and Sec'y of Agric. v. Cent. Roig Ref. Co., 338 U.S. 604, 616 (1950)). *But see* Thomas B. Colby, *Revitalizing the Forgotten Uniformity Constraint on the Commerce Power*, 91 VA. L. REV. 249 (2005) (arguing that the Interstate Commerce Clause, originally understood, required Congress to comply with a uniformity requirement). The congressional-approval exception to the dormant commerce principle (see Chapter 5) supports Professor Metzger's point. If Congress can approve state discrimination against interstate commerce, it need not itself treat states uniformly.

[137] Richard H. Pildes, *Why the Center Does Not Hold: The Causes of Hyperpolarized Democracy in America*, 99 CAL. L. REV. 273, 290–94 (2011) (explaining how the Voting Rights Act transformed American politics).

[138] U.S. CONST. amend. XIII, § 2; amend. XIV, § 5; amend. XV, § 2. Chapter 9 discusses these enforcement clauses.

350   THE COLLECTIVE-ACTION CONSTITUTION

This language self-consciously invokes the deference logic of *McCulloch*, which Chapter 1 discussed.

Yet, the Admissions Clause makes no distinction among states in protecting them from involuntary dismemberment or fusion.[139] Nor, with one exception (discussed below), does the Constitution anywhere distinguish the authority (and limits on authority) of new states from those of the original thirteen. For example, all receive two senators, and no state can be denied equal voting rights in the Senate without its consent. All are subject to the same population formula for representation in the House. All are protected by the prohibitions on export taxes and port preferences in Article I, Section 9. All are subject to the limitations in Article I, Section 10. All possess one vote in the Article V amendment process. And all are protected by the principle of enumerated powers and so enjoy the same reserved powers, as the Tenth Amendment underscores.[140] State equality along these key dimensions partially motivates this book's conceptualization of states as individual actors that must often act collectively to act effectively and that have equal power out of Congress (and in the Senate) to choose whether to do so.

The one textual exception to state equality is the provision in Article I, Section 9, providing that "[t]he Migration or importation of such Persons [i.e., enslaved people] as *any of the States now existing* shall think proper to admit, shall not be prohibited by the Congress prior to [1808]" (emphasis added).[141] This provision presumably meant that Congress could have prohibited the international slave trade before 1808 in states admitted to the Union after 1788. This clause implies that new states are not on an equal footing with the original thirteen for all purposes. Still, this provision is the only one that deems new states differently situated from the original ones. Overall, the soundest conclusion is probably that the Constitution views the states as equals upon admission to the Union unless Congress indicates otherwise in a manner not foreclosed by the constitutional text.

Structurally, a rebuttable presumption in favor of state equality makes sense given the potential described above for strict equality to compromise national

---

[139] *See* Metzger, *supra* note 48, at 1518 ("While the [Admissions] Clause does not expressly require that states enter on equal terms, the restrictions it imposes on Congress's ability to carve up or consolidate existing states embody state equality concerns.").

[140] U.S. CONST. art. I, § 3, cl. 1 (specifying, *inter alia*, that the Senate "shall be composed of two Senators from each State" and "each Senator shall have one Vote"); amend. V (providing, *inter alia*, that "no State, without its Consent, shall be deprived of its equal Suffrage in the Senate"); art. I, § 2, cl. 3 (providing, *inter alia*, that "[r]epresentatives . . . shall be apportioned among the several States which may be included within this Union, according to their respective Numbers"); art. I, § 9, cl. 5 (prohibiting the taxation of exports "from any State"); art. I, § 9, cl. 6 (prohibiting, *inter alia*, commerce or revenue regulations that prefer "the Ports of one State over those of another"). Chapter 10 discusses the Article V amendment process.

[141] U.S. CONST. art. I, § 9, cl. 1 (emphasis added).

loyalty and unity on one hand, and the potential for state inequality to foment conflict among states on the other hand. In *Coyle*, the Court defended the "equal footing" doctrine, which provides that "when a new State is admitted into the Union, it is so admitted with all of the powers of sovereignty and jurisdiction which pertain to the original States." In its opinion, the Court stated that "the constitutional equality of the States is essential to the harmonious operation of the scheme upon which the Republic was organized."[142] This rhetoric oversimplifies the difficulty of discerning the purposes for which states are equal and does not capture past practice, but the Court's linkage of state equality to the harmonious functioning of the constitutional system remains apt. As Madison anticipated, the younger Western states might not have been willing to abide a regime in which they wielded much less power than Eastern states for no good democratic reason. If Congress had acted over time to realize Madison's fear, the predictions by nationalist Founders of sectional conflict absent a strong Union might have been validated horizontally (between East and West), not just vertically (between North and South). "The existence of second-class states," Professor David Currie writes, "is a recipe for recrimination."[143]

Even so, the Roberts Court erred in subjecting a key provision of the Voting Rights Act of 1965 to heightened judicial scrutiny. In *Shelby County v. Holder* (2013), the Court invoked what it called the "fundamental principle of equal state sovereignty" to justify applying heightened scrutiny to—and invalidating— the Act's coverage formula, which identified the states or subdivisions of states that had to pre-clear changes to their voting rules with the federal government because of their histories of racial discrimination in voting.[144] The Court quoted *Coyle* as support for its principle of equal state sovereignty.[145] The foregoing discussion of multiple modalities of interpretation—including structural, collective-action reasoning—shows that there is no such principle. Instead, there is a rebuttable presumption of state equality. Congress has not historically had to meet heightened scrutiny to rebut the presumption, nor should it when using Section Two of the Fifteenth Amendment. Again, the enforcement clauses of the Civil War Amendments self-consciously invoke the deference logic of *McCulloch*.

---

[142] 221 U.S. 559, 573, 580 (1911). The Court first announced the equal-footing doctrine in *Pollard's Lessee v. Hagan*, 44 U.S. (3 How.) 212 (1845), where it held that states own the beds of their navigable waters, and new states secure such ownership when they join the Union because they are admitted on an equal footing with older states.

[143] CURRIE, *supra* note 135, at 243.

[144] 570 U.S. 529 (2013) (invalidating the coverage formula in Section 4(b) of the Voting Rights Act).

[145] *Id.* at 545.

352 THE COLLECTIVE-ACTION CONSTITUTION

The Democratic Deficit of American Territorial Empire

Not all federal territories have become states, and the collective-action theory developed in this book cannot justify the democratic illegitimacy of American territorial empire. The placement of the Admissions Clause in the same section as the Territory Clause arguably reflects an original expectation that US territories would not remain territories forever—they would eventually become states.[146] Original expectations by themselves are not law, but their frustration in this instance raises troubling questions about the seemingly endless duration of American empire. These questions are more troubling given the long-standing, racialized rulings in *The Insular Cases* that certain American territories such as Puerto Rico are "unincorporated," meaning that they are not part of the United States for certain legal purposes. The legal consequence of this status is that Congress determines whether constitutional provisions, including limitations on taxation and rights protections, apply in them.[147] The territories are where the United States hides its less-than-democratic empire.[148]

The indefinite existence of American territories suggests that it is oversimplified to think of the Union as composed only of the federal government and the states, as almost all contemporary scholarship on American federalism does.[149] Because residents of American territories are not represented in Congress, the federal-state paradigm misses the extent to which collective action by states in Congress lacks democratic legitimacy when it regulates American territories. For example, residents of Puerto Rico have never been represented in the House, the Senate, or the Electoral College, and residents of the District of Columbia are represented only in the Electoral College.[150] This is not an adequate substitute for representation in Congress for all the reasons explained in this book that Congress, relative to the president, possesses superior democratic legitimacy and authority to solve collective-action problems for the states (and the District). This is a regime of national collective action without national representation.

---

[146] AMAR, *supra* note 32, at 274 ("[T]he fact that Article IV addressed both federal territory and new states in a single integrated section both reflected and reinforced a general expectation that territories would indeed mature into new states that in due course would be admitted on equal terms.").

[147] *The Insular Cases* were thirty-five cases decided by the Court beginning in 1901. *See, e.g.*, Downes v. Bidwell, 182 U.S. 244 (1901) (holding that Puerto Rico is not part of the United States for purposes of the uniformity requirement of the Taxing Clause, *see* U.S. CONST. art. I, § 8, cl. 1); Balzac v. Puerto Rico, 258 U.S. 298 (1922) (holding that whether constitutional protections apply in Puerto Rico is a political question). On the invention of "unincorporated territories," see SAM ERMAN, ALMOST CITIZENS: PUERTO RICO, THE U.S. CONSTITUTION, AND EMPIRE (2019).

[148] The idea of "hiding" American empire is borrowed from DANIEL IMMERWAHR, HOW TO HIDE AN EMPIRE: A HISTORY OF THE GREATER UNITED STATES (2019).

[149] For an alternative to the conventional paradigm, see Green, *supra* note 130.

[150] U.S. CONST. amend. XXIII.

Conclusion

The structural logics of collective action illuminate both the constitutional limits on state authority imposed in Article IV and the congressional powers enumerated or implied in Article IV. By barring states from causing certain races to the bottom, coordination problems, or cost-benefit collective-action problems, and by empowering Congress to address such problems, the Full Faith and Credit Clause, the Effects Clause, the Extradition Clause, the Territory Clause, and the Admissions Clause advance the Constitution's project of securing an integrated political and economic union.

Two other provisions of Article IV—the Privileges and Immunities Clause, which opens Section 2, and the Guarantee Clause, which closes Article IV—do so as well. How they do so will be explained in the next chapter. It develops the relationship of the Collective-Action Constitution to the protection of constitutional rights beyond the discussions of Article III in the previous chapter and the Fugitive Slave Clause in this one.

9

Constitutional Rights, Collective Action, and Individual Action

Introduction

A primary role of the Constitution in modern America is to protect individual rights. Most Americans today, if asked what the Constitution does, would likely cite this purpose of the Constitution, not its purposes to soundly divide and mix government powers both vertically and horizontally. Protecting individual rights from infringement by the states was not, however, a primary purpose of the original Constitution, even after the Bill of Rights was added in 1791. Few rights named in the original Constitution applied against the states.[1] Moreover, the Bill of Rights limited the federal government only, and the provisions of these first ten amendments performed a structural, states' rights function at least as much as they performed a rights-protecting function.[2]

For several reasons, however, the nature of the Constitution and the Bill of Rights changed over time. The nation fought an epic Civil War over slavery in the territories. After the war, three nationalizing constitutional amendments were added to the Constitution whose provisions applied expressly to the states, and the Supreme Court and Congress eventually enforced them. Moreover, the Court slowly came to understand part of one of these amendments to incorporate almost all the Bill of Rights, meaning that most of its provisions, too, would apply to the states. And several rights-protecting amendments followed the Reconstruction Amendments in the twentieth century. The parts of the Constitution that are charged with protecting individuals from their own state governments can be called the Reconstruction Constitution. This chapter examines the relationship of this Constitution to the Collective-Action Constitution.

Because the Collective-Action Constitution seeks primarily to describe and justify the Constitution's federal structure, this chapter does not bear the burden

---

[1] For individual rights that applied against the states in the original Constitution, see the first clause of Article I, Section 10, which provides that "[n]o State shall," among other things, "pass any bill of attainder, ex post facto law, or law impairing the obligation of contracts."

[2] For a structural, "agency costs" account of the original Bill of Rights that emphasizes its role in controlling self-dealing by federal officials, see AKHIL REED AMAR, THE BILL OF RIGHTS: CREATION AND RECONSTRUCTION (1998).

The Collective-Action Constitution. Neil S. Siegel, Oxford University Press. © Neil S. Siegel 2024.
DOI: 10.1093/oso/9780197760963.003.0010

356   THE COLLECTIVE-ACTION CONSTITUTION

of accounting for the many constitutional rights that Americans possess today. It is nonetheless the case that collective-action reasoning can help justify some constitutional rights, including ones that have already appeared in this book: those protected by the dormant commerce principle, which individual businesspeople, corporations, and consumers can invoke; the Full Faith and Credit Clause, which litigants who have won court judgments in sister states can invoke; and, disgracefully, the Fugitive Slave Clause, which slaveowners once could invoke. This chapter identifies several additional rights that not only protect the liberty or equality of individuals but also prevent states from causing collective-action problems. They are the rights protected by the Privileges and Immunities Clause[3] and the Republican Form of Government Clause,[4] as well as the unenumerated right to enter and leave another state. Certain rights in the Bill of Rights must also be protected for Americans to be and feel safe traveling through sister states. Given the extent to which the vertical constitutional structure dominated the proceedings in Philadelphia and during the ratification debates, it should not be surprising that collective-action rationales help illuminate the functions of some constitutional rights.

Judicial and legislative enforcement of most constitutional rights does not, however, primarily reflect the logics of collective action. Most notably, the main structural significance of the Reconstruction Amendments, the slow and steady judicial process of incorporation of almost every right in the Bill of Rights into Section One of the Fourteenth Amendment, and several later amendments was to empower the federal courts and Congress to regulate the internal policy choices of states on certain subjects regardless of collective-action problems facing the states. That said, a collective-action theory of the Constitution can help account for many constitutional rights that protect the integrity of the democratic process at both the state and national levels. A democratically legitimate national political process justifies giving Congress, not the states, authority to decide whether there are collective-action problems in need of solving when the states disagree, and the legitimacy of the national process is significantly impacted by the legitimacy of state processes. The Collective-Action Constitution can also provide a secondary explanation for antidiscrimination commitments, which must be protected to make the right to travel through sister states meaningful for members of racial and other minority groups.

This chapter begins by discussing several constitutional rights that a collective-action account can explain well. They can be called "collective-action rights," meaning that, in addition to protecting people's liberty or equality, they play the structural role of helping prevent collective-action problems for the

---

[3] U.S. CONST. art. IV, § 2, cl. 1.
[4] U.S. CONST. art. IV, § 4.

CONSTITUTIONAL RIGHTS AND INDIVIDUAL ACTION 357

states. The distinguishing feature of a collective-action right is that this structural role is a primary purpose of the right, not a secondary purpose; as a result, collective-action reasoning helps define the scope of the right. The chapter then contrasts the basic logic of rights protection against one's own state government from the logics of collective action. Most constitutional rights can be called 'individual-action rights," meaning that they exist mainly to protect people from unconstitutional individual action by their home state governments, not to prevent states from causing collective-action problems; as a result, collective-action reasoning does not help define their scope. The Constitution is more than one thing, so the Collective-Action Constitution must be combined with the Reconstruction Constitution to capture the Constitution's vital role in protecting human liberty, equality, and dignity. This chapter discusses the Reconstruction Constitution at some length because the contrast with the Collective-Action Constitution helps clarify the domain, functions, and limitations of the latter Constitution. The chapter closes by discussing individual-action rights for which a collective-action theory can offer supplemental justification—those protecting the integrity of the democratic process and constitutional equality rights.

Collective-Action Rights Protected by the Collective-Action Constitution

Several constitutional rights serve dual purposes: they protect the individuals who invoke them and prevent the states from causing collective-action problems. For example, as Chapter 5 explained, the dormant commerce principle combats state protectionism and helps maintain a national free-trade zone. The principle also confers rights on out-of-state businesspeople and corporations not to be discriminated against, or unduly burdened, by in-state regulations of commerce. Similarly, the principle confers rights on in-state consumers, who must pay more for goods and services when protectionist measures succeed. In litigation, these individuals and corporations can invoke their rights under the dormant commerce principle, even though the Court does not tend to characterize the principle as vindicating individual rights. Similarly, the Full Faith and Credit Clause addresses itself directly to the states, but individuals can assert their rights under this clause to ensure that a state court recognizes a judgment in their favor issued by a sister-state court. Likewise, the Fugitive Slave Clause sought both to prevent collective-action problems for the states and to give slaveowners a constitutional right. The dual nature of such constitutional principles or provisions is especially evident in Article IV's Privileges and Immunities Clause.

358   THE COLLECTIVE-ACTION CONSTITUTION

The Privileges and Immunities Clause

The Privileges and Immunities Clause of Article IV is succinct: "The Citizens of each State shall be entitled to all Privileges and Immunities of Citizens in the several States."[5] This provision is illuminated by its more loquacious predecessor in Article IV of the Articles of Confederation:

> The better to secure and perpetuate mutual friendship and intercourse among the people of the different states in this union, the free inhabitants of each of these states, paupers, vagabonds and fugitives from Justice excepted, shall be entitled to all privileges and immunities of free citizens in the several states; and the people of each state shall have free ingress and regress to and from any other state, and shall enjoy therein all the privileges of trade and commerce, subject to the same duties, impositions and restrictions as the inhabitants thereof respectively . . . .[6]

According to Madison in *Federalist 42*, the Framers cleaned up the "confusion of language" in this provision and eliminated redundancies. It "cannot easily be determined," Madison wrote, "[w]hy the terms *free inhabitants* are used in one part of the article, *free citizens* in another, and *people* in another; or what was meant by superadding to 'all privileges and immunities of free citizens,' 'all the privileges of trade and commerce.' "[7] The Constitution's Privileges and Immunities Clause "generated little discussion and debate during the Founding era" because it mostly reaffirmed what had already been established; the two privileges and immunities guarantees have the same basic purpose, nature, and content.[8] Each aspect is discussed in turn below.

---

[5] U.S. CONST. art. IV, § 2, cl. 1.

[6] The balance of this clause added qualifications:

> provided that such restrictions shall not extend so far as to prevent the removal of property [enslaved people, probably] imported into any state, to any other State of which the Owner is an inhabitant; provided also that no imposition, duties or restrictions shall be laid by any state, on the property of the united states, or either of them.

Notably, the Constitution did not guarantee slaveowners this right. *See* Ariela Gross & David P. Upham, *Article IV, Section 2: Movement of Persons Throughout the Union*, NATIONAL CONSTITUTION CENTER: INTERACTIVE CONSTITUTION, https://perma.cc/DPY5-L3AG (observing that "[t]he probable purpose of this provision was to protect nonresident slaveholders against local antislavery law," and "[o]ver the objection of South Carolina's Charles Pinckney and some other slaveholding delegates, the Convention approved the omission of this guarantee").

[7] THE FEDERALIST NO. 42, at 269–70 (James Madison) (Clinton Rossiter ed., 1961). The reference to "all the privileges of trade and commerce" is noteworthy given the debate canvassed in Chapter 5 over the original meaning of the word "Commerce" in the Commerce Clauses. If "commerce" originally meant only "trade," then the reference to "trade and commerce" is redundant.

[8] Gross & Upham, *supra* note 6. The major difference was reflected in Madison's concern—which Chapter 6 discussed in the section on the Naturalization Clause, U.S. CONST. art. I, § 8, cl. 4—that the initial reference to free inhabitants instead of citizens in the version in the Articles of Confederation

CONSTITUTIONAL RIGHTS AND INDIVIDUAL ACTION 359

The purpose of the Privileges and Immunities Clause is the purpose of the Collective-Action Constitution more generally: political and economic union. As the Articles put it, the purpose is "[t]he better to secure and perpetuate mutual friendship and intercourse among the people of the different states in this union." In *Federalist 80*, Hamilton wrote that the Privileges and Immunities Clause "may be esteemed the basis of the Union," and he defended federal diversity jurisdiction as necessary to enforce it—"[t]o secure the full effect of so fundamental a provision against all evasion and subterfuge" by state courts that were biased against "another state or its citizens."[9] Writing after the Civil War, the Court in *Paul v. Virginia* (1869) observed of the Privileges and Immunities Clause that "no provision in the Constitution has tended so strongly to constitute the citizens of the United States one people as this," for "without some provision of the kind removing from the citizens of each State the disabilities of alienage in the other States, and giving them equality of privilege with citizens of those States, the Republic would have constituted little more than a league of States."[10]

The nature of the guarantee secured by the Privileges and Immunities Clause is that of an equality right, not a substantive right. If out-of-state citizens want to know which privileges and immunities they enjoy in a particular state, they need to inquire about the privileges and immunities enjoyed by citizens of this state. "If the rights of local citizens change, the rights of visitors under the clause change derivatively," Professor Douglas Laycock explains. "This is an equality right." Implicit in the comparative logic of the clause is that interstate privileges and immunities are defined by state law.[11]

The content of the guarantee protected by the Privileges and Immunities Clause is "those privileges and immunities which are fundamental," as Justice Bushrod Washington (a nephew of George Washington) wrote in his famous circuit court opinion in *Corfield v. Coryell* (1823).[12] The idea of fundamental rights had (and retains) a special meaning in this Article IV context, one that differs

---

allowed an alien to seek naturalization in a state with permissive naturalization policies, move to a state with more restrictive policies, and still be entitled to all the rights of naturalized citizens in the more restrictive state. The Constitution solved this problem by federalizing the naturalization power. Another difference between the two clauses is that the version in the Constitution omitted the Articles' reference to "paupers, vagabonds and fugitives from Justice excepted," thereby removing a class distinction discussed later in this chapter and addressing criminal suspects in the Extradition Clause.

[9] THE FEDERALIST No. 80, at 478 (Alexander Hamilton) (Clinton Rossiter ed., 1961).

[10] 75 U.S. (8 Wall.) 168, 180 (1869).

[11] Douglas Laycock, *Equal Citizens of Equal and Territorial States: The Constitutional Foundations of Choice of Law*, 92 COLUM. L. REV. 249, 262 (1992).

[12] 6 F. Cas. 546, 551 (C.C.E.D. Pa. 1823) (No. 3,230); *see* Baldwin v. Fish & Game Comm'n, 436 U.S. 371, 383, 388 (1978) (describing fundamental rights for purposes of the Privileges and Immunities Clause as those "bearing upon the vitality of the Nation as a single entity" and those that are "basic to the maintenance or well-being of the Union").

360   THE COLLECTIVE-ACTION CONSTITUTION

from other constitutional contexts, including the Fourteenth Amendment.[13] Under the Privileges and Immunities Clause, fundamental rights would come in the nineteenth century to be called "civil rights," in contrast to "political rights." Civil rights include the right to own and sell property within a state; to contract within a state; to sue and testify in state courts; to not pay higher taxes than state citizens who engage in the same taxable conduct within the state; and to equal protection of the state's laws. Political rights include voting in elections, running for office, and, perhaps, serving on juries.[14]

Much, although not all, of the conduct protected by the Privileges and Immunities Clause is economic in nature. The Court has applied heightened scrutiny to discrimination against out-of-staters that makes it more difficult for them to earn a living.[15] The Court has invalidated, for example, a state residency requirement for membership in the state bar;[16] a state's imposition of much higher fees upon out-of-staters for commercial shrimping licenses;[17] a state requirement that in-staters be preferred in employment;[18] and a state law that in effect taxed the incomes only of out-of-staters working in the state.[19] The Court has upheld a state's imposition of much higher fees on out-of-staters for elk-hunting licenses, reasoning that leisure activities are beyond the Privileges and Immunities Clause.[20] Moreover, the Court has said that "the States can require that voters be bona fide residents of the relevant political subdivision," reasoning that "[a]n appropriately defined and uniformly applied requirement of bona fide

---

[13] See, e.g., Gillian E. Metzger, Congress, Article IV, and Interstate Relations, 120 HARV. L. REV. 1468, 1486 n.61 (2007) (noting that economic rights are fundamental under the Privileges and Immunities Clause but not under the Due Process and Equal Protection Clauses).

[14] For discussions of nineteenth-century distinctions between civil and political rights, see Mark Tushnet, The Politics of Equality in Constitutional Law, 74 J. AM. HIST. 884 (1987); JACK M. BALKIN, LIVING ORIGINALISM 221–26 (2011); RICHARD A. PRIMUS, THE AMERICAN LANGUAGE OF RIGHTS 154–56 (1999).

[15] The Court described its test in Supreme Court of New Hampshire v. Piper, writing that the Privileges and Immunities Clause allows discrimination against out-of-state citizens when "there is a substantial reason for the difference in treatment" and "the discrimination practiced against nonresidents bears a substantial relationship to the State's objective." Moreover, "[i]n deciding whether the discrimination bears a close or substantial relationship to the State's objective, the Court has considered the availability of less restrictive means." 470 U.S. 274, 285 (1985).

[16] Id.

[17] Toomer v. Witsell, 334 U.S. 385, 403 (1948).

[18] See, e.g., Hicklin v. Orbeck, 437 U.S. 518, 526 (1978) (invalidating an Alaska law mandating that Alaska residents be preferred in employment on oil and gas projects to reduce unemployment in the state).

[19] Austin v. New Hampshire, 420 U.S. 656, 665 (1975) (holding that, "[a]gainst this background establishing a rule of substantial equality of treatment for the citizens of the taxing State and non-resident taxpayers, the New Hampshire Commuters Income Tax cannot be sustained," because "[t]he overwhelming fact, as the State concedes, is that the tax falls exclusively on the income of nonresidents; and it is not offset even approximately by other taxes imposed upon residents alone").

[20] Baldwin v. Fish & Game Comm'n, 436 U.S. 371, 388 (1978) ("Equality in access to Montana elk is not basic to the maintenance or well-being of the Union.").

CONSTITUTIONAL RIGHTS AND INDIVIDUAL ACTION 361

residence may be necessary to preserve the basic conception of a political community, and therefore could withstand close constitutional scrutiny."[21]

So, the Privileges and Immunities Clause gives out-of-state citizens an equality right within a limited domain. But the clause is also a structural provision that aims to help make of states a union, and the Collective-Action Constitution explains it well.[22] Like the other clauses in Section 2 of Article IV examined in the previous chapter, the Privileges and Immunities Clause prevents destructive races to the bottom among states. States that do not allow citizens of other states to practice a trade or profession within their borders on equal terms with in-state citizens are likely to provoke retaliation. The same is true of states that do not give citizens of other states equal ability to hold and sell property within their borders, or to access state courts, or to obtain police or fire protection. Treating citizens of other states not as welcome visitors but as foreigners in these realms, which are essential to people's livelihoods and pursuit of "happiness and safety," to quote Justice Washington again,[23] is tantamount to treating sister states as foreign nations. It is the antithesis of being a part of a federal *union*.[24]

By contrast, state discrimination against out-of-staters regarding recreational activities poses less of a threat to union, although such discrimination poses some threat given the importance of certain leisure activities to individual identity and happiness. More importantly, prohibiting out-of-state citizens from voting in elections within the state, running for state office, or serving on state juries is consistent with—indeed, essential to—being part of a *federal* union. Such a union requires maintenance of the states as separable political communities, which would be impossible if Americans could live in one state and vote, hold office, or serve on juries in another state—or multiple other states. Equality of political rights between in-state citizens and out-of-state citizens would severely undermine federal union. Equality of civil rights maintains union without compromising its federal structure.[25]

---

[21] Dunn v. Blumstein, 405 U.S. 330, 343–44 (1972).

[22] Laycock, *supra* note 11, at 263 (calling the Privileges and Immunities Clause "first and foremost a national unity provision, eliminating a source of interstate divisiveness," but adding that "the Clause also appears to be an individual liberty provision, protecting individual American citizens from discrimination by sister states").

[23] Corfield v. Coryell, 6 F. Cas. 546, 551 (C.C.E.D. Pa. 1823) (No. 3,230).

[24] "Any discrimination against visiting citizens of sister states harms the victim and strikes a small blow against national unity," Professor Laycock writes. "Discrimination against citizens of sister states, justified only by a preference for locals or a view that the state has no interest in protecting outsiders, undermines our tendency to think of ourselves as a single people and leaves the victims with a legitimate sense of raw injustice." Laycock, *supra* note 11, at 264.

[25] *See id.* at 270 ("The most fundamental exception to the rule of equal treatment is that each state can reserve the exercise of government power, including the vote, to its own citizens. This exception is consistent with, and required by, the Founders' dual purpose of achieving national unity and preserving the states as separate polities" (footnote omitted).); Jonathan D. Varat, *State Citizenship and Interstate Equality*, 48 U. CHI. L. REV. 487, 520 (1981) ("If the states are to be representative

362 THE COLLECTIVE-ACTION CONSTITUTION

Another major area of state activity is beyond the Privileges and Immunities Clause, and it can be explained powerfully by the logic of cooperation or cost-benefit collective-action problems. As with the market-participant exception to the dormant commerce principle, states are generally permitted to limit the provision of subsidized social-welfare services to their own residents. Examples include state welfare benefits and low-cost higher education at state universities. Part of the rationale has to do with the relative tax burdens of in-staters and out-of-staters. It is often said that subsidized social-welfare services are funded by state taxes on residents, but that is not entirely true—some state residents do not pay state taxes and some out-of-state residents do pay state taxes for in-state activities. Registering these imperfections in this rationale, Professor Jonathan Varat offers the more nuanced argument that "[t]he vulnerabilities of residents [to state taxation] and the immunities of nonresidents [from taxation] together support the use of residence classifications as a proxy for determining who provided the resources to create the state's public goods."[26]

Perhaps, but regardless of how good a proxy residence classifications are for this purpose, Professor Laycock identifies a structural, collective-action rationale for state power to restrict subsidized services to in-staters that is more foundational:

> If Americans were entitled to subsidized services in every state, whole states could be free riders. A state could decide there was no need to create a state university so long as its students could be educated at the expense of taxpayers elsewhere, and no need to pay welfare benefits so long as its citizens could claim benefits in any state they might choose.[27]

The likely result of applying the Privileges and Immunities Clause to many subsidized social services would be to largely eviscerate them at the state level and force their near-complete provision at the federal level—beyond what federal programs like Medicaid already achieve to combat free riding by states. Granted, unlike applying the Privileges and Immunities Clause to residence restrictions for voting, applying it to subsidized services would not destroy the states as political communities. But it would significantly reduce the efficacy of their police powers.

Out-of-staters must, however, have an equal right to access state roads, police protection, fire protection, and emergency medical care. Although these

governments exercising their powers within the state's boundaries, their constituencies must surely be defined by the line between those who make their home in the state and those who do not.").

[26] Varat, *supra* note 25, at 528.
[27] Laycock, *supra* note 11, at 272.

CONSTITUTIONAL RIGHTS AND INDIVIDUAL ACTION 363

too are subsidized social-welfare services, the inhabitants of sister states require them to travel interstate and participate in commerce broadly conceived. Union demands that the equal provision of these services be protected by the Privileges and Immunities Clause and the dormant commerce principle, and, in any event, "states collect substantial sums from travelers through neutral taxes on gasoline, hotels, and retail sales." Accordingly, "this restriction on state power does not threaten the separate existence of the states or their ability to make policy choices and fund services."[28]

The Privileges and Immunities Clause overlaps significantly with the dormant commerce principle discussed in Chapter 5. As interpreted by the Court, however, there are differences between the two. For example, the Privileges and Immunities Clause does not protect corporations; the dormant commerce principle does.[29] As Professor Metzger observes, this is "an anachronistic rule at odds with many modern decisions, but one that remains settled law today."[30] Also, there are two exceptions to the dormant commerce principle—congressional approval and market participation—both of which Chapter 5 discussed. Most commentators do not believe that either exception applies to the Privileges and Immunities Clause.[31] But the de facto exception to the Privileges and Immunities Clause for subsidized social-welfare services does some of the same work as the market-participant exception.

Regarding congressional approval, Professor Metzger has argued that "congressional authority over the dormant commerce clause and Article IV's Privileges and Immunities Clause should be interpreted in tandem; whatever authority Congress enjoys to authorize violations of the former it should also enjoy with respect to the latter."[32] Structurally, her position is defensible. The dormant commerce principle and the Privileges and Immunities Clause are both concerned with preventing collective-action problems for the states and with protecting individual rights. Both overlap substantially by protecting economic activities in which out-of-staters engage to make a living. Thus, it is unclear why Congress can override the Court in one case but not the other, and the answer probably cannot be the text of the Privileges and Immunities Clause, which limits state power and does not expressly limit congressional power. The Interstate Commerce Clause covers much of the same subject matter as the Privileges and Immunities Clause, so Congress typically has available an enumerated power to authorize state violations of the Privileges and Immunities Clause. It is also worth

---

[28] *Id.* at 273.

[29] *Paul*, 75 U.S. at 180.

[30] Metzger, *supra* note 13, at 1487–88.

[31] *See, e.g.*, Erwin Chemerinsky, Constitutional Law: Principles and Policies 490 (6th ed. 2019) ("[T]here are two exceptions to the dormant Commerce Clause that do not apply to the Privileges and Immunities Clause.").

[32] Metzger, *supra* note 13, at 1488–89.

364   THE COLLECTIVE-ACTION CONSTITUTION

recalling that the Court construed the other two clauses in Article IV, Section 2, to permit federal legislation. Finally, the structural logic that would permit Congress to authorize violations of the Privileges and Immunities Clause would not let Congress generally authorize violations of individual-rights provisions, because such provisions are not concerned with preventing multistate collective-action problems in the economic sphere.

The Republican Form of Government Clause

Article IV closes by obliging the federal government to ensure each state a republican (meaning democratic) form of government, as opposed to a monarchical or aristocratic one: "The United States shall guarantee to every State in this Union a Republican Form of Government, and shall protect each of them against Invasion; and on Application of the Legislature, or of the Executive (when the Legislature cannot be convened) against domestic Violence."[33] Like the Privileges and Immunities Clause, the so-called Guarantee Clause, or Republican Form of Government Clause, has both an individual-rights component and a collective-action component. The collective-action component has, moreover, both a horizontal dimension and a vertical one.

The Republican Form Clause expresses a commitment to individual rights against one's own state by championing popular sovereignty, or government by the people. Although the concepts of individual rights and popular sovereignty conflict when popular majorities violate individual rights, the two may also be mutually supporting. Most relevant here, today the values of full and equal citizenship animating popular sovereignty imply voting rights for a state's adult citizens. For example, Professor John Hart Ely argues that resort to the Equal Protection Clause may be unnecessary in voter-qualification and malapportionment cases because "[w]hatever additional content Article IV's Republican Form of Government Clause may have, at a bare minimum it means that states must hold popular elections."[34] Professor Ely's point about the

---

[33] U.S. CONST. art. IV, § 4. In his *Vices Memo*, with Shay's Rebellion in mind, Madison decried the "want of Guaranty to the States of their Constitutions & laws against internal violence." JAMES MADISON, *Vices of the Political System of the United States* (Apr. 1787), *in* 2 THE WRITINGS OF JAMES MADISON 363 (Gaillard Hunt ed., 1904). Shay's Rebellion was a popular insurgency in Massachusetts that began in late August 1786 and ended in early February 1787. The insurgents violently demanded, but did not receive, paper money and relief from taxation and debt. "The principal lasting effect of Shay's Rebellion was that it persuaded a sufficient number of staunch Massachusetts federalists that the Confederation needed reform to enable it to protect their state against a future popular insurgency." GEORGE WILLIAM VAN CLEVE, WE HAVE NOT A GOVERNMENT: THE ARTICLES OF CONFEDERATION AND THE ROAD TO THE CONSTITUTION 242 (2017).

[34] JOHN HART ELY, DEMOCRACY AND DISTRUST: A THEORY OF JUDICIAL REVIEW 118 n* (1980). The general point is defensible regardless of whether there are exceptions. One issue is whether felons may constitutionally be disenfranchised given Section 2 of the Fourteenth Amendment, which may

CONSTITUTIONAL RIGHTS AND INDIVIDUAL ACTION 365

minimum content of the Republican Form Clause is sound regardless of whether the Court has been right to deem nonjusticiable the issue of whether a state has a republican form of government.[35] Justiciability concerns suggest, however, that resort to the Equal Protection Clause remains necessary.[36]

Daniel Korobkin calls the individual-rights component of the clause "republicanism on the inside," because "the principles of government are rooted in popular sovereignty, and these virtues are *internal* to the polity in which they are practiced." Put differently, "the values of republicanism are held by the citizens" of a state, and "the benefits of republicanism flow to those citizens." Citizens "who live *inside* unrepublican states have reason to complain because they are denied the virtues of republican government, namely the right to partake in collective self-government as a free and equal member of society together with others who are free and equal."[37] Korobkin is inspired by Professor Amar, who writes that "the Constitution would offer a kind of democratic insurance policy," meaning that "[i]f any individual state system of self-government fell sick and needed help, sister republics would come to its aid."[38]

"Republicanism on the inside" implies the existence of "republicanism on the outside," which Korobkin defines in national-security terms along two structural axes that should be familiar to readers of this book. The first concerns the relationship of an unrepublican state to sister states, and the second concerns the relationship of an unrepublican state to the federal government. "Republican government," Korobkin writes, "is guaranteed to protect the geostrategic security of each state from unrepublican aggressors next door, and to protect the

---

countenance disenfranchisement for criminal activity by excepting "participation in rebellion, or other crime" from its requirements regarding "the right to vote." Another issue, which is moot given the Nineteenth Amendment, is whether women were properly viewed as lacking constitutional voting rights at the Founding and throughout the nineteenth century even though they were citizens. *See* Minor v. Happersett, 88 U.S. (21 Wall.) 162 (1875) (holding that the limitation of suffrage to men did not violate the Republican Form Clause).

[35] Luther v. Borden, 48 U.S. (7 How.) 1 (1849) (declining to decide which of two governments was the proper republican government of Rhode Island and instead deeming conclusive the determination of this question by the political branches). Professor Ely writes that this case "did involve a situation whose political tangle the Court probably was wise to leave to Congress" but that it was "a gross mistake of logic to infer, as subsequent cases did, that all cases brought under the Republican Form Clause must therefore also present political questions." In his view, "the right to vote in state elections is a rather special constitutional prerogative, a view that cannot be teased out of the language of equal protection alone and in textual terms is most naturally assignable to the Republican Form Clause." ELY, *supra* note 34, at 118.

[36] For an argument that the modern political question doctrine lacks the historical pedigree that legal scholars attribute to it and was instead created in the mid-twentieth century as an instrument of judicial supremacy, see Tara Leigh Grove, *The Lost History of the Political Question Doctrine*, 90 N.Y.U. L. REV. 1908 (2015).

[37] Daniel S. Korobkin, *Republicanism on the Outside: A New Reading of the Reconstruction Congress*, 41 SUFFOLK U. L. REV. 487, 492–93 (2008).

[38] AKHIL REED AMAR, AMERICA'S CONSTITUTION: A BIOGRAPHY 280 (2005).

366   THE COLLECTIVE-ACTION CONSTITUTION

structural security of the United States from unrepublican member states." In other words, "[t]he republican virtues of the Guarantee Clause are *external*; the relevant values of republicanism are held by *other* states, and the relevant benefits of republicanism flow to *other* states and to the Union as a whole." People "who live *outside* an unrepublican state have reason to complain, not because of the unrepublican suffering of their neighbors as such, but because their neighbors' unrepublican government poses a threat to the security of other states and the integrity of the Union as a whole."[39]

Similarly, Professor Amar conveys the horizontal-federalism worry by writing that "[a] monarch or tyrant in any one state would pose a geostrategic threat to each and every neighboring state," which is why "Article IV not only guaranteed that each state would honor the basics of republican government, but also promised to protect each state from any 'Invasion' or 'domestic Violence,' instigated by a neighbor state or otherwise." Amar captures the vertical-federalism concern by emphasizing that "an unrepublican state government might tend to undermine the republican character of the *federal* government, whose own institutions would rest largely on state-law pillars." For example, "a warped state government might corrupt the integrity of that state's elections to the House, Senate, and electoral college."[40]

Korobkin and Professor Amar do not frame their sound structural points as collective-action problems facing the states. Their two structural arguments can, however, readily be expressed by leveraging respectively the logic of cost-benefit collective-action problems (or, possibly, cooperation problems) and the democratic preconditions for legitimate collective action by the states in Congress. First, regarding the relationship of unrepublican states to republican sister states, the clause obliges the government of "this Union" to engage in regime change in states should authoritarian governments arise in them. Such governments are especially likely to impose negative externalities on neighboring states, including by invading them or encouraging violent disturbances within them. These actions impose very high costs, whether measured in terms of lives lost or money spent, and so cause a cost-benefit collective-action problem. Moreover, such actions can invite retaliation—which can result in war—and so cause a cooperation problem. An ancient example cited during the ratification debates was the despotic king of Macedon, who first used political cunning to get admitted to the joint government of the Greek city-states and then gained control of each of them.[41]

[39] Korobkin, *supra* note 37, at 496.
[40] AMAR, *supra* note 38, at 280.
[41] *See, e.g.,* THE FEDERALIST NO. 43, at 275 (James Madison) (Clinton Rossiter ed., 1961) (quoting Montesquieu as writing that "Greece was undone as soon as the king of Macedon obtained a seat among the Amphictyons").

CONSTITUTIONAL RIGHTS AND INDIVIDUAL ACTION   367

Second, regarding the relationship of unrepublican states to the federal government, recall that the composition of the federal political branches is determined by elections within the states and that the states take the lead in setting voting qualifications for federal elections.[42] Thus, democratically illegitimate state governments will likely undermine the legitimacy of federal actions, including the solutions to collective-action problems that Congress imposes after concluding, amid disagreements among states, that such problems exist and warrant a regulatory response.

Congress's democratic legitimacy has been corrupted more frequently than many Americans may realize. In the decades before the Civil War, "[a]ggressive slavocrats had flouted basic democratic freedoms within their own states, menaced [and sought to muzzle] freedom-lovers in neighboring states [and in Congress], and begun to corrupt the character of federal institutions that rested on state-law foundations."[43] Beginning in the late nineteenth century and continuing until enforcement of the Voting Rights Act of 1965, Southern states disenfranchised Black people (and many poor white people) on a massive scale, notwithstanding the Fifteenth Amendment, which had banned racial discrimination in voting.[44] The federal government would have been fully justified in declaring Southern state governments in violation of the Republican Form Clause as well as Section Two of the Fourteenth Amendment, which directed Congress to reduce the representation of states that denied adult male citizens the right to vote. But the political branches lacked the will to intervene due in part to Southern members of Congress and presidents who ascended to office via undemocratic elections in Southern states.

But is it a stretch to think that the Collective-Action Constitution can explain the Republican Form Clause? One might object, for example, that race-based disenfranchisements throughout the Jim Crow South, although deeply unjust and unconstitutional, did not threaten the existence of the Union or sister states any more than the efforts of certain states today to limit the franchise threaten the existence of the Union or sister states. According to this objection, the internal composition of a state government may have effects outside the borders of the state in question, but such effects do not imperil the Union or other states.

---

[42] U.S. Const. art. I, § 2, cl. 1 (providing that "the Electors in each State" in elections for members of the House of Representatives "shall have the Qualifications requisite for Electors of the most numerous Branch of the State Legislature"); art. II, § 1, cl. 2 (providing that "[e]ach State shall appoint, in such Manner as the Legislature thereof may direct, a Number of Electors" in elections for president); amend. XVII (providing that "[t]he electors in each State" in elections for members of the Senate "shall have the qualifications requisite for electors of the most numerous branch of the State legislatures").

[43] Amar, *supra* note 38, at 372.

[44] U.S. Const. amend. XV (providing that the right of US citizens to vote "shall not be denied or abridged by the United States or by any State on account of race").

368   THE COLLECTIVE-ACTION CONSTITUTION

This objection does not appreciate the concerns expressed at the Founding that it is difficult for a state to remain a democracy if it is surrounded by monarchies—that democracies are less likely to go to war with one another than monarchies are to go to war with democracies or with one another. "In a confederacy founded on republican principles, and composed of republican members," Madison wrote in *Federalist 43*, "the superintending government ought clearly to possess authority to defend the system against aristocratic or monarchical innovations."[45] "The more intimate the nature of such a union may be," he continued, "the greater interest have the members in the political institutions of each other; and the greater right to insist that the forms of government under which the compact was entered into should be *substantially* maintained."[46] To reiterate Professor Ely's point, if the Republican Form Clause has any substantive content, it at least means that states must hold popular elections. In other words, the clause announces a no-monarchies principle that is, in significant part, structural in nature. The Republican Form Clause is therefore linked to the eighth clause of Article I, Section 9, which provides in part that "[n]o Title of Nobility shall be granted by the United States."

In addition, the Republican Form Clause is concerned with more than preventing states from going to war with one another or with the federal government—from posing an existential threat to them. The authoritarian political regimes of the Jim Crow South violated the Republican Form Clause precisely because they were authoritarian—because they disenfranchised a large percentage of their adult populations for no Constitution-respecting reason. Southern states should have been held accountable for warping the composition of the political branches throughout this long period of time, just as state governments should be held accountable today if they do the same.

In sum, one component of the Republican Form Clause concerns the relationship of a state to its citizens. But the collective-action component best explains why the clause is housed in Article IV, which primarily concerns interstate relations; why "every State in this Union" is its beneficiary, not the inhabitants of each state; and why the United States (the states collectively) is the guarantor of state republicanism. Unrepublican state governments threaten—or threaten to warp—both sister states and the federal government. It is part of the Constitution's structural DNA to prevent states from causing such collective-action problems

---

[45] THE FEDERALIST NO. 43, at 274 (James Madison) (Clinton Rossiter ed., 1961).

[46] *Id.* Madison had skeptics in his own day. "It may possibly be asked what need there could be of such a precaution," he noted, and he responded in part with this question: "But who can say what experiments may be produced by the caprice of particular States, by the ambition of enterprising leaders, or by the intrigues and influence of foreign powers?" *Id.* at 275. Madison's question remains worth asking today.

or from undermining the democratic legitimacy of federal solutions to such problems.

Although not in Article IV, the Elections Clause also provides for federal protection against state sabotage of the democratic legitimacy of the federal government. It permits state legislatures to prescribe "[t]he Times, Places and Manner of holding Elections for Senators and Representatives," but it also provides that "the Congress may at any time by Law make or alter such Regulations."[47] This congressional-override provision serves as backup should a state, for example, make it effectively impossible for some or all of its electorate to choose representatives to Congress.

The Right to Enter and to Leave Another State

Article IV's Privileges and Immunities Clause protects one component of the right to travel. In *Saenz v. Roe* (1999), the Court described this component as "the right to be treated as a welcome visitor rather than an unfriendly alien when temporarily present in the second State."[48] It is the right to exercise the same civil rights that state citizens enjoy.

Another component of the right to travel "protects the right of a citizen of one State to enter and to leave another State," to again quote the Court in *Saenz*.[49] This component was expressly protected in Article IV of the Articles of Confederation, which declared that "the people of each state shall have free ingress and regress to and from any other state." This right is not stated in the text of the Constitution, but it went without saying; the Constitution did not weaken the bonds of union relative to the regime established by the Articles. As Justice Potter Stewart wrote for the Court in *United States v. Guest* (1966), the right to enter and leave states is not in the text because "a right so elementary was conceived from the beginning to be a necessary concomitant of the stronger Union the Constitution created."[50] The Court in *Guest* upheld a federal indictment for conspiracy to violate the right of African Americans to travel interstate.

In *The Passenger Cases* (1849), the Court held unconstitutional a state law imposing a tax on aliens arriving in the United States from foreign ports. Although

---

[47] U.S. Const. art. I, § 4, cl. 1. The only limitation on congressional authority to override state election rules concerns "the Places of chusing Senators." *Id.*

[48] 526 U.S. 489, 500 (1999). As discussed in the next section, the Court in *Saenz* held that the Privileges or Immunities Clause of Section One of the Fourteenth Amendment was violated by a California law providing welfare benefits at the same level as the applicants' prior state of residence for their first year of residence in California.

[49] *Id.*

[50] 383 U.S. 745, 758 (1966) (citing Zechariah Chafee, Three Human Rights in the Constitution of 1787, at 185 (1956)).

370 THE COLLECTIVE-ACTION CONSTITUTION

dissenting, Chief Justice Roger Taney forcefully embraced the right of Americans to enter and leave every state:

> For all the great purposes for which the Federal government was formed we are one people, with one common country. We are all citizens of the United States; and, as members of the same community, must have the right to pass and repass through every part of it without interruption, as freely as in our own States. And a tax imposed by a State for entering its territories or harbours is inconsistent with the rights which belong to the citizens of other States as members of the Union, and with the objects which that Union was intended to attain. Such a power in the States could produce nothing but discord and mutual irritation, and they very clearly do not possess it.[51]

Taney referenced not only the individual-rights aspect of the right to enter and leave other states, but the collective-action dimension as well: "discord and mutual irritation" concerns the relationship of states to one another. States that banned entry or exit, or charged for either, would likely provoke similar responses from other states, and all states would likely regard themselves as worse off in most circumstances as one extended the time horizon. Even if a co-operation problem did not exist because some states would not regard themselves as worse off, states that banned entry or exit would almost certainly be externalizing greater costs than the benefits they were internalizing, creating a cost-benefit collective-action problem.[52] Relatedly, under such a state of affairs, the states could not fairly be described as part of one nation. Absent extraordinary circumstances, like a deadly flu pandemic ravaging an unvaccinated population, freedom of movement through subnational states may be constitutive of nationhood.

After the Civil War, the Court continued to protect the right of (most) Americans to enter and leave sister states.[53] In *Crandall v. Nevada* (1868), the Court rejected "the right of a State to levy a tax [of any amount] upon persons residing in the State who may wish to get out of it, and upon persons not residing in it who may have occasion to pass through it." In this purely structural opinion, the Court reasoned in part that "[i]f one State can do this, so can every other

---

[51] 48 U.S. 283, 492 (1849) (Taney, C.J., dissenting).

[52] Before the Civil War, Southern states effectively prohibited free Black people and white abolitionists from entering their jurisdictions and speaking their minds notwithstanding the right to enter and leave states, a right that Southern jurisdictions did not believe free Black people possessed. Gross & Upham, *supra* note 6. Such states may have regarded themselves as better off with such a barrier to entry, although at least some of them may have rethought their position had Northern states banned slaveowners from entering their jurisdictions.

[53] As explained below, poor Americans did not possess this right throughout the eighteenth and nineteenth centuries.

CONSTITUTIONAL RIGHTS AND INDIVIDUAL ACTION   371

State," which would mean that "one or more States covering the only practicable routes of travel from the east to the west, or from the north to the south, may totally prevent or seriously burden all transportation of passengers from one part of the country to the other."[54] The Court thought that such state power would, like the collective-action problem caused by state overtaxation of the national bank in *McCulloch v. Maryland* (1819), effectively undermine the functioning of the federal government. "That government has a right to call . . . any or all of its citizens to aid in its service," the Court reasoned, and "no power can exist in a State to obstruct this right that would not enable it to defeat the purposes for which the government was established."[55]

In *Edwards v. California* (1941), the Court invalidated a state law that criminalized bringing a nonresident into California knowing that the person was indigent. Although the Court relied on the dormant commerce principle instead of the right to enter or leave other states, it remained concerned about a race to the bottom. In effect, the Court characterized the interstate movement of indigent people as a NIMBY ("not in my backyard") problem:

> [T]here are . . . boundaries to the permissible area of State legislative activity. . . . And none is more certain than the prohibition against attempts on the part of any single State to isolate itself from difficulties common to all of them by restraining the transportation of persons and property across its borders. It is frequently the case that a State might gain a momentary respite from the pressure of events by the simple expedient of shutting its gates to the outside world. But, in the words of Mr. Justice Cardozo: "The Constitution was framed under the dominion of a political philosophy less parochial in range. It was framed upon the theory that the peoples of the several States must sink or swim together, and that in the long run prosperity and salvation are in union and not division."

The Court added that "[t]he prohibition against transporting indigent nonresidents into one State is an open invitation to retaliatory measures, and the burdens upon the transportation of such persons become cumulative."[56]

California effectively agreed that there was a NIMBY cooperation problem but disagreed that it was the cause. The state "assert[ed] that the huge influx of migrants into California in recent years has resulted in problems of health, morals, and especially finance, the proportions of which are staggering."[57] From

[54] 73 U.S. (6 Wall.) 35, 39, 46 (1868).
[55] *Id.* at 43–44.
[56] 314 U.S. 160, 173–74, 176 (1941). The quotation of Justice Cardozo is from *Baldwin v. Seelig*, 294 U.S. 511, 523 (1935).
[57] *Edwards*, 314 U.S. at 173.

372   THE COLLECTIVE-ACTION CONSTITUTION

its perspective, states that did not take adequate care of their indigent residents (as it defined adequacy) incentivized them to leave, thereby externalizing costs onto sister states, which would respond in kind and produce a race to the bottom. Recall the exclusion of the provision of social-welfare services from the scope of the Privileges and Immunities Clause.

Perhaps the Court was unsympathetic to California's assignment of responsibility to sister states because the state invoked "health" and "morals" in addition to "finance." California was thereby relying on the principle of settlement and removal, which had a long history in English and American law. Historian Kate Masur observes that state "laws designed to address challenges of poverty and dependency . . . dated back to the sixteenth century and the English tradition of managing the poor."[58] Professor Roderick Hills explains that, according to the idea of settlement, "one could claim support only from that unique community in which one had spent a considerable period of one's life as a contributing taxpayer, family member, or property owner." As for removal, "indigent persons who were not settled in a community were removed from it by force." During the 1800s, the dominant view in American politics and law was that "local communities had the power to protect themselves from . . . unfamiliar 'paupers' by expelling them."[59]

This tradition was reflected in the exclusion of "paupers" and "vagabonds" from the protections in Article IV of the Articles of Confederation. The Constitution omitted this exclusion, but the tradition continued long after ratification. In *Mayor of New York v. Miln* (1837), the Court sustained a state law barring "paupers" from entering New York City on ships:

> We think it as competent and as necessary for a state to provide precautionary measures against the moral pestilence of paupers, vagabonds, and possibly convicts; as it is to guard against the physical pestilence, which may arise from unsound and infectious articles imported, or from a ship, the crew of which may be labouring under an infectious disease.[60]

The Court in *Edwards*, after noting that "[t]his language has been casually repeated in numerous later cases up to the turn of the century," rejected "the

---

[58] Kate Masur, Until Justice Be Done: America's First Civil Rights Movement, from the Revolution to Reconstruction 5 (2021); *see id.* ("The core idea in the English poor-law tradition was that families and communities were obliged to provide for their own dependent poor, but not for transients and strangers.").

[59] Roderick M. Hills Jr., *Poverty, Residency, and Federalism: States' Duty of Impartiality toward Newcomers*, 1999 Sup. Ct. Rev. 277, 317–18.

[60] 36 U.S. (11 Pet.) 102, 142–43 (1837).

CONSTITUTIONAL RIGHTS AND INDIVIDUAL ACTION 373

contention that the limitation upon State power to interfere with the interstate transportation of persons is subject to an exception in the case of 'paupers.'" "Whatever may have been the notion . . . prevailing" when *Miln* was decided, the Court wrote, "we do not think it will now be seriously contended that because a person is without employment and without funds he constitutes a 'moral pestilence.' Poverty and immorality are not synonymous."[61]

In sum, the right to enter and leave other states, like the component of the right to travel protected by the Privileges and Immunities Clause, has both an individual-rights aspect and a collective-action dimension. The collective-action dimension seeks to prevent Pareto cooperation problems or cost-benefit collective-action problems for the states that are caused when states impose barriers to entry, even if similar problems may be caused when other states—through neglect of vulnerable members of their population—provide incentives to exit. States cannot invoke an exception to the principle of free interstate movement for impoverished individuals, even though such an exception was reflected in historical practice and judicial precedent until the New Deal. The demise of this exception is best explained not by structural reasoning but by a change in societal morality, which the Court has partially reflected and partially endeavored to shape.

For the same reason that the Collective-Action Constitution helps explain and justify the right to travel throughout the Union, this Constitution helps account for those rights in the Bill of Rights that must be protected for Americans to safely exercise this component of the right to travel. For example, if the Fourth Amendment's protections against unreasonable searches and seizures did not apply in some states and these states did not offer similar protections under their own constitutions, many Americans might be hesitant to travel through these states. A collective-action theory cannot, however, identify which rights must be protected to make meaningful the right to enter and leave sister states, and it would likely be impossible to generate consensus on this question. For example, more socially conservative Americans may emphasize religious liberty (the Free Exercise Clause) and the possession of firearms for purposes of self-defense (the Second Amendment), whereas more liberal Americans may emphasize constitutional criminal procedure rights (the Fourth, Fifth, and Sixth Amendments) and protection against cruel and unusual punishments (the Eighth Amendment). More libertarian Americans may emphasize all the foregoing rights. It seems likely that more than nothing and less than everything in the Bill of Rights would need to be protected for Americans to be and feel reasonably safe traveling interstate.

---

[61] *Edwards*, 314 U.S. at 176, 177.

374   THE COLLECTIVE-ACTION CONSTITUTION

Individual-Action Rights Protected by
the Reconstruction Constitution

Most constitutional rights do not exist mainly to serve collective-action ends. Most rights can be called "individual-action rights" because they exist primarily to protect people from unconstitutional individual action by their home state governments, not to prevent states from causing collective-action problems. This section first illustrates the idea of individual-action rights by examining the right to move to another state, the third component of the right to travel. The Court has deemed this right protected by part of the Fourteenth Amendment, and it has rejected collective-action arguments in interpreting its scope. The section then generalizes the logic of individual-action rights. This generalization justifies the rejection of collective-action rationales in limiting the scope of rights protected by the Reconstruction Amendments.

The Right of Indigent Individuals to Move to Another State

The difference between collective-action rights and individual-action rights is well illustrated by the distinction between how the Court views the first two components of the right to travel (discussed above) and how it enforces the third component to protect indigent people. In *Saenz v. Roe* (1999), the Court described this component as protecting "those travelers who elect to become permanent residents" and named it "the right to be treated like other citizens of that State."[62] Professor Ely called it "the right, if you will, to relocate."[63] In *Saenz*, the Court held that the right to move to another state is protected by the Privileges or Immunities Clause of the Fourteenth Amendment. It provides that "[n]o State shall make or enforce any law which shall abridge the privileges or immunities of citizens of the United States." The Court so held even though it almost entirely eviscerated this clause in *The Slaughter-House Cases* (1872).[64]

In *Saenz*, the Court relied on the right to move to another state in invalidating a durational residency requirement—a California law providing that new state residents, during their first year of residence, would receive the same amount of welfare benefits that they had received in their prior state of residence. The lower courts had concluded that the "apparent purpose of [the law] was to deter

---

[62] Saenz v. Roe, 526 U.S. 489, 500 (1999).

[63] ELY, *supra* note 34, at 178.

[64] 83 U.S. (16 Wall.) 36 (1872) (implausibly limiting the Privileges or Immunities Clause, U.S. CONST. amend. XIV, § 1, to rights already protected before the clause was ratified); *see Saenz*, 526 U.S. at 503 ("[I]t has always been common ground that this Clause protects the third component of the right to travel" (citation omitted).).

CONSTITUTIONAL RIGHTS AND INDIVIDUAL ACTION   375

migration of poor people to California."[65] The Court deemed this purpose "unequivocally impermissible" given the Court's decision in *Shapiro v. Thompson* (1969), which invalidated several state and DC laws that imposed a one-year residency requirement as a condition of eligibility for welfare benefits.[66] The states in *Shapiro* defended their laws as ensuring the fiscal viability of their welfare programs given the incentive of other states to free ride on them by offering less generous benefits to their own residents, thereby incentivizing them to leave. The Court responded that "the purpose of inhibiting migration by needy persons into the State is constitutionally impermissible," declaring that "a State may no more try to fence out those indigents who seek higher welfare benefits than it may try to fence out indigents generally."[67]

Congress had approved the durational residency requirement at issue in *Saenz*, and the solicitor general argued that the Court "should recognize the congressional concern addressed in the legislative history . . . that the 'States might engage in a "race to the bottom" in setting the benefit levels in their [welfare] programs.' " The Court dismissed this concern as speculative and suggested that "the savings resulting from the discriminatory policy, if spread equitably throughout the entire program, would have only a miniscule impact on benefit levels."[68] But these responses were beside the point given the Court's conclusion that California could not permissibly seek to deter the migration of poor people to the state.

These responses were also questionable on their own terms. As for the allegedly speculative nature of the state's concern, it does not seem consistent to endorse the plausibility of collective-action rationales when they are invoked to uphold key pieces of New Deal taxing-and-spending legislation that sought to help economically vulnerable Americans (see Chapter 4's discussions of *Steward Machine Company v. Davis* (1937)[69] and *Helvering v. Davis* (1937)[70]), and then to dismiss these rationales as speculative when invoked to justify durational residency requirements that harm certain indigent individuals. Perhaps selective deference logic can do some distinguishing work given the different contexts of enumerated powers and individual rights, but such logic cannot do all the work if one aims to be consistent about the potential existence—as opposed to the

---

[65] *Saenz*, 526 U.S. at 506 n.19.

[66] 394 U.S. 618 (1969).

[67] *Id.* at 629, 631. The Court in *Shapiro* applied strict scrutiny to the states' discrimination against new residents because "the classification here touches on the fundamental right of interstate movement," and the Court invalidated the one-year waiting periods under the Equal Protection Clause. *Id.* at 638. Less important than which clause the Court deemed violated is the fact that the Court viewed the states' invocation of collective-action reasoning as constitutionally irrelevant.

[68] *Saenz*, 526 U.S. at 521.

[69] 301 U.S. 548 (1937).

[70] 301 U.S. 619 (1937).

376   THE COLLECTIVE-ACTION CONSTITUTION

constitutional relevance—of interstate movements caused by differences in state legal regimes that may generate collective-action problems for the states.

The Court's cost-spreading reply was also nonresponsive to the state's free-rider concern, unless one views surrender to a free-rider problem as a solution to it.[71] Chief Justice William Rehnquist thus emphasized in dissent that a key question was whether Congress and some states could act to prevent other states from causing cost-benefit collective-action problems or cooperation problems by incentivizing the interstate exodus of indigent people:

> The National Legislature, where people from Mississippi as well as California are represented, has recognized the need to protect state resources in a time of experimentation and welfare reform. As States like California revamp their total welfare packages, they should have the authority and flexibility to ensure that their new programs are not exploited.[72]

In rejecting the rights claim and crediting the collective-action problem, Rehnquist was reasoning from the perspective of states like California, which were more generous than most of their sister states in providing welfare benefits. In validating the rights claim, the Court was in essence rejecting the relevance of collective-action reasoning. Thus, the Court's strongest point was that the nature of the right disables states from deterring the migration of poor people to them regardless of collective-action problems facing the states.

Notably, the Court in *Saenz* did not argue that states that disincentivized poor people from relocating to their jurisdictions might trigger responses in kind from sister states. Any such argument would have been strained because states that offered lower welfare benefits than sister states like California had little to gain from imposing a durational residency requirement. The Court's wise decision not to invoke collective-action reasoning can be contrasted with its sound decisions to invoke such reasoning in *The Passenger Cases* and *Edwards*.

The point here is not whether *Saenz*, *Shapiro*, and other cases invalidating durational residency requirements for new indigent residents to obtain important benefits (including medical care[73]) are correctly decided on balance. The point, rather, is to illustrate the difference between the logic of a collective-action right and the logic of an individual-action right. The Court does not view the right

---

[71] Hills, *supra* note 59, at 309 ("When a generous state cuts its welfare payments to match the welfare cuts of its stingier neighbors, then society loses the benefit of the more generous state's tax effort.").

[72] *Saenz*, 526 U.S. at 509–10 (Rehnquist, C.J., dissenting) (citation omitted).

[73] Memorial Hospital v. Maricopa County, 415 U.S. 250, 261–62 (1974) (invalidating an Arizona durational residency requirement for free nonemergency hospitalization or medical care as like the laws invalidated in *Shapiro* because the Arizona law "penalizes indigents for exercising their right to migrate to and settle in that state").

of indigent individuals to move to another state as a collective-action right. This view contrasts with the rights protected by the Article IV Privileges and Immunities Clause and the right to enter and leave other states. When indigent people invoke the right to move, the Court rejects arguments that states need to distinguish new indigent residents from older ones to continue providing the social-welfare service in question. This position is unlike prevailing doctrine under the Privileges and Immunities Clause and the market-participant exception to the dormant commerce principle, both of which permit distinctions between state residents and nonresidents regarding the provision of social-welfare services.

In short, the rights to be treated like a welcome visitor and to enter and leave states are collective-action rights. The right of indigent individuals to move to another state and obtain welfare benefits on equal terms with older residents is an individual-action right. It is not true that collective-action dynamics do not arise in the latter context. It *is* true that the Court does not care about them when states render new indigent residents less eligible for welfare benefits or medical care than more established residents. In the Court's view, the rights of indigents trump concerns (including by Congress) about a race to the bottom by states or a cost-benefit collective-action problem for the states.[74]

Finally, even regarding the right to move to another state, the Court has been inconsistent about the constitutionality of durational residency requirements, which is why the above analysis has focused on the right to relocate when such requirements are applied to indigent individuals. When the Court does not perceive the rights of indigents or other highly valued rights (like voting[75]) to be at stake, and when it perceives the public treasury or other valid state concerns to be at issue, the Court has been more responsive to collective-action reasoning.

---

[74] "This Court long ago recognized," the Court wrote in *Shapiro*, "that the nature of our Federal Union and our constitutional concepts of personal liberty unite to require that all citizens be free to travel throughout the length and breadth of our land uninhibited by statutes, rules, or regulations which unreasonably burden or restrict this movement." 394 U.S. at 629. The Court's reference to "the nature of our Federal Union" might suggest that the Court viewed the right to relocate as a collective-action right. In so observing, however, the Court quoted Chief Justice Taney's dissenting opinion in *The Passenger Cases* and Justice Stewart's majority opinion in *Guest*, both of which were discussed in the previous section. Thus, in this part of its opinion, the Court in *Shapiro* focused on the right to enter and leave other states, which has both collective-action and individual-liberty dimensions, not on the right to move to another state, which was at issue in *Shapiro*.

[75] *See* Dunn v. Blumstein, 405 U.S. 330, 338 (1972) (invalidating a one-year residency requirement for eligibility to vote because it penalizes exercise of the right to travel). For qualifications of this holding, see *Marston v. Lewis*, 410 U.S. 679 (1973) (upholding a durational residency requirement as long as fifty days for voting to enable the state government to check election rolls and prevent fraud), and *Rosario v. Rockefeller*, 410 U.S. 752 (1973) (sustaining a state law that permitted voters to participate in primary elections only if they registered for the relevant political party thirty days before the previous general election, which was typically more than a year before the next primary—meaning that new residents effectively had to satisfy a roughly one-year durational residency requirement to vote in state primary elections—because the parties had a valid interest in guaranteeing that only previously registered members could vote in their primaries).

378   THE COLLECTIVE-ACTION CONSTITUTION

Regarding subsidized college education, free public education, and divorce, the Court has walked back its egalitarian commitments in *Shapiro* and *Saenz*.

For example, in *Vlandis v. Kline* (1973), the Court invalidated a state law providing that students who had a legal address outside Connecticut before they applied to the state university were irrebuttably presumed not to be bona fide state residents during their entire period of attendance. Such students would thus be charged twice as much for tuition as residents. This holding is consistent with *Shapiro* and *Saenz*, but the Court reassured the state that it could adopt more reasonable criteria for bona fide residence that would be both constitutional and "certainly sufficient to *prevent abuse of the lower, in-state rates* by students who come to Connecticut *solely to obtain an education*."[76] Such reasoning diverges from the Court's insistence in *Shapiro* and *Saenz* that California could not try to "prevent abuse" of its more generous welfare system by indigents who come to the state "solely to obtain" welfare benefits.

Similarly, in *Martinez v. Bynum* (1983), the Court distinguished residency requirements from durational residency requirements and upheld the constitutionality of a law denying free public education to students who lived apart from their parents and were in the school district primarily to attend school.[77] The apparent purpose of the residency requirement was "to prevent newcomers from free-riding on the tax effort of old-timers," Professor Hills observes, just like the state laws that limited in-state tuition to state residents. In *Martinez*, "[t]he Court was silent on whether this fiscal motivation was legitimate," but "even *Martinez's* central holding tends to undermine both *Shapiro* and *Saenz*," because "*Martinez* squarely holds that, as part of the test for domicile, a state could require a person to show that they had a reason to enter the state other than receipt of benefits from the state."[78]

Likewise, in *Sosna v. Iowa* (1975), the Court upheld the constitutionality of a law requiring a year of state residence to obtain a divorce decree in the state's courts. The Court reasoned in part that "[a] state such as Iowa may reasonably decide it does not wish to become a divorce mill for unhappy spouses."[79] The Court in *Shapiro* and *Saenz* deemed it anathema to regard states that provide generous welfare benefits or medical care to indigent residents as welfare "mills" or "magnets" to out-of-state poor people, including new indigent residents.

A collective-action account cannot explain the Court's selectivity in viewing the right to move to another state as an individual-action right, as opposed to a

---

[76] 412 U.S. 441, 451–52 (1973) (emphases added); *see* Starns v Malkerson, 401 U.S. 985 (1971), *aff'g without opinion* 326 F. Supp. 234 (D. Minn. 1970) (upholding a one-year residency requirement for in-state tuition at state universities).

[77] 461 U.S. 321 (1983).

[78] Hills, *supra* note 59, at 294–95.

[79] 419 U.S. 393, 407 (1975).

CONSTITUTIONAL RIGHTS AND INDIVIDUAL ACTION   379

collective-action right. The primary reason seems to be the special status of poor migrants, perhaps in part because of the Court's emphatic rejection of the long tradition of settlement and removal in *Edwards*.[80] The Court has never offered a persuasive rationale, which is not easy to provide doctrinally, given the Court's rejection of poverty status as a suspect classification in *San Antonio Independent School District v. Rodriguez* (1974).[81]

Professor Hills offers a thoughtful account—one partially responsive to the logic of cooperation problems. He argues that the constitutional definition of bona fide residence should guard against attempts by states to undermine the common national citizenship of Americans by trying to make themselves socially homogenous "affective communities" through laws that view newcomers as unwelcome strangers to be met with hostility. Yet, he argues, the Court should credit the legitimate interest of states in limiting eligibility for their redistributive programs to new residents whose relocation to the state was not motivated by a desire to access the programs, so as not to undermine state incentives to maintain such programs. His "affective communities" idea accounts for decisions not concerning poor new residents that invalidated state laws giving benefits to new residents less generous than the benefits received by older residents.[82]

Although Professor Hills does not suggest as much, his "affective communities" account also reflects the nation's eventual repudiation of the denials of civil rights to free Black Americans by colonies and then states in the antebellum United States. "From the colonial period until the Civil War, white northerners regularly characterized free African Americans, as a group, as dependents, vagrants, or criminals who lowered the moral standards of the community," Professor Masur explains. "The poor-law tradition and the nation's federated structure itself, combined with antiblack racism, gave racist laws legitimacy and made them difficult to dislodge."[83] The principle of settlement and removal in antebellum America was not just about poverty; it was also about race. Federalism was also about race.

---

[80] 314 U.S. at 173–74, 176.

[81] 411 U.S. 1 (1973).

[82] Hills, *supra* note 59, at 299–326. *See* Zobel v. Williams, 457 U.S. 55 (1982) (holding unconstitutional an Alaska law that gave oil revenues to state residents based upon the length of their residence within the state); Hooper v. Bernalillo County Assessor, 472 U.S. 612 (1985) (holding unconstitutional a state law that provided a property-tax exemption to Vietnam veterans who had become state residents before a specified date, but not afterwards); Attorney General of New York v. Soto-Lopez, 476 U.S. 898 (1986) (holding unconstitutional a state law that offered a hiring preference to veterans who were state residents when they began military service, but not to veterans who were residents of other states when they began serving).

[83] MASUR, *supra* note 58, at 12; *see id.* at xviii (identifying a commitment to racial equality regarding civil rights, not political rights, as uniting the different groups that constituted the nation's first civil rights movement during the antebellum period).

380   THE COLLECTIVE-ACTION CONSTITUTION

The combined power of these three forces made it very difficult for free Black Americans to live in some free states and move to others. In the early 1850s, an article in the official publication of the American Colonization Society, which promoted the migration of free Black Americans to Liberia, "warned that exclusionary measures in the Old Northwest would drive African Americans into free states that had no such restrictions and that whites, in turn, would leave those states, 'to avoid the inconveniences of the preponderance of that race.' "[84] Today, states may not seek social homogeneity, and collective-action rationales will not help them do so.

A Generalization of the Logic of Individual-Action Rights

The logic of individual-action rights differs from the logic of collective-action rights. This difference reflects the truth that both the Constitution and the federal government it creates perform more than one function. Thus, this book's collective-action theory cannot explain the entire Constitution or every role of the national government in the federal structure, let alone the entire constitutional scheme. Most importantly, the theory cannot provide the primary explanation for the role of the federal government—the federal courts and Congress—in protecting many constitutional rights of individuals against violations by their home states.

At the Founding, Madison presciently anticipated the rights-protecting purpose of the Constitution and the federal government in three ways. First, at the Constitution Convention, he sought to empower Congress to veto (or "negative") state laws that it deemed unconstitutional. As Chapter 7 explained, Resolution VI of the Virginia Plan provided in part that "the National Legislature ought to be impowered . . . to negative all laws passed by the several States, contravening in the opinion of the National Legislature the articles of Union."[85] Madison failed to persuade his colleagues, who rejected his proposed federal negative on state laws, and the original Constitution provided merely that "[n]o state shall . . . pass any bill of attainder, ex post facto law, or law impairing the obligation of contracts."[86] Most rights provisions in the original Constitution bound the federal government.[87]

---

[84] *Id.* at 236–37 (quoting an article in the *African Repository*).

[85] 1 THE RECORDS OF THE FEDERAL CONVENTION OF 1787, at 21 (Max Farrand ed., rev. ed. 1966) (May 29).

[86] U.S. Const. art. I, § 10, cl. 1.

[87] U.S. Const. art. I, § 9, cl. 2 (Habeas Suspension Clause); art. I, § 9, cl. 3 (ban on federal bills of attainder and ex post facto laws); art. III, § 2 (right of a jury trial in federal criminal cases); art. III, § 3, cl. 1 (narrow definition of the crime of treason and evidentiary protections); art. III, § 3, cl. 2 (authorizing and limiting congressional power to punish treason).

CONSTITUTIONAL RIGHTS AND INDIVIDUAL ACTION 381

Second, Madison articulated his theory of the extended republic in his *Vices Memo*, at the Convention, in *Federalist 10* and *51*, and in private correspondence before and after the Convention.[88] He reasoned—theoretically and abstractly—that local majorities would likely be disempowered by extending the sphere of republican government and so diversifying the number of interests represented in the national legislature relative to the state legislatures:

> The smaller the society, the fewer probably will be the distinct parties and interests composing it; the fewer the distinct parties and interests, the more frequently will a majority be found of the same party; and the smaller the number of individuals composing a majority, and the smaller the compass within which they are placed, the more easily will they concert and execute their plans of oppression. Extend the sphere, and you take in a greater variety of parties and interests; you make it less probable that a majority of the whole will have a common motive to invade the rights of other citizens; or if such a common motive exists, it will be more difficult for all who feel it to discover their own strength, and to act in unison with each other.[89]

Madison there sought to protect citizens from abuses by their state governments, not to protect their state governments or the federal government from abuses by other state governments or foreign nations. Most nationalist Founders did not share (or even understand) Madison's structural solution to the problem of minority rights given majority rule.[90]

Madison appeared to be imagining politics as a majority-rule game of redistribution in which local majorities can outvote (and oppress) local minorities at the state level but not at the federal level due to the inclusion at the national level of local majorities from other states. All these local majorities become national minorities in Congress, Madison reasoned, and they must bargain with one another to avoid endless cycling because every possible majority coalition can be undone by another majority coalition.[91] For example, if three legislators must divide a dollar by majority rule and two of them propose to split the dollar evenly between them, the excluded legislator can offer a member of the majority

---

[88] *Vices Memo, supra* note 33, at 365–69; 1 THE RECORDS OF THE FEDERAL CONVENTION OF 1787, *supra* note 85, at 134–36 (Jun. 6). *Federalist 10* and *Federalist 51* are discussed below. On Madison's private correspondence with Jefferson, Randolph, and Washington, see Larry Kramer, *Madison's Audience*, 112 HARV. L. REV. 611, 635–36 (1999).

[89] THE FEDERALIST NO. 10, at 83 (James Madison) (Clinton Rossiter ed., 1961).

[90] Kramer, *supra* note 88 (finding that Madison's argument for an extended republic effectively played no part in influencing the framing or ratification of the Constitution).

[91] For this social-choice interpretation of Madison's argument, see Neil S. Siegel, Intransitivities Protect Minorities: Interpreting Madison's Theory of the Extended Republic (2001) (unpublished PhD dissertation, Jurisprudence & Social Policy Program, University of California, Berkeley) (on file with U.C. Berkeley Library).

382 THE COLLECTIVE-ACTION CONSTITUTION

coalition more than fifty cents to form a new majority coalition, and this fact is endlessly true.[92] To stop the cycling, legislators must craft broad compromises, such as dividing the dollar by giving the three legislators one-third each. "In the extended republic of the United States, and among the great variety of interests, parties, and sects which it embraces," Madison wrote toward the end of *Federalist 51*, "a coalition of a majority of the whole society could seldom take place on any other principles than those of justice and the general good."[93]

Madison's argument for an extended republic is problematic for several reasons. He did not anticipate the creation of political parties and the establishment of committees, rules, and practices by the House of Representatives and the Senate. Political parties and institutions help solve the social-choice problem.[94] As for group members "act[ing] in unison with each other," Madison did not register the advantages that small, cohesive minorities may have over large, diffuse majorities in overcoming impediments to collective action and influencing the federal legislative process.[95] There is also more to democratic politics that majority-rule games of redistribution, as Madison understood in advocating the creation of a federal government to solve pressing collective-action problems for the states.

Madison anticipated the rights-protecting purpose of the Constitution and the federal government in a third way. In the first Congress, he did not rely exclusively on his prior theorizing. Responding to the demands of state ratifying conventions and then constituents for a bill of rights to limit federal power, he sought to also require states to respect certain rights. A congressional committee of which he was a member recommended that in "Article 1, section 10, between the first and second paragraph," an amendment should "insert 'no State shall infringe the equal rights of conscience, nor the freedom of speech, or of the press, nor of the right of trial by jury in criminal cases.'" Madison told his colleagues that he "conceived this to be the most valuable amendment in the whole list."[96] Again,

---

[92] Technically, because every coalition can be blocked by another coalition, majority-rule games of redistribution have an empty core. *See* ROBERT D. COOTER, THE STRATEGIC CONSTITUTION 58–60 (2000).

[93] THE FEDERALIST NO. 51, at 325 (James Madison) (Clinton Rossiter ed., 1961).

[94] On the rise of political parties to solve certain social-choice problems within Congress, see JOHN H. ALDRICH, WHY PARTIES? A SECOND LOOK 35–43, 67–101 (2d ed. 2011) (arguing that Hamilton, Jefferson, Madison, and others formed the first two political parties to solve the social-choice problem of forming durable majority coalitions to address "the 'great principle'—how large and active the new central government would be, and in their competing views *must* be—to make the great experiment in republican democracy viable," *id.* at 67). On the importance of political institutions in producing legislative stability, see Kenneth A. Shepsle & Barry R. Weingast, *Structure-Induced Equilibrium and Legislative Choice*, 37 PUB. CHOICE 503 (1981).

[95] THE FEDERALIST NO. 10, at 83 (James Madison) (Clinton Rossiter ed., 1961). On the advantages that cohesive minorities have over diffuse majorities in overcoming free-rider problems, see MANCUR OLSON, THE LOGIC OF COLLECTIVE ACTION: PUBLIC GOODS AND THE THEORY OF GROUPS (1965); *see also* Bruce A. Ackerman, *Beyond* Carolene Products, 98 HARV. L. REV. 713 (1985).

[96] 1 ANNALS OF CONGRESS 755 (Aug. 13, 1789). Regarding Madison's membership in the committee of eleven, see 1 ANNALS OF CONGRESS 665 (Jul. 21, 1789).

CONSTITUTIONAL RIGHTS AND INDIVIDUAL ACTION 383

however, he failed to persuade. The rights protected in the first ten amendments were widely understood—within and outside Congress—to apply only to the federal government; to a significant extent, the Bill of Rights performed a structural, states' rights function.[97] Some abolitionists later argued that rights in the Bill of Rights applied to the states, but this was a minority view in antebellum America.[98] In perceiving the potential threat that state governments posed to their own inhabitants, as opposed to one another or to the federal government, Madison was ahead of his time.

Accomplishing structurally what Madison could not achieve in his own day required several developments that repudiated Madison's own views on race and slavery. The first was the Union's victory in a savage Civil War after politics had failed to settle the issue of slavery in the territories.[99] The second was the ratification of the Reconstruction Amendments. Section One of the Thirteenth Amendment ended slavery in the United States. Section One of the Fourteenth Amendment established birthright citizenship and provided that "[n]o state shall make or enforce any law which shall abridge the privileges or immunities of citizens of the United States; nor . . . deprive any person of life, liberty, or property, without due process of law; nor deny to any person within its jurisdiction the equal protection of the laws." Section One of the Fifteenth Amendment prohibited racial discrimination in voting by both the states and the United States.

All three amendments ended with enforcement clauses, which empowered Congress to enforce the foregoing rights against state governments "by appropriate legislation."[100] This formulation self-consciously invoked the deference logic of *McCulloch*, which Chapter 1 discussed. Recall the rule of law that Chief Justice Marshall announced for the Court: "Let the end be legitimate, . . . and all means which are *appropriate* . . . are constitutional."[101] In all likelihood, the Reconstruction Congress thrice used the word "appropriate," not the term "proper" from the Necessary and Proper Clause, because the Court had

---

[97] *See* AMAR, *supra* note 2.

[98] *See, e.g.*, Barron ex rel. Tiernan v. Mayor & City Council of Baltimore, 32 U.S. (7 Pet.) 243 (1833) (holding that only the federal government is capable of violating the Takings Clause of the Fifth Amendment). Some abolitionists argued that slavery, which was authorized by state law, violated the Due Process Clause of the Fifth Amendment, the Republican Form Clause, and other clauses. Ariela Gross, *Slavery, Anti-Slavery, and the Coming of the Civil War, in* II CAMBRIDGE HISTORY OF LAW IN AMERICA: THE LONG NINETEENTH CENTURY (1789–1920) 280, 302 (Michael Grossberg & Christopher Tomlins eds., 2008) ("Within anti-slavery politics, radical constitutional abolitionists such as Frederick Douglas and Lysander Spooner began to argue after 1840 that, rather than endorse slavery, the Constitution in fact made slavery illegitimate everywhere, in the South as well as in the territories. Theirs was a minority position . . . .").

[99] R. Craig Green, *Beyond States: A Constitutional History of Territory, Statehood, and Nation-Building*, 90 U. CHI. L. REV. 813 (2023) (arguing that the Civil War was caused by intractable sectional conflict over slavery in the territories).

[100] U.S. CONST. amend. XIII, § 2; amend. XIV, § 5; amend. XV, § 2.

[101] McCulloch v. Maryland, 17 U.S. (4 Wheat.) 316, 421 (1819) (emphasis added). Chief Justice Marshall used the word "appropriate" six times in *McCulloch*. *Id.* at 408, 410, 415, 421, 422, 423.

384   THE COLLECTIVE-ACTION CONSTITUTION

repeatedly used the word "appropriate" in liberally construing this clause in *McCulloch*, and because "[i]n the antebellum period, no Court opinion—with the arguable exception of the malodorous Taney opinion in *Dred Scott*—had ever held that a congressional statute flunked *McCulloch's* deferential test of congressional power."[102] The modern Court's decisions in *City of Boerne v. Flores* (1997) and its progeny, which narrowly construe congressional power under Section Five of the Fourteenth Amendment, contravene the original intent behind, and the original meaning of, the enforcement clauses.[103]

As Chapter 5 explained, in *United States v. Morrison* (2000), the Court held that Congress could not use the Interstate Commerce Clause to authorize victims of gender-motivated violence to sue their assailants for money damages in federal court. The Court also held this provision beyond Section Five, reasoning that Congress may not authorize suits against private actors using this power because Section One is limited to prohibitions on state action, not private action.[104] The Court thereby reaffirmed *The Civil Rights Cases* (1883), which had held broadly that Congress could not use Section Five to prohibit racial discrimination by places of public accommodation because Congress may not target private discrimination using Section Five.[105]

Morrison may have been a difficult commerce-power case given the question of whether Congress rationally found that gender-motivated violence deterred women from traveling interstate. But for at least two reasons, a properly deferential Court would have upheld the law under Section Five. Even if Congress may target only state action when using Section Five, Congress was targeting state action with the civil-damages remedy: unconstitutional sex discrimination in the administration of state criminal-justice systems. An "appropriate" congressional remedy need not run against a state actor just because the constitutional violator must be a state actor. Remedies exist to make a victim whole (or less un-whole), and this one did that.[106]

---

[102]   AMAR, *supra* note 38, at 362; *see id.* at 361 (suggesting that the Reconstruction Congress likely followed the language of *McCulloch*, which had been interpreted broadly in the decades before the Civil War).

[103]   521 U.S. 507 (1997). *See* Jack M. Balkin, *The Reconstruction Power*, 85 N.Y.U. L. REV. 1801, 1805 (2010) ("[M]odern doctrine has not been faithful to the text, history, and structure of the Thirteenth, Fourteenth, and Fifteenth Amendments.").

[104]   529 U.S. 598 (2000).

[105]   109 U.S. 3 (1883). The Court also deemed the Civil Rights Act of 1875 beyond the scope of Section Two of the Thirteenth Amendment, reasoning that Congress may ensure only an end to slavery; it may not seek to eliminate private racial discrimination. *See id.* at 24–25 ("It would be running the slavery argument into the ground to make it apply to every act of discrimination which a person may see fit to make as to the guests he will entertain, or as to the people he will take into his coach or cab or car, or admit to his concert or theatre, or deal with in other matters of intercourse or business."). This holding was overruled in the cases cited *infra* note 108.

[106]   *See Morrison*, 529 U.S. at 665 (Breyer, J., dissenting) (emphasizing "the relation between remedy and violation—the creation of a federal remedy to substitute for constitutionally inadequate state remedies").

CONSTITUTIONAL RIGHTS AND INDIVIDUAL ACTION 385

More broadly, Congress may target certain forms of private gender discrimination under Section Five because Section One is not limited to prohibiting various forms of state action; it also contains the Citizenship Clause, as the first Justice John Marshall Harlan emphasized in dissent in *The Civil Rights Cases*.[107] Just as the modern Court permits Congress to use Section Two of the Thirteenth Amendment to target the badges and incidents of slavery in addition to slavery itself, so a properly deferential Court should allow Congress to use Section Five to protect the badges and incidents of citizenship and not just citizenship itself.[108] Although it may not always be clear what is a badge and incident of citizenship, protection against gender-motivated violence by public and private actors should qualify. It is difficult to regard women as full and equal citizens of the United States if their own state officials—police, prosecutors, judges, and juries—do not take seriously private, gender-motivated crimes of violence against them.

The third development needed to accomplish Madison's structural goal of requiring states to respect federal constitutional rights was the slow and steady judicial process of holding that almost every right in the Bill of Rights protects Americans from violations by their state governments. Whether or not the Court has been correct as a textualist and originalist matter to use the Due Process Clause, as opposed to the Privileges or Immunities Clause, as the vehicle of incorporation, the result has been the modern American conception of constitutional rights, which exist against government at every level.[109] Critically, the structural logic of the federal government's role in protecting constitutional rights within the states is distinct from the logics of its roles in enabling collective action by states and preventing states from causing collective-action problems. The primary structural change accomplished by the Civil War, Reconstruction, and later judicial interpretation and civil rights legislation was to empower the federal courts and Congress to regulate the internal policy choices of states regarding certain subjects—including, but not limited to, racial subordination—regardless of multistate collective-action problems. Thus, an important limitation of the collective-action account offered in this book is that it cannot serve as the main justification for the federal government's role in protecting most constitutional rights through adjudication and legislation, which many constitutional

---

[107] 109 U.S. at 44–57 (Harlan, J., dissenting). For elaboration of Justice Harlan's position, see Akhil Reed Amar, *Intratextualism*, 112 HARV. L. REV. 747, 821–27 (1999).

[108] Amar, *supra* note 107, at 824–26. Decisions broadly construing congressional power under Section Two of the Thirteenth Amendment include *Runyon v. McCrary*, 427 U.S. 160 (1976) (permitting Congress to prohibit private racial discrimination in private contracting), and *Jones v. Alfred H. Mayer Company*, 392 U.S. 409 (1968) (permitting Congress to prohibit private racial discrimination in selling and leasing property). The Court reaffirmed these decisions in *Patterson v. McLean Credit Union*, 491 U.S. 164 (1989).

[109] For a moving telling of this story, see SANFORD LEVINSON ET AL., PROCESSES OF CONSTITUTIONAL DECISIONMAKING: CASES AND MATERIALS 558–67 (8th ed. 2022). For a longer version, see AMAR, *supra* note 2.

386 THE COLLECTIVE-ACTION CONSTITUTION

provisions seek to facilitate. The Reconstruction Constitution best explains this function.

Consider this thought experiment. Imagine that, instead of appending constitutional amendments to the end of the original Constitution, we followed Madison's idea of incorporating them within the body of the original text.[110] If that were standard American practice, where would the Reconstruction Amendments go? Would they go in Article IV, Section 2, just after the Privileges and Immunities Clause? Or would they go in Article I, Section 10, just after the Contracts Cause? Article I, Section 10, seems the better home. Textually, a portion of Section One of the Fourteenth Amendment ("No State shall") reproduces verbatim a portion of Section Ten. But the deeper point is structural: the prohibitions in the opening sections of all three amendments, like the Citizenship Clause of the Fourteenth Amendment, primarily concern how a state government may constitutionally relate to its own inhabitants; they do not mainly concern how a state government may relate to sister states or to the federal government. For example, slavery is categorically barred regardless of whether doing so will prevent multistate collective-action problems, and states must have very good reasons for discriminating on certain bases—again, regardless of collective-action logics.

True, the Court did hold in *Metropolitan Life Insurance Company v. Ward* (1985) that the Equal Protection Clause was violated by an Alabama law that taxed out-of-state insurance companies at a higher rate than in-state insurance companies, notwithstanding the fact that a federal statute permitted such discrimination.[111] The Court purported to apply only rational basis review to the state law.[112] It actually applied heightened scrutiny, however, by collapsing the separate means and ends prongs of rational basis review into one and holding that "promotion of domestic business within a State, by discriminating against foreign corporations that wish to compete by doing business there, is not a legitimate state purpose."[113] The Court thought that "Alabama's aim to promote

---

[110] In the first Congress, Madison presented his proposed amendments as insertions in the text of the Constitution. *See supra* note 96 and accompanying text. Madison's method underscores that, where possible, constitutional provisions should be read as part of an integrated whole, not as a series of unrelated provisions.

[111] 470 U.S. 869 (1985).

[112] Western & S. Life Ins. Co. v. State Bd. of Equalization, 451 U.S. 648, 668 (1981) (requiring discrimination against out-of-state corporations to bear merely "a rational relation to a legitimate state purpose").

[113] *Metropolitan Life Ins. Co.*, 470 U.S. at 880; *see id.* at 884 (O'Connor, J., dissenting) (criticizing the majority for "melding the proper two-step inquiry regarding the State's purpose and the classification's relationship to that purpose into a single unarticulated judgment," which "enables the Court to characterize state goals that have been legitimated by Congress itself as improper solely because it disagrees with the concededly rational means of differential taxation selected by the legislature"); *see also Northeast Bancorp, Inc. v. Board of Governors of the Federal Reserve System*, 472 U.S.

CONSTITUTIONAL RIGHTS AND INDIVIDUAL ACTION   387

domestic industry is purely and completely discriminatory, designed only to favor domestic industry within the State," and "constitutes the very sort of parochial discrimination that the Equal Protection Clause was intended to prevent."[114]

Alabama's law was parochial, but one wonders which history of the Equal Protection Clause the Court has in mind—and why, if its historical understanding is correct, it purports to apply only rational basis review in equal-protection cases involving economic discrimination against out-of-state corporations. The Equal Protection Clause does not stand for the principle that parochial state economic legislation is constitutionally suspect. Such discrimination *is* a major concern of the Privileges and Immunities Clause, but recall that, under the Court's doctrine, this clause does not protect out-of-state corporations. Such discrimination is also a major concern of the dormant commerce principle, but as Chapter 5 explained, this principle drops out when Congress approves of the discrimination, which reflects its judgment that there are not collective-action problems facing the states that warrant federal intervention. Congress possesses the democratic legitimacy to render such a judgment; the Court does not. It is thus not clear what warrant the Court has to displace Congress's judgment by shifting analysis to the Equal Protection Clause when this clause polices the relationship of a state government to its own inhabitants (including its own corporations), not the relationship of a state government to sister states or to the federal government. The clause does not police the potential generation of multistate collective-action problems caused by state parochialism.

This conclusion may seem surprising in a book devoted to reading the structural Constitution as preventing state governments from causing collective-action problems. To reiterate, however, the Constitution has more than one purpose, and if the Collective-Action Constitution purports to account for every function of the Constitution, it likely accounts for none. In any event, this book does not aim to prevent states from causing collective-action problems in every context. In the economic realm, if Congress approves of state parochialism, the Court lacks authority to invalidate it under the Equal Protection Clause because out-of-state corporations are disadvantaged.

159, 180 (1985) (O'Connor, J., concurring) ("Especially where Congress has sanctioned the barriers to commerce that fostering of local industries might engender, this Court has no authority under the Equal Protection Clause to invalidate classifications designed to encourage local businesses because of their special contributions.").

[114] *Metropolitan Life Ins. Co.*, 470 U.S. at 878.

388 THE COLLECTIVE-ACTION CONSTITUTION

Individual-Action Rights Protected by Both Constitutions

Although the logics of collective-action rights and individual-action rights differ, there is an important category of individual-action rights that the Collective-Action Constitution can help explain. This category can be called "democratic-process rights" because it encompasses rights that help secure the integrity of the democratic process at the state and federal levels. Examples include free political speech, expression, and association, a free press, peaceful assembly, a right to petition the government for a redress of grievances, voting rights, the apportionment principle of one-person, one-vote, and, arguably, protection from extreme partisan gerrymanders (despite the Court's ruling that challenges to them are nonjusticiable political questions[115]). The Court has deemed these rights protected by the First Amendment as incorporated into the Due Process Clause of the Fourteenth Amendment,[116] by several Amendments protecting voting rights,[117] and by the Equal Protection Clause.[118]

Beyond the doctrine, some of these rights are also implied in the constitutional structure as theorized in this book. For example, even if the Constitution did not expressly protect free speech, a free press, or any voting rights for anyone, state officials would not be members of a democratically legitimate government if they entrenched themselves in power by suppressing core political speech, criminalizing all press not run by the state government, and disenfranchising a significant share of its adult citizens. Moreover, elections for federal offices in the state would all be corrupted by the state's authoritarianism. The more states that turned authoritarian, the more corrupt the composition of the federal political branches would become. In addition, federal officials that entrenched themselves in power through the same means would directly corrupt the federal government. Whether indirectly via state corruption of the state democratic process or directly via their own corruption of the federal democratic process, elected federal officials would lack the democratic legitimacy to act. They would therefore lack the democratic legitimacy to decide, when states

---

[115] Rucho v. Common Cause, 139 S. Ct. 2484 (2019).

[116] *See, e.g.*, New York Times Co. v. Sullivan, 376 U.S. 254 (1964) (holding that a state cannot, under the First and Fourteenth Amendments, award damages to public officials for defamatory falsehoods relating to their official conduct unless they prove "actual malice"—i.e., that the statements were made with knowledge of their falsity or with reckless disregard of whether they were true or false).

[117] See the Fifteenth Amendment's ban on racial discrimination in voting in federal and state elections, the Seventeenth Amendment's provision for direct election of US senators, the Nineteenth Amendment's prohibition of sex-based disenfranchisements, the Twenty-Third Amendment's extension of representation in the Electoral College to the District of Columbia, the Twenty-Fourth Amendment's prohibition on federal or state poll taxes in federal elections, and the Twenty-Sixth Amendment's extension of the franchise to eighteen-year-olds.

[118] *See, e.g.*, Reynolds v. Sims, 377 U.S. 533, 568 (1964) (extending the principle of population equality to state legislative districts).

CONSTITUTIONAL RIGHTS AND INDIVIDUAL ACTION   389

disagreed, whether there were collective-action problems facing the states that should be addressed.[119]

In *United States v. Carolene Products Company* (1938), in its famous footnote four, the Court asked "whether legislation which restricts those political processes which can ordinarily be expected to bring about repeal of undesirable legislation, is to be subjected to more exacting judicial scrutiny under the general prohibitions of the Fourteenth Amendment than are most other types of legislation."[120] Professor Ely fleshed out this footnote and developed a theory of judicial review. According to part of his "participation-oriented, representation-reinforcing approach to judicial review," a democratic "[m]alfunction occurs when the *process* is underserving of trust, when . . . the ins are choking off the channels of political change to ensure that they will stay in and the outs will stay out." Professor Ely was incorrect that judges who followed his theory would avoid making substantive value choices, but he was correct that rights like "free speech, publication, and association," "whether or not they are explicitly mentioned [in the constitutional text], must nonetheless be protected, strenuously so, because they are critical to the functioning of an open and effective democratic process." He was also correct that "the right to vote seems equally central to a right of participation in the democratic process."[121]

By contrast, the second part of Professor Ely's theory concerns individual-action rights that do not seem best described as democratic-process rights. Professor Ely thought that the process also malfunctions when, "though no one is actually denied a voice or a vote, representatives beholden to an effective majority are systematically disadvantaging some minority out of simple hostility or a prejudiced refusal to recognize commonalities of interest, and thereby denying that minority the protection afforded other groups by a representative system."[122] Professor Ely was again tracking footnote four, which asked "whether similar considerations enter into the review of statutes directed at particular religious,

---

[119] The category of democratic-process rights was partially anticipated earlier in this chapter in part of the discussion of the Republican Form of Government Clause, which the chapter described as protecting collective-action rights. Democratic-process rights are nonetheless best viewed as individual-action rights, not collective-action rights, because their role is not to solve or prevent collective-action problems for the states, and so collective-action reasoning is not relevant to their scopes. Democratic-process rights intersect with the theory developed in this book because they help ensure the democratic legitimacy of congressional determinations that multistate collective-action problems exist and warrant a federal response.

[120] 304 U.S. 144, 152 n.4 (1938) (citing decisions concerning "restrictions upon the right to vote," "restraints upon the dissemination of information," "interferences with political organizations," and "prohibition of peaceable assembly").

[121] ELY, *supra* note 34, at 87, 103, 105, 116. For critiques of Ely's claim to be offering a value-neutral approach to constitutional adjudication, see, for example, Paul Brest, *The Substance of Process*, 42 OHIO St. L.J. 131 (1981); and Laurence H. Tribe, *The Puzzling Persistence of Process-Based Constitutional Theories*, 89 YALE L.J. 1063 (1980).

[122] ELY, *supra* note 34, at 103.

390 THE COLLECTIVE-ACTION CONSTITUTION

or national, or racial minorities: whether prejudice against discrete and insular minorities may be a special condition, which tends seriously to curtail the operation of those political processes ordinarily to be relied upon to protect minorities, and which may call for a correspondingly more searching judicial inquiry."[123]

It is difficult, however, to distinguish hostility or prejudice on one hand from moral opposition on the other, as illustrated by past debates over race and contemporary debates over sexual orientation and gender identity. Yet, Professor Ely regarded hostility or prejudice as a failure of the democratic process while not finding "anything unconstitutional about outlawing an act due to a bona fide feeling that it is immoral."[124] Constitutional antidiscrimination commitments seem better defended as individual-action rights that do not protect the integrity of the democratic process but rather vindicate other vitally important values, especially human dignity and equality. These rights also facilitate interstate travel, as discussed earlier in this chapter. Members of racial and other minority groups would be loath to travel to and through states in which invidious discrimination against them was promoted or tolerated. Thus, the Collective-Action Constitution can provide a secondary explanation for constitutional equality rights, just as Chapter 5 explained why Congress was justified in using the Interstate Commerce Clause to combat racial subordination.

Conclusion

This chapter has shown that a structural, collective-action theory of the Constitution can help justify and define some important constitutional rights. The dormant commerce principle, the Full Faith and Credit Clause, the Privileges and Immunities Clause, the Republican Form of Government Clause, and the unenumerated right to enter and leave other states all have both collective-action dimensions and individual-rights dimensions. The Collective-Action Constitution can also partially account for various democratic-process rights, including political speech, political expression, political association, a free press, peaceful assembly, voting, and the principle of one-person-one-vote. The theory requires that federal interventions to solve or prevent multistate collective-action problems be democratically legitimate. Finally, the Collective-Action Constitution provides a supplemental justification for constitutional antidiscrimination law.

The most important lesson of this chapter is, however, that this book's structural theory, like any structural theory, is incomplete. As illustrated by

---

[123] *Carolene Products*, 304 U.S. at 152 n.4.
[124] ELY, *supra* note 34, at 256 n.14.

the right of indigent individuals to relocate and the rights protected by the Citizenship Clause, the Privileges or Immunities Clause, the Due Process Clause, and the Equal Protection Clause, the logic of rights protection against one's own state government differs from the logics of collective action. Rights protection concerns how a state relates to its own inhabitants; this is a different question from how a state relates to sister states or to the federal government. As a result, the Collective-Action Constitution must be combined with the Reconstruction Constitution to capture the Constitution's functions more fully in modern America.

PART III

PERFECTING THE COLLECTIVE-ACTION CONSTITUTION

10

The Collective Costs of Strict Supermajority Requirements

Introduction

The foregoing chapters have identified numerous instances in which sound interpretation of the Constitution requires more than collective-action reasoning. This is primarily because the Constitution is charged with accomplishing a number or purposes, not just one. As a result, the constitutional values associated with achieving collective action by states in Congress can trade off with other values. These include the preservation of state autonomy and individual liberty through the dispersion of government power, and the protection of human freedom and equality through the vindication of constitutional rights.

Although rights protection trumps structural concerns, Chapter 1 defended a rebuttable presumption that collective-action commitments supersede other structural considerations when they conflict and the text does not settle the matter. Regarding some of these tradeoffs, however, the text does settle the matter: several structural restraints that make collective action more difficult are hardwired into the text. When this is so, the constitutional purpose of facilitating collective action by states must give way.

Even when the text defeats collective-action reasoning about the constitutional structure, the account developed in this book remains relevant due to its critical acuity. An important part of constitutional debates has always been critical, not interpretive. Critique of the Constitution can serve several purposes. It can caution Americans against relating to their Constitution and its drafters with blind reverence. It can strive to persuade others of the need for constitutional amendments. It can seek to justify workarounds to hardwired portions of the text that ill serve the nation. It can lay the groundwork for proposing new workarounds or advising changes in subconstitutional rules that exacerbate problems caused by certain rules in the constitutional text. This final part of the book turns from interpreting the Constitution to perfecting it by making it easier for congressional majorities to solve collective-action problems for the states in modern times. With this objective in hand, Part III assesses the wisdom of certain constitutional provisions and subconstitutional rules given historical practice, modern developments, and contemporary political conditions.

The Collective-Action Constitution. Neil S. Siegel, Oxford University Press. © Neil S. Siegel 2024.
DOI: 10.1093/oso/9780197760963.003.0011

396 THE COLLECTIVE-ACTION CONSTITUTION

This chapter first analyzes two supermajority voting requirements in the constitutional text that significantly constrain the exercise of vitally important powers: (1) proposing and then approving constitutional amendments, which typically requires the agreement of both two-thirds of each house of Congress and three-fourths of the states; and (2) concluding treaties, which requires the approval of two-thirds of the Senate.[1] As noted in earlier chapters, there is a tradeoff between facilitating collective action by states and preventing the exploitation of a minority of states by the majority of states, and the Constitution usually negotiates this tension by authorizing the use of federal powers by majority vote in each chamber of Congress. This is the Constitution's default voting rule—the one that goes without saying unless the text indicates otherwise. The result of the foregoing two supermajority requirements has been to make use of the associated powers increasingly rare and to prompt the development of workarounds. Constitutional change in the United States almost always occurs through state building by the political branches and judicial interpretation, not constitutional amendments. In addition, executive agreements, not treaties, are almost always made with other countries. Although the logics of collective action by states in Congress cannot identify the appropriate voting rule for amending the Constitution and concluding treaties, it can illuminate the tradeoffs involved and explain why Article V overrepresents the states, effectively letting them vote twice. Moreover, the development of workarounds, combined with other considerations, suggests that these supermajority rules are incompatible with the perceived needs of modern American governance.

This chapter next turns to two other strict supermajority voting rules in the Constitution that empower presidents to undermine congressional solutions to multistate collective-action problems. They are the two-thirds vote required in each house of Congress to override a presidential veto and the two-thirds vote required in the Senate to convict impeached presidents.[2] If presidents conclude that Congress is encroaching on their office, they can respond by vetoing the bills in question. This is the main reason why presidents were given the veto power. By contrast, if Congress concludes that a president is encroaching on its authority—for instance, by legislating via executive order or acting despite what Congress views as a valid congressional prohibition—it can pass a bill with clear language to address the matter, but the president will almost certainly veto the bill, in which case the bill will not become law unless two-thirds supermajorities in each house vote to override the veto. The Framers did not anticipate that presidents might usurp or disregard the powers of Congress and not just be potential

---

[1] U.S. Const. art. V. (proposing and approving amendments); U.S. Const. art. II, § 2, cl. 2 (concluding treaties).

[2] U.S. Const. art. I, § 7, cl. 2 (veto override); U.S. Const. art. I, § 3, cl. 6 (conviction by Senate).

victims of congressional aggrandizement, and so the Framers did not perceive the difficulty in this scenario of overriding a presidential veto by a two-thirds vote in each legislative chamber. Nor did the Framers anticipate expansive executive power and political parties, let alone polarized parties and a closely divided polity. These developments make it extraordinarily challenging both to override vetoes and to remove impeached presidents by securing the support of two-thirds of the Senate. In an America with political parties, policy-based vetoes, expansive executive power, partisan polarization, partisan animosity, and political divisions of roughly equal strength, these strict supermajority voting rules likely make collective action by members of Congress too difficult to accomplish, particularly given the impossibility of developing satisfactory workarounds.

To see how this chapter fits within the overall architecture of the book, it is important to understand the relationship between collective-action problems facing members of Congress and collective-action problems facing the states. States act in Congress through their elected members, including when these members vote for constitutional amendments and when senators decide whether to approve proposed treaties. Collective action by members of Congress is also what potentially protects federal statutes that solve collective-action problems for the states when presidents ignore, violate, or decline to enforce such statutes. In other words, collective action by members of Congress helps protect collective action by states in Congress.

This chapter begins at the beginning, with a sensible instance of a strict supermajority voting rule in the constitutional text: Article VII's two-thirds requirement for ratification of the original Constitution. Identifying the key features of this rule is useful in assessing other supermajority requirements in the text. The chapter then considers constitutional change, international agreements, and the adequacy of constraints on executive actions that may undermine congressional solutions to multistate collective-action problems. As the discussion will reveal, the supermajority rules in Article V and the Treaty Clause have always been regrettable but have grown more problematic over time, while the supermajority votes required to override vetoes and convict impeached presidents have come to be regrettable under modern political conditions that the Framers did not anticipate.

Ratifying the Constitution

Rarely noticed today, Article VII concerns the requirements for ratification of the Constitution. The Framers understood from experience that requiring the approval of all thirteen states would mean that the Constitution would not be ratified. Article XIII of the Articles of Confederation had required unanimity

398 THE COLLECTIVE-ACTION CONSTITUTION

for amendments, which had made it impossible for the states to act collectively to amend the Articles even on such vital matters as funding the national government, regulating commerce, and raising troops to defend the states collectively. Rhode Island refused even to send delegates to the Philadelphia Convention. Relative to this baseline, Article VII facilitated collective action by declaring self-referentially that "[t]he Ratification of the Conventions of nine States shall be sufficient for the Establishment of this Constitution between the States so ratifying the Same."[3] In *Federalist 40*, Madison explained the Convention's rejection of a unanimity requirement to ratify the Constitution by emphasizing—with Rhode Island in mind—"the absurdity of subjecting the fate of twelve States to the perverseness or corruption of the thirteenth."[4] From a collective-action standpoint, Article VII followed a much longer historical pattern. Professor Melissa Schwartzberg has explained that supermajority voting rules emerged in other cultures in earlier times to facilitate collective action relative to unanimity rule, not to limit collective action relative to majority rule.[5]

For purposes of analyzing other supermajority requirements in the Constitution, three features of Article VII are noteworthy. First, as just noted, Article VII significantly enhanced the ability of the states to act collectively compared with what came before it: there is a world of difference between a two-thirds requirement (nine states) and a unanimity requirement (all thirteen). The Constitution would not have been ratified had North Carolina's and Rhode Island's decisions to hold out proven decisive. (When Washington took the oath of office on April 30, 1789, the Union consisted of eleven states.) Moreover, had unanimity been required, additional states would likely have voted no or held out for changes that they wanted. The decisions of state conventions to ratify depended in part on the decisions of other conventions to ratify and on the overall number of "yes" votes needed for ratification. Even many opponents of the Constitution did not want their states fending for themselves as separate nations should enough other states vote to abandon the Articles by ratifying the Constitution. The choice was not between voting to ratify the Constitution and voting to keep the Articles, but between voting to ratify and running the risk

---

[3] There are other important differences between Article VII of the Constitution and Article XIII of the Articles. Whereas Article XIII required that amendments "be agreed to in a Congress of the United States, and be afterwards confirmed by the legislatures of every State," Article VII eliminated any role for the Confederation Congress and required ratification by state conventions instead of state legislatures. Both changes did not just address the matters of democratic principle discussed in Chapters 1 and 3. These changes also facilitated collective action because they prevented the Confederation Congress or state legislatures from blocking ratification of the Constitution, which eliminated the Confederation Congress and limited state regulatory power in significant ways.

[4] THE FEDERALIST NO. 40, at 251 (James Madison) (Clinton Rossiter ed., 1961).

[5] MELISSA SCHWARTZBERG, COUNTING THE MANY: THE ORIGINS AND LIMITS OF SUPERMAJORITY RULE 6, 17–102 (2014) (tracing the origins of supermajority rule as a remedy for the problems of unanimity rule in the ancient world, the Middle Ages, and eighteenth-century France).

of going it alone or with other states that did not ratify. "Given the recognized need to be in the Union," Professor Mark Graber writes, "Article VII practically guaranteed a process of increasing returns in which the ratification of each additional state increased the odds that every remaining state would ratify."[6]

Because the practical stakes were so high, there is substantially less difference between one aspect of Article VII and other supermajority voting rules in the Constitution than a formal analysis of Article VII would suggest. If the two-thirds requirement for ratification of the Constitution could be satisfied, Article VII purported to bind only those states that agreed to be bound. In theory, there is less risk of disadvantaging a minority of states when they are not formally bound by the decision of the (super)majority. No other supermajority rule discussed in this chapter, including the Article V process for amendments, possesses this formal quality. Practically, however, Article VII was not significantly different from other supermajority voting rules in the Constitution. Rhode Island and North Carolina would not likely have thrived as independent nations, and they were unwilling to risk finding out. Thus, although these states were not formally bound, they were under enormous pressure to ratify.

The Framers and delegates to the state ratifying conventions were aware of these collective-action dynamics. The Federalists viewed a nine-state threshold as a means to the end of a thirteen-state union. Neither Madison in *Federalist 40* (which, as noted above, defended a twelve-state union), nor Hamilton in his early *Federalist* essays, nor other Federalists defended a nine-state union. They argued against a partial union as a recipe for destructive conflict at home and abroad.[7] Tellingly, no one seemed to think that all four states that ratified after New Hampshire (Massachusetts, New York, North Carolina, and Rhode Island), or the two states that ratified after Washington's inauguration (again, North Carolina and Rhode Island), could be admitted into the Union only pursuant to the Admissions Clause.[8] Thirteen states was always the idea, and so no time limit was placed on when each state could ratify.

A second feature of Article VII is that it concerned formal constitutional change, not ordinary legislative change or even change to a constitution in practice (or "small-c" constitution, a topic discussed below). It is plausible to believe that formal constitutional change should be more difficult to accomplish than these other kinds of change. Constitutions cannot well accomplish their purposes of structuring, enabling, and limiting ordinary politics if constitutions can be altered by ordinary politics.[9] Given the constitutive nature of the question

---

[6] Mark A. Graber, *Why Nine Meant Thirteen*, NATIONAL CONSTITUTION CENTER, INTERACTIVE CONSTITUTION (2016), https://perma.cc/F5XK-D3UU.

[7] *See* Chapter 3 (quoting *Federalist 6* and *Federalist 7*).

[8] Art. IV, § 3, cl. 1 (discussed in Chapter 8).

[9] Why formal constitutional change should be harder to achieve than legislative change implicates complex debates over the purposes of a constitution, written versus unwritten constitutions, and how

400   THE COLLECTIVE-ACTION CONSTITUTION

whether to replace the Articles of Confederation with the Constitution, it arguably made structural sense for the Framers to require more than a majority of state conventions to ratify the Constitution, even as the delegates to each convention voted by majority rule.

But how much more demanding? There were practical and practice-based reasons for imposing a two-thirds requirement instead of the less demanding threshold of three-fifths (eight states). A new regime might not have had enough people, territory, and wealth to be viable with only eight states joining, particularly because such a union might not have included one or more key states (Virginia, New York, and Massachusetts). More importantly, given the increasing-returns dynamic noted above, setting the threshold at nine likely exerted gravitational pull. As Chapter 4 discussed, under Article IX of the Articles, at least nine states had to agree before Congress could requisition the states for taxes or troops, conclude treaties, or engage in war.[10]

A three-fourths requirement (ten states) for ratification lacked this foundation in practice. Such a requirement would have also diminished the force of the increasing-returns dynamic. Most importantly, a ten-state rule might have made collective action sufficiently difficult that it was deemed inappropriate in principle. It is already very demanding to require at least twice as many states to approve formal constitutional change than to oppose it before such change can occur. Requiring at least three times as many states is even more demanding.

The third feature of Article VII, which will be especially relevant in the analyses below, is that ratification was a one-time decision. Without future ratification decisions, there was no risk that collective action would later become too difficult formally or practically. Specifically, there could be no reasonable concern that Article VII's two-thirds requirement, which (as noted above) was crafted with knowledge of the relevant players and current conditions, would prove shortsighted, given subsequent experience and changes in the perceived needs of American governance. The same cannot be said of the supermajority requirements analyzed below, and this fact is critical to assessing their normative desirability.

---

the US Constitution compares with those of other democracies and state constitutions. Engaging these issues is not possible here. Canonical discussions of the nature and purposes of the US Constitution include *Marbury v. Madison*, 5 U.S. (1 Cranch) 137 (1803), and *McCulloch v. Maryland*, 17 U.S. (4 Wheat.) 316 (1819).

[10] *See* AKHIL REED AMAR, AMERICA'S CONSTITUTION: A BIOGRAPHY 594 n.50 (2005) (noting several times during the Constitutional Convention when Charles Pinckney or Edmund Randolph suggested that the requisite number of states should be nine).

Amending the Constitution

Article V sets forth the procedural requirements for formally amending the Constitution. It identifies two ways of proposing amendments and two ways of ratifying them. Whichever methods are used, proposals must meet a two-thirds voting threshold and ratifications require at least three-fourths support.

The proposal method used for all twenty-seven amendments to date is a two-thirds affirmative vote in each house of Congress. The alternative method allows state legislatures to sidestep Congress. "[O]n the Application of two thirds of the Legislatures of the several States," Article V provides, Congress "shall call a Convention for proposing amendments," and this convention can offer proposals regardless of whether Congress supports them. Article V also authorizes Congress to choose between the two ratification methods. Twenty-six amendments were ratified by at least three-fourths of the state legislatures. The Twenty-First Amendment, which repealed prohibition (the Eighteenth Amendment), was ratified by at least three-fourths of the state ratifying conventions that Congress directed the states to call for the sole purpose of deciding whether to ratify this amendment.

This section begins by drawing from Chief Justice Marshall's theory in *McCulloch v. Maryland* (1819) of the superior democratic legitimacy of the federal government, which this book has invoked to justify letting Congress decide whether there are multistate collective-action problems in need of solving when the states are divided. A comparison of how Article V and other parts of the Constitution view the relationship between the federal government and the states reveals that Article V overrepresents the states—essentially letting them vote twice—which suggests that the Constitution is too difficult to formally amend and that any amendment to Article V should count the states once. This conclusion is buttressed by analyzing Article V's supermajority voting rules from several other perspectives, including the development of workarounds to avoid these rules. Finally, the section examines the portion of Article V that entrenches part of the Constitution—today, the equal representation of states in the Senate—against constitutional change even via the typical Article V process.

Letting the States Vote Twice

Article V, like Article VII, concerns formal constitutional change, not politics as usual, and so there is a good argument for supermajority voting rules of some kind. Also like Article VII, Article V makes collective action substantially less difficult to accomplish than did Article XIII of the Articles of Confederation, whose unanimity requirement for amendments made it effectively impossible to amend the Articles. As detailed above, however, Article V imposes substantially more demanding supermajority requirements than Article VII did: one vote of two-thirds support to propose amendments, and one vote of three-fourths support to ratify them. Article V does so even though it concerns an indefinite number of future decisions, not a one-time decision, so the risk of shortsightedness is much higher than it is regarding Article VII.

Professors John McGinnis and Michael Rappaport argue that, like the requirements for constitutional amendments, the Constitution was proposed and ratified through a multistage supermajoritarian process. In addition to the Article VII ratification process, they reason, a supermajority of states in the Confederation Congress had to approve the decision to call for the Constitutional Convention, then a supermajority of states sent delegates to the Convention, and then a supermajority of Convention delegates supported the Constitution they proposed.[11]

Unlike Article V, however, the process they describe was not set out in advance as requirements; doing so could have affected the proposals made and the voting on them along the way.[12] Regarding the particulars, the Confederation Congress approved a convention that would propose certain revisions to the Articles, not one that would shred the Articles and craft a new Constitution.[13] Likewise, the decision of twelve states to send delegates to the Convention was not a specific endorsement of how the Convention proceeded or what it drafted. Moreover, the fact that a certain supermajority of delegates, as opposed to a smaller supermajority or a majority, supported the Constitution as finally drafted seems difficult to describe as a threshold of support that had to be reached. Further, the Confederation Congress submitted the proposed Constitution to the states to begin the ratification process without approving or disapproving it.[14] Finally, Article VII imposed a two-thirds voting requirement for ratification, not a three-fourths rule. Given how close ratification was in key states and the interdependence of voting in multiple states, this difference was potentially significant.

Article V's more demanding requirements are difficult to defend in terms of the difference between formally binding states in the minority (Article V) and not binding them but placing existential pressure on them (Article VII). If

---

[11] See JOHN O. MCGINNIS & MICHAEL B. RAPPAPORT, ORIGINALISM AND THE GOOD CONSTITUTION 13, 77–78 (2013).

[12] See supra note 3 (explaining that Article VII excluded the Confederation Congress from playing any formal role in the ratification process).

[13] NATIONAL ARCHIVES, THE FORMATION OF THE UNION 50 (1970) (Publication No. 70–13) (approving a convention "for the sole and express purpose of revising the Articles of Confederation and reporting to Congress and the several legislatures such alterations and provisions therein as shall when agreed to in Congress and confirmed by the States render the federal constitution adequate to the exigencies of Government & the preservation of the Union").

[14] Scott Bomboy, On This Day, the Confederation Congress Agrees to a New Constitution, NATIONAL CONSTITUTION CENTER, CONSTITUTION DAILY (Sept. 28, 2020), https://perma.cc/598G-WEJX.

Article V gave states the choice between being bound by amendments they had voted against and not being bound but being excluded from the Union, the risk of disadvantaging these states from their own perspectives would almost certainly not decline in almost all situations. As discussed below, ex-Confederate states ratified the Fourteenth Amendment rather than be excluded from Congress. True, many states had sought to leave the Union less than a decade earlier, but this is the major exception to the overwhelming likelihood that the states would not generally view themselves as better off if they left the Union than if they accepted terms of continued inclusion that they deemed distasteful.

Comparing Article V to Article VII suggests not only that Article V makes the Constitution too difficult to amend, but also, in part, how it does so. The same problem is revealed by comparing Article V to other key constitutional provisions. Article V permits state legislatures to bypass Congress in proposing amendments, and it permits Congress to avoid state legislatures in specifying the approval process. Relative to other parts of the Constitution, these bypass maneuvers reflect greater distrust of Congress and state legislatures, and greater concern about disagreements between them.

Article V seems animated in part by the worry that Congress may fail to represent either state legislatures or the American people. As a result, Article V prevents Congress from amending the Constitution on its own and from being the sole gatekeeper of amendment proposals. As noted, congressional proposals must be ratified by state legislatures or state conventions, and Article V permits state legislatures to initiate—or threaten to initiate—the amendment process when they do not regard themselves or the American people as adequately represented in Congress.[15] Likewise, Article V reflects the concern that state legislatures may fail to represent their own citizens. Article V thus authorizes Congress to require state conventions, not state legislatures, to complete the formal process of constitutional change.

One can imagine hypotheticals in which such distrust would be warranted. Members of Congress might seek to give themselves—or a demagogic president—dictatorial powers, although an amendment would likely be unnecessary to do so if the country were that far down the road to authoritarianism. Less arrestingly, members of Congress might seek to raise their salaries excessively or, for self-interested reasons, oppose term limits that would apply to them. Similarly, state legislators might seek to increase their powers or those of the governor in troubling ways, and they might pursue unwarranted salary increases or vote against term limits for bad reasons. Such concerns are not baseless, but

---

[15] AMAR, *supra* note 10, at 290 (explaining how and why Article V limits congressional power to amend the Constitution).

404 THE COLLECTIVE-ACTION CONSTITUTION

they are validated in Article V to a much greater extent than in other parts of the Constitution, which suggests that they are likely overstated.

Recall that Chief Justice Marshall's theory of the superior democratic legitimacy of the federal government rests upon the view that every state and all the people are better represented in Congress (however imperfectly) than anywhere else. Recall also that the Interstate Compacts Clause, the Interstate Commerce Clause, and the congressional-consent exception to the dormant commerce principle all authorize Congress to determine, amid disagreements among states, whether there is a multistate collective-action problem that warrants solving. For example, the proper inquiry under the Interstate Commerce Clause asks only whether Congress rationally concluded that the states face a collective-action problem in the commercial realm; the inquiry does not also ask whether a certain number of state legislatures share this objective separate and apart from the representation of states in Congress. By contrast, Article V effectively lets the states vote twice—first in Congress, and then in the state legislatures or ratifying conventions. Moreover, Article V lets the states vote twice for purposes of determining first whether there is two-thirds support and then whether there is three-fourths support. Comparing Article V with other parts of the Constitution, it is no wonder that the Constitution has proven so difficult to amend.

It is one thing to conclude that formal constitutional change should require a higher threshold of support than ordinary legislative change. In this regard, as already noted, Article V is indeed different from the other parts of the Constitution just mentioned. But it is another thing to say that formal constitutional change requires multiple supermajority thresholds of support to be satisfied—first by an entity in which the Constitution generally deems the states to be adequately represented, and then by the states themselves. The difference between formal constitutional change and ordinary legislative change does not justify this framework.

Historical practice suggests that, for purposes of amending the Constitution, state legislatures and the American people are reasonably well represented in Congress, just as state citizens are reasonably well represented in their state legislatures. As noted, Congress has always been the entity to propose constitutional amendments, and state legislatures have nearly always been the entities to ratify them. The sole exception was the repeal of prohibition. This amendment occurred, however, well before the Court's one-person, one-vote decision in *Reynolds v. Sims* (1964), which required all state legislative districts to be roughly equal in population.[16] Because popular support for the repeal of prohibition was strongest in urban areas, which were underrepresented in most state legislatures,

---

[16] 377 U.S. 533 (1964).

the issue did implicate a potential disconnect between malapportioned state legislatures and statewide public opinion.[17]

Past practice lends support to the Marshallian account, even if one could quibble with drawing such an inference. Perhaps the threat of a state-initiated process has helped prompt or deter Congress, which (as discussed below) may have been true regarding the Bill of Rights. Maybe state legislatures would have made good on this threat more often if not for concerns about "runaway conventions"—the fear that if state legislatures voted to require Congress to call a convention for proposing amendments, such a convention could consider any proposals, including those not contemplated by the state legislatures themselves.[18] But the practice need not be dispositive to be suggestive, and the representation of state legislatures in Congress (and state citizens in state legislatures) is suggested by the facts that (1) only six amendment proposals have passed Congress only to be rejected by state legislatures (although one cannot know how many more would have passed Congress had the states not been part of the process), and, as noted, (2) Congress has only once bypassed state legislatures.[19]

This comparison of Article V with both the Marshallian theory of democratic legitimacy and certain parts of the Constitution does not compel a particular amendment process that would be superior to Article V. But the above analysis does suggest that, when formally amending the Constitution, states should not be overrepresented out of distrust of Congress or state

---

[17] Congress chose the convention method of ratification for the Twenty-First Amendment mainly due to concerns that state legislators might not track public opinion. John C. Gebhart, *Movement Against Prohibition*, 163 ANNALS. AM. ACAD. POL. & SOC. SCI. 172, 180 (1932) (observing that "[t]he chief arguments for submitting the proposed amendment to popular state conventions are: (1) urban sections, where repeal sentiment is strongest, are inadequately represented in most state legislatures; [and] (2) delegates to state conventions would be elected solely on the question of repeal or retention of the Eighteenth Amendment"). State conventions avoided both the malapportionment of state legislatures at the time and the demands placed on legislators by single-issue interest groups like the temperance lobby. Given the first concern, Congress might have chosen state legislatures had it proposed the amendment after *Reynolds v. Sims*.

[18] Michael B. Rappaport, *The Constitutionality of a Limited Convention: An Originalist Analysis*, 81 CONST. COMMENT. 53, 55–56 (2012). In addition to making this predictive claim, Professor Rappaport seeks to refute the arguments of Professors Bruce Ackerman, Charles Black, Walter Dellinger, Gerald Gunther, and Michael Paulsen that a limited convention would violate Article V. *Id.* at 62.

[19] CONG. RSCH. SERV., THE CONSTITUTION OF THE UNITED STATES OF AMERICA, ANALYSIS AND INTERPRETATION, S. Doc. No. 112-9, at 49–51 (2013), https://perma.cc/BH7T-PWVM. The proposals that passed Congress but went unratified by enough states would have (1) more closely regulated the number of representatives in the House rather than leaving Congress with more discretion (1789); (2) barred citizens who had accepted titles of nobility or related honors from foreign governments from holding office and remaining citizens (1810); (3) prohibited amendments that permitted congressional interference with slavery in the states (1861); (4) permitted Congress to regulate child labor (1924); (5) added the Equal Rights Amendment (ERA) (1971); and (6) treated Washington, DC, as a state for purposes of representation in Congress, the election of the president, and Article V. Whether the failure to ratify these proposals suggests that the Constitution is too difficult to formally amend depends on how one evaluates them normatively and in terms of their significance.

406 THE COLLECTIVE-ACTION CONSTITUTION

governments. One possible alternative to Article V would require two-thirds support in each House of Congress, where all states and interests are represented, to propose and ratify amendments. Imposing a separate process of state ratification effectively lets the states vote twice, and requiring the second vote to command three-fourths support adds to the overkill. Another possible alternative to Article V would permit state action as a supplement to congressional action—that is, a system in which Congress could propose and ratify amendments by a two-thirds vote in each House, but state legislatures or conventions could also propose and ratify amendments by a two-thirds vote outside Congress. Permitting states to amend the Constitution outside Congress might be helpful if what is needed are amendments to provisions that benefit sitting members of Congress.

Article V's Supermajority Rules in Numerical and Comparative Perspective

The foregoing collective-action analysis and conclusion is buttressed by examining Article V's multiple supermajority rules from several other perspectives. The first is numerical. The impact of supermajority voting rules on the ability of the states to act collectively was likely less severe during the Article VII ratification process, when the number of states was thirteen, than during the process of deciding whether to ratify an amendment today, when the number of states is fifty. When the Constitution was drafted, the difference between majority rule (seven states) and a two-thirds requirement (nine states) was a difference of two states. The difference between a two-thirds requirement (again, nine states) and a three-fourths requirement (ten states) was a difference of one state. Today, the collective-action dynamics are different. As Chapter 2 discussed, as the number of states that must agree to act collectively grows, so do the number of states that can increase their bargaining power by holding out, which increases the overall costs of bargaining and so (all else equal) makes collective action harder to accomplish.

Bargaining and holding out can occur during the amendment-proposal process within Congress, among state legislatures when deciding whether to require Congress to call a convention, or within such a convention itself. Less intuitively, bargaining and holding out can also occur during the ratification process. This happened during the Article VII process when certain state conventions that voted for the Constitution demanded amendments. Put differently, the constitutional politics of ratification may entail more than a simple vote on an amendment proposal. Thus, regardless of whether the Framers realized this tendency and regardless of how much work they expected the Admissions Clause to do, the process of formally amending the Constitution then likely imposed fewer impediments to collective action than it does now.

Today, two-thirds of the 100-member Senate is 67 members. Two-thirds of the 435-member House of Representatives is 290 members. Two-thirds of the states is 34 states, and three-fourths is 38 states. Article V's procedural requirements mean that even proposed amendments supported by significant supermajorities in Congress and the nation will be defeated. They will be defeated if one-third plus one member of the House of Representatives opposes the proposed amendment (145 members opposed, 289 in favor); *or* if one-third plus one member of the Senate opposes the amendment (34 members opposed, 66 in favor); *or* if 13 state legislative chambers oppose the amendment (13 chambers opposed, 86 in favor).[20]

Comparative experience also suggests that the Article V process is extraordinarily demanding. Article V makes formal constitutional change more difficult to accomplish than any US state constitution. In a healthy federal system, learning flows in both directions, not just from the national constitutional experience to the states. Further, Article V makes constitutional change more challenging to produce than almost every other democratic constitution in the world. State constitutions and other national constitutions are formally amended at a much higher rate than the US Constitution—roughly once every year or two.[21] Granted, formal requirements are not all that determine the frequency of amendments. For example, partisan polarization, which is examined below and in the next chapter, significantly affects the ability of Congress and the states to satisfy Article V's requirements. But multiple supermajority voting rules of increasing strength also matter.[22]

---

[20] There are ninety-nine state legislative chambers, not one hundred, because Nebraska has a unicameral legislature.

[21] JACK M. BALKIN, LIVING ORIGINALISM 113–14 (2011) (noting that among national constitutions, "the American Constitution is one of the most difficult to amend" and "the constitutions of the individual states, and those of many other democratic nations have much less arduous procedures"); Richard Albert, *The World's Most Difficult Constitution to Amend?*, 110 CALIF. L. REV. 2005, 2007–08 (2022) (explaining that comparative legal scholars have long "situated the U.S. Constitution at the high end of constitutional rigidity," and concluding that "the Constitution may be the world's most difficult to amend"); Eric Posner, *The U.S. Constitution Is Impossible to Amend*, SLATE (May 5, 2014), https://perma.cc/VMD3-QBNE (noting that "Germany amends its Basic Law almost once per year," "France [does so] a bit more than once every two years," and "most *states in the U.S.* amend their constitutions every couple of years").

[22] Professor Posner writes that amendment procedures "in states and most liberal democracies are much easier than they are for the U.S Constitution. For example, in Germany, an amendment requires a two-thirds majority in each House, and that's it." Posner, *supra* note 21. *See* Marcia Coyle, *Scalia, Ginsburg Offer Amendments to the Constitution*, LEGAL TIMES (Apr. 17, 2014), https://www.law.com/nationallawjournal/almID/1202651605161/?/, on file with author at https://perma.cc/7VPK-2GPG (reporting that Justice Scalia said "he once calculated what percentage of the population could prevent an amendment to the Constitution and found it was less than 2 percent," and quoting Scalia as then stating that "[i]t ought to be hard, but not that hard").

408   THE COLLECTIVE-ACTION CONSTITUTION

Historical Practice

Past practice further illustrates the great difficulty of amending the Constitution. By the start of 2019, roughly 11,848 constitutional amendments had been proposed in Congress. Yet in more than 235 years of enormous changes in social conditions and values, the Constitution has been amended only 27 times, a success rate of 0.228 percent.[23] Moreover, even this low number likely understates the difficulty of running the Article V gauntlet once the new constitutional regime had been established. To defend the severity of Article V's supermajority requirements while also accounting for existing amendments, one must believe that Article V's requirements can permissibly be avoided or evaded in certain high-stakes situations. One must also believe that constitutional change should not occur unless one of two situations exists: (1) where such change is supported by an overwhelming consensus within American society because the transformation in popular values and expectations of government has already occurred, because overwhelming support exists in response to relatively recent events, or a combination of the two; or (2) where a relatively uncontroversial coordination problem must be solved.

Added in 1791, the first ten amendments were essentially an extension of the Article VII ratification process; several state ratifying conventions conditioned their votes for the Constitution on the addition of amendments. Madison and others in the first Congress honored this demand, which was easier to do because there were many proposals from which to choose. Members of Congress were motivated in part by the promises they had made to their state ratifying conventions or constituents, and in part by the possibility that state legislatures would initiate the process of calling a convention if Congress failed to act.[24]

The Eleventh and Twelfth Amendments are also fairly deemed part of the process of establishing the new constitutional regime; they addressed an arguable oversight and a definite lack of foresight that was widely recognized to require attention. The Eleventh Amendment reflected vehement and widespread opposition to the early Supreme Court's understanding of the scope of state sovereign immunity from lawsuits by private parties, a long-standing doctrine that the original text of the Constitution did not expressly reference.[25] The Twelfth Amendment remedied the Framers' failure to anticipate political parties, which

---

[23] *Measures Proposed to Amend the Constitution*, U.S. Senate, https://perma.cc/LUM5-92NK (last visited Jun. 1, 2021) (stating that "[a]pproximately 11,848 measures have been proposed to amend the Constitution from 1789 through January 3, 2019").

[24] Amar, *supra* note 10, at 317–18.

[25] Chisholm v. Georgia, 2 U.S. (2 Dall.) 419 (1793) (reasoning that Article III, Section 2, overrode state sovereign immunity by permitting the federal courts to hear all suits between states and citizens of other states, including diversity suits in which states are defendants). The Eleventh Amendment overrules *Chisholm*, providing that "[t]he Judicial power of the United States shall not be construed to extend to any suit in law or equity, commenced or prosecuted against one of the United States by Citizens of another State, or by Citizens or Subjects of any Foreign State." The modern scope of state

arose soon after the Constitution was established. The original Constitution did not instruct electors to cast separate votes for president and vice-president, and these rules had twice resulted in the election of a president and vice-president who were political opponents.[26] The Twelfth Amendment, which requires electors to cast separate votes for president and vice-president, was ratified in 1804, and the Constitution would not again be amended until after the Civil War.

Of the remaining fifteen amendments, three survived the Article V process because they did not follow it in any conventional sense. The Thirteenth Amendment, Professor David Strauss explains, "received crucial ratification votes from state legislatures in ex-Confederate states that were controlled by governments installed by the North." In addition, the Fourteenth Amendment would not have been approved if ex-Confederate states had not been "required to ratify [it] to be readmitted to the Union," and "those states still outside the Union were required to ratify the Fifteenth Amendment."[27] Commentators debate whether some of these maneuvers were legally justified under the circumstances,[28] but it is less debatable whether the Civil War Amendments illustrate the general viability of amending the Constitution. Aptly named, the Civil War Amendments resulted primarily from the military settlement of the most fundamental, enduring disagreement among Americans during the Constitution's first seventy-plus years of existence: slavery in the territories, as Chapter 8 discussed.

Several other amendments were ratified primarily because they formalized changes that had mostly occurred and so mainly policed outliers. For example, the Seventeenth Amendment provided for the direct election of senators and so overrode the original Constitution's requirement of appointment by state legislatures.[29] As Professor Strauss explains, "[t]he change occurred, for all practical purposes, before the Amendment was adopted; the effect of the Amendment was to ratify a change that had already taken place." States responded to popular demands for direct election of US senators by, among other things, requiring candidates for the state legislature to declare whether they would vote for the

---

sovereign immunity extends well beyond the text of the amendment, and commentators dispute the soundness of the Court's doctrine. For further discussion, see the Conclusion to this book.

[26] U.S. CONST. art. II, § 1, cl. 3. Democratic-Republican Thomas Jefferson was vice-president when Federalist John Adams was president, and Aaron Burr was vice-president during President Thomas Jefferson's first term.

[27] David A. Strauss, *The Irrelevance of Constitutional Amendments*, 114 HARV. L. REV. 1457, 1479 (2001). Professor Strauss likely means "readmitted to Congress," not "the Union." The congressional theory of Reconstruction was that secessionist states had never left the Union.

[28] *Compare* BRUCE ACKERMAN, 2 WE THE PEOPLE: TRANSFORMATIONS 99–119, 207–34 (1998) (concluding that the Fourteenth Amendment is not an Article V amendment), *with* AMAR, *supra* note 10, at 364–80 (disagreeing).

[29] U.S. CONST. art. I, § 3, cl. 1.

410 THE COLLECTIVE-ACTION CONSTITUTION

US Senate candidate who received the most popular votes in the state-held election.[30] The Twenty-Fourth Amendment also mostly formalized changes that had already occurred. When it was proposed, "only five states had poll taxes," and the amendment "forbade those states from using the poll tax in federal elections—a clear example of an amendment that has the effect only of suppressing outliers."[31] One can appreciate the role of such amendments in bringing about national uniformity, enhancing access to the franchise, and preventing backsliding while still accepting Professor Strauss's point that the amendments were much more the effect than the cause of transformations in social values.

Two amendments responded to relatively recent events that aroused strong opposition. As Chapter 4 discussed, the Sixteenth Amendment overruled the Court's aberrant decision in *Pollock v. Farmers' Loan & Trust Company* (1895), which held that federal taxation of income derived from real or personal property—in *Pollock*, rental or dividend income—was direct taxation and so subject to the constitutional requirement of apportionment, in contrast to income taxes on wages (among other things), which were not.[32] This decision was in tension with both public sentiment and the Court's jurisprudence before and after it was rendered.[33] In a similar vein, the Twenty-Second Amendment, which prohibits individuals from being elected president more than twice, responded to an aberration.[34] Ratified in 1951, this amendment constitutionalized the apparent constitutional convention against presidents serving more than two terms, which had been set by President Washington and respected until President Franklin Delano Roosevelt ran for and won a third and then a fourth term.[35]

The story of the Nineteenth Amendment, which prohibits denials of the franchise on account of sex, is complex. On one hand, Americans debated women's suffrage, and women's citizenship more broadly, for more than a half-century before the amendment was ratified in 1920. During this period, suffragists such as Susan B. Anthony, Elizabeth Cady Stanton, and others sought to rebut arguments

---

[30] Strauss, *supra* note 27, at 1496; *see id.* at 1496–98.

[31] *Id.* at 1481.

[32] 158 U.S. 601 (1895).

[33] Strauss, *supra* note 27, at 1491.

[34] Section One of the Twenty-Second Amendment also prohibits anyone who has acted as president for more than two years of another elected president's term from being elected president more than once.

[35] JAMES ALBERT WOODBURN, THE AMERICAN REPUBLIC AND ITS GOVERNMENT 115 (2d ed. 1916) ("[I]t may now be said to be a part of the unwritten constitution that no President is eligible to a third term."). *But see* HERBERT W. HORWILL, THE USAGES OF THE AMERICAN CONSTITUTION 99 (1925) ("The usage, if usage it be, is not so firmly established as absolutely to deter an ambitious man from making the venture."). Before Roosevelt, presidents and their supporters at times contemplated a possible third term. *See* MICHAEL J. KORZI, PRESIDENTIAL TERM LIMITS IN AMERICAN HISTORY: POWER, PRINCIPLES & POLITICS 43–78 (2011); Bruce G. Peabody & Scott E. Gant, *The Twice and Future President: Constitutional Interstices and the Twenty-Second Amendment*, 83 MINN. L. REV. 565, 579–84 (1999).

that enfranchising women was: (1) unnecessary because women were virtually represented by their husbands; (2) a threat to the American family because it would sow marital discord (an argument inconsistent with the idea of virtual representation); and (3) a danger to the federal system because an amendment would undermine state control over domestic relations law. Such arguments had long and passionately been advanced by powerful opponents of women's suffrage, who did not need to worry about alienating women for most of this era because they did not need their votes.[36] The fact that such arguments, which had succeeded for so many decades, did not ultimately prevail might support an inference that the Nineteenth Amendment validated a transformation in popular values that was a long time in the making. Additional support for such a conclusion might be found in the fact that the amendment policed outliers, especially in the South, where opposition was strongest.[37] Moreover, in the years following ratification of the Nineteenth Amendment, there were no significant attempts to evade it, in stark contrast to the shameful history of the Fifteenth Amendment.

On the other hand, the situation looked very different only a decade before the Nineteenth Amendment was ratified. The political momentum moved strongly in the direction of the suffragists only beginning in 1910, when more states than the previous few in the West began giving women full or partial voting rights. Numerous considerations help explain the change in momentum and the ultimate ratification of the amendment. They include the examples set by first-moving states, which corroborated that neither calamity nor political transformation resulted when women voted; the ability of suffragists—but not their opponents—to fight again (and again) when they lost in a state; the need for federal and state politicians to be on the right side of the issue once women were voting in their states or close to becoming enfranchised; the ethos of good government during the Progressive Era; America's entry into World War I, including women's support for the war effort and President Wilson's eventual insistence that the amendment was part of the democratic project Americans were fighting to advance; and Congress's decision to send the proposed amendment to state legislatures (whose members had reason to fear losing the support of current or future women voters), not state ratifying conventions (whose delegates did not need to worry about such matters).[38] The late-breaking and partially contingent movement in favor of the Nineteenth Amendment might suggest that it was not

---

[36] Reva B. Siegel, *She the People: The Nineteenth Amendment, Sex Equality, Federalism, and the Family*, 115 Harv. L. Rev. 947 (2002); *see* Alexander Keyssar, The Right to Vote: The Contested History of Democracy in the United States 172–221 (2000).

[37] Gerald L. Ingalls, Gerald R. Webster, & Jonathan I. Leib, *Fifty Years of Political Change in the South: Electing African Americans and Women to Public Office*, 37 Se. Geographer 140, 141 (1997).

[38] Amar, *supra* note 10, at 419–25; Neil S. Siegel, *Why the Nineteenth Amendment Matters Today: A Guide for the Centennial*, 27 Duke J. Gender L. & Pol'y 235, 242–45, 250 (2020).

412   THE COLLECTIVE-ACTION CONSTITUTION

simply the result of a social transformation that had already occurred or would have soon occurred absent the amendment.

Thus, it may not be clear how best to categorize the Nineteenth Amendment. Most likely, it resulted from a combination of both longer-term changes and shorter-term events. Regardless, the mission of the suffragists was long and arduous, and it benefited from not just hard work and smart strategy but also good fortune. The Nineteenth Amendment illustrates the great difficulty, not the viability, of amending the Constitution. It should not have taken 132 years for the Constitution to protect women from sex-based disenfranchisements.

Professors McGinnis and Rappaport argue that the Seventeenth and Nineteenth Amendments "provid[e] compelling evidence that the amendment process is not too strict." According to them, these amendments "show that social and technological change can generate the consensus required by Article V to make necessary constitutional transformations even when they strike at interests powerfully vested in the amendment process itself." The interests to which they refer were those of members of state legislatures and members of Congress, who were either cut out of the process of choosing US senators by the Seventeenth Amendment (members of state legislatures); or who would be elected by a different method once the Seventeenth Amendment was ratified (US senators); or who would dilute the voting power of the men they represented by voting for the Nineteenth Amendment (members of Congress and state legislatures).[39] As explained, however, the relevant changes had mostly occurred when state legislators and US senators voted for the Seventeenth Amendment; the "interests powerfully vested in the amendment process itself" had already been largely divested. Given elections, politicians almost never have an interest in preserving personal powers when doing so alienates their electorate. As also explained, those who voted for the Nineteenth Amendment had reason to fear current or future women voters, not just men. In any event, the voting power of men would be diluted by the amendment only to the extent that women as a group would vote differently from men as a group on important issues, creating a new cleavage in American politics. As noted above, and as Professor Alexander Keyssar shows, experience prior to passage of the amendment demonstrated that this would not occur, and such a cleavage never materialized after ratification.[40]

The Eighteenth Amendment, which imposed national prohibition, is the only amendment that has been repealed (by the Twenty-First). Professors McGinnis and Rappaport contend that the existence of an amendment that was (and is)

[39] MCGINNIS & RAPPAPORT, *supra* note 11, at 69.
[40] KEYSSAR, *supra* note 36, at 219 ("The victories of the suffrage drive were built in part on the ever-widening perception among men that the enfranchisement of women would not significantly transform politics or policy. ... Sex, thus, did not prove to be a significant line of cleavage in the American electorate ....").

perceived to have been a mistake "illustrat[es] the dangers of a less stringent amendment process."[41] It seems unlikely, however, that an optimal amendment process is one that will generate no errors of inclusion or exclusion. Perfection is not something that can reasonably be expected of structural arrangements. The fact that there has been only one error of inclusion in 235 years suggests that there have been many more errors of exclusion—that the Constitution is too hard to amend, not too easy or just right.

Still other amendments primarily solved coordination problems that did not generate significant disagreements in American society regarding how to do so. An example is the Twentieth Amendment, which moved Inauguration Day from March 4 to January 20; specified January 3 as the day when the terms of members of Congress would end and Congress would presumptively convene; and addressed presidential succession if a president-elect or presidential candidate died. Another example is the Twenty-Fifth Amendment, which primarily explains how to proceed in cases of potential presidential disability. Still another example is the Twenty-Sixth Amendment, which provides that eighteen-year-olds may not be denied the right to vote in any election on account of age. As Professor Strauss explains, this amendment addressed an unworkable situation. In the Voting Rights Act, Congress had prohibited states from denying eighteen-year-olds the right to vote, but the Court had upheld this part of the legislation only as applied to federal elections.[42] Rather than have the states conduct elections with two different electorates, Congress and the states quickly agreed to lower the voting age to eighteen in all elections.[43]

These three amendments are all important, just like deciding which side of the road everyone must drive on saves many lives. The point is not relative importance, but the difficulty of amending the Constitution. It is far easier to amend the Constitution when doing so will solve pure coordination problems than when coordination problems involve strong disagreements—or when the amendment will have to resolve disagreements apart from coordination problems.

It is difficult to characterize the sui generis Twenty-Seventh Amendment, which prohibits congressional pay changes from going into effect until after the next elections for the House of Representatives. The amendment was proposed in 1789, ignored for long stretches of time, and not ratified until 1992, more than two hundred years later. Whatever else can be said of this low-stakes, oddball amendment, the time required to ratify it does not illustrate the feasibility of amending the Constitution. This amendment aside, the Constitution has not been amended since 1971—for more than half a century.

---

[41] McGINNIS & RAPPAPORT, *supra* note 11, at 72.
[42] Oregon v. Mitchell, 400 U.S. 112 (1970).
[43] Strauss, *supra* note 27, at 1486–89.

414 THE COLLECTIVE-ACTION CONSTITUTION

During this period, the Equal Rights Amendment (ERA) was almost ratified. First introduced in Congress in 1923, the ERA would have provided that "[e]quality of rights under the law shall not be denied or abridged by the United States or by any state on account of sex."[44] The ERA received far more than two-thirds support in each House of Congress and more than two-thirds support in the states—thirty-five in all. As a countermobilization against the ERA gained momentum, however, five states purported to rescind their ratifications and, attempted rescissions aside, the amendment did not meet the three-fourths requirement for ratification within the ten-year extended deadline set by Congress. Between 2017 and 2020, Nevada, Illinois, and Virginia ratified the ERA, leading some ERA advocates to argue that Article V's three-fourths requirement of thirty-eight states had been reached. The legal soundness of this claim turns on whether the deadline set by Congress is binding, whether Congress can waive the deadline after it has expired, and whether the state rescissions are valid.[45]

These complex issues will not be addressed here. What is clear is that the ERA was not ratified in the 1970s despite more than two-thirds support in Congress and the states, and Congress has not proposed it again. Whatever one thinks of the ERA's merits, its story is in part about the difficulty of amending the Constitution. The failure to ratify the ERA is not explicable mainly on the ground that opponents deemed it unnecessary given the Court's gender-equality rulings, or that opponents feared it would be interpreted in a non-originalist fashion.[46] These arguments were never the main objections of opponents, nor can they account for the intensity of the opposition. The ERA has mainly been a fight about gender roles in the family and social life. In her first published attack on the ERA, Phyllis Schlafly, who led the countermobilization against it, stated that "[w]omen's lib is a total assault on the role of the American woman as wife and mother, and on the family as the basic unit of society."[47]

Evaluating Past Practice

In sum, to defend Article V's supermajority rules while also accounting for existing amendments, one must believe that Article V's requirements can appropriately be avoided or circumvented when the stakes are high enough. One must also believe that constitutional change should not occur unless such change is

---

[44] Brennan Center for Justice, The Equal Rights Amendment Explained, https://perma.cc/6Y57-36KR.

[45] Id.

[46] MCGINNIS & RAPPAPORT, supra note 11, at 93–94.

[47] Reva B. Siegel, Constitutional Culture, Social Movement Conflict and Constitutional Change: The Case of the de facto ERA, 94 CAL. L. REV. 1323, 1391 (2006) (quoting Phyllis Schlafly, What Is Wrong with "Equal Rights" for Women, 5 PHYLLIS SCHLAFLY REP. 4 (Feb. 1972)).

supported by an overwhelming consensus within American society, or where a relatively pure coordination problem must be solved. Such a view of legitimate constitutional change can be evaluated normatively and positively.

Normatively, it does not seem persuasive to defend the strictness of legal requirements by identifying measures to avoid or circumvent them, in which case the requirements may not be well described as strict. Article V's defenders do not make this argument. Likewise, few people would argue that constitutional change should be limited to solving coordination problems, and Article V's defenders do not make this argument either. Constitutional change also exists to impose value choices amid at least some normative dissensus regardless of coordination difficulties. The strongest of the above arguments for Article V's demands is that constitutional change should not occur until an overwhelming societal consensus supports the change. Waiting for such a consensus can perhaps best be defended as promoting social stability, encouraging bipartisanship, and protecting minorities from majorities.[48]

This claim can be critiqued by drawing from a rich literature in the history of political thought and modern political science concerning the vulnerabilities of strong supermajority voting rules.[49] First, there are times when political communities require change more than they require stability. For example, certain kinds of constitutional change might be needed to reflect major changes in social circumstances and values and consequent alterations in most Americans' expectations of government—and waiting for an overwhelming societal consensus might take many years or decades. How long, one might ask, should Americans living during the Great Depression have had to wait for societal consensus to be reached on a much-expanded conception of Congress's enumerated powers? How long should people of color have had to wait for *Brown v. Board of Education* (1954)?[50] One cannot persuasively avoid the force of such questions by arguing long after the fact that government-mandated racial segregation violates

---

[48] McGinnis & Rappaport, *supra* note 11, at 12–13, 33–61. Other arguments for strict supermajority voting rules are less persuasive. One is that supermajorities will not approve rules that oppress minorities because the rules cannot easily be repealed and supermajorities fear being minorities in the future. *Id.* at 13. This idea fails to explain, *inter alia*, the supermajority of state conventions that ratified a constitution protecting slavery. Another argument is that supermajority rules produce good outcomes in the present no matter how long ago the votes were cast. *Id.* at 81–99. Goodness depends upon many considerations, including what one means by goodness. Assuming goodness can be defined as some broadly held conception of human well-being (and that this conception can be broadly held in the contemporary United States), such goodness is unlikely to be produced by supermajority rules when the supermajorities voted centuries ago without knowledge of dramatic changes in social conditions, values, problems, and expectations of government. For example, US Supreme Court justices would likely lack life tenure had the Founders understood the Court's future power and increased human longevity. Only supermajorities of overwhelming strength can change this arrangement.

[49] For an impressive treatment, see Schwartzberg, *supra* note 5.

[50] 347 U.S. 483 (1954).

416 THE COLLECTIVE-ACTION CONSTITUTION

the original meaning of the Equal Protection Clause. Few people thought so at the time.

Second, when maintaining the status quo is deemed most attractive by a sufficiently large minority of decision-makers (because, say, a bill can be left unenacted or a nominee can go unconfirmed), strict supermajority voting rules are as likely to result in paralysis as consensus. For example, the modern filibuster, which effectively requires sixty votes to pass most bills in the Senate, has not tended to produce bipartisan cooperation. As a result, the filibuster has been abandoned by majority vote as to judicial appointments, and it may be abandoned as to legislation in the years ahead.[51] As supermajority rules go, the filibuster is substantially less onerous than a two-thirds or three-fourths threshold, and still it has not produced consensus.

Third, a strong presumption against change will affect different groups differently and in potentially troubling ways. Generally, privileged groups are most likely to benefit from strong status-quo bias, and members of traditionally excluded groups are most likely to be harmed by major impediments to change. Although supermajority rules are often touted as protecting minorities from exploitation by the majority, they do not accomplish this task when minorities are being exploited in the status quo. In this situation, supermajority rules make it harder for coalitions of minorities to combat their oppression.[52] A similar concern is raised by the argument that the nation's allegiance to the Constitution would be threatened by constitutional changes vehemently opposed by a small minority of the country.[53] This defense of strict supermajority rules misses the threats to allegiance caused by strong opposition to the status quo.

It is difficult, however, to gain traction over these normative questions at a relatively high level of abstraction. First, constitutional change can do more harm than good. A relatively uncontroversial example is the Eighteenth Amendment. In addition, examples such as the Great Depression and *Brown* do not identify just how much less supermajoritarian constitutional change should be relative to Article V. Second, when certain conditions are met, such as a willingness to exhibit ideological self-restraint and a shared perception that action is required, supermajority rules can be conducive to compromise, not paralysis.[54] Third, there have been periods in American history in which constitutional change

---

[51] Neil S. Siegel, *After the Trump Era: A Constitutional Role Morality for Presidents and Members of Congress*, 107 GEO. L.J. 109, 141–43 (2018) (discussing the Senate's partisan handling of judicial nominations, including the role of each party in ending the filibuster as to all judicial appointments). The legislative filibuster is discussed in Chapter 11.

[52] Anthony J. McGann, *The Tyranny of the Supermajority: How Majority Rule Protects Minorities*, 16 J. THEOR. POL. 53 (2004).

[53] McGINNIS & RAPPAPORT, *supra* note 11, at 12.

[54] Siegel, *supra* note 51, at 141 (writing that "the filibuster as to appointments or legislation will promote bipartisanship . . . when the majority and the minority parties participate in the political process with ideological self-restraint").

outside the Article V process exacerbated social subordination. The Taney Court made the Constitution more pro-slavery than it originally was,[55] and the Court during the Republican Era, reflecting cultural currents, made the Reconstructed Constitution more racist than it was in 1868 or 1870.[56]

Matters are less speculative, however, if one asks whether Americans have been willing to abide the strength of Article V's presumption in favor of the status quo. Americans have largely been unwilling to wait for a small minority to agree to constitutional change. This conclusion makes the most sense of the fact that the constitutional text (called the "Big-C" Constitution by constitutional theorists) has been left unaltered by dramatic changes over time in the basic political institutions of the United States, the powers exercised by them, and the rights protected by them. These institutions can be described as the "small-c" constitution, the American constitutional regime or order, or the Constitution in practice.[57]

Two related examples are the Court's acceptance, beginning in 1937, of the dramatic expansion of congressional authority, and the Court's simultaneous rejection of the long-standing deregulatory doctrine that protected freedom of contract.[58] These changes provided the constitutional foundations for the post-New Deal regulatory and welfare state, which undergirds federal and state protection of economically vulnerable Americans, workers, public health, public safety, the market, the environment, and civil rights. As Chapter 5 discussed, these protections persist with relatively modest constitutional pushback to date. A third example, related to the first two, is the entrenchment of the modern administrative state, which does not appear in the text and could be viewed as in some tension with the separation-of-powers system created by the first three articles.[59] Still another (related) example is the power flow from Congress to

---

[55] *See, e.g.,* Prigg v. Pennsylvania, 41 U.S. (16 Pet.) 539 (1842) (questionably concluding that Congress had an exclusive obligation to regulate the rendition process); Abelman v. Booth, 62 U.S. (21 How.) 506 (1859) (similar); Dred Scott v. Sandford, 60 U.S. (19 How.) 393 (1857) (implausibly concluding that Congress lacked the authority to regulate slavery in the territories).

[56] As the first Justice John Marshall Harlan argued in dissent, the original understanding of the Civil War Amendments did not require the reasoning or results in *The Civil Rights Cases,* 109 U.S. 3 (1883) (invalidating a federal ban on racial discrimination in public accommodations), or *Plessy v. Ferguson,* 163 U.S. 537 (1896) (upholding government-mandated racial segregation in railroad cars). *See* Ernest A. Young, *Dying Constitutionalism and the Fourteenth Amendment,* 102 MARQUETTE L. REV. 949, 959–60, 969–71 (2019).

[57] For work distinguishing between the "small-c" constitution and the "Big-C" Constitution, see WILLIAM N. ESKRIDGE, JR. & JOHN FEREJOHN, A REPUBLIC OF STATUTES: THE NEW AMERICAN CONSTITUTION 1–28 (2010); Curtis A. Bradley & Neil S. Siegel, *Constructed Constraint and the Constitutional Text,* 64 DUKE L.J. 1213, 1215–16, 1268, 1274, 1277 (2015); Richard Primus, *Unbundling Constitutionality,* 80 U. CHI. L. REV. 1079, 1082–83 (2013); Frederick Schauer, *Amending the Presuppositions of a Constitution, in* RESPONDING TO IMPERFECTION: THE THEORY AND PRACTICE OF CONSTITUTIONAL AMENDMENT 145, 156–57 (Sanford Levinson ed., 1995); and Strauss, *supra* note 27, at 1459–60, 1468, 1505.

[58] On economic substantive due process, see, for example, *Lochner v. New York,* 198 U.S. 45 (1905).

[59] Strauss, *supra* note 27, at 1472–73. Among other potential tensions with the constitutional text, agencies combine the functions of all three branches of government.

418   THE COLLECTIVE-ACTION CONSTITUTION

the president beginning in the twentieth century via delegations to executive-branch agencies and in other ways, especially in the areas of foreign affairs and war powers.[60] A final example is the rise in the constitutional status of members of several racial and ethnic minority groups, women, members of the LGBTQ+ community, religious Americans, and gun owners.[61]

With Americans' demand for constitutional change far surpassing the quantity that Article V can supply, Americans have elected representatives who have passed laws and appointed executive-branch officials and judges who have developed two constitutional workarounds. First, elected representatives and government officials have engaged in acts of state (re)building by passing laws and creating institutions that serve constitutional purposes.[62] Second, and perhaps more commonly recognized, judicial interpretations of the powers and rights provisions in the Constitution—which have mostly approved these laws and institutions—have helped produce a constitutional regime that past generations of Americans would not have recognized and that current generations have required to regard the Constitution as their own.[63]

These two workarounds are not, however, perfect substitutes for Article V amendments. Many hardwired provisions of the Constitution—like the Electoral College method of electing the president, the various supermajority voting rules discussed in this chapter, the age requirements for holding federal offices, and the lengths of various terms of office—have meanings too determinate to work around, at least absent extraordinary, likely fanciful circumstances.[64] Moreover, the fact that workarounds can be produced more easily than Article V permits means that they can be abandoned more readily than Article V allows. The current Court's major changes in legal doctrine in many areas of law exemplify this point, and these changes are less democratic than Article V because they are accomplished by the Court alone. As workarounds go, however, state-building and

---

[60] BALKIN, *supra* note 21, at 5 (observing that "Congress has created the various parts of the executive branch—like the Defense Department and the Justice Department—to help the president carry out his duties to faithfully execute the laws and perform other constitutional functions," with the result that "the president is far more powerful today than anyone could have imagined in 1787").

[61] *See, e.g.*, Brown v. Bd. of Educ., 347 U.S. 483 (1954) (race); United States v. Virginia, 518 U.S. 515 (1996) (gender); Obergefell v. Hodges, 576 U.S. 644 (2015) (gay rights); Burwell v. Hobby Lobby Stores, Inc., 573 U.S. 682 (2014) (religious liberty); District of Columbia v. Heller, 554 U.S. 570 (2008) (gun rights).

[62] BALKIN, *supra* note 21, at 5–6, 33. For discussion of several purposes of the Constitution and of reasoning from constitutional purposes, see Chapter 1 and Siegel, *supra* note 51, at 126, 149–50.

[63] On the contingent nature of the public legitimacy of the Constitution and constitutional law, see BARRY FRIEDMAN, THE WILL OF THE PEOPLE: HOW PUBLIC OPINION HAS INFLUENCED THE SUPREME COURT AND SHAPED THE MEANING OF THE CONSTITUTION (2009); Richard H. Fallon, *Legitimacy and the Constitution*, 118 HARV. L. REV. 1787 (2005); and Neil S. Siegel, *The Virtue of Judicial Statesmanship*, 86 TEX. L. REV. 959 (2008).

[64] Bradley & Siegel, *supra* note 57, at 1285 n.383 ("Hypothesizing an unlikely scenario in which the text would be disregarded does not show that the text is unconstraining. Rather, it shows only that the text is not infinitely constraining.").

judicial review have proven reasonably effective. For example, it is probably too late to significantly shrink Congress's power, dismantle the administrative state, or terminate certain rights. As noted, pushback from politicians, administrators, and judges tends to be directed at the margins, although there is no guarantee that this trend will continue.[65]

One might seek to defend Article V's requirements by arguing, as Professors McGinnis and Rappaport do, that Article V would have produced more constitutional change had judges, elected officials, and federal administrators not been so impatient—if they had waited for an overwhelming societal consensus to emerge before taking assertive action by amending the Constitution.[66] It is plausible to think that there would be more Article V amendments had Article V been the exclusive avenue of constitutional change. But the foregoing discussion has not argued that Article V makes the Constitution effectively unamendable in any situation. It has contended that most Americans have demanded far more constitutional change than Article V could ever provide. Because the defense of Article V under consideration criticizes various federal actors for not waiting for an overwhelming societal consensus, the defense concedes that using Article V as the exclusive means of constitutional change would not have produced nearly as much change as has occurred. Indeed, significantly reducing the amount of constitutional change appears to be a main point of defending exclusive use of Article V.

It also seems unlikely that (super)majorities of Americans would have routinely tolerated federal actors who waited several or many decades longer than they did for an overwhelming societal consensus to possibly be achieved. For example, it might have taken decades longer before at least three-fourths of state legislatures or conventions would have freely approved an amendment ending government-mandated racial segregation and other forms of invidious discrimination against non-white Americans. The Court's racial-equality decisions and federal civil rights statutes have been the workarounds. A similar concern could be raised about gender equality, given that the ERA has not been ratified and the Court's gender-equality cases and certain federal laws have substituted for it. It is questionable to assume that Article V would have been used within a time horizon acceptable to a (super)majority of Americans—or used at all— had the Court waited however long it took for recalcitrant Americans to come around. Lest these concerns be deemed unduly pessimistic, it is worth noting

---

[65] For possible indications that the trend will not continue, see, for example, *Students for Fair Admissions, Inc. v. President and Fellows of Harvard College*, 143 S. Ct. 2141 (2023) (effectively overruling forty-five years of precedent permitting limited use of racial classifications in university admissions to increase the racial and ethnic diversity of the student body); and *Dobbs v. Jackson Women's Health Organization*, 142 S. Ct. 2228 (2022) (overruling, *inter alia*, Roe v. Wade, 410 U.S. 113 (1973), and Planned Parenthood of Se. Pa. v. Casey, 505 U.S. 833 (1992)).

[66] McGinnis & Rappaport, *supra* note 11, at 88–94.

420   THE COLLECTIVE-ACTION CONSTITUTION

that racism, sexism, misogyny, and other bigotry remain present in America today. Moreover, political leadership affects popular values on matters of race and gender, and exclusive reliance on Article V would have limited the efficacy of progressive leadership.[67]

Constitutional Theory and Article V

Important work in constitutional theory responds to the need to account for the reality of constitutional change absent Article V amendments. Rather than deny the legal legitimacy of change outside the Article V process and call for exclusive reliance on Article V, many commentators have offered theories that seek to explain why at least some of this change has been constitutionally permissible. Professor Bruce Ackerman has developed the influential theory that the Constitution can be amended outside the Article V process as a result of certain "constitutional moments."[68] By contrast, most theorists reject the idea of unwritten amendments to the text and instead emphasize changing interpretations of an unchanging text (until properly amended via Article V). Reflecting this view, some commentators have distinguished constitutional interpretation, which focuses on the original meaning of the text, from constitutional construction, which takes place when the text is unclear.[69]

Other theorists have been less concerned to tie their accounts to the text. They have defended the idea of an "unwritten Constitution,"[70] or developed a theory

---

[67] Cf. Peter K. Enns & Ashley Jardina, Complicating the Role of Racism and Anti-Immigrant Sentiment in the 2016 U.S. Presidential Election, 85 PUB. OP. Q. 539 (2021) (finding, inter alia, that the strong connection between white attitudes toward African Americans and support for Donald Trump during the 2016 presidential campaign . . . is probably due as much to Trump supporters' updating their survey answers to express opinions more consistent with Trump's as it is to Trump's gaining support from racially hostile voters).

[68] BRUCE ACKERMAN, 1 WE THE PEOPLE: FOUNDATIONS (1991); ACKERMAN, supra note 28; BRUCE ACKERMAN, 3 WE THE PEOPLE: THE CIVIL RIGHTS REVOLUTION (2014).

[69] BALKIN, supra note 21, at 3–6, 341 n.2; KEITH E. WHITTINGTON, CONSTITUTIONAL CONSTRUCTION: DIVIDED POWERS AND CONSTITUTIONAL MEANING 5–9 (1999); Randy E. Barnett, Interpretation and Construction, 34 HARV. J.L. & PUB. POL'Y 65 (2011); Mitchell N. Berman, Constitutional Constructions and Constitutional Decision Rules: Thoughts on the Carving of Implementation Space, 27 CONST. COMMENT. 39 (2010); Mitchell N. Berman, Constitutional Decision Rules, 90 VA. L. REV. 1 (2004); Lawrence B. Solum, Originalism and Constitutional Construction, 82 FORDHAM L. REV. 453 (2013).

[70] Thomas C. Grey, Do We Have an Unwritten Constitution?, 27 STAN. L. REV. 703 (1975); Thomas C. Grey, Origins of the Unwritten Constitution, 30 STAN. L. REV. 843 (1978); Thomas C. Grey, The Constitution as Scripture, 37 STAN. L. REV. 1 (1984); Thomas C. Grey, The Uses of an Unwritten Constitution, 64 CHI.-KENT L. REV. 211 (1988). For more recent discussions, see AKHIL REED AMAR, AMERICA'S UNWRITTEN CONSTITUTION: THE PRECEDENTS AND PRINCIPLES WE LIVE BY (2012); LAURENCE H. TRIBE, THE INVISIBLE CONSTITUTION (2008); Stephen E. Sachs, The "Unwritten Constitution" and Unwritten Law, 2013 U. ILL. L. REV. 1797; and Lawrence B. Solum, Originalism and the Unwritten Constitution, 2013 U. ILL. L. REV. 1935.

of common law constitutionalism,[71] or emphasized the role of unwritten "constitutional conventions."[72] Still other commentators have included materials like major federal statutes within a broader view of what counts as constitutional law, thereby reducing pressures to develop theories (like Professor Ackerman's) of how the Constitution can change absent Article V amendments.[73] Another group of scholars has destabilized the foregoing distinctions by explaining how the constitutional text itself is partially constructed by extratextual modalities of constitutional argument.[74] Notwithstanding all that divides these approaches, they recognize the reality of constitutional change absent Article V amendments and, to different extents, they seek to legitimate it.

Summary

The foregoing subsections have not proven that the Constitution is too difficult to amend. Such a claim, like its antithesis, is ultimately unprovable. But these subsections have offered substantial evidence for the soundness of this conclusion, which flows from a comparison of Article V with how other parts of the Constitution conceive of the relationship between the federal government and the states. Only Article V effectively lets the states vote twice, and the ill effects are suggested by numerical analysis, comparative experience at home and abroad, past practice, normative inquiry, the positive development of workarounds, and modern constitutional theory.

A defender of Article V could, however, respond in several ways. In addition to the counterarguments already discussed, perhaps every state and other countries are wrong according to some normative theory. Maybe, according to the same theory, Americans have also been wrong to demand so much constitutional change, or perhaps the amount of such change has been an elite-driven phenomenon that has taken Americans for a ride. Although more could be said in response to such claims, this subsection has offered reasons to doubt

[71] DAVID A. STRAUSS, THE LIVING CONSTITUTION (2010); David A. Strauss, *Common Law Constitutional Interpretation*, 63 U. CHI. L. REV. 877 (1996).

[72] Curtis A. Bradley & Neil S. Siegel, *Historical Gloss, Constitutional Conventions, and the Judicial Separation of Powers*, 105 GEO. L.J. 255 (2017); Michael C. Dorf, *How the Written Constitution Crowds Out the Extraconstitutional Rule of Recognition, in* THE RULE OF RECOGNITION AND THE U.S. CONSTITUTION 69 (Matthew D. Adler & Kenneth Einar Himma eds., 2009); Tara Leigh Grove, *The Origins (and Fragility) of Judicial Independence*, 71 VAND. L. REV. 465 (2018); David E. Pozen, *Self-Help and the Separation of Powers*, 124 YALE L.J. 2 (2014); Adrian Vermeule, *Conventions of Agency Independence*, 113 COLUM. L. REV. 1163 (2013).

[73] ESKRIDGE & FEREJOHN, *supra* note 57, at 1–28; MARK TUSHNET, WHY THE CONSTITUTION MATTERS 6–9 (2010); Ernest A. Young, *The Constitution Outside the Constitution*, 117 YALE L.J. 408 (2007); Karl N. Llewellyn, *The Constitution as an Institution*, 34 COLUM. L. REV. 1 (1934).

[74] Bradley & Siegel, *supra* note 57; Richard H. Fallon, Jr., *A Constructivist Coherence Theory of Constitutional Interpretation*, 100 HARV. L. REV. 1189 (1987).

422 THE COLLECTIVE-ACTION CONSTITUTION

that Article V—an extreme outlier by US state and world standards that has not benefited from more than 235 years of national and world experience with constitutionalism—correctly answers the question of how difficult formal constitutional change should be. It also seems unlikely that most Americans have generally opposed the constitutional changes wrought by their elected representatives, whether directly through state-building or indirectly through appointments.[75]

Article V's Entrenchment of Certain Provisions

The discussion so far has not mentioned the most draconian impediments to constitutional change that Article V imposes. It originally entrenched certain provisions against change even via the formal process specified in the article. Two provisions concerned slavery and were declared unamendable until 1808 (when Congress banned the international slave trade), and a third concerned the equal state representation in the Senate, which remains in force today.[76] For most Americans then and almost all commentators now, there was no working around the Constitution's entrenched protection of the international slave trade from federal interference until 1808, and today there appears to be no working around Article V's entrenched guarantee that no state can be denied equal suffrage in the Senate without its consent.[77] Whether this latter provision is a virtue or a vice depends on one's views on the nature of the Union, a topic discussed at the start of Chapter 3.[78] For Americans who regard equal state representation in the Senate as a large and consequential democratic failure, the most that can be done to reduce the potential disconnect between a Senate majority and a national popular majority is to add certain states to the Union, a fact recognized by both political parties in debates over statehood for Puerto Rico and Washington, DC.[79]

---

[75] The current Court may be an exception to this general point. For the first time in American history, a president who lost the popular vote (Donald Trump) successfully nominated a decisive number of justices (Neil Gorsuch, Brett Kavanaugh, and Amy Coney Barrett) who were confirmed by a Senate majority that represents a minority of the nation. *See* Steven Levitsky & Daniel Ziblatt, *The Crisis of American Democracy*, 44 AMERICAN EDUCATOR 6, 11 (Fall 2020) (No. 3).

[76] U.S. CONST. art. V (stating partly that no amendment made before 1808 shall affect the first clause in Article I, Section 9, which prohibited Congress from banning the importation of enslaved people into existing states until 1808, and the fourth clause in the same section, which concerned direct taxes; and providing that "no State, without its Consent, shall be deprived of its equal Suffrage in the Senate"). As Chapter 4 explained, the second Direct Tax Clause (the fourth clause of Article I, Section 9) was part of compromises over slavery at the Constitutional Convention.

[77] For ingenious arguments to the contrary, see AMAR, *supra* note 10, at 292–95.

[78] This subject is further discussed in the Postscript on Methodology.

[79] *See, e.g.*, Emily Cochrane, *House Approves D.C. Statehood, but Senate Obstacles Remain*, N.Y. TIMES (Apr. 22, 2021), https://www.nytimes.com/2021/04/22/us/politics/dc-statehood-vote.html, on file with author at https://perma.cc/6768-BYKA. Democrats who favor statehood for Puerto Rico and Washington, DC, reason that their residents would disproportionately vote Democratic.

Concluding Treaties

Another supermajority voting rule is in the Treaty Clause of Article II, Section 2, which requires the approval of two-thirds of the Senate to conclude treaties. The subject of treaties was closely related to foreign commerce at the Founding. But whereas the Constitution changed the voting threshold for regulating foreign commerce in the Articles of Confederation from unanimity rule to majority rule (see Chapter 5), the Constitution kept the voting threshold for concluding treaties at two-thirds. It did so even though the subject of treaty-making does not involve constitutional change, as Article VII did and Article V does, and even though treaty-making does not involve a one-time decision, as Article VII did. Due to experience-based anxieties about uses of the treaty power to advantage one section of the nation at the expense of another, the Framers failed to anticipate the perceived future needs of American governance. Their lack of foresight is evidenced by the development of workarounds in the form of executive agreements, which facilitate collective action by the states in Congress relative to supermajority rule.

Historical Background

In authorizing the president, "by and with the Advice and Consent of the Senate, to make Treaties," the Treaty Clause requires "two thirds of the Senators present [to] concur."[80] As examined in Chapter 7, empowering the president (who is one person), instead of Congress (which is many people), to take the lead in foreign affairs facilitates collective action. But the two-thirds requirement for concluding treaties is effectively the same as the nine-state threshold in Article IX of the Articles of Confederation. The Framers were less concerned to enable collective action by the states in Congress and more worried about preventing the exploitation of a minority of states. So, they gave a minority of states, or a section of the nation, effective veto power over proposed treaties.

Context clarifies why. During the Jay-Gardoqui treaty controversy of the mid-1780s, northern and southern states fractured along sectional lines over whether the states' navigation rights to the Mississippi River should be exchanged for a commercial treaty with Spain. The Southern states were vehemently opposed because they saw their future—slavery, their power in the Union, and their extended

---

Admitting them as states would reduce the malapportionment of the Senate because of the largely partisan distribution of American geography today. Low-population states benefit from the Senate's malapportionment, and residents of such states disproportionately vote Republican.

[80] U.S. Const. art. II, § 2, cl. 2.

424 THE COLLECTIVE-ACTION CONSTITUTION

family members—in the West,[81] and occupation of the West required access to the Mississippi to export products via the ocean.[82] The Northern states were strongly supportive because commercial conditions there were deteriorating due to Great Britain's punishing trade restrictions, and they believed that trade with Spain would help rehabilitate Northern industry. When the Confederation Congress voted on whether John Jay, who was negotiating with Don Diego de Gardoqui of Spain, should be reinstructed to permit Jay to surrender American claims to the Mississippi River, Massachusetts, New Hampshire, Rhode Island, Connecticut, New York, Pennsylvania, and New Jersey voted for reinstruction, while Maryland, Virginia, North Carolina, South Carolina, and Georgia voted against it. (Delaware's delegates were absent when Congress voted.) Although the reinstruction was apparently valid based on majority approval, it authorized Jay to negotiate an agreement that he knew would never be ratified because Southern states opposed it. Negotiations between the countries broke down before there was a proposed agreement on which the states in Congress could vote.[83]

Treaties versus Executive Agreements

Looking back with the benefit of 235-plus years of experience, the question arises whether the Founders were wise to privilege the prevention of minority exploitation by imposing a two-thirds requirement for treaties, or whether it was shortsighted to deviate so significantly from the Constitution's typical collective-action threshold of majority rule. It is especially important to consider this issue from the perspective of the perceived needs of the United States since World War II. Relevant to this question is the fact that almost all international agreements entered into by the United States since 1939 are not Article II treaties but executive agreements, which are concluded without resort to the treaty process specified in Article II. The large majority of modern executive agreements are congressional-executive agreements, which are either authorized ex ante or approved ex post by

[81] MICHAEL J. KLARMAN, THE FRAMERS' COUP: THE MAKING OF THE UNITED STATES CONSTITUTION 54 (2016) (observing that most Western settlers were from southern states and "many southerners hoped that westward expansion ultimately would lead to the creation of several western states, which would increase the South's weight within the union"); see JACK N. RAKOVE, ORIGINAL MEANINGS: POLITICS AND IDEAS IN THE MAKING OF THE CONSTITUTION 27 (1996). Professor Klarman explains, however, that not all southerners (or northerners) agreed regarding access to the Mississippi River. KLARMAN, supra, at 54–55.

[82] Charles Warren, The Mississippi River and the Treaty Clause of the Constitution, 2 GEO. WASH. L. REV. 271, 276–77 (1934).

[83] GEORGE WILLIAM VAN CLEVE, WE HAVE NOT A GOVERNMENT: THE ARTICLES OF CONFEDERATION AND THE ROAD TO THE CONSTITUTION 161–85 (2017); Warren, supra note 82, at 282–87.

Period	# of Treaties	# of Exec. Agreements	% of Exec. Agreements
1789–1839	60	27	31
1839–1889	215	238	53
1889–1939	524	917	64
1939–1989	702	11,698	94
1989–2016	378	6,423	94

Figure 10.1 Treaties and Executive Agreements Over Time

[a] For data from 1789 to 1989, see CONG. RSCH. SERV., S. PRT. 106-71, TREATIES AND OTHER INTERNATIONAL AGREEMENTS: THE ROLE OF THE UNITED STATES SENATE 39 (2001). For data from 1989 to 2016, see Jeffrey S. Peake, The Decline of Treaties? Obama, Trump, and the Politics of International Agreements (Apr. 6, 2018), at 40, *available at* SSRN: https://perma.cc/VKH7-LD8T. According to Professor Peake, his data for 2013–16 are preliminary and represent significant undercounts.

majorities in both Houses of Congress. The minority of executive agreements are "sole" executive agreements, which are made by presidents alone based on their Article II powers. Like treaties, both categories of executive agreements impose binding international legal obligations on the United States.[84]

Figure 10.1 records the number of treaties and executive agreements, and the percentage of all agreements that are executive agreements, over fifty-year periods beginning in 1789 and ending in 1989. The final column covers the twenty-seven-year period from 1989 to 2016.

These data reveal that the number of binding international agreements has exploded since 1939, indicating that the nation's demand for international agreements has been high. This is unsurprising given the nation's military, diplomatic, and economic activities around the globe, reflecting a degree of power and influence that even Hamilton likely could not have imagined. Roughly 94 percent of all such agreements since 1939 have been executive agreements.

Why has there been such a strong preference for executive agreements over treaties? A complete answer likely includes the Senate's acceptance that most agreements can be concluded without the supermajority treaty process, partly because there are so many of them; the Senate would not have the time or the desire to process them all. The Senate has demanded that the treaty-making process be used regarding only certain subjects. For example, arms-control

[84] CURTIS A. BRADLEY ET AL., FOREIGN RELATIONS LAW: CASES AND MATERIALS 383, 390–91 (7th ed. 2020). There are also nonbinding political commitments that presidents may make. An example is the Iran Nuclear Agreement concluded by President Barack Obama. This agreement "lifted international and domestic sanctions against Iran in exchange for Iran's dismantling of its nuclear weapons development program." Curtis A. Bradley & Jack L. Goldsmith, *Presidential Control over International Law*, 131 HARV. L. REV. 1201, 1203–04 (2018).

426   THE COLLECTIVE-ACTION CONSTITUTION

agreements, human-rights agreements, and extradition agreements are almost always concluded as treaties, which indicates some perceived limits on the use of executive agreements based on historical practice.[85] It is also noteworthy that the House of Representatives has long insisted on playing a role in the process, given the connection between many international agreements and its prerogatives— for example, over appropriations and commerce. Moreover, the treaty-making process has not generally been viewed as constitutionally required. Although some scholars disagree for plausible reasons, "the prevailing view," maintained by the Restatement (Third) of Foreign Relations Law, "is that the Congressional-Executive agreement can be used as an alternative to the treaty method in every instance," and "which procedure should be used is a political judgment, made in the first instance by the President."[86]

It seems likely, however, that a main part of the story concerns the perceived need for collective action by states in Congress to conclude international agreements in a globalized world and the severe impediments imposed by the two-thirds requirement for Senate treaty ratification. This voting threshold requires a high level of bipartisanship because neither party in contemporary American politics is likely to win anywhere near sixty-seven seats. The Treaty Clause probably makes collective action too hard to achieve, and federal officials appear to have increasingly used workarounds that better facilitate collective action—except when the Senate has been especially insistent that the Article II process be used.

As with the Article V amendment process, comparative evidence suggests that the Constitution's supermajority requirement to ratify treaties is too demanding. Professor Oona Hathaway compiled a comprehensive database of the treaty-making practices of every nation that had a constitution in the year 2007.

---

[85] For an example, see BRADLEY ET AL., *supra* note 84, at 389–90 (excerpting a 2002 letter from the senior Democratic and Republican members of the Senate Foreign Relations Committee to the secretary of state demanding submission to the Senate of an arms control agreement with Russia, which happened); *see id.* at 395 (reporting comments of Harold Koh, then-legal advisor to the State Department, on why the executive branch sometimes attempts to conclude international agreements through the Article II process even though "it is so hard to get sixty-seven votes for a treaty").

[86] Restatement (Third) of the Foreign Relations Law of the United States § 303 cmt. 2 (1987). For discussion, see BRADLEY ET AL., *supra* note 84, at 393. The Restatement's position may require qualification. Even supporters of broad power to create congressional-executive agreements accept that such agreements, unlike treaties, cannot regulate activities domestically beyond Congress's other enumerated powers. *See, e.g.,* Oona A. Hathaway, *Treaties' End: The Past, Present, and Future of International Lawmaking in the United States,* 117 YALE L.J. 1236, 1339 (2008) ("In contrast with Article II treaties, congressional-executive agreements cannot exceed the bounds placed by the Constitution on congressional authority."). If that is correct, there is not complete interchangeability. The challenge is to explain why congressional majorities (and the president) can reach activities that do not fall within Congress's enumerated powers when, but only when, another nation agrees to also regulate such activities. A persuasive answer would include the perceived need to solve multination and multistate collective-action problems and the frequent inability of the United States to participate in doing so through the treaty-making process given the two-thirds requirement for Senate ratification, which overprotects the states.

She found that "[o]nly five other countries in the world—Algeria, Burundi, Iraq, Micronesia, and the Philippines—require a supermajority vote in their legislature in order for the country to ratify a treaty." Most nations "require that international law be made through a simple or absolute majority vote in the legislature."[87]

This collective-action analysis suggests that congressional-executive agreements derive their legal legitimacy not only from enduring practice but also from structural reasoning and prudential considerations.[88] In addition, the foregoing analysis supports the conventional position that congressional-executive agreements are largely interchangeable with treaties. Strikingly, treaties are an area in which the Constitution mimics the supermajority rule of the Articles of Confederation, and over time the United States has used majoritarian substitutes.[89] More precisely, the practice has been dominated by roughly majoritarian alternatives—not mostly the collective-action extreme of the president's acting alone through sole executive agreements, but the ordinary collective-action threshold of the president's acting with legislative majorities. Collective-action reasoning helps explain why such agreements are likely essential to meet the perceived needs of modern American governance.

That said, the story of executive agreements is not all positive; it is partly a story of executive aggrandizement. Professors Curtis Bradley and Jack Goldsmith observe that there "has been a long accretion of presidential control over international law since the constitutional Founding," and "much presidential control over international law is the result of broad delegations of authority from Congress and accretions of executive branch practice in the face of congressional inaction."[90] For example, within the category of congressional-executive agreements, ex ante agreements are the most common and give the president substantially more discretion than ex post agreements.[91] So, the practice has not set an ideal balance between enabling collective action and ensuring sufficient democratic warrant for such action. As noted, however, executive

[87] Hathaway, *supra* note 86, at 1271–72.

[88] On the historical practice, see BRADLEY ET AL., *supra* note 84, at 390. The constitutional text might seem to favor treaties over executive agreements, but the Treaty Clause does not indicate that treaties are the only forms of international agreements that the United States can conclude. Moreover, the Foreign Compacts Clause, located in the third clause of Article I, Section 10, recognizes other international agreements by permitting states, only with congressional consent, to "enter into any Agreement or Compact . . . with a foreign Power." Because the Constitution gives the federal government exclusive or ultimate control over foreign affairs, majorities in Congress can almost certainly conclude the same international agreements that such majorities can permit states to enter.

[89] *Cf.* VAN CLEVE, *supra* note 83, at 289 (writing that "to reach agreement and make ratification possible, . . . the Convention had no political alternative but to make concessions to persistent sectional jealousies and states' sovereignty claims," including by agreeing that treaty adoption would require "supermajority consent").

[90] Bradley & Goldsmith, *supra* note 84, at 1204, 1206.

[91] BRADLEY ET AL., *supra* note 84, at 391–92.

428   THE COLLECTIVE-ACTION CONSTITUTION

aggrandizement is invited by unduly burdensome voting rules in Congress, whether the two-thirds supermajority requirement in the Senate to ratify treaties or the three-fifths supermajority requirement in the chamber to end a filibuster.

Other Treaty Power Puzzles

Another controversy that a collective-action lens can help illuminate is whether the treaty power can be used to regulate conduct that Congress cannot reach using its enumerated powers. The Court in *Missouri v. Holland* (1920) so held (when congressional power was judicially interpreted to be far more limited than it is today), and in doing so the Court registered the existence of a multistate and multination externality problem being addressed by a migratory bird treaty:

> Here a national interest of very nearly the first magnitude is involved. It can be protected only by national action in concert with that of another power. The subject-matter is only transitorily within the State and has no permanent habitat therein. *But for the treaty and the statute there soon might be no birds for any powers to deal with.* We see nothing in the Constitution that compels the Government to sit by while a food supply is cut off and the protectors of our forests and our crops are destroyed. It is not sufficient to rely upon the States. The reliance is vain, and were it otherwise, the question is whether the United States is forbidden to act.[92]

Birds have nonmarket value that spills across jurisdictions as they migrate. If states want to protect them, they must coordinate their efforts. Moreover, states may destroy animal habitat for profit and hope that other states will preserve it, resulting in a race to the bottom. Alternatively, some states may not value protecting animal habitat and externalize costs onto sister states that do want to protect animal habitat. Protecting birds thus combines an externality problem and three potential collective-action problems, which is why the states are separately incompetent to protect migratory birds.[93] Unless the only level

---

[92]   252 U.S. 416, 435 (1920) (emphasis added).

[93]   Robert D. Cooter & Neil S. Siegel, *Collective Action Federalism: A General Theory of Article I, Section 8*, 63 STAN. L. REV. 115, 177–78 & n.227 (2010) (noting the externality discussion in *Holland* and identifying one collective-action problem); *see* Solid Waste Agency of Northern Cook Cty. (SWANCC) v. United States Army Corps of Engineers, 531 U.S. 159, 195 (2001) (Stevens, J., dissenting) ("The destruction of aquatic migratory bird habitat, like so many other environmental problems, is an action in which the benefits (*e.g.*, a new landfill) are disproportionately local, while many of the costs (*e.g.*, fewer migratory birds) are widely dispersed and often borne by citizens living in other States. In such situations, described by economists as involving 'externalities,' federal regulation is both appropriate and necessary.").

of government that can address a problem is the one that cannot do so effectively, then at least when a collective-action problem likely exists (as it did in *Holland*),[94] there is a structural argument for permitting treaties to reach conduct that would otherwise be beyond Congress's enumerated powers.[95] There is also a structural argument, albeit not necessarily a decisive one, for permitting executive agreements to do the same.[96] By contrast, a treaty regulating, say, traffic safety or guns in schools could not be justified on collective-action grounds.

A related question about the Treaty Clause and executive agreements that a collective-action framework helps clarify is the kinds of agreements that they permit federal officials to enter. Do they grant the United States the power to join other countries in addressing multi*nation* collective-action problems (e.g., climate change or the migratory birds in *Holland*)? Do they permit treaties and agreements that focus mainly on the internal policy choices of the parties to the agreement (e.g., many international human-rights treaties)?[97] Permitting agreements that address multination collective-action problems is generally uncontroversial in part because it makes deep structural sense to imagine the Constitution as a collective-action layer cake: just as the federal government is structurally better situated than the states to address multistate collective-action problems, so international bodies created by international agreements are better situated than the federal government, which is better situated than the states, to address less multination collective-action problems—although, as explained at the end of Chapter 1, international institutions may not possess as much democratic legitimacy as the federal government. One might argue that the United States may not conclude an international agreement addressing the problem of, say, global warming because one nation acting with a few other nations cannot significantly ameliorate a global collective-action problem. But one could also argue that the United States has discretion to address such a problem partially and to take the lead by acting in anticipation of eventual negotiations with many countries.

---

[94] For those who believe that *Holland* was wrongly decided, the multination and multistate collective-action problems that were present could be used to limit the Court's holding.

[95] Far less controversial is the holding in *Holland* that if a treaty is constitutional, Congress can use the Necessary and Proper Clause to pass a statute implementing it, even if such legislation would be beyond congressional power absent the treaty. BRADLEY ET AL., *supra* note 84, at 314–15. This holding is sensible from a collective-action perspective insofar as the treaty being implemented through federal legislation solves collective-action problems for the states or nations. For a challenge to this holding in *Holland*, see Nicholas Quinn Rosenkranz, *Executing the Treaty Power*, 118 HARV. L. REV. 1867 (2005) (arguing that federal legislation can help facilitate only the making of treaties, not their implementation); Bond v. United States, 572 U.S. 844, 874–76 (2014) (Scalia, J., concurring in judgment) (same).

[96] Few commentators would accept this argument. *See supra* note 86 (discussing this issue).

[97] *Cf.* Cooter & Siegel, *supra* note 93, at 151 n.36 (asking whether the logics of collective action inform the scope of the treaty power).

430   THE COLLECTIVE-ACTION CONSTITUTION

Such structural reasoning may be available regarding some human-rights treaties—there can be concerns, for example, about regional stability, spillover refugee problems, and related issues. Collective-action reasoning may play a supporting role in justifying some human-rights treaties for reasons similar to those that partially justify federal legislative and judicial power to enforce certain constitutional rights—those that Chapter 9 called collective-action rights and democratic-process rights. Also recall that the Republican Form of Government Clause is based in part on the idea that democracies are less likely to go to war with one another than monarchies are to go to war with democracies or with other monarchies. To the extent that human-rights treaties promote democracy around the globe, there may be a collective-action justification for them.

Collective-action rationales seem largely unavailable for many human-rights treaties, however, just as Chapter 9 explained that collective-action logics are largely unavailable when Congress uses its enforcement powers under the Civil War Amendments. Such human-rights treaties must find their primary justification elsewhere. Early and modern historical practice is pertinent to the question of their permissibility. So is the fact that there is no collective-action-type language or subject-matter limitation in the Treaty Clause, in contrast to the "general Welfare" language in the Spending Clause and the phrase "among the several States" in the Interstate Commerce Clause.

Preventing Presidents from Undermining Solutions to Collective-Action Problems

Imagine that a president decided to govern by executive order in ways that were not grounded either in Article II or a delegation of legislative authority from Congress. Or imagine that a president used imaginative statutory interpretation to act in the face of a valid congressional prohibition of executive conduct. How might Congress respond? It could pass a clearly worded bill to override the presidential action, but the president would presumably veto the bill, in which case it would not become law unless two-thirds majorities in each house of Congress approved it.[98] If the president's conduct were sufficiently egregious—for example, if the president routinely refused to enforce valid federal statutes to which the president objected on policy grounds—the House of Representatives could

---

[98] U.S. CONST. art. I, § 7, cl. 2. This clause gives the president ten days, excluding Sundays, either to sign a bill into law, or to do nothing and have the bill become law without the president's signature, or to veto the bill and return it to Congress for potential override, which requires two-thirds of each House to vote in favor. The fourth possibility is a "pocket veto," which occurs when Congress sends the president a bill at the end of a legislative session and "Congress by their Adjournment prevent its Return." The president can do nothing—put the bill in the president's "pocket"—and the bill dies.

impeach the president by simple majority vote, but conviction in the Senate would require a two-thirds vote.[99] These two supermajority voting rules in the Constitution make it effectively impossible for simple majorities in Congress to prevent presidents from undermining congressional solutions to multistate collective-action problems. These supermajority rules likely make collective action by members of Congress—which helps protect collective action by states in Congress—too difficult to accomplish in modern America.

In *Federalist 51*, Madison argued that the best way to prevent or remedy usurpations of power by one political branch is to arm each branch with sufficient defensive powers and incentives to use them. "The great security against a gradual concentration of the several powers in the same department," he wrote, "consists in giving to those who administer each department the necessary constitutional means and personal motives to resist encroachments of the others." Invoking martial imagery of clashing armies, Madison added that "[t]he provision for defense must in this, as in all other cases, be made commensurate to the danger of attack."[100]

The modern system of separation of powers and checks and balances does not function in the way that Madison described. Heavily influenced by prior experience, he and other Founders incorrectly predicted how the institutions they were creating—especially Congress—would operate. They did not anticipate that presidents would defend their office from congressional encroachments more strenuously than Congress would defend itself from presidential incursions.[101] But Madison did usefully, even if unwittingly, identify two ways in which the system could malfunction. First, members of a branch might be unable to resist encroachments by another branch—they might lack "the necessary constitutional means." Second, members of a branch might lack sufficient incentive to act—they might lack "personal motives to resist encroachments of the others."

Today, lack of motivation is an important reason why congressional majorities do not consistently push back against encroaching presidents, and this section will discuss why members generally lack incentive to defend their branch or chambers. But inability continues to play a major role, and the Constitution's

---

[99] Four constitutional provisions govern the impeachment process. *See* U.S. CONST. art. I, § 2, cl. 5 (giving the House "the sole Power of Impeachment"); art. I, § 3, cl. 6 (giving the Senate "the sole Power to try all Impeachments" and providing that "no Person shall be convicted without the Concurrence of two thirds of the Members present"); art. I, § 3, cl. 7 (providing that "Judgment in Cases of Impeachment shall not extend further than to removal from Office, and disqualification to hold and enjoy any Office of honor, Trust or Profit under the United States"); art. II, § 4 (providing that "[t]he President, Vice President and all civil Officers of the United States, shall be removed from Office on Impeachment for, and Conviction of, Treason, Bribery, or other high Crimes and Misdemeanors").

[100] THE FEDERALIST No. 51, at 321–22 (James Madison) (Clinton Rossiter ed., 1961).

[101] Curtis A. Bradley & Trevor W. Morrison, *Historical Gloss and the Separation of Powers*, 126 HARV. L. REV. 411, 438–47 (2012) (developing this point and citing the political science and legal literatures).

432   THE COLLECTIVE-ACTION CONSTITUTION

supermajority rules for overriding vetoes or convicting impeached presidents are primary reasons why Congress is unable to adequately defend itself. These two sources of dysfunction are discussed below. Also examined are potential substitutes *by* Congress—tools that require only majority support to use—and potential substitutes *for* Congress—courts, elections, criminal prosecutions, and states. The inadequacies of these substitutes underscore the significance of the two-thirds voting rules in the legislative and impeachment processes. Although possible alternatives to these rules will be suggested, the rules are hardwired into the constitutional text and so would require an Article V amendment to change.

This section does not claim, and it does not demonstrate, that the presidency has become too powerful. Whether this proposition is valid depends on many considerations, including an assessment of what Americans can justifiably expect of the federal government; whether executive power must be as expansive as it is to meet these expectations; whether Congress could do more if executive power were reduced; and how much presidential power is limited in ways other than by the constitutional separation of powers. Instead of arguing that modern presidents are too powerful, this section contends that two supermajority voting rules in the Constitution, along with other factors, likely make it too difficult for Congress to police presidential abuses of power in today's world. Some of these abuses can damage the efficacy of federal statutes that solve collective-action problems for the states.

The Inability of Congressional Majorities to Act

The Founders were not equally worried about the ability of each branch to protect itself. They had seen state legislatures dominate state executives during the 1780s, and, because of this experience, they were more concerned that Congress would overwhelm presidents than the other way around. The Constitution reflects these asymmetric concerns. The Framers gave presidents the veto power primarily to enable them to oppose congressional encroachments on their office and likely also to empower them to oppose bills that they thought were unconstitutional.[102]

---

[102] *See* Chapter 11; ROBERT J. SPITZER, THE PRESIDENTIAL VETO: TOUCHSTONE OF THE AMERICAN PRESIDENCY 15–16 (1988) ("Again and again in the convention's consideration of the veto power, one central theme persistently surfaced: the veto as a device of executive self-protection against encroachments of the legislature. This had indisputably been the lesson gleaned from state experiences."); Charles L. Black, Jr., *Some Thoughts on the Veto*, 40 Law & CONTEMP. PROBS. 87, 89 (1976) ("The prime original purpose for the inclusion of this power was that it was thought to give the President the means of protecting his office from Congressional encroachment. There may have been an anticipation that it would be used to vindicate the President's own constitutional views, by being interposed against legislation he considered unconstitutional."); *see* Bradley & Morrison, *supra* note 101, at 440 n.120 ("The President's veto power and certain other features of the Constitution were included in part as a reaction by the Founders to the dominance of state legislatures under the Articles of Confederation.").

STRICT SUPERMAJORITY REQUIREMENTS 433

The veto power creates a substantial asymmetry between executive and congressional power. If presidents believe that Congress is encroaching on their office or acting unconstitutionally, they can respond by vetoing the bill, in which case the bill will not become law unless two-thirds of each house of Congress votes to override the veto.[103] By contrast, if congressional majorities believe that the president is encroaching on Congress's powers or acting unconstitutionally, their primary way of push backing is to enact legislation limiting the president's authority. But such legislation will almost certainly be met with a veto, in which case there will be no pushback unless two-thirds of each chamber supports it. In this scenario, the Constitution in essence requires compliance with the two-thirds requirement of Article IX of the Articles of Confederation, except that Article IX required only one supermajority vote, not two.[104] If congressional majorities are correct about the president's conduct, the veto power facilitates usurpation or unconstitutionality rather than combatting it.

Unfortunately, presidential overreach is the more likely scenario today than the Founding fear that Congress would encroach on the presidency.[105] Presidents can act unilaterally to a greater extent than Congress can, and presidents head a more powerful branch of government than Congress.[106] (Although the relative power of the political branches is difficult to assess, one rough way to get at the issue is to ask whether most Americans would want their political party to control the presidency or both houses of Congress if control of both were impossible.) The relationship between modern veto practice and the status of the modern presidency does not appear coincidental. There are many reasons why presidents are likely more powerful than Congress today, but widespread use of the veto power and veto threats—

and congressional anticipations of veto threats—are an important part of the story. The Constitution's two-thirds supermajority rules for overriding

---

[103] U.S. CONST. art. I, § 7, cl. 2.

[104] ARTICLES OF CONFEDERATION of 1781, art. IX ("The united states in congress assembled shall never engage in a war, nor grant letters of marque and reprisal in time of peace, nor enter into any treaties or alliances, nor coin money, nor regulate the value thereof, nor ascertain the sums and expences necessary for the defence and welfare of the united states, or any of them, nor emit bills, nor borrow money on the credit of the united states, nor appropriate money, nor agree upon the number of vessels of war, to be built or purchased, or the number of land or sea forces to be raised, nor appoint a commander-in-chief of the army or navy, unless nine states assent to the same . . . .").

[105] THE FEDERALIST No. 48, at 309 (James Madison) (Clinton Rossiter ed., 1961).

[106] *Cf.* Bradley & Morrison, *supra* note 101, at 440 (observing that "Presidents sit atop a vast executive branch and [can] take a wide variety of actions unilaterally," including by issuing executive orders and directives, ordering the use of military force, and concluding international agreements without congressional approval). For work theorizing unilateral presidential action and offering empirical evidence, see WILLIAM G. HOWELL, POWER WITHOUT PERSUASION: THE POLITICS OF DIRECT PRESIDENTIAL ACTION (2003); and Terry M. Moe & William G. Howell, *The Presidential Power of Unilateral Action*, 15 J. LAW ECON. & ORG. 132 (1999). For limits on executive unilateralism imposed by ideological diversity within and across agencies, see *infra* note 148 and accompanying text.

434 THE COLLECTIVE-ACTION CONSTITUTION

vetoes have contributed to the dramatic expansion of executive power.[107] Commentators and jurists can reasonably disagree about the desirability of robust executive power generally, but all should worry about presidential abuses of power.

Several constitutional-design alternatives would likely be preferable to the veto power as it exists in the constitutional text and long-standing practice. Perhaps presidents should not possess the veto power at all. Perhaps less than a two-thirds majority in both houses of Congress should be required to override vetoes. Congress could instead be required to vote again on a bill by simple majority rule in each chamber after considering the president's objections to it. Or Congress could be required to override a veto by a three-fifths vote in each chamber, which would shift the balance of power in Congress's direction by making collective action in this body easier to accomplish. These potential alternatives are not offered in the conviction that they would be viable as constitutional amendments, but in the spirit of constructive critique animating this chapter.

The foregoing concerns are less significant if viable alternatives to legislation exist that Congress can use to push back against encroaching or unconstitutional conduct by presidents. One possible substitute is impeachment and conviction of presidents, which requires majority support in the House to impeach and two-thirds support in the Senate to convict.[108] Conviction results in the removal of presidents from office if they remain in office when convicted, and it results in their disqualification from holding future office if the Senate votes separately—by majority rule—for this result.[109] Removal from office, or rendering former

---

[107] SPITZER, *supra* note 102, at xvi (arguing that "[t]he rise of the veto power . . . is symptomatic of the rise of the modern strong presidency, and indeed has also been a major building-presidency tool"); Black, *supra* note 102, at 97 ("The asymmetry-of-veto may go far to explain the growth of the President's powers through history.").

[108] *See supra* note 99 (quoting constitutional provisions governing the impeachment and conviction of presidents).

[109] The constitutional text does not specify the voting rule for disqualification, but past practice suggests majority rule, although the practice is limited and results only from the Senate's own determination. Only three individuals, all federal judges, have been disqualified from holding future office following conviction in a Senate trial. In 1862, 1912, and 2010, the Senate imposed disqualification (on West H. Humphreys, Robert W. Archbald, and G. Thomas Porteous Jr.) by a simple majority vote after the two-thirds vote to convict. AMAR, *supra* note 10, at 199; JOSH CHAFETZ, CONGRESS'S CONSTITUTION: LEGISLATIVE AUTHORITY AND THE SEPARATION OF POWERS 149 (2017); Jennifer Steinhauer, *Senate for Just the Eighth Time, Votes to Oust a Federal Judge*, N.Y. TIMES (Dec. 8, 2010), https://www.nytimes.com/2010/12/09/us/politics/09judge.html, on file with author at https://perma.cc/NFV2-W2QT. Senate practice is supported by the fact that disqualification is discretionary, unlike removal upon conviction. Further, the text expressly requires a two-thirds vote only for conviction, not disqualification, and majority rule is the Constitution's default voting rule. But Professor Michael Gerhardt argues that a two-thirds vote should be required for disqualification "given the framers' expectation that the two-thirds vote requirement would make it less likely for impeached officials to be convicted and punished for improper motives." MICHAEL J. GERHARDT, THE FEDERAL IMPEACHMENT PROCESS: A CONSTITUTIONAL AND HISTORICAL ANALYSIS 81 (3d ed. 2019). Notably from a collective-action perspective, the Senate has narrowly interpreted the two-thirds requirement in the text.

presidents ineligible to run again in the future, is the ultimate congressional weapon for unconstitutional behavior or other abuses of power by presidents. But it is no substitute for legislation precisely because it is the ultimate weapon. When used properly, impeachment and conviction are limited to instances of grave presidential misconduct, as indicated (among other ways) by the textual limitation of impeachable offenses to "Treason, Bribery, or other high Crimes and Misdemeanors."[110]

Moreover, impeachment and removal are not a viable substitute for legislation when Congress cannot enact legislation over a veto. Both actions require two-thirds support in the Senate. There has never been a situation in which two-thirds of the Senate was unwilling to override a veto but willing to convict a president of impeachable offenses. A willingness to impeach and convict likely implies a willingness to legislate. For example, after president Richard Nixon resigned because he concluded that he would otherwise be impeached and convicted, Congress enacted significant legislation limiting executive power.[111]

Just as impeachment and conviction are not a viable substitute for legislation, the above analysis implies that legislation may not be an adequate substitute for impeachment and conviction. If Congress seeks to punish already committed abuses of power by a particular president, prospective legislation will not accomplish its objective. (The Ex Post Facto Clause prohibits legislation that punishes conduct after the fact, and the Bill of Attainder Clause prohibits legislation that singles out specific individuals for punishment.[112]) In this situation too, the two-thirds requirement makes it very difficult for the Senate to convict. In four impeachment trials (of Andrew Johnson, Bill Clinton, and Donald Trump twice), there has never been two-thirds support in the Senate to convict.

Granted, the number of data points is small, and the data do not include past presidents who committed impeachable offenses (however determined) but were not impeached. Moreover, the data cannot determine whether an impeached president committed impeachable offenses and should have been convicted. And Nixon resigned rather than likely be removed. Yet—especially after the two impeachment trials of Donald Trump for his egregious misconduct

---

[110] U.S. CONST. art. II, § 4.

[111] Supporting Nixon's conclusion is Brian R. Fry & John S. Stolarek, *The Nixon Impeachment Vote: A Speculative Analysis*, 11 PRES. STUD. Q. 387, 392 (1981) ("[N]o combination of lists adds up to the thirty-four votes required for the President to escape conviction in the Senate."). Post-Watergate legislation included the Federal Election Campaign Act Amendments of 1974, Pub. L. No. 93-443, 88 Stat. 1263; the Ethics in Government Act of 1978, Pub. L. No. 95-521, 92 Stat. 1824; a statute amending the Freedom of Information Act, Act of Nov. 21, 1974, Pub. L. No. 93-502, 88 Stat. 1561; and the Government in the Sunshine Act of 1976, Pub. L. No. 94-409, 90 Stat. 1241.

[112] U.S. CONST. art. I, § 9, cl. 3.

436 THE COLLECTIVE-ACTION CONSTITUTION

in office[113]—there is scant evidence that a president who warrants conviction will be convicted.[114]

Although the two-thirds requirement makes collective action in the Senate significantly more difficult than majority rule, collective-action reasoning cannot identify what the threshold should be. Because impeachment and removal should not be politics as usual, majority rule in the Senate, as in the House, does not seem appropriate. Perhaps a three-fifth rule (sixty senators out of one hundred) would be preferable to a two-thirds requirement. A three-fifths supermajority rule might not have made a decisive difference in Trump's case, but it is impossible to know; a different voting rule might have affected the calculus for some senators, just as a different voting rule for ratification of the Constitution might have affected the vote in some state conventions. Whatever the outcomes of past trials might have been, the prospective point is that a sixty-vote requirement would typically require bipartisanship while still likely causing presidents to worry about removal if their conduct were sufficiently grave. In this context, sixty is a much lower number than sixty-seven. An amendment changing the voting rule in the Senate is, however, very unlikely to succeed.

Other Tools Available to Congressional Majorities

Notwithstanding the above concerns, simple majorities in one or both houses of Congress possess powers to resist presidential abuses of authority. Senators could end the filibuster by majority vote.[115] Congressional majorities can pass nonbinding resolutions, which let them express their views without requiring the president's signature. They can conduct oversight hearings or investigations that publicly disclose information and compel witnesses to testify or turn over documents, and they can hold in contempt those who refuse. Congress can leverage its control over annual appropriations, which expire at the end of each year (and so effectively have sunset provisions), to "pull the plug" on presidential

[113] Curtis A. Bradley, *Trump Provided a Road Map for Stealing an Election: Next Time Could Be Worse*, WASH. POST (Nov. 30, 2020), https://www.washingtonpost.com/outlook/2020/11/30/trump-election-institutions-coup-electors/, on file with author at https://perma.cc/EN87-C93T; Maureen Groppe, *"I will keep the oath I made": Pence Defies Trump, Says He Won't Block Congress from Certifying Biden's Win*, USA TODAY (Jan. 7, 2021), https://perma.cc/HE7D-3TWK.

[114] Necessary and sufficient conditions for impeachment will not be offered here. Doing so would require working through difficult, nuanced questions of constitutional law and prudence and would take this chapter too far afield. For discussions of past impeachments and the impeachment process generally, see CHARLES L. BLACK, JR., IMPEACHMENT: A HANDBOOK (1974); GERHARDT, *supra* note 109; MICHAEL J. GERHARDT, IMPEACHMENT: WHAT EVERYONE NEEDS TO KNOW (2018); RICHARD A. POSNER, AN AFFAIR OF STATE: THE INVESTIGATION, IMPEACHMENT, AND TRIAL OF PRESIDENT CLINTON (2000); CASS R. SUNSTEIN, IMPEACHMENT: A CITIZEN'S GUIDE (2017); and LAURENCE TRIBE & JOSHUA MATZ, TO END A PRESIDENCY: THE POWER OF IMPEACHMENT (2018).

[115] *See* Chapter 11.

activities or force presidents to (re)negotiate with Congress.[116] Congressional majorities can pass omnibus appropriations bills or use riders, which make it less likely that presidents will veto the bills.[117] They can delegate less authority to presidents where delegation is not essential given the complexity of modern problems and governance. Senators can leverage their confirmation power regarding executive-branch and judicial nominees to extract concessions from presidents or influence the composition of the executive branch.[118] Congress can limit presidential power to remove the heads of most independent agencies, although the scope of its authority is disputed, and congressional majorities require presidents to sign bills imposing such limits.[119]

These tools ameliorate the consequences for collective action by members of Congress—who, to repeat, protect collective action by states in Congress—of the two-thirds supermajority rules for overriding vetoes and convicting impeached presidents. Congressional majorities should use these powers where appropriate, and courts should consider them in determining whether Congress has acquiesced in an assertion of executive authority.[120] As Chapter 1 explained, acquiescence is relevant to deciding whether to credit historical practice in constitutional interpretation. Congressional silence should not be used to validate otherwise unconstitutional exercises of executive power when presidents, by vetoing bills, are mostly responsible for such silence.[121] Put differently, in considering acquiescence, courts should view "Congress" as consisting of simple majorities, not two-thirds supermajorities.

---

[116] CHAFETZ, *supra* note 109, at 61–62. A sunset provision provides that a statute will cease having legal effect after a specified termination date. Absent a sunset provision, attempts by congressional majorities to amend a statute will likely trigger a presidential veto if the president prefers the original statute. With a sunset provision, there is no original statute for the president to potentially prefer, so the president is more likely to negotiate with, and make concessions to, congressional majorities if the president prefers new legislation to no legislation.

[117] U.S. CONST. art. I, § 9, cl. 7 (providing that "[n]o Money shall be drawn from the Treasury, but in Consequence of Appropriations made by Law"). An omnibus bill combines two or more appropriations bills into one bill. The purpose of combining bills is to reduce objections from the floor and to increase the likelihood that the president will not veto the omnibus bill (because the president prefers part or most of it). A rider is a provision added to a bill, such as an appropriations bill, that has little to do with the bill's substance. Because presidents may favor the bill as a whole, they may not veto it notwithstanding their objections to the rider and to the use of appropriations bills as vehicles for substantive legislation. Craig Goodman, *The Power to Appropriate Money and to Budget, in* THE POWERS OF CONGRESS: WHERE CONSTITUTIONAL AUTHORITY BEGINS AND ENDS 201, 208–13 (Brien Hallett ed., 2016).

[118] U.S. CONST. art. I, § 2, cl. 2 (authorizing the president to nominate and, if a Senate majority "Consent[s]," to appoint diplomats, judges, and other principal officers).

[119] For discussion of the congressional powers discussed in this paragraph and other powers, see CHAFETZ, *supra* note 109. For discussion of some of these powers and their limits, see DANIEL A. FARBER & NEIL S. SIEGEL, UNITED STATES CONSTITUTIONAL LAW 215–22, 241–42 (2d ed. 2024).

[120] Bradley & Morrison, *supra* note 101, at 448–52.

[121] Black, *supra* note 102, at 98–99.

438 THE COLLECTIVE-ACTION CONSTITUTION

The foregoing tools also have significant limits, however, and two are especially important here. First, enacting legislation is Congress's most significant power—it is the primary reason why Congress exists—and none of these tools empower congressional majorities to resist presidents by passing major substantive legislation that is veto-proof. Second, none of these tools can result in a president's removal from office or disqualification from holding future office.[122] Thus, although congressional majorities are not helpless when presidents overreach, the two-thirds requirements to overcome vetoes or convict impeached presidents are structurally significant. No president would likely support getting rid of either two-thirds rule, and no defender of congressional authority would likely dismiss them as inconsequential.

The Unwillingness of Congressional Majorities to Act

For several reasons, however, it is also true that congressional majorities are often unwilling, as opposed to unable, to hold presidents accountable.[123] First, members face collective-action problems. They internalize all the costs of protecting their institution (e.g., the expenditure of their time and political capital), and they externalize most of the benefits onto other members. This interaction has the structure of a Prisoner's Dilemma, and the result is insufficient investment by individual members in institutional goals.

Second, and relatedly, most members have greater motivation to be reelected than to be institutionalists.[124] They internalize not just the costs of running for office but also the benefits. They therefore spend most of their time doing what their constituents most want: securing benefits, not trying to maintain the system of separation of powers. It does not help that Congress is unpopular and so members are incentivized to disidentify with their institution. Members who want to be president also lack much incentive to defend Congress.

Third, presidents are the leaders of their political party in Congress and typically hold sway with the base of the party. These facts about contemporary American politics discourage members of Congress of a president's own party from crossing the president if they want to be reelected.[125] This dynamic is

[122] U.S. CONST. art. I, § 3, cl. 7 (providing that "Judgment in Cases of Impeachment shall not extend further than to removal from Office, and disqualification to hold and enjoy any Office of honor, Trust or Profit under the United States").

[123] For discussion of factors that help explain the unwillingness of most members of Congress to defend their institution, see Bradley & Morrison, *supra* note 101, at 441–44.

[124] For the classic work that assumes members of Congress are "single-minded seekers of reelection," see DAVID R. MAYHEW, CONGRESS: THE ELECTORAL CONNECTION (1974).

[125] NOLAN MCCARTY, POLARIZATION: WHAT EVERYONE NEEDS TO KNOW 135 (2019) ("[A]s legislative partisanship has increased, legislators of the president's party are often forced to act as advocates of the administration rather than as defenders of the prerogatives of a co-equal branch.").

STRICT SUPERMAJORITY REQUIREMENTS   439

especially significant if their constituents are unconcerned about, or applaud, potential abuses of power by the president. For example, given President Trump's hold over the base of his party, Republican members of Congress mostly feared him.[126]

Fourth, party elites began moving farther apart ideologically during the late 1970s, and American voters have potentially polarized since the 1990s.[127] The existence of polarized parties that regard each other with animosity and distrust increases the chances that members of Congress will place greater value on partisan considerations or their likely agreement with what a president wants to do than on the implications for their institution of how the president means to do it.[128] Moreover, as political scientist Frances Lee has shown, the motivation of members of Congress to act for partisan reasons is much higher during periods like the current one, in which partisan control of the White House, Senate, and House is perceived to be up for grabs in nearly every election cycle.[129] The tools discussed above are most likely to be used during divided government, as Professors Daryl Levinson and Richard Pildes explain.[130]

These four factors are generalizations. Members of Congress sometimes overcome their own collective-action problems and defend their chamber's powers. One example, discussed earlier in this chapter, is the Senate's bipartisan insistence that certain international agreements be concluded as treaties, not executive agreements.[131] Members also have motivations other than being re-elected, and they sometimes defy presidents of their own party.[132] In general, however, members of Congress face serious collective-action problems in defending their institutional interests; reelection is ordinarily their primary motivation; and partisan motivations typically dominate institutional interests in dealing with presidents of their own party. When members do push back against same-party

---

[126] Bradley, *supra* note 113.

[127] *See* Chapter 11.

[128] Neal Devins, *Presidential Unilateralism and Political Polarization: Why Today's Congress Lacks the Will and the Way to Stop Presidential Initiatives*, 45 WILLAMETTE L. REV. 395, 396–97, 398 (2009) (arguing that "[u]nless and until party polarization diminishes, Congress is unlikely to assert its institutional prerogatives" and "[t]oday's Congress, unlike the Watergate-era, has neither the will nor the way to check presidential initiatives").

[129] FRANCES E. LEE, INSECURE MAJORITIES: CONGRESS AND THE PERPETUAL CAMPAIGN (2016).

[130] Daryl J. Levinson & Richard H. Pildes, *Separation of Parties, Not Powers*, 119 HARV. L. REV. 2311 (2006) (arguing that during periods of partisan polarization, the amount and nature of competition between Congress and the president will change substantially, and potentially evaporate, depending on whether party control of the political branches is divided or unified).

[131] *See supra* note 85 and accompanying text.

[132] For discussion with examples, see CHAFETZ, *supra* note 109, at 28–41. According to the political science literature, many members of Congress have motivations other than reelection, including a desire to promote sound public policy, to be influential while in office, and to obtain private gain afterwards. *See* Bradley & Morrison, *supra* note 101, at 442 (describing the findings of political science scholarship). But the motivation to be reelected has significant explanatory power, perhaps because it is both an end and a means to these other ends.

440 THE COLLECTIVE-ACTION CONSTITUTION

presidents, it is typically due more to policy disagreements than to their willingness to defend the institutional interests of their chambers. Moreover, there is no public-regarding reason why Congress should play much less of a role in holding the executive branch accountable when government is unified. Unified government is probably when it is most critical for Congress to provide effective oversight.

The point of the foregoing collective-action analysis of supermajority voting rules in Congress is not to discount, let alone dismiss, the importance of these four factors, especially when some action by congressional majorities is possible. The point, rather, is that these factors offer an incomplete explanation of why Congress does not function as Madison and other Founders expected. For example, although high levels of bipartisanship are often impossible in contemporary politics, it is the two-thirds supermajority requirements in the Constitution that often trigger the need for high levels of bipartisanship in the first place. These supermajority rules—not just insufficient motivation— also explain the great difficulty that Congress has legislating against executive encroachments and that the Senate has convicting an impeached president. Under simple majority rule or a three-fifths supermajority rule, there would likely be more such legislation and a higher probability of convicting an impeached president.

Put differently, Congress is not well positioned to combat presidential overreach today due to the interaction of supermajority voting rules and political conditions that the Framers did not anticipate. These conditions include the collective-action problems besetting members of Congress; their dominant incentive to be reelected; the development of the party system in the United States in the late eighteenth and early nineteenth centuries; the rise of policy-based vetoes in the nineteenth century and the dramatic expansion of executive power since the start of the twentieth century; the rise of partisan polarization in the latter decades of that century; and the existence today of partisan animosity and a national polity that is divided roughly equally. Neither party will likely control two-thirds of either legislative chamber any time soon, nor is a two-thirds bipartisan supermajority likely to impose significant discipline on a president.

Potential Substitutes for Congress

The effects of the supermajority rules discussed in this section are less concerning insofar as viable substitutes for Congress exist. Courts play a role in limiting executive power, but they are not an adequate substitute for legislation. As illustrated by the political question doctrine, some executive actions are not subject to judicial review.[133] Moreover, absent already existing legislation barring the president's conduct, courts are often unwilling to significantly constrain executive power.[134] When individual rights are not at stake, the judiciary's reticence is often justified: Congress may have greater institutional capacity and democratic legitimacy than courts to determine the severity of certain presidential encroachments or to render some constitutional judgments, such as whether a president's introduction of troops into hostilities is constitutionally permissible.[135] Finally, members of Congress take an oath "to support this Constitution" and so should not offload constitutional judgments to judges, even if they often do so in an America in which the institution of judicial review is firmly established.[136]

Judicial review is an even poorer alternative to the impeachment process. Unlike what is typically true of judicial review, impeachment proceedings involve more than legal judgments. The process takes place in the political branches in part because the proceedings appropriately include prudential judgments—which should not be confused with partisanship—about grave political misconduct.[137] Moreover, conviction may result in a president's removal from office and disqualification from holding future office. Courts cannot provide these remedies.

Nor are presidential elections an adequate replacement for legislation or impeachment proceedings. Democratic elections are profoundly important; they are the primary way to confer democratic legitimacy on the decisions made by elected officials, including presidential decisions to issue vetoes and congressional judgments about the existence and seriousness of collective-action problems facing the states. Democratic elections are also an essential way in which to hold politicians accountable for their conduct. But presidents who will not run for reelection will not be disciplined by the desire to retain their office, and presidents who will run for reelection may succeed in gaining sufficient support among the voting population notwithstanding their abuses of power and constitutional violations. Further, the next election is no substitute when presidents, due to misconduct, should not be permitted to complete their terms.

---

[133] Oetjen v. Central Leather Co., 246 U.S. 297, 302 (1918) ("The conduct of the foreign relations of our Government is committed by the Constitution to the Executive and Legislative—'the political'—Departments of the Government, and the propriety of what may be done in the exercise of this political power is not subject to judicial inquiry or decision.").

[134] *Cf.* Youngstown Sheet & Tube Co. v. Sawyer, 343 U.S. 579, 635–38 (1952) (Jackson, J., concurring) (identifying three zones into which presidential action may fall and describing presidential "power [a]s at its lowest ebb" when the president acts despite a congressional prohibition).

[135] *See, e.g.*, War Powers Resolution of 1973, Pub. L. No. 93-148, *codified at* 50 U.S.C. § 1541 et. seq. (2018).

[136] U.S. CONST. art. VI, § 1, cl. 3 (oath requirement). *See* Paul Brest, *The Conscientious Legislator's Guide to Constitutional Interpretation*, 27 STAN. L. REV. 585 (1975).

[137] AMAR, *supra* note 10, at 198–204.

442   THE COLLECTIVE-ACTION CONSTITUTION

The Founders did not view popular elections for members of the House (or members of state legislatures, who appointed senators before the Seventeenth Amendment) as sufficient to prevent Congress from dominating the president. The same holds for preventing domination in the opposite direction. "A dependence on the people is, no doubt, the primary control on the government," Madison wrote in *Federalist 51*, "but experience has taught mankind the necessity of auxiliary precautions."[138]

Criminal prosecution of a sitting president is also no substitute for legislation or impeachment proceedings. First, the prevailing view among constitutional law scholars, which accords with the position of the US Department of Justice, is that presidents may not be criminally prosecuted while they remain in office.[139] It would be problematic to render every current president vulnerable to prosecution by every (perhaps politically motivated) prosecutor's office in the nation, particularly because prosecution can wait until after the individual is no longer president. Second, the prevailing view among such scholars is that presidential conduct need not be criminal to be impeachable. A president who did not respond to an invasion of the country by a foreign military would not be behaving criminally, but such a president should be impeached, convicted, and removed immediately. In short, criminal prosecution is not available while the individual remains president, and prosecution would not be appropriate anyway if the impeachable conduct were not criminal.[140]

Finally, states can act in certain ways to police presidential abuses of power. State governments are less likely than Congress to have supermajority voting rules (whether to override vetoes or to break filibusters), and a number of states have less strict veto-override requirements than the two-thirds rule that applies to Congress.[141] Moreover, state government is unified far more frequently than the federal government.[142] These facts suggest that states may sometimes have greater ability and motivation to check presidential abuses of power than Congress. For example, states can sue over certain executive actions they deem unlawful, and, as Professors Jessica Bulman-Pozen and Heather Gerken argue,

---

[138] THE FEDERALIST NO. 51, at 322 (James Madison) (Clinton Rossiter ed., 1961).

[139] A Sitting President's Amenability to Indictment and Criminal Prosecution, 24 Op. O.L.C. 222, 222 (2000) (reaffirming the Department of Justice's conclusion in 1973 that "[t]he indictment or criminal prosecution of a sitting President would unconstitutionally undermine the capacity of the executive branch to perform its constitutionally assigned functions").

[140] For discussion of both positions described in the text, see AMAR, *supra* note 10, at 200–02.

[141] McCARTY, *supra* note 125, at 147.

[142] *Id.*; Jessica Bulman-Pozen, *Partisan Federalism*, 127 HARV. L. REV. 1077, 1092–93 (2014) ("The same partisan dynamics that yield gridlock in Washington may . . . yield differentiated action in the states."); *id.* at 1097 n.69 ("At the state level, unified party government is currently prevalent."); Jacob M. Grumbach, *From Backwaters to Major Policymakers: Policy Polarization in the States, 1970-2014*, 16 PERSPECTIVES ON POL. 416 (2018) (finding that from 1970 to 2014, the federal government was unified 27 percent of the time while states on average were unified 50 percent of the time).

states can leverage their role as administrators of federal policies to resist their implementation or extract concessions from the federal government.[143] In principle, such resistance can be a way of voicing concerns about presidential encroachments on congressional authority or unconstitutional presidential conduct. These actions are potentially important, especially when courts support them.

Under the Supremacy Clause, however, states cannot enact legislation that structures or prohibits presidential conduct; only Congress can.[144] Further, states cannot remove presidents from office or bar them from holding future office. Thus, while it is plausible to argue that states can act based on partisan or policy disagreements with the executive branch,[145] it is less plausible to contend that states have generally effective ways of preventing presidents from encroaching on Congress or acting unconstitutionally, especially when states would lack standing to sue.[146] States seem as likely to be victimized by congressional inaction when presidents abuse their powers vis-à-vis Congress than to viably substitute for Congress, because states can no longer rely on Congress to (1) protect federal statutes that solve collective-action problems for them or (2) check presidential encroachments on state authority.[147]

There are other potential substitutes. Within government, administrative agencies and even the military have some ability to resist unlawful or otherwise dangerous exercises of presidential power, particularly given ideological diversity within and across agencies in an administration.[148] Outside government, the news media, academic institutions, and other participants in civil society can call out troubling presidential conduct. But it is difficult to see how these alternatives can sufficiently replace a national legislature with the way and the will to impose legal limitations on presidential conduct, to remove presidents from office, or to render them ineligible to hold public office again.

Unfortunately, there are no generally effective substitutes for federal legislation that would respond to encroachments on congressional powers and constitutional violations by presidents. There are also no substitutes for the impeachment process. The Founders did not realize that presidents could veto legislation not

---

[143] Jessica Bulman-Pozen & Heather K. Gerken, *Uncooperative Federalism*, 118 YALE L.J. 1256 (2009).

[144] U.S. CONST. art. VI, § 1, cl. 2 (discussed in Chapters 1 and 7).

[145] Bulman-Pozen, *supra* note 142.

[146] The ability of states to challenge federal action is limited by the rule of *Massachusetts v. Mellon*, 262 U.S. 447 (1923), that states may not sue the federal government in their capacity as *parens patriae*—i.e., as representatives of their citizens.

[147] McCARTY, *supra* note 125, at 146.

[148] Joshua Clinton et al., *Separated Powers in the United States: The Ideology of Agencies, Presidents, and Congress*, 56 AM. J. POL. SCI. 341, 345–49 (2012) (finding significant ideological differences between political appointees and civil servants within agencies and significant ideological differences across agencies within an administration).

444 THE COLLECTIVE-ACTION CONSTITUTION

only to prevent abuses by Congress but also to insulate abuses from Congress. Nor did the Founders anticipate how difficult it would be for the Senate to convict even impeached presidents who pose grave danger to the nation. As a result of these and other failures of foresight, the Founders approved supermajority voting rules for overriding vetoes and convicting presidents that are very difficult to meet under contemporary political conditions. It is likely not a coincidence that the modern presidency, depending on who occupies the office, poses the greatest threat to American democracy—the greatest risk of authoritarianism.[149] In this instance, it is easier to identify the constitutional problem than to solve it, and the primary role of the Collective-Action Constitution is critique, not construction.

Conclusion

This chapter has analyzed supermajority voting rules in the Constitution that— either in and of themselves or under modern political conditions—differ in questionable ways from Article VII's sensible two-thirds requirement to ratify the Constitution. Unlike Article VII, Article V does not involve a one-time decision. Yet, it places a three-fourths requirement atop a two-thirds requirement, thereby effectively letting the states, which are reasonably represented in Congress, vote twice. Unlike Article VII, the treaty-making process involves neither a one-time decision nor formal constitutional change. Yet, Article II retains the two-thirds requirement imposed by the Articles of Confederation, which severely impedes collective action by states in Congress. Unlike Article VII, neither the federal legislative process nor the impeachment process involves a one-time decision or formal constitutional change. Yet, by giving presidents veto authority that expanded over time and by requiring two-thirds supermajorities in each house to override vetoes, the text effectively retains the strict supermajority voting rule for most legislation under Article IX of the Articles when congressional legislation seeks to resist abuses of executive power, including efforts by the president to undermine statutory solutions to multistate collective-action problems. Moreover, by requiring the approval of two-thirds of the Senate, the Constitution makes it extraordinarily difficult to convict impeached presidents in contemporary circumstances.

Workarounds have developed for the Article V process and the treaty-making process, and they have proven reasonably effective. No such substitutes have

---

[149] STEVEN LEVITSKY & DANIEL ZIBLATT, HOW DEMOCRACIES DIE 203 (2018) (analyzing former President Trump's conduct during his first year in office and concluding that even if he "does not break the hard guardrails of our constitutional democracy, he has increased the likelihood that a future president will").

been developed to overcome the two-thirds requirements to override presidential vetoes or to convict presidents of impeachable offenses. As a partial result, executive power has dramatically expanded over time. It cannot be proven that deviating so substantially from the Constitution's default baseline of majority rule makes collective action by members of Congress—which protects collective action by states in Congress—too difficult to accomplish regarding these subjects. But in a country with political parties, policy-based vetoes, expansive executive power, partisan polarization, partisan animosity, and a closely divided polity, these strict supermajority voting rules have likely become dysfunctional and counterproductive.

11

The Problem of Congressional Gridlock

Introduction

One primary goal of the Founders, this book has argued, was to make it easier for the states to act collectively in Congress than it was under the Articles of Confederation. Recall that Article IX had required two-thirds of the states in Congress to agree before it could exercise its most potent powers, and Article XIII had required all states to agree before Congress could be given additional powers, such as to regulate commerce. By contrast, the Constitution ordinarily permits Congress to legislate if majorities in both chambers approve, and it grants Congress more formidable powers, including commercial ones. As Professor George William Van Cleve concludes, the Constitution emerged from "the states' and sections' willingness to confer fundamental new powers on the national government and to permit them to be exercised by majority vote."[1]

Today, however, it is typically very difficult for Congress to legislate—far more difficult than one would generally expect from the operation of majority voting rules. This chapter's first objective is to explain why. It identifies five main causes that interact to frequently produce congressional gridlock. The first two are closely connected to the original constitutional text; they are defensible considered by themselves because they advance important constitutional objectives without standing as immovable obstacles to collective action by states in Congress. The third has a footing in both text and practice; it is normatively questionable but firmly established. The last two have been produced by later developments; one should likely be abandoned, and the other is a fact of contemporary political life in the United States.

First, the Constitution creates a bicameral national legislature with chambers that enjoy equal power to block legislation. Requiring majorities in two chambers to pass bills obviously makes it more difficult to legislate than requiring one majority in a unicameral legislature. Second, the Constitution does not establish a system of parliamentary supremacy, in which the legislature chooses the executive (guaranteeing that they are of the same political party), and courts cannot hold legislation unconstitutional. The Constitution instead creates a

---

[1] GEORGE WILLIAM VAN CLEVE, WE HAVE NOT A GOVERNMENT: THE ARTICLES OF CONFEDERATION AND THE ROAD TO THE CONSTITUTION 286–87 (2017).

The Collective-Action Constitution. Neil S. Siegel, Oxford University Press. © Neil S. Siegel 2024.
DOI: 10.1093/oso/9780197760963.003.0012

separation-of-powers system, in which the president is separately elected and courts possess the power of judicial review. Third, the text of the Veto Clause licenses presidential veto power that is far broader than the Founders intended it to be, and presidents eventually embraced a maximally broad reading of the text.

Fourth, the Senate's filibuster rule requires three-fifths of its membership to agree before it passes most bills. This subconstitutional "veto-gate" impedes Congress's ability to legislate and empowers the president. Fifth, the Founders failed to anticipate political parties, let alone the polarized and hostile parties that exist today in a nation so closely split that divided government is the norm. Although partisan polarization is not necessarily harmful and does not generally produce gridlock in two-party parliamentary systems, it does so in a separation-of-powers system that routinely results in divided government. The cumulative consequences of these five causes have typically been frequent congressional inaction despite serious social problems of broad geographic scope, and frequent unilateral action by the president or state governments that Congress seldom overrides. A gridlocked Congress also increases the power of the federal courts relative to Congress.

Understanding the causes of congressional inaction in contemporary political times enables critique—this chapter's second objective. The Constitution presupposes a functioning Congress to achieve key constitutional purposes— including solving collective-action problems for the states, preventing states from causing such problems, deciding whether to allow states to solve or cause such problems, protecting individual rights, and holding the executive and the federal judiciary accountable. Today, however, Congress is often not up to the task. This disconnect between institutional assumptions and realities is probably the single-greatest defect of the Constitution in modern America.

The effect of congressional gridlock on the relative power of other branches and the states points toward potential workarounds, although they are partial and raise concerns of their own. One primary workaround, as noted above, has been greater exercises of unilateral power by the president. Presidential governance can be warranted when the alternative is no federal response to problems requiring such a response. As Chapter 10 argued, however, executive unilateralism can also undermine congressional solutions to multistate collective-action problems, and it poses greater risks of democratic deficits and authoritarianism than congressional power. In any event, executive orders are easier than statutes for the next president to undo, and the president cannot "legislate" by executive order to anywhere near the extent that Congress can legislate by statute.

Another possible workaround is "statutory updating" by federal judges, who may alter the meaning of federal laws to help the US Code reflect major changes in social circumstances and values. This potential workaround is at best partial, however, because Congress is also charged with passing new laws to address

THE PROBLEM OF CONGRESSIONAL GRIDLOCK 449

new problems, not just with updating old laws to address long-standing, related problems. Further, it is controversial whether statutory updating is ever within the judicial role, let alone whether it is routinely so. Federal courts possess far less democratic legitimacy than the political branches.

A more frequent potential workaround has been greater exercises of state regulatory power, which is preempted less often when Congress passes fewer laws. States may try to partially address interstate or international problems by passing individual legislation or forming interstate compacts. As Chapter 3 explained, however, states are no substitute for Congress when they would need to act collectively to meet a regulatory challenge. Individual action by states is unlikely to significantly address national or international problems, and it is almost certainly more difficult for states to form interstate compacts involving most or all states than it is for Congress to legislate. Compacts require the unanimous agreement of the states involved and may require Congress's approval, given the constitutional text and the concern that compacts may harm the federal government or state nonparties to the compacts. As hard as it is for Congress to legislate today, it is not *that* difficult, which explains why there have been relatively few interstate compacts involving large numbers of states while there have been many federal laws. Even amid current polarization and a closely divided polity, Congress has passed a good number of significant statutes.

Congress could change certain subconstitutional rules, especially the legislative filibuster, which this book reluctantly advises. But veto practice is very unlikely to change; amending the Constitution to make it easier to legislate is practically impossible; and political realignments do not often occur. Thus, congressional gridlock is likely to endure. Americans are still better off than they would be, however, if they had to rely on the states acting through unanimity rule to solve collective-action problems or to fulfill Congress's other regulatory functions.

Bicameralism

Under Article V of the Articles of Confederation, state governments sent delegations to the unicameral Confederation Congress to cast one vote each for one-year terms, and state governments paid these delegates and could recall them at will.[2] As several earlier chapters explained, Congress's powers were strictly limited, and under Article IX, exercising the most important of them required the support of two-thirds of the state delegations and the willingness of state governments to honor treaty obligations and congressional requisitions

---

[2] ARTICLES OF CONFEDERATION of 1781, art. V.

450   THE COLLECTIVE-ACTION CONSTITUTION

for money and troops. Moreover, under Article XIII, Congress could not exercise additional powers unless every state agreed to grant them. As for the states themselves, prominent Federalists like Hamilton and Madison concluded by the late 1780s that state legislatures often encroached on the constitutional powers of state executives and judiciaries.[3]

Under the US Constitution, things would be different. Under Article I, Section 8, Congress would enjoy substantially greater powers, and under the second clause of Article I, Section 7, it would ordinarily be able to exercise them by majority vote in each chamber. Members would serve for longer terms (two years for House members and six for senators); House members would not be chosen or paid by state legislatures and would not be subject to recall; senators, although chosen by state legislatures, would not be paid by them or subject to recall; and all members would vote as individuals, not as members of state delegations.[4] Further, Congress would not need state governments to regulate individuals and enforce federal law. Congress could regulate individual behavior directly, and under Articles II and III, the federal executive and judiciary would enforce federal law, including treaty obligations.

The foregoing facts suffice to explain why the Framers chose bicameralism over unicameralism. They were creating a substantially more powerful legislature that would be substantially less dependent on state governments at a time when legislatures were thought to exceed constitutional boundaries and encroach on coordinate branches. "In republican government," Madison explained in *Federalist 51*, "the legislative authority necessarily predominates." "The remedy for this inconveniency," he insisted, "is to divide the legislature into different branches; and to render them, by different modes of election and different principles of action, as little connected with each other as the nature of their common functions and their common dependence on the society will admit." Bicameralism, like the veto power discussed in Chapter 10, partially served to keep Congress from encroaching on the other branches. Just "[a]s the weight of legislative authority requires that it should be thus divided," Madison reasoned, "the weakness of the executive may require, on the other hand, that it should be fortified."[5] Moreover, by reducing the likelihood that bills exceeding congressional power would pass, bicameralism would protect state governments.

Bicameralism impedes collective action relative to unicameralism by requiring two majorities to enact legislation. If different political parties control

---

[3] AKHIL REED AMAR, AMERICA'S CONSTITUTION: A BIOGRAPHY 59 (2005) (discussing the views of Hamilton and Madison).

[4] U.S. CONST. art. I, § 2, cl. 1 (composition of the House); art. I, § 3, cl. 1 (composition of the Senate); art. I, § 6, cl. 1 (compensation of members of Congress). For additional differences between the Confederation Congress and the US Congress, see AMAR, *supra* note 3, at 58.

[5] THE FEDERALIST No. 51, at 322–23 (James Madison) (Clinton Rossiter ed., 1961).

THE PROBLEM OF CONGRESSIONAL GRIDLOCK   451

each chamber, then at least one chamber must muster a bipartisan majority, which in many cases will be a supermajority. This is a cost of having a two-house legislature, which is presumably why most countries do not have them (although larger ones tend to have them), and why those nations with bicameral parliaments rarely give both chambers equal authority to block legislation.[6] Still, enabling Congress to encroach on other branches (or states) or to violate the Constitution is not why Congress is given powers to solve collective-action problems and to perform other functions. True, bicameralism makes it harder for Congress to pass all laws, not just encroaching or unconstitutional ones. But this part of the structure is partially justified by its role in limiting Congress's ability to render other branches or states subservient to it.

From a collective-action perspective, American-style bicameralism can also be defended as enhancing the democratic legitimacy of congressional determinations that there are collective-action problems in need of solving when the states are divided on the matter. Such legitimacy, Chapter 1 explained, depends on the plausibility of the claim that the interests of all states and all people are better represented in Congress than anywhere else. (As noted above, members of Congress are less dependent on state governments than were members of the Confederation Congress, but state "peoples" are equally represented in the Senate). Relative to a unicameral legislature organized around either equal representation of states or equal representation of individuals, the plausibility of this claim is arguably enhanced by equal representation of states in one chamber (even after ratification of the Seventeenth Amendment) and equal representation of individuals in the other. Strongly federal nations, including the United States, Germany, Switzerland, Canada, and Australia, characteristically have bicameral legislatures.[7]

Bicameralism can be defended in other ways. Depending on the length of the terms of members of the upper house relative to members of the lower house, bicameralism may better insulate Congress from passing passions. Again, senators serve for six years. Depending on the number of members of the upper house relative to the lower one, bicameralism may render Congress less parochial than it otherwise would be. The average senator represents many more people than the average House member. Every state legislature but Nebraska's is bicameral, and "almost all upper houses differ from the lower houses either by length of term or by the number of people represented."[8] But these arguments are somewhat

---

[6] SANFORD LEVINSON, OUR UNDEMOCRATIC CONSTITUTION: WHERE THE CONSTITUTION GOES WRONG (AND HOW WE THE PEOPLE CAN CORRECT IT) 30 (2006); see id. ("Not since 1911 ... has the House of Lords enjoyed any real parity of power with the House of Commons, and it has become ever weaker in the almost full century since.").

[7] Id.; see id. ("Bicameralism to some extent may be a proxy for the degree that one is committed to preferring the dispersion of loyalties and identities attached to federalism as against focusing more strongly on a single *national* identity.").

[8] Id. at 34.

452　THE COLLECTIVE-ACTION CONSTITUTION

speculative because the ability and willingness of legislators to take the longer view and be more broadminded also depends on other factors. The level of partisan polarization, discussed later in this chapter, may also affect the time horizon and geographic perspective of legislators, and "polarization in the House and the Senate turned sharply upward at approximately the same time in the middle of the 1970s."[9]

Finally, bicameralism can be defended as promoting policy stability and a more consensual form of governance relative to pure majority rule.[10] The same could be said of supermajority rules writ large. In evaluating the structural Constitution, however, the key question is not whether to choose bicameralism, a supermajority requirement for legislation, or pure majority rule. Rather, given the role of bicameralism in increasing the chances that the use of congressional power will be constitutionally permissible, democratically legitimate from the perspectives of both states and individuals, and not purely majoritarian, the issue is whether to impose additional impediments to legislating. Unfortunately, the separation of powers, policy-based vetoes or veto threats, and the Senate's filibuster rule, all on top of bicameralism, impose a cumulative burden that is very high, especially during periods of partisan polarization. As will be shown, it is no virtue that the Constitution gives Congress formidable powers to solve serious problems that Congress is frequently unable to exercise.

The Separation of Powers

Most democracies have a parliamentary system in which the head of government, usually called the prime minister, is chosen by the national legislature. In a two-party system such as Great Britain's (called the Westminster system), this form of government thereby guarantees that the same party controls both the executive and the legislature, which diminishes conflict between the two branches.[11] By contrast, in the separation-of-powers (or presidential) system created by the Framers, the president is elected separately from members of Congress, so there is no guarantee that the executive and the legislature are of the same party. In the modern United States, divided government is the norm, which increases conflict between the branches.[12]

---

[9] NOLAN MCCARTY, POLARIZATION: WHAT EVERYONE NEEDS TO KNOW 32 (2019); *see id.* at 31–32 ("While currently the House is more polarized than the Senate, there is no general pattern. In earlier periods, the Senate was the more polarized.").

[10] LEVINSON, *supra* note 6, at 31–34.

[11] In a multiparty parliamentary system, the situation is more complex because selecting the head of government requires forming a coalition, which in turn can require giving different parties a role in policymaking.

[12] Dean Lacy et al., *Measuring Preferences for Divided Government: Some Americans Want Divided Government and Vote to Create It*, 41 POL. BEHAVIOR 79, 80 (2019) ("Relatively rare in earlier periods

THE PROBLEM OF CONGRESSIONAL GRIDLOCK   453

In addition, although members of the federal judiciary are nominated by the president and confirmed by the Senate, federal judges serve for life absent impeachment and conviction, so they enjoy a very high degree of independence from the political branches.[13] As Chapter 7 explained, federal judges wield the power of judicial review, which means that they can both invalidate laws they adjudge to be unconstitutional in cases properly before them and interpret statutes to avoid constitutional doubts about them. The Constitution contains no judicial review clause, but strong textual, structural, and originalist arguments support the inference that the federal courts possess this power, as does acquiescence in the practice by the political branches and the states and more than two centuries of judicial precedent.[14] Courts in modern parliamentary systems often possess the power of judicial review, but they lack this authority in systems of parliamentary supremacy that follow the British Westminster model.[15]

Much has been written for and against parliamentary and presidential systems, and these arguments will not be rehearsed here.[16] The debate is complex in part because there are many variations among parliamentary and presidential systems. Instead, this section will focus on the impediments to legislation produced by the presidential system in the United States relative to most modern parliamentary systems. Regarding the legislative process, the strongest argument for the US separation of powers is that it enables the executive (through the veto power) and the courts (through judicial review) to resist encroachments and to

in US history, divided government has become the new normal. The party of the president failed to control at least one house of Congress in eighteen of the twenty-five congresses between 1969 and 2017.").

[13] U.S. CONST. art. II, § 2, cl. 2 (appointment of federal judges); art. III, § 1 (federal judicial service "during good Behaviour"). As Chapter 7 discussed, Hamilton interpreted Article III's "good Behaviour" language to mean life tenure, and this language has long been glossed by practice to mean life tenure absent impeachment and conviction.

[14] *Marbury v. Madison*, 5 U.S. (1 Cranch) 137 (1803), offered classic formal arguments for judicial review.

[15] The principle of parliamentary supremacy makes parliament the supreme legal authority in a country by granting it the power to enact or repeal any law. Many modern parliamentary systems constrain the powers of parliament by granting independence to institutions—often including a constitutional court—that can check parliament. *See* Bruce Ackerman, *The New Separation of Powers*, 113 HARV. L. REV. 633 (2000).

[16] For an argument that the presidential system generates impasses between the political branches, tempts the president to act unilaterally, and produces a "cult of personality" surrounding the president that injures democratic politics, see *id.* at 643–64. For historical discussion of parliamentary critics of the presidential system starting in the nineteenth century, see Thomas O. Sargentich, *The Limitations of the Parliamentary Critique of the Separation of Powers*, 34 WM. & MARY L. REV. 679, 684–706 (1993). For an argument that the presidential system is "more democratic, more stable, less ideological, more protective of judicial review, and more libertarian than will be parliamentary regimes, all else being equal," see Steven G. Calabresi, *The Virtues of Presidential Government: Why Professor Ackerman Is Wrong to Prefer the German to the U.S. Constitution*, 18 CONST. COMMENT. 51, 56 (2001). For a critique of parliamentary systems as leaving the prime minister potentially unchecked and unaccountable because the same party controls the executive and legislature, see Sargentich, *supra*, at 723–27.

454   THE COLLECTIVE-ACTION CONSTITUTION

prevent unconstitutional bills from becoming or remaining law—including bills that encroach on the powers of state governments.

This rationale for the separation of powers is implicit in the letter that begins this book. In submitting the draft Constitution to the Confederation Congress, Washington explained on behalf of the Philadelphia Convention why its architecture had to differ from the Articles:

> The friends of our country have long seen and desired, that the power of making war, peace and treaties, that of levying money and regulating commerce, and the correspondent executive and judicial authorities should be fully and effectually vested in the general government of the Union: but the impropriety of delegating such extensive trust to one body of men is evident—Hence results the necessity of a different organization.[17]

The separation of powers was intended to serve much the same Constitution-enforcing function as bicameralism. As Professor Akhil Amar writes, the purpose of the separation of powers was not to minimize the quantity of federal statutes but "to minimize the likelihood that an *arguably unconstitutional* federal law would pass and take effect."[18]

Because they share a common purpose, discussions of bicameralism and the separation of powers are often lumped together. They are split apart here to underscore that a constitutional system could have just one and that having both makes it more difficult to legislate than having one. The greatest potential concern with the US separation of powers is that it makes it too difficult for Congress to address pressing problems through legislation. Holding constant whether the legislature is bicameral or unicameral, the extent to which it is more difficult to legislate under a presidential system than a parliamentary system with judicial review turns primarily on whether presidents limit their use of the veto power to encroachments on their office or good-faith constitutional concerns. A presidential system will make it challenging to legislate insofar as presidents routinely veto (or threaten to veto) bills based on policy objections or Congress avoids proposing or passing bills that presidents oppose on policy grounds. Unfortunately, the modern practice is for presidents to use or threaten vetoes for any of these reasons and for Congress to anticipate their policy views in deciding whether to propose or enact legislation.

---

[17] 2 THE RECORDS OF THE FEDERAL CONVENTION OF 1787, at 666–67 (Max Farrand ed., 1911) (Sept. 17, 1787).

[18] AMAR, *supra* note 3, at 62; *see id.* at 62–64 (arguing that the separation of powers also promotes the rule of law, specialization of labor, and "a more accurate and more stable composite sketch of deliberate public opinion").

The Overbroad Veto Power

Recall that the second clause of Article I, Section 7, gives the president power to veto bills passed by majorities in both houses of Congress. A veto prevents the bills from becoming law unless two-thirds of each chamber votes to override it.[19] The grant of such power to the president poses a puzzle. As Chapter 4 discussed, a key way in which the Constitution is designed to facilitate collective action by states is by letting Congress legislate by majority vote in each chamber, not by the two-thirds requirement in Article IX of the Articles of Confederation. Yet, a veto requires not just one two-thirds vote to overcome it, but two. It is therefore worth asking why the Constitution allows the president to impose a voting rule more demanding than the one in the Articles—and whether, given modern problems and expectations of government, this arrangement makes sense.

Founding Rationale

As Chapter 10 explained, at the Founding, a functional logic supported giving the president the veto power. During the 1780s, state legislatures had dominated state executives, so many Founders feared that Congress would overwhelm the president. For example, in *Federalist 48*, Madison argued that "in a representative republic where the executive magistracy is carefully limited," the power wielded by the legislature is most to be feared. "The legislative department," he warned, "is everywhere extending the sphere of its activity and drawing all power into its impetuous vortex."[20]

The Framers gave presidents the veto power mainly so that they could defend their office against congressional encroachments. In *Federalist 73*, Hamilton reminded the reader that "[t]he propensity of the legislative department to intrude upon the rights, and to absorb the powers, of the other departments has been already more than once suggested," and he tied the Framers' general concerns about legislative aggrandizement to a specific defense of the veto power.[21] Without this power, Hamilton argued, the president "would be absolutely unable to defend himself against the depredations" of Congress.[22]

The veto power likely had a secondary purpose. Professor Charles Black, after stressing the primary original objective noted above, suggested that the Founders may have expected that presidents would use the veto to resist bills

---

[19] U.S. Const. art. I, § 7, cl. 2.

[20] The Federalist No. 48, at 309 (James Madison) (Clinton Rossiter ed., 1961).

[21] The Federalist No. 73, at 442 (Alexander Hamilton) (Clinton Rossiter ed., 1961).

[22] *Id.*; *see id.* at 443 (observing that "[t]he primary inducement to conferring the power in question upon the executive is to enable him to defend himself").

456   THE COLLECTIVE-ACTION CONSTITUTION

that they concluded were unconstitutional. Such an expectation seems especially likely at a time when courts did not play a major role in declaring legislation unconstitutional and the Founders did not anticipate that they would.[23] Hamilton did not mention this purpose, and Professor Black could not find it in the preratification materials. But political scientist Robert Spitzer found it in his study of the veto power,[24] and Professor Black emphasized that this "theme ... appears very early in veto practice and veto messages," including one that alluded to the Presidential Oath Clause.[25] Use of the veto power to express presidential concerns about constitutionality may have been thought to derive from this clause because it requires presidents to swear or affirm that they will do their best to "preserve, protect and defend the Constitution of the United States."[26] Honoring this oath arguably requires presidents to interpret the Constitution in executing their responsibilities.

Hamilton did write of "a further use" of the veto power, which was to "furnish[] an additional security against the enaction of improper laws"—to reduce the likelihood of passing "bad laws, through haste, inadvertence, or design."[27] Hamilton was there justifying use of the veto power based on certain policy objections, but he added that presidents would veto bills only when "the public good was evidently and palpably sacrificed." "The superior weight and influence of the legislative body in a free government and the hazard to the executive in a trial of strength with that body," he explained, "afford a satisfactory security that the negative would generally be employed with great caution." Hamilton even wrote that the president would be more cautious than the British king, who by then had stopped exercising the right to negative legislation approved by Parliament.[28] Here, as elsewhere in *The Federalist*, Hamilton's words were partially polemical. But "even in its exaggeration," Professor Black emphasized, Hamilton's defense "underscores an original understanding that the veto would be used only rarely, and certainly not as a means of systematic policy control over

[23] After *Marbury v. Madison*, 5 U.S. (1 Cranch) 137 (1803), the Court did not again invalidate a federal law until *Scott v. Sandford*, 60 U.S. (19 How.) 393 (1857). By comparison, and as explained below, presidents during this era vetoed more than twenty bills on constitutional grounds. For sympathetic discussion of the greater use of the constitutional veto than of judicial review during this period, see AMAR, *supra* note 3, at 179–81, 184–85.

[24] ROBERT J. SPITZER, THE PRESIDENTIAL VETO: TOUCHSTONE OF THE AMERICAN PRESIDENCY 17 (1988) (noting, for example, a 1788 letter to Jefferson in which Madison wrote that "[a] revisionary power is meant as a check to precipitate, to unjust, and to unconstitutional laws").

[25] Charles L. Black, Jr., *Some Thoughts on the Veto*, 40 Law & CONTEMP. PROBS. 87, 89 (1976) (writing that "[t]here may have been an anticipation that it would be used to vindicate the President's own constitutional views, by being interposed against legislation he considered unconstitutional," a "theme ... [that] appears very early in veto practice and veto messages," including President Washington's first veto and President Tyler's first veto message, the latter of which alluded to the Oath Clause).

[26] U.S. CONST. art. II, § 1, cl. 8.

[27] THE FEDERALIST NO. 73, at 443 (Alexander Hamilton) (Clinton Rossiter ed., 1961).

[28] *Id.* at 444–45.

THE PROBLEM OF CONGRESSIONAL GRIDLOCK   457

the legislative branch, on matters constitutionally indifferent and not menacing the President's independence."[29]

Professor Spitzer disagrees. He argues that "the circumstances of veto use . . . in the minds of the founders were extremely broad" and "[e]ssentially, the president was free, in constitutional terms, to veto any bill that crossed his desk." In Professor Spitzer's view, "Hamilton's defense of the veto represents a prediction *of its likely use*, not a prescription *for its intended use*."[30] This proposed distinction is questionable, however, because Hamilton was offering a normative defense of the veto power in *Federalist 73*, not a positive analysis of how presidents were likely to use it. He was seeking to persuade his audience that the Constitution should be ratified. Tellingly, he did not imply that his prediction of presidential behavior was much narrower than the intended scope of the president's authority to veto bills. Thus, the most reasonable inference to draw from Hamilton's discussion was that the convention's intent, and the understanding of his readers, aligned with his prediction of rare use.

Beyond Hamilton, Spitzer concludes that "[a]gain and again in the convention's consideration of the veto power, one central theme persistently surfaced: the veto as a device of executive self-protection against encroachments of the legislature."[31] This more narrowly focused veto power makes substantially more structural sense of the original Constitution than a robust veto power, but Professor Spitzer does not consider the structural implications of broad veto authority for the likelihood of enabling the kinds of collective action that mainly explain the Constitution's creation. The best conclusion is probably Professor Black's: the Framers intended for presidents to veto bills almost always to protect their office or to enforce the Constitution, and rarely to voice policy objections based on a special justification, like national-security concerns.

A much earlier analysis supports Professor Spitzer. Edward Campbell Mason disagreed that the objections assigned to a bill by a vetoing president must be "to the intrinsic merits of a bill," because "[t]his restriction would narrow the plain wording of the Constitution," which "sets no limit upon the nature of the objections stated by the President, nor is it generally assumed that there are any limits." "If there be none," Mason continued, "the President has a constitutional right to veto a bill simply because undue influence had been used in securing its passage, or for any other reason that seems good to him." Mason later noted the "well-settled principle that a President is the sole judge of the nature of the reasons which shall be assigned for a veto." Although Mason correctly identified the breadth of de facto presidential power, he did

---

[29] Black, *supra* note 25, at 90.
[30] SPITZER, *supra* note 24, at 18.
[31] *Id.* at 15.

458   THE COLLECTIVE-ACTION CONSTITUTION

not show that the Framers' intent or original understanding was as broad as practice would later become or that presidents' constitutional obligations were as narrow as what they could get away with. Nor does it seem true that policy-based vetoes increased over time and Constitution-based vetoes decreased just because the issues changed—because "the era of great constitutional debates has passed."[32]

If the account offered here is correct, it is necessary to explain why the Framers approved such an open-ended veto provision instead of specifying that vetoes were to be limited to certain permissible uses. Part of the answer may be the difficulty of crafting such a provision, which would need to cover not only bills that the president deems unconstitutional but also bills that encroach on the institutional independence of the presidency and perhaps rare policy-based vetoes that raise national security concerns. Another part of the answer is likely that the Framers did not think it was necessary to craft such textual limitations. They could not imagine that the presidency, as opposed to Congress, would come to dominate American politics.

Early Historical Practice and Collective Action

Early historical practice largely followed original expectations. Until Andrew Johnson, presidents vetoed bills sparingly—fifty-nine times. (This number, like all numbers reported in this section, includes both regular vetoes and pocket vetoes.[33]) Although some of these vetoes were based on policy disagreements with Congress, most reflected either constitutional scruples or national-security concerns.[34] Vetoes based on national security can often be viewed as presidential defenses of their office. Presidents play the dominant role in protecting the nation from attack, as indicated by the Presidential Oath Clause and especially by the Commander in Chief Clause.[35]

Washington vetoed only two bills in eight years, one based on constitutional objections and the other on national-security grounds.[36] He also did not sign the bill creating the first Bank of the United States until he heard arguments about its constitutionality from his cabinet.[37] John Adams and

---

[32] EDWARD CAMPBELL MASON, THE VETO POWER: ITS ORIGIN, DEVELOPMENT AND FUNCTION IN THE GOVERNMENT OF THE UNITED STATES 114, 130–31 (1789–1889) (1890).

[33] A pocket veto occurs when Congress sends the president a bill at the end of a legislative session and "Congress by their Adjournment prevent its Return." U.S. CONST. art. I, § 7, cl. 2. Presidents can do nothing—put the bill in their "pocket"—and the bill dies.

[34] Black, *supra* note 25, at 90–92; AMAR, *supra* note 3, at 183.

[35] U.S. CONST. art. II, § 2, cl. 1.

[36] Black, *supra* note 25, at 90.

[37] Daniel A. Farber, *The Story of* McCulloch: *Banking on National Power, in* CONSTITUTIONAL LAW STORIES 33, 39–44 (Michael C. Dorf ed., 2004).

THE PROBLEM OF CONGRESSIONAL GRIDLOCK   459

Thomas Jefferson vetoed no bills. Most of Madison's seven vetoes were Constitution-based, but he was the first president to veto a bill on policy grounds—the one to create the second bank. Even there, however, Madison objected that the bill did not sufficiently provide for successfully prosecuting a war and circulating currency in wartime.[38] James Monroe vetoed one bill in two terms, and it was based on constitutional objections. John Quincy Adams vetoed no bills, and Martin Van Buren vetoed only one. In between, Andrew Jackson vetoed twelve bills, but almost all were constitutional. William Henry Harrison vetoed none.[39]

True, Congress did not pass many laws early on. But this early practice also likely reflects the view that presidents must use the veto power sparingly to facilitate accomplishment of the Constitution's collective-action objectives.[40] When presidents limit vetoes overwhelmingly to sincere defenses of the presidency and the Constitution, Congress retains its predominant role in the legislative process—majority votes in each chamber determine whether bills become law (putting aside for now subconstitutional rules that chambers may impose on themselves). Majority rule does not apply when presidents have constitutional objections or concerns about institutional self-preservation, but there is a good argument that such considerations should ordinarily trump collective action as long as presidents act in good faith. Collective action should occur constitutionally and without undermining the structural integrity of another branch.

One could view this enterprise cynically because policy-based objections can masquerade as constitutional or institutional concerns. But the Framers did not operate under such premises, which is why they produced constitutional text far broader than their intentions regarding proper uses of the veto power. As a result, they made it potentially harder to legislate than it was under the Articles of Confederation, when they had intended to make it easier.

There is another reason that the veto power must play a limited role to render it compatible with collective action in Congress. The representation of all states in Congress furnishes the democratic justification for letting Congress determine, amid potential disagreements among states, that there is a multistate collective-action problem in need of solving. Because states are not as well represented in

---

[38] 28 ANNALS OF CONG. 189–91 (Jan. 30, 1815) (message of James Madison to the Senate).

[39] Black, *supra* note 25, at 90–91; U.S. House of Representatives, Presidential Vetoes (last visited Jun. 8, 2021), https://perma.cc/VW6X-LYA4.

[40] *Cf.* LEVINSON, *supra* note 6, at 41–42 (observing that early veto practice "may be explained simply by reference to the fact that Congress at the time passed relatively little legislation," but that "[i]t may also be explained at least in part by a tension in the very notion of the veto as part of the constitutional system" and the idea that "a president could properly veto a bill only if he believed that it raised constitutional questions").

460 THE COLLECTIVE-ACTION CONSTITUTION

the executive branch as in Congress, turning the president into the third legislative chamber undermines the democratic legitimacy of federal decisions regarding whether collective action is needed.[41]

One response is that presidents represent the American people as a whole—they are the "people's choice" or, as Professor Sanford Levinson puts the idea before rejecting it, the "tribune of the people."[42] Representing people and representing states are not, however, the same thing. Moreover, even as to representing people, a victory in the Electoral College does not ensure that the president has earned a plurality of the popular vote, let alone a majority—or even that the current president, who may have started the term as vice-president, has received any votes to be president.[43] And in practice, presidential campaigns focus on battleground states.[44]

More fundamentally, the presidency involves an up-or-down choice every four years followed by the losing voters having no real voice until the next election. Put differently, the president in modern America represents members of just one political party, not two. There are seriously unrepresentative features of the House (especially partisan gerrymandering) and the Senate (especially the equal representation of the states).[45] But generally, all—or almost all—Americans are better represented in Congress than in the presidency. Congress is a broadly representative body; it is where both political parties are present and where competing interests are weighed. A large majority of Americans can find at least one member of Congress who speaks for them on the issues they care about most.

The constitutional text reflects this difference between Congress and the presidency, and not just by listing the legislative branch first. Since ratification of the Seventeenth Amendment in 1913, the Constitution has required democratic elections for members of both houses of Congress. The text does not require such elections before presidents are chosen. Rather, it provides that "[e]ach State

---

[41] On the better representation of states in Congress than in the executive branch, see Margaret H. Lemos & Ernest A. Young, *State Public Law Litigation in an Age of Polarization*, 97 TEX. L. REV. 43, 63–64 (2018).

[42] LEVINSON, *supra* note 6, at 46–49.

[43] Five presidents lost the popular vote: John Quincy Adams (1824), Rutherford B. Hayes (1876), Benjamin Harrison (1888), George W. Bush (2000), and Donald J. Trump (2016). Four presidents in five elections failed to win a popular majority: Harry Truman (1948), John F. Kennedy (1960), Richard Nixon (1968), and Bill Clinton (1992 and 1996). Nine presidents did not receive any votes when they became president because they were vice-presidents who ascended to the presidency due to the death (eight times) or resignation (once) of the prior president: John Tyler (1841), Millard Fillmore (1850), Andrew Johnson (1865), Chester A. Arthur (1881), Theodore Roosevelt (1901), Calvin Coolidge (1923), Harry S. Truman (1945), Lyndon B. Johnson (1963), and Gerald Ford (1974).

[44] LEVINSON, *supra* note 6, at 87–89.

[45] For discussions of political branch countermajoritarianism, see *id.* at 25–122; and Corinna Barrett Lain, *Upside-Down Judicial Review*, 101 GEO. L.J. 113, 144–57 (2012).

THE PROBLEM OF CONGRESSIONAL GRIDLOCK 461

shall appoint, *in such Manner as the Legislature thereof may direct*, a Number of Electors."[46]

Later Historical Practice and Collective (In)action

Veto practice began to change with John Tyler, who served from 1841 to 1845 and became president upon the death of President William Henry Harrison. Tyler was the first president to veto bills freely based on policy objections.[47] This practice did not take off, however, until later. Starting with Andrew Johnson and ending with Donald Trump, presidents have issued 2,525 vetoes. Along the way, Grover Cleveland issued 584 vetoes over two nonconsecutive terms, and Franklin D. Roosevelt issued 636 vetoes over his three-plus terms.[48] Harry Truman vetoed 250 bills, and Dwight D. Eisenhower vetoed 181.[49] These vetoes have prevented passage of more than 90 percent of the bills at issue. Of the 2,584 vetoes in history, only 112 have been overridden, for a congressional success rate of 4.33 percent. Excluding pocket vetoes (which cannot be overridden), the number of regular vetoes is 1,518 and Congress's success rate is 7.38 percent.[50]

Although part of the large upward trend in vetoes is attributable to Congress's passing more bills over time, these numbers are still impressive, and they significantly understate the president's impact. First, there likely would have more vetoes had presidents disagreed with many more bills on policy grounds. The likelihood of a veto turns in part on whether political forces are aligned in Congress and the White House. Second, and critically, once policy-based vetoes became firmly established—a practice whose legitimacy Congress, the political opposition, and the public accepted—an unknowably large number of bills were never drafted or voted on even though majorities supported them in both houses of Congress. Absent two-thirds support in each chamber, bills were strangled at birth (or before it) by a veto threat or knowledge of the president's opposition on policy grounds.[51]

---

[46] U.S. CONST. art. II, § 1, cl. 2 (emphasis added). *Compare* U.S. CONST. art. I, § 2 (House elections), *and* amend. XVII (Senate elections), *with* art. II, § 1, cl. 2 (presidential elections).

[47] Black, *supra* note 25, at 91.

[48] For both President Cleveland and FDR, the largest number of vetoes were of distributive bills, especially those concerning private pensions. SPITZER, *supra* note 24, at 66–67. Such vetoes can be defended as protecting the public treasury from depletion caused by a collective-action problem among members of Congress—namely, their tendency to overspend US Treasury funds, a common pool resource. It is not clear, however, why the president possesses greater constitutional authority or democratic legitimacy than Congress to make these fiscal calls. Congress, not the president, has the power of the purse, and states and people are better represented in Congress than in the White House.

[49] U.S. House of Representatives, Presidential Vetoes, *supra* note 39.

[50] *Id.*

[51] Derek Jinks & Neal Kumar Katyal, *Disregarding Foreign Relations Law*, 116 YALE L.J. 1230, 1255 (2007) (observing that the president's "veto power functions ex ante as a disincentive to even begin

462 THE COLLECTIVE-ACTION CONSTITUTION

Veto practice since President Eisenhower is consistent with this interpretation. The number of vetoes declined after his presidency, from a high of 78 by President Ronald Reagan to a low of 10 by President Donald Trump.[52] But presidential involvement in the policymaking process has not declined. It may also be true, however, that "the president's greatly expanded role in budget-making and the legislative process" makes it somewhat less necessary to issue or threaten vetoes than it used to be.[53]

Modern practice, in which presidents can veto bills or threaten vetoes just because they disagree with Congress on policy grounds, is difficult to reconcile with the Constitution's general strategy of making it easier, not harder, for the states to act collectively in Congress than it was under the Articles of Confederation. Depending on whether presidents agree with congressional majorities, the veto power potentially imposes a stronger status-quo bias than the Articles did. There is little indication that the Framers intended this result or that the ratifying public expected it. From their perspective, the result is likely perverse. It should be viewed this way from ours.

One might respond that congressional majorities can readily avoid the problem of having to override presidential vetoes. Congressional majorities can package bill provisions that the president opposes with bill provisions that the president needs, thereby significantly reducing—if not eliminating—the likelihood that the president will veto the overall bill. Although the potential availability of this maneuver suggests that the veto power (as well as the threat of it) does not inevitably matter, it still matters. This maneuver is not always feasible, as evidenced by the vetoes (and veto threats) that still occur.

It must be acknowledged, however, that this section's criticisms of policy-based vetoes are swimming against the tide. The constitutional text permits such vetoes, as does much historical practice. In addition, both political parties and the American public broadly accept the legitimacy of policy-based vetoes.

---

the legislative reform process, as Senators [and House members] are likely to spend their resources and time on projects that are likely to pass").

[52] U.S. House of Representatives, Presidential Vetoes, *supra* note 39. The veto numbers in the text have limitations. More illuminating comparisons would need to account for several independent variables, including the amount of congressional legislation during a given presidency, the existence of unified or divided government, the degree of partisan polarization in the political branches, the filibuster norms in the Senate, and the other powers available to each president to influence the legislative process. For a methodologically pluralistic study of how presidents use veto threats and vetoes—especially during divided government—to extract policy concessions, see CHARLES M. CAMERON, VETO BARGAINING: PRESIDENTS AND THE POLITICS OF NEGATIVE POWER (2000).

[53] SPITZER, *supra* note 24, at 75; *see* JOSH CHAFETZ, CONGRESS'S CONSTITUTION: LEGISLATIVE AUTHORITY AND THE SEPARATION OF POWERS 63–66 (2017) (explaining that, under the Budget and Accounting Act of 1921, the president initiates the annual appropriations process by submitting a budget proposal to Congress, but that Congress countered presidential domination of the process by passing the Budget Act of 1974).

THE PROBLEM OF CONGRESSIONAL GRIDLOCK   463

Moreover, Article I, Section 7, provides for a presentment process (with a veto) that is arguably just as central to federal lawmaking as bicameralism in the American constitutional system. It is easy enough to dismiss the foregoing concerns about policy-based vetoes with the suggestion that such concerns are more of a problem for a collective-action account of the Constitution than they are for the Constitution itself. Even so, bicameralism and the separation of powers are more compatible with democratically legitimate collective action by states in Congress than are policy-based vetoes. The president represents only one party and potentially represents a minority of the nation and a minority of the states. It is normatively questionable that one such individual should be empowered to block legislation solving collective-action problems for the states that garners majority support—and, typically, bipartisan majority support—in both the House and the Senate.

In any event, presidential use of veto threats and vetoes is very unlikely to change. A constitutional amendment limiting or eliminating presidential vetoes—or their procedural effects—will not happen within a foreseeable time horizon, just as similar amendment proposals by members of Congress repeatedly failed during the nineteenth century.[54] Nor are modern presidents likely to restrain themselves from issuing or threatening vetoes when it is politically advantageous for them to use this power. Politicians do not often surrender formidable powers absent demands from their electorate that they do so, and Americans do not view policy-based vetoes as inappropriate, likely because they have become so accustomed to them. Nor is a norm likely to develop in Congress that would oblige members to vote to override policy-based vetoes regardless of members' views of the bills in question or the reelection effects of defying the leader of their party on matters important to the president. As Chapter 10 explained, members typically privilege partisan or policy considerations over institutional ones.

Subconstitutional Rules

Although congressional majorities cannot legislate around the president's veto power, they can consider their own role in making the legislative process even more supermajoritarian. Among the "veto-gates" through which bills must pass, each chamber's committee structure places obstacles in the path of legislation, as evidenced by the many bills that never make it out of committee.[55]

---

[54] SPITZER, *supra* note 24, at 38 (noting twelve instances between 1833 and 1884 in which members of Congress proposed constitutional amendments limiting the impact of the veto power, including by permitting vetoes to be overridden by a simple majority vote).

[55] Terry M. Moe & William G. Howell, *The Presidential Power of Unilateral Action*, 15 J. LAW ECON. & ORG. 132, 146 (1999) ("A bill must pass through subcommittees, full committees, and floor votes in

464 THE COLLECTIVE-ACTION CONSTITUTION

Because even bills with majority support may die in committee, this structure effectively imposes a supermajority voting rule. Congressional majorities could change the structure, but given deeply rooted practice and the complexity of modern problems, Congress may need it—meaning that the structure may actually help Congress solve multistate collective-action problems on balance. Still, this structure has been adjusted in the past to make it harder or easier to legislate.[56]

The Senate need not retain Rule 22, which requires three-fifths of the chamber to support most bills before they can pass.[57] Terminating the legislative filibuster would end the Senate's practice of enhancing presidential power to impede legislation and move policymaking to the executive branch.[58] As noted, the original plan, which remains desirable, was to facilitate collective action by enabling Congress to legislate by majority rule in each chamber. The plan was not to lower the collective-action threshold slightly from two-thirds (or ten-fifteenths), as the Articles of Confederation usually required, to three-fifths (or nine-fifteens), as the filibuster demands.

Terminating the filibuster would be costly. By preventing the majority party from legislating however it wants during unified government, the filibuster lowers the costs of losing elections.[59] This effect matters in a polarized country in which the political parties increasingly view one another with distrust and disdain. Lowering the costs of losing elections is conducive to regime stability and can potentially help limit the degree of partisan polarization and ill will. At its best, the filibuster promotes both collective action and bipartisanship, which happens "when the majority and the minority parties participate in the political process with ideological self-restraint, meaning that the majority party avoids giving the minority party reason to filibuster bills routinely and the minority party uses the filibuster sparingly."[60]

---

the House and the Senate; it must be endorsed in identical form by both houses; and it is threatened along the way by party leaders, rules committees, filibusters, holds, and other roadblocks. Every single veto point must be overcome if Congress is to act.").

[56] CHAFETZ, *supra* note 53, at 282–96 (canvassing the history of committees, including changes to their structure, from the first Congress to the present era).

[57] Under Rule 22.2, a motion to end debate "shall be decided . . . by three-fifths of the Senators duly chosen and sworn—except on a measure or motion to amend the Senate rules, in which case the necessary affirmative vote shall be two-thirds of the Senators duly present and voting." COMM. ON RULES AND ADMIN., SENATE MANUAL, S. Doc. No. 116-1, at 21 (2020).

[58] CHAFETZ, *supra* note 53, at 296 (observing that "[o]ne significant effect of th[e] routinization of the filibuster was to transfer power away from Congress and to the executive").

[59] *Cf.* Samuel Issacharoff, *Populism versus Democratic Governance*, *in* CONSTITUTIONAL DEMOCRACY IN CRISIS? 458 (Mark A. Graber et al. eds., 2018) ("[P]opulism does not accept that the challenge of democratic politics is to allow the electoral victors to prevail, but not too much.").

[60] Neil S. Siegel, *After the Trump Era: A Constitutional Role Morality for Presidents and Members of Congress*, 107 GEO. L.J. 109, 141 (2018).

THE PROBLEM OF CONGRESSIONAL GRIDLOCK 465

In practice, however, the filibuster has promoted far more paralysis than bipartisanship. This effect is at least partly due to increasing partisan polarization and animosity, which decrease the appetite of party voters, activists, donors, other elites, and members of Congress for the compromises that enable bipartisanship.[61] Thus, the main issue during an era of polarization is whether it is generally more important to ensure that any legislative action is bipartisan or that such action occurs even if partisan. Choosing between the two is likely context-sensitive and requires the balancing of incommensurable values, which is why reasonable people may set the balance differently depending on their institutional and substantive commitments. But from the standpoint of accomplishing the Constitution's structural objective of facilitating collective action that is democratically legitimate, the answer is majority rule, the default baseline set by the Constitution considered both originally and traditionally.[62]

One might respond that the filibuster does not just diminish Congress's ability to address collective-action problems facing the states. It also impedes the repeal of such legislation. Although this observation accurately identifies the effects of the filibuster, repeals are likely to occur only when states disagree about the need for collective action, so that a potential cost-benefit collective-action problem exists. When states disagree, the perspective of the current Congress, not a prior one, should govern in a national democracy.

Both political parties, when they control Congress and the White House, appear to be privileging partisan action over bipartisan inaction. Both played a role in ending the filibuster as to all judicial appointments.[63] Moreover, to avoid the filibuster and thus paralysis, the majority party in the Senate regularly uses the reconciliation process to pass taxing and spending bills.[64] Also to avoid paralysis,

---

[61] CHAFETZ, *supra* note 53, at 296 (noting the history of efforts to reform both chambers when obstructionist tactics threatened their functioning, and observing that the Senate's decision in 1975 to lower the threshold for ending a filibuster from two-thirds to three-fifths backfired by routinizing the filibuster instead of reducing obstruction); *id.* (explaining that "[b]y the turn of the twenty-first century . . . the filibuster had come to operate as a standing supermajority requirement for doing business, rather than as a debate- or deliberation-forcing device").

[62] AKHIL REED AMAR, AMERICA'S UNWRITTEN CONSTITUTION: THE PRECEDENTS AND PRINCIPLES WE LIVE BY 360 (2012) ("[I]n a wide range of constitutional contexts, majority rule went without saying. For the same reason that this background rule applied to [the state] ratifying conventions and to each house of Congress, it also applied to the [Supreme] Court."); *id.* at 357 (noting that, although "the written Constitution does not textually specify the master voting rule that operates inside these three chambers," "two centuries of actual practice make clear that the bedrock constitutional principle within each is simple majority rule").

[63] In 2013, a Democratic Senate ended the filibuster as to nominees for the lower federal courts after alleging Republican obstruction. In 2017, a Republican Senate ended the filibuster as to Supreme Court nominees to overcome a Democratic filibuster of Republican nominee Neil Gorsuch. Siegel, *supra* note 60, at 142.

[64] David Wessel, *What Is Reconciliation in Congress?*, BROOKINGS INSTITUTION (Feb. 5, 2021), https://perma.cc/RR42-HUPC ("Reconciliation is, essentially, a way for Congress to enact legislation on taxes, spending, and the debt limit with only a majority (51 votes, or 50 if the vice president breaks a tie) in the Senate, avoiding the threat of a filibuster . . . .").

466   THE COLLECTIVE-ACTION CONSTITUTION

presidents of both parties govern by executive order when they lawfully can, and presidents sometimes push the legal limits of their authority. Moreover, as Chapter 10 explained, Democratic and Republican Congresses alike pass omnibus appropriations bills and use riders to reduce the likelihood of a veto. All these actions reflect a shared belief that Congress and the president are not adequately addressing pressing problems by legislating. True, the filibuster still stands, even though both parties have had the opportunity to end it. But its future is uncertain. To facilitate collective action by states in the form of federal legislation, the filibuster should probably be terminated by majority vote in the Senate.[65]

One can be more confident in this conclusion if one takes the broader structural context into account. The issue is not merely whether to keep or discard the filibuster. It is, rather, whether the filibuster should continue to impose a serious impediment to legislation above and beyond bicameralism, the separation of powers, and a broad understanding of the veto power. The question is whether one party should have to control the presidency, the House, and three-fifth of the Senate for the US separation-of-powers system to approximate the Westminster model's requirements for legislating. An affirmative answer is difficult to reconcile with the reasons why the Constitution replaced the Articles of Confederation and with the expectations that modern Americans have of the federal government.

The issue can be framed more precisely if one also takes the broader political context into account. The issue is whether to continue imposing the filibuster as an obstacle to legislation on top of bicameralism, the separation of powers, and a broad view of the veto power amid partisan polarization and animosity. Polarization and related phenomena amplify the effects of all four impediments to the capacity of congressional majorities to legislate.

Partisan Polarization, Sorting, and Dislike: Bitribalism and the Separation of Parties

There are two main reasons why this book has repeatedly referenced the implications of partisan polarization for the functioning of the constitutional system. First, such polarization and associated political developments are the defining features of contemporary American politics. As political scientists Steven Levitzky and Daniel Ziblatt write, "the fundamental problem facing American democracy remains extreme partisan divisions—one fueled not just by policy

---

[65] See AMAR, *supra* note 62, at 361–69 (arguing that the Senate's filibuster rule is unconstitutional if it cannot be changed by a simple majority vote).

differences but by deeper sources of resentment, including racial and religious differences."[66] Second, partisan divisions profoundly affect Congress's ability to exercise its core responsibility in the constitutional scheme: legislating. This section defines partisan polarization and related concepts; clarifies that their normative desirability depends on their degree and the constitutional structure within which they operate; and explains why in the United States, as opposed to Westminster systems, they make it much harder for Congress to legislate than it already is.

"Polarization" refers to the increasing adoption over time of more extreme policy positions and ideological orientations by groups of people.[67] In the United States, "partisan polarization" exists when such relatively more extreme views are increasingly adopted by members of the Republican and Democratic Parties, whether party elites or party members more broadly. There is strong evidence, resulting in a consensus among political scientists, that political elites have increasingly polarized since the late 1970s.[68] As explained below, political scientists debate whether, and to what extent, the mass public has become polarized since the 1990s, which is when potential evidence of polarization began appearing in most longitudinal studies of voter opinions.

Political scientists often use the term "partisan polarization" more generally to describe situations in which policy or ideological differences between members of the two parties have increased. This more encompassing definition is questionable, however, because it conflates partisan polarization with "partisan sorting." If there is increasing policy or ideological divergence between liberals (who are characteristically Democrats) and conservatives (who are characteristically Republicans), polarization is the relevant phenomenon. But if liberals and conservatives are increasingly sorting themselves into the Democratic and Republican Parties without an overall increase in policy or ideological divergence, partisan sorting is occurring.[69]

Professor Morris Fiorina argues that voters have sorted themselves into the parties in response to the polarization of the parties. Among other evidence, he points to the moderate or centrist policy positions that most Americans have consistently expressed on surveys over the past several decades without any increase in the expression of extreme positions.[70] Professor Alan Abramowitz disagrees,

---

[66] STEVEN LEVITSKY & DANIEL ZIBLATT, HOW DEMOCRACIES DIE 220 (2018).

[67] MCCARTY, *supra* note 9, at 8–11.

[68] Keith T. Poole & Howard Rosenthal, *D-Nominate after 10 years: A Comparative Update to Congress: A Political-Economic History of Roll-Call Voting*, 26 LEG. STUD. Q. 5, 18–19 (2001); MCCARTY, *supra* note 9, at 17, 22–49 (discussing both qualitative accounts that combine historical research with participant observation or that study the results of intraparty battles among partisan elites, and quantitative work that uses measures of elite polarization related to roll-call voting, campaign contributions, the contents of congressional speeches, and the use of social media).

[69] MCCARTY, *supra* note 9, at 11–12.

[70] MORRIS P. FIORINA (with SAMUEL J. ABRAMS & JEREMY C. POPE), CULTURE WAR?: THE MYTH OF A POLARIZED AMERICA (2005).

468   THE COLLECTIVE-ACTION CONSTITUTION

emphasizing the partisan polarization of the mass public. He argues, among other things, that the Americans who voice moderate positions on surveys are not especially knowledgeable about politics and do not tend to participate in it, whereas engaged voters increasingly express more extreme positions and align themselves with the party that advocates them.[71] It is unnecessary to choose between these two perspectives to explain why it is so difficult for the contemporary Congress to legislate. In the discussion below, the term "polarization/sorting" will be used to capture both possibilities or a combination of them.[72]

Although most political-science research on partisan polarization has examined whether the policy positions and ideological orientations of voters have become more extreme, other scholarship has focused on "affective polarization," which refers to the tendency of voters in one party to dislike and distrust voters in the other. This work suggests that the partisan affiliation of voters is becoming a significant social identity. In 1960, "only five percent of Republicans and four percent of Democrats felt 'displeased' if their son or daughter married outside their political party." By contrast, when respondents were asked in 2010 "whether they felt somewhat or very unhappy at the prospect of inter-party marriage," 49 percent of Republicans and 33 percent of Democrats chose one of these two options. These percentages have since grown and converged.[73] There is disagreement in the literature, however, regarding whether partisanship is the most important identity driving affective polarization (an earlier finding), or whether the sorting of voters into the parties by social group and ideology is primarily causing hostility between members of the parties (a more recent finding).[74]

---

[71] ALAN ABRAMOWITZ, THE DISAPPEARING CENTER: ENGAGED CITIZENS, POLARIZATION, AND AMERICAN DEMOCRACY (2010).

[72] Another phenomenon related to partisan polarization is "ideological consistency" or "belief constraint," which is the tendency of voters to have entirely liberal, moderate, or conservative views. See Philip E. Converse, The Nature of Belief Systems in Mass Publics, in IDEOLOGY AND DISCONTENT 206 (David Apter ed., 1964). The impact of ideological consistency on Congress's ability to legislate is like that of partisan polarization and sorting.

[73] Shanto Iyengar, Gaurav Sood, & Yphtach Lelkes, Affect, Not Ideology: A Social Identity Perspective on Polarization, 76 PUB. OPIN. Q. 405, 415–18 (2012). See Lynn Vavreck, A Measure of Identity: Are You Wedded to Your Party?, N.Y. TIMES (Jan. 31, 2017), https://www.nytimes.com/2017/01/31/upshot/are-you-married-to-your-party.html, on file with author at https://perma.cc/6HPA-284Y ("In 1958, 33 percent of Democrats wanted their daughters to marry a Democrat, and 25 percent of Republicans wanted their daughters to marry a Republican. But by 2016, 60 percent of Democrats and 63 percent of Republicans felt that way.").

[74] Compare, e.g., Iyengar, Sood, & Lelkes, supra note 73 (arguing that partisanship is the key social identity causing affective polarization), with, e.g., Steven W. Webster & Alan I. Abramowitz, The Ideological Foundations of Affective Polarization in the US Electorate, 45 AM. POLITICS RESEARCH 621 (2017) (arguing that affective polarization is caused mostly by the views of partisans regarding the ideological orientations of the parties rather than by partisan social identity), and Lilliana Mason, "I Disrespectfully Agree": The Differential Effects of Partisan Sorting on Social and Issue Polarization, 59 AM. J. POL. SCI. 128 (2015) (arguing that affective polarization is caused by the sorting of partisans by both social group identification and ideological orientation).

Finally, "partisanship" is a general term that captures any favoritism individuals have toward their party regardless of the basis for such favoritism.[75] The source of the favoritism could be polarized policy preferences or ideological commitments, polarized social identities, inherited family tradition, a desire to obtain patronage, or (for politicians) a desire to be elected. For example, politicians can act for partisan reasons that are inexplicable based on disagreements with the other party over policy, ideology, or affect, but instead are focused on winning control of a legislative chamber or the presidency. It can be difficult to distinguish one source of partisan behavior by politicians from another, particularly as one extends the time horizon. But partisanship can cause politicians to behave in ways that partisan polarization, sorting, and dislike cannot explain.

As the above discussion reveals, partisan sorting, affective polarization, and partisanship are related to partisan polarization and distinct from it. Whether one should lump them together or split them apart depends on the question one is asking. For example, the distinction between polarization and sorting is relevant to whether polarization between party elites has produced the sorting of the public, or whether polarization of the public has caused elite polarization.[76] By contrast, to understand the relative difficulty of legislating, the most important point is what these phenomena share. All tend to reinforce, and increase, divisions between the parties.

Whether this consequence is desirable depends on numerous factors, including the extent to which party divisions exist and the constitutional structure of the political system in which they operate. According to the "responsible party theory," distinct and coherent parties empower voters to choose between genuinely contrasting party positions on issues, and such parties provide voters with accurate partisan cues regarding the candidates for whom they should vote. Distinct party positions also enhance political accountability by enabling voters to identify, amid blame-shifting, which party is responsible when a policy is adopted and succeeds or fails from the voters' perspectives. It is much harder for voters to influence legislation and public policy when both parties offer a mushy mix of moderate positions on the issues of the day.[77] Moreover, in two-party parliamentary systems, polarization/sorting and related phenomena do not significantly impede the ability to legislate. One party controls the legislature and the executive.

In the contemporary United States, however, the level of partisan polarization/sorting and animosity appear well beyond what is necessary

---

[75] McCarty, *supra* note 9, at 12.
[76] *Id.* at 58.
[77] *Id.* at 19–20.

470   THE COLLECTIVE-ACTION CONSTITUTION

to achieve a desirable degree of differentiation between the parties. As Professor Nolan McCarty writes in summarizing the political-science literature, "there is considerable evidence that the level of polarization among the elites and the public is well to the warm side of the Goldilocks point."[78] The objective, as he implies, is to achieve an optimal level of differentiation between the parties, not a maximal one. The goal of enabling meaningful voter choice and accountability must be balanced against the goal of ensuring that Congress can legislate.

High levels of partisan polarization/sorting and ill will, combined with the real chance that each party routinely possesses to win the presidency, House, and Senate,[79] make it much harder for Congress to legislate than it already is due to the impediments imposed by the constitutional and subconstitutional rules discussed above. Because the nation is closely divided, unified government is rare, and a filibuster-proof Senate majority is very rare on major issues. As a result, legislation typically requires bipartisanship and compromise. But polarization/sorting and distrust make it very difficult for bipartisan coalitions and compromises to form. Especially with aggressive partisan gerrymandering of congressional districts, the partisan divides outside Congress produce a more extreme nomination process and, therefore, more polarized members. Such members begin far apart on most issues and so are less able to compromise. They are also less interested in trying to compromise, given the increasing time it takes and the lower payoffs it produces. Moreover, if they join bipartisan coalitions, they risk being punished ("primaried") by the polarized/sorted groups on which they depend for reelection.[80]

In other words, polarization/sorting, animosity, razor's-edge elections, and extreme partisan gerrymandering supercharge the power of the horizontal constitutional structure and the filibuster to prevent Congress from performing its primary role. When each party controls one chamber, bicameralism veers toward bitribalism. And when divided government exists, the separation of powers becomes the separation of parties—as Professors Daryl Levinson and Richard Pildes memorably put it.[81] This reasoning is supported by important theorizing in political science, including Professor Keith Krehbiel's theory of "pivotal politics." Under this theory, the pivotal vote on a bill in Congress does not generate a simple majority but enables its supporters to overcome a potential veto or filibuster, which is why winning coalitions are usually bipartisan supermajorities.[82]

---

[78] *Id.* at 20.

[79] FRANCES E. LEE, INSECURE MAJORITIES: CONGRESS AND THE PERPETUAL CAMPAIGN (2016).

[80] MCCARTY, *supra* note 9, at 58, 67.

[81] Daryl J. Levinson & Richard H. Pildes, *Separation of Parties, Not Powers*, 119 HARV. L. REV. 2311 (2006).

[82] KEITH KREHBIEL, PIVOTAL POLITICS: A THEORY OF U.S. LAWMAKING (1998).

THE PROBLEM OF CONGRESSIONAL GRIDLOCK   471

As just explained, polarization/sorting makes it harder to form such coalitions. This reasoning is also supported by empirical studies finding that, controlling for other factors, "the least polarized congressional term produces 111% more legislation than the most polarized."[83]

One might respond that legislating should be hard when the nation is polarized/sorted and closely divided. Divided government can reflect divided public opinion, so representatives of roughly half the nation should not legislate much for the whole nation. As Professor Josh Chafetz writes, "unified versus divided government [depends] on the will of the people, as expressed through electoral mechanisms," and divided government "indicates that the American people have not seen fit to entrust the entirety of governmental operations to a single party."[84] The result is, however, that problems deemed significant and urgent by most Americans often go unaddressed by Congress—the government institution with the most constitutional authority, democratic legitimacy, regulatory power, and geographic reach to address them.

The situation is worse. These problems go unaddressed in nontrivial part for reasons of partisanship other than differences in policy, ideology, or identity. Partisanship warps how the system was designed to function amid differences along these dimensions. Because of the partisan calculations of officeholders, which are exacerbated by the perception that the political branches are nearly always up for grabs, one party wants the president to fail so that it will have a greater chance to capture the White House and Congress. This goal, which motivates congressional behavior, has nothing to do with policy merits or differences in ideology or identity. Yes, some disagreements are non-negotiable, and compromise is impossible. But this is not true for many issues, including controversial ones. In a system that could plausibly be described as functional, one would expect frequent negotiation and compromise among various policy, ideological, and identity-based divisions. Instead, the US system usually produces gridlock and paralysis. Because members of Congress are motivated by partisan calculations at least as much as differences over policy, ideology, or identity, there is scant reason to think that divided government produces the optimal level of policymaking amid partisan divides.

The situation is still worse. As polarization/sorting and evenly matched parties make bipartisan compromise more necessary and more difficult, "political fragmentation" renders it even harder to achieve. As Professor Pildes

---

[83] McCarty, *supra* note 9, at 140; *see* Nolan McCarty, *The Policy Effects of Political Polarization*, *in* THE TRANSFORMATION OF AMERICAN POLITICS: ACTIVIST GOVERNMENT AND THE RISE OF CONSERVATISM 211 (Paul Pierson & Theda Skocpol eds., 2007).

[84] CHAFETZ, *supra* note 53, at 34, 35.

472 THE COLLECTIVE-ACTION CONSTITUTION

explains, fragmentation refers most importantly to "the diffusion of power in government away from the leadership of the major political parties to their more extreme factions." In contrast to party leaders in parliamentary systems, leaders in Congress "have less capacity to force party members to toe the party line." Because "[m]embers of the House and Senate are much better able to function as independent entrepreneurs and free agents," compromise is more difficult to forge not just between party caucuses but also within them. It may seem strange that weak parties exacerbate the gridlock that is caused in significant part by polarization/sorting. But this causal story makes sense because even polarized/sorted parties are a "they," not an "it," and members may care more about their own interests than legislating. They can also access funding and mass-communication technologies that are not controlled by the parties.[85]

Power Shifts and Partial Workarounds

A gridlocked Congress increases the relative power of other branches or levels of government—the executive branch, the federal judiciary, and state governments. This is because such a Congress is less able to legislatively "overrule" their decisions. Whether partisan polarization/sorting increases the absolute authority of these government institutions, as opposed to their relative authority vis-à-vis Congress, is a more complex question that turns primarily on whether and how polarization/sorting affects their own ability to exercise power and on how much help they need from Congress to do so. Generally, Congress is less able both to stop and to support them. Because the focus here is on institutional power shifts and potential workarounds for the problem of congressional gridlock, it is unnecessary to determine whether polarization/sorting has a net positive or negative effect on the overall power of other institutions.

This section first explains how congressional gridlock enhances the relative power of the executive branch, the federal judiciary, and state governments. It then examines whether they can and should help fill the void left by Congress's diminished capacity to act.

---

[85] Richard H. Pildes, *Romanticizing Democracy, Political Fragmentation, and the Decline of American Government*, 124 YALE L.J. 804, 830 (2014). Fragmentation also refers to "the diffusion of the power in elections away from the formal campaigns and the political parties" to Super PACS and related organizations that have narrower ideological and policy objectives than the parties. *Id.* For other work on fragmentation, see Nolan McCarty, *Reducing Polarization by Making Parties Stronger*, *in* SOLUTIONS TO POLITICAL POLARIZATION IN AMERICA 136 (Nathaniel Persily ed., 2015); and, in that volume, Richard H. Pildes, *Focus on Political Fragmentation, Not Polarization: Re-Empower Party Leadership*, at 146.

Presidential Governance

As the last chapter discussed, presidents enjoy substantially more authority and ability to engage in unilateral policymaking than Congress. For example, presidents can issue executive orders based on constitutional or statutory authority; initiate military operations without congressional authorization in at least some situations; conclude certain international agreements without Congress's approval; and exercise prosecutorial discretion on more than a case-by-case basis.[86] Scholars and jurists dispute the scope of these powers and others, but presidents use them to engage in unilateral policymaking, and (to reiterate) they may push the legal limits of these powers.

Congress enjoys substantial authority to override unilateral executive action. For example, where presidents do not have exclusive constitutional authority to act—and they seldom do—legislation can trump executive orders.[87] Congress can also override policymaking by federal agencies as they implement federal statutes. But authority is one thing; willingness and ability are others. Amid partisan polarization/sorting, statutory overrides are less likely to be passed by congressional majorities, let alone by the supermajorities needed to override vetoes. Further, presidents can invoke Congress's inaction as rhetorical justification for bold, unilateral executive action.[88] Thus, like bicameralism, the separation of powers, a robust veto power, and the filibuster, partisan polarization/sorting enhances executive power relative to Congress.

Unilateral executive action, otherwise known as presidential governance, can partially be viewed as a workaround for congressional gridlock, not just as a problematic consequence of it. From this perspective, at least one branch with a potentially national constituency can respond to significant problems— including multistate collective-action problems such as immigration—and action may be better than inaction even if the branch doing the acting is not ideal. There is force to this argument: presidential governance may sometimes be the second-best solution in a world in which Congress is unable to execute its legislative responsibilities in the constitutional scheme. Still, unilateral executive action is less enduring than federal statutes, and executive unilateralism is (to repeat) less democratically legitimate than congressional action and poses

[86] Curtis A. Bradley & Trevor W. Morrison, *Historical Gloss and the Separation of Powers*, 126 HARV. L. REV. 411, 440 (2012).

[87] As Chapter 7 explained, Justice Jackson's canonical three-zone analysis of congressional-executive relations in the *Youngstown* steel seizure case reflects the principle of congressional priority: with few exceptions, the lawmaker (Congress) gets to control the law enforcer (the president). *See* Youngstown Sheet & Tube Co. v. Sawyer, 343 U.S. 579, 635–38 (1952) (Jackson, J., concurring).

[88] CHAFETZ, *supra* note 53, at 296–301 (explaining how the filibuster's blocking of legislation with majority support has shifted policymaking to the executive, including by giving presidents the rhetorical power to justify unilateral executive action based upon congressional inaction despite serious problems).

474   THE COLLECTIVE-ACTION CONSTITUTION

greater potential risks of democratic backsliding depending on who is president. Further, executive orders must rest on the president's constitutional authority or lawfully delegated legislative authority, which means that presidents cannot lawfully regulate via executive order nearly as much as Congress can regulate via statute. Generally, presidential governance is a partial workaround for reduced congressional ability to legislate. It is also an effect of gridlock that raises its own concerns.

The Federal Courts

Congressional gridlock empowers the federal courts for at least two reasons. First, as Professor Richard Hasen has shown, their interpretations of federal statutes are less likely to be overruled by Congress.[89] Second, their interpretations of the Constitution are less likely to be met with federal statutes stripping their jurisdiction or packing them with judges who are ideologically more congenial to Congress. In modern America, however, unlike in some past periods,[90] the chances of such forceful congressional responses to constitutional decisions by federal judges, especially the justices, are low to begin with. For example, notwithstanding unified Democratic government and widespread Democratic anger in Congress over what they viewed as Republicans' abuse of the confirmation process to install a six-justice conservative supermajority on the Court, the political branches from 2020 to 2022 did not come close to meeting the demands of certain liberal groups to add any seats to the Court, let alone four. Thus, although the situation may change in the future, most of the power shift from Congress to the federal courts likely occurs regarding questions of statutory interpretation. With a gridlocked Congress, however, statutory-interpretation decisions can be at least as important as many constitutional rulings.

For example, the Court has recently created a freestanding "major questions doctrine" to limit the power of federal administrative agencies to use democratically enacted, broadly worded statutes that have been around for decades to respond flexibly to new problems. These problems include the dire effects of

---

[89] Richard L. Hasen, *End of the Dialogue? Political Polarization, the Supreme Court, and Congress*, 86 So. CAL. L. REV. 205, 217–18, 228–42 (2013) (reporting only 2.8 congressional overrides of Supreme Court statutory-interpretation decisions per Congress from 2001 to 2012, in contrast to 12 overrides per Congress from 1975 to 1990, and arguing that the reduction is due significantly to partisan polarization in Congress, not just to a decrease in the number of cases or to their ideological orientation).

[90] *See* BARRY FRIEDMAN, THE WILL OF THE PEOPLE: HOW PUBLIC OPINION HAS INFLUENCED THE SUPREME COURT AND SHAPED THE MEANING OF THE CONSTITUTION (2009) (discussing past instances in which federal judgeships were abolished, the Court's jurisdiction was stripped, and seats on the Court were added or subtracted at least partly for political reasons).

THE PROBLEM OF CONGRESSIONAL GRIDLOCK 475

climate change and the spread of COVID-19 in large workplaces.[91] The states cannot adequately address these collective-action problems on their own, and Congress previously overcame all the obstacles to collective action canvassed in this chapter and legislated. Congress responded to perceptions of public need, during periods of substantial democratic agreement, to establish agencies that were expressly empowered through discretion-conferring language to address wide ranges of policy, including new and unexpected perils.

For instance, Section 111 of the Clean Air Act expansively authorized the Environmental Protection Agency (EPA) to choose the "best system of emission reduction" for power plants.[92] The Court has not given the words of such statutes their ordinary meaning. Nor has the Court granted deference to agencies like the EPA or the Occupational Safety and Health Administration under the *Chevron* doctrine, which directs courts to defer to reasonable agency interpretations of ambiguous statutory language that the agency is charged with administering. The Court has instead imposed an anti-*Chevron* presumption that each agency's ordinary-language interpretation of its statutory authority is unacceptable and can be sustained only if supported by "clear congressional authorization."[93] According to the Court's major questions doctrine, there are " 'extraordinary cases' . . . in which the 'history and the breadth of the authority that [the agency] has asserted,' and the 'economic and political significance' of that assertion, provide a 'reason to hesitate before concluding that Congress' meant to confer such authority."[94]

---

[91] West Virginia v. Env't. Prot. Agency, 142 S. Ct. 2587 (2022) (holding that, in Section 111(d) of the Clean Air Act, Congress did not grant the Environmental Protection Agency the authority to devise emissions caps based on the generation-shifting approach that the Agency took in the Obama Administration's Clean Power Plan); NFIB v. Dep't of Labor, Occupational Safety & Health Admin., 142 S. Ct. 661 (2022) (per curiam) (granting the applications to stay the challenged rule of the Occupational Safety & Health Administration mandating that employers with at least one hundred employees require covered workers to receive a COVID-19 vaccine, unless workers wear a mask each workday and obtain a medical test each week). *But see* Biden v. Missouri, 142 S. Ct. 647 (2022) (granting the applications to stay the two injunctions barring the regulation issued by the Secretary of Health and Human Services requiring facilities that participate in Medicare and Medicaid to ensure that their employees are vaccinated against COVID-19 unless they are eligible for a medical or religious exemption). For another invocation of the major questions doctrine, see *Biden v. Nebraska*, 143 S. Ct. 2355 (2023) (holding that the secretary of education lacked authority under federal law to create a student loan forgiveness program that would cancel approximately $430 billion in debt principal and affect almost all borrowers).

[92] 42 U.S.C. § 7411(a)(1).

[93] *West Virginia*, 142 S. Ct. at 2609 (internal quotation marks and citation omitted). *See* Craig Green, *Greenhouse Gaslighting: Deceptive Moderation and* West Virginia v. EPA, JUST SECURITY (Jul. 5, 2022), https://perma.cc/W29W-RBLQ. On hostility to *Chevron U.S.A. v. Natural Resources Defense Council, Inc.*, 467 U.S. 837 (1984), and to the administrative state more generally, see Craig Green, *Deconstructing the Administrative State:* Chevron *Debates and the Transformation of Constitutional Politics*, 101 B.U. L. REV. 619 (2021); and Gillian E. Metzger, *Foreword: 1930s Redux: The Administrative State Under Siege*, 131 HARV. L. REV. 1 (2017).

[94] *West Virginia*, 142 S. Ct. at 2608 (quoting FDA v. Brown & Williamson Tobacco Corp., 529 U.S. 120, 159–60 (2000)).

476   THE COLLECTIVE-ACTION CONSTITUTION

The theory offered in this book might be thought to support these decisions: agencies lack the democratic legitimacy of Congress, and the Court is requiring Congress to make the judgment call that there is a multistate collective-action problem in need of solving. The force of this defense of the doctrine turns on whether Congress has already made the call, and ordinary statutory interpretation focused on the text and purpose of the statute at issue should decide the question. The Court's imposition of a clear-statement requirement does not help resolve this issue; rather, it loads the dice against the exercise of federal power for no structurally defensible reason. Congress has long possessed constitutional power to pass generously worded statutes that authorize agencies to confront serious problems that are unforeseeable at the time of enactment; the "non-delegation" concerns that may underlie the major questions doctrine undermine, rather than advance, the capacity of Congress to solve collective-action problems for the states.

Further, agencies possess more democratic legitimacy than the Court. The Court is diminishing democratically enacted statutes, and threatening others, by newly minting a no-broad-language rule in areas that the Court determines, after exercising substantial discretion, to be of great "economic and political significance."[95] The Court is doing so even though that is not what the statutes say; the states cannot address such problems on their own; and Congress is too gridlocked to override any decision that the Court renders.

To help fill the regulatory void left by congressional inaction, willing federal courts could try to engage in "statutory updating." This practice entails assigning meanings to federal statutes that cannot be derived from either their text or the purposes of the Congress that passed them. The goal of judicial updating of statutes is to help the US Code "keep up with the times," where Congress is unable to perform this function. But even a full-throated effort by judges to update federal statutes would be a poor substitute for a more functional Congress, which is also charged with crafting new laws to address distinct problems, not just with updating old laws to solve related problems. And no serious person argues that federal judges can pass federal statutes.

Moreover, it is controversial whether courts should ever simply make law in statutory interpretation cases as if they are a legislative body, let alone whether they should do so routinely. Statutory updating can potentially be defended on (perhaps counterintuitive) democratic grounds when Congress, over long periods, does not update major statutes despite sea changes in public opinion.[96] A possible example would be Congress's failure to amend federal employment

[95] *West Virginia*, 142 S. Ct. at 2608.
[96] *Cf.* Lain, *supra* note 45 (emphasizing times when the Court is more aligned with the constitutional values held by most Americans than are the political branches).

discrimination law (Title VII) to expressly prohibit sexual-orientation discrimination in the workplace, notwithstanding the views of increasingly large supermajorities of Americans for decades that such discrimination is wrong.[97] But statutory updating is in significant tension with the ideal and expectation that, as far as statutory interpretation is concerned, the judicial role is to interpret statutory language insofar as its meaning is discernible, not to craft such language. This is because courts possess far less democratic legitimacy than Congress. Although the potential distinction between what judges say and what they do must be held in mind, it is indicative of the expectations of the legal community and the public that few sitting judges would write in a judicial opinion that they were updating a federal law.

For example, in an opinion for himself alone, Judge Richard Posner wrote that his en banc appellate court (the US Court of Appeals for the Seventh Circuit) should have admitted that it was appropriately updating the meaning of Title VII to include a ban on sexual-orientation discrimination in the workplace. Unsurprisingly, his other colleagues in the majority instead grounded the same result in Supreme Court precedent and logical reasoning based on the text of the statute—language prohibiting employment discrimination "because of sex."[98] A few years later, in different cases, a six-justice majority engaged in logical reasoning based on the semantic meaning of this same language in concluding that Title VII banned workplace discrimination based on sexual orientation or gender identity. Like Judge Posner's colleagues in the majority, the Court reasoned that one cannot discriminate on either basis without taking the sex of the employee into account, and all Title VII requires is that sex be a motivating factor in the adverse employment decision. The Court might have further, or alternatively, followed the Seventh Circuit by emphasizing Title VII's purpose to combat gender subordination in the workplace and the Court's related precedents prohibiting gender stereotyping by employers.[99] In dissent, Justice

---

[97] *Gay and Lesbian Rights, Gallup Historical Trends, LGBT Rights*, Gallup, https://perma.cc/DY66-2GMK (last visited Aug. 30, 2021) (asking whether "gays or lesbians should or should not have equal rights as non-gays or non-lesbians in terms of job opportunities," and reporting affirmative answers of 56 percent in 1977, 71 percent in 1989, 83 percent in 1999, 89 percent in 2008, and 93 percent in 2019).

[98] *Compare* Hively v. Ivy Tech Cmty. Coll., 853 F. 3d 339, 357 (2017) (Posner, J., concurring) ("I would prefer to see us acknowledge openly that today we, who are judges rather than members of Congress, are imposing on a half-century-old statute a meaning of 'sex discrimination' that the Congress that enacted it would not have accepted."), *with id.* at 350–51 (majority opinion) (en banc) ("The logic of the Supreme Court's decisions, as well as the common-sense reality that it is actually impossible to discriminate on the basis of sexual orientation without discriminating on the basis of sex, persuade us that the time has come to overrule our previous cases that have endeavored to find and observe that line.").

[99] *Id.* at 342, 344–45, 349 (majority opinion) (discussing Price Waterhouse v. Hopkins, 490 U.S. 228 (1989), and Oncale v. Sundowner Offshore Servs., Inc., 523 U.S. 75 (1998)).

478 THE COLLECTIVE-ACTION CONSTITUTION

Alito predictably tarred the Court for "sail[ing] a textualist flag" but updating the law.[100]

Whatever one thinks of occasional judicial updating of old, landmark statutes that consistent supermajorities of Americans support amending to no avail, it would be difficult to argue that courts should routinely update statutes—rule of law and democratic values be damned. Judge Posner himself wrote that "judicial interpretive updating . . . presupposes a lengthy interval between enactment and (re)interpretation," because "[a] statute when passed has an understood meaning; it takes years, often many years, for a shift in the political and cultural environment to change the understanding of the statute."[101] It also seems unlikely that judicial legitimacy could be maintained if judges routinely engaged in statutory updating. Presidents or state legislatures might wonder aloud why they should abide the destructive decisions of another political body whose members have never been elected but who serve for life.

State Governments

Partisan polarization/sorting increases the regulatory power of state governments relative to Congress. This is because polarization/sorting generally makes it more difficult for Congress to legislate than for states to legislate. Recall from Chapter 10 that state governments are less likely than Congress to have supermajority voting rules (whether to override vetoes or to break filibusters) and that some states have veto-override requirements that are less strict than the two-thirds threshold applicable to Congress. Also recall that state governments are unified far more frequently than the national government. As a result, polarization/sorting is less likely to reduce the ability of states to pursue policy initiatives—or to resist implementation of federal ones[102]—than it is to decrease Congress's capacity to preempt such state activities.

---

[100] *Compare* Bostock v. Clayton Cnty., Georgia, 140 S. Ct. 1731, 1737 (2020) ("An employer who fires an individual for being homosexual or transgender fires that person for traits or actions it would not have questioned in members of a different sex. Sex plays a necessary and undisguisable role in the decision, exactly what Title VII forbids."), *with id.* at 1755–56 (Alito, J., dissenting) ("The Court's opinion is like a pirate ship. It sails under a textualist flag, but what it actually represents is a theory of statutory interpretation that Justice Scalia excoriated—the theory that courts should 'update' old statutes so that they better reflect the current values of society. If the Court finds it appropriate to adopt this theory, it should [like Judge Posner] own up to what it is doing" (citation omitted).).

[101] *Hively*, 853 F. 3d at 353 (Posner, J., concurring).

[102] For discussion of how states can resist federal policy—practice "uncooperative federalism"—by refusing to enforce federal laws based on constitutional objections, leveraging their power to implement federal laws to pressure the federal government to alter its position, and administering federal programs in ways that undermine their purposes, see Jessica Bulman-Pozen & Heather K. Gerken, *Uncooperative Federalism*, 118 YALE L.J. 1256 (2009).

The power shift from Congress to the states amid polarization/sorting raises the possibility that state regulation can serve as a workaround for congressional gridlock. As Chapter 3 discussed, state legislation and interstate compacts are potential ways in which states can help solve collective-action problems that are interstate in scope (like boundary disputes and interstate infrastructure) or even international in scope (like state efforts to combat climate change). As explained in earlier chapters and as examined below, however, states are no substitute for Congress when they would need to act collectively to meet a regulatory challenge.

Congressional Regulation versus State Regulation

Even if Congress is structurally better situated than the states to solve multistate or multination collective-action problems, one could argue that at least the states are able to act, which is frequently not true of Congress. What it means for states to act must, however, be specified. It may often be easier for states acting individually or in small groups to regulate than it is for Congress to regulate. But generally, individual action by states is unlikely to contribute significantly to the solution of problems that are national or international in scope, and such action is likely to affect the federal government or sister states. States must act collectively, not individually, and states cannot generally form interstate compacts involving most or all states more easily than Congress can legislate. To form an interstate compact, Chapter 3 explained, all relevant players within each state must agree; the compacting states must unanimously agree; and Congress may need to consent given the potential for compacts to harm the federal government or state nonparties. There have been relatively few such compacts throughout American history. As difficult as the federal legislative process is to negotiate, it does not operate under unanimity rule. Moreover, amid polarization/sorting, it is especially difficult for "red" and "blue" states to agree on many important matters, so polarization/sorting further decreases the probability that compacts involving many states will form.

The hardwired constitutional structure, veto practice, and the filibuster likely make it too difficult for Congress to legislate, and partisan polarization/sorting makes it harder still. But there would almost certainly be greater, not fewer, multistate collective-action problems that went unaddressed if Americans had to rely on the ability of states to form compacts concerning, say, national defense, foreign relations, health-care access, financial regulation, immigration policy, disaster relief, infrastructure spending, and pandemic responses. Nor is it likely that states would be better able than Congress to perform Congress's other major functions, including protecting individual rights nationally and ensuring that presidents and federal courts operate within the law.

480   THE COLLECTIVE-ACTION CONSTITUTION

Conclusion

By creating a two-house Congress and a separately elected president, the original Constitution established a sensible, even if imperfect, balance between empowering Congress to solve multistate collective-action problems and making such legislative power safe for other constitutional goals. Today, however, bicameralism, the separation of powers, policy-based veto practice, the filibuster, and partisan polarization/sorting—along with affective polarization, razor's-edge elections, partisan gerrymandering, partisanship, and political fragmentation—combine to explain why it is so difficult for Congress to legislate. These causes of gridlock do not merely qualify the exercise of the formidable powers that the Constitution gives Congress. Rather, these forces often make it very difficult for Congress to use them at all. Ending the filibuster by majority vote in the Senate, although costly, would improve Congress's capacity to legislate, especially under unified government, but the other causes of gridlock are not going anywhere. Modern veto practice is deeply entrenched, and the nation will remain closely divided for the foreseeable future. In addition, constitutional amendments are effectively impossible.

Regarding the vertical constitutional structure, Congress's most important responsibility is to solve collective-action problems for the states. Yet, the rules and practices associated with the horizontal structure, combined with partisan polarization/sorting and related phenomena, make it very challenging for Congress to execute this responsibility. This is likely the Constitution's most significant defect today. The collective-action account offered in this book cannot solve this problem, but it does help illuminate the disconnect between structural design and legislative performance.

Still, Congress passes major legislation today. Since 2000, Congress has passed laws on many subjects, including national security, education, campaign finance, energy policy, the 2008 financial crisis, financial regulation, health insurance and health care, tax cuts, the environment, the economic and public-health consequences of the COVID-19 pandemic, the epidemic of gun violence, corporate taxation, prescription drug-price reform, IRS tax enforcement, climate change, individual rights, and the statutory debt ceiling.[103] The states acting

---

[103] *See* Authorization for Use of Military Force, Pub. L. No. 107-40, 115 Stat. 224 (2001); No Child Left Behind Act of 2001, Pub. L. No. 107-110, 115 Stat. 1425; Uniting and Strengthening America by Providing Appropriate Tools Required to Intercept and Obstruct Terrorism (USA PATRIOT) Act of 2001, Pub. L. No. 107-56, 115 Stat. 272; Bipartisan Campaign Reform Act of 2002, Pub. L. No. 107-155, 116 Stat. 81; Homeland Security Act of 2002, Pub. L. No. 107-296, 116 Stat. 2135; Detainee Treatment Act of 2005, Pub. L. No. 109-148, §§ 1001–1006, 119 Stat. 2680, 2739–2744; Energy Policy Act of 2005, Pub. L. No. 109-58, 119 Stat. 594; Military Commissions Act of 2006, Pub. L. No. 109-366, 120 Stat. 2600; Energy Independence and Security Act of 2007, Pub. L. No. 110-140, 121 Stat. 1492; Emergency Economic Stabilization Act of 2008, Pub. L. No. 110-343, 122 Stat. 3765; American Recovery and Reinvestment Act of 2009, Pub. L. No. 111-5, 123 Stat. 115; Dodd-Frank Wall Street

individually could not solve many aspects of the problems addressed by such statutes, and the states trying to act collectively via proposed compacts would be less likely to agree than would congressional majorities and the president. The ability of the Collective-Action Constitution to fulfill its mission through Congress is diminished in current times, but the mission is not impossible, and it is more feasible than relying on the states.

Reform and Consumer Protection Act, Pub. L. No. 111-203, 124 Stat. 1376 (2010); Patient Protection and Affordable Care Act, Pub. L. No. 111-148, 124 Stat. 119 (2010); Every Student Succeeds Act, Pub. L. No. 114-95, 129 Stat. 1802 (2015); Tax Cuts and Jobs Act, Pub. L. No. 115-97, 131 Stat. 2054 (2017); America's Water Infrastructure Act of 2018, Pub. L. No. 115-270, 132 Stat. 3765; Coronavirus Aid, Relief, and Economic Security (CARES) Act, Pub. L. No. 116-136, 134 Stat. 281 (2020); Paycheck Protection Program and Health Care Enhancement Act, Pub. L. No. 116-139, 134 Stat. 620 (2020); American Rescue Plan Act of 2021, Pub. L. No. 117-2, 135 Stat. 4; Bipartisan Safer Communities Act, Pub. L. No. 117-159, 135 Stat. 1313 (2022); Inflation Reduction Act of 2022, Pub. L. No. 117-169, 136 Stat. 1818; Respect for Marriage Act, Pub. L. No. 117-228, 136 Stat. 2305 (2022); Fiscal Responsibility Act of 2023, Pub. L. No. 118-5, 137 Stat. 10.

Conclusion

The US Constitution is, to a significant extent, the Collective-Action Constitution. Structurally, the Constitution's main purpose is to authorize Congress to solve collective-action problems for the states and to prevent state governments from undercutting these solutions or producing such problems. Some multistate collective-action problems are Pareto problems, in which all states prefer mutual cooperation to mutual noncooperation or coordination to noncoordination. But the vast majority are cost-benefit collective-action problems, in which some states internalize all the benefits of the activities they engage in or permit within their borders and externalize most of the costs, and externalized costs exceed internalized benefits. The federal executive and judicial branches also play pivotal roles in achieving the Constitution's collective-action goals. Among other activities, they enforce federal laws that solve multistate collective-action problems, and they vindicate constitutional provisions and principles that prevent states from generating them.[1]

The collective-action theory developed in this book cannot fully explain and justify every function of the Constitution. Most importantly, the theory can only partially capture the Constitution's role in protecting constitutional rights. This limitation is not, however, simply a weakness of the theory; the US Constitution is too multifaceted for any one theory to explain it completely, and an account that purports to do so is likely to prove unpersuasive. As Professor John Hart Ely wrote of his own theory, "our Constitution is too complex a document to lie still for *any* pat characterization."[2] The limits of the Collective-Action Constitution help define the idea of collective action and give it greater descriptive and normative power where it does apply. Moreover, the theory's critical acuity enables it to identify vulnerabilities of the Constitution in contemporary times. Notwithstanding its limitations, the collective-action account offered here is fundamental to illuminating the Constitution's roles in sustaining—and authorizing the federal government to sustain—political and economic union. This is true originally, traditionally, and today.

---

[1] *Cf.* AKHIL REED AMAR, THE WORDS THAT MADE US: AMERICA'S CONSTITUTIONAL CONVERSATION, 1760–1840, at 194 (2021) ("As human instruments go, the Constitution had an impressive inner logic, coherence, and systematicity to it.").

[2] JOHN HART ELY, DEMOCRACY AND DISTRUST: A THEORY OF JUDICIAL REVIEW 101 (1980).

The Collective-Action Constitution. Neil S. Siegel, Oxford University Press. © Neil S. Siegel 2024.
DOI: 10.1093/oso/9780197760963.003.0013

484   THE COLLECTIVE-ACTION CONSTITUTION

The critique that the Collective-Action Constitution is social science, not constitutional law, is historically inaccurate and generally misguided. Some justices and scholars occasionally suggest that constitutional law is fully autonomous of knowledge in other disciplines (except, perhaps, history), including political science and economics. This suggestion would have astonished Madison, who widely consulted academic work when drafting his *Vices Memo* and the Virginia Plan. The notion also would have surprised Hamilton, Wilson, Washington, and Marshall, whose constitutional views were informed by their political and economic ambitions for the young nation.

Embedded in the above paragraphs are several lessons that this study of the Constitution offers. First, when states disagree, collective-action problems do not simply exist or not in a technical, scientific way. Cost-benefit collective-action problems have a certain objective structure, but their existence and significance require assessing the extent to which states are externalizing costs that are greater than the benefits they are internalizing.

Second, the assessor that matters most for constitutional purposes is either the Constitution itself or the government institution with the most democratic legitimacy to make such judgment calls. This institution is Congress—the first branch of government—where all states and all Americans are represented, in contrast to individual state governments, where only one state and some Americans are represented. In *McCulloch v. Maryland*, Chief Justice John Marshall explained this key difference between the democratic legitimacy of the states and the people collectively in Congress and the democratic legitimacy of the states individually outside it.[3] Congress is also more broadly representative of all the states and all the people than is the presidency, which does not balance interests and include both political parties at a given time to anywhere near the same extent that Congress does.

Third, precisely because the Constitution privileges Congress's assessment of costs and benefits, it does not have the structural purpose of preventing the federal government from causing collective-action problems for the states. For example, as Chapter 5 discussed, federal price supports for farmers may solve a cost-benefit collective-action problem by helping states with many farmers. But from the perspective of states with no farmers and many consumers of agricultural products, federal price supports may create a cartel that limits production and thereby commands higher prices than could be obtained absent federal intervention. Such a cartel may or may not be sound policy, but the Constitution says nothing about the matter because Congress is entitled to its point of view regarding how the externalized costs compare with the internalized benefits in deciding whether there is a collective-action problem and whether to address

---

[3] McCulloch v. Maryland, 17 U.S. (4 Wheat.) 316, 407 (1819).

CONCLUSION 485

it. Whatever Congress rationally decides regarding the advisability of price supports based on its assessment of the relative costs and benefits, the system is functioning constitutionally as it should.

Fourth, if it is acting within its enumerated powers, Congress need only comply with the majority or supermajority voting rules set forth in the Constitution; Congress need not first establish that all or most states agree that a collective-action problem exists and is sufficiently serious to warrant federal regulation. In other words, Congress need not poll the states apart from establishing sufficient support in the federal legislative process. Because states are represented in Congress—because congressional majorities represent (albeit imperfectly) the constitutionally relevant views of the states collectively—proceeding otherwise would overrepresent the states, effectively letting them vote twice. One main reason that the Constitution is too difficult to amend is that Article V essentially lets the states vote twice.

Fifth, Congress's central role in deciding whether and how to solve collective-action problems for the states connects constitutional provisions, principles, and ideas that may otherwise seem to have little to do with one another. These include, for example, the Interstate Compacts Clause, the Interstate Commerce Clause, the congressional-approval exception to the dormant commerce principle, Article III's opening clause (which instantiates the Madisonian Compromise), Article IV's provisions expressly or implicitly authorizing Congress to legislate, and democratic-process rights and theory.

Sixth, the values animating a collective-action approach to the Constitution are not limited to efficiency in the economic sense of Pareto optimality or cost-benefit analysis.[4] Rather, the main point of empowering the Constitution or Congress to solve collective-action problems for the states, and of preventing states from interfering with these solutions or causing collective-action problems, is more inspiring: a more integrated union both politically and economically. If Congress lacked this authority, and if states could externalize significant costs onto sister states with impunity, the Union might well have fractured into several warring sections long ago—just as Hamilton had warned.[5] And no civil war might have put it back together again.

Recall Article II of the Articles of Confederation: "Each State retains its sovereignty, freedom, and independence, and every power, jurisdiction, and right, which is not by this Confederation expressly delegated to the United States in Congress assembled." The Collective-Action Constitution creates a substantially

---

[4] As Chapter 2 explained, collective-action problems that harm all states are Pareto inefficiencies, and collective-action problems that harm some states a lot and benefit others a little are cost-benefit inefficiencies.

[5] THE FEDERALIST No. 6, at 54 (Alexander Hamilton) (Clinton Rossiter ed., 1961); THE FEDERALIST No. 7, at 65–66 (Alexander Hamilton) (Clinton Rossiter ed., 1961).

486 THE COLLECTIVE-ACTION CONSTITUTION

more nationalist constitutional regime, albeit not a completely centralized one. "It is obviously impracticable in the foederal government of these States, to secure all rights of independent sovereignty to each, and yet provide for the interest and safety of all," George Washington explained in his letter accompanying submission of the draft Constitution to the Confederation Congress. "In all our deliberations on this subject," he added, "we kept steadily in our view, that which appears to us the greatest interest of every true American, the consolidation of our Union, in which is involved our prosperity, felicity, safety, perhaps our national existence."[6]

Different audiences can benefit from accepting the central claims of this book. Constitutionally conscientious legislators and executive-branch officials, both federal and state, may better execute their responsibilities if they are more mindful of the collective-action logics that explain and justify much of the Constitution. These logics inform the expanse and limits of their own powers. Similarly, concerned citizens may reorient elements of their civic participation— what they demand of different levels of government—if they bear these logics in mind. For example, the geographic scope of a regulatory problem should inform which level of government voters hold primarily responsible for (not) addressing the problem.

Moreover, this book has privileged breadth of coverage of the Constitution and judge-made constitutional law over depth. As a result, scholars can examine more closely the collective-action dimensions (or not) of the specific clauses, sections, principles, decisions, ideas, and debates that have been explored in the foregoing chapters. Room remains for work on these subjects that is theoretical, doctrinal, historical, or empirical.

Room also remains to analyze topics neglected here. For example, personal jurisdiction is an individual right with a structural component, and the structural component should arguably prohibit a state from conditioning the ability of a company to do business in the state on the waiver of this right. When states "impose a blanket claim of authority over controversies with no connection to [them]," they "intrude[] on the prerogatives of other States—domestic and foreign—to adjudicate the rights of their citizens and enforce their own laws," thereby likely externalizing costs that are greater than the benefits they internalize.[7] Such cost externalization can create either a race to the bottom or a cost-benefit collective-action problem.

---

[6] 2 THE RECORDS OF THE FEDERAL CONVENTION OF 1787, at 666–67 (Max Farrand ed., 1911).

[7] Mallory v. Norfolk So. R. Co., 143 S. Ct. 2028, 2058 (2023) (Barrett, J., dissenting). Contrary to the reasoning in the text, the Court in this case held that a Pennsylvania law requiring out-of-state companies that register to do business in Pennsylvania to agree to appear in Pennsylvania courts on "any cause of action" against them comports with the Due Process Clause under *Pennsylvania Fire Insurance Company of Philadelphia v. Gold Issue Mining & Milling Company*, 243 U.S. 93 (1917).

CONCLUSION 487

Or consider the states' sovereign immunity from suit by private parties without their consent. Although one's view of the Founding history matters, the Supreme Court's position that states enjoy immunity from suit even when claims arise under federal law—and that Congress can abrogate this immunity when using only a select few of its enumerated powers in Article I, Section 8—is difficult to reconcile with the collective-action logics underlying the Constitution's federal structure.[8] The notion that states retain the authority to secede from the Union is even more fundamentally at odds with the collective-action rationales for creating a powerful national government and limiting state authority. State secession, by literally blowing holes in the territory composing the Union, wars with the aspirations for national security, domestic peace, effective diplomacy, revenue collection, and economic development that were responsible for the Constitution's creation.[9]

Finally, the book cautions the US Supreme Court and other federal courts—both of which can be far more aggressive than the Founders envisioned—not to substantially restrict federal authority in the years ahead, whether through constitutional-law rulings concerning congressional power or administrative-law rulings regarding agency power. The nation will continue to face many serious problems that spill across state (or national) borders, so federal intervention will be needed to address them successfully. In general, there is ample constitutional warrant for the federal government to act. And given the horizontal structure and the partisan polarization and animosity that will persist, there are already significant impediments to the ability and desire of members of Congress to overcome their own collective-action problems and legislate. Especially in such an era, judicial doctrine should facilitate, not impede, realization of the Constitution's main structural purpose—its commitment to collective action.

[8] Torres v. Texas Dept. of Pub. Safety, 142 S. Ct. 2455 (2022) (observing that the Court has allowed Congress to abrogate state sovereign immunity when using its bankruptcy and eminent-domain powers, and holding that Congress may also do so when using its powers to raise and support the armed forces).

[9] AMAR, *supra* note 1, at 262 ("If any state at any time could take its land and waters and ally with some foreign European power, the Constitution's entire system—promising the permanent elimination of international borders from Georgia to Maine—would make no sense.").

Postscript on Methodology

This brief methodological postscript to *The Collective-Action Constitution* explains why the book has identified the states, as opposed to individual Americans, as the group members whose collective-action problems potentially justify intervention by the government of the group as a whole—the federal government. The two approaches do not have significantly different implications for the scope of federal power, but they do have different implications for judging the legitimacy of the American constitutional system and, relatedly, for institutional design. This book's decision to focus mostly on the states as experiencing collective-action problems reflects the author's judgment that the most convincing arguments for federal authority are those that do not demand agreement on a strong normative preference for nationalism. The book has articulated a robust view of federal power that is consistent with both We the People and We the States by adopting, methodologically, the perspective that one would presume is less congenial to such a view. This is no small thing in the United States today: the greatest challenges to the American constitutional system as it has operated for a long time now are from those advocating for a substantially weaker federal government. During a challenging era of American politics, in which some powerful jurists and influential academics seek to significantly shrink federal authority, this book has sought to preserve and perfect it by proceeding from structural premises that assign prime importance to the states as units of constitutional analysis.

U.S. Constitution, federal power, collective action, state compact theory, constitutional design, constitutional legitimacy, constitutional federalism, John Marshall, James Madison, *McCulloch*

This book has defended robust, albeit not limitless, federal power by claiming to rest substantially on Chief Justice John Marshall's canonical decision in *McCulloch v. Maryland* (1819). One could argue, however, that the book's analytical framework is not as nationalist, or as reliant on *McCulloch*, as it could be. As Chapter 1 explained, Marshall argued in *McCulloch* that the American people as a whole were sovereign and—in their sovereign capacity—ratified the Constitution, thereby creating the federal government. Marshall further argued in effect that the sovereign American people as principals had two agents—the federal government and the state governments—and that, when there was a regulatory conflict between the former and one of the latter that the constitutional

490 POSTSCRIPT ON METHODOLOGY

text did not settle, the federal government must prevail because it represents all the people, whereas each state government represents only some of the people.

If the American people are sovereign—if they are the principals in the American constitutional system—then perhaps individual Americans are the "players" in the "games" modeling collective-action problems discussed throughout this book. On this understanding, Americans want good government and so prefer governance at the state or local level where it is effective to secure various values of federalism, but they turn to the federal government where it provides a superior way of solving their collective-action problems, such as obtaining national public goods. By contrast, this book has viewed the "players" facing collective-action problems as the states, whether state governments or state political communities, and it has conceptualized the federal government as the primary means by which the states solve their own collective-action problems. At the same time, the book has insisted that not only all the states but also (almost) all the people and interests in the nation are better represented in Congress than in a single state legislature. This brief methodological postscript explains why the book has elected to proceed in this fashion.

The two approaches do not have significantly different implications for the scope of federal power. Whether the participants in the strategic interactions examined in this book are state governments, state electorates, or individual Americans, the argument remains that governance problems are presumptively best dealt with locally but that collective-action problems make local resolution infeasible or unattractive in a variety of situations, with the implications for federal power that this book has elaborated. Likewise, regardless of who the actors are, the argument remains that their collective-action problems are not being adequately addressed in the contemporary United States for the reasons discussed in Part III of the book. Tellingly, Marshall insisted on refuting the state-compact theory of the Constitution, but as Chapter 1 noted, he himself was not sure whether anything of substance in *McCulloch* turned on who was right about whether the Constitution was created by the American people as a whole or by the state peoples one by one.

The two approaches do, however, have different implications for judging the legitimacy of the American constitutional system and, relatedly, for institutional design. Marshall's approach justifies proportional representation in the House of Representatives much more persuasively than it justifies the equal representation of the states in the Senate. This book's formulation easily accounts for the equal representation of the states in the Senate; it frequently has added that (almost) all people and interests in the nation are better represented in Congress than in a state legislature to also capture the structure of representation in the House. In addition, a pure Marshallian (or a Californian) might disagree with this book's insistence that Congress is more democratically legitimate than the presidency.

If democratic legitimacy is measured only in terms of voting power (a claim this book has denied) and only in terms of the voting power of individuals and not of state peoples as well (a claim this book has neither defended nor denied), then the Senate is the worst offender among the elected institutions of the federal government.

Judging from the different structures of representation in the two houses of Congress, the Constitution seems a compromise among these two competing visions of it. Both We the People and We the States as sovereign principals created the Constitution and are represented in the national legislature that it establishes. Indeed, Marshall himself insisted that these competing descriptions of the Constitution are reconcilable. In a newspaper essay he wrote defending *McCulloch* the month following the decision, Marshall argued that his opinion's identification of the American people as "the source from which the government of the Union derives its powers" was identical in substance to Madison's description, in the Virginia Report of 1800, of "the compact to which the states are parties" as the basis of the federal government's powers. "This celebrated report," he wrote, "concurs exactly with the Supreme Court, in the opinion that the constitution is the act of the people."[1]

This book's decision to focus mostly on the states as experiencing collective-action problems reflects the author's judgment that these two views are complementary, and that the most convincing arguments for federal power are those that do not demand agreement on a strong normative preference for nationalism. The book has articulated a robust view of federal authority that is consistent with both We the People and We the States by adopting, methodologically, the perspective that one would presume is less congenial to such a view. This is no small thing in the United States today: the greatest challenges to the American constitutional system as it has operated for a long time now are from those advocating for a substantially weaker federal government. During a challenging era of American politics, in which some powerful jurists and influential academics seek to significantly shrink federal authority, this book has sought to preserve and perfect it by proceeding from structural premises that assign prime importance to the states as units of constitutional analysis.

---

[1] A Friend to the Union [John Marshall], No. 1 (Apr. 24, 1819), *in* 8 THE PAPERS OF JOHN MARSHALL 287, 295 (Charles F. Hobson ed., 1995). In the Report of 1800, a resolution that Madison drafted and the Virginia General Assembly adopted in opposition to the Alien and Sedition Acts, Madison defined the word "States" as "the people composing those political societies, in their highest sovereign capacity," and he wrote that "in that sense of the term 'States,' they are . . . parties to the compact from which the powers of the Federal Government result." James Madison, Report on the Resolutions (1800), *in* 6 THE WRITINGS OF JAMES MADISON 341, 348 (Gaillard Hunt ed., 1906).

Index of Constitutional Provisions

For the benefit of digital users, indexed terms that span two pages (e.g., 52–53) may, on occasion, appear on only one of those pages.

Admiralty Clause (Art. III, section 2, cl.1), 283
Admissions Clause (Art. IV, section 3, cl. 1), 16–17, 314, 323, 341–42, 345, 346–47, 348–49, 350, 352, 353, 399, 406–7
Amendment of the Constitution (Art. V), 401–2, 405–6, 407–8, 409
Appointments Clause (Art. II, section 2, cl. 2), 270

Bankruptcy Clause (Art. I, section 8, cl. 4), 247, 250–55
Borrowing Clause (Art. I, section 8, cl. 2), 167

Citizenship Clause (Amend. XIV, section 1), 356
Coinage Clause (Art. I, section 8, cl. 5), 259
Congress, lower federal courts and (Art. I, section 8, cl. 9 & Art. III, section 1), 261
Congressional enforcement power (Amend. XIV, section 5), 383–84
Contracts Clause, (Art. I, section 10, cl. 1), 105–6
Counterfeiting Clause (Art. I, section 8, cl. 6), 260–61
Criminal procedure rights (Amend. VI), 373
Cruel and Unusual Punishments Clause (Amend VIII), 373

Debts and Engagements Clause (Art. VI, section 1, cl. 1), 306–7
Define and Punish Clause (Art. I, section 8, cl. 10), 230
Democratic elections for Congress (Amend. XVII), 183n.33, 460–61
Due Process Clause (Amend. XIV, section 1), 390–91

Effects Clause (Art. IV, section 1), 16
Elections Clause (Art. I, section 4, cl. 1), 369
Enclave Clause (Art. I, section 8, cl. 17), 15
Equal Protection Clause (Amend. XIV, section 1), 174
Expressly/implicitly authorizing Congress to legislate (Art. IV), 485

Extradition Clause (Art. IV, section 2, cl. 2), 16

Foreign Commerce Clause (Art. I, section 8, cl. 3), 220
Foreign Compacts Clause (Art. I, section 10, cl. 3), 105–6, 105n.40
Free Exercise Clause (Amend. I), 373
Fugitive Slave Clause (Art. IV, section 2, cl. 3), 16, 17
Full Faith and Credit Clause (Art. IV, section 1), 16, 17

General Welfare Clause (Art. I, section 8, cl. 1), 15
Guarantee Clause (Art. IV, section 4), 17

House of Representatives (Art. 1, section 2, cl. 1), 183n.33

Income tax apportionment overruled (Amend. XVI), 410
Indian Commerce Clause (Art. I, section 8, cl. 3), 220–21
Intellectual Property Clause (Art. I, section 8, cl. 8), 83n.69
Interstate Commerce Clause (Art. I, section 8, cl. 3), 11, 128, 223, 259, 283, 288, 485
Interstate Compacts Clause (Art. I, section 10, cl. 3), 97, 105–6, 105n.40

Judicial power
 Judicial independence provisions (Art. III, section 1), 279, 293–95, 421n.72
 Heads of federal jurisdiction (Art. III, section 2, cl. 1), 281
 Jurisdiction of Supreme Court (Art. III, section 2, cl. 2), 301–2

Military powers of Congress (Art. I, section 8, cl. 11 to cl. 14), 234
 Eighteen clauses in Article I, Section 8 (Art. 1, section 8, cl. 15 & cl. 16), 145*f*

494 INDEX OF CONSTITUTIONAL PROVISIONS

Military powers of Congress (Art. I, section 8, cl. 11 to cl. 14) (*cont.*)
National security (Art. II, section 2, cl.1), 273–74

Naturalization Clause (Art. I, section 8, cl. 4), 247–48, 249–50
Necessary and Proper Clause (Art. I, section 8, cl. 18), 9–10, 12–13, 13n.48, 25, 28–29, 30, 45, 46, 259, 260–61, 264, 283, 285, 301–2, 336–37, 383–84

Oaths of Office Clause (Art. VI, section 1, cl. 3), 310n.159
Offenses Clause (Art. I, section 8, cl. 10), 230
Origination Clause (Art. 1, section 7, cl. 1), 154–55

Poll taxes (Amend. XXIV), 409–10
Possession of firearms (Right to Bear Arms Clause, Amend. II), 373
Postal Clause (Art. I, section 8, cl. 7), 235–36, 238, 240, 247
President
convene both/either Houses on extraordinary occasions (Art. II, section 3), 274
election amendment (Amend. XII), 183n.33, 408–9
election, Electoral College method of (Art. II, section 1, cl. 2), 275–76
election, four-year term (Art. II, section 1, cl. 1), 275
eligibility (Art. II, section 1, cl. 5), 274–75
federal judges & foreign affairs (Art. II, section 2, cl. 2), 273
protect nation from attack (Art. II, section 2, cl. 1), 273–74
removal from office (Art. II, section 4), 275–76
salaries & emoluments (Emolument Clause, Art. II, section 1, cl. 7), 275–76
State of the Union address (Art. II, section 3), 276

succession to (Art. II, section 1, cl. 6), 274
temporary appointments during Senate recesses (Art. II, section 2, cl. 3), 274
veto power (Art. I, section 7, cl. 2), 275, 276
Presidential Oath Clause (Art. II, section 1, cl. 8), 273–74
Privileges and Immunities Clause (Art. IV, section 2, cl. 1), 17, 217, 313, 314, 355–56, 357, 362–63, 364, 369, 371–72, 373, 376–77

Racial discrimination in voting prohibited (Amend. XV, section 1), 383
Ratification (Art. VII), 406–7
Republican Form of Government Clause (Art. IV, section 4), 17

Scope of state sovereign immunity (Amend. XI), 408
Slavery ban (abolition of slavery, Amend. XIII, section 1), 383
Spending Clause (Art. I, section 8, cl. 1), 15, 42–43, 143–44, 146, 155, 198, 232, 306–7, 352
Supremacy Clause (Art. VI, section 1, cl. 2), 15–16, 223

Take Care Clause (Art. II, section 3), 269–70
Takings Clause (Amend. V), 208
Taxing Clause (Art. I, section 8, cl. 1), 306–7
Territory Clause (Art. IV, section 3, cl. 2), 16–17, 314, 345, 346, 353, 384
Treaty Clause (Art. II, section 2, cl. 2), 269–70, 273, 276, 278, 301–2, 396, 423, 453
Two-term presidential limit (Amend. XXII), 410

Unreasonable searches and seizures (Amend. IV), 373

Washington D.C. voting rights (Amend. XXIII), 352

Index of Cases

For the benefit of digital users, indexed terms that span two pages (e.g., 52–53) may, on occasion, appear on only one of those pages.

Alaska Packers Association v. Industrial Accident Commission (1935), 321–22
Allstate Insurance Company v. Hague (1981), 321–22
American Insurance Association v. Garamendi (2003), 224–25, 226n.188
Attorney General of New York v. Soto-Lopez (1986), 379n.82

Bailey v. Drexel Furniture Company (Child Labor Tax Case) (1922), 152–53n.84, 154–55
Baldwin v. G.A.F. Seelig, Inc. (1935), 210
Balzac v. Puerto Rico (1922), 352n.147
Brown v. Board of Education (1954), 101n.20, 418n.61
Burwell v. Hobby Lobby Stores, Inc. (2014), 418n.61

California v. Superior Court (1987), 331n.62
California v. Texas (2021), 152n.82
Carter v. Carter Coal Company (1936), 6–7, 176–78
Chevron U.S.A. v. Natural Resources Defense Council, Inc. (1984), 475n.93
Chicago & Alton Railroad Company v. Wiggins Ferry Company (1887), 321
Chisholm v. Georgia (1793), 408–9n.25
Chy Lung v. Freeman (1875), 220–21
Civil Rights Cases (1883), 185–86, 384, 385
Cohens v. Virginia (1821), 308–9n.157
Cooley v. Board of Wardens (1852), 208–9n.122
Corfield v. Coryell (1823), 359–60
Crandall v. Nevada (1868), 370–71
Crosby v. National Foreign Trade Council (2000), 224–25

Daniel v. Paul (1969), 188n.51, 363n.29
District of Columbia v. Heller (2008), 418n.61
Dobbs v. Jackson Women's Health Organization (2022), 202, 334–35
Downes v. Bidwell (1901), 352n.147

Edwards v. California (1941), 371, 372–73

FERC v. Mississippi (1982), 99n.10, 100n.11
Franchise Tax Board of California v. Hyatt (2016), 321–22

Gade v. National Solid Wastes Management Association (1992), 223n.178
Gibbons v. Ogden (1824), 6, 40, 175, 191, 209n.125, 223–24, 327
Gonzales v. Raich (2005), 9–10, 49n.91, 190, 193–94, 195–96, 223–24
Granholm v. Heald (2004), 211–12
Gregory v. Ashcroft (1991), 99n.10, 100n.11

Hammer v. Dagenhart (Child Labor Case) (1918), 6–7, 8–9, 176–78
Heart of Atlanta Motel, Inc. v. United States (1964), 171
Helvering v. Davis (1937), 152–53, 375–76
Hodel v. Virginia Surface Mining & Reclamation Association (1981), 8–9, 181
Hooper v. Bernalillo County (1985), 379n.82
Houston, East & West Texas Railway Company v. United States (Shreveport Rate Cases) (1914), 188n.49
H.P. Hood & Sons, Inc. v. Du Mond (1949), 212
Hughes v. Alexandra Scrap Corporation (1976), 216n.150

Katzenbach v. McClung (1964), 171
Kentucky v. Dennison (1861), 330–31, 332–33

Lochner v. New York (1905), 116n.92, 417n.58

Mallory v. Norfolk Southern Railway Company (2023), 486n.7
Marbury v. Madison (1803), 302–3
Martin v. Hunter's Lessee (1816), 308–9n.157
Martinez v. Bynum (1983), 378
Massachusetts v. Mellon, (1923), 443n.146
Mayor of New York v. Miln (1837), 372–73
McCulloch v. Maryland (1819), 85, 212–13
McDonald v. Board of Election Commissioners of Chicago (1964), 303n.142

496 INDEX OF CASES

Memorial Hospital v. Maricopa County (1974), 376n.73

Metcalf & Eddy v. Mitchell (1926), 85n.79

Metropolitan Life Insurance Company v. Ward (1985), 386–87n.113

Missouri v. Holland (1920), 6–7

Murphy v. National Collegiate Athletic Association (2018), 207

National Pork Producers Council v. Ross (2023), 209n.123

New Hampshire v. Maine (1976), 114

New York Times Company v. Sullivan (1964), 388n.116

New York v. New Jersey (2023), 121n.113

New York v. United States (1992), 83n.68, 113n.75, 205n.108, 206–7, 208, 216

NFIB v. Sebelius (2012), 193–94, 199

NLRB v. Jones & Laughlin Steel Corporation (1937), 7–8, 181

Northeast Bancorp, Inc. v. Board of Governors of the Federal Reserve System (1985), 115

Obergefell v. Hodges (2015), 101n.18

Panhandle Oil Company v. Mississippi ex rel. Knox (1928), 50n.96

Passenger Cases (1849), 369–70

Paul v. Virginia (1869), 359

Perez v. United States (1971), 332

Pennsylvania Fire Insurance Company of Philadelphia v. Gold Issue Mining & Milling Company (1917), 486n.7

Philadelphia v. New Jersey (1978), 209n.124

Pike v. Bruce Church, Inc. (1970), 214–15

Planned Parenthood of Southeastern Pennsylvania v. Casey (1992), 202

Pollock v. Farmers' Loan & Trust Company (1895), 410

Prigg v. Pennsylvania (1842), 53, 336–37, 340, 416–17

Printz v. United States (1997), 207, 208

Prize Cases (1863), 273–74

Prudential Insurance Company v. Benjamin (1946), 216n.146

Puerto Rico v. Franklin California Tax-Free Trust (2016), 226n.185

Reynolds v. Sims (1964), 388n.118

Rhode Island v. Massachusetts (1838), 107n.52

Roe v. Wade (1973), 202

Romero v. International Terminal Operating Company (1959), 283

Rucho v. Common Cause (2019), 388n.115

Sabri v. United States (2004), 49n.91

Scott v. Emerson (1852), 339

Scott v. Sandford (1857), 302–3

Slaughter-House Cases (1872), 374

Sosna v. Iowa (1975), 378

South Carolina State Highway Department v. Barnwell Brothers (1938), 209n.124, 212–13

South-Central Timber Development, Inc. v. Wunnicke (1984), 216n.149

South Dakota v. Dole (1987), 85n.78

Steward Machine Company v. Davis (1937), 152–53, 375–76

Swift & Company v. United States (1905), 177n.16

Texas v. New Mexico (2018), 121n.112

United States v. Butler (1936), 158–59

United States v. Carolene Products Company (1938), 51, 389, 390n.123

United States v. Comstock (2010), 9–10, 45, 48, 49n.91

United States v. Darby (1941), 8–9, 49–50, 181

United States v. Guest (1966), 369

United States v. Harris (1883), 303n.142

United States v. Lopez (1995), 9–10, 190, 192, 193–96, 200–1

United States v. Morrison (2000), 174n.8, 175n.10, 190, 384

United States v. Nagarwala (2018), 193n.72

United States v. Railroad Company (1893), 85n.79

United States v. South-Eastern Underwriters Association (1944), 199n.89

United States v. Gettysburg Electric Railway Company (1896), 84n.77

Virginia v. Tennessee (1893), 106n.42, 114

Vlandis v. Kline (1973), 378

Ware v. Hylton (1796), 302–3

Western & Southern Life Insurance Company v. State Board of Equalization (1981), 386n.112

West Virginia v. Environmental Protection Agency (2022), 475n.91, 475–76nn.93–95

Wickard v. Filburn (1942), 190, 193–94

Willson v. Black Bird Creek Marsh Company (1829), 208–9n.122

Youngstown Sheet & Tube Company v. Sawyer (1952) *(Steel Seizure Case)*, 33n.30, 34

Zivotofsky v. Kerry (Zivotofsky II) (2015), 273n.22

Zobel v. Williams (1982), 379n.82

General Index

For the benefit of digital users, indexed terms that span two pages (e.g., 52–53) may, on occasion, appear on only one of those pages.

Figures are indicated by *f* following the page number.

abolitionist, 336–37, 382–83
abortion
  access to, 202
  Center for Reproductive Rights and, 202–3
  Congressional intervention and, 202–3
  financial means and, 204
  future litigation over, 334–35
  insurance coverage of, 215
  national ban on, 204
  negative interstate externalities and, 203
  opponents of, 204
  pro-choice regime and, 203
  restriction of, 127
  rights, 334–35
  state regulations of, 322–23
admiralty jurisdiction
  Admiralty Clause and, 283
  collective-action reasoning in, 282–83
  historical practice and, 282–83
Admissions Clause
  American empire and, 16–17
  collective action and, 348
  Congress' exclusive power, 314
  consent requirements, 263
  constraint, 345
  design, 341–42
  enumerated power, an, 346
  implications of, 348–49
  integrated union and, 353
  majority voting rule of, 346
  new states, 16–17, 346–47
  placement of, 352
  pursuant to, 399
  state equality, 323, 349, 350
Affordable Care Act (ACA; Obamacare)
  debate on, 2
  effects theory and, 153–54
  individual mandate and, 199
  Interstate Commerce Clause and, 199–200, 201

"job lock" and, 200
  Medicaid and, 162
  negative interstate externalities, 200
  shared responsibility payment and, 152–53
  spillover effects and, 200–1
Agricultural Adjustment Act (1933), 158–59
Alaska, 346
Amar, Akhil Reed, 10–11, 46, 198, 220–21, 271–72, 286–87, 288, 454
amendment proposal process
  collective action in, 406–7
  comparative experience and, 407
  supermajorities and, 407
American Revolution, counterfeiting during, 259–60
American territories
  democratic legitimacy of, 352
  expansion of, 345
  unincorporated status and, 352
Annapolis Conference (1786), 137
anti-commandeering doctrine
  collective-action approach, 227
  commandeering, 205, 206, 207, 208
  Congress and, 205
  cost-benefit collective-action problem, 207
  expanded federal power and, 205
  government coercion and, 206–7
  market participant & regulator distinction in, 114–15
  power to regulate and, 332
  regulatory alternatives to, 171–72
  scope of, 15, 83–84
  structural sense of, 206
  uncompromising nature of, 205
antidiscrimination commitments, 356, 390
Articles of Confederation
  Article IV of, 358, 369, 372
  Articles IX & XIII of, 447
  collective action and, 444, 464
  consolidation and, 485–86

498 GENERAL INDEX

Articles of Confederation (*cont.*)
  Constitution, the, and, 330
  context and, 466
  democratic legitimacy and, 346
  federal law unenforceable under, 46
  federal territories and, 342–43
  legislate under, 459
  nine-state threshold in, 423
  states' tension & hostility and, 345
  status-quo bias in, 462
  structural sense in, 399–400
  supermajority rule of, 427, 433
  two-thirds requirement and, 455
  unanimity and, 397–98, 401–2
  unicameral Congress in, 449–50

Balkin, Jack M., 10–11, 35, 198, 220–21
Bank of North America, 135–36
Bedford, Gunning, 139–40
Biber, Eric, 347, 348
Black, Charles, 30, 455–57
Black Americans (African Americans)
  characterized as free, 379
  denials of civil rights to, 379
  federalism & race and, 379
  settlement & removal and, 372
Bork, Judge Robert H., 10–11
Borrowing Clause, 167
Brennan, Justice William, 183–84
Bridge or Seaway game
  inequality problem in, 71
  outcomes in, 70–71
  two Nash equilibria in, 72
Brown, Roger H., 104
Brownlee, W. Elliot, 154–55

Calabresi, Steven G., 10–11
California, 214–15, 220–21, 224–25, 321–22,
  346–47, 371–72, 374–75, 376, 378
Canada, 342–43
Chevron doctrine, 475
Civil Rights Act (CRA), 1964
  collective & individual action and, 171
  decisions upholding and, 9
  Interstate Commerce Clause and, 171
  public accommodation and, 49
Civil War
  African Americans and, 379
  change accomplished by, 385–86
  collective-action logics and, 430
  Congress's resolution of disputes and, 285–86
  Constitution amended after, 408–9
  counterfeiting during, 259–60

  disagreement and, 409
  enter & leave states and, 370–71
  failed politics and, 383
  integrated union and, 485
  interstate compacts and, 111
  "slavocrats" and, 367
Clean Air Act, Section 111 of, 475
Cleveland, Grover, 461
Coinage Clause, 259
"Collective-Action Constitution"
  ability of, 480–81
  antidiscrimination commitments and, 356
  critique and, 443–44, 484
  goals of, 483
  history and, 484
  idea of, 483
  limitations of, 270
  logics of, 211
  nationalist regime and, 485–86
  political science & economics in, 484
  primary focus of, 270
  purpose of, 359
  "Reconstruction Constitution" and, 355,
    390–91
  Republican Form Clause and, 367
  rights and, 353, 356–57, 361, 373, 390
  state parochialism and, 387
  theory of, 483
  transportation cases and, 211
collective-action problems. *See also* Pareto
  cost-benefit, 13–14, 210, 212–13, 224, 328–29
  multistate, 14–15, 48, 224, 226
"Commerce," 197–98, 220–21
Confederation Congress, 138, 233–34, 342–43
conflict preemption, 223, 224–25
Congress
  collective-action problems and, 26–27, 185
  democratic legitimacy of, 352
  federal laws and branches of government
    and, 46–47
  focus of, 184
  legislative powers of, 4
  majorities in, 182–83
  state governments & political communities
    and, 184
Congressional-approval exception to dormant
    commerce principle
  Collective-Action Constitution and, 309
  collective-action reasoning and, 171–72
  multistate cooperation problem and, 216, 404
Congressional consent
  federalism and, 82–83
  Madisonian negative and, 106–7

GENERAL INDEX 499

Marshallian theory of democratic legitimacy and, 120
provisions, principles, & ideas in, 485
Connecticut, 103–4, 115, 139, 172, 218–19, 250, 256, 378, 423–24
Constitution, the
  Fugitive Slave Clause in, 338
  horizontal structure of, 470–71
  new regime of, 408–9
  provisions, principles, & ideas in, 485
  structural theory of, 11
Constitutional Convention, 281–82, 343
Consumer Credit Protection Act, 181–82
Contracts Clause, judicially enforceable contracts under, 105–6
Controlled Substances Act, 223–24
cooperation, 13, 45, 210, 212–13
coordination, 13, 212–13
Cooter, Robert D., 10–11
cost-benefit
  collective-action problem, 90f
  efficiency, 91
  improvement, 90
  inefficiencies, 92
cost-benefit concept
  Congress and, 328–29
  democratic-process theory and, 212–13
  economic & political union and, 212
  field preemption and, 224
  multistate collective-action phenomena and, 91
  negative interstate externalities and, 210
  structural purpose of, 13–14
cost externalization, benefits internalized and, 14–15, 486
Counterfeiting Clause, 260–61
COVID-19 (pandemic), 1–3, 474–75, 480–81
criminal law enforcement, 195
criminal procedure rights, 373
Currie, David P., 350–51

Delaware, 139, 423–24
democratic-legitimacy theory
  American-style, 39
  authority & Congress and, 42–43
  decision-making and, 41
  interests in, 41
  states and, 56
democratic-process theory
  Congress's central role in, 485
  dormant commerce principle in, 212–13
democratic warrant
  collective action and, 427–28

Congress's powers and, 277–78
Court (the Supreme) and, 184
dormant commerce doctrine and, 210–11
multistate collective-action problems and, 224–25
state nonparties and, 127
value judgments and, 247
diplomacy & national-security operations, 15–16
disaster relief, compacts concerning, 479
District of Columbia
  compacts & less formal agreements and, 105–6
  residents of, 352
doctrine
  collective-action dimensions of, 390
  individual-rights dimensions of, 390
dormant-commerce principle
  democratic-process theory of, 212–13
  originalist case for, 209–10
  structural principle and, 210, 390
  tradeoff and, 223, 224–25
Due Process Clause, rights protected by, 211–12

Eisenhower, President Dwight D, 461
Ely, John Hart, 51, 212–13, 364–65, 374, 390
embargo, least-preferred outcome and, 69–70
enter & leave other states, unenumerated right to, 390
Environmental Protection Agency (EPA), 475
Equal Protection Clause, rights protected by, 211–12
Equal Rights Amendment (ERA), 414
externalities, 163–65, 198, 232
Extradition Act, 331–32
Extradition Clause, 16

Fair Labor Standards Act (FLSA), 1938, 181, 183–84
federal courts, lower
  domestic peace and, 15–16
  establishment of, 291
  foreign relations and, 15–16
  Madisonian Compromise and, 291–92, 485
  national security and, 15–16
  uniform interpretation of federal law in, 15–16, 293
Federalist Papers, The, 106–7, 173, 220, 234, 251–52
federal judicial power
  controversies between states and, 287–88
  court's doctrine concerning, 119
  federal institutions and, 281–82

500 GENERAL INDEX

federal judicial power (*cont.*)
  federal law and, 281–82, 285
  federal-question jurisdiction in, 281–82
  foreign affairs & national security and, 281–82
  nine categories of cases or controversies and, 281
federal taxing authority, theory of, 15
female genital mutilation (FGM), 192–93
Field, Justice Stephen, 114
Field preemption, 223, 224
Financial regulation, compacts concerning, 479
Finkel, Jacob, 106–7
firearms, possession of, 373
Foreign relations, compacts concerning, 479
Frankfurter, Felix, 104–5
Franklin, Benjamin, 133, 235–36
Fugitive Slave Act (1793), 330–31
Fugitive Slave Act (1850), 336–37
Fugitive Slave Clause
  Amendment XIII and, 16n.55
  collective-action rationale for, 16
  slaveowners and, 17
Full Faith and Credit Clause, 16, 17

game theory. *See also* mutual cooperation
  assumption, 59–60
  Assurance game, 71
  Asymmetric Dilemma, 67, 68, 69
  Chicken game, 71–72, 86
  collective-action problems, 57–58
  cooperation & coordination problems, 13
  cost-benefit collective-action problem, 92
  cost-benefit optimality, 5
  cost sharing, 90
  most preferred outcome, 62–63, 67, 69, 70
  mutual noncooperation, 73–74
  Nash equilibrium, the, 65
  no collective action problem, 92*f*
  Prisoners' Dilemma, the, 64, 67
  Pure Coordination game, 70
  unanimity, 124
Georgia, 423–24
Gettysburg battlefield, 84
Gibbons v. Ogden, 1824 (*Gibbons* case)
  canonical federalism decision in, 6
  Constitution in, 223
  federal navigation license in, 223–24
  internal concerns in, 327
  Interstate Commerce Clause and, 40
  interstate commerce in, 175
  regulate navigation and, 6
Ginsburg, Justice Ruth Bader, 1–2, 200–1

Government regulation, cooperation & coordination and, 87
Great Britain, 69, 104–5, 132–36, 217–18, 219–20, 237–38, 247–48, 302–3, 423–24
Greene, Jamal, 340
Greve, Michael S., 106–7

Hamilton, Alexander, 6, 57, 135, 157, 158–59, 167–68, 172–73, 209–10, 274–75, 278, 282, 345, 485
Harrison, William Henry, 461
Hart, H.L.A., 80
Hawaii, 326–27, 328–29, 346
health care access, compacts concerning, 479
Hills, Roderick M. Jr., 372
Holmes, Justice Oliver Wendell, 6–7, 50–51, 116–17, 158
horizontal allocation of authority, 470–71
Huq, Aziz, 183–84

Illinois, 414
immigration policy, compacts concerning, 479
individual rights, 355, 355n.1
infrastructure spending, compacts concerning, 479
Insular Cases, 352
internalization principle, 83–84
Interstate and Foreign Commerce Clauses, preemption issues, 223
Interstate Commerce Clause
  admiralty legislation and, 283
  Congress's authority under, 259
  exceeding enumerated powers and, 288
  Interstate Compacts Clause and, 128
  externalities and, 11
  preemption issues and, 223
Interstate Compacts Clause
  colonial & postcolonial history of, 107
  Congress and, 485
  differing views of, 116–17
  federal authority and, 106–7
  general skepticism in, 128
  market participant/regulator distinction 114–15
  Marshallian theory of democratic legitimacy in, 120
  nationalist resolution of, 107
  one-shot game of chicken and, 107*f*–8
  political power in, 114
  text of, 121–22
  tradeoffs in, 127–28
Iredell, Justice James, 260

GENERAL INDEX 501

Jackson, President Andrew, 157–58
Jackson, Justice Robert, 38
Jay-Gardoqui treaty, 423–24
Jay, John, 423–24
Jefferson, Thomas, 241–42
Johnson, President Andrew, 461
Johnson, William, 250
judicial review
    democratic legitimacy and legal authority
      in, 307
    Framers never debated, 295
    human dignity & equality, 390
    obligation of state courts to enforce federal
      law; 307
    responsibility of state & federal courts, 307
    rights and, 388–89
    state taxation authority development of, 51
    supremacy of federal law over state law; 307
    vertical, 296–97

Kansas-Nebraska Act (1854), 343–44, 345
Kennedy, Justice Anthony, 200–1
Koppelman, Andrew, 10–11
Krehbiel, Keith, 470–71

Landis, James M., 104–5
LeBoeuf, Jacques, 10–11
Levinson, Daryl J., 470–71
Levinson, Sanford, 35
Levy, Richard E., 10–11
Livingston Robert, 146
Louisiana Purchase, 343–44

Madison, James, 135–36, 146, 157–58, 173,
    209–10, 291, 342–43, 358, 380–83, 484
Madisonian negative, 106–7
majority. *See also* supermajority
    Congress by, 92
    constitutional-design alternatives and, 434
    executive encroachments and, 424*f*–25, 440
    impeach president by, 430–31
    pivotal vote on a bill and, 470–71
    power to borrow by, 167
Maltz, Earl, 212
market-participant exception
    indigent people and, 376–77
    permits states to discriminate, 216–17
    subsidized social-welfare services and, 362,
      363, 376–77
Marshall, Chief Justice John
    Congress's enumerated powers and, 28–29
    Constitution's purpose and, 44–45
    democratic legitimacy and, 401, 484

"enumeration presupposes something not
    enumerated," 191
greatest opinion by, 25–26
"more States than one," 40, 175
proportional representation and, 490–91
reasoning and, 29
rule of law and, 44
sovereign American people and, 489–90
Martin, Luther, 44
Maryland, 25, 30, 44, 50–51, 54, 102–3, 106–7,
    236, 263, 334, 345, 423–24
Massachusetts, 1–2, 8–9, 115, 148–49, 159,
    200–1, 212, 218–19, 220, 399, 400, 423–24
Masur, Kate, 379
McConnell, Michael W., 10–11
McCulloch v. Maryland (1819) (*McCulloch* case)
    canonical federalism decision in, 6
    effective powers and, 44–45
    exigencies and, 34, 37
    legitimate end and, 44, 383–84
    modern Court and, 47
    pretextual purpose and, 49
    "sword and the purse," 40
    values of federalism, 40
Metzger, Gillian E., 363–64
Michigan, 211–12
militia, 48, 234, 273–74
Missouri Compromise (1820), 343–44
Monroe, President James, 343–44
Morris, Gouverneur, 343, 349
Mutual cooperation
    collective action and, 66–67
    collective optimum, the, 65
    pareto optimum and, 66–67*f*

Nadelmann, Kurt H., 250, 252–53, 318–19
national defense, compacts concerning, 479
national uniformity
    bankruptcy, 15
    coinage, 15
    counterfeiting, 15
    naturalization, 15
    standards, 15
Necessary and Proper Clause
    authorize Congress, 9–10, 301–2
    collective action and, 12–13, 46
    Congress & implied power and, 25, 28–29, 264
    Counterfeiting Clause and, 260–61
    currency and, 259
    deference logic and, 383–84
    exclusive state regulation, 336–37
    federalism and, 46
    Marshallian interpretation of, 45

502 GENERAL INDEX

Necessary and Proper Clause (*cont.*)
  separation of powers and, 46, 283, 285
  structural inference, 283
  "whole instrument," the, 30
Nevada, 414
Newark (NJ), 112
New Hampshire, 236, 399, 423–24
New Jersey, 112, 121, 172, 423–24
New Jersey Plan, 138
New York, 8–9, 42, 102–3, 121, 135, 136, 146,
  172, 182–83, 210, 211–12, 270–71, 314,
  399, 400, 423–24
New York City, 112, 372
New York Port Authority, 112
North Carolina, 399, 423–24
Northwest Ordinance (1787), 343–44

Oaths of Office Clause, 310
Office of Legal Counsel (OLC), 120–21
Olson, Mancur, 62–63
originalism, 31–32, 209–10

pandemic responses, compacts concerning, 479
Pareto
  2 × 2 matrix games, 92–93
  basis to intervene and, 91
  collective-action problems, 5, 45
  cooperation problems, 210, 212–13
  externalized costs less than internalized
    benefits, 91*f*
  fifty states (not thirteen) and, 89
  justifies intervention of federal courts,
    212–13
  limiting principle & collective-action
    reasoning in, 89–90
  logics of, 43
  more integrated union, 485
  Nash equilibrium, 65
  optimal or efficient, 59
  payoffs associated with, 86
  potential differences, 13
  potential solutions, 13
  strategic environment and, 58
Patterson, William, 138
Pennsylvania, 53, 103–4, 106–7, 141, 204, 219,
  231, 248–49, 262–63, 280, 330–31, 332–33,
  336–37, 340, 423–24
Pettit, Philip, 80
Pfander, James E., 247, 248–49
Philadelphia Convention, the, 349
Pildes, Richard H., 470–71
Pinckney, Charles Cotesworth, 338
pivotal politics, 470–71
polarization/sorting, 470–71

political philosophy
  NIMBY ("not in my backyard"), 371–72
  principle of settlement and removal, 372
  people of states must sink or swim together, 371
preemption
  conflict, 223, 224–25
  doctrine, 223–26
  express, 225–26
  field, 223, 224
  implied, 223, 225–26
  presumption against, 225–26
President, the, office of, 276
presumption-against-federal-preemption canon
  historical practice for guidance, 226
  statutory construction and, 225–26
price supports
  states with many farmers and, 484–85
  states with no farmers and, 484–85
Prigg v. Pennsylvania (1842)
  federal exclusivity, assertion of, 338
  Northern states, fugitives free in, 339
  recover enslaved individuals and, 338
  slaveholders, abolitionists and, 336–37
  structural arguments for federal power and, 53
  system of regulations and, 338–39
  textually questionable decision in, 338
Privileges and Immunities Clause
  application of, 217
  dormant commerce principle and, 313, 357,
    362–63
  individual rights and, 314, 355–56, 357, 364
  naturalization and, 249
  right to travel and, 369, 373
  social-welfare services and, 363, 371–72, 376–77
pro-democratic norms, 183
Puerto Rico, 167–68, 334, 345, 352, 422

Rakove, Jack, 140–41
Randolph, Edmund, 138, 140
Reconstruction Amendments (Civil War
  Amendments)
  birthright citizenship, 356
  collective-action logics and, 430
  congressional power, 383–84
  enforcement clauses in, 383–84
  racial discrimination prohibited, 383
Reconstruction Congress, 383–84
Reconstruction Constitution
  adjudication & legislation and, 385–86
  Collective-Action Constitution and, 356–57,
    390–91
  individual rights and, 17–18
  nationalizing, 355
Regan, Donald H., 139–40, 211–12

GENERAL INDEX   503

Republican Form of Government Clause, rights
  protected by, 355–56
Rhode Island, 42, 182–83, 399, 423–24
Roberts, Chief Justice John, 152–53, 162
Roosevelt, President Franklin D., 7–8, 177–78,
  302–3, 410, 461

Secret Service, the, counterfeiting and, 259–60
Sherman, Roger, 139
simple majority. *See* majority
slavery
  Extradition & Fugitive Slave Clauses and,
    330–31
  federal regulation of rendition and, 339
  Fugitive Slave Act (1850) and, 336–37
  human beings claimed as property and,
    335–36
  individuals & states and, 339
  structural arguments and, 340
  territories in, 341
South Carolina, 423–24
Spitzer, Robert, 455–56, 457–58
state power, federal power to create and, 50
state regulatory autonomy, 216–17
state welfare benefits, 362
Stearns, Maxwell L., 10–11
Stern, Robert L., 7–8, 140–41
Stewart, Justice Potter, 369
Stone, Justice Harlan Fiske, 212–13
Story, Justice Joseph, 274–75, 286–87, 288,
  336–37, 338, 340
Strauss, David A., 409
structural theory, 211–12
structure of executive and judicial branches, 46
subsidiarity, law & scholarship of, 10–11
supermajority
  Article V's procedural requirements and, 407
  collective-action dynamics and, 406
  comparative experience with, 407
  voting rules of increasing strength and, 407
Supremacy Clause
  categories of federal law and, 269
  constitutional principle and, 223
  democratic legitimacy and, 301
  federal law & state judges and, 270–71
  legal authority, hierarchy of, 307
  leverage, states, and, 302–3
  pursuance of the Constitution in, 308
  standing to sue and, 443
  structural argument for, 39, 308–9
  structural inference from, 296

superior democratic legitimacy of, 309
vertical judicial review and, 295

Taney, Chief Justice Roger, 340
Taney Court, the
  Congress's dominion & sovereignty and, 344
  Scott v. Sandford and, 342
  slave & free state permanent balance and, 343–44
Taxing Clause
  coerciveness of, 152–53
  confers authority, 146–47
  Congress and, 37, 146
  effects theory of, 153–54
  interstate-commerce power and, 198–99
  limits federal taxation and, 147
  mandates and, 201
  misuse of, 151–52
  regulatory purposes in, 154–55
Territory Clause
  Admissions Clause and, 346
  collective-action rationale for, 384
  Congress and, 16–17, 314, 345
  integrated political & economic union and, 353
Tribe, Laurence, 216–17
Truman, President Harry, 461
Trump, President Donald, 461
Tuck, Richard, 41–42, 60–61
Tyler, President John, 461

Uniform Criminal Extradition Act (UCEA), 334
US territories. *See* American territories

Van Cleve, George William, 14–15, 104
Varat, Jonathan, 362
Vermont, 236
vertical allocation of authority, counterfeiting
  and, 260
vesting theory, 286–87, 288
Virginia, 42, 102–3, 219, 263, 302–3, 332–33,
  343–44, 345, 400, 414, 423–24
Virginia Plan, the, 138, 141, 169, 196–97, 232,
  236, 249–50, 281, 295, 297, 315, 327,
  330–31, 380, 484

Wardon, Theresa R., 247, 248–49
Washington, George, 6
Washington, Justice Bushrod, 359–60
Wechsler, Herbert, 308–9
"Welfare," 198
Wilson, James, 6, 133, 139, 140, 141, 142, 250,
  255–56, 282–83, 291